The Philosophy of Sex

Also by Alan Soble

Pornography, Sex, and Feminism
Sexual Investigations
The Philosophy of Sex and Love: An Introduction
The Structure of Love
Pornography: Marxism, Feminism, and the Future of Sexuality
Sex, Love, and Friendship (editor)
Eros, Agape, and Philia (editor)

The Philosophy of Sex
Contemporary Readings

Fourth Edition

Edited by
Alan Soble

ROWMAN & LITTLEFIELD PUBLISHERS, INC.
Lanham • Boulder • New York • Oxford

ROWMAN & LITTLEFIELD PUBLISHERS, INC.

Published in the United States of America
by Rowman & Littlefield Publishers, Inc.
4720 Boston Way, Lanham, Maryland 20706

www.rowmanlittlefield.com
12 Hid's Copse Road
Cumnor Hill, Oxford OX2 9JJ, England

British Library Cataloguing in Publication Information Available

Library of Congress Cataloging-in-Publication Data Available

ISBN 0–7425-1345–9 (alk. paper)
ISBN 0–7425-1346–7 (pbk : alk. paper)

Printed in the United States of America

♾™ The paper used in this publication meets the minimum requirements of
American National Standard for Information Sciences—Permanence of Paper
for Printed Library Materials, ANSI/NISO Z39.48–1992.

For Rachel Emőke,
"the finest girl"
Love always from your Daddy

CONTENTS

PREFACE

I have been teaching undergraduate courses in and writing about the philosophy of sex and love since 1976. That comes to more than twenty-five years: a good portion of my adult life (almost half) and all my post-graduate professional life. You might think that I would be sick of the subject, if not of sex itself, by now—say, by a kind of excitatory habituation. To some extent that has happened.[1] Nevertheless, I still experience a scholarly-sensuous frisson whenever I open an envelope or an e-mail in which a colleague has sent to me, for comments or perusal, a new piece on sexual morality (most recently, when Igor Primoratz sent me his enticing "Sexual Morality: Is Consent Enough?");[2] or whenever I page through a professional journal or an anthology and unexpectedly find an exploration of sexuality (for example, Louise Collins's unfortunately somewhat tedious "Emotional Adultery: Cybersex and Commitment");[3] or whenever, browsing through a university press catalogue or the *New York Review of Books*, I discover yet another scholar bringing innovative ideas and a fresh perspective to the field (David Archard's *Sexual Consent* comes to mind immediately).[4] This revised, fourth edition of *The Philosophy of Sex: Contemporary Readings* contains the kind of philosophical investigations of sexuality that have sustained my interest in the field during all these years in the face of a suspicion (and the fact) that some philosophers, theologians, and other writers have, in their published work, been merely repeating the same old tired formulas over and over again.

The second edition of *The Philosophy of Sex* (1991) was an 80-percent revision of the first edition (1980); the third edition (1997) was also an 80-percent revision of the second. By contrast, this fourth edition (2002) is about a quarter or so revision of the third edition—which is supposed to inform you, my students, colleagues, and other readers, that I was happy with the third edition, although not *perfectly* happy with it. This fourth edition is the largest *Philosophy of Sex* ever published, containing thirty chapters (or thirty-one, depending on how you do the counting), thereby providing, in the resulting mixture, more substance and variety for students studying the philosophy of sexuality and for researchers working in the field. It newly contains, for example, my introductory essay "The Fundamentals of the Philosophy of Sex," written to ease students into, and provoke them about, the subject matter. This edition also contains other essays that are appearing in the collection for the first time, plus a much-expanded "Suggested Readings" section. Once again the core theoretical and historically important essays that are central to contemporary philosophy of sex are included (four of which were originally and surprisingly published in the dignified pages of the *Journal of Philosophy*): Thomas Nagel's "Sexual Perversion," Robert Solomon's "Sexual Paradigms," Janice Moulton's "Sexual Behavior: Another Position," Robert Gray's "Sex and Sexual Perversion," and Alan Goldman's "Plain Sex" (from the prestigious journal *Philosophy and Public Affairs*).

The bulk of the fourth edition of *Philosophy of Sex* falls properly in the area of applied philosophy of sex or, more generally, applied philosophy, applied ethics, and gender studies (so the book could be used in those sorts of courses as well as in courses that concentrate on the philosophy of sex). Some of the essays I have chosen to include in this volume are very good, even excellent; others, I think, are probably wrong, even if provocative. But this latest version of *Philosophy of Sex* would be an extraordinarily boring book were I to assemble together only what I personally like, find compelling, or sympathize with ideologically. Such a monistic collection, furthermore, would not serve well the interests of students who are attempting to learn about the philosophy of sex or of scholars who utilize this text for research, and it would not do justice to the richness of sexual philosophy. Hence there are essays in this anthology that are critical *and* supportive of homosexuality, abortion, prostitution, and pornography, which makes the book unlike a large number of recent collections in sex and gender studies that are merely platforms for partisan views.[5]

The section on conceptual analysis (Part 1) begins with a sweet and sour essay by Greta Christina, who exhibits how the paradigmatically philosophical task of providing criteria for the identification of sexual acts also arises in (some of) our sexual lives.[6] "What is sex?" (definitionally and descriptively) is the question addressed in the other essays of Part 1: Thomas Nagel focuses on the sophisticated psychological nature of human sexual interaction; Robert Solomon explores the expressive functions of sexual behavior; Janice Moulton exposes what is false and misleading, from a woman's perspective, in Nagel's and Solomon's accounts of human sexuality; Alan Goldman attempts to define "sexual desire" and "sexual activity" by discovering the lowest common denominator of all sexual events; Robert Gray illuminates the conceptual relationship between sexual activity and sexual pleasure and explains how this bears on our understanding of sexual perversion; and in my contribution to Part 1, I examine conceptually and ethically the much-maligned yet nearly universally practiced (among males, at least) act of masturbation. (You might remember Woody Allen's joke: "Why are you such a good lover?" Answer: "I practice a lot when I'm alone.")

In Part 2, the pieces by John Finnis and Michael Levin express severe doubts about the morality, wisdom, and normality of homosexuality,[7] while those of Martha Nussbaum and John Corvino offer defenses of gay and lesbian sexuality. Ed Vacek's prescient paper presents an early statement of a position that has lately been growing in popularity and visibility, namely, that the tenets of Christianity do not entail that loving and consummated homosexual relationships are morally wrong.[8] Cheshire Calhoun, in her recent essay "Defending Marriage," critically analyzes several arguments that attempt to defend same-sex marriage, and concludes that such marriages are essential for the full citizenship of gay men and lesbians. Of course the analytic essays of Part 1 of this volume on the nature of sex and perversion have implications for these disagreements over homosexuality, as they do for all the other topics discussed later in the volume.

Both abortion and sexuality have been written about abundantly, but largely independently of each other. For this reason, I have reserved Part 3 of the book for two essays that nicely examine an issue that has been, among philosophers, relatively neglected: Sidney Callahan and Ellen Willis explore the logical, psychological, and social connections between the abortion controversy and contemporary sexual norms.[9]

In Part 4, which is new to this fourth edition of *Philosophy of Sex,* the important concept (and practice) of the "sexual use" of one person by another is investigated. Part 4 begins with a classic statement by the German philosopher Immanuel Kant (1724–1804) about the essentially objectifying or instrumental nature of human sexual interaction. (This chapter is the only one in the book that cannot be called a "contemporary reading," in violation of the book's subtitle. I include it because there has lately been a good deal of writing about Kant and sexuality—see the "Suggested Readings"—and it is helpful to have some of what Kant wrote about sex conveniently available.) Thomas Mappes and I explore, in separate essays, what is implied about the morality of sexual behavior if we take Kant's metaphysics of human sexuality seriously (or semiseriously) and also hold to some version of the Second Formulation of Kant's Categorical Imperative. Thus both essays ask how and when sexual activity could be morally permissible if the persons involved wanted to follow Kant's injunction never to use another person sexually merely as a means. (This is a topic brought up briefly earlier in the volume by Alan Goldman).[10] An essay by Irving Singer closes Part 4, in which he registers strong disagreement with Kant's characterization of sex as inherently instrumental and objectifying.[11] Clearly, the theoretical and practical discussion of sexual use and sexual objectification in Part 4 is especially relevant to the topics addressed in Parts 5 and 6 of this book: rape, harassment, pornography, and prostitution.

Part 5 is devoted to questions that arise about rape, date rape, and sexual harassment. Robin Warshaw, by carefully presenting case studies of possibly sexually harassing behavior, shows us that analytic tangles, and hence legal and social uncertainties, plague this phenomenon. Mane Hajdin tries to clear up this perplexing territory by suggesting how a demarcation criterion, one that reliably distinguishes acceptable from unacceptable sexual advances, might be devised. H. E. Baber compares the harms caused by work in our society and the harms caused by rape or sexual assault and reaches a surprising conclusion. Robin West explores another problematic distinction, that between nonconsensual sexual activity and sexual activity that is consensual yet still engaged in under some sort of pressure and is in that way harmful, especially to women's autonomy. Two additional essays have been added to Part 5 of this edition. My essay on Antioch University's "Sexual Offense Policy" analyzes the school's procedures designed to reduce or eliminate date rape on college campuses. And Alan Wertheimer's essay insightfully ponders and questions the meaning, moral power, and even the relevance of "consent" in sexual contexts. Note that Wertheimer and Mappes discuss similar cases in probing the influence of coercion and deception on the morality of sexual relations.

Prostitution and pornography—which both involve, in their own way, performing sexual acts for compensation, and arguably involve the sexual use and objectification of (mostly) women—are the last of the special topics, analyzed by two sets of three essays each in Part 6. In her essay, Sallie Tisdale presents a feisty and enlightening look at pornography from a woman's perspective.[12] Martha Nussbaum tackles the enormous and difficult task of distinguishing, both analytically and morally, the various kinds of sexual objectification that are represented in or carried out by pornography and literature (and, by extension, the objectification that also occurs in our lives). My contribution to this section is an essay that investigates empirically and conceptually the connection between pornography and harm to women. (This essay had appeared in the second edition, but not the third, of *Philosophy of Sex.*) The final three essays are concerned with prostitution. Laurie Shrage presents a unique feminist view of prostitution, a position that not only is highly critical of prostitution as it is currently practiced in our society but also suggests ways of improving prostitution. Igor Primoratz, in part replying to Shrage's essay, finds in prostitution—from his libertarian perspective— much less about which to complain, even as prostitution is currently practiced.[13] Closing this section is an iconoclastic essay by Pat Califia,

"Whoring in Utopia," which unabashedly defends prostitution by pointing out its many useful benefits.

I have dedicated this edition of *Philosophy of Sex* to my daughter Rachel, who is the supreme love of my life (and now eight years old). Rachel has brought to me, and made me feel, a kind of exquisite joy I did not, earlier in my life, ever anticipate experiencing—and surely something that even sexual activity at its best has never provided.

Notes

1. This is partly why I took several breaks from the philosophy of sex and love and pursued other research matters. One break occurred in 1994, when I immersed myself in the writings of Francis Bacon, inspired to do so by those feminists who found obnoxious allusions to "rape" in Bacon's philosophy of science. The result was "In Defense of Bacon," *Philosophy of the Social Sciences* 25, 2 (1995): 192–215; a revised version appears in *A House Built on Sand: Exposing Postmodernist Myths about Science,* ed. Noretta Koertge (New York: Oxford University Press, 1998), 195–215. The second break occurred in 1998, and resulted in my exposé of some excesses of feminist scholarship: "Bad Apples: Feminist Politics and Feminist Scholarship," *Philosophy of the Social Sciences* 29, 3 (1999): 354–88. But even these publications deal tangentially or directly with sexual issues (for example, see my critique of Rae Langton on pornography in "Bad Apples," 370–77). These essays (and others) are available on my Website, <www.uno.edu/~asoble>.

2. *Ethical Theory and Moral Practice* 4, 3 (2001): 201–18.

3. *Social Theory and Practice* 25, 2 (1999): 243–70. There is much that is valuable in Collins's groundbreaking essay, but I found unconvincing and confusing her reliance on the writings of the conservative sexual philosopher Vincent Punzo (*Reflective Naturalism* [New York: Macmillan, 1969], chap. 6) in arguing that a feminist can, and perhaps should, embrace a thesis about the significance of the connection between sex and love (see 249 and 266, n. 21).

4. *Sexual Consent* (Boulder, Colo.: Westview, 1998). Many other articles and books that have made important contributions to the field are listed at the end of this volume in the "Suggested Readings" section.

5. See, for example, my review of the third edition of Marilyn Pearsall's *Women and Values: Readings in Recent Feminist Philosophy* (Belmont, Calif.: Wadsworth, 1999), which appeared in *Teaching Philosophy* 23, 2 (2000): 215–20.

6. Christina's essay was reprinted by the magazine *Ms.* in its "Feminism and Sex" issue of November/December 1995 (60–62). But, strangely, the essay's last two paragraphs are missing from that reprint (but not from this volume), and my inspection of that issue of *Ms.* could find no editorial warning that the essay had been abridged. Those paragraphs of Christina's essay are perhaps the most provocative—and the least feminist—parts of the essay: she admits to finding some sadomasochist sex "tremendously erotic," and she relates that when working as a nude dancer inside a peep show booth she had a "fabulous time" sexually with one of her quarter-laden customers.

7. For an early essay by Levin on homosexuality, see his "Why Homosexual-

ity Is Abnormal," *The Monist* 67, 2 (1984): 251–83; reprinted in Alan Soble, ed., *The Philosophy of Sex,* 3rd edition (Lanham, Md.: Rowman & Littlefield, 1997), 95–127. A detailed critique of Levin's *Monist* essay can be found in Timothy Murphy, "Homosexuality and Nature: Happiness and the Law At Stake," *Journal of Applied Philosophy* 4, 2 (1987): 195–204.

8. See also the defense of homosexual marriage in Patricia Jung and Ralph Smith, *Heterosexism: An Ethical Challenge* (Albany: State University of New York Press, 1993), which book I briefly reviewed in *Ethics* 105, 4 (1995): 975–76.

9. See also Roger Paden, "Abortion and Sexual Morality" (229–36), and my essay "More on Abortion and Sexual Morality" (239–44), both of which appear in my edited collection *Sex, Love, and Friendship* (Amsterdam: Editions Rodopi, 1997). Although Judith Jarvis Thomson's well-known and widely reprinted essay "A Defense of Abortion" (*Philosophy and Public Affairs* 1, 1 [1971]: 47–66) is often read as a statement about the implications for the morality of abortion of a woman's right to control what happens to and in her own body, I think the essay is usefully probed for its implications about the relationship between the morality of abortion and the morality of sexual activity. See also David Boonin-Vail, "A Defense of 'A Defense of Abortion': On the Responsibility Objection to Thomson's Argument," *Ethics* 107, 2 (1997): 286–313.

10. See "Plain Sex," in this volume, pages 39–55, at 51.

11. On the striking similarity between the views of Kant on sexuality and those of the contemporary feminists Catharine MacKinnon and Andrea Dworkin, see Barbara Herman, "Could It Be Worth Thinking about Kant on Sex and Marriage?" in *A Mind of One's Own: Feminist Essays on Reason and Objectivity,* ed. Louise M. Antony and Charlotte Witt (Boulder, Colo.: Westview, 1993), 49–67.

12. The essay by Tisdale contained in this volume was published in *Harper's* in February 1992. Afterward, she gave her thoughts on sexuality more complete treatment in *Talk Dirty to Me: An Intimate Philosophy of Sex* (New York: Doubleday, 1994). See the review of her book by James Wolcott, "Position Papers," *The New Yorker* (21 November 1994), 115–19; don't miss the color comic of Tisdale in a pornography store (115). Readers' letters of reply to her *Harper's* essay, as well as her responses to them, appeared in the May 1992 issue of that magazine (4–7, 72–73, and 76–78).

13. Shrage continues the debate with Primoratz in her *Moral Dilemmas of Feminism: Prostitution, Adultery, and Abortion* (New York: Routledge, 1994); see chap. 5 and 207, n. 22. Some thoughts about Shrage and Primoratz can be found in my *Sexual Investigations* (New York: New York University Press, 1996), 33–34 and 125–26. More recent criticism of Primoratz, in an essay that defends a tart-with-a-heart type of prostitution, can be found in S. E. Marshall, "Bodyshopping: The Case of Prostitution," *Journal of Applied Philosophy* 16, 2 (1999): 139–50.

Introduction

THE FUNDAMENTALS OF THE PHILOSOPHY OF SEX

Alan Soble

Only when you [have sex] . . . are you most cleanly alive and most cleanly yourself. . . . Sex isn't just friction and shallow fun. Sex is also the revenge on death. Don't forget death. Don't ever forget it. Yes, sex too is limited in its power. . . . But tell me, what power is greater?
　—Philip Roth, *The Dying Animal*

When a great deal of material has been written on a subject, by many different writers of various persuasions and backgrounds, eventually it will be possible to assemble a collection of assertions about the subject that are bound to be silly. (The principle I have just put forward reverses a well-known story, according to which a group of monkeys equipped with typewriters will eventually produce a Shakespearian sonnet.) This principle holds for the topics of love and human sexuality, and perhaps especially for these loaded and emotional subjects. I have over the years collected a number of apparently absurd or ridiculous claims made by in-

This essay is a revision of my "Philosophy of Sexuality," an entry in the *Internet Encyclopedia of Philosophy* (<www.utm.edu/research/iep/>). It is reprinted by permission of the editor of the encyclopedia, James Fieser. This encyclopedia entry is a descendent of three earlier pieces: "Sexuality and Sexual Ethics," in *Encyclopedia of Ethics,* ed. Lawrence and Charlotte Becker (New York: Garland, 1992), 1141–47 (rev. version in *Encyclopedia of Ethics,* 2nd ed. [N.Y.: Routledge, 2001], 1570–77); "La morale et la sexualité," in *Dictionnaire d'éthique et de philosophie morale,* ed. Monique Canto-Sperber (Paris: Presses Universitaires de France, 1996), 1387–91; and "Sexuality, Philosophy of," in *Routledge Encyclopedia of Philosophy,* ed. Edward Craig (London: Routledge, 1998), vol. 8, 717–30.

telligent people about sex and love. Let me share a few with you. Of course, that this is *my* list of silly assertions may say more about my own biases and prejudices than about the thoughtfulness of their authors.

For example, the theologian Gilbert Meilaender has written, in his very fine book *The Limits of Love,* that heterosexual coitus (penis-vagina intercourse), in particular, is "the act in which human beings are present most fully and give themselves most completely to another"[1]—as if during homosexual sexual activity, the partners do not or cannot give themselves totally to each other.[2] Moreover, to think that a sexual act, of all things, whether heterosexual or homosexual, forms the stuff of the greatest intimacy is to overestimate or exaggerate the strength and meaning of an exceedingly common and often trite physical act that has no more important implications than passing gas.

The contemporary American secular philosopher Robert Nozick, who is deservedly well respected for his brilliant books and articles, has described sexual activity as a "metaphysical exploration, knowing the body and person of another as a map or microcosm of the very deepest reality, a clue to its nature and purpose"[3]—as if investigating carefully the pimples on your partner's bottom supplies a reflection of cosmic order. (Actually, I don't have the foggiest idea what Nozick is saying in the first place. Surely we expect something less obscure from one of our premier analytic philosophers.) Nozick also thinks, along the lines of Meilaender, that "the most intense way we relate to another person is sexually."[4] Apparently Nozick has never experienced the enormous intensity of the relationship between some people who play chess with each other. And he has overlooked that reciprocal bursts of anger can be extraordinarily intense, even if brief (like a brief and intense mutual orgasm), and that fervent mutual hatred can last nearly a lifetime. Further, we should not forget the lamentable fact that there is not much intensity in the dull coitus routinely performed by a long-married couple.

The world-famous psychologist Rollo May denies that the key "moment" in sexual activity is the orgasm (which makes good sense). Instead, however, May thinks that the key "moment" is the precise instant of the penetration of the erect penis of the man into the vaginal opening of the woman[5]—as if that brief event never eventuated in a premature ejaculation depressing to both partners. And is the key "moment" for homosexual lovers exactly when the penis enters the anus, pushing its way through that tight muscular ring? (Victory! Scoring!) I am suspicious of any talk about the key "moment" in the sexual activity of two people. Sometimes it is the very first light kiss, or the very first time we hold hands, realizing at that moment that we are *going to* engage in sexual activity, that makes the biggest sexual impression—and afterward all is sadly downhill. (May does acknowledge that the event of penetration may be "disappointing," but still considers it the moment of "greatest significance" in sex. But if the act of penetration is a disappointment, then why insist that it "is the moment of union and the realization that we have won the other"? "Won," indeed.)

The biomedical ethicist Timothy Murphy has proffered the idea (reminiscent of Nozick's) that sex, whether straight or gay, "is a rich and fertile language for discovering and articulating the meanings of human life"[6]— as if English or Hungarian weren't good enough, or even better, for that purpose. Sex as a rich and fertile language, indeed, precisely for "articulating the meanings of human life." What makes Murphy think he is advancing our understanding of sex, or the philosophy of sex, by describing sex in such overblown and pretentious terms? Come on, guy, get a hold of yourself: sex is most of the time just fornicating or *plain sex* (to use Alan Goldman's term from his contribution to this collection), whether it is straight or gay, nothing metaphysically or linguistically finer than that.

The philosopher Janice Moulton writes in this volume, in a very perceptive essay, that "sexual behavior differs from other behavior by virtue of its unique feelings and emotions and its unique ability to create shared intimacy"[7]—as if a platoon of soldiers, buddies one and all, while fired upon in battle, didn't experience profound shared intimacy. Moulton pays insufficient attention to those relationships, such as that between John Stuart Mill and Harriet Taylor, in which their deep, shared intimacy was created not by sexual activity but by their common interests in philosophy and political economy and their writing projects (probably a more firm foundation for shared intimacy than sexual activity). But the married-to-each-other philosophers Hilde Lindemann Nelson and James Lindemann Nelson win the syrup award for their generalization that after two people get married their "idealizations give way to a better understanding of what's really admirable about one's partner."[8] Quite the opposite, I should have thought, at least some if not most of the time: idealizations do give way after marriage, but we discover how rotten the other person really is. At least we can raise the question: Do we, after marriage, discover mostly the good and admirable *or* the bad, nasty, and worthless?

As does Moulton, Roger Scruton thinks that sexuality is unique; but whereas Moulton thinks that sexuality's uniqueness lies in something good (the shared intimacy it creates), Scruton identifies something obnoxious in sexuality that makes it special: "it is in the experience of sexual desire that we are most vividly conscious of the distinction between virtuous and vicious impulses"[9]—between, say, a tendency to lavish caring, devoted attention upon the object of our sexual desire and the wild impulse just to have our way with her or him, which occasionally is victorious. But Scruton is myopic is focusing on sex in this regard (unlike St. Augustine, who found the consciousness of the pull of virtue and of viciousness in all human endeavors). The contrast between our virtuous and vicious impulses can force itself upon our consciousness just as often, perhaps more strongly, and frequently with more disastrous consequences, in matters of politics, ambition, and money (for example, being pulled between generosity and stinginess).

I could go on and on with similar examples. But please do not take my sarcasm all that seriously. What I mostly want to urge is that the reader should take much of what is written about sexuality with a grain of salt, including this introduction and the essays that have been collected together in this anthology. Try to approach the philosophy of sex, even when it seems to be at its most intense and threatening, with a light heart and a willingness to poke holes in bubbles. (The first and last articles in this book, Greta Christina's piece on figuring out what sex *is,* and Pat Califia's essay on the possible future of prostitution, have already taken this advice, as does Sallie Tisdale's essay on pornography, which accounts for why these three are, in some ways, the most entertaining and absorbing papers in this collection.) Now, then, let us get down to the business of the philosophy of sex.

Among the many topics explored by the philosophy of sex are procreation, contraception, celibacy, marriage, adultery, casual sex, flirting, prostitution, homosexuality, masturbation, seduction, rape, sexual harassment, sadomasochism, pornography, bestiality, and pedophilia. What do all these various things have in common? All are related in various ways to the vast domain of human sexuality. That is, they are related, on the one hand, to the human desires and activities that involve the search for and attainment of sexual pleasure or satisfaction and, on the other hand, to the human desires and activities that involve the creation of new human beings. For it is a natural feature of human beings that certain sorts of behaviors and certain bodily organs are and can be employed either for pleasure or for reproduction, or for both.

The philosophy of sexuality explores these topics both conceptually and normatively. Conceptual analysis is carried out in the philosophy of sex in order to clarify the fundamental notions of the discipline, including *sexual desire* and *sexual activity.* Conceptual analysis is also carried out in attempting to arrive at satisfactory definitions of specific sexual practices, for example, adultery, rape, and prostitution. Conceptual analysis (for example: What are the distinctive features of a desire that make it sexual desire instead of something else? In what ways does seduction differ from nonviolent rape?) is often difficult and seemingly picky, but proves rewarding in unanticipated and surprising ways. Although Part 1 of this collection focuses on conceptual matters about the nature of sex, the reader will find that many other articles in the other parts of the book also pay attention to conceptual matters (most notably, the essays by Thomas A. Mappes on "sexual use," Mane Hajdin's essay on "sexual harassment," and Alan Wertheimer's essay on "consent").

Normative philosophy of sexuality inquires about the value of sexual activity and sexual pleasure and of the various forms they take. Thus normative philosophy of sexuality is concerned with the perennial questions of sexual morality and constitutes a large branch of applied ethics. It investigates what contribution is made to the good or virtuous life by sexuality, and tries to determine what moral obligations we have to refrain from performing certain sexual acts and what moral permissions we have to engage in others. Parts 2 through 6 of this anthology concentrate on normative matters in the philosophy of sex, discussing homosexuality, abortion, sexual use, rape, harassment, pornography, and prostitution. Clearly, what is written about the morality of sexual behavior in one of these parts will have implications for the topics discussed in the other parts. For example, the investigation of Kantian sexual ethics and of the notions of sexual use and objectification in Part 4 has important connections with the issues of prostitution and pornography addressed in Part 6.

Some philosophers of sexuality carry out conceptual analysis and the normative study of sexual ethics separately. They believe that it is one thing to *define* a sexual phenomenon (such as masturbation, rape, or adultery) and quite another thing to *evaluate* the phenomenon as being morally right or wrong. Other philosophers of sexuality believe that a robust distinction between defining a sexual phenomenon and arriving at moral evaluations of it cannot be made, that analyses of sexual concepts and moral evaluations of sexual acts necessarily influence each other. Whether there actually is a tidy distinction between values and morals, on the one hand, and natural, social, or conceptual facts, on the other hand, is one of those fascinating, endlessly debated issues in philosophy, and is not limited to the philosophy of sexuality. One thing to think about while reading the essays in this book is to what extent the authors keep distinct the conceptual and the normative or imply, to the contrary, that this distinction is an impediment to the doing of the philosophy of sex.

The Metaphysics of Sex

Our moral evaluations of sexual activity are likely to be affected by what we view the nature of the sexual impulse, or of sexual desire, to be in human beings. In this regard there is a deep divide between those philosophers that we might call the metaphysical sexual optimists and those we might call the metaphysical sexual pessimists.

The pessimists in the philosophy of sexuality, such as St. Augustine, Immanuel Kant, and, sometimes, Sigmund Freud, perceive the sexual impulse and acting on it to be something nearly always, if not necessarily, unbefitting the dignity of the human person. They see the essence and the results of the sexual drive to be incompatible with more significant and lofty goals and aspirations of human existence. They fear that the power and demands of the sexual impulse make it a danger to harmonious civilized life. And they find in a person's sexuality a severe threat not only to his or her proper relations with, and moral treatment of, other persons, but also to his or her own humanity.

On the other side of the divide are the metaphysical sexual optimists—Plato, in some of his works, sometimes Sigmund Freud, Bertrand Russell, and many contemporary philosophers—who perceive nothing especially obnoxious in the sexual impulse. They frequently view human sexuality as just another and mostly innocuous dimension of our existence as embodied or animal-like creatures (like the impulses to eat and find shelter). They judge that sexuality, which in some measure has been given to us by evolution, cannot but be conducive to our well-being without detracting from our intellectual propensities. And they praise rather than fear the power of an impulse that can lift us to various high forms of happiness.

The particular sort of metaphysics of sex one holds will likely influence one's subsequent judgments about the value and role of sexuality in the good or virtuous life and about what sexual activities are morally wrong and which ones are morally permissible. Let's explore some of these implications.

An extended version of metaphysical pessimism might make the following claims. (1) In virtue of the nature of sexual desire, a person who sexually desires another person objectifies that other person, both before and during sexual activity. Sex, says the German philosopher Immanuel Kant, "makes of the loved person an Object of appetite. . . . Taken by itself it is a degradation of human nature."[10] That is, our sexual desire for another person tends to make us view him or her merely as a thing, as a sexual object. And when one person sexually desires another, the other person's body is primarily desired, distinct from the person.

(2) Further, certain types of deception seem required prior to engaging in sex with another person. We go out of our way, for example, to make ourselves look more physically attractive and socially desirable to the other person than we really are, and we go to great lengths to conceal our physical and personality defects. We are never our true selves on a first date, trying to make a good (and hence misleading) impression. While it might be the case that men sexually objectify women more than women objectify men, it is undeniable that both men and women engage in deception in trying to elicit a positive response from the other person.

(3) The sexual act itself is peculiar, with its uncontrollable arousal, in-

voluntary jerkings, and its yearning to master and consume the other person's body. This is part of what St. Augustine had in mind when he wrote: "lust . . . is the more shameful in this, that the soul does neither rule itself . . . nor the body either, so that the will rather than lust might move these parts."[11] During the act, a person both loses control of himself or herself and loses regard for the humanity of the other person. Our sexuality is a threat to the other's personhood; but the one who is in the grip of desire is also on the verge of losing his or her personhood.

(4) Moreover, a person who gives in to another's sexual desire makes a tool of himself or herself. As Kant makes the point, "For the natural use that one sex makes of the other's sexual organs is *enjoyment*, for which one gives oneself up to the other. In this act a human being makes himself into a thing."[12] Those engaged in sexual activity make themselves willingly into objects for each other merely for the sake of sexual pleasure. Hence both persons are reduced to the animal level.

(5) Finally, due to the insistent nature of the sexual impulse, once things get going it is often hard to stop them in their tracks, and as a result we often end up doing things sexually that we had never planned or wanted to do. Sexual desire is also powerfully inelastic, one of the passions most likely to challenge reason, compelling us to seek satisfaction even when doing so involves obvious physical and psychological dangers. The one who desires depends on the whims of another person to gain satisfaction, and thereby becomes susceptible to the demands of the other. People who are caught up in sexual desire can be easily exploited and manipulated.

Given such a pessimistic metaphysics of human sexuality, one might well conclude that acting on the sexual impulse is always morally wrong, or that for purely prudential reasons one would do best by being celibate. That might, indeed, be precisely the right conclusion to draw, even if it implies the end of Homo sapiens. (This doomsday result was not fearsome to St. Augustine; it is also implied by St. Paul's praising, in 1 Corinthians 7, sexual celibacy as the ideal spiritual state.) More often, however, the pessimistic metaphysicians of sexuality conclude that sexual activity is morally permissible and prudentially wise only within marriage (of the lifelong, monogamous, heterosexual sort) and only or primarily for the purpose of procreation. Regarding the bodily acts that are both procreative and produce sexual pleasure, it is their procreative potential that is singularly significant and bestows value on these activities; seeking pleasure apart from procreation is an impediment to morally virtuous sexuality, and is something that should not be undertaken deliberately or for its own sake. Sexual pleasure at most has instrumental value, in inducing us to engage in an act that has procreation as its main purpose. Such views have long been common among Christians, for example, St. Augustine: "A man turns to good use the evil of concupiscence, and is not overcome by it, when he bridles and restrains its rage . . . and never relaxes his hold upon it except when intent on offspring, and then controls and applies it to the carnal generation of children . . . , not to the subjection of the spirit to the flesh in a sordid servitude."[13]

Metaphysical sexual optimists suppose that sexuality is a natural bonding mechanism that happily joins people together both sexually and nonsexually. Sexual activity involves pleasing the self and the other at the same time, and these exchanges of pleasure generate both gratitude and affection, which in turn deepen human relationships and make them more satisfying and emotionally substantial. Further, and this may be the most important point, sexual pleasure is, for a metaphysical optimist, a valuable thing in its own right, something to be cherished and promoted because it has intrinsic and not merely instrumental value. Hence the pursuit of sexual pleasure does not require much intricate justification; sexual activity surely need not be confined to marriage or directed at procreation. The good and virtuous life, while including much else, can also include a wide variety and extent of sexual relations.[14] Irving Singer is a contemporary philosopher of sexuality who expresses well one form of metaphysical optimism: "For though sexual interest resembles an appetite in some respects, it differs from hunger or thirst in being an *interpersonal* sensitivity, one that enables us to delight in the mind and character of other persons as well as in their flesh. Though at times people may be used as sexual objects and cast aside once their utility has been exhausted, this is no[t] . . . definitive of sexual desire. . . . By awakening us to the living presence of someone else, sexuality can enable us to treat this other being as just the person he or she happens to be. . . . There is nothing in the nature of sexuality as such that necessarily . . . reduces persons to things. On the contrary, sex may be seen as an instinctual agency by which persons respond to one another *through* their bodies."[15]

The character Pausanias, in Plato's dramatic dialogue *Symposium,* asserts that sexuality in itself is neither good nor bad.[16] He recognizes that there can therefore be morally bad and morally good sexual activity, and proposes a corresponding distinction between what he calls "vulgar" eros and "heavenly" eros. A person who has vulgar eros is one who experiences promiscuous sexual desire, has a lust that can be satisfied by nearly any other person (male or female), and selfishly seeks only for himself or herself the pleasures of sexual activity. By contrast, a person who has heavenly eros experiences a sexual desire that attaches to a particular person; the heavenly erotic lover is as much interested in the other person's virtue, personality and well-being as he or she is concerned to have physical contact with and sexual satisfaction by means of the other person. A similar distinction between sexuality per se and eros is described by C. S. Lewis in his book *The Four Loves*,[17] and it is perhaps what Allan Bloom had in mind when he wrote, "Animals have sex and human beings have eros, and no accurate science [or philosophy of sex] is possible without making this distinction."[18] The divide between metaphysical optimists and metaphysical pessimists might, then, in part be understood this way: metaphysical pessimists think that sexuality, unless it is rigorously constrained by religious or social norms that have become psychologically internalized, will tend to be governed by vulgar eros, while metaphysical optimists think that sexuality, by itself, does not lead to or become vulgar, that by its own nature it can easily be and often is heavenly.

Moral versus Nonmoral Evaluations

Of course, we can and often do evaluate sexual activity *morally:* we inquire whether a sexual act—either a particular occurrence of a sexual act (the act we are doing or want to do right now) or a general type of sexual act (say, all instances of homosexual fellatio)—is morally good or right or morally bad or wrong. More specifically, we evaluate or judge sexual acts to be morally obligatory, morally permissible, morally wrong, or even morally supererogatory. For example: one spouse might have a *moral obligation* to engage in sex with the other spouse; it might be *morally permissible* for married couples to employ contraception while engaging in coitus; rape, prostitution, and some forms of incest are commonly thought to be *morally wrong* (or *immoral*); and one person's agreeing to have sexual relations with another person when the former has no sexual desire of his or her own but wants to please the latter might be *morally supererogatory*. "Morally supererogatory" sexual activity is a category that is not often discussed by sexual ethicists. Raymond Belliotti has this to say about it: "We cannot fully describe this type of sex, but we can say generally that it goes above and beyond the call of moral duty. It is sex that is not merely morally permissible, but morally exemplary. It would involve some extraordinary moral benefits to others not attainable in merely morally permissible sex."[19]

Note that if a specific type of sexual act is immoral (say, homosexual fellatio), then every instance of that type of act will be morally wrong. However, from the fact that the particular sexual act we are now doing or contemplate doing is morally wrong, it does not follow that the specific type of act we are performing is morally wrong; the sexual act that we are contemplating might be wrong for lots of reasons having nothing to do with the type of sexual act it is. For example, suppose we are engaging in heterosexual coitus, and that this particular sexual act is wrong because it is adulterous. The wrongfulness of our sexual activity does not imply that heterosexual coitus in general, as a type of sexual act, is morally wrong. In some cases, of course, a particular sexual act will be wrong for several reasons at once: not only is it wrong because it is of a specific type (say, it is an instance of homosexual fellatio), but it is also wrong because at least one of the participants is married to someone else (it is wrong also because it is adulterous).

We can also evaluate sexual activity (again, either a particular occurrence of a sexual act or a specific type of sexual activity) *nonmorally* instead of morally: *nonmorally good* sex is sexual activity that provides pleasure to the participants or is physically or emotionally satisfying, while *nonmorally bad* sex is unexciting, tedious, boring, unenjoyable, or even unpleasant. (Be careful: *nonmoral* is not the same term as *immoral,* and *nonmorally bad sexual activity* does not mean *immoral sexual activity.*) An analogy will clarify the difference between morally evaluating something as good or bad and nonmorally evaluating it as good or bad. This radio on my desk is a good radio, in the nonmoral sense, because it does what I expect from a radio: it consistently provides clear tones. If, instead, the radio hissed and cackled most of the time, it would be a bad radio, nonmorally speaking, but it would be senseless for me to blame (morally) the radio for its faults and threaten it with a trip to hell if it did not improve its behavior. Similarly, sexual activity can be nonmorally good if it provides for us what we expect sexual activity to provide, which is usually sexual pleasure, and this fact has no necessary moral implications.

It is not difficult to see that the fact that a sexual activity is perfectly nonmorally good, by abundantly satisfying both persons, does not mean by itself that the act is morally good: some adulterous sexual activity might well be very pleasing to the participants, yet be morally wrong. Further, the fact that a sexual activity is nonmorally bad, that is, does not produce pleasure for the persons engaged in it, does not by itself mean that the act is morally bad. Unpleasant sexual activity might occur between persons who have little experience engaging in sexual activity (they do not yet know how to do sexual things, or have not yet learned what their likes and dislikes are), but their failure to provide pleasure for each other does not mean by itself that they perform morally wrongful acts.

Thus the moral evaluation of sexual activity is distinct from the nonmoral evaluation of sexual activity, even if there do remain important connections between them. For example, the fact that a sexual act provides pleasure to both participants, and is thereby nonmorally good, might be taken (especially by a metaphysical sexual optimist) as a strong, but only prima facie good, reason for thinking that the act is morally good or at least has some degree of moral value. Indeed, utilitarian philosophers such as Jeremy Bentham and John Stuart Mill might claim that, in general, the nonmoral goodness of sexual activity goes a long way toward justifying it. Another example: if one person never attempts to provide sexual pleasure to his or her partner, but selfishly insists on experiencing only his or her own pleasure, then that person's contribution to their sexual activity is morally suspicious. But that judgment rests not simply on the fact that he or she did not provide pleasure for the other person, that is, on the fact that the sexual activity was for the other person nonmorally bad. The moral judgment rests, more precisely, on his or her motives for not providing any pleasure, for not making the experience nonmorally good for the other person.

It is one thing to point out that as evaluative categories, moral goodness/badness is quite distinct from nonmoral goodness/badness. It is another thing to wonder, nonetheless, about the emotional or psychological connections between the moral quality of sexual activity and its nonmoral quality. Perhaps morally good or right sexual activity tends also to be the most satisfying sexual activity, in the nonmoral sense. Whether that is true likely depends on what we mean by morally "good" or "right" sexuality and on certain features of human moral psychology. What would our lives be like, if there were always a neat correspondence between the moral quality of a sexual act and its nonmoral quality? I am not sure what such a human sexual world would be like. But examples that violate such a neat correspondence are at the present time, in this world, easy to come by. A sexual act might be both morally and nonmorally good: consider the exciting and joyful sexual activity of a newly married couple. But a sexual act might be morally good and nonmorally bad: consider the routine sexual acts of this couple after they have been married for ten years. A sexual act might be morally bad yet nonmorally good: one spouse in that couple, married for ten years, commits adultery with another married person and finds their sexual activity to be extraordinarily satisfying. And, finally, a sexual act might be both morally and nonmorally bad: the adulterous couple get tired of each other, eventually no longer experiencing the excitement they once knew. A world in which there was little or no discrepancy between the moral quality and the nonmoral quality of sexual activity might be a better world than ours, or it might be a worse world. I would refrain from making such a judgment unless I were pretty sure what the moral goodness and badness of sexual activity amounted to in the first place, and until I knew a lot more about human psychology. Sometimes that a sexual activity is acknowledged to be morally wrong by its participants actually contributes by itself to its being, for them, nonmorally good, that is, exciting and pleasurable. In this sense, the metaphysical sexual pessimists, by issuing myriad prohibitions of sexual activity, might, ironically, keep our sexual lives happy or satisfying. St. Augustine, on such a view, was not the worst thing that happened to the history of sex, but the best.

The Dangers of Sex

Whether a particular sexual act, or a specific type of sexual act, provides sexual pleasure is not the only factor in arriving at a judgment of its non-moral quality: pragmatic and prudential considerations also figure in to whether a sexual act, all things considered, has a preponderance of non-moral goodness or badness. Many sexual activities can be physically or psychologically risky, dangerous, or harmful. Anal coitus, for example, whether carried out by a heterosexual couple or by two gay males, can damage delicate tissues and is a mechanism for the potential transmission of various HIV viruses (as can heterosexual genital intercourse). Thus in evaluating whether a sexual act will be overall nonmorally good or bad, not only its anticipated pleasure or satisfaction must be counted, but also all sorts of negative (undesired) side effects: whether the sexual act is likely to damage the body, as in some sadomasochistic acts, or to transmit any one of a number of venereal diseases, or to result in an un-wanted pregnancy, or even whether one might feel regret, anger, or guilt afterward as a result of having engaged in a sexual act with this person, or in this location, or under these conditions, or of a specific type. Indeed, all these pragmatic and prudential factors can also figure into the moral evaluation of sexual activity: intentionally causing unwanted pain or discomfort to one's partner, or not taking adequate precautions against the possibility of pregnancy, or not informing one's partner of a suspected case of genital infection, might very well be morally wrong.[20] Thus, depending on what particular sexual moral principles one embraces, the various ingredients that constitute the nonmoral quality of sexual acts can influence one's moral judgments.

Sexual Perversion

In addition to inquiring about the moral and nonmoral quality of a given sexual act or a type of sexual activity, we can also ask whether the act or type is natural or unnatural (that is, "perverted"). Natural sexual acts, to provide merely a broad definition, are those acts that flow naturally from human sexual nature, or at least do not frustrate, counteract, or interfere with sexual tendencies that flow naturally from human sexual desire. An account of what is natural in human sexual desire and activity is part of a philosophical account of human nature in general, what we might call philosophical anthropology, which is a rather large undertaking.

Evaluating a particular sexual act or a specific type of sexual activity as being natural or unnatural can very well be distinct from evaluating the act or type either as being morally good or bad or as being nonmorally good or bad. Suppose we assume, for the sake of discussion only, that heterosexual coitus is a natural human sexual activity and that homosexual fellatio is not natural, or is a sexual perversion. Even so, it would not follow from these judgments alone that all heterosexual coitus is morally good or right (some of it might be adulterous, or constitute rape); nor would it follow that all homosexual fellatio is morally bad or wrong (some of it, engaged in by consenting adults in the privacy of their homes, might be morally permissible). Further, from the fact that heterosexual coitus is natural, it does not follow that acts of heterosexual coitus will be nonmorally good, that is, pleasurable; nor does it follow from the fact that homosexual fellatio is not natural that it does not or cannot produce sexual pleasure for those people who engage in it. Of course, both natural and unnatural sexual acts can be medically or psychologically risky or dangerous. There is no reason to assume that natural sexual acts are in general more safe than unnatural sexual acts; for example, unprotected (sans condom) heterosexual intercourse is more dangerous, in several ways, than mutual homosexual masturbation.

Since there are no necessary connections between the naturalness or unnaturalness of a particular sexual act or a specific type of sexual activity and its moral and nonmoral quality, why would we wonder whether a particular sexual act or a type of sexual activity was natural or perverted? (Indeed, many philosophers suggest that we should abandon the term *perversion* in talking about sexually unnatural acts, or about sexuality in general.)[21] One reason for continuing the discussion of the natural and the unnatural (or perverted) in sexuality is simply that understanding what is sexually natural and unnatural helps complete our picture of human nature in general and allows us to understand our species more fully. With such deliberations, the human self-reflection about humanity and the human condition that is the heart of philosophy becomes more complete. A second reason is that an account of the difference between the natural and the unnatural in human sexuality might be useful for the discipline of psychology, if we assume that a desire or tendency to engage (exclusively) in unnatural or perverted sexual activities is a sign or symptom of an underlying mental pathology. (By the way, the American Psychiatric Association no longer considers homosexuality to be a "sexual disorder.")[22] Finally, a third reason: even though natural sexual activity is not on that score alone morally good or right and unnatural sexual activity is not necessarily morally bad or wrong, it is still possible to argue that whether a particular sexual act or a specific type of sexuality is natural or unnatural does *influence,* to a greater or lesser extent, whether the act is morally good or morally bad. Just as whether a sexual act is nonmorally good, that is, produces pleasure for the participants, may be a factor, sometimes an important one, in our evaluating the act morally, whether a sexual act or type of sexual expression is natural or unnatural may also play a role, sometimes a large one, sometimes not, in deciding whether the act is morally good or bad.

Aquinas's Natural Law versus Nagel's Secular Philosophy

A comparison of the sexual philosophy of the medieval Catholic theologian St. Thomas Aquinas (ca. 1225–1275) with that of the contemporary secular philosopher Thomas Nagel is, in this matter, instructive. Both Aquinas and Nagel make the relatively innocuous assumptions that what is unnatural in human sexual behavior is perverted, and that what is unnatural (or perverted) in human sexuality is simply that which does not conform with or is inconsistent with natural human sexuality. But beyond these trivial areas of general agreement, there are deep differences between the views of Aquinas and Nagel.

Based on a comparison of the sexuality of humans and the sexuality of lower animals (birds, dogs, etc.), Aquinas concludes that what is natural in human sexuality is the impulse to engage in heterosexual coitus. Heterosexual coitus is the mechanism designed by the Christian God to ensure the preservation of animal species, including the human species, and hence engaging in this activity is the primary natural expression of human sexual nature. Further, this God designed each of the parts of the human body to carry out specific functions, and on Aquinas's view God designed the male penis to implant sperm into the female's vagina for the purpose of effecting procreation. It follows, for Aquinas, that depositing the sperm elsewhere than inside a human female's vagina is unnatural: it is a violation of God's design, contrary to the natural order of the world as established by God. For this reason alone, on Aquinas's view, such activities are immoral, a grave offense to the sagacious plan of the Almighty.

Sexual intercourse with lower animals (bestiality), sexual activity with members of one's own sex (homosexuality), and masturbation, for Aquinas, are unnatural sexual acts and immoral exactly for that reason. If they are committed intentionally, according to one's will, they disrupt deliberately the natural order of the world as created by God and which God commanded to be respected.[23] In none of these activities is there any possibility of procreation, and the sexual and other organs are used, or misused, for purposes other than that for which they were designed. Although Aquinas does not say so explicitly, but only hints in this direction, it follows from his philosophy of sexuality that fellatio, even when engaged in by heterosexuals, is also unnatural and morally wrong. At least in those cases in which orgasm occurs by means of this act, the sperm is not being placed where it should be placed and procreation is therefore not possible.[24] If the penis entering the vagina is the paradigmatic natural act, then any other combination of anatomical connections will be unnatural and hence immoral; for example, the penis, tongue, or fingers entering the anus. Aquinas's criterion of a sexually natural act, that it must be procreative in form or potential, and hence must involve a penis inserted into a vagina, makes no mention of human psychology. Aquinas's line of thought yields an anatomical or physiological criterion of natural and perverted sexuality that refers only to bodily organs, to where they are, or are not, put in relation to each other, and what they might accomplish as a result.

Thomas Nagel denies Aquinas's presupposition that in order to discover what is natural in human sexuality we should emphasize what is common sexually between humans and lower animals. Applying this formula, Aquinas concludes that the purpose of sexual activity and the sexual organs in humans is procreation, as it is in the lower animals. Everything else in Aquinas's sexual philosophy follows more or less logically from this assumption. Nagel, by contrast, argues that to discover what is distinctive about natural human sexuality, and hence, derivatively, what is unnatural or perverted for humans, we should focus, instead, on what humans and lower animals do *not* have in common. We should emphasize the ways in which humans are different from animals, the ways in which humans and their sexuality are special. Thus Nagel argues that sexual perversion in humans should be understood as a *psychological* phenomenon rather than, as in Aquinas's treatment, as an anatomical and physiological phenomenon. For it is human psychology that makes us different from other animals, and hence an account of natural human sexuality must acknowledge the uniqueness of human psychology and its role in sexuality.

Nagel proposes that sexual interactions in which each person responds with sexual arousal to noticing the sexual arousal of the other person exhibit the psychology that is natural to human sexuality. In such an encounter, each person becomes aware of himself or herself and the other person as both the subject and the object of their joint sexual experiences. I am sexually aroused not only by your physical attractiveness or your touch, but also by the fact that you are aroused by me and my touches; we become sexually aroused by recognizing that we are aroused. Nothing as complex as this occurs among the lower animals. Perverted sexual encounters are, on Nagel's view, those in which this mutual recognition of arousal is absent, and hence in which a person remains fully a subject or fully an object of the sexual interaction. Sexual perversion, then, is a departure from or a truncation of a psychologically "complete" pattern of arousal and consciousness.[25] Nothing in Nagel's psychological account of the natural and the perverted refers to bodily organs or physiological processes. That is, for a sexual encounter to be natural, it need not be procreative in form, as long as the requisite psychology of mutual recognition is present. Whether a sexual activity is natural or perverted does not depend, on Nagel's view, on what organs are used or where they are put, but only on the character of the psychology of the sexual encounter. Thus Nagel disagrees with Aquinas that homosexual activities, as a specific type of sexual act, are unnatural, for homosexual fellatio and anal intercourse can be accompanied by the mutual recognition of and response to the other person's sexual arousal.

It is illuminating to compare what the views of Aquinas and Nagel imply about fetishism, for example, the usually male practice of masturbating while fondling women's shoes or panties. Aquinas and Nagel agree that such activities are unnatural, but they disagree about the *grounds* of that evaluation. For Aquinas, masturbating while fondling shoes or undergarments is unnatural because the sperm is not deposited where it should be, by God's design, and the act thereby has no procreative potential. For Nagel, masturbatory fetishism is perverted for a different reason: in this activity, there is no possibility of one persons' noticing and being aroused by the arousal of another person. The arousal of the fetishist is, from the perspective of natural human psychology, defective. Note, in this example, one more difference between Aquinas and Nagel: Aquinas would judge the sexual activity of the fetishist to be immoral precisely because it is unnatural (it violates a natural pattern established by God), while Nagel would not conclude that it must be morally wrong—after all, a fetishistic sexual act might be carried out quite harmlessly and be quite pleasurable. The move historically and socially away from a Thomistic moralistic account of sexual perversion toward a morality-free psychological account such as Nagel's represents a more widespread trend: the gradual replacement of moral or religious judgments, about all sorts of deviant behavior, by medical, legal, psychiatric, or psychological judgments and interventions.[26] But, as we have seen, even psychiatry has lately been narrowing the extent of the "perverted."

A different kind of disagreement with Aquinas is registered by Christine Gudorf, a Christian theologian who otherwise has much in common with Aquinas. Gudorf agrees that the study of human anatomy and physiology yields insights into God's plan and design, and that human sexual behavior should conform with God's creative intentions. Gudorf's philosophy is, therefore, squarely within the Thomistic Natural Law tradition. But Gudorf argues that if we take a more careful look at the anatomy and physiology of the female sexual organs, and especially the clitoris, instead of focusing exclusively on the male's penis (which is what Aquinas did), we can arrive at very different conclusions about God's plan and design and, as a result, Christian sexual ethics turns out to be less restrictive. In particular, Gudorf claims that the female's clitoris is an organ whose only purpose is the production of sexual pleasure and, unlike the mixed or dual functional of the penis, has no connection with procreation. Gudorf concludes that the existence of the clitoris in the female body suggests that God intended that the purpose of sexual activity was as much for sexual pleasure for its own sake as it was for procreation. Therefore, according to Gudorf, pleasurable sexual activity apart from procreation (at least for women) does not violate God's design, is not unnatural, and hence is not necessarily morally wrong, as long as it occurs in the context of a monogamous marriage (including, even, a homosexual monogamous marriage).[27] Gudorf, it seems, is advancing a kind of Christian semioptimistic sexual metaphysics. Today we are not as confident as Aquinas was that God's plan and design could be discovered by a straightforward examination of human and animal bodies; but this healthy skepticism about our ability to discern God's intentions from facts of the natural or biological world would seem to apply to Gudorf's proposal as well. That the clitoris, through its ability to provide pleasure, can play a crucial role in sexuality that is eventually procreative, is not obviously false.

Debates in Sexual Ethics

The ethics of sexual behavior, as a branch of applied ethics, is no more and no less contentious than the ethics of anything else that is usually included within the area of applied ethics. Think, for example, of the notorious debates over euthanasia, welfare entitlements, capital punishment, abortion, environmental pollution, and our treatment of lower animals for food, clothing, entertainment, and in medical research. So it should come as no surprise that even though a discussion of sexual ethics might well result in the removal of some confusions and a clarification of the issues, very few final or absolute answers to questions about the morality of sexual activity are likely to be forthcoming from the philosophy of sexuality. (Of course, all parties, except maybe the Marquis de Sade, agree that rape is seriously morally wrong. Yet debates remain even here: what exactly is a case of rape? How can its occurrence be reliably identified? And most ethical systems conclude that adultery is morally wrong or at least morally suspect. But, again, what counts as adultery? Is it merely having lustful thoughts, as claimed by Jesus in Matthew 5:28?) As far as I can tell by surveying the literature on sexual ethics, there are several major topics that have received much attention by philosophers of sex and provide arenas for continual debate.

We have already encountered one of these debates: the dispute between a Natural Law approach to sexual morality and a more liberal or secular outlook that denies that there is a tight connection between what is unnatural in human sexuality and what is immoral. The secular or liberal philosopher emphasizes the values of autonomous choice, self-determination, and pleasure in arriving at moral judgments about sexual behavior, in contrast to the Thomistic tradition that justifies a more restrictive sexual ethics by invoking a divinely imposed scheme to which human action must conform. For a secular or liberal philosopher of sexuality, rape is the paradigmatically morally wrong sexual act, in which one person forces himself or herself upon another or uses powerful threats to coerce the other to engage in sexual activity. By contrast, for the liberal, anything done voluntarily between two or more people is generally morally permissible. For the secular or liberal philosopher, then, a sexual act would be immoral only if it were coercive, dishonest, or manipulative. Natural Law theory would agree, except to add, importantly, that the sexual act's merely being unnatural is another, independent reason for condemning it morally. Kant, for example, held that "Onanism . . . is abuse of the sexual faculty. . . . By it man sets aside his person and degrades himself below the level of animals. . . . Intercourse between *sexus homogenii* . . . too is contrary to the ends of humanity."[28] The sexual liberal, however, usually finds nothing morally wrong or non-morally bad about either masturbation or homosexual sexual activity. These activities might be unnatural, and perhaps in some ways prudentially unwise, but in many if not most cases they can be carried out without harm being done either to anyone else or to the participants. But Natural Law is alive and well today among some philosophers of sex, even if the details do not precisely match Aquinas's original version.[29]

Consent

Another debate is about whether, when there is no harm done to third parties (that is, nonparticipants), to be concerned about the fact that two people engage in sexual activity voluntarily, with their own free and informed consent, is both necessary and sufficient for satisfying the demands of sexual morality. Of course, those in the Natural Law tradition deny that consent is sufficient, since on their view willingly engaging in unnatural sexual acts is morally wrong, but they are not alone in reducing the moral significance of consent. Sexual activity between two persons might be harmful to one or both participants, and a moral paternalist or perfectionist would claim that it is wrong for one person to harm another person, or for the latter to allow the former to engage in this harmful behavior, even when both persons provide free and informed consent to their joint activity. Consent in this case is not sufficient, and as a result some forms of sadomasochistic sexuality turn out to be morally wrong. The denial of the sufficiency of consent is also frequently asserted by those philosophers who claim that only in a committed relationship is sexual activity between two people morally permissible. The free and informed consent of both parties may be a necessary condition for the moral goodness of their sexual activity, but in the absence of some other magical ingredient (love, marriage, devotion, and the like) their sexual activity remains mere mutual use or objectification and hence morally objectionable.

About casual sex, for example, it might be said that two persons are merely using each other for their own separate sexual pleasure; even when genuinely consensual, these mutual sexual uses do not yield a virtuous sexual act. Kant and Karol Wojtyła (Pope John Paul II) take this position: willingly allowing oneself to be used sexually by another person makes an object of oneself. Hence mutual consent is not sufficient for the moral rightness of sexual acts. For Kant, sexual activity avoids treating a person merely as a means only in marriage, since in such a state both persons have surrendered their bodies and souls to each other.[30] For Wojtyła, "only love can preclude the use of one person by another," since love is a unification of persons resulting from a mutual gift of their selves.[31] Note, however, that the thought that a unifying love is the ingredient that justifies sexual activity (beyond consent) has an interesting implication: gay and lesbian sexual relations would seem to be permissible if they occur within homosexual marriages that are loving, committed, and monogamous. At this point in the argument, defenders of the view that sexual activity is justifiable only in marriage commonly appeal to Natural Law to rule out homosexual marriage.

On another view of these matters, the fact that sexual activity is carried out voluntarily by all persons involved means, assuming that no harm to third parties exists, that the sexual activity is morally permissible. In defending the sufficiency of consent for the moral goodness of sexual activity, Thomas Mappes writes that "respect for persons entails that each of us recognize the rightful authority of other persons (as rational beings) to conduct their individual lives as they see fit."[32] Allowing the other person's consent to control when the other engages in sexual activity with me is to respect that person by taking his or her autonomy, his or her ability to reason and make choices, seriously, while not to allow the other to make the decision about when to engage in sexual activity with me is disrespectful (if not also officiously paternalistic). According to such a view of the power of consent, there can be no moral objection in principle to casual sexual activity, to sexual activity with strangers, or to promiscuity, as long as the persons involved in the activity genuinely agree to engage in their chosen sexual activities.[33]

Even if Mappes's free and informed consent criterion of the moral rightness of sexual activity is correct, we would still have to address several difficult questions. How *specific* must consent be? When one person agrees vaguely, and in the heat of the sexual moment, with another person, "yes, let's have sex," has the speaker consented to every type of sexual caress or coital position the second person might have in mind? And how *explicit* must consent be? Can consent be reliably implied by involuntarily behavior (moans, for example), and do nonverbal cues (erection, lubrication) decisively show that another person has consented to sex? Some insist that consent must be exceedingly specific as to the sexual acts to be carried out, and some would permit only explicit verbal consent, denying that body language by itself can do an adequate job of expressing the participant's desires and intentions.[34]

Another debate concerns the meaning of "voluntary" or "free," in the expression "free and informed consent." Whether consent is only necessary for the moral goodness of sexual activity, or also sufficient, any principle that relies on consent to make moral distinctions among sexual events presupposes a clear understanding of the "voluntary" aspect of consent. It is safe to say that participation in sexual activity ought not to be physically forced upon one person by another. But this obvious truth leaves matters wide open. The philosopher Onora O'Neill, for example, believes that casual sex, much or most of it, is morally wrong because the consent it involves is not likely to be sufficiently voluntary, in light of subtle pressures people commonly put on each other to engage in sexual activity. She argues that, if so, people who engage in casual sex are merely using each other, not treating each other with respect as persons, in a Kantian sense.[35]

One moral ideal is that genuinely voluntary or consensual participation in sexual activity requires not a hint of coercion or pressure of any sort. Because engaging in sexual activity can be risky or dangerous in many ways, physically, psychologically, and metaphysically, we would like to be sure, according to this moral ideal, that anyone who engages in sexual activity does so with perfectly voluntarily consent. Some philosophers have argued that this ideal can be realized only when there is substantial economic and social equality between the persons involved in a given sexual encounter. For example, a society that exhibits disparities in the incomes or wealth of its various members is one in which some people will be exposed to economic coercion. If some groups of people (women and members of ethnic minorities, in particular) have less economic and social power than others, members of these groups will be exposed to sexual coercion in particular, among other kinds. One immediate application of this thought is that prostitution, which to many sexual liberals is a business bargain made by a provider of sexual services and a client and is largely characterized by adequately free and informed consent, may be morally wrong, if the economic situation of the prostitute acts as a kind of pressure that negates the voluntary nature of his or her participation. Further, women with children who are economically dependent on their husbands may find themselves in the position of having to engage in sexual activity with their husbands, whether they want to or not, for fear of being abandoned; these women, too, may not be engaging in sexual activity fully voluntarily. The woman who allows herself to be nagged into sex by her husband worries that if she says "no" too often, she will suffer economically, if not also physically and psychologically.

The view that the presence of any kind of pressure at all is coercive, negates the voluntary nature of participation in sexual activity, and hence is morally objectionable has been expressed by, among others, Charlene Muehlenhard and Jennifer Schrag.[36] They list—to provide just two of their examples—"status coercion" (women are coerced into sexual activity or marriage by a man's occupation) and "discrimination against lesbians" (which compels women into having sexual relationships only with men) as forms of coercion that undermine the voluntary nature of participation by women in sexual activity with men. But depending on the kind of case we have in mind, it might be more accurate to say either that some pressures are not coercive and do not appreciably undermine voluntariness, or that some pressures are coercive but are nevertheless not morally objectionable. Is it always true that the presence of any kind of pressure put on one person by another amounts to coercion that negates the voluntary nature of consent, so that subsequent sexual activity is morally wrong? I wonder whether a woman who says to her husband, "buy me that mink coat or you will sleep on the couch for a month," is engaging in any objectionable behavior.

Conceptual Analysis

Conceptual philosophy of sexuality is concerned to clarify concepts that are central in this area of philosophy, including *sexual activity* and *sexual desire*. It also attempts to define less abstract concepts, such as prostitution, pornography, sexual harassment, and rape. Consider, for example, the concept *sexual activity* and how that concept is related to another central concept, *sexual pleasure*. One lesson to be learned from the following conceptual exploration is that conceptual philosophy of sex can be just as contentious as normative philosophy of sexuality, and that, as a result, firm conceptual conclusions are also hard to come by.

According to a notorious study published in 1999 in the *Journal of the American Medical Association*,[37] a large percent of undergraduate college students, about 60 percent, do not think that engaging in oral sex (fellatio and cunnilingus) is "having sex." This finding is at first glance very surprising, but it is not difficult to comprehend sympathetically. To be sure, philosophers easily conclude that oral sex is a specific type of sexual activity. But "sexual activity" is a philosopher's technical concept, while "having sex" is an ordinary language concept, which usually refers primarily to heterosexual intercourse. Thus when Monica Lewinsky told her confidant Linda Tripp that she did not "have sex" with William Jefferson Clinton, she was not necessarily self-deceived, lying, or pulling a fast one. She was merely relying on the ordinary language definition or criterion of "having sex," which is not identical to the philosopher's concept of "sexual activity," does not always include oral sex, and usually requires genital intercourse.

Another conclusion might be drawn from the *JAMA* survey. *If* heterosexual coitus by and large, or in many cases, produces more pleasure for the participants than does heterosexual oral sex, or at least in heterosexual intercourse there is greater mutuality of sexual pleasure than in one-directional heterosexual oral sex, and this is why ordinary thought and language tend to discount the ontological significance of oral sex, then perhaps we can use this insight to fashion a philosophical account of "sexual activity" that is consistent with ordinary thought.

In ordinary thought, whether a sexual act is nonmorally good or bad is often associated with whether it is judged to be a sexual act at all. Sometimes we derive little or no pleasure from a sexual act (say, we are primarily giving pleasure to another person, or we are selling it to the other person, or what we are doing just doesn't feel very good), and we think that even though the other person might have had a sexual experience, we didn't. Or the other person did try to provide us with sexual pleasure but failed miserably, whether from ignorance of technique or sheer sexual crudity. In such a case it would not be implausible to say that we did not undergo a sexual experience and so did not engage in a sexual act. If Ms. Lewinsky's performing oral sex on President Clinton was done only for his sake, for his sexual pleasure, and Lewinsky did it out of consideration for his needs and not hers, then perhaps she did not herself, after all, engage in a sexual act, even if he did.

Robert Gray is one philosopher who has taken up this line of ordinary thought and has argued that "sexual activity" should be analyzed in terms of the production of sexual pleasure. He asserts that "any activity might become a sexual activity" if sexual pleasure is derived from it, and "no activity is a sexual activity unless sexual pleasure is derived from it"— which together assert that the production of sexual pleasure is both necessary and sufficient for an act to be sexual.[38] Perhaps Gray is right, since we tend to think that holding hands is a sexual activity when sexual pleasure is produced by doing so, but otherwise holding hands is not (very) sexual. A handshake is normally not a sexual act, and usually does not yield sexual pleasure; but two lovers caressing each other's fingers can be a sexual act when it produces sexual pleasure for them.

There is another reason for taking seriously the idea that sexual activities are exactly those that produce sexual pleasure. What is it about a sexually perverted activity that makes it *sexual?* The act is unnatural, we might say, because it has no connection with one common purpose of sexual activity, that is, procreation. But the only thing that would seem to make the act a *sexual* perversion is that it does, on a fairly reliable basis, nonetheless produce sexual pleasure. Undergarment fetishism is a sexual perversion, and not, say, a "fabric" perversion, because it involves sexual pleasure. Similarly, what is it about homosexual sexual activities that makes them sexual? All such acts are nonprocreative, yet they share something very important in common with procreative heterosexual activities: they produce sexual pleasure, and the same sort of sexual pleasure.

Suppose I were to ask you, "How many sexual partners have you had during the last five years"? If you were on your toes, you would ask me, before answering, "What counts as a sexual partner?" (Maybe you are suspicious of my question because you have already read the essay by Greta Christina on this topic.)[39] At this point I should give you an adequate analysis of "sexual activity," and tell you to count anyone with whom you engaged in sexual activity according to the definition I provide. What I should definitely *not* do is to tell you to count only those people with whom you had a pleasing or satisfactory sexual experience, forgetting about, and not counting, those partners with whom you had disappointing, nonmorally bad sex. But if we accept Gray's analysis of sexual activity, according to which sexual acts are exactly those and only those that produce sexual pleasure, I should of course urge you not to count, over those five years, any person with whom you had a nonmorally bad sexual experience. You will end up reporting to me fewer sexual partners than you in fact had. (Maybe that will make you feel better about yourself.)

The general point is this. If "sexual activity" is logically dependent on "sexual pleasure," if sexual pleasure is thereby the criterion of sexual activity itself, then sexual pleasure cannot be the gauge of the nonmoral quality of sexual activities. That is, this analysis of "sexual activity" in terms of "sexual pleasure" conflates what it is for an act to *be* a sexual activity with what it is for an act to be a *nonmorally good* sexual activity. On such an analysis, procreative sexual activities, when the penis is placed into the vagina, would be sexual activities only when they produce sexual pleasure, and not when they are as boring as a common handshake. Further, the victim of a rape, who has not experienced nonmorally good sex, cannot claim that he or she was forced to engage in *sexual* activity, even if the act compelled on him or her was penis-vagina or penis-anus intercourse.

I would prefer to say that the couple who have lost sexual interest in each other, and who engage in routine sexual activities from which they derive no pleasure, are still performing a sexual act. But we are forbidden, by Gray's proposed analysis, from saying that they engage in nonmorally bad sexual activity, for on his view they have not engaged in any sexual activity at all. Rather, we could say at most that they tried to engage in sexual activity but failed to do so. It may be a sad fact about our sexual lives that we can engage in sexual activity and not derive any or much pleasure from it, but that fact should not give us reason for refusing to call these unsatisfactory events "sexual."

Notes

1. *The Limits of Love* (University Park: Pennsylvania State University Press, 1987), 47.

2. See Robert Mapplethorpe's 1978 photograph *Helmut and Brooks,* reproduced in Richard Mohr, *Gay Ideas* (Boston, Mass.: Beacon Press, 1992), 189.

3. *The Examined Life* (New York: Simon and Schuster, 1989), 67.

4. *The Examined Life,* 61.

5. *Love and Will* (New York: Norton, 1969), 75.

6. "Homosex/Ethics," in Timothy Murphy, ed., *Gay Ethics* (Binghamton, N.Y.: Haworth Press, 1994), 9–25, at 10. For more on sex as language, see Robert Solomon, "Sexual Paradigms," in this volume, 21–29.

7. "Sexual Behavior: Another Position," in this volume, 31–38, at 37.

8. "An Unromantic Reply to 'Marital Friendship'," in Alan Soble, ed., *Sex, Love, and Friendship* (Amsterdam: Editions Rodopi, 1997), 429–32, at 432.

9. Roger Scruton, *Sexual Desire: A Moral Philosophy of the Erotic* (New York: Free Press, 1986), 337.

10. *Lectures on Ethics,* trans. Louis Infield (New York: Harper and Row, 1963), 163 (in this volume, 200). On Kant, see the essays in Part 4 of this collection.

11. *The City of God,* vol. 2, trans. John Healey (London: J. M. Dent, 1945), bk. 14, sect. 23, page 53.

12. Kant, *The Metaphysics of Morals,* trans. Mary Gregor (Cambridge, Eng.: Cambridge University Press, 1996), 62.

13. *On Marriage and Concupiscence,* in *The Works of Aurelius Augustine, Bishop of Hippo,* vol. 12, ed. Marcus Dods (Edinburgh, Scot.: T. & T. Clark, 1874), bk. 1, chap. 9, page 107.

14. See Russell Vannoy's spirited defense of the value of sexual activity for its own sake, in *Sex without Love: A Philosophical Exploration* (Buffalo, N.Y.: Prometheus, 1980).

15. *The Nature of Love,* vol. 2: *Courtly and Romantic* (Chicago, Ill.: University of Chicago Press, 1984), 382. See also Singer's contribution to this volume, "The Morality of Sex: Contra Kant," 259–72.

16. *Symposium,* trans. Michael Joyce, in *The Collected Dialogues of Plato,* ed. E. Hamilton and H. Cairns (Princeton, N.J.: Princeton University Press, 1961), 526–74; see (in any edition of the *Symposium*), sections 181a-e, 183e, 184d.

17. *The Four Loves* (New York: Harcourt Brace Jovanovich, 1960), chap. 5.

18. *Love and Friendship* (New York: Simon and Schuster, 1993), 19. The "or philosophy of sex" is my editorial addition.

19. *Good Sex: Perspectives on Sexual Ethics* (Lawrence: University Press of Kansas,

1993), 210. On Belliotti's *Good Sex,* see my "Book Note" in *Ethics* 105, 2 (1995): 447–48.

20. The philosopher David Mayo is possibly unique in arguing that we do not necessarily have a moral obligation to reveal our HIV status to potential sexual partners. See his provocative essay "An Obligation to Warn of HIV Infection?" in Soble, ed., *Sex, Love and Friendship,* 447–53.

21. Michael Slote argues that "sexual perversion" is an "inapplicable concept" ("Inapplicable Concepts and Sexual Perversion," in *Philosophy and Sex,* 1st edition, ed. Robert Baker and Frederick Elliston [Buffalo, N.Y.: Prometheus, 1975], 261–67, at 266); Graham Priest also calls it "inapplicable" and adds that "the notion of sexual perversion makes no sense" any longer ("Sexual Perversion," *Australasian Journal of Philosophy* 75, 3 [1997], 360–72, at 370, 371); Igor Primoratz thinks that "sexual perversion" is "a concept best discarded" (*Ethics and Sex* [London: Routledge, 1999], 63–66); Linda LeMoncheck wants to replace "sexual perversion" with "sexual difference" (*Loose Women, Lecherous Men: A Feminist Philosophy of Sex* [New York: Oxford University Press, 1997], 72, 80, 82–83); and Robert Gray submits that "sexual perversion" should "be dropped from our sexual vocabulary altogether" ("Sex and Sexual Perversion," in this volume, 57–66, at 66.

22. See the *Diagnostic and Statistical Manual of Mental Disorders,* 4th edition (Washington, D.C.: American Psychiatric Association, 1994), 493–538.

23. See Thomas Aquinas, *Summa Theologiae,* 60 vols. [1265–1273] (Cambridge: Blackfriars, 1964–76), vol. 43, 2a2ae, questions 153–154, passim.

24. Aquinas condemns sexual acts in which "the natural style of intercourse is not observed, as regards the proper organ or according to rather beastly and monstrous techniques" (question 154, article 11, 245). He might have meant this claim to apply to oral sex.

25. Thomas Nagel, "Sexual Perversion," in this volume, 9–20, at 16–17.

26. See, for discussion, Alan Soble, *Sexual Investigations* (New York: New York University Press, 1996), chap. 4.

27. *Sex, Body, and Pleasure: Reconstructing Christian Sexual Ethics* (Cleveland, Ohio: Pilgrim Press, 1994), 65. See Gudorf on my Website at <http://www.uno.edu/~asoble>; scroll to "Snippets." For a Christian defense of homosexual marriage, see also Patricia Jung and Ralph Smith, *Heterosexism: An Ethical Challenge* (Albany: State University of New York Press, 1993), as well as the suggestive remarks of Edward Vacek, "A Christian Homosexuality?" in this volume, 127–33. For a other perspectives on homosexual marriage, see Cheshire Calhoun, "Defending Marriage," in this volume, 147–73.

28. *Lectures on Ethics,* 170; in this volume, 204.

29. See, for example, John Finnis's contribution to John Finnis and Martha C. Nussbaum, "Is Homosexual Conduct Wrong? A Philosophical Exchange," in this volume, 97–100; and Finnis's "Law, Morality, and 'Sexual Orientation,'" *Notre Dame Law Review* 69, 5 (1994), 1049–76. For discussion of Finnis, see my "Masturbation: Conceptual and Ethical Matters," in this volume, 67–94, at 84–87.

30. *Lectures on Ethics,* in this volume, 202–3.

31. *Love and Responsibility* (New York: Farrar, Straus and Giroux, 1981), 30.

32. "Sexual Morality and the Concept of Using Another Person," in this vol-

ume, 207–23, at 208. Also defending the sufficiency of consent is Bernard Baumrin's "Sexual Immorality Delineated," in *Philosophy and Sex,* 2nd edition, ed. Robert Baker and Frederick Elliston (Buffalo, N.Y.: Prometheus, 1984), 300–11. For discussion of Mappes, see my "Sexual Use and What to Do about It: Internalist and Externalist Sexual Ethics," in this volume, 225–58, at 235–39.

33. Robin West argues that even when sexual activity is perfectly consensual, it can be harmful, especially to the women who participate in it. See her essay "The Harms of Consensual Sex," in this volume, 317–22.

34. For discussion of these topics, see my "Antioch's 'Sexual Offense Policy': A Philosophical Exploration," in this volume, 323–40.

35. "Between Consenting Adults," in her *Constructions of Reason: Explorations of Kant's Practical Philosophy* (Cambridge: Cambridge University Press, 1989), 105–25.

36. "Nonviolent Sexual Coercion," in *Acquaintance Rape: The Hidden Crime,* ed. Andrea Parrot and Laurie Bechhofer (New York: John Wiley, 1991), 115–28.

37. Stephanie Sanders and June Reinisch, "Would You Say You 'Had Sex' If . . . ?" *Journal of the American Medical Association* 281, 3 (20 January 1999), 275–77.

38. "Sex and Sexual Perversion," in this volume, 57–66, at 61.

39. "Are We Having Sex Now or What?" in this volume, 3–8.

PART 1

CONCEPTUAL ANALYSIS

Chapter 1

ARE WE HAVING SEX NOW OR WHAT?

Greta Christina

When I first started having sex with other people, I used to like to count them. I wanted to keep track of how many there had been. It was a source of some kind of pride, or identity anyway, to know how many people I'd had sex with in my lifetime. So, in my mind, Len was number one, Chris was number two, that slimy awful little heavy metal barbiturate addict whose name I can't remember was number three, Alan was number four, and so on. It got to the point where, when I'd start having sex with a new person for the first time, when he first entered my body (I was only having sex with men at the time), what would flash through my head wouldn't be "Oh, baby, baby you feel so good inside me," or "What the hell am I doing with this creep," or "This is boring, I wonder what's on TV." What flashed through my head was "Seven!"

Doing this had some interesting results. I'd look for patterns in the numbers. I had a theory for a while that every fourth lover turned out to be really great in bed, and would ponder what the cosmic significance of the phenomenon might be. Sometimes I'd try to determine what kind of person I was by how many people I'd had sex with. At eighteen, I'd had sex with ten different people. Did that make me normal, repressed, a total slut, a free-spirited bohemian, or what? Not that I compared my numbers with anyone else's—I didn't. It was my own exclusive structure, a game I played in the privacy of my own head.

Then the numbers started getting a little larger, as numbers tend to do, and keeping track became more difficult. I'd remember that the last one was *seventeen* and so this one must be *eighteen,* and then I'd start having doubts about whether I'd been keeping score accurately or not. I'd lie awake at night thinking to myself, well, there was Brad, and there was that guy on my birthday, and there was David and . . . no, wait, I forgot that guy I got drunk with at the social my first week at college . . . so that's seven, eight, nine . . . and by two in the morning I'd finally have it figured out. But there was always a nagging suspicion that maybe I'd missed someone, some dreadful tacky little scumball that I was trying to forget about having invited inside my body. And as much as I maybe wanted to forget about the sleazy little scumball, I wanted more to get that number right.

It kept getting harder, though. I began to question what counted as sex and what didn't. There was that time with Gene, for instance. I was pissed off at my boyfriend, David, for cheating on me. It was a major crisis, and Gene and I were friends and he'd been trying to get at me for weeks and I hadn't exactly been discouraging him. I went to see him that night to gripe about David. He was very sympathetic of course, and he gave me a backrub, and we talked and touched and confided and hugged, and then we started kissing, and then we snuggled up a little closer, and then we started fondling each other, you know, and then all heck broke loose, and we rolled around on the bed groping and rubbing and grabbing and smooching and pushing and pressing and squeezing. He never did actually get it in. He wanted to, and I wanted to too, but I had this thing about being faithful to my boyfriend, so I kept saying, "No, you can't do that, Yes, that feels so good, No, wait that's too much, Yes, yes, don't stop, No, stop that's enough." We never even got our clothes off. Jesus Christ, though, it was some night. One of the best, really. But for a long time I didn't count it as one of the times I'd had sex. He never got inside, so it didn't count.

Later, months and years later, when I lay awake putting my list together, I'd start to wonder: Why doesn't Gene count? Does he not count because he never got inside? Or does he not count because I had to preserve my moral edge over David, my status as the patient, ever-faithful, cheated-on, martyred girlfriend, and if what I did with Gene counts then I don't get to feel wounded and superior?

Years later, I did end up fucking Gene and I felt a profound relief because, at last, he definitely had a number, and I knew for sure that he did in fact count.

Then I started having sex with women, and, boy, howdy, did *that* ever shoot holes in the system. I'd always made my list of sex partners by defining sex as penile-vaginal intercourse—you know, screwing. It's a pretty simple distinction, a straightforward binary system. Did it go in or didn't it? Yes or no? One or zero? On or off? Granted, it's a pretty arbi-

trary definition, but it's the customary one, with an ancient and respected tradition behind it, and when I was just screwing men, there was
no compelling reason to question it.

But with women, well, first of all there's no penis, so right from the
start the tracking system is defective. And then, there are so many ways
women can have sex with each other, touching and licking and grinding
and fingering and fisting—with dildoes or vibrators or vegetables or
whatever happens to be lying around the house, or with nothing at all
except human bodies. Of course, that's true for sex between women and
men as well. But between women, no one method has a centuries-old tradition of being the one that counts. Even when we do fuck each other
there's no dick, so you don't get that feeling of This Is What's Important,
We Are Now Having Sex, objectively speaking, and all that other stuff is
just foreplay or afterplay. So when I started having sex with women the
binary system had to go, in favor of a more inclusive definition.

Which meant, of course, that my list of how many people I'd had sex
with was completely trashed. In order to maintain it I would have had to
go back and reconstruct the whole thing and include all those people I'd
necked with and gone down on and dry-humped and played touchy-
feely games with. Even the question of who filled the all-important Number One slot, something I'd never had any doubts about before, would
have to be re-evaluated.

By this time I'd kind of lost interest in the list anyway. Reconstructing
it would be more trouble than it was worth. But the crucial question remained: What counts as having sex with someone?

It was important for me to know. You have to know what qualifies as
sex because when you have sex with someone your relationship changes.
Right? *Right?* It's not that sex itself has to change things all that much.
But knowing you've had sex, being conscious of a sexual connection,
standing around making polite conversation with someone while thinking to yourself, "I've had sex with this person," that's what changes
things. Or so I believed. And if having sex with a friend can confuse or
change the friendship, think how bizarre things can get when you're not
sure whether you've had sex with them or not.

The problem was, as I kept doing more kinds of sexual things, the line
between *sex* and *not-sex* kept getting more hazy and indistinct. As I
brought more into my sexual experience, things were showing up on the
dividing line demanding my attention. It wasn't just that the territory I
labeled *sex* was expanding. The line itself had swollen, dilated, been
transformed into a vast gray region. It had become less like a border and
more like a demilitarized zone.

Which is a strange place to live. Not a bad place, just strange. It's like
juggling, or watchmaking, or playing the piano—anything that demands
complete concentrated awareness and attention. It feels like cognitive

dissonance, only pleasant. It feels like waking up from a compelling and realistic bad dream. It feels like the way you feel when you realize that everything you know is wrong, and a bloody good thing too, because it was painful and stupid and it really screwed you up.

But, for me, living in a question naturally leads to searching for an answer. I can't simply shrug, throw up my hands, and say, "Damned if I know." I have to explore the unknown frontiers, even if I don't bring back any secret treasure. So even if it's incomplete or provisional, I do want to find some sort of definition of what is and isn't sex.

I know when I'm *feeling* sexual. I'm feeling sexual if my pussy's wet, my nipples are hard, my palms are clammy, my brain is fogged, my skin is tingly and super-sensitive, my butt muscles clench, my heartbeat speeds up, I have an orgasm (that's the real giveaway), and so on. But feeling sexual with someone isn't the same as having sex with them. Good Lord, if I called it sex every time I was attracted to someone who returned the favor I'd be even more bewildered than I am now. Even *being* sexual with someone isn't the same as *having* sex with them. I've danced and flirted with too many people, given and received too many sexy, would-be-seductive backrubs, to believe otherwise.

I have friends who say, if you thought of it as sex when you were doing it, then it was. That's an interesting idea. It's certainly helped me construct a coherent sexual history without being a revisionist swine: redefining my past according to current definitions. But it really just begs the question. It's fine to say that sex is whatever I think it is; but then what do I think it *is*? What if, when I was doing it, I was *wondering* whether it counted?

Perhaps having sex with someone is the conscious, consenting, mutually acknowledged pursuit of shared sexual pleasure. Not a bad definition. If you are turning each other on and you say so and you keep doing it, then it's sex. It's broad enough to encompass a lot of sexual behavior beyond genital contact/orgasm; it's distinct enough *not* to include every instance of sexual awareness or arousal; and it contains the elements I feel are vital—acknowledgment, consent, reciprocity, and the pursuit of pleasure. But what about the situation where one person consents to sex without really enjoying it? Lots of people (myself included) have had sexual interactions that we didn't find satisfying or didn't really want and, unless they were actually forced on us against our will, I think most of us would still classify them as sex.

Maybe if *both* of you (or all of you) think of it as sex, then it's sex whether you're having fun or not. That clears up the problem of sex that's consented to but not wished-for or enjoyed. Unfortunately, it begs the question again, only worse: now you have to mesh different people's vague and inarticulate notions of what is and isn't sex and find the place where they overlap. Too messy.

How about sex as the conscious, consenting, mutually acknowledged pursuit of sexual pleasure of *at least one* of the people involved. That's better. It has all the key components, and it includes the situation where one person is doing it for a reason other than sexual pleasure—status, reassurance, money, the satisfaction and pleasure of someone they love, etc. But what if *neither* of you is enjoying it, if you're both doing it because you think the other one wants to? Ugh.

I'm having trouble here. Even the conventional standby—sex equals intercourse—has a serious flaw: it includes rape, which is something I emphatically refuse to accept. As far as I'm concerned, if there's no consent, it ain't sex. But I feel that's about the only place in this whole quagmire where I have a grip. The longer I think about the subject, the more questions I come up with. At what point in an encounter does it *become* sexual? If an interaction that begins nonsexually turns into sex, was it sex all along? What about sex with someone who's asleep? Can you have a situation where one person is having sex and the other isn't? It seems that no matter what definition I come up with, I can think of some real-life experience that calls it into question.

For instance, a couple of years ago I attended (well, hosted) an all-girl sex party. Out of the twelve other women there, there were only a few with whom I got seriously physically nasty. The rest I kissed or hugged or talked dirty with or just smiled at, or watched while they did seriously physically nasty things with each other. If we'd been alone, I'd probably say that what I'd done with most of the women there didn't count as having sex. But the experience, which was hot and sweet and silly and very, very special, had been created by all of us, and although I only really got down with a few, I felt that I'd been sexual with all of the women there. Now, when I meet one of the women from that party, I always ask myself: Have we had sex?

For instance, when I was first experimenting with sadomasochism, I got together with a really hot woman. We were negotiating about what we were going to do, what would and wouldn't be ok, and she said she wasn't sure she wanted to have sex. Now we'd been explicitly planning all kinds of fun and games—spanking, bondage, obedience—which I strongly identified as sexual activity. In her mind, though, *sex* meant direct genital contact, and she didn't necessarily want to do that with me. Playing with her turned out to be a tremendously erotic experience, arousing and stimulating and almost unbearably satisfying. But we spent the whole evening without even touching each other's genitals. And the fact that our definitions were so different made me wonder: Was it sex?

For instance, I worked for a few months as a nude dancer at a peep show. In case you've never been to a peep show, it works like this: the customer goes into a tiny, dingy black box, kind of like a phone booth, puts in quarters, and a metal plate goes up; the customer looks through a window at a little room/stage where naked women are dancing. One time, a guy came into one of the booths and started watching me and masturbating. I came over and squatted in front of him and started masturbating too, and we grinned at each other and watched each other and masturbated, and we both had a fabulous time. (I couldn't believe I was being paid to masturbate—tough job, but somebody has to do it . . . .) After he left I thought to myself: Did we just have sex? I mean, if it had been someone I knew, and if there had been no glass and no quarters, there'd be no question in my mind. Sitting two feet apart from someone, watching each other masturbate? Yup, I'd call that sex all right. But this was different, because it was a stranger, and because of the glass and the quarters. Was it sex?

I still don't have an answer.

Chapter 2

SEXUAL PERVERSION

Thomas Nagel

There is something to be learned about sex from the fact that we possess a concept of sexual perversion. I wish to examine the idea, defending it against the charge of unintelligibility and trying to say exactly
what about human sexuality qualifies it to admit of perversions. Let me
begin with some general conditions that the concept must meet if it is to
be viable at all. These can be accepted without assuming any particular
analysis.

First, if there are any sexual perversions, they will have to be sexual desires or practices that are in some sense unnatural, though the explanation of this natural/unnatural distinction is of course the main problem.
Second, certain practices will be perversions if anything is, such as shoe
fetishism, bestiality, and sadism; other practices, such as unadorned sexual intercourse, will not be; about still others there is controversy. Third,
if there are perversions, they will be unnatural sexual *inclinations* rather
than just unnatural practices adopted not from inclination but for other
reasons. Thus contraception, even if it is thought to be a deliberate perversion of the sexual and reproductive functions, cannot be significantly
described as a *sexual* perversion. A sexual perversion must reveal itself in
conduct that expresses an unnatural *sexual* preference. And although
there might be a form of fetishism focused on the employment of contraceptive devices, that is not the usual explanation for their use.

© Cambridge University Press, 1979. Reprinted, with the permission of Thomas Nagel
and Cambridge University Press, from Thomas Nagel, *Mortal Questions,* pp. 39–52. This is
a revised version of the essay that appeared in *Journal of Philosophy* 66:1 (1969), pp. 5–17.

The connection between sex and reproduction has no bearing on sexual perversion. The latter is a concept of psychological, not physiological, interest, and it is a concept that we do not apply to the lower animals, let alone to plants, all of which have reproductive functions that can go astray in various ways. (Think of seedless oranges.) Insofar as we are prepared to regard higher animals as perverted, it is because of their psychological, not their anatomical, similarity to humans. Furthermore, we do not regard as a perversion every deviation from the reproductive function of sex in humans: sterility, miscarriage, contraception, abortion.

Nor can the concept of sexual perversion be defined in terms of social disapprobation or custom. Consider all the societies that have frowned upon adultery and fornication. These have not been regarded as unnatural practices, but have been thought objectionable in other ways. What is regarded as unnatural admittedly varies from culture to culture, but the classification is not a pure expression of disapproval or distaste. In fact it is often regarded as a *ground* for disapproval, and that suggests that the classification has independent content.

I shall offer a psychological account of sexual perversion that depends on a theory of sexual desire and human sexual interactions. To approach this solution I shall first consider a contrary position that would justify skepticism about the existence of any sexual perversions at all, and perhaps even about the significance of the term. The skeptical argument runs as follows:

"Sexual desire is simply one of the appetites, like hunger and thirst. As such it may have various objects, some more common than others perhaps, but none in any sense 'natural'. An appetite is identified as sexual by means of the organs and erogenous zones in which its satisfaction can be to some extent localized, and the special sensory pleasures which form the core of that satisfaction. This enables us to recognize widely divergent goals, activities, and desires as sexual, since it is conceivable in principle that anything should produce sexual pleasure and that a nondeliberate, sexually charged desire for it should arise (as a result of conditioning, if nothing else). We may fail to empathize with some of these desires, and some of them, like sadism, may be objectionable on extraneous grounds, but once we have observed that they meet the criteria for being sexual, there is nothing more to be said on *that* score. Either they are sexual or they are not: sexuality does not admit of imperfection, or perversion, or any other such qualification—it is not that sort of affection."

This is probably the received radical position. It suggests that the cost of defending a psychological account may be to deny that sexual desire is an appetite. But insofar as that line of defense is plausible, it should make us suspicious of the simple picture of appetites on which the skepticism depends. Perhaps the standard appetites, like hunger, cannot be classed as pure appetites in that sense either, at least in their human versions.

Can we imagine anything that would qualify as a gastronomical perversion? Hunger and eating, like sex, serve a biological function and also play a significant role in our inner lives. Note that there is little temptation to describe as perverted an appetite for substances that are not nourishing: we should probably not consider someone's appetite *perverted* if he liked to eat paper, sand, wood, or cotton. Those are merely rather odd and very unhealthy tastes: they lack the psychological complexity that we expect of perversions. (Coprophilia, being already a sexual perversion, may be disregarded.) If on the other hand someone liked to eat cookbooks, or magazines with pictures of food in them, and preferred these to ordinary food—or if when hungry he sought satisfaction by fondling a napkin or ashtray from his favorite restaurant—then the concept of perversion might seem appropriate (it would be natural to call it gastronomical fetishism). It would be natural to describe as gastronomically perverted someone who could eat only by having food forced down his throat through a funnel, or only if the meal were a living animal. What helps is the peculiarity of the desire itself, rather than the inappropriateness of its object to the biological function that the desire serves. Even an appetite can have perversions if in addition to its biological function it has a significant psychological structure.

In the case of hunger, psychological complexity is provided by the activities that give it expression. Hunger is not merely a disturbing sensation that can be quelled by eating; it is an attitude toward edible portions of the external world, a desire to treat them in rather special ways. The method of ingestion: chewing, savoring, swallowing, appreciating the texture and smell, all are important components of the relation, as is the passivity and controllability of the food (the only animals we eat live are helpless mollusks). Our relation to food depends also on our size: we do not live upon it or burrow into it like aphids or worms. Some of these features are more central than others, but an adequate phenomenology of eating would have to treat it as a relation to the external world and a way of appropriating bits of that world, with characteristic affection. Displacements or serious restrictions of the desire to eat could then be described as perversions, if they undermined that direct relation between man and food which is the natural expression of hunger. This explains why it is easy to imagine gastronomical fetishism, voyeurism, exhibitionism, or even gastronomical sadism and masochism. Some of these perversions are fairly common.

If we can imagine perversions of an appetite like hunger, it should be possible to make sense of the concept of sexual perversion. I do not wish to imply that sexual desire is an appetite—only that being an appetite is no bar to admitting of perversions. Like hunger, sexual desire has as its characteristic object a certain relation with something in the external world; only in this case it is usually a person rather than an omelet, and the relation is considerably more complicated. This added complication allows scope for correspondingly complicated perversions.

The fact that sexual desire is a feeling about other persons may encourage a pious view of its psychological content—that it is properly the expression of some other attitude, like love, and that when it occurs by itself it is incomplete or subhuman. (The extreme Platonic version of such a view is that sexual practices are all vain attempts to express something they cannot in principle achieve: this makes them all perversions, in a sense.) But sexual desire is complicated enough without having to be linked to anything else as a condition for phenomenological analysis. Sex may serve various functions—economic, social, altruistic—but it also has its own content as a relation between persons.

The object of sexual attraction is a particular individual, who transcends the properties that make him attractive. When different persons are attracted to a single person for different reasons—eyes, hair, figure, laugh, intelligence—we nevertheless feel that the object of their desire is the same. There is even an inclination to feel that this is so if the lovers have different sexual aims, if they include both men and women, for example. Different specific attractive characteristics seem to provide enabling conditions for the operation of a single basic feeling, and the different aims all provide expressions of it. We approach the sexual attitude toward the person through the features that we find attractive, but these features are not the objects of that attitude.

This is very different from the case of an omelet. Various people may desire it for different reasons, one for its fluffiness, another for its mushrooms, another for its unique combination of aroma and visual aspect; yet we do not enshrine the transcendental omelet as the true common object of their affections. Instead we might say that several desires have accidentally converged on the same object: any omelet with the crucial characteristics would do as well. It is not similarly true that any person with the same flesh distribution and way of smoking can be substituted as object for a particular sexual desire that has been elicited by those characteristics. It may be that they recur, but it will be a new sexual attraction with a new particular object, not merely a transfer of the old desire to someone else. (This is true even in cases where the new object is unconsciously identified with a former one.)

The importance of this point will emerge when we see how complex a psychological interchange constitutes the natural development of sexual attraction. This would be incomprehensible if its object were not a particular person, but rather a person of a certain *kind*. Attraction is only the beginning, and fulfillment does not consist merely of behavior and contact expressing this attraction, but involves much more.

The best discussion of these matters that I have seen appears in part III of Sartre's *Being and Nothingness*.[1] Sartre's treatment of sexual desire and of love, hate, sadism, masochism, and further attitudes toward others, depends on a general theory of consciousness and the body which we can neither expound nor assume here. He does not discuss perversion, and this is partly because he regards sexual desire as one form of the perpetual attempt of an embodied consciousness to come to terms with the existence of others, an attempt that is as doomed to fail in this form as it is in any of the others, which include sadism and masochism (if not certain of the more impersonal deviations) as well as several nonsexual attitudes. According to Sartre, all attempts to incorporate the other into my world as another subject, i.e. to apprehend him at once as an object for me and as a subject for whom I am an object, are unstable and doomed to collapse into one or other of the two aspects. Either I reduce him entirely to an object, in which case his subjectivity escapes the possession or appropriation I can extend to that object; or I become merely an object for him, in which case I am no longer in a position to appropriate his subjectivity. Moreover, neither of these aspects is stable; each is continually in danger of giving way to the other. This has the consequence that there can be no such thing as a *successful* sexual relation, since the deep aim of sexual desire cannot in principle be accomplished. It seems likely, therefore, that the view will not permit a basic distinction between successful or complete and unsuccessful or incomplete sex, and therefore cannot admit the concept of perversion.

I do not adopt this aspect of the theory, nor many of its metaphysical underpinnings. What interests me is Sartre's picture of the attempt. He says that the type of possession that is the object of sexual desire is carried out by "a double reciprocal incarnation" and that this is accomplished, typically in the form of a caress, in the following way: "I make myself flesh in order to impel the Other to realize *for herself* and *for me* her own flesh, and my caresses cause my flesh to be born for me in so far as it is for the Other *flesh causing her to be born as flesh*" (*Being and Nothingness*, p. 391; Sartre's italics). This incarnation in question is described variously as a clogging or troubling of consciousness, which is inundated by the flesh in which it is embodied.

The view I am going to suggest, I hope in less obscure language, is related to this one, but it differs from Sartre's in allowing sexuality to achieve its goal on occasion and thus in providing the concept of perversion with a foothold.

Sexual desire involves a kind of perception, but not merely a single perception of its object, for in the paradigm case of mutual desire there is a complex system of superimposed mutual perceptions—not only perceptions of the sexual object, but perceptions of oneself. Moreover, sexual awareness of another involves considerable self-awareness to begin with—more than is involved in ordinary sensory perception. The experience is felt as an assault on oneself by the view (or touch, or whatever) of the sexual object.

Let us consider a case in which the elements can be separated. For clarity we will restrict ourselves initially to the somewhat artificial case of desire at a distance. Suppose a man and a woman, whom we may call Romeo and Juliet, are at opposite ends of a cocktail lounge, with many mirrors on the walls which permit unobserved observation, and even mutual unobserved observation. Each of them is sipping a martini and studying other people in the mirrors. At some point Romeo notices Juliet. He is moved, somehow, by the softness of her hair and the diffidence with which she sips her martini, and this arouses him sexually. Let us say that X *senses* Y whenever X regards Y with sexual desire. (Y need not be a person, and X's apprehension of Y can be visual, tactile, olfactory, etc., or purely imaginary; in the present example we shall concentrate on vision). So Romeo senses Juliet, rather than merely noticing her. At this stage he is aroused by an unaroused object, so he is more in the sexual grip of his body than she of hers.

Let us suppose, however, that Juliet now senses Romeo in another mirror on the opposite wall, though neither of them yet knows that he is seen by the other (the mirror angles provide three-quarter views). Romeo then begins to notice in Juliet the subtle signs of sexual arousal, heavy-lidded stare, dilating pupils, faint flush, etc. This of course intensifies her bodily presence, and he not only notices but senses this as well. His arousal is nevertheless still solitary. But now, cleverly calculating the line of her stare without actually looking her in the eyes, he realizes that it is directed at him through the mirror on the opposite wall. That is, he notices, and moreover senses, Juliet sensing him. This is definitely a new development, for it gives him a sense of embodiment not only through his own reactions but through the eyes and reactions of another. Moreover, it is separable from the initial sensing of Juliet; for sexual arousal might begin with a person's sensing that he is sensed and being assailed by the perception of the other person's desire rather than merely by the perception of the person.

But there is a further step. Let us suppose that Juliet, who is a little slower than Romeo, now senses that he senses her. This puts Romeo in a position to notice, and be aroused by, her arousal at being sensed by him. He senses that she senses that he senses her. This is still another level of arousal, for he becomes conscious of his sexuality through his awareness of its effect on her and of her awareness that this effect is due to him. Once she takes the same step and senses that he senses her sensing him, it becomes difficult to state, let alone imagine, further iterations, though they may be logically distinct. If both are alone, they will presumably turn to look at each other directly, and the proceedings will continue on another plane. Physical contact and intercourse are natural extensions of this complicated visual exchange, and mutual touch can involve all the complexities of awareness present in the visual case, but with a far greater range of subtlety and acuteness.

Ordinarily, of course, things happen in a less orderly fashion—sometimes in a great rush—but I believe that some version of this overlapping system of distinct sexual perceptions and interactions is the basic framework of any full-fledged sexual relation and that relations involving only part of the complex are significantly incomplete. The account is only schematic, as it must be to achieve generality. Every real sexual act will be psychologically far more specific and detailed, in ways that depend not only on the physical techniques employed and on anatomical details, but also on countless features of the participants' conceptions of themselves and of each other, which become embodied in the act. (It is a familiar enough fact, for example, that people often take their social roles and the social roles of their partners to bed with them.)

The general schema is important, however, and the proliferation of levels of mutual awareness it involves is an example of a type of complexity that typifies human interactions. Consider aggression, for example. If I am angry with someone, I want to make him feel it, either to produce self-reproach by getting him to see himself through the eyes of my anger, and to dislike what he sees—or else to produce reciprocal anger or fear, by getting him to perceive my anger as a threat or attack. What I want will depend on the details of my anger, but in either case it will involve a desire that the object of that anger be aroused. This accomplishment constitutes the fulfillment of my emotion, through domination of the object's feelings.

Another example of such reflexive mutual recognition is to be found in the phenomenon of meaning, which appears to involve an intention to produce a belief or other effect in another by bringing about his recognition of one's intention to produce that effect. (That result is due to H. P. Grice,[2] whose position I shall not attempt to reproduce in detail.) Sex has a related structure: it involves a desire that one's partner be aroused by the recognition of one's desire that he or she be aroused.

It is not easy to define the basic types of awareness and arousal of which these complexes are composed, and that remains a lacuna in this discussion. In a sense, the object of awareness is the same in one's own case as it is in one's sexual awareness of another, although the two awarenesses will not be the same, the difference being as great as that between feeling angry and experiencing the anger of another. All stages of sexual perception are varieties of identification of a person with his body. What is perceived is one's own or another's *subjection* to or *immersion* in his body, a phenomenon which has been recognized with loathing by St. Paul and St. Augustine, both of whom regarded "the law of sin which is in my members" as a grave threat to the dominion of the holy will.[3] In sexual desire and its expression the blending of involuntary response with deliberate control is extremely important. For Augustine, the revolution launched against him by his body is symbolized by erection and the other involuntary physical components of arousal. Sartre too stresses the fact that the penis is not a prehensile organ. But mere involuntariness characterizes other bodily processes as well. In sexual desire the involuntary responses are combined with submission to spontaneous impulses: not only one's pulse and secretions but one's actions are taken over by the body; ideally, deliberate control is needed only to guide the expression of those impulses. This is to some extent also true of an appetite like hunger, but the takeover there is more localized, less pervasive, less extreme. One's whole body does not become saturated with hunger as it can with desire. But the most characteristic feature of a specifically sexual immersion in the body is its ability to fit into the complex of mutual perceptions that we have described. Hunger leads to spontaneous interactions with food; sexual desire leads to spontaneous interactions with other persons, whose bodies are asserting their sovereignty in the same way, producing involuntary reactions and spontaneous impulses in *them*. These reactions are perceived, and the perception of them is perceived, and that perception is in turn perceived; at each step the domination of the person by his body is reinforced, and the sexual partner becomes more possessible by physical contact, penetration, and envelopment.

Desire is therefore not merely the perception of a pre-existing embodiment of the other, but ideally a contribution to his further embodiment which in turn enhances the original subject's sense of himself. This explains why it is important that the partner be aroused, and not merely aroused, but aroused by the awareness of one's desire. It also explains the sense in which desire has unity and possession as its object: physical possession must eventuate in creation of the sexual object in the image of one's desire, and not merely in the object's recognition of that desire, or in his or her own private arousal.

Even if this is a correct model of the adult sexual capacity, it is not plausible to describe as perverted every deviation from it. For example, if the partners in heterosexual intercourse indulge in private heterosexual fantasies, thus avoiding recognition of the real partner, that would, on this model, constitute a defective sexual relation. It is not, however, generally regarded as a perversion. Such examples suggest that a simple dichotomy between perverted and unperverted sex is too crude to organize the phenomena adequately.

Still, various familiar deviations constitute truncated or incomplete versions of the complete configuration, and may be regarded as perversions of the central impulse. If sexual desire is prevented from taking its full interpersonal form, it is likely to find a different one. The concept of perversion implies that a normal sexual development has been turned aside by distorting influences. I have little to say about this causal condition. But if perversions are in some sense unnatural, they must result from interference with the development of a capacity that is there potentially.

It is difficult to apply this condition, because environmental factors play a role in determining the precise form of anyone's sexual impulse. Early experiences in particular seem to determine the choice of a sexual object. To describe some causal influences as distorting and others as merely formative is to imply that certain general aspects of human sexuality realize a definite potential whereas many of the details in which people differ realize an indeterminate potential, so that they cannot be called more or less natural. What is included in the definite potential is therefore very important, although the distinction between definite and indeterminate potential is obscure. Obviously a creature incapable of developing the levels of interpersonal sexual awareness I have described could not be deviant in virtue of the failure to do so. (Though even a chicken might be called perverted in an extended sense if it had been conditioned to develop a fetishistic attachment to a telephone.) But if humans will tend to develop some version of reciprocal interpersonal sexual awareness unless prevented, then cases of blockage can be called unnatural or perverted.

Some familiar deviations can be described in this way. Narcissistic practices and intercourse with animals, infants, and inanimate objects seem to be stuck at some primitive version of the first stage of sexual feeling. If the object is not alive, the experience is reduced entirely to an awareness of one's own sexual embodiment. Small children and animals permit awareness of the embodiment of the other, but present obstacles to reciprocity, to the recognition by the sexual object of the subject's desire as the source of his (the object's) sexual self-awareness. Voyeurism and exhibitionism are also incomplete relations. The exhibitionist wishes to display his desire without needing to be desired in return; he may even fear the sexual attention of others. A voyeur, on the other hand, need not require any recognition by his object at all: certainly not a recognition of the voyeur's arousal.

On the other hand, if we apply our model to the various forms that may be taken by two-party heterosexual intercourse, none of them seem clearly to qualify as perversions. Hardly anyone can be found these days to inveigh against oral-genital contact, and the merits of buggery are urged by such respectable figures as D. H. Lawrence and Norman Mailer. In general, it would appear that any bodily contact between a man and a woman that gives them sexual pleasure is a possible vehicle for the system of multi-level interpersonal awareness that I have claimed is the basic psychological content of sexual interaction. Thus a liberal platitude about sex is upheld.

The really difficult cases are sadism, masochism, and homosexuality. The first two are widely regarded as perversions and the last is controversial. In all three cases the issue depends partly on causal factors: do these dispositions result only when normal development has been prevented? Even the form in which this question has been posed is circular, because of the word 'normal'. We appear to need an independent criterion for a distorting influence, and we do not have one.

It may be possible to class sadism and masochism as perversions because they fall short of interpersonal reciprocity. Sadism concentrates on the evocation of passive self-awareness in others, but the sadist's engagement is itself active and requires a retention of deliberate control which may impede awareness of himself as a bodily subject of passion in the required sense. De Sade claimed that the object of sexual desire was to evoke involuntary responses from one's partner, especially audible ones. The infliction of pain is no doubt the most efficient way to accomplish this, but it requires a certain abrogation of one's own exposed spontaneity. A masochist on the other hand imposes the same disability on his partner as the sadist imposes on himself. The masochist cannot find a satisfactory embodiment as the object of another's sexual desire, but only as the object of his control. He is passive not in relation to his partner's passion but in relation to his nonpassive agency. In addition, the subjection to one's body characteristic of pain and physical restraint is of a very different kind from that of sexual excitement: pain causes people to contract rather than dissolve. These descriptions may not be generally accurate. But to the extent that they are, sadism and masochism would be disorders of the second stage of awareness—the awareness of oneself as an object of desire.

Homosexuality cannot similarly be classed as a perversion on phenomenological grounds. Nothing rules out the full range of interpersonal perceptions between persons of the same sex. The issue then depends on whether homosexuality is produced by distorting influences that block or displace a natural tendency to heterosexual development. And the influences must be more distorting than those which lead to a taste for large breasts or fair hair or dark eyes. These also are contingencies of sexual preference in which people differ, without being perverted.

The question is whether heterosexuality is the natural expression of male and female sexual dispositions that have not been distorted. It is an unclear question, and I do not know how to approach it. There is much support for an aggressive–passive distinction between male and female sexuality. In our culture the male's arousal tends to initiate the perceptual exchange, he usually makes the sexual approach, largely controls the course of the act, and of course penetrates whereas the woman receives. When two men or two women engage in intercourse they cannot both adhere to these sexual roles. But a good deal of deviation from them occurs in heterosexual intercourse. Women can be sexually aggressive and men passive, and temporary reversals of role are not uncommon in heterosexual exchanges of reasonable length. For these reasons it seems to be doubtful that homosexuality must be a perversion, though like heterosexuality it has perverted forms.

Let me close with some remarks about the relation of perversion to good, bad, and morality. The concept of perversion can hardly fail to be evaluative in some sense, for it appears to involve the notion of an ideal or at least adequate sexuality which the perversions in some way fail to achieve. So, if the concept is viable, the judgment that a person or practice or desire is perverted will constitute a sexual evaluation, implying that better sex, or a better specimen of sex, is possible. This in itself is a very weak claim, since the evaluation might be in a dimension that is of little interest to us. (Though, if my account is correct, that will not be true.)

Whether it is a moral evaluation, however, is another question entirely—one whose answer would require more understanding of both morality and perversion than can be deployed here. Moral evaluation of acts and of persons is a rather special and very complicated matter, and by no means all our evaluations of persons and their activities are moral evaluations. We make judgments about people's beauty or health or intelligence which are evaluative without being moral. Assessments of their sexuality may be similar in that respect.

Furthermore, moral issues aside, it is not clear that unperverted sex is necessarily *preferable* to the perversions. It may be that sex which receives the highest marks for perfection *as sex* is less enjoyable than certain perversions; and if enjoyment is considered very important, that might outweigh considerations of sexual perfection in determining rational preference.

That raises the question of the relation between the evaluative content of judgments of perversion and the rather common *general* distinction between good and bad sex. The latter distinction is usually confined to sexual acts, and it would seem, within limits, to cut across the other: even someone who believed, for example, that homosexuality was a perversion could admit a distinction between better and worse homosexual sex, and might even allow that good homosexual sex could be better *sex* than not very good unperverted sex. If this is correct, it supports the position that, if judgments of perversion are viable at all, they represent only one aspect of the possible evaluation of sex, even *qua sex*. Moreover it is not the only important aspect: sexual deficiencies that evidently do not constitute perversions can be the object of great concern.

Finally, even if perverted sex is to that extent not so good as it might be, bad sex is generally better than none at all. This should not be controversial: it seems to hold for other important matters, like food, music, literature, and society. In the end, one must choose from among the available alternatives, whether their availability depends on the environment or on one's own constitution. And the alternatives have to be fairly grim before it becomes rational to opt for nothing.

Notes

1. *L'Etre et le Néant* (Paris: Gallimand, 1943), translated by Hazel E. Barnes (New York: Philosophical Library, 1956).

2. 'Meaning', *Philosophical Review*, LXVI, no. 3 (July, 1957), 377–88.

3. See Romans, VII, 23; and the *Confessions*, bk VIII, pt V.

Chapter 3

SEXUAL PARADIGMS

Robert Solomon

It is a cocktail lounge, well-lit and mirrored, not a bar, martinis and not beer, two strangers—a furtive glance from him, shy recognition from her. It is 1950's American high comedy; boy arouses girl, both are led through ninety minutes of misunderstandings of identity and intention, and, finally, by the end of the popcorn, boy kisses girl with a clean-cut fade-out or panned clip of a postcard horizon. It is one of the dangers of conceptual analysis that the philosopher's choice of paradigms betrays a personal bias, but it is an exceptional danger of sexual conceptual analysis that one's choice of paradigms also betrays one's private fantasies and personal obsessions.[1] No doubt that is why, despite their extraprofessional interest in the subject, most philosophers would rather write about indirect discourse than intercourse, the philosophy of mind rather than the philosophy of body.

In Tom Nagel's pioneering effort[2] there are too many recognizable symptoms of liberal American sexual mythology. His analysis is cautious and competent, but absolutely sexless. His Romeo and Juliet exemplify at most a romanticized version of the initial phases of (hetero)-sexual attraction in a casual and innocent pickup. They "arouse" each other, but there is no indication to what end. They "incarnate each other as flesh," in Sartre's awkward but precise terminology, but Nagel gives us no clue as to why they should indulge in such a peculiar activity. Presumably a pair of dermatologists or fashion models might have a similar effect on

Reprinted, with the permission of Robert Solomon and the *Journal of Philosophy*, from *Journal of Philosophy* 71:11 (1974), pp. 336–45.

each other, but without the slightest hint of sexual intention. What makes this situation paradigmatically sexual? We may assume, as we would in a Doris Day comedy, that the object of this protracted arousal is sexual intercourse, but we are not told this. Sexuality without content. Liberal sexual mythology takes this Hollywood element of "leave it to the imagination" as its starting point and adds the equally inexplicit suggestion that whatever activities two consenting adults choose as the object of their arousal and its gratification is "their business." In a society with such secrets, pornography is bound to serve a radical end as a vulgar valve of reality. In a philosophical analysis that stops short of the very matter investigated, a bit of perverseness may be necessary just in order to refocus the question.

Sexual desire is distinguished, like all desires, by its aims and objects. What are these peculiarly sexual aims and objects? Notice that Nagel employs a fairly standard "paradigm case argument" in his analysis; he begins,

> . . . certain practices will be perversions if anything is, such as shoe fetishism, bestiality, and sadism; other practices, such as unadorned sexual intercourse, will not be. (9)

So we can assume that the end of Romeo and Juliet's tryst will be intercourse—we do not know whether "adorned" or not. But what is it that makes intercourse the paradigm of sexual activity—its biological role in conception, its heterosexuality, its convenience for mutual orgasm? Would Nagel's drama still serve as a sexual paradigm if Juliet turns out to be a virgin, or if Romeo and Juliet find that they are complementarily sado-masochistic, if Romeo is in drag, if they are both knee-fetishists? Why does Nagel choose two *strangers*? Why not, as in the days of sexual moralism, a happily married couple enjoying their seventh anniversary? Or is not the essence of sex, as Sartre so brutally argues, Romeo and Juliet's mutual attempts to possess each other, with each's own enjoyment only a secondary and essentially distracting effect? Are we expected to presume the most prominent paradigm, at least since Freud, the lusty ejaculation of Romeo into the submissive, if not passive, Juliet? Suppose Juliet is in fact a prostitute, skillfully mocking the signs of innocent arousal: is this a breach of the paradigm, or might not such subsequent "unadorned" intercourse be just the model that Nagel claims to defend?

To what end does Romeo arouse Juliet? And to what end does Juliet become affected and in turn excite Romeo? In this exemplary instance, I would think that "unadorned" intercourse would be perverse, or at least distasteful, in the extreme. It would be different, however, if the paradigm were our seven-year married couple, for in such cases "adorned" intercourse might well be something of a rarity. In homosexual encounters, in the frenzy of adolescent virginal petting, in cases in which intercourse is restricted for temporary medical or political reasons, arousal may be no different, even though intercourse cannot be the end. And it is only in the crudest cases of physiological need that the desire for intercourse is the sole or even the leading component in the convoluted motivation of sexuality. A nineteen-year-old sailor back after having discussed nothing but sex on a three-month cruise may be so aroused, but that surely is not the nature of Juliet's arousal. Romeo may remind her of her father, or of her favorite philosophy professor, and he may inspire respect, or fear, or curiosity. He may simply arouse self-consciousness or embarrassment. Any of these attitudes may be dominant, but none is particularly sexual.

Sexuality has an essential bodily dimension, and this might well be described as the "incarnation" or "submersion" of a person into his body. The end of this desire is interpersonal communication; but where Sartre gives a complex theory of the nature of this communication, Nagel gives us only an empty notion of "multi-level interpersonal awareness." Presumably the mutual arousal that is the means to this awareness is enjoyable in itself. But it is important that Nagel resists the current (W.) Reichian-American fetish for the wonders of the genital orgasm, for he does not leap to the facile conclusion that the aim of sexual activity is mutual or at least personal orgasm. It is here that Nagel opens a breach with liberal sexual mythology, one that might at first appear absurd because of his total neglect of the role of the genitalia and orgasm in sexuality. But we have an overgenitalized conception of sexuality, and, if sexual satisfaction involves and even requires orgasm, it does not follow that orgasm is the goal of the convoluted sexual games we play with each other. Orgasm is the "end" of sexual activity, perhaps, but only in the sense that swallowing is the "end" of tasting a Viennese torte.

There was a time, and it was not long ago and may come soon again, when sexuality required defending. It had to be argued that we had a right to sex, not for any purpose other than our personal enjoyment. But that defense has turned stale, and sexual deprivation is no longer our problem. The "swollen bladder" model of repressed sexuality may have been convincing in sex-scared bourgeois Vienna of 1905, but not today, where the problem is not sexual deprivation but sexual dissatisfaction. The fetishism of the orgasm, now shared by women as well as men, threatens our sex lives with becoming antipersonal and mechanical, anxiety-filled athletic arenas with mutual multiple orgasm its goal. Behind much of this unhappiness and anxiety, ironically, stands the liberal defense of sexuality as enjoyment. It is one of the virtues of Nagel's essay that he begins to overcome this oppressive liberal mythology. But at the same time he relies upon it for his support and becomes trapped in it, and the result is an account which displays the emptiness we have pointed out and the final note of despair with which he ends his essay.

Liberal sexual mythology appears to stand upon a tripod of mutually supporting platitudes: (1) and foremost, that the essential aim (and even the sole aim) of sex is enjoyment; (2) that sexual activity is and ought to be essentially private activity; and (3) that any sexual activity is as valid as any other. The first platitude was once a radical proposition, a reaction to the conservative and pious belief that sexual activity was activity whose end was reproduction, the serving of God's will or natural law. Kant, for example, always good for a shocking opinion in the realm of normative ethics, suggests that sexual lust is an appetite with an end intended by nature, and that any sexual activity contrary to that end is "unnatural and revolting," by which one "makes himself an object of abomination and stands bereft of all reverence of any kind."[3] It was Sigmund Freud who destroyed this long-standing paradigm, in identifying sexuality as "discharge of tension" (physical and psychological), which he simply equated with "pleasure," regardless of the areas of the body or what activities or how many people happened to be involved. Sex was thus defined as self-serving, activity for its own sake, with pleasure as its only principle. If Freud is now accused of sexual conservatism, it is necessary to remind ourselves that he introduced the radical paradigm that is now used against him. Since Freud's classic efforts, the conception of sexuality as a means to other ends, whether procreation or pious love, has become bankrupt in terms of the currency of opinion. Even radical sexual ideology has confined its critique to the social and political *abuses* of this liberal platitude without openly rejecting it.

The second platitude is a hold-over from more conservative days, in which sexual activity, like defecation, menstruation, and the bodily reactions to illness, was considered distasteful, if not shameful and to be hidden from view. Yet this conservative platitude is as essential as the first, for the typically utilitarian argument in defense of sexuality as enjoyment is based on the idea that sex is private activity and, when confined to "consenting adults," should be left as a matter of taste. And sex is, we are reminded by liberals, a natural appetite, and therefore a matter of taste.

The platitude of privacy also bolsters the third principle, still considered a radical principle by many, that any sexual activity is as valid as any other. Again, the utilitarian argument prevails, that private and mutually consented activity between adults, no matter how distasteful it might be to others and no matter how we may think its enthusiasts to be depraved, is "their own business."

Nagel's analysis calls this tri-part ideology to his side, although he clearly attempts to go beyond it as well. The platitude of enjoyment functions only loosely in his essay, and at one point he makes it clear that sexuality need not aim at enjoyment. ("It may be that . . . perfection *as sex* is less enjoyable than certain perversions; and if enjoyment is considered very important, that might outweigh considerations of sexual perfection in determining rational preference" (19). His central notion of "arousal," however, is equivocal. On the one hand, arousal is itself not necessarily enjoyable, particularly if it fails to be accompanied with expectations of release. But on the other hand, Nagel's "arousal" plays precisely the same role in his analysis that "tension" (or "cathexis") plays in Freud, and though the arousal itself is not enjoyable, its release is, and the impression we get from Nagel, which Freud makes explicit, is that sexual activity is the intentional arousal both of self and other in order to enjoy its release. On this interpretation, Nagel's analysis is perfectly in line with post-Freudian liberal theory.

Regarding the second platitude, Nagel's analysis does not mention it, but rather it appears to be presupposed throughout that sexuality is a private affair. One might repeat that the notion of privacy is more symptomatic of his analysis itself. One cannot imagine J. L. Austin spending a dozen pages describing the intentions and inclinations involved in a public performance of making a promise or christening a ship without mentioning the performance itself. Yet Nagel spends that much space giving us the preliminaries of sexuality without ever quite breaching the private sector in which sexual activity is to be found.

The third platitude emerges only slowly in Nagel's essay. He begins by chastising an approach to that same conclusion by a radical "skeptic," who argues of sexual desires, as "appetites,"

> Either they are sexual or they are not: sexuality does not admit of imperfection, or perversion, or any other such qualification. (10)

Nagel's analysis goes beyond this "skepticism" in important ways, yet he does conclude that "any bodily contact between a man and a woman that gives them sexual *pleasure* [italics mine] is a possible vehicle for the system of multi-level interpersonal awareness that I have claimed is the basic psychological content of sexual interaction" (17). Here the first platitude is partially employed to support the third, presumably with the second implied. Notice again that Nagel has given us no indication what distinguishes "sexual pleasure" from other pleasures, whether bodily pleasures or the enjoyment of conquest or domination, seduction or submission, sleeping with the president's daughter or earning thirty dollars.

To knock down a tripod, one need kick out only one of its supporting legs. I for one would not wish to advocate, along with several recent sexual pundits, an increased display of fornication and fellatio in public places, nor would I view the return of "sexual morality" as a desirable state of affairs. Surprisingly, it is the essential enjoyment of sex that is the least palatable of the liberal myths.

No one would deny that sex is enjoyable, but it does not follow that sexuality is the activity of "pure enjoyment" and that "gratification," or "pure physical pleasure," that is, orgasm, is its end. Sex is indeed pleasurable, but, as Aristotle argued against the hedonists of his day, this enjoyment accompanies sexual activity and its ends, but is not that activity or these ends. We enjoy being sexually satisfied; we are not satisfied by our enjoyment. In fact, one might reasonably hypothesize that the performance of any activity, pleasurable or not, which is as intensely promoted and obsessively pursued as sex in America would provide tremendous gratification. [One might further speculate on the fact that recent American politics shows that "every (white, male Christian) American boy's dream of becoming President" seems to encourage the exploitation of all three sexual platitudes of enjoyment, privacy, and "anything goes." (Cf. H. Kissinger, "Power is the ultimate aphrodisiac.")]

If sexuality does not essentially aim at pleasure, does it have any purpose? Jean-Paul Sartre has given us an alternative to the liberal theory in his *Being and Nothingness*, in which he argues that our sexual relations with others, like all our various relationships with others, are to be construed as *conflicts*, modeled after Hegel's parable of master and slave. Sexual desire is not desire for pleasure, and pleasure is more likely to distract us from sexuality than to deepen our involvement. For Sartre, sexual desire is the desire to possess, to gain recognition of one's own freedom at the expense of the other. By "incarnating" and degrading him/her in flesh, one reduces him/her to an object. Sadism is but an extension of this domination over the other. Or one allows himself to be "incarnated" as a devious route to the same end, making the other his/her sexual slave. Sexual activity concentrates its attention on the least personal, most inert parts of the body—breasts, thighs, stomach, and emphasizes awkward and immobile postures and activities. On this model, degradation is the central activity of sex, to convince the other that he/she is a slave, to persuade the other of one's own power, whether it be through the skills of sexual technique or through the passive demands of being sexually served. Intercourse has no privileged position in this model, except that intercourse, particularly in these liberated times in which it has become a contest, is ideal for this competition for power and recognition. And no doubt Sartre, who, like Freud, adopts a paradigmatically male perspective, senses that intercourse is more likely to be degrading to the woman, who thus begins at a disadvantage.

Sartre's notion of sexuality, taken seriously, would be enough to keep us out of bed for a month. Surely, we must object, something has been left out of account, for example, the two-person *Mitsein* that Sartre himself suggests in the same book. It is impossible for us to delve into the complex ontology that leads Sartre into this pessimistic model, but its essential structure is precisely what we need to carry us beyond the liberal mythology. According to Sartre, sexuality is interpersonal communication with the body as its medium. Sartre's mistake, if we may be brief, is his narrow constriction of the message of that communication to mutual degradation and conflict. Nagel, who accepts Sartre's communication model but, in line with the liberal mythology, seeks to reject its pessimistic conclusions, makes a mistake in the opposite direction. He accepts the communication model, but leaves it utterly without content. What is communicated, he suggests, is arousal. But, as we have seen, arousal is too broad a notion; we must know arousal of what, for what, to what end. Nagel's notion of "arousal" and "interpersonal awareness" gives us an outline of the grammar of the communication model, but no semantics. One might add that sexual activity in which what is aroused and intended are pleasurable sensations alone is a limiting and rare case. A sensation is only pleasurable or enjoyable, not in itself, but in the context of the meaning of the activity in which it is embedded. This is as true of orgasm as it is of a hard passion-bite on the shoulder.

This view of sexuality answers some strong questions which the liberal model leaves a mystery. If sex is pure physical enjoyment, why is sexual activity between persons far more satisfying than masturbation, where, if we accept recent physiological studies, orgasm is at its highest intensity and the post-coital period is cleansed of its interpersonal hassles and arguments? On the Freudian model, sex with other people ("objects") becomes a matter of "secondary process," with masturbation primary. On the communication model, masturbation is like talking to yourself; possible, even enjoyable, but clearly secondary to sexuality in its broader interpersonal context. (It is significant that even this carnal solipsism is typically accompanied by imaginings and pictures; "No masturbation without representation," perhaps.) If sex is physical pleasure, then the fetish of the genital orgasm is no doubt justifiable, but then why in our orgasm-cluttered sex lives are we so dissatisfied? Because orgasm is not the "end" of sex but its resolution, and obsessive concentration on reaching climax effectively overwhelms or distorts whatever else is being said sexually. It is this focus on orgasm that has made Sartre's model more persuasive; for the battle over the orgasm, whether in selfish or altruistic guise ("my orgasm first" or "I'll *give* you the best ever") has become an unavoidable medium for conflict and control. "Unadorned sexual intercourse," on this model, becomes the ultimate perversion, since it is the sexual equivalent of hanging up the telephone without saying anything. Even an obscene telephone caller has a message to convey.

Sexual activity consists in speaking what we might call "body language." It has its own grammar, delineated by the body, and its own phonetics of touch and movement. Its unit of meaningfulness, the bodily equivalent of a sentence, is the *gesture*. No doubt one could add considerably to its vocabulary, and perhaps it could be possible to discuss world politics or the mind-body problem by an appropriate set of invented gestures. But body language is essentially expressive, and its content is limited to interpersonal attitudes and feelings—shyness, domination, fear, submissiveness and dependence, love or hatred or indifference, lack of confidence and embarrassment, shame, jealousy, possessiveness. There is little value in stressing the overworked point that such expressions are "natural" expressions, as opposed to verbal expressions of the same attitudes and feelings. In our highly verbal society, it may well be that verbal expression, whether it be poetry or clumsy blurting, feels more natural than the use of our bodies. Yet it does seem true that some attitudes, e.g., tenderness and trust, domination and passivity, are best expressed sexually. Love, it seems, is not best expressed sexually, for its sexual expression is indistinguishable from the expressions of a number of other attitudes. Possessiveness, mutual recognition, "being-with," and conflict are expressed by body language almost essentially, virtually as its deep structure, and here Sartre's model obtains its plausibility.

According to Nagel, "perversion" is "truncated or incomplete versions of the complete configuration" (16). But again, his emphasis is entirely on the form of "interpersonal awareness" rather than its content. For example, he analyzes sadism as "the concentration on the evocation of passive self-awareness in others . . . which impedes awareness of himself as a bodily subject of passion in the required sense." But surely sadism is not so much a breakdown in communication (any more than the domination of a conversation by one speaker, with the agreement of his listener, is a breach of language) as an excessive expression of a particular content, namely the attitude of domination, perhaps mixed with hatred, fear, and other negative attitudes. Similarly, masochism is not simply the relinquishing of one's activity (an inability to speak, in a sense), for the masochist may well be active in inviting punishment from his sadistic partner. Masochism is excessive expression of an attitude of victimization, shame, or inferiority. Moreover, it is clear that there is not the slightest taint of "perversion" in homosexuality, which need differ from heterosexuality only in its mode of resolution. Fetishism and bestiality certainly do constitute perversions, since the first is the same as, for example, talking to someone else's shoes, and the second like discussing Spinoza with a moderately intelligent sheep.

This model also makes it evident why Nagel chose as his example a couple of strangers; one has far more to say, for one can freely express one's fantasies as well as the truth, to a stranger. A husband and wife of seven years have probably been repeating the same messages for years, and their sexual activity now is probably no more than an abbreviated ritual incantation of the lengthy conversations they had years before. One can imagine Romeo and Juliet climbing into bed together each with a spectacular set of expectations and fantasies, trying to overwhelm each other with extravagant expressions and experiments. But it may be, accordingly, that they won't understand each other, or, as the weekend plods on, sex, like any extended conversation, tends to become either more truthful or more incoherent.

Qua body language, sex admits of at least two forms of perversion: one deviance of form, the other deviance in content. There are the techniques of sexuality, overly celebrated in our society, and there are the attitudes that these techniques allegedly express. Nagel and most theorists have concentrated on perversions in technique, deviations in the forms of sexual activity. But it seems to me that the more problematic perversions are the semantic deviations, of which the most serious are those involving insincerity, the bodily equivalent of the lie. Entertaining private fantasies and neglecting one's real sexual partner is thus an innocent semantic perversion, while pretended tenderness and affection that reverses itself soon after orgasm is a potentially vicious perversion. However, again joining Nagel, I would argue that perverse sex is not necessarily bad or immoral sex. Pretense is the premise of imagination as well as of falsehood, and sexual fantasies may enrich our lives far more than sexual realities alone. Perhaps it is an unfortunate comment on the poverty of contemporary life that our fantasies have become so confined, that our sexuality has been forced to serve needs which far exceed its expressive capacity. That is why the liberal mythology has been so disastrous, for it has rendered unconscious the expressive functions of sex in its stress on enjoyment and, in its platitude of privacy, has reduced sexuality to each man's/woman's private language, first spoken clumsily and barely articulately on wedding nights and in the back seats of Fords. It is thus understandable why sex is so utterly important in our lives, and why it is typically so unsatisfactory.

Notes

1. I confess, for example, that certain male biases infiltrate my own analysis. I thank Janice Moulton for pointing this out to me.

2. "Sexual Perversion," *The Journal of Philosophy* 66, no. 1 (1969), pp. 5–17. (This volume, pp. 9–20.)

3. *Metaphysics of Ethics*, trans. Semple (Edinburgh: Clark, 1971) IV, pt. I, ch. 1, sec. 7.

Chapter 4

SEXUAL BEHAVIOR: ANOTHER POSITION

Janice Moulton

We can often distinguish behavior that is sexual from behavior that is not. Sexual intercourse may be one clear example of the former, but other sexual behaviors are not so clearly defined. Some kissing is sexual; some is not. Sometimes looking is sexual; sometimes *not* looking is sexual. Is it possible, then, to *characterize* sexual behavior?

Thomas Nagel in "Sexual Perversion"[1] and Robert Solomon in "Sexual Paradigms"[2] each offer an answer to this question. Nagel analyzes sexual desire as a "complex system of superimposed mutual perceptions" (13). He claims that sexual relations that do not fit his account are incomplete and, consequently, perversions.

Solomon claims that sexual behavior should be analyzed in terms of goals rather than feelings. He maintains that "the end of this desire is interpersonal communication" (23) and not enjoyment. According to Solomon, the sexual relations between regular partners will be inferior to novel encounters because there is less remaining to communicate sexually.

I believe that sexual behavior will not fit any single characterization; that there are at least two sorts of sexual behavior to characterize. Both Nagel and Solomon have interesting things to say about one sort of sexual behavior. However, both have assumed that a model of flirtation and

Reprinted, with the permission of Janice Moulton and the *Journal of Philosophy*, from *Journal of Philosophy* 73:16 (1976), pp. 537–46.

seduction constitutes an adequate model of sexual behavior in general. Although a characterization of flirtation and seduction can continue to apply to a relationship that is secret, forbidden, or in which there is some reason to remain unsure of one's sexual acceptability, I shall argue that most sexual behavior does not involve flirtation and seduction, and that what characterizes flirtation and seduction is not what characterizes the sexual behavior of regular partners. Nagel takes the development of what I shall call "sexual anticipation" to be characteristic of all sexual behavior and gives no account of sexual satisfaction.[3] Solomon believes that flirtation and seduction are different from regular sexual relationships. However, he too considers only characteristics of sexual anticipation in his analysis and concludes that regular sexual relationships are inferior to novel ones because they lack some of those characteristics.

Flirtation, seduction, and traditional courtship involve sexual feelings that are quite independent of physical contact. These feelings are increased by anticipation of success, winning, or conquest. Because what is anticipated is the opportunity for sexual intimacy and satisfaction, the feelings of sexual satisfaction are usually not distinguished from those of sexual anticipation. Sexual satisfaction involves sexual feelings which are increased by the other person's knowledge of one's preferences and sensitivities, the familiarity of their touch or smell or way of moving, and not by the novelty of their sexual interest.

It is easy to think that the more excitement and enthusiasm involved in the anticipation of an event, the more enjoyable and exciting the event itself is likely to be. However, anticipation and satisfaction are often divorced. Many experiences with no associated build-up of anticipation are very satisfying, and others, awaited and begun with great eagerness, produce no feelings of satisfaction at all. In sexual activity this dissociation is likely to be frequent. A strong feeling of sexual anticipation is produced by the uncertainty, challenge, or secrecy of novel sexual experiences, but the tension and excitement that increase anticipation often interfere with sexual satisfaction. The comfort and trust and experience with familiar partners may increase sexual satisfaction, but decrease the uncertainty and challenge that heighten sexual anticipation. Given the distinction between anticipation and satisfaction, there is no reason to believe that an increase of trust and love ought to increase feelings of sexual anticipation nor that sexual anticipation should be a prerequisite for any long-term sexual relationship.

For some people the processes that create sexual anticipation, the exchange of indirect signals, the awareness of the other person's sexual interest, and the accompanying sexual anticipation may be *all* that is valued in sexual behavior. Satisfaction is equated with release, the end of a good time, and is not considered a process in its own right. But although flirtation and seduction are the main objects of sexual fantasy and fiction, most people, even those whose sexual relations are frequently casual, seek to continue some sexual relationships after the flirtation and seduction are over, when the uncertainty and challenge are gone. And the motives, goals, and feelings of sexual satisfaction that characterize these continued sexual relations are not the same as the motives, goals, and feelings of sexual anticipation that characterize the novel sexual relations Nagel and Solomon have tried to analyze. Let us consider their accounts.

Nagel's account is illustrated by a tale of a Romeo and a Juliet who are sexually aroused by each other, notice each other's arousal and become further aroused by that:

> He senses that she senses that he senses her. This is still another level of arousal, for he becomes conscious of his sexuality through his awareness of its effect on her and of her awareness that this effect is due to him. Once she takes the same step and senses that he senses her sensing him, it becomes difficult to state, let alone imagine, further iterations, though they may be logically distinct. If both are alone, they will presumably turn to look at each other directly, and the proceedings will continue on another plane. Physical contact and intercourse are natural extensions of this complicated visual exchange, and mutual touch can involve all the complexities of awareness present in the visual case, but with a far greater range of subtlety and acuteness.
>
> Ordinarily, of course, things happen in a less orderly fashion—sometimes in a great rush—but I believe that some version of this overlapping system of distinct sexual perceptions and interactions is the basic framework of any full-fledged sexual relation and that relations involving only part of the complex are significantly incomplete. (14–15)

Nagel then characterizes sexual perversion as a "truncated or incomplete version" (16) of sexual *arousal,* rather than as some deviation from a standard of subsequent physical interaction.

Nagel's account applies only to the development of sexual anticipation. He says that "the proliferation of levels of mutual awareness . . . is . . . a type of complexity that typifies human interactions" (15), so he might argue that his account will cover Romeo and Juliet's later relationship as well. Granted that levels of mutual awareness exist in any close human relationship. But it does not follow that the development of levels of awareness *characterize* all human relationships, particularly sexual relationships between familiar partners. In particular, the sort of awareness Nagel emphasizes—"a desire that one's partner be aroused by the recognition of one's desire that he or she be aroused" (15)—does not seem essential to regular sexual relationships. If we accept Nagel's account for sexual behavior in general, then we must classify as a perversion the behavior of an intimate and satisfying sexual relation begun without any preliminary exchange of multilevel arousals.[4]

Sexual desire can be generated by many different things—a smell, a phrase in a book, a familiar voice. The sexual interest of another person is only on occasion novel enough to be the main cause or focus of sexual arousal. A characterization of sexual behavior on other occasions should describe the development and sharing of sexual pleasure—the creation of sexual satisfaction. Nagel's contribution lies in directing our attention to the analysis of sexual behavior in terms of its perceptions and feelings. However, he characterizes only a limited sort of sexual behavior, flirtation and seduction.

Solomon characterizes sexual behavior by analogy with linguistic behavior, emphasizing that the goals are the same. He says:

> Sexual activity consists in speaking what we might call "body language." It has it own grammar, delineated by the body, and its own phonetics of touch and movement. Its unit of meaningfulness, the bodily equivalent of a sentence, is the *gesture*. . . . [B]ody language is essentially expressive, and its content is limited to interpersonal attitudes and feelings. (27–28)

The analogy with language can be valuable for understanding sexual behavior. However, Solomon construes the goals of both activities too narrowly and hence draws the wrong conclusions.

He argues that the aim of sexual behavior is to communicate one's attitudes and feelings, to express oneself, and further, that such self-expression is made less effective by aiming at enjoyment:

> That is why the liberal mythology has been so disastrous, for it has rendered unconscious the expressive functions of sex in its stress on enjoyment. . . .
> It is thus understandable why sex is so utterly important in our lives, and why it is typically so unsatisfactory. (29)

Does stress on enjoyment hinder self-expression? Trying to do one thing, X, may interfere with trying to do another, Y, for some Xs and Ys. For example, trying to eat peanut butter or swim under water may interfere with vocal self-expression. But enjoyment is a different sort of goal. One isn't trying to do both Y and something else when aiming at Y and enjoyment, but to do one sort of thing, Y, a certain way. Far from interfering, one is more likely to be successful at a venture if one can manage to enjoy oneself during the process.

Solomon claims to refute that enjoyment is the essential aim of sexual activity, but he erroneously identifies enjoyment with orgasm:[5]

> No one would deny that sex is enjoyable, but it does not follow that sexuality is the activity of "pure enjoyment" and that "gratification," or "pure physical pleasure," that is, orgasm, is its end. (26)

and consequently he shows merely that orgasm is not the only aim of sexual activity. His main argument is:

> If sex is pure physical enjoyment, why is sexual activity between persons far more satisfying than masturbation, where, if we accept recent physiological

studies, orgasm is at its highest intensity and the post-coital period is cleansed of its interpersonal hassles and arguments? (27)

One obvious answer is that, even for people who have hassles and arguments, interpersonal sexual activity is more enjoyable, even in the "pure physical" sense.[6] Solomon's argument does not show that enjoyment is not the appropriate aim of sexual activity, only that maximum-intensity orgasm is not. As those recent physiological studies pointed out, participants report interpersonal sexual activity as more enjoyable and satisfying even though their orgasms are less intense.[7] Only someone who mistakenly equated enjoyment with orgasm would find this paradoxical.

One need not claim that orgasm is always desired or desirable in sexual activity. That might be like supposing that in all conversations the participants do, or should, express their deepest thoughts. In sexual, as in linguistic, behavior, there is great variety and subtlety of purpose. But this is not to say that the desire for orgasm should be ignored. The disappointment and physical discomfort of expected but unachieved orgasm is only faintly parallel to the frustration of not being able to "get a word in edgewise" after being moved to express an important thought. It is usually rude or boorish to use language with indifference to the interests and cares of one's listeners. Sexual behavior with such indifference can be no better.

Solomon does not need these arguments to claim that enjoyment is not the only or the essential goal of sexual behavior. His comparison of sexual behavior with linguistic (or other social) behavior could have been used to do the job. The same social and moral distinctions and evaluations can be applied to both behaviors: hurting and humiliating people is bad; making people happy is good; loyalty, kindness, intelligence, and wit are valued; stupidity, clumsiness, and insincerity are not. The purpose of contact, sexual or otherwise, with other people is not just to produce or receive enjoyment—there are times of sadness, solace, and anguish that are important and meaningful to share, but not enjoyable.

Is self-expression, then, the essential goal of sexual behavior? Solomon lists a number of feelings and attitudes that can be expressed sexually:

- love, tenderness and trust, "being-with," mutual recognition

- hatred, indifference, jealousy, conflict

- shyness, fear, lack of confidence, embarrassment, shame

- domination, submissiveness, dependence, possessiveness, passivity

He claims "some attitudes, e.g., tenderness and trust, domination and passivity, are best expressed sexually" (28), and says his account

. . . makes it evident why Nagel chose as his example a couple of strangers; one has far more to say, for one can freely express one's fantasies as well as the truth, to a stranger. A husband and wife of seven years have probably been repeating the same messages for years, and their sexual activity now is probably no more than an abbreviated ritual incantation of the lengthy conversations they had years before. (28)

A glance at the list of feelings and attitudes above will show that its items are not independent. Shame, for example, may include components of embarrassment, lack of confidence, fear, and probably mutual recognition and submissiveness. To the extent that they can be conveyed by sexual body language,[8] a mere grunt or whimper would be able to express the whole range of the attitudes and feelings as well, if not better, than sexual gestures. Moreover, it is not clear that some attitudes are best expressed sexually. Tenderness and trust are often expressed between people who are not sexual partners. The tenderness and trust that may exist between an adult and a child is not best expressed sexually. Even if we take Solomon's claim to apply only to sexual partners, a joint checking account may be a better expression of trust than sexual activity. And domination, which in sado-masochistic sexual activity is expressed most elaborately with the cooperation of the partner, is an attitude much better expressed by nonsexual activities[9] such as beating an opponent, firing an employee, or mugging a passerby, where the domination is real, and does not require the cooperation of the other person. Even if some attitudes and feelings (for example, prurience, wantonness, lust) are best expressed sexually, it would be questionable whether the primary aim of sexual activity should be to express them.

The usual conversation of strangers is "small talk": cautious, shallow, and predictable because there has not been time for the participants to assess the extent and nature of common interests they share. So too with sexual behavior; first sexual encounters may be charged with novelty and anticipation, but are usually characterized by stereotypic physical interactions. If the physical interaction is seen as "body language," the analogy with linguistic behavior suggests that first encounters are likely to consist of sexual small talk.

Solomon's comparison of sexual behavior with linguistic behavior is handicapped by the limited view he has about their purposes. Language has more purposes than transmitting information. If all there were to sexual behavior was the development of the sexual anticipation prominent in flirtation and seduction, then Solomon's conclusions might be correct. The fact that people will continue sexual relations with the same partners even after the appropriate attitudes and feelings from Solomon's list have been expressed indicates that sexual behavior, like linguistic behavior, has other functions that are important. Solomon's analogy with linguistic behavior is valuable not because communication is the main goal of sexual behavior but because he directs attention to the social nature of sexual behavior. Solomon's analogy can be made to take on new importance by considering that sexual behavior not only transmits information about feelings and attitudes—something any activity can do—but also, like language, it has a *phatic* function to evoke feelings and attitudes.

Language is often used to produce a shared experience, a feeling of togetherness or unity. Duets, greetings, and many religious services use language with little information content to establish or reaffirm a relation among the participants. Long-term sexual relationships, like regular musical ensembles, may be valued more for the feelings produced than the feelings communicated. With both sexual and linguistic behavior, an interaction with a stranger might be an enjoyable novelty, but the pleasures of linguistic and sexual activity with good friends are probably much more frequent and more reliable.

Solomon's conclusion that sexually one should have more to "say" to a stranger and will find oneself "repeating the same messages for years" to old acquaintances,[10] violates the analogy. With natural language, one usually has more to say to old friends than to strangers.

Both Nagel and Solomon give incomplete accounts because they assume that a characterization of flirtation and seduction should apply to sexual behavior in general. I have argued that this is not so. Whether we analyze sexual behavior in terms of characteristic perceptions and feelings, as Nagel does, or by a comparison with other complex social behavior, as Solomon does, the characteristics of novel sexual encounters differ from those of sexual relationships between familiar and recognized partners.

What about the philosophical enterprise of characterizing sexual behavior? A characterization of something will tell what is unique about it and how to identify a standard or paradigm case of it. Criteria for a standard or paradigm case of sexual behavior unavoidably have normative implications. It is my position that normative judgments about sexual behavior should not be unrelated to the social and moral standards that apply to other social behavior. Many people, in reaction to old standards, avoid disapproving of sexual behavior that involves deceit or humiliation to another, but will condemn or ridicule sexual behavior that hurts no one yet fails to conform to a sexual standard. Both Nagel and Solomon classify sexual behavior that does not fit their characterizations as perversion, extending this strong negative judgment to behavior that is neither morally nor socially condemned (i.e., sex without multilevel awareness of arousal; sex without communication of attitudes and feelings). Yet perversion can be more accurately accounted for as whatever makes people frightened or uncomfortable by its bizarreness.[11]

Sexual behavior differs from other behavior by virtue of its unique feelings and emotions and its unique ability to create shared intimacy. These unique features of sexual behavior may influence particular normative judgments, but they do not justify applying *different* normative principles to sexual behavior.[12]

Notes

1. *The Journal of Philosophy* 66, No. 1 (1969), pp. 5–17. (In this volume, pp. 9–20. All references are to this volume.)

2. *The Journal of Philosophy* 71, No. 11 (1974), pp. 336–45. (In this volume, pp. 21–29. All references are to this volume.)

3. Satisfaction includes the good feelings of intimacy, warm friendship, the pleasure of being appreciated and of giving pleasure. 'Satisfaction' is not intended as a euphemism for orgasm, although the physical and social discomforts of the absence of orgasm often make a feeling of satisfaction impossible.

4. This was first pointed out to me by Sara Ketchum.

5. Solomon also claims that aiming at *orgasm* "overwhelms or distorts whatever else is being said sexually" (27). In this case there might be interference. However, if one is trying to express feelings and attitudes through the giving or having of an orgasm, then "aiming at self-expression" and "aiming at orgasm" will describe the same activity and there will be no interference. It should be pointed out that whatever else is being said sexually should have been said before orgasm is imminent or should be postponed because one will not do a very good job of transmitting or receiving any other communication during orgasm. Instead of an objection to aiming at orgasm, the potential interference raises an objection to aiming at self-expression during the time that orgasm is the goal.

6. Several theories of motivation in psychology (e.g., McClelland's) easily incorporate this fact: Creatures find moderate discrepancies from predicted sensation more pleasurable than sensations that are completely expected. Sensations produced by a sexual partner are not as adequately predicted as autoerotic stimulation.

7. William Masters and Virginia Johnson, *Human Sexual Response* (Boston: Little, Brown, 1966), p. 113.

8. More than gestures must be employed to communicate such feelings as love, trust, hatred, shame, dependence, and possessiveness. I doubt that jealousy or a distinction between "one's fantasies [and] the truth" (28) can be communicated by sexual body language at all.

9. In her comments on a relative of this paper at the 1976 Pacific Division APA meetings, Sara Ketchum pointed out that I have completely overlooked one sort of sexual activity in which the domination *is* real and the cooperation of the other person is not required: rape.

10. Repeated messages about one's feelings are not merely redundant; they convey new information: the continuation, renewal, or salience of those feelings.

11. See Mary Douglas, *Purity and Danger* (London: Routledge & Kegan Paul, 1966).

12. This paper has been greatly improved by the discussions and careful criticisms of G. M. Robinson and Helen Heise, the suggestions of Tim Binkley and Jay Rosenberg that it be expanded, and the comments from audiences of The Society for Women in Philosophy and the American Philosophical Association.

Chapter 5

PLAIN SEX

Alan Goldman

I

Several recent articles on sex herald its acceptance as a legitimate topic for analytic philosophers (although it has been a topic in philosophy since Plato). One might have thought conceptual analysis unnecessary in this area; despite the notorious struggles of judges and legislators to define pornography suitably, we all might be expected to know what sex is and to be able to identify at least paradigm sexual desires and activities without much difficulty. Philosophy is nevertheless of relevance here if for no other reason than that the concept of sex remains at the center of moral and social consciousness in our, and perhaps any, society. Before we can get a sensible view of the relation of sex to morality, perversion, social regulation, and marriage, we require a sensible analysis of the concept itself; one which neither understates its animal pleasure nor overstates its importance within a theory or system of value. I say "before," but the order is not quite so clear, for questions in this area, as elsewhere in moral philosophy, are both conceptual and normative at the same time. Our concept of sex will partially determine our moral view of it, but as philosophers we should formulate a concept that will accord with its proper moral status. What we require here, as elsewhere, is "reflective equilibrium," a goal not achieved by traditional

Goldman, Alan, "Plain Sex," *Philosophy and Public Affairs* 6:3 (1977), pp. 267–87. Copyright © 1977 by Princeton University Press. Reprinted by permission of Princeton University Press.

and recent analyses together with their moral implications. Because sexual activity, like other natural functions such as eating or exercising, has become imbedded in layers of cultural, moral, and superstitious superstructure, it is hard to conceive it in its simplest terms. But partially for this reason, it is only by thinking about plain sex that we can begin to achieve this conceptual equilibrium.

I shall suggest here that sex continues to be misrepresented in recent writings, at least in philosophical writings, and I shall criticize the predominant form of analysis which I term "means-end analysis." Such conceptions attribute a necessary external goal or purpose to sexual activity, whether it be reproduction, the expression of love, simple communication, or interpersonal awareness. They analyze sexual activity as a means to one of these ends, implying that sexual desire is a desire to reproduce, to love or be loved, or to communicate with others. All definitions of this type suggest false views of the relation of sex to perversion and morality by implying that sex which does not fit one of these models or fulfill one of these functions is in some way deviant or incomplete.

The alternative, simpler analysis with which I will begin is that sexual desire is desire for contact with another person's body and for the pleasure which such contact produces; sexual activity is activity which tends to fulfill such desire of the agent. Whereas Aristotle and Butler were correct in holding that pleasure is normally a byproduct rather than a goal of purposeful action, in the case of sex this is not so clear. The desire for another's body is, principally among other things, the desire for the pleasure that physical contact brings. On the other hand, it is not a desire for a particular sensation detachable from its causal context, a sensation which can be derived in other ways. This definition in terms of the general goal of sexual desire appears preferable to an attempt to more explicitly list or define specific sexual activities, for many activities such as kissing, embracing, massaging, or holding hands may or may not be sexual, depending upon the context and more specifically upon the purposes, needs, or desires into which such activities fit. The generality of the definition also represents a refusal (common in recent psychological texts) to overemphasize orgasm as the goal of sexual desire or genital sex as the only norm of sexual activity (this will be hedged slightly in the discussion of perversion below).

Central to the definition is the fact that the goal of sexual desire and activity is the physical contact itself, rather than something else which this contact might express. By contrast, what I term "means-end analyses" posit ends which I take to be extraneous to plain sex, and they view sex as a means to these ends. Their fault lies not in defining sex in terms of its general goal, but in seeing plain sex as merely a means to other separable ends. I term these "means-end analyses" for convenience, although "means-separable-end analysis," while too cumbersome, might be more fully explanatory. The desire for physical contact with another person is a minimal criterion for (normal) sexual desire, but is both necessary and sufficient to qualify normal desire as sexual. Of course, we may want to express other feelings through sexual acts in various contexts; but without the desire for the physical contact in and for itself, or when it is sought for other reasons, activities in which contact is involved are not predominantly sexual. Furthermore, the desire for physical contact in itself, without the wish to express affection or other feelings through it, is sufficient to render sexual the activity of the agent which fulfills it. Various activities with this goal alone, such as kissing and caressing in certain contexts, qualify as sexual even without the presence of genital symptoms of sexual excitement. The latter are not therefore necessary criteria for sexual activity.

This initial analysis may seem to some either over- or underinclusive. It might seem too broad in leading us to interpret physical contact as sexual desire in activities such as football and other contact sports. In these cases, however, the desire is not for contact with another body per se, it is not directed toward a particular person for that purpose, and it is not the goal of the activity—the goal is winning or exercising or knocking someone down or displaying one's prowess. If the desire is purely for contact with another specific person's body, then to interpret it as sexual does not seem an exaggeration. A slightly more difficult case is that of a baby's desire to be cuddled and our natural response in wanting to cuddle it. In the case of the baby, the desire may be simply for the physical contact, for the pleasure of the caresses. If so, we may characterize this desire, especially in keeping with Freudian theory, as sexual or protosexual. It will differ nevertheless from full-fledged sexual desire in being more amorphous, not directed outward toward another specific person's body. It may also be that what the infant unconsciously desires is not physical contact per se but signs of affection, tenderness, or security, in which case we have further reason for hesitating to characterize its wants as clearly sexual. The intent of our response to the baby is often the showing of affection, not the pure physical contact, so that our definition in terms of action which fulfills sexual desire *on the part of the agent* does not capture such actions, whatever we say of the baby. (If it is intuitive to characterize our responses as sexual as well, there is clearly no problem here for my analysis.) The same can be said of signs of affection (or in some cultures polite greeting) among men or women: these certainly need not be homosexual when the intent is only to show friendship, something extrinsic to plain sex although valuable when added to it.

Our definition of sex in terms of the desire for physical contact may appear too narrow in that a person's personality, not merely her or his body, may be sexually attractive to another, and in that looking or conversing in a certain way can be sexual in a given context without bodily contact. Nevertheless, it is not the contents of one's thoughts per se that are sexually appealing, but one's personality as embodied in certain manners of behavior. Furthermore, if a person is sexually attracted by another's personality, he or she will desire not just further conversation, but actual sexual contact. While looking at or conversing with someone can be interpreted as sexual in given contexts it is so when intended as preliminary to, and hence parasitic upon, elemental sexual interest. Voyeurism or viewing a pornographic movie qualifies as a sexual activity, but only as an imaginative substitute for the real thing (otherwise a deviation from the norm as expressed in our definition). The same is true of masturbation as a sexual activity without a partner.

That the initial definition indicates at least an ingredient of sexual desire and activity is too obvious to argue. We all know what sex is, at least in obvious cases, and do not need philosophers to tell us. My preliminary analysis is meant to serve as a contrast to what sex is not, at least not necessarily. I concentrate upon the physically manifested desire for another's body, and I take as central the immersion in the physical aspect of one's own existence and attention to the physical embodiment of the other. One may derive pleasure in a sex act from expressing certain feelings to one's partner or from awareness of the attitude of one's partner, but sexual desire is essentially desire for physical contact itself: it is a bodily desire for the body of another that dominates our mental life for more or less brief periods. Traditional writings were correct to emphasize the purely physical or animal aspect of sex; they were wrong only in condemning it. This characterization of sex as an intensely pleasurable physical activity and acute physical desire may seem to some to capture only its barest level. But it is worth distinguishing and focusing upon this least common denominator in order to avoid the false views of sexual morality and perversion which emerge from thinking that sex is essentially something else.

II

We may turn then to what sex is not, to the arguments regarding supposed conceptual connections between sex and other activities which it is necessary to conceptually distinguish. The most comprehensible attempt to build an extraneous purpose into the sex act identifies that purpose as reproduction, its primary biological function. While this may be "nature's" purpose, it certainly need not be ours (the analogy with eating, while sometimes overworked, is pertinent here). While this identification may once have had a rational basis which also grounded the identification of the value and morality of sex with that applicable to reproduction and childrearing, the development of contraception rendered the connection weak. Methods of contraception are by now so familiar and so widely used that it is not necessary to dwell upon the changes wrought by these developments in the concept of sex itself and in a rational sexual ethic dependent upon that concept. In the past, the ever present possibility of children rendered the concepts of sex and sexual morality different from those required at present. There may be good reasons, if the presence and care of both mother and father are beneficial to children, for restricting reproduction to marriage. Insofar as society has a legitimate role in protecting children's interests, it may be justified in giving marriage a legal status, although this question is complicated by the fact (among others) that children born to single mothers deserve no penalties. In any case, the point here is simply that these questions are irrelevant at the present time to those regarding the morality of sex and its potential social regulation. (Further connections with marriage will be discussed below.)

It is obvious that the desire for sex is not necessarily a desire to reproduce, that the psychological manifestation has become, if it were not always, distinct from its biological roots. There are many parallels, as previously mentioned, with other natural functions. The pleasures of eating and exercising are to a large extent independent of their roles in nourishment or health (as the junk-food industry discovered with a vengeance). Despite the obvious parallel with sex, there is still a tendency for many to think that sex acts which can be reproductive are, if not more moral or less immoral, at least more natural. These categories of morality and "naturalness," or normality, are not to be identified with each other, as will be argued below, and neither is applicable to sex by virtue of its connection to reproduction. The tendency to identify reproduction as the conceptually connected end of sex is most prevalent now in the pronouncements of the Catholic church. There the assumed analysis is clearly tied to a restrictive sexual morality according to which acts become immoral and unnatural when they are not oriented towards reproduction, a morality which has independent roots in the Christian sexual ethic as it derives from Paul. However, the means-end analysis fails to generate a consistent sexual ethic: homosexual and oral-genital sex is condemned while kissing or caressing, acts equally unlikely to lead in themselves to fertilization, even when properly characterized as sexual according to our definition, are not.

III

Before discussing further relations of means-end analyses to false or inconsistent sexual ethics and concepts of perversion, I turn to other examples of these analyses. One common position views sex as essentially an expression of love or affection between the partners. It is generally recognized that there are other types of love besides sexual, but sex itself is taken as an expression of one type, sometimes termed "romantic" love.[1] Various factors again ought to weaken this identification. First, there are other types of love besides that which it is appropriate to express sexually, and "romantic" love itself can be expressed in many other ways. I am not denying that sex can take on heightened value and meaning when it becomes a vehicle for the expression of feelings of love or tenderness, but so can many other usually mundane activities such as getting up early to make breakfast on Sunday, cleaning the house, and so on. Second, sex itself can be used to communicate many other emotions besides love, and, as I will argue below, can communicate nothing in particular and still be good sex.

On a deeper level, an internal tension is bound to result from an identification of sex, which I have described as a physical-psychological desire, with love as a long-term, deep emotional relationship between two individuals. As this type of relationship, love is permanent, at least in intent, and more or less exclusive. A normal person cannot deeply love more than a few individuals even in a lifetime. We may be suspicious that those who attempt or claim to love many love them weakly if at all. Yet, fleeting sexual desire can arise in relation to a variety of other individuals one finds sexually attractive. It may even be, as some have claimed, that sexual desire in humans naturally seeks variety, while this is obviously false of love. For this reason, monogamous sex, even if justified, almost always represents a sacrifice or the exercise of self-control on the part of the spouses, while monogamous love generally does not. There is no such thing as casual love in the sense in which I intend the term "love." It may occasionally happen that a spouse falls deeply in love with someone else (especially when sex is conceived in terms of love), but this is relatively rare in comparison to passing sexual desires for others; and while the former often indicates a weakness or fault in the marriage relation, the latter does not.

If love is indeed more exclusive in its objects than is sexual desire, this explains why those who view sex as essentially an expression of love would again tend to hold a repressive or restrictive sexual ethic. As in the case of reproduction, there may be good reasons for reserving the total commitment of deep love to the context of marriage and family—the normal personality may not withstand additional divisions of ultimate commitment and allegiance. There is no question that marriage itself is best sustained by a deep relation of love and affection; and even if love is not naturally monogamous, the benefits of family units to children provide additional reason to avoid serious commitments elsewhere which weaken family ties. It can be argued similarly that monogamous sex strengthens families by restricting and at the same time guaranteeing an outlet for sexual desire in marriage. But there is more force to the argument that recognition of a clear distinction between sex and love in society would help avoid disastrous marriages which result from adolescent confusion of the two when sexual desire is mistaken for permanent love, and would weaken damaging jealousies which arise in marriages in relation to passing sexual desires. The love and affection of a sound marriage certainly differs from the adolescent romantic variety, which is often a mere substitute for sex in the context of a repressive sexual ethic.

In fact, the restrictive sexual ethic tied to the means-end analysis in terms of love again has failed to be consistent. At least, it has not been applied consistently, but forms part of the double standard which has curtailed the freedom of women. It is predictable in light of this history that some women would now advocate using sex as another kind of means, as a political weapon or as a way to increase unjustly denied power and freedom. The inconsistency in the sexual ethic typically attached to the sex-love analysis, according to which it has generally been taken with a grain of salt when applied to men, is simply another example of the impossibility of tailoring a plausible moral theory in this area to a conception of sex which builds in conceptually extraneous factors.

I am not suggesting here that sex ought never to be connected with love or that it is not a more significant and valuable activity when it is. Nor am I denying that individuals need love as much as sex and perhaps emotionally need at least one complete relationship which encompasses both. Just as sex can express love and take on heightened significance when it does, so love is often naturally accompanied by an intermittent desire for sex. But again love is accompanied appropriately by desires for other shared activities as well. What makes the desire for sex seem more intimately connected with love is the intimacy which is seen to be a natural feature of mutual sex acts. Like love, sex is held to lay one bare psychologically as well as physically. Sex is unquestionably intimate, but beyond that the psychological toll often attached may be a function of the restrictive sexual ethic itself, rather than a legitimate apology for it. The intimacy involved in love is psychologically consuming in a generally healthy way, while the psychological tolls of sexual relations, often including embarrassment as a correlate of intimacy, are too often the result of artificial sexual ethics and taboos. The intimacy involved in both love and sex is insufficient in any case in light of previous points to render a means-end analysis in these terms appropriate.

IV

In recent articles, Thomas Nagel and Robert Solomon, who recognize that sex is not merely a means to communicate love, nevertheless retain the form of this analysis while broadening it. For Solomon, sex remains a means of communicating (he explicitly uses the metaphor of body language), although the feelings that can be communicated now include, in addition to love and tenderness, domination, dependence, anger, trust, and so on.[2] Nagel does not refer explicitly to communication, but his analysis is similar in that he views sex as a complex form of interpersonal awareness in which desire itself is consciously communicated on several different levels. In sex, according to his analysis, two people are aroused by each other, aware of the other's arousal, and further aroused by this awareness.[3] Such multileveled conscious awareness of one's own and the other's desire is taken as the norm of a sexual relation, and this model is therefore close to that which views sex as a means of interpersonal communication.

Solomon's analysis is beset by the same difficulties as those pointed out in relation to the narrower sex-love concept. Just as love can be communicated by many activities other than sex, which do not therefore become properly analyzed as essentially vehicles of communication (making breakfast, cleaning the house, and so on), the same is true of the other feelings mentioned by Solomon. Domination can be communicated through economic manipulation, trust by a joint savings account. Driving a car can be simultaneously expressing anger, pride, joy, and so on. We may, in fact, communicate or express feelings in anything we do, but this does not make everything we do into language. Driving a car is not to be defined as an automotive means of communication, although with a little ingenuity we might work out an automotive vocabulary (tailgating as an expression of aggression or impatience; beating another car away from a stoplight as expressing domination) to match the vocabulary of "body language." That one can communicate various feelings during sex acts does not make these acts merely or primarily a means of communicating.

More importantly, to analyze sex as a means of communication is to overlook the intrinsic nature and value of the act itself. Sex is not a gesture or series of gestures, in fact not necessarily a means to any other end, but a physical activity intensely pleasurable in itself. When a language is used, the symbols normally have no importance in themselves; they function merely as vehicles for what can be communicated by them. Furthermore skill in the use of language is a technical achievement that must be carefully learned; if better sex is more successful communication by means of a more skillful use of body language, then we had all better be well schooled in the vocabulary and grammar. Solomon's analysis, which uses the language metaphor, suggests the appropriateness of a sex-manual approach, the substitution of a bit of technological prowess for the natural pleasure of the unforced surrender to feeling and desire.

It may be that Solomon's position could be improved by using the analogy of music rather than that of language, as an aesthetic form of communication. Music might be thought of as a form of aesthetic communicating, in which the experience of the "phonemes" themselves is generally pleasing. And listening to music is perhaps more of a sexual experience than having someone talk to you. Yet, it seems to me that insofar as music is aesthetic and pleasing in itself, it is not best conceived as primarily a means for communicating specific feelings. Such an analysis does injustice to aesthetic experience in much the same way as the sex-communication analysis debases sexual experience itself.[4]

For Solomon, sex that is not a totally self-conscious communicative act tends toward vulgarity,[5] whereas I would have thought it the other way around. This is another illustration of the tendency of means-end analyses to condemn what appears perfectly natural or normal sex on my account. Both Solomon and Nagel use their definitions, however, not primarily to stipulate moral norms for sex, as we saw in earlier analyses, but to define norms against which to measure perversion. Once again, neither is capable of generating consistency or reflective equilibrium with our firm intuitions as to what counts as subnormal sex, the problem being that both build factors into their norms which are extraneous to an unromanticized view of normal sexual desire and activity. If perversion represents a breakdown in communication, as Solomon maintains, then any unsuccessful or misunderstood advance should count as perverted. Furthermore, sex between husband and wife married for several years, or between any partners already familiar with each other, would be, if not perverted, nevertheless subnormal or trite and dull, in that the communicative content would be minimal in lacking all novelty. In fact the pleasures of sex need not wear off with familiarity, as they would if dependent upon the communicative content of the feelings. Finally, rather than a release or relief from physical desire through a substitute imaginative outlet, masturbation would become a way of practicing or rehearsing one's technique or vocabulary on oneself, or simply a way of talking to oneself, as Solomon himself says.[6]

Nagel fares no better in the implications of his overintellectualized norm. Spontaneous and heated sex between two familiar partners may well lack the complex conscious multileveled interpersonal awareness of which he speaks without being in the least perverted. The egotistical desire that one's partner be aroused by one's own desire does not seem a primary element of the sexual urge, and during sex acts one may like one's partner to be sometimes active and aroused, sometimes more passive. Just as sex can be more significant when love is communicated, so it can sometimes be heightened by an awareness of the other's desire. But at other times this awareness of an avid desire of one's partner can be merely distracting. The conscious awareness to which Nagel refers may actually impede the immersion in the physical of which I spoke above, just as may concentration upon one's "vocabulary" or technique.

Sex is a way of relating to another, but primarily a physical rather than intellectual way. For Nagel, the ultimate in degeneration or perversion would have to be what he calls "mutual epidermal stimulation"[7] without mutual awareness of each other's state of mind. But this sounds like normal, if not ideal, sex to me (perhaps only a minimal description of it). His model certainly seems more appropriate to a sophisticated seduction scene than to the sex act itself,[8] which according to the model would often have to count as a subnormal anticlimax to the intellectual foreplay. While Nagel's account resembles Solomon's means-end analysis of sex, here the sex act itself does not even qualify as a preferred or central means to the end of interpersonal communication.

V

I have now criticized various types of analysis sharing or suggesting a common means-end form. I have suggested that analyses of this form relate to attempts to limit moral or natural sex to that which fulfills some purpose or function extraneous to basic sexual desire. The attempts to brand forms of sex outside the idealized models as immoral or perverted fail to achieve consistency with intuitions that they themselves do not directly question. The reproductive model brands oral-genital sex a deviation, but cannot account for kissing or holding hands; the communication account holds voyeurism to be perverted but cannot accommodate sex acts without much conscious thought or seductive nonphysical foreplay; the sex-love model makes most sexual desire seem degrading or base. The first and last condemn extra-marital sex on the sound but irrelevant grounds that reproduction and deep commitment are best confined to family contexts. The romanticization of sex and the confusion of sexual desire with love operate in both directions: sex outside the context of romantic love is repressed; once it is repressed, partners become more difficult to find and sex becomes romanticized further, out of proportion to its real value for the individual.

What all these analyses share in addition to a common form is accordance with and perhaps derivation from the Platonic-Christian moral tradition, according to which the animal or purely physical element of humans is the source of immorality, and plain sex in the sense I defined it is an expression of this element, hence in itself to be condemned. All the analyses examined seem to seek a distance from sexual desire itself in attempting to extend it conceptually beyond the physical. The love and communication analyses seek refinement or intellectualization of the desire; plain physical sex becomes vulgar, and too straightforward sexual encounters without an aura of respectable cerebral communicative content are to be avoided. Solomon explicitly argues that sex cannot be a "mere" appetite, his argument being that if it were, subway exhibitionism and other vulgar forms would be pleasing.[9] This fails to recognize that sexual desire can be focused or selective at the same time as being physical. Lower animals are not attracted by every other member of their species, either. Rancid food forced down one's throat is not pleasing, but that certainly fails to show that hunger is not a physical appetite. Sexual desire lets us know that we are physical beings and, indeed, animals; this is why traditional Platonic morality is so thorough in its condemnation. Means-end analyses continue to reflect this tradition, sometimes unwittingly. They show that in conceptualizing sex it is still difficult, despite years of so-called revolution in this area, to free ourselves from the lingering suspicion that plain sex as physical desire is an expression of our "lower selves," that yielding to our animal natures is subhuman or vulgar.

VI

Having criticized these analyses for the sexual ethics and concepts of perversion they imply, it remains to contrast my account along these lines. To the question of what morality might be implied by my analysis, the answer is that there are no moral implications whatever. Any analysis of sex which imputes a moral character to sex acts in themselves is wrong for that reason. There is no morality intrinsic to sex, although general moral rules apply to the treatment of others in sex acts as they apply to all human relations. We can speak of a sexual ethic as we can speak of a business ethic, without implying that business in itself is either moral or immoral or that special rules are required to judge business practices which are not derived from rules that apply elsewhere as well. Sex is not in itself a moral category, although like business it invariably places us into relations with others in which moral rules apply. It gives us opportunity to do what is otherwise recognized as wrong, to harm others, deceive them or manipulate them against their wills. Just as the fact that an act is sexual in itself never renders it wrong or adds to its wrongness if it is wrong on other grounds (sexual acts towards minors are wrong on other grounds, as will be argued below), so no wrong act is to be excused because done from a sexual motive. If a "crime of passion" is to be excused, it would have to be on grounds of temporary insanity rather than sexual context (whether insanity does constitute a legitimate excuse for certain actions is too big a topic to argue here). Sexual motives are among others which may become deranged, and the fact that they are sexual has no bearing in itself on the moral character, whether negative or exculpatory, of the actions deriving from them. Whatever might be true of war, it is certainly not the case that all's fair in love or sex.

Our first conclusion regarding morality and sex is therefore that no conduct otherwise immoral should be excused because it is sexual conduct, and nothing in sex is immoral unless condemned by rules which apply elsewhere as well. The last clause requires further clarification. Sexual conduct can be governed by particular rules relating only to sex itself. But these precepts must be implied by general moral rules when these are applied to specific sexual relations or types of conduct. The same is true of rules of fair business, ethical medicine, or courtesy in driving a car. In the latter case, particular acts on the road may be reprehensible, such as tailgating or passing on the right, which seem to bear no resemblance as actions to any outside the context of highway safety. Nevertheless their immorality derives from the fact that they place others in danger, a circumstance which, when avoidable, is to be condemned in any context. This structure of general and specifically applicable rules describes a reasonable sexual ethic as well. To take an extreme case, rape is always a sexual act and it is always immoral. A rule against rape can therefore be considered an obvious part of sexual morality which has no bearing on nonsexual conduct. But the immorality of rape derives from its being an extreme violation of a person's body, of the right not to be humiliated, and of the general moral prohibition against using other persons against their wills, not from the fact that it is a sexual act.

The application elsewhere of general moral rules to sexual conduct is further complicated by the fact that it will be relative to the particular desires and preferences of one's partner (these may be influenced by and hence in some sense include misguided beliefs about sexual morality itself). This means that there will be fewer specific rules in the area of sexual ethics than in other areas of conduct, such as driving cars, where the relativity of preference is irrelevant to the prohibition of objectively dangerous conduct. More reliance will have to be placed upon the general moral rule, which in this area holds simply that the preferences, desires, and interests of one's partner or potential partner ought to be taken into account. This rule is certainly not specifically formulated to govern sexual relations; it is a form of the central principle of morality itself. But when applied to sex, it prohibits certain actions, such as molestation of children, which cannot be categorized as violations of the rule without at the same time being classified as sexual. I believe this last case is the closest we can come to an action which is wrong *because* it is sexual, but even here its wrongness is better characterized as deriving from the detrimental effects such behavior can have on the future emotional and sexual life of the naive victims, and from the fact that such behavior therefore involves manipulation of innocent persons without regard for their interests. Hence, this case also involves violation of a general moral rule which applies elsewhere as well.

Aside from faulty conceptual analyses of sex and the influence of the Platonic moral tradition, there are two more plausible reasons for thinking that there are moral dimensions intrinsic to sex acts per se. The first is that such acts are normally intensely pleasurable. According to a hedonistic, utilitarian moral theory they therefore should be at least prima facie morally right, rather than morally neutral in themselves. To me this seems incorrect and reflects unfavorably on the ethical theory in question. The pleasure intrinsic to sex acts is a good, but not, it seems to me, a good with much positive moral significance. Certainly I can have no duty to pursue such pleasure myself, and while it may be nice to give pleasure of any form to others, there is no ethical requirement to do so, given my right over my own body. The exception relates to the context of sex acts themselves, when one partner derives pleasure from the other and ought to return the favor. This duty to reciprocate takes us out of the domain of hedonistic utilitarianism, however, and into a Kantian moral framework, the central principles of which call for such reciprocity in human relations. Since independent moral judgments regarding sexual activities constitute one area in which ethical theories are to be tested, these observations indicate here, as I believe others indicate elsewhere, the fertility of the Kantian, as opposed to the utilitarian, principle in reconstructing reasoned moral consciousness.

It may appear from this alternative Kantian viewpoint that sexual acts must be at least prima facie wrong in themselves. This is because they invariably involve at different stages the manipulation of one's partner for one's own pleasure, which might appear to be prohibited on the formulation of Kant's principle which holds that one ought not to treat another as a means to such private ends. A more realistic rendering of this formulation, however, one which recognizes its intended equivalence to the first universalizability principle, admits no such absolute prohibition. Many human relations, most economic transactions for example, involve using other individuals for personal benefit. These relations are immoral only when they are one-sided, when the benefits are not mutual, or when the transactions are not freely and rationally endorsed by all parties. The same holds true of sexual acts. The central principle governing them is the Kantian demand for reciprocity in sexual relations. In order to comply with the second formulation of the categorical imperative, one must recognize the subjectivity of one's partner (not merely by being aroused by her or his desire, as Nagel describes). Even in an act which by its nature "objectifies" the other, one recognizes a partner as a subject with demands and desires by yielding to those desires, by allowing oneself to be a sexual object as well, by giving pleasure or ensuring that the pleasures of the acts are mutual. It is this kind of reciprocity which forms the basis for morality in sex, which distinguishes right acts from wrong in this area as in others. (Of course, prior to sex acts one must gauge their effects upon potential partners and take these longer range interests into account.)

VII

I suggested earlier that in addition to generating confusion regarding the rightness or wrongness of sex acts, false conceptual analyses of the means-end form cause confusion about the value of sex to the individual. My account recognizes the satisfaction of desire and the pleasure this brings as the central psychological function of the sex act for the individual. Sex affords us a paradigm of pleasure, but not a cornerstone of value. For most of us it is not only a needed outlet for desire but also the most enjoyable form of recreation we know. Its value is nevertheless easily mistaken by being confused with that of love, when it is taken as essentially an expression of that emotion. Although intense, the pleasures of sex are brief and repetitive rather than cumulative. They give value to the specific acts which generate them, but not the lasting kind of value which enhances one's whole life. The briefness of the pleasures contributes to their intensity (or perhaps their intensity makes them necessarily brief), but it also relegates them to the periphery of most rational plans for the good life.

By contrast, love typically develops over a long term relation; while its pleasures may be less intense and physical, they are of more cumulative value. The importance of love to the individual may well be central in a rational system of value. And it has perhaps an even deeper moral significance relating to the identification with the interests of another person, which broadens one's possible relationships with others as well. Marriage is again important in preserving this relation between adults and children, which seems as important to the adults as it is to the children in broadening concerns which have a tendency to become selfish. Sexual desire, by contrast, is desire for another which is nevertheless essentially self-regarding. Sexual pleasure is certainly a good for the individual, and for many it may be necessary in order for them to function in a reasonably cheerful way. But it bears little relation to those other values just discussed, to which some analyses falsely suggest a conceptual connection.

VIII

While my initial analysis lacks moral implications in itself, as it should, it does suggest by contrast a concept of sexual perversion. Since the concept of perversion is itself a sexual concept, it will always be defined relative to some definition of normal sex; and any conception of the norm will imply a contrary notion of perverse forms. The concept suggested by my account again differs sharply from those implied by the means-end analyses examined above. Perversion does not represent a deviation from the reproductive function (or kissing would be perverted), from a loving relationship (or most sexual desire and many heterosexual acts would be perverted), or from efficiency in communicating (or unsuccessful seduction attempts would be perverted). It is a deviation from a norm, but the norm in question is merely statistical. Of course, not all sexual acts that are statistically unusual are perverted—a three-hour continuous sexual act would be unusual but not necessarily abnormal in the requisite sense. The abnormality in question must relate to the *form of the desire* itself in order to constitute sexual perversion; for example, desire, not for contact with another, but for merely looking, for harming or being harmed, for contact with items of clothing. The concept of sexual abnormality is that suggested by my definition of normal sex in terms of its typical desire. However, not all unusual desires qualify either, only those with the typical physical sexual effects upon the individual who satisfies them. These effects, such as erection in males, were not built into the original definition of sex in terms of sexual desire, for they do not always occur in activities that are properly characterized as sexual, say, kissing for the pleasure of it. But they do seem to bear a closer relation to the definition of activities as perverted. (For those who consider only genital sex sexual, we could build such symptoms into a narrower definition, then speaking of sex in a broad sense as well as "proper" sex.)

Solomon and Nagel disagree with this statistical notion of perversion. For them the concept is evaluative rather than statistical. I do not deny that the term "perverted" is often used evaluatively (and purely emotively for that matter), or that it has a negative connotation for the average speaker. I do deny that we can find a norm, other than that of statistically usual desire, against which all and only activities that properly count as sexual perversions can be contrasted. Perverted sex is simply abnormal sex, and if the norm is not to be an idealized or romanticized extraneous end or purpose, it must express the way human sexual desires usually manifest themselves. Of course not all norms in other areas of discourse need be statistical in this way. Physical health is an example of a relatively clear norm which does not seem to depend upon the numbers of healthy people. But the concept in this case achieves its clarity through the connection of physical health with other clearly desirable physical functions and characteristics, for example, living longer. In the case of sex, that which is statistically abnormal is not necessarily incapacitating in other ways, and yet these abnormal desires with sexual effects upon their subject do count as perverted to the degree to which their objects deviate from usual ones. The connotations of the concept of perversion beyond those connected with abnormality or statistical deviation derive more from the attitudes of those likely to call

certain acts perverted than from specifiable features of the acts themselves. These connotations add to the concept of abnormality that of *sub-
normality*, but there is no norm against which the latter can be measured
intelligibly in accord with all and only acts intuitively called perverted.

The only proper evaluative norms relating to sex involve degrees of
pleasure in the acts and moral norms, but neither of these scales coin-
cides with statistical degrees of abnormality, according to which perversion is to be measured. The three parameters operate independently
(this was implied for the first two when it was held above that the pleasure of sex is a good, but not necessarily a moral good). Perverted sex
may be more or less enjoyable to particular individuals than normal sex,
and more or less moral, depending upon the particular relations involved. Raping a sheep may be more perverted than raping a woman,
but certainly not more condemnable morally.[10] It is nevertheless true
that the evaluative connotations attaching to the term "perverted" derive
partly from the fact that most people consider perverted sex highly immoral. Many such acts are forbidden by long standing taboos, and it is
sometimes difficult to distinguish what is forbidden from what is immoral. Others, such as sadistic acts, are genuinely immoral, but again
not at all because of their connection with sex or abnormality. The principles which condemn these acts would condemn them equally if they
were common and nonsexual. It is not true that we properly could continue to consider acts perverted which were found to be very common
practice across societies. Such acts, if harmful, might continue to be condemned properly as immoral, but it was just shown that the immorality
of an act does not vary with its degree of perversion. If not harmful,
common acts previously considered abnormal might continue to be
called perverted for a time by the moralistic minority; but the term when
applied to such cases would retain only its emotive negative connotation
without consistent logical criteria for application. It would represent
merely prejudiced moral judgments.

To adequately explain why there is a tendency to so deeply condemn
perverted acts would require a treatise in psychology beyond the scope
of this paper. Part of the reason undoubtedly relates to the tradition of
repressive sexual ethics and false conceptions of sex; another part to the
fact that all abnormality seems to disturb and fascinate us at the same
time. The former explains why sexual perversion is more abhorrent to
many than other forms of abnormality; the latter indicates why we tend
to have an emotive and evaluative reaction to perversion in the first
place. It may be, as has been suggested according to a Freudian line,[11]
that our uneasiness derives from latent desires we are loathe to admit,
but this thesis takes us into psychological issues I am not competent to
judge. Whatever the psychological explanation, it suffices to point out
here that the conceptual connection between perversion and genuine

or consistent moral evaluation is spurious and again suggested by misleading means-end idealizations of the concept of sex.

The position I have taken in this paper against those concepts is not totally new. Something similar to it is found in Freud's view of sex, which of course was genuinely revolutionary, and in the body of writings deriving from Freud to the present time. But in his revolt against romanticized and repressive conceptions, Freud went too far—from a refusal to view sex as merely a means to a view of it as the end of all human behavior, although sometimes an elaborately disguised end. This pansexualism led to the thesis (among others) that repression was indeed an inevitable and necessary part of social regulation of any form, a strange consequence of a position that began by opposing the repressive aspects of the means-end view. Perhaps the time finally has arrived when we can achieve a reasonable middle ground in this area, at least in philosophy if not in society.

Notes

1. Even Bertrand Russell, whose writing in this area was a model of rationality, at least for its period, tends to make this identification and to condemn plain sex in the absence of love: "sex intercourse apart from love has little value, and is to be regarded primarily as experimentation with a view to love." *Marriage and Morals* (New York: Bantam, 1959), p. 87.

2. Robert Solomon, "Sex and Perversion," *Philosophy and Sex*, ed. R. Baker and F. Elliston (Buffalo: Prometheus, 1975), 268–87.

3. Thomas Nagel, "Sexual Perversion," *The Journal of Philosophy* 66, No. 1 (1960), pp. 5–17. (This volume, pp. 9–20.)

4. Sex might be considered (at least partially) as communication in a very broad sense in the same way as performing ensemble music, in the sense that there is in both ideally a communion or perfectly shared experience with another. This is, however, one possible ideal view whose central feature is not necessary to sexual acts or desire per se. And in emphasizing the communication of specific feelings by means of body language, the analysis under consideration narrows the end to one clearly extrinsic to plain and even good sex.

5. Solomon, pp. 284–85.

6. *Ibid.*, p. 283. One is reminded of Woody Allen's rejoinder to praise of his technique: "I practice a lot when I'm alone."

7. Nagel, p. 15. [This passage is not in the version of Nagel's essay reprinted above.]

8. Janice Moulton made the same point in a paper at the Pacific APA meeting, March 1976. (This volume, pp. 31–38.)

9. Solomon, p. 285.

10. The example is like one from Sara Ruddick, "Better Sex," *Philosophy and Sex*, p. 96.

11. See Michael Slote, "Inapplicable Concepts and Sexual Perversion," *Philosophy and Sex*, 261–67.

Chapter 6

SEX AND SEXUAL PERVERSION

Robert Gray

Sara Ruddick has suggested, what seems probable, that intrinsic to the notion of perversion is that of unnaturalness.[1] That and only that sexual activity which is unnatural is perverted. There are, of course, difficulties with the notion of naturalness itself. 'Natural' may be used synonymously with 'usual' or 'ordinary', in which case perversion would appear to be entirely culturally relative. (We should have, perhaps, to except such things as adultery, which seem to be common to virtually all human societies.) On the other hand, 'natural' may be used to describe particular activities as the outcomes of naturally occurring processes. Ignoring the circularity in this, such a definition would have as a consequence that all perversions are natural, since the fetishes of the coprophiliac are as much the outcome of his natural desires and propensities as those of the "normal" heterosexual. Even if it were argued that there has been some sort of breakdown in the control mechanisms governing the behavior of the coprophiliac, still that breakdown itself could be accounted for ultimately only by an appeal to naturally occurring events, in this case, perhaps, biological laws. There is, however, a sense of 'natural' which may allow an argument such as Ruddick's to get off the ground.

Typically, by 'unnatural' we mean not just "unusual," but something more like "contrary to nature." The question is, in what sense anything may be regarded as contrary to nature. To this, the best answer would

Reprinted, with the permission of Robert Gray and the *Journal of Philosophy*, from *Journal of Philosophy* 75:4 (1978), pp. 189–99.

appear to be that something is contrary to (its own) nature if it is counterproductive. What this requires, of course, is that there be some end or
function of a given kind of behavior in terms of which we may say that a
particular behavior is counterproductive or contrary to its nature as an
instance of behavior of that kind, and the question is, "How do we fix
that end or function in a noncircular way?" The way Ruddick would
seem to favor, and the only way I see if we are to avoid cultural relativism,
is in terms of evolutionary theory. If, then, we are able to show that there
is some adaptive function or end that sexual activity evolved to fulfill, we
may speak of sexual activity that departs from that function and, more
clearly, of sexual activity that, by departing from that function, is maladaptive, as counterproductive and, in that sense, contrary to nature or
unnatural. Thus, if reproduction is the adaption function of sexual activity, those forms of sexual activity which are nonreproductive and,
more clearly, those which are inimical to successful reproduction (for
example, any nonreproductive sexual obsession) would be unnatural
and perverted; they would constitute, as it were, a twisting of sexual activity away from its "natural" object or function. Put more simply, those
forms of sexual activity would be perverted which, in evolutionary terms,
are dysfunctional.

This would, in fact, seem to be Ruddick's position. On her view, the
adaptive function or, if one prefers, the natural end of sexual activity is
reproduction, and she concludes that all and only those forms of sexual
activity which may, under normal conditions, be expected to fulfill this
end are natural (24). All others are unnatural and perverted. However,
this view raises some problems.

In the first place, one might ask how sexual activities are to be identified. If, for example, the natural function of sexual activity is reproduction, an end to which coprophilia has no relation at all, would that not
by itself be ground for suggesting that the activities of the coprophiliac
are not *sexual* activities at all, and so, of course, not sexual perversions?
The problem may not be one whose solution is difficult, but for our
question it is important, for in order to elucidate the notion of sexual
perversion it would seem crucial that we be able to specify just what it is
about an activity that makes it an instance of sexual activity. The coprophiliac's activities might well be perverted, but there need be nothing
about them in virtue of which they are sexually perverted. I might, for
example, have developed some sort of penchant for eating cow dung,
doubtless disgusting, doubtless nonnutritive, almost certainly perverted,
but what has this to do with sex? Clearly, if I regard the eating of manure
simply as the only means of fulfilling my appetite for food, if in other
words, I eat because I am hungry and because it tastes good or better
than the available alternatives, or, if it tastes worse, because it leaves me
feeling less hungry, my perversion is not sexual. Sexually, I might be

entirely normal. Now the only thing I can see in this example that would constitute it as a nonsexual form of coprophilia and the only thing whose change could conceivably make it an example of coprophilia in the sexual sense, is the motive assigned. Hunger is a fairly distinct, clearly recognizable form of displeasure; as such, it gives rise, circumstances permitting, to activities that will remove or assuage it. In the same way, sexual desire (although, unlike hunger, it may be in itself pleasant or partially so) is a distinct, recognizable appetite, typically unpleasant if unfulfilled, which gives rise to activities that will remove or assuage it.

What is to be noted here is that neither hunger nor sexual desire is in itself a desire for a particular (kind of) object. In itself, each is a feeling which, all things considered, it would, at the time, be better not to have, or, better, which one would, when circumstances permit, so act as to remove. Hunger seems to be a desire for food because, typically, it is food that relieves it, and it is therefore food that the hungry person seeks. But it is entirely possible that someone should develop a food fetish for the coprolites of cattle; that is to say, it is entirely possible that, for whatever reason, someone's feeling of hunger might be relieved only by the ingestion of manure. Such a person we might well call a food pervert. But we would not call him a sexual pervert. The difference lies in his motive. His motive is hunger, not sex. On the other hand, if what he had eaten gave him sexual pleasure, his perversion, and therefore his activity, would have been sexual. Since the activities I have described here are otherwise identical (need the coprophiliac who is sexually perverted display any overt signs of sexual excitement?), I see no other way by which the one might be classed as sexual and the other not. Those activities, accordingly, are sexual which serve to relieve sexual feeling or, alternatively put, which give rise to sexual pleasure.

Of course, it might well be objected that sexual activity does not, in fact, serve so much to relieve, as to heighten sexual feeling (which, for purposes of this discussion, we may take to refer, at least initially, to a physiological state, although many emotional and cognitive states may, and typically do, come to be intimately associated with it). The objection has some force; however, I believe it may be fairly easily answered, for, in much the same way, food, which typically serves to relieve hunger, may also serve to heighten it. There is, of course, a point at which the analogy between hunger and sexual feeling breaks down, for sexual feeling is typically relieved by intensifying it. Whereas a little food may, in some cases, be very satisfying, a little bit of sex often leaves an individual feeling less satisfied than he might otherwise have been. Accordingly, I prefer to speak of sexual activity in terms of sexual pleasure. The activities by which sexual feeling is removed are experienced as (an intensification of) pleasurable sexual feeling. When they cease to be pleasurable, that is to say, when the sexual feeling has been removed, the activities lose their specifically sexual character, and, unless there is some other reason for continuing, the behavior ceases.

Sexual perversions, then, will be all and only those activities which are dysfunctional (in the sense given above) in terms of sexual pleasure, or, as Thomas Nagel expresses it, "A sexual perversion must reveal itself in conduct that expresses an unnatural *sexual* preference" (9). However, as the quotation from Nagel shows, this is not quite adequate. Perversion, as a category, applies not only to activities, but to persons, in which case the perversion must reveal itself in an unnatural sexual *preference*. There are many sorts of activities from which we might derive sexual pleasure, some of which are undoubtedly perverted, but it is not the fact that a person might derive sexual pleasure from a given activity that makes him perverted; it is, rather, that he desires or prefers to engage in such sexual activities. We may say, accordingly, that a person will be sexually perverted if his sexual desires are for, or lead him to perform, activities which, given the adaptive function(s) of sexual activity (e.g., that it ends in reproduction), are counterproductive or maladaptive.

The definitions given here have some interesting implications, which may be best seen by contrasting them with the views taken by Ruddick. Ms. Ruddick is concerned, not so much with sexual perversion, as with what she calls "better sex," of which, on her account, pleasure, naturalness (nonpervertedness), and "completeness" are the three criteria (18). As I have developed the notion of sexual activity, however, it is clear that pleasure is a criterion not so much of better sex as of sex itself. Those activities not serving to relieve sexual feeling, or from which no sexual pleasure is derived, would thus not be sexual activities at all. This at first sight seems counterintuitive, since we often speak, for example, of a person's not enjoying (in the sense of deriving pleasure from) sexual relations with his or her spouse. In this case, the difficulty lies, I think, with ordinary language. Sexual intercourse is thought to be, and is spoken of as, sexual activity, because it is that activity to which sexual desire paradigmatically leads. The unacceptability of the ordinary-language criterion is best shown, however, by the fact that, if we accept it, we are led to the unhappy conclusion that the rape victim has engaged in sexual activity, although, from her point of view, the activity may not have been sexual at all. It may make the analysis of sexual relations more difficult, but there is nothing intrinsically objectionable in the suggestion that what is, from the point of view of one of the participants, a sexual activity, may not be so from the point of view of the other. In fact, it would seem that ordinary language itself recognizes sexual pleasure as a criterion of sexual activity, at least implicitly and on some occasions. For example, ordinary persons are fond of bewailing the amount of sex and violence shown on commercial television. Just what constitutes sex in this case, however, is not clear, since neither nudity nor the portrayal of it is, in itself, a sexual activity. Were it so, the ordinary man, it seems to me, would be forced to conclude that he engages in sexual activities far more frequently than he might otherwise think, e.g., in taking a bath or changing his clothes. The only thing I can see in this example in virtue of which televised nudity might be called sexual is the fact that it is intended to, and in fact does, arouse sexual feelings. The fact that it is so intended, however, may not be crucial. To take another example, Dr. David Reuben relates that, in the early days of the garment industry, women found that the operation of treadle sewing machines could be employed as a masturbatory technique,[2] and, to the extent that they so employed it, I think it is clear that they would, in ordinary parlance, be said to be engaging in sexual activity. We must assume, however, that at some point the sexual possibilities of operating a treadle sewing machine must have been discovered, presumably, at least in some cases, by accident. Those women who made this discovery would then have found themselves engaging in sexual activity quite unintentionally. They may or may not have found this a welcome discovery, but that is quite beside the point.

If these examples are compelling, and taken in sum I think they are, we are forced to the conclusion that what makes an activity a sexual activity, even in terms of ordinary language, is just the sexual nature of the pleasure deriving from it. Accordingly, it is quite possible that any activity might become a sexual activity and, as the last example shows, that it might become a sexual activity unintentionally. And, of course, it would follow too that no activity is a sexual activity unless sexual pleasure is derived from it. And, since no activity could be sexually perverted unless it were also a sexual activity, the same thing would hold for sexual perversion.

Although pleasure would thus seem to enter the analysis of sexual activity only as a matter of degree, as one means of determining the comparative worth, in sexual terms, of any given sexual experience, the notion of completeness would not appear to enter at all. Ruddick, who seems to take the notion principally from Nagel, defines it in this way:

> A sex act is complete if each partner (1) allows himself to be "taken over" by desire, which (2) is desire not merely for the other's body but also for *his* desire, and (3) where each desire is occasioned by a response to the partner's desire (20).

Though she offers a defense of sorts for the claim that, in a complete sex act, the participant is "taken over" or "embodied" by his or her desire, Ruddick would seem to have no real argument in support of the other elements of her definition. In fact, she goes so far as to say at the end of her discussion of completeness that "incompleteness does not disqualify a sex act from being fully sexual" (23). Presumably, these other aspects

of the completeness of a sex act are just accidental components, characteristics which may or may not be present but which serve to make the
sex act "better" when they are. It should be noted, however, that when
Ruddick comes to discuss the contribution that completeness makes to
the sex act, it is not the sex act itself that is said to be improved. (This will
not hold for the condition of "embodiment.") She argues, rather, that
completeness contributes to the psychological and social well-being of
the participants (29–30).

For Nagel, on the other hand, completeness would appear to be, at
least partially, constitutive of sexual activity. Completeness, on his view,
would appear to consist in a complex interaction between the desires of
the two participants ("It is important that the partner be aroused, and
not merely aroused, but aroused by the awareness of one's desire"—16),
and he writes accordingly that

> . . . this overlapping system of distinct sexual perceptions and interactions
> is the basic framework of any full-fledged sexual relation and that relations
> involving only part of the complex are significantly incomplete. (15)

That Nagel should have attached such significance to the notion of completeness (a perversion is, for him, simply an incomplete sex act—16) is
fairly easily explained. Nagel has incorrectly assumed that "sexual desire
is a feeling about other persons." It "has its own content as a relation between persons." Accordingly, "it is only by analyzing that relation that we
can understand the conditions of sexual perversion" (12). This mistake,
as has already been pointed out, is understandable and is, furthermore,
one we commonly make. Copulation is the paradigmatic object of sexual desire; it is just such a relation between persons that sexual desire has
as its "characteristic object." But it is a mistake to go from this to the view
that sexual desire has such an object as its content (or to the view that,
in the analysis of sexual activity, the nature of sexual desire is in any way
fundamental). A given desire is sexual, not because it has a particular object, but because it arises from a particular kind of feeling. Put differently, it is the desire (or feeling) itself that is sexual, and it is in terms of
this that the activity it has as its object is perceived as a sexual activity. The
relationship is not the other way around. If it were, it would be difficult,
if not impossible, to see how many of the more exotic perversions could
be considered sexual. One might characterize an activity such as masturbation (which Nagel apparently regards as a perversion—17) as sexual on the basis of some sort of family relation with coital activity, but this
seems unlikely as a means of categorizing all sexual activities as sexual.
Even in the case of masturbation this approach would raise problems
(one could, for example, conceive a situation in which a person might
masturbate, while feeling nothing at all—perhaps by using anesthetic

ointments—for reasons having nothing to do with sexual desire or grat-ification—as part of a medical experiment, for instance. Would this ac-tivity in that case be sexual?), but one wonders what the family resemblance might be in the, admittedly strange, case of coprophilia de-scribed earlier.

This, however, is not the only difficulty with Nagel's notion of com-pleteness, although I think it is the most serious. As Janice Moulton has argued, both Nagel and Robert Solomon (who sees the specific content of sexual desire in terms of interpersonal communication—sexual activ-ity is a kind of "body language")³ have "assumed that a model of flirta-tion and seduction constitute an adequate model of sexual behavior in general," whereas, as she argues, "most sexual behavior does not involve flirtation and seduction, and . . . what characterizes flirtation and se-duction is not what characterizes the sexual behavior of regular part-ners."⁴ This itself, however, leads Moulton into difficulties. She is forced to conclude that it is impossible to characterize sexual behavior, because there are two kinds of it: "sexual anticipation," which includes "flirtation, seduction, and traditional courtship," and "sexual satisfaction," which "involves sexual feelings which are increased by the other person's knowledge of one's preferences and sensitivities, the familiarity of their touch or smell or way of moving, and not by the novelty of their sexual interest" (32). "However, anticipation and satisfaction are often di-vorced" (32). But even this classification is too narrow, for, to the extent that satisfaction is here defined in interpersonal terms, "the *other* per-son's knowledge . . . the familiarity of *their* touch," etc., masturbation and related types of sexual activities would, again, be excluded from the pos-sible range of sexual behaviors. However, there is, as we have seen, a means, if not of characterizing, at least of identifying behavior as sexual, and the ground here, sexual feeling, is independent of any particular model of sexual activity. Note that this is not equivalent to saying that, as Solomon puts it, "sex is pure physical enjoyment" (27). To put it in Solomon's words again, "this enjoyment accompanies sexual activity and its ends, but is not that activity or these ends" (26). Sexual activity may have many ends, interpersonal communication among them, but if we take the view that it is the end that identifies it as sexual, then we are left squarely facing the problem that any sexual activity that does not have that specific end is not, in fact, sexual activity or is somehow less than fully sexual. Thus, on Solomon's communication model, masturbation turns out to be like "talking to yourself" and therefore "clearly secondary to sexuality in its broader interpersonal context." And " 'Unadorned sex-ual intercourse' . . . becomes the ultimate perversion, since it is the sex-ual equivalent of hanging up the telephone without saying anything" (27). One is inclined to take the view, in fact, that, if Solomon has con-centrated too narrowly on one model of sexuality, it is not that of anticipation, but of satisfaction. Like most men, Solomon seems to be fully persuaded of the fundamental role of genital-genital intercourse (which is entirely satisfactory from a male point of view) in human sexuality. There is evidence, however, to show that, at least from the female point of view, it is not (this sort of) intercourse, but masturbation that is crucial.[5] This may, of course, take place in an interpersonal context, and it may be preferable when it does. All it shows is that our models must not be so constructed as to exclude it.

* * *

What the foregoing discussion will show is that the classification of a given (type of) sexual behavior as perverted is purely descriptive. Which activities are and are not perverted will depend on what we ultimately discover the natural adaptive function of sexual activity to be, and this is a question whose answer must be given by the scientist whose business it is to study such things. Of course, if reproduction were, as some think, the sole function of sexual activity, the scientist would have no further questions to ask about the matter, and all nonreproductive sexual activity might correctly be described as perverted. However, it would seem that this is not the case. "Reproduction" is, as Nagel claims, a biological concept. As such, it includes such biological functions as conception, gestation, and birth, and, if men were fruit flies, sexual behavior might have been just that behavior minimally sufficient to ensure reproduction in this limited sense. Copulation, then, might have been enough to ensure conception; conception, enough to ensure gestation; and gestation, enough to ensure birth. The fact is, however (and the world may or may not be better off for it), that men are not fruit flies, and reproduction in man includes far more than just the production of new individuals. Reproductive activity in man must be construed as the sum of all those activities minimally necessary to bring those new individuals themselves to reproductive maturity. Among other things, this would seem to include the formation and maintenance of well-organized, stable societies and the establishment and maintenance of fairly stable male-female reproductive pairs. Since the latter would seem ultimately to depend on sexual attraction and since there is substantial evidence to show that many characteristics of human sexual behavior contribute as well to the former, it would seem probable at least that maintenance of that degree (and kind) of social organization and stability requisite to the maintenance of human society is a function that human sexual behavior has evolved to fulfill, and, if this is so, it is clear that the range of nonperverted sexual activity will be much broader than it has traditionally been taken to be. It may turn out, too, that the natural adaptive functions of human sexual activity are not culturally independent. In this case, a behavior that is maladaptive in one society may not be so in another. Thus, for example, male homosexual behavior may be maladaptive in a society with a high ratio of females to males and a birth rate too low to make the society viable. In another society, however, where the sex ratios are reversed, male homosexual behavior, by reducing sexual rivalry, might be adaptive. A similar argument would serve to demonstrate the possible adaptive character of such activities as masturbation, whatever the techniques used, including "intercourse with . . . inanimate objects," which Nagel classes as a perversion. We could, perhaps, say then that variability of sexual objects is a natural characteristic, or natural adaptive function, of human sexual desire and that, where it contributes to (or, at least, does not detract from) the maintenance of the over-all social order, or to the long-term viability of society, such variability is adaptive (or, at least, not maladaptive) and nonperverted.

Of course, it may well be that, as many stalwarts claim, all and only those sexual activities traditionally approved in our society are natural (or adaptive) and nonperverted, and what the discussion so far will show is that those who agitate against the increasing sexual permissiveness of contemporary society on the ground that it is destructive of the family, presumably the bulwark of modern social institutions, are at least on the right track. However, if the view of the nature of sexual perversion taken here is correct, to uphold the claim that such practices are sexually perverted, it will be necessary to show that societies that encourage divergent sexual behaviors are, for that reason, substantially less viable than our own (since evolutionary theory regards the reproductive group rather than the individual, it should be noted, too, that a particular practice detrimental to a given group or institution may benefit the society as a whole), or that our own society, with its peculiar institutions, would be made substantially less viable, and not merely different, if it permitted or encouraged other sexual practices. In any case, the judgment whether or not a given activity is sexually perverted, to the extent that it is properly an answer to the factual question whether the behavior is or is not consonant with the natural adaptive function(s) of sexual activity, would be descriptive and nonevaluative and need not, therefore, carry any moral connotations.

This, of course, is not to say that sexual perversion is not immoral. In fact, depending on the moral view we take, there may well be ground for claiming that any and all sexual perversion is immoral. For example, one might adopt a moral view according to which the natural is the moral. This would not automatically brand sexual perversion as immoral, since it may be the case, as we have seen, that human sexual activity is naturally variable. If, however, this theory were cast in evolutionary terms, so that natural is taken to mean the naturally adaptive function of given behavior, sexual perversion would, by definition, be immoral. I am not myself inclined to such a moral view. I am, rather, inclined to take a somewhat

Hobbesian view, according to which morality is the sum of those rules minimally necessary to social cohesion. On this view, all sexual activities that are perverted by virtue of the fact that they disrupt the cohesiveness of society, assuming social cohesion is a natural function of human sexual activity, would be immoral. But it should be noted that this judgment is logically independent of the judgment that those activities are perverted. One might, therefore, make the suggestion, since 'perversion' has acquired such a strong pejorative connotation in our society, that the term be dropped from our sexual vocabulary altogether. Other clearer and less emotive terms may just as easily be substituted for it.

But, whatever the moral implications, this much seems clear. If we have correctly defined what it is for behavior to be sexually perverted and, in that sense, "contrary to nature," as any practice or activity from which sexual pleasure is derived and which, given the natural adaptive function(s) of sexual activity, is counterproductive or maladaptive, we will at least have succeeded in putting the question, "What specific activities are and are not perverted?" in terms amenable to investigation by the behavioral sciences. In such questions as these, no more really can be asked of the philosopher.

Notes

1. "On Sexual Morality," in James Rachels, ed., *Moral Problems,* 2nd ed. (New York: Harper & Row, 1975), pp. 23–24. See also Thomas Nagel, "Sexual Perversion," *The Journal of Philosophy* 66, No. 1 (1969), pp. 5–17. (This volume, pp. 9–20.)

2. *Everything You Always Wanted to Know About Sex* (New York: Bantam, 1971), pp. 201–202. (Originally: McKay, 1969.)

3. "Sexual Paradigms," *The Journal of Philosophy* 71, No. 1 (1974), pp. 336–45, p. 343. (This volume, pp. 21–29; p. 27.)

4. "Sexual Behavior: Another Position," *The Journal of Philosophy* 73, No. 16 (1976), pp. 537–46, p. 538 (This volume, pp. 31–38; p. 32.)

5. Shere Hite, *The Hite Report* (New York: Macmillan, 1976), pp. 229–52.

Chapter 7

MASTURBATION: CONCEPTUAL AND ETHICAL MATTERS

Alan Soble

This vice, which shame and timidity find so convenient, has a particular attraction for lively imaginations. It allows them to dispose, so to speak, of the whole female sex at their will, and to make any beauty who tempts them serve their pleasure without the need of first obtaining her consent.

—Jean-Jacques Rousseau[1]

My philosophical writing on masturbation has a long history. The first piece I wrote on the topic, "Sexual Desire and Sexual Objects," was a paper I presented, not long out of graduate school, at the Pacific Division meetings of the American Philosophical Association (held in San Francisco, March 1978). Soon after that I published an essay on the topic, "Masturbation," which appeared in *Pacific Philosophical Quarterly* 61 (1980): 233–44. I resisted the kind advice of the editors of the journal to alter the title; they reasonably feared that some readers would unfairly take its title to be descriptive of the essay's content. (The essay has been reprinted, unchanged, in Igor Primoratz, ed., *Human Sexuality* [Dartmouth Publishing Co., 1997], 139–150.) A greatly revised, mostly new, version of that early essay, "Masturbation and Sexual Philosophy," was included eleven years later in the second edition of *The Philosophy of Sex: Contemporary Readings* (1991). I continued to read and think about masturbation and sexuality and the results of my additional research emerged in *Sexual Investigations* (New York University Press, 1996), chap. 2, 59–110. Part of that chapter, of course revised, was included the next year as "Masturbation" in the third edition of *The Philosophy of Sex* (1997); it was further changed in various ways to form the less technical "Philosophies of Masturbation," which is to appear in Martha Cornog, ed., *Self-Love/Self-Abuse* (Down There Press). The article included in this fourth edition of *Philosophy of Sex* is an amalgam, modification, correction, and expansion of some of the work mentioned in this note. For more ruminations on the issues discussed in this paper, see my *The Philosophy of Sex and Love: An Introduction* (St. Paul, Minn.: Paragon House, 1998).

[I]f your right hand causes you to sin, cut it off and throw it away. It is better for you to lose one part of your body than for your whole body to go into
hell.
        —Jesus [Matthew 5:30]

Masturbation mocks, even "deconstructs," the categories and concepts of both our everyday (ordinary) and technical (scientific)
sexual discourses. Masturbation, like sex that can occur in a good marriage or with an admired and intimate lover, is sex with someone I care
about and to whose satisfaction and welfare I am devoted. Masturbation
is incestuous, since it happens with someone to whom I am blood-
related, someone within my own family. If I am married, my masturbating is adulterous, since it is sex with someone who is not my spouse, to
whom I am not married. Masturbation is homosexual: a man sexually
pleases a man or a woman sexually pleases a woman. Masturbation is
pederastic, when it is engaged in by a youngster. Masturbation is sex we
occasionally fall into inadvertently or nonconsciously ("if you shake it
more than twice, you're playing with it"), and hence masturbation is sex
that is not completely voluntary or consensual; it is not quite against my
will, yet not fully with my will either. And masturbation with fantasies—
to rely on Rousseau's insight—is the promiscuous rape of every man,
woman, or beast to whom I take a fancy. Given the queer nature of masturbation, it is no wonder that we advertise our marriages and brag
about our affairs and conquests, but silently keep our masturbatory practices to ourselves. The sexual revolution has made having sex and living
together outside matrimony perfectly socially acceptable; it has encouraged the toleration, if not also the celebration, of homosexual lifestyles;
it has even breathed respectable life into the colorful practices of the
sons and daughters of the Marquis de Sade.[2] But to call a man a jerk off
is still strongly derogatory (and an accusation that masturbating women
somehow avoid). Masturbation, at least the male variety, is the black
sheep of the family of sex,[3] scorned, as we shall see, by both the Right
and the Left.

The Concept

Conceptual questions about masturbation arise when we critically examine the paradigm or central case: a person in a private place or space
manually rubs the penis or clitoris and eventually reaches an orgasm
(perhaps aided by fantasy, pornography, or by nothing at all). But most
of the salient features of the paradigm case are conceptually unnecessary. (1) One can masturbate in the crowded waiting room of a bus terminal (hardly a private space), with erect penis displayed for all to see or

with fingers conspicuously rubbing the clitoris. (Of course, this masturbatory behavior might lead to being arrested by the police.) (2) The hands do not have to be used, as long as the sexually sensitive areas of the body can be pressed against a suitably shaped object of comfortable composition: the back of a horse or its saddle, the seat of a bicycle or motorcycle, a rug or pillows. (3) Orgasm need not be attained for the act to be masturbatory, nor need orgasm even be the goal. Prolonged sexual pleasure itself is often the point of masturbation, pleasure that can be curtailed by the orgasm, which might occur too soon. (4) The clitoris or penis need not receive the most or any attention. There are other sexually sensitive areas one can touch and press for masturbatory pleasure: the anus, nipples, thighs, and lips. What little remains in the paradigm case of masturbation does seem necessary, however: (5) the person who, by touching or pressing the sexually sensitive areas of the body causally produces the sensations, is exactly the same person who experiences them. The rubber is the rubbed. On this account, the "solitary vice" of "self-abuse" looks logically reflexive.

But *mutual* masturbation would be conceptually impossible if masturbation were logically solitary, and we have a paradigm case of mutual masturbation: two persons rubbing each other between the legs (which act we do often call "mutual masturbation"). Now, if it is conceptually possible for two persons *X* and *Y* to masturbate each other, it must also be conceptually possible for *X* to masturbate *Y*, while *Y* simply relaxes and receives this attention, not doing anything to or for *X*. For example, to give to another person, or to receive from another person, what is sometimes called a "hand job" is to engage in a masturbatory sexual act.[4] "To masturbate," then, is both an intransitive and a transitive verb or concept. Similarly, I can, conceptually, both respect (or deceive) myself and respect (or deceive) another person. Reflexivity, then, may be a sufficient condition, but it does not seem to be necessary, for a sexual act to be masturbatory.

But, if so, an analytic problem arises: explaining why mutual masturbation *is* masturbation. This turns out to be a difficult task. For example, saying that the paradigm case of mutual masturbation and the two-person hand job are masturbatory just because they are sexual acts that involve the hands and genitals is awkward. We would end up claiming that all solitary sex acts are masturbatory, even those that do not involve the hands and the genitals, while paired sexual acts are masturbatory exactly when they do involve the hands and the genitals. This seems arbitrary and ad hoc. Further, on this view, *X*'s tweaking her own nipples when she is alone *is* masturbatory, *Y*'s doing it to or for *X* when they are together is *not* masturbatory, yet *Y*'s manually tweaking *X*'s clitoris *is* masturbatory. These implications are chaotic; there must be (we optimistically hope) a better way to differentiate paired masturbatory from paired nonmasturbatory sexual acts, if there is a distinction at all.

One way to distinguish paired masturbatory sexual acts (that is, mutual masturbation) from paired nonmasturbatory sexual acts might be to contrast sexual acts that do not involve any insertion and those that do. The idea is that without the bodily insertion of something, somewhere, no mixing together of two fleshes occurs, and the participants in some sense remain isolated in their private place (the way the solitary masturbator carries out his or her sexual activity). On this view, the paradigm case of mutual masturbation, in which the persons rub each other between the legs, and the two-person hand job, both turn out to be masturbatory because no insertion occurs. And male-female coitus and male-male anal coitus would not be masturbatory because they do involve insertion. Further, on this view, X's fellating Y is not a case of masturbation, which seems correct, and the view plausibly implies that coitus between a human male and a female animal (a sheep), or between a human female and a male animal (a dog), is not masturbatory (assuming that the man or the woman is not engaged in a *solitary* activity if an animal is involved). These sexual acts are not masturbatory because some sort of insertion occurs. The view also implies that frottage in a crowded subway car is masturbatory, even though it requires the presence of another person, the unwilling victim, and that tribadism is a mutually masturbatory sexual activity, because there is no insertion in either case. But distinguishing between paired masturbatory and paired nonmasturbatory sexual activity by referring to acts that do not and acts that do involve insertion is inadequate. In the paradigm case of mutual masturbation, insertion of one person's fingers into the vagina of the other person might very well occur, and the fact that some insertion takes place would not seem to imply that the act was no longer mutual masturbation. To appreciate the point another way, consider cunnilingus. This sexual act might or might not involve insertion, in this case of the tongue, lips, or nose into another person's vagina. To claim that cunnilingus is masturbatory when and only when it does not involve insertion implies that one continuous act of cunnilingus would change from not masturbatory to masturbatory and back again often within a few minutes. That, too, is a chaotic and counterintuitive implication. And what about a male who punctures a hole in a watermelon to make room for his erect penis, or a female who reaches for her g-spot with a zucchini inside her vagina? These acts are masturbatory yet involve insertion of a genital organ into something or of something into a genital organ.

Some of these problem examples can be avoided by narrowing what counts as an "insertion." Masturbation might be characterized more specifically as sexual activity not involving the insertion of a real penis into a hole or cavity of a living being. Then the problem caused by the watermelon and the zucchini examples mentioned above is solved. But it seems to follow that all paired lesbian sexuality, which does not involve a penis, is masturbatory,[5] while many paired sexual acts (oral sex, anal coitus) engaged in by male homosexuals are not masturbatory. This conclusion doesn't make any sense at all. Were we to decide, for which there is good reason, that a male having intercourse with a sheep is, after all, engaging in a masturbatory act—that is, if we perceive no significant difference between this bestial sexual act and a man's rubbing his penis with a pair of woman's panties (using "solitary" to mean being away from other people)—we could define masturbation even more specifically as sexual activity not involving the insertion of a real penis into a hole or cavity of a human being. This refined, scholastic account of masturbation is literally phallocentric in characterizing sexual acts with reference to the male organ. As a result, the analysis implies an implausible *conceptual* double standard: fellatio, oral sex done on a male (whether by a male or a female), is not masturbatory, but cunnilingus, oral sex done on a female (by a male or a female), is always masturbatory. An *evaluative* double standard looms when to this analysis the usual disparagement of masturbation is added: fellatio is "real sex," cunnilingus is a fraud, merely masturbation. This refined view (which is sexist but not heterosexist, because its point does not depend on the sex or gender of the fellator) is similar to the claim (which is heterosexist but not necessarily sexist) that the paradigm case of a natural, normal, acceptable, or proper sexual act is male-female coitus. What is conceptually and normatively emphasized in this latter view—the most specific we can get about "insertion"—is the insertion of a real penis not into any hole of a human being, but its insertion into a particular hole, the vagina. This view suggests that masturbation should be understood as any sexual act that is not procreative in its form or potential, whether solitary or paired. Socially, biologically, or theologically useless sexual acts, those that do not aim at, or do not have at least the potential of, perpetuating the species, and whose purpose is, instead, only or primarily to produce pleasure for the participant(s), are masturbatory. If so, our sexual lives contain a *lot* more masturbation than we had thought. Maybe, as we shall see, this is the right conclusion to draw, that most of our paired sexual acts (in addition to our solitary sexual acts) are masturbatory, but we would like more convincing grounds for it. Maybe, also, we should abandon the attempt to distinguish paired masturbatory from paired nonmasturbatory sexual acts, and jettison the notion of "mutual masturbation" from our sexual discourse as being archaic, misleading, and a misnomer. But let us stubbornly press forward.

There is usually a clear distinction between solitary and paired sexual activity, and to this extent, at least, there is a clear way to identify some masturbatory sexual acts. But suppose a person X is engaging in some sexual activity with another person Y, and X's arousal is sustained during this physical interaction by X's having private fantasies. This sexual act is solitary and hence masturbatory in the sense that Y is absent from X's sexual consciousness. It is as if X were really alone. That which would be arousing X during solitary masturbation (X's fantasies) is doing the same thing for X while X rubs his penis or her clitoris on or with Y's body instead of with X's own hand. Paired sex, then, even heterosexual genital intercourse, might be seen as masturbation pure and simple, depending on certain "mental" components of the sexual act. Consider, further, that under certain descriptions of paired sexual activity, no difference exists between it and solitary masturbation. Listen to the young, precocious, helpful Alexander Portnoy offer his cheating father an exculpating redescription of adultery:

> What after all does it consist of? You put your dick some place and moved it back and forth and stuff came out the front. So, Jake, what's the big deal?[6]

Adulterous coitus is redescribed, defined "downward," as if it were solitary masturbation: you put your penis someplace—in your fist—and move it back and forth until it ejaculates. Portnoy's sarcasm also suggests why there is no essential difference between mutual masturbation and heterosexual genital or homosexual (or heterosexual) anal intercourse: *every* paired sexual act is masturbatory because the mutual rubbing of sensitive areas, the friction of skin against skin, that occurs during mutual masturbation is, from a physical perspective, the same as the mutual rubbing of skin against skin that occurs during coitus. The only difference is that different parts of the body or patches of skin may be involved in the rubbings; but, of course, no one patch or set of patches of skin has any sexual privilege over any other. Further, there is only one difference between solitary and paired masturbation or between solitary sexual activity and any type of paired sexual activity: the number of people who accomplish these same physical rubbings. We might now have a better reason for concluding that *all* sex is masturbatory.

Reflecting on what Immanuel Kant has written on human sexuality may be useful here. For Kant, sexual interaction by its nature involves one person merely using another person for the sake of achieving sexual pleasure:

> [T]here is no way in which a human being can be made an Object of indulgence for another except through sexual impulse. . . . Sexual love . . . by itself . . . is nothing more than appetite. Taken by itself it is a degradation of human nature. . . . [A]s an Object of appetite for another a person becomes a thing.[7]

Kant is not asserting the physical indistinguishability of mutual masturbation and other paired sexual acts. He is suggesting that the desire involved in all sexual activity is the desire to get sexual pleasure for oneself through the vehicle of the other's body and the other's compliance with one's wishes, and that the other person is just a means for the satisfaction of this desire. (Solitary masturbation would involve the desire to get sexual pleasure for oneself by using one's own body, or oneself, as a thing.) In portraying all sexual acts as by their nature objectifying and instrumental, Kant makes us wonder: Is not celibacy required? Kant answers in the negative:

> The sole condition on which we are free to make use of our sexual desire depends upon the right to dispose over the person as a whole. . . . [I] obtain these rights over the whole person . . . [o]nly by giving that person the same rights over the whole of myself. This happens only in marriage. . . . In this way the two persons become a unity of will. . . . Thus sexuality leads to a union . . . and in that union alone its exercise is possible.[8]

I do not think that Kant is claiming that the marital pledge assures that even though the spouses are a means to each other's sexual pleasure in the marriage bed, they do not treat each other merely as means to their sexual pleasure but also as ends, as persons to whom respect and consideration are due during sex, as well as before and after. Perhaps, instead, Kant justifies marital sexual acts by abolishing the conceptual possibility of instrumentality altogether; by literally uniting two persons into one person by marriage, he makes the sexual use of one person by another conceptually impossible.[9] I do not think that this is what Kant had in mind.[10] But if this view is right, Kant would in effect be justifying sexual activity in marriage by reducing or equating it to solitary masturbation, the sexual activity of a single, even if metaphysically larger or more complex, person.[11]

Kant's notion (if it is Kant's) that the marital union of two persons into one person cleanses sexuality of instrumentality apparently has two radical implications: that marriage between two homosexual persons would similarly cleanse same-sex sexuality[12] and that masturbation must be permissible. Kant himself, however, resists both implications, asserting that masturbation and homosexuality are immoral because they are *crimina carnis contra naturam:*

> [O]nanism . . . is abuse of the sexual faculty without any object. . . . By it man sets aside his person and degrades himself below the level of animals. . . . [I]ntercourse between *sexus homogenii* . . . too is contrary to the ends of humanity; for the end of humanity in respect of sexuality is to preserve the species.[13]

Kant culminates his denouncement of these sexual aberrations nastily: "He," the masturbator or the homosexual, "no longer deserves to be a person."

Kant has not provided a criterion for distinguishing paired masturbatory from paired nonmasturbatory sexual activity (quite the opposite, actually). Nor was that an issue that concerned him. But Kant's thought
suggests a criterion that concedes to Portnoy the *physical* similarity of
solitary masturbation, mutual masturbation, and paired intercourse,
and focuses instead on a *mental*, or attitudinal, difference: sexual activity
between two persons, each of whom is concerned not only (or not at all)
with her or his own sexual pleasure but also (or only) with the sexual
pleasure of the other person, is not masturbatory (no matter what physical acts they engage in), while sexual activity in which a person is concerned solely with her or his own pleasure is masturbatory. Conceiving
of and treating another person merely as a means to the satisfaction of
one's sexual desires might be, as argued throughout Kant's ethical writings, an important mark of the immoral. Here it is being regarded, instead, as the criterion of the masturbatory. This view implies, plausibly,
that inconsiderate husbands and rapists are the authors of masturbatory
acts. It also implies that mutual masturbation is not masturbatory, as
long as the touches are meant to produce sexual pleasure not only for
the toucher but also for the one being touched.

A weakness of this Kant-inspired analysis is that it does not sufficiently
keep distinct the definition and the evaluation of masturbation, for if we
assume the correctness of Kantian ethics, to call a sexual act masturbatory without also condemning it morally or raising doubts about its
moral status would be difficult if not impossible. It is philosophically desirable that the mere definition of masturbation should not entail a negative (or positive) moral judgment about it. One solution to this tangle
is to reject Kantian ethics (as, after all, many do), while retaining a Kant-
inspired definition of masturbation. This might entail that not all selfish,
self-centered, or self-interested paired sexual acts are for that reason
alone immoral, even if they are for that reason alone masturbatory. What
seems to lie at the heart of masturbation on this Kant-inspired account
is the effort to bring about sexual pleasure for the self—full stop. It is not
part of the core idea of masturbation, then, that masturbation is solitary;
for the attempt to produce sexual pleasure for the self might causally involve other people, animals, the whole universe. Hence that masturbation is logically reflexive—X acts on himself or herself to produce sexual
pleasure for X—must not be taken to entail that masturbation is "solitary." Acting on oneself does not exclude, that is, acting on oneself by
acting on others. In light of the kind of physical creatures we are, attempting to please the self by acting on oneself is easier, even if not always successful. Because our own bodies are handy, and usually more
accessible than the bodies of others, we misleadingly associate masturbation entirely with one form of it, the case in which X touches and sexually pleases X. But the attempt to produce one's own pleasure can

involve other people. Solitary and paired sexual acts are masturbatory, then, to the extent that the actor attempts to produce pleasure for the actor; paired sexual activity is not masturbatory when one person (or both?) attempts to produce pleasure for the other. This notion of masturbation is descriptive, not normative; by itself, it neither praises nor condemns masturbation. But I am not convinced that all the maneuvering that is required philosophically to make this Kant-inspired criterion of masturbation hang together is worth it. Maybe the philosophy of sex would benefit from simply abandoning the idea that there is such a thing as mutual masturbation.

Fulfilling Desire

Three contemporary philosophical accounts of sexuality, proffered by thinkers within the sexually liberal tradition, yield the conclusions that solitary masturbation is not a sexual activity at all (Alan Goldman), is perverted sexuality (Thomas Nagel), or is "empty" sexuality (Robert Solomon). These conclusions are surprising, given the pedigree of these philosophers.[14] I propose to take a careful look at their claims and arguments.

Let's begin with Alan Goldman's definitions of *sexual desire* and *sexual activity*:[15]

> [S]exual desire is desire for contact with another person's body and for the pleasure which such contact produces; sexual activity is activity which tends to fulfill such desire of the agent. (40)

On Goldman's view, sexual desire is strictly the desire for the pleasure of physical contact itself, nothing else, and so does not include a component desire for, say, things such as love, communication, emotional expression, or progeny. Goldman thus takes himself to be offering a liberating analysis of sexuality that does not tether sex normatively or conceptually to love, the emotions, or procreation. But while advocating the conceptual and normative superiority of his notion of "plain sex," Goldman apparently forgot that masturbation needed protection from the same, usually conservative, philosophy that requires sexual activity to occur within a loving marriage or to be procreative in form or potential in order for it to be morally acceptable. On Goldman's analysis, solitary masturbation is not a sexual activity to begin with, for it does not "tend to fulfill" sexual desire, that is, the desire for contact with another person's body. Solitary masturbation, on this view, is quite unlike mutual masturbation, which does tend to fulfill the desire for contact, since it does involve the desired contact and hence is fully sexual. Goldman seems not to be troubled that in his view solitary masturbation is not a sexual act. But it is funny that masturbation is, for Goldman, not sexual, for the conservative philosophy that he rejects could reply to his account somewhat like this: by *reducing* sexuality entirely to the meaningless desire for the pleasure of physical contact ("meaningless" since divorced from love, marriage, commitment, and procreation), what Goldman has analyzed as being the sexual is merely a form of masturbation, even if it occurs between two people.

The vague "tends to fulfill" in Goldman's analysis of sexual activity presents problems. Goldman intended, I think, a narrow causal reading of this phrase: actually touching another person's body is a sexual act just because by the operation of a simple mechanism the act fulfills the desire for that contact and its pleasure. The qualification "tends to" functions to allow, for example, bungled kisses to count as sexual acts, even though they did not do what they were intended to do. Kisses "tend to fulfill" desire in the sense that they normally and effectively produce pleasure, prevented from doing so only by the odd interfering event (the braces get tangled; the hurrying lips land on the chin). The qualification also functions to allow disappointing sexual activity, which does not bring what anticipation promised, to count as sex. In this sense of "tends to fulfill," solitary masturbation is not sex. Suppose that X sexually desires Y, but Y declines X's invitations, and so X masturbates thinking about Y. Goldman's view is not that X's masturbation satisfies X's desire for contact with Y at least a little bit and hence is a sexual act, even if an inefficient one. X's solitary masturbation is not a sexual act at all, despite the sexual pleasure it yields for X, unlike the not pleasurable but still sexual bungled kiss. X's masturbation cannot "tend to fulfill" X's desire for contact with Y, since that contact is excluded.

Suppose we read "tends to fulfill" in a causally broader way. Then giving money to a prostitute—the act of taking bills out of a wallet and handing them to her—might be a sexual act (even if no sexual arousal accompanies the act), because doing so allows the patron to (tend to) fulfill his desire for contact with her body. Handing over $100 would be a *more efficient* sexual act than handing over a ten. Even on this broader reading, however, solitary masturbation would not be a sexual activity; despite the causal generosity, masturbation is still precluded from fulfilling sexual desire in Goldman's sense. (For similar reasons, someone masturbating while looking at erotic photographs is not engaged in a sexual act.) Indeed, solitary masturbation would be a *contrasexual* act, on Goldman's view, if the more X masturbates, the less time, energy, or interest X has for fulfilling the desire for contact with someone else's body.

Goldman does, though, acknowledge one sense in which solitary masturbation is a sexual activity:

Voyeurism or viewing a pornographic movie qualifies as a sexual activity, but only as an imaginative substitute for the real thing (otherwise a deviation from the norm as expressed in our definition). The same is true of masturbation as a sexual activity without a partner. (42)

As I read Goldman, he seems to be claiming that masturbation done for its own sake, done only for the specific pleasure it yields, is *not* sexual, since it is not connected with a desire for contact with another person's body. On his view, masturbation is a sexual act only when done as a substitute for the not available "real thing." But on what grounds could he claim that masturbation's being an "imaginative substitute" for a sexual act makes it a sexual act? In general, being a *substitute for* a certain kind of act does not make something an occurrence of that kind of act. To eat soy burger as a beef substitute in a vegetarian restaurant is not to eat hamburger, even if the soy burger tastes exactly like hamburger. Eating a hamburger as a substitute for the sex I want but cannot have does not make my going to Burger King a sexual event, not even if out of frustration I gorge myself on burgers and fries as compensation.

Given Goldman's analyses of sexual desire and activity, the claim that masturbation done for its own sake is not sexual makes sense. If the solitary masturbator desires the pleasure of physical contact, and masturbates trying (in vain) to get that pleasure, the act, by a stretch, is sexual, because it at least involves genuine sexual desire. By contrast, if the masturbator wants only to experience pleasurable genital sensations, then the masturbator does not have sexual desire in Goldman's sense, and activity engaged in to fulfill this (on his view) nonsexual desire is not sexual activity. But now we have a different problem: what are we to call the act of this masturbator? In what category does it belong, if not the sexual? Note that Goldman argues (41), along the same lines, that if a parent's desire to cuddle a baby, to have some physical contact with it, is only a desire (for example) to show affection and not a desire for the pleasure of physical contact itself, then the parent's act is not sexual. Goldman seems to assume that if the *desire* that causes or leads to an act is not sexual, then neither is the *act* sexual. But if so, a woman who performs fellatio on a man just for the money she gets from doing so is not performing a sexual act. It does not fulfill the sexual desire "of the agent," for, like the baby-cuddling parent, she has no sexual desire to begin with. Thus the prostitute's contribution to fellatio must be called, instead, a "rent paying" or "food gathering" act, since it tends to fulfill her desires to have shelter and eat. Actually, this is an interesting idea, that we should classify an act in part by its motive and not only in terms of its physical characteristics. Still, what Goldman's account implies about a prostitute's participation in a sexual act—it is not sexual, because it is not tied to the appropriate desire—is counterintuitive, flying in the face of common definitions of prostitution as having sex in exchange for money. What the prostitute does is to pay the rent *by* engaging in sex.

Completeness

Thomas Nagel designed his theory of sexuality in order to distinguish, in human sexuality, between the natural and the unnatural (or the perverted).[16] Human sexuality differs from animal sexuality in the role played by a spiral phenomenon that depends on our consciousness. Suppose (1) X looks at Y or hears Y's voice or smells Y's hair—that is, X "senses" Y—and as a result becomes sexually aroused. Also suppose (2) Y senses X, too, and as a result becomes aroused. X and Y are at the earliest or lowest stage of human sexual interaction: the animal level of awareness and arousal. But if (3) X becomes aroused further by noticing ("sensing") that Y is aroused by sensing X, and (4) Y becomes further aroused by noticing that X is aroused by sensing Y, then X and Y have reached a level of distinctively natural human sexuality. Higher iterations of the pattern are also psychologically characteristic of human sexuality: (5) X is aroused even further by noticing (4), that is, Y has become further aroused by noticing that X has been aroused by sensing Y. We might express Nagel's view of human sexuality this way: when X senses Y at the purely animal stage of sexual interaction, X is in X's own consciousness a subject and only a subject of a sexual experience; while Y is for X at this stage only an object of sexual attention. When X advances to the distinctively human level of sexuality, by noticing that Y is aroused by sensing X, X then becomes in X's own consciousness also an object (X sees himself or herself through the eyes—through the desire and arousal—of Y), and so at this level X experiences X as both subject and object. If Y, too, progresses up the spiral, Y's consciousness also recognizes Y as both subject and object. For Nagel, consciousness of oneself as *both subject and object* in a sexual interaction marks it as "complete," as psychologically natural.

Nagel's theory, because it is about natural sexuality and not about the essence (or the definition) of the sexual, does not entail that masturbation is not sexual. However, the judgment that solitary masturbation is perverted *seems* to follow from Nagel's account. Mutual masturbation can, but solitary masturbation cannot, exhibit the completeness of natural sexuality; it lacks the combination of an awareness of the embodiment of another person and an awareness of being sensed as embodied, in turn, by that person. This explains, apparently, why Nagel claims that "narcissistic practices"—which for him seem to include solitary masturbation—are "stuck at some primitive version of the first stage" (17) of the spiral of arousal; "narcissistic practices" are sexually perverted because they are "truncated or incomplete versions of the complete configuration" (16). However, there is a world of difference between narcissism in some special, technical sense and solitary masturbation, so even if looking upon one's own body in a mirror with delight is a sexual perversion, a theorist of sex should not feel compelled for that reason to judge perverted the prosaic practice of solitary masturbation. Nagel also claims that shoe fetishism is perverted (9); "intercourse with . . . inanimate objects" is incomplete (17). But just because shoe fetishism might be a sexual perversion that involves masturbation, a theory of sex need not also conclude that shoeless masturbation is perverted.

A case can be made that the nature of sexual fantasy allows masturbation to be complete enough to be natural in Nagel's sense, and hence not a sexual perversion. Consider someone who is masturbating while looking at erotic photographs. This sexual act avoids incompleteness insofar as the person is aroused not only by sensing the model's body (the animal level), but by being aware of the model's intention to arouse the viewer or by sensing her real or feigned arousal (the human level), as much as these things are captured by the camera (or read into the photograph by the masturbator). Completeness seems not to require that X's arousal as a result of X's awareness of Y's arousal occur at the same time as Y's arousal. Nor does completeness require that X and Y be in the same place: X and Y can cause each other pleasure by talking over the telephone, ascending without any trouble into the spiral of arousal. Further, if X masturbates while fantasizing, sans photograph, about another person, X might be aroused by the intentions expressed or arousal experienced by the imagined partner. (Nagel does say [14] that X might become aroused in response to a "purely imaginary" Y, but does not explain this observation or explore its implications.) A masturbator can imagine, conjure up, these details and experience heightened pleasure as a result. If the masturbator is aroused not only by sensing, in imagination, the other's body, but aroused also by noticing (having created the appropriate fantasy) that the other is aroused by sensing X, then X can be conscious of X as both subject and object, which is the mark of complete, and hence not perverted, sexuality.

I think that this way of arguing that masturbation can be psychologically complete sexuality exposes a complication in Nagel's account. Consider a sexual encounter between a man and a female prostitute. The woman, in order to spend as little time as possible engaging in coitus with her client (she is, after all, a business person, for whom time is money; and, besides, she might be repulsed by him), would like the client to achieve his orgasm quickly, and then she is done with him. She knows, by intuition or experience (she did not read Nagel to discover this feature of human sexual psychology), that her feigning being aroused both at the lowest animal level and at Nagel's human level will greatly increase the sexual arousal of her client and thereby instigate his orgasm. And she knows, equivalently, that failing to express her own arousal—lying mute and motionless on the bed—will impede his becoming aroused and postpone his orgasm. So the smart prostitute pretends, first, to be at the lowest animal level of human sexuality and then *pretends* to enter the spiral of arousal distinctive of human sexuality, while her client *really does* enter the spiral of arousal. The client is not responding with arousal to her being aroused, but only to his false belief that she is aroused. (The woman must carry out the feigning in a credible way, without histrionics.) He experiences himself as both subject and object of the sexual encounter, even though the prostitute remains altogether a sexual object. Thus, in order for one person X to ascend in the spiral of arousal, it need not be the case that the other person ascend as well; X need only *believe* that the other person is ascending. Whether this phenomenon (which, by the way, is not confined to prostitution, but can occur as well during marital sexual activity) confirms Nagel's account of human sexual psychology, or shows that his notion of psychological completeness is not all that complete, is unclear. My guess is that both are true.

Communication

Robert Solomon, as does Nagel, thinks that it is important to distinguish between animal and human sexuality.[17] On Solomon's view, human sexuality is differentiated by its being "primarily a means of communicating with other people" (*SAP*, 279). Sensual pleasure is important in sexual activity, but pleasure is not the main point of sexual interaction or its defining feature (*SP*, 26; *SAP*, 277–79). Sexuality is, instead, "first of all language" (*SAP*, 281). As "a means of communication, it is . . . *essentially* an activity performed with other people" (*SAP*, 279). Could such a view of human sexuality be kind to solitary masturbation? Apparently not:

> If sexuality is essentially a language, it follows that masturbation, while not a perversion, is a deviation. . . . Masturbation is not "self-abuse" . . . but it is, in an important sense, self-denial. It represents an inability or a refusal to say what one wants to say. . . . Masturbation is . . . essential as an ultimate retreat, but empty and without content. Masturbation is the sexual equivalent of a Cartesian soliloquy. (*SAP*, 283)

If sexuality is communicative, as Solomon claims, solitary masturbation can *be* a sexual activity, for conversing with oneself is not impossible, even if it is not the paradigm case of a communicative act. The distinctive flaw of masturbation, for Solomon, is that with respect to other people, communicative intent, success, or content is missing from masturbation. Hence solitary masturbation is "empty" and a "deviation," a conclusion that seems to follow naturally from the proposition that sexuality is "essentially" a way persons communicate *with each other.*

Solomon's denouncing masturbation as a "refusal to say what one wants to say," however, slights the fact that a person might not have, at a given time, something to say to someone else (without thereby being dull); or that there might be nothing worthy of being said, and so silence toward another person is appropriate. Solomon's communication model of sexuality seems to force people to have sexual activity with each other, to talk with each other—in order to avoid the "deviation" of masturbation—even when they have nothing special to say (now *that* looks like "empty" sex). Further, even if the masturbator is merely babbling to himself or herself, he or she still enjoys this harmless pastime as much as does the baby who, for the pure joy if it, makes noises having no communicative intent or meaning. This is not to say that the masturbator is just an infant, in some derogatory sense. The point is that just as the baby who babbles confirms and celebrates its own existence, the person who masturbates can accomplish the same valuable thing, at the same time that he or she experiences the sheer physical pleasure of the act. Thus for Solomon to call masturbation "self-denial" is wrongheaded (it would be self-denial only if the masturbator had something to say to another person, and fled the opportunity to do so), but at least the accusation is a change from the popular conservative criticism of masturbation (which is implicit in Kant) as being a *failure* of self-denial, as being a giving-in to distracting temptations, an immersing of the self in the hedonistic and animalistic excess of self-gratification.

There is little warrant to conclude, within a model of sexuality that likens it to communicative or linguistic behavior, that masturbation is inferior.[18] Solomon meant his analogy between masturbation and a "Cartesian soliloquy" to reveal the shallowness of solitary sexuality (or maybe it was just a thoughtless joke). But René Descartes's philosophical soliloquies are hardly uninteresting; even if we reject, as many philosophers today do, the foundationalism of Cartesian epistemology, we must admit the huge significance of what Descartes accomplished. I suspect, then, that many people would be proud to masturbate as well as the *Meditations* does philosophy. Diaries—which provide another analogy with masturbation, in that a person speaks only to himself or herself—are not often masterpieces of literature, but that does not make them "empty." Indeed, some of the most fruitful discussions one can have are precisely with oneself, not as a substitute for dialogue with another person, and not as compensation for lacking opportunity for conversing with another person, but exactly to explore one's mind, to get one's thoughts straight. This is the stuff from which intellectual integrity emerges and is not necessarily just a preparation for polished public utterances.

Solomon acknowledges that not only do "children, lunatics, and hermits" talk to themselves; "poets and philosophers" do so too (*SAP*, 283). This misleading concession has obvious derogatory implications for solitary masturbation. It plays upon the silly notion that philosophers and poets are a type of lunatic. Where are the bus drivers, the cooks, and the accountants? Solomon's abuse of solitary masturbation trades unfairly on the fact that talking to oneself has always received undeservedly bad publicity—unfair because we all do it, lips moving and heads bouncing, without thereby damning ourselves.

Solomon admits, in light of the fact that philosophers and others do speak to themselves—a counterexample to his argument that "sexuality is a language . . . and primarily communicative" and, hence, masturbation must be deviant—that "masturbation might, *in different contexts,* count as wholly different extensions of language" (*SAP*, 283; italics added). This crucial qualification implies that Solomon's negative judgment of masturbation is, after all, unjustified. Sometimes we want to converse with another person; sometimes we want to have that conversation sexually. In other contexts—in other moods, with other people, in different settings—we want only the pleasure of touching the other's body or of being touched and no serious messages are communicated. To turn around one of Solomon's points: sometimes pleasure alone is the goal of sexual activity, and even though communication might occur it is not the desired or intended result but only an unremarkable or merely curious side effect. In still other contexts or moods, we will not want to talk with anyone at all, but spend time alone. We might want to avoid intercourse, of both types, with human beings, those hordes from whose noisy prattle we try to escape by running off to Montana—not an "ultimate retreat," but a blessed haven, a sanctuary. For Solomon to call masturbation "empty" or inferior in the face of such facts about the importance of context to human sexuality in its many forms is to confess that he did not understand the implications of his own crucial qualification.

Men's Liberation

One of the conspicuous curiosities of the late twentieth century and early twenty-first century is that deciding who is liberal and who is conservative is no longer easy. (Was it ever?) Consider, as an example, the views of John Stoltenberg, a student of the feminist writers and activists Catharine MacKinnon and Andrea Dworkin. Stoltenberg rightly complains about our "cultural imperative," which asserts that men in our society must "fuck" in order to *be* men, and he rightly calls "baloney" the idea that "if two people don't have intercourse, they have not had real sex."[19] Stoltenberg also observes that "sometimes men have coital sex . . . not because they particularly feel like it but because they feel they *should* feel like it." This is a reasonable philosophy of men's liberation and men's feminism, and supplies part of an answer to Solomon. But from these observations Stoltenberg fails to draw the almost obvious conclusion about the value of men's solitary masturbation. Indeed, it is jolting to behold him, in an argument reminiscent of religious objections to contraception (viz., its use makes women into sexual objects), laying a guilt trip on those men who masturbate with the aid of pornography:

> Pay your money and imagine. Pay your money and get real turned on. Pay your money and jerk off. That kind of sex helps . . . support an industry committed to making people with penises believe that people without [penises] are sluts who just want to be ravished and reviled—an industry dedicated to maintaining a sex-class system in which men believe themselves sex machines and men believe women are mindless fuck tubes. (35–36)

In light of Kant's dismal view of human sexual interaction as essentially instrumental, and Stoltenberg's criticism of the obnoxious social imperative that men must fuck women to be men, surely *something* can be said on behalf of men's solitary masturbation. The men's movement attack on oppressive cultural definitions of masculinity, in hand with feminist worries about the integrity of sexual activity between unequally empowered men and women, suggests that men's masturbation is at least a partial solution to a handful of problems. A man pleasing himself by masturbating is not taking advantage of economically and socially less powerful women; he is not refurbishing the infrastructure of his fragile ego at the expense of womankind. He is, instead, flouting cultural standards of masculinity that instruct him that he must perform sexually with women in order to be a man.

Yet, for Stoltenberg, it is fantasizing and the heightened sexual pleasure that the imagination makes possible (44), the things I mentioned while arguing that masturbation is psychologically complete, in Nagel's sense, that constitute wrongful sexual objectification. Stoltenberg does not merely condemn masturbating with pornography (35–36, 42–43, 49–50). Fantasy per se is at fault: Stoltenberg condemns men's masturbating with memories of and passing thoughts about women, even when these fantasies are not violent (41–44). A man's conjuring up a mental image of a woman, her body, or its various parts, is to view the woman as an object, as a thing. Stoltenberg thus takes Jesus and Kant *very* seriously. He answers Robert Nozick's deconstructive or sarcastic question—"In getting pleasure from seeing an attractive person go by, does one use the other solely as a means? Does someone so use an object of sexual fantasies?"[20]—with "yes."

The mental sexual objectification involved in sexual fantasy is both a cause and a result of our social system of "male supremacy," according to Stoltenberg (51, 53–54). Further, mental sexual objectification makes its own contribution to violence against women (54–55). Stoltenberg's reason for thinking this is flimsy. He supposes that when a man fantasizes sexually about women, he reduces them from persons to objects. Further, when a man thinks of women as things, he has given himself carte blanche in his behavior toward them, including violence: regarding an object, "you can do anything to it you want" (55). Of course the last claim is false. There are innumerable lifeless objects to which I would never lay a hand, because other people value them, and I value these people, or because I myself dearly value the objects. Therefore, reducing a woman to a thing—or, to describe it more faithfully to men's experiences than Stoltenberg is willing to do: emphasizing for a while the beauty of only one aspect of a person's existence—does not mean, either logically or psychologically, that she can or will be tossed around the way a young girl slings her Barbie or a young boy tosses his Buzz Lightyear.

Stoltenberg vastly underestimates the nuances of men's fantasies about women; his phenomenological account of what occurs in the minds of fantasizing men—the purported reduction of persons to things—is crude. Her smile, the way she moves down the stairs, the bounce of her tush, the sexy thoughts in her own mind, her lusty yearning for me—these are mere parts of her. But fantasizing or imagining them while masturbating, or driving my car, or having coffee, need not amount to, indeed is *the opposite of,* my reducing her to plastic. These are fantasies about people, not things, and they remain people during the fantasy. My fantasy of her (having a) fantasy of me (or of her having a fantasy of my [having a] fantasy of her) is structurally too sophisticated to be called crude objectification. The fantasizer makes himself in his consciousness both subject and object and imagines his partner as both subject and object. Recognizing the imagined person ontologically as a person is hardly a superfluous component of men's—or women's—fantasies. That Stoltenberg overlooks the complex structure of men's fantasies about women is not surprising; the primitive idea that men vulgarly reduce women to objects in their fantasies is precisely what would occur to someone (Stoltenberg) who has already objectified men, who has reduced men from full persons having intricate psychologies to robots with penises.

Conjugal Union

The conservative Catholic philosopher and legal scholar John Finnis claims, plausibly, that there are morally worthless sexual acts in which "one's body is treated as instrumental for the securing of the experiential satisfaction of the conscious self."[21] Out of context, this claim seems to be condemning rape, the use of a person and his or her body by another person for mere "experiential satisfaction." But rape is the farthest thing from Finnis's mind, for he is talking not about coerced sex, but sexual activity that is fully voluntary. When is sex instrumental, and hence worthless, even though consensual? Finnis immediately mentions, creating the impression that these sexual activities are his primary targets, that "in masturbating, as in being . . . sodomized," the body is merely a tool of satisfaction. As a result of one's body being used, a person undergoes "disintegration": in masturbation and homosexual anal intercourse "one's choosing self [becomes] the quasi-slave of the experiencing self which is demanding gratification." We should ask—since Finnis sounds remarkably like the Kant who claims that sex by its nature is instrumental and objectifying—how sexual acts other than masturbation and sodomy avoid this problem. The answer Finnis provides is that they don't; the worthlessness and disintegration that attach to masturbation and sodomy attach to "all extramarital sexual gratification." The physical nature of the act is not the decisive factor, after all; the division between the sexually wholesome and the sexually worthless is, on Finnis's view, between potentially procreative "conjugal activity" and everything else. (Nevertheless, Finnis uses a broad notion of "masturbation," which perhaps explains why he mentions that practice as his first example of a disintegrating and worthless sexual act: for Finnis, even a married couple that performs anal intercourse, coitus interruptus, or fellatio—nonprocreative sexual acts—are engaging in *masturbatory* sex.)[22]

The question then arises: what is so special about the conjugal bed that allows marital sex to avoid promoting disintegration? Finnis replies that worthlessness and disintegration attach to masturbation and sodomy in virtue of the fact that in these activities "one's conduct is not the actualizing and experiencing of a real common good." Marriage, on the other hand,

> with its double blessing—procreation and friendship—is a real common good . . . that can be both actualized and experienced in the orgasmic union of the reproductive organs of a man and a woman united in commitment to that good.

Being married is, we can grant, often conducive or contributes to the value of sexual activity. Even so, what is objectionable about sexual activity between two single consenting adults who care about and enjoy pleasing each other? Does not this mutual pleasing avoid shamefulness and worthlessness? No: the friends might only be seeking pleasure for its own sake, as often occurs in sodomy and masturbation. And although

Finnis thinks that "pleasure is indeed a good," he qualifies that concession with "*when* it is the experienced aspect of one's participation in
some intelligible good" (italics added). For Finnis's argument to work,
however, he must claim that pleasure is good *only when* it is an aspect of
the pursuit or achievement of some other good. This is not what Finnis
says. Perhaps he does not say it because he fears his readers will reject
such an extreme reservation about the value of pleasure; or, perhaps, he
doesn't say it because he realizes it is false: the pleasure of tasting food is
good in itself, regardless of whether the eating is part of the goods of securing nutrition or sharing table.

What if the friends say that they do have a common good, their friendship, the same way a married couple has the common good that is their
marriage? If "their friendship is not marital . . . activation of their reproductive organs cannot be, in reality, an . . . actualization of their friendship's common good," replies Finnis. The claim is obscure. Finnis tries
to explain, and in doing so reveals the crux of his sexual philosophy:

> the common good of friends who are not and cannot be married (man and
> man, man and boy, woman and woman) has nothing to do with their hav-
> ing children by each other, and their reproductive organs cannot make
> them a biological (and therefore a personal) unit.

Finnis began with the Kantian intuition that sexual activity involves treating the body instrumentally, and he concludes with the Kantish intuition
that sex in marriage avoids disintegrity since the couple is a biological
"unit," or insofar as "the orgasmic union of the reproductive organs of
husband and wife really unites them biologically." In order for persons
to be part of a genuine union, their sexual activity must be both marital
and procreative. The psychic falling apart each person would undergo
in nonmarital sex is prevented in marital sex by their joining into one;
this bolstering of the self against a metaphysical hurricane is gained by
the tempestuous orgasm, of all things.

At the heart of Finnis's philosophy is a scientific absurdity, if not also
an absurdity according to common sense, and further conversation with
him becomes difficult. But Finnis's argument, even if it shows the worthlessness of sterile homosexuality and solitary masturbation, seems to
have no relevance for heterosexual friends, for those who are not, but
could be, married. After all, if marriage has the "double blessing" of procreation and friendship, the same double blessing is available to heterosexual friends. Would Finnis want to claim, in reply, that if these friends
are committed to each other and plan to, or do, have children with each
other, they are in effect *married* and hence their sexual interactions are
fine? That claim might be true, but others in Finnis's school of thought
make it clear that marriage requires more than an informal agreement

between people to spend their lives together indefinitely. No genuine commitment (or love, or union) exists without a formal compact; a promise too easily fled is no promise at all.[23]

Transcendental Illusions

For Finnis, the self is so fragile metaphysically that engaging in sexual activity for the sheer pleasure of it threatens to burst it apart. For Roger Scruton, another conservative who condemns masturbation, the ephemeral self is in continual danger of being exposed as a fraud: "In my [sexual] desire [for you] I am gripped by the illusion of a transcendental unity behind the opacity of [your] flesh."[24] We are not really transcendental selves but fully material beings, which is why "excretion is the final 'no' to all our transcendental illusions" (151). We are redeemed only through "a metaphysical illusion residing in the heart of sexual desire" (95). Our passions make it *appear* that we are ontologically more than we really are. Sexuality must be treated with kid gloves, then, lest we lose the spiritually uplifting and socially useful reassurance that we humans are the ontological pride of the universe.

The requirement that human sexuality be approached somberly translates, for Scruton, not only into the ordinary claim that the sexual impulse must be educated or tamed to be the partner of heterosexual love, but also into a number of silly judgments. While discussing the "obscenity" of masturbation, Scruton offers this example:

> Consider the woman who plays with her clitoris during the act of coition. Such a person affronts her lover with the obscene display of her body, and, in perceiving her thus, the lover perceives his own irrelevance. She becomes disgusting to him, and his desire may be extinguished. The woman's desire is satisfied at the expense of her lover's, and no real union can be achieved between them. (319)

The obvious reply to how Scruton handles this example is to say that without the woman's masturbation, *her* desire might be extinguished and *his* desire satisfied at the expense of hers, and still no union is achieved. Further, her masturbating can even help the couple attain the very union Scruton hopes for as the way to perpetuate our metaphysical illusion, by letting them experience and recognize the mutual pleasure, perhaps the mutual orgasm, that results. Scruton's claim is false, I think, that most men would perceive a woman's masturbating during coitus as "disgusting." But even if there is some truth in this, we could, instead of blessing this disgust, offer the pastoral advice to the man who "perceives his own irrelevance" that he become more involved in his partner's pleasure by helping her massage her clitoral region or doing the rubbing for her; even when they are linked together coitally, he will find the arms long and the body flexible.

Why does Scruton judge the woman's masturbation an "obscene display"? Here is one part of his thought. When masturbation is done in public (for example, a bus station), it is obscene; it "cannot be witnessed without a sense of obscenity." Scruton then draws the astounding conclusion that *all* masturbation is obscene, even when done privately, on the grounds that "that which cannot be witnessed without obscene perception is itself obscene" (319). Scruton seems not to notice that his argument proves too much; it implies that coitus engaged in by a loving, heterosexual, married couple in private is also obscene, if we assume—as I think he would—that this act "cannot be witnessed," in public, "without obscene perception." The fault lies in the major premise of Scruton's syllogism. Whether an act is obscene might turn exactly on whether it is done publicly or privately. Scruton has failed to acknowledge the difference between exposing oneself to anonymous spectators and opening oneself to the gaze of a lover.

All masturbation is obscene, for Scruton, also because the act "involves a concentration on the body and its curious pleasures" (319). Obscenity, on his view, is an "obsession . . . with the organs themselves and with the pleasures of sensation" (154), and even if the sexual acts that focus on the body and its pleasures are paired sexual acts, they are nonetheless "masturbatory." (Recall how the religious conservative criticized Goldman's notion of "plain sex.") "In obscenity, attention is taken away from embodiment towards the body" (32), and there is "a 'depersonalized' perception of human sexuality, in which the body and its sexual function are uppermost in our thoughts" (138). A woman's masturbation during coitus is obscene since it leads the couple to focus too sharply on their physical features; she is a depersonalized body instead of a person-in-a-body. Thus, for Scruton, this obscene masturbation cannot sustain and, indeed, it threatens the couple's metaphysical illusion. But if a woman's masturbating during coitus is greeted with delight by her male partner, rather than with disgust, and increases the pleasure they realize and recognize in the act together, then, contrary to Scruton, either not all masturbation is obscene (the parties have not been reduced altogether to flesh) or obscenity, all things considered, is not a sexual, normative, or metaphysical disaster.

Two Models of Sexuality

It might not be surprising that the conservatives, Finnis and Scruton, are suspicious about the value and morality of masturbation. But our more liberal philosophers, who are unconventional enough to reject traditional or religious views about sexuality, have also scorned masturbation, in their own ways. Why? Here is a diagnosis. Even as they reject particular conservative or religious judgments about sexual behavior, these liberal thinkers still hold the deepest global assumption of their ideological foes. Their accounts of sexuality, that is, exemplify a *binary model:* reference to an interaction between two persons occurs in their accounts of the essence of sexuality or in their description of the best sex or its paradigm case. They thereby bestow normative, logical, or ontological primacy on paired sexual activity and evaluate the rest of the sexual world from this perspective. The sexually conservative or religious theorist embraces a binary model either by taking seriously the Genesis story, in which God deliberately created the human pair, or by assimilating human sexuality to the sexuality of the animal kingdom, where they find paired sex galore. But there is no obvious reason why liberal theorists must embrace a binary model. Because both Solomon and Nagel want to distinguish sharply between animal and human sexuality, it is disappointing that they construed human sexuality as only a variant of the paired, albeit less sophisticated, sexuality of animals.

The binary model is plainly exhibited in Goldman's definition of *sexual desire* as the "desire for contact with another person's body" (40). He claims that sexual desire is directed at and hence depends, conceptually, on another *body.* In Nagel, sexual desire is directed at another *person:* it is "a feeling about other persons"; the sexual "has its own content as a relation between persons" (12). Solomon, too, assumes a binary model. For Solomon, sexual desire "is not desire for pleasure" (*SP,* 26). Rather, "the end of this desire is interpersonal communication" (*SP,* 23); sex "is essentially an activity performed with other people" (*SAP,* 279). While for Solomon, sexual desire is a binary desire to talk with other people, for Goldman it is a binary desire simply to touch them.

Accounts of sexuality that presuppose a binary model will not illuminate the full range of human sexuality. Ordinary, everyday sexuality includes a desire for physical contact with another person (anyone at all or a specific person). And, we know as clearly, much paired sexual activity occurs. But we should still ask: *Why* is paired sexual activity so commonly practiced and so commonly desired? In trying to fathom these facts, we formulate a theory of sex. But a theory that presupposes a binary model will not help. It is trivial to say that people commonly behave in a paired sexual way because sexuality by its essence is paired, in the same way that the dormitive power of morphine does not explain why it knocks us out. An alternative account of sexuality is worth exploring, one that exemplifies a *unitary model,* in which sexuality is not by its nature a relation between persons and sexual desire does not attach necessarily to other persons or their bodies. According to a unitary model, sexual desire is the desire for certain pleasurable sensations, period. In contrast to Goldman's view, sexual desire is conceived as aiming at particular sensations that are both developmentally and analytically "detachable from [their] causal context" (40). Hence a unitary model does not entail that solitary masturbation is logically secondary or peripheral in the domain of sexual acts. If a theorist of sexuality wanted to distinguish sharply between the instinctual, routine paired sexuality of animals and the endlessly varied behaviors of human sexuality, presupposing a unitary model seems an effective way to achieve that. Further, a unitary model leaves room for constructing interesting explanations of the desire to engage in paired sexual activity that refer to the desire of persons for pleasurable sensations. The expression and development of that desire within specific social and cultural contexts would be invoked to explain why people want, even prefer, physical contact with persons of the other biological sex, or the same sex, or contact with both, or contact with neither. The value of a unitary model is that it encourages the exploration of the etiology of our sexual preferences, which seem to be highly contingent. It is a drawback of a binary model that it tends to obscure these questions.

How are we to decide whether the deep nature of sexual desire is "really" captured by a unitary or a binary model? Is Freud right that infants desire pleasure and discover that the mother and her breast provide that pleasure; or are the object-relations psychoanalysts right that infants have a primitive desire for contact with the mother and her breast and discover willy-nilly that satisfying that desire yields pleasure? This intriguing philosophical puzzle is a kind of chicken-and-egg conundrum. But it can be ignored. The central question concerns the research advantages of the competing models. A unitary model seems better suited for providing a framework for studying, in the various empirical disciplines, all the manifestations of human sexuality.

Within a unitary model, the desire for pleasurable sensations is logically primary, and the task is to explain the common paired pattern of sexuality as well as other behaviors. Whatever it is that we as individuals or as societies eventually cathect is open to explanation: all aims, objects, and targets of sexual desire, and the means of satisfying it, are seen as contingent facts requiring investigation. By contrast, within Nagel's binary model, for example, the psychologically complete configuration is taken as logically primitive and as part of human nature; hence the common paired pattern does not *require* explanation, indeed is not *susceptible* to explanation. In this approach, only deviations from the complete configuration require explanation. Of course, when we ask for an explanation of valium's calming effect, we are disappointed if we are told it is an antianxiety agent. We are let down because we think that the calming nature of valium is explainable in terms of the *deeper nature* of the drug, its chemistry, and the biological system with which it interacts. This kind of "deep nature" of human sexuality is what Nagel must be attempting to provide in his account of the psychologically complete configuration. I think, however, that Nagel candidly recognizes the problem that this causes. Given that the complete configuration is primitively natural, the task is to explain the existence of deviations, patterns of sexuality that result from factors that interfere with the normal or automatic blossoming of the natural, paired pattern of sexuality. Speaking about this task, Nagel writes, "We appear to need an independent criterion for a distorting influence, and we do not have one" (18).[25] A unitary model, by contrast, seems to need no such criterion: it does not claim that departures from the paired pattern are necessarily "deviations" or that factors that influence their development are "distorting."

In order to highlight the difference between the two models, consider a fanciful example that has been made plausible by technological advances in virtual reality. Suppose there is a life-size doll whose covering feels like skin, whose genitals have the odor and flavor of the genitals of either sex, and which is programmed to rub, to squirm in response to being rubbed, and to emit soft noises. An account of sexuality that presupposes a binary model would say that any event between a human and this doll does not count as *bona fide* sexual activity—it is either not sexual activity at all, or perverted sexuality (no different from masturbating on a shoe), or "empty" sexuality (no different from talking to a can of baked beans). Or the account might say that *to the extent* that there is anything sexual about an event between a human and the doll, it is because the doll *reminds us* of a person (which is like saying that solitary masturbation is sexual to the extent that it involves fantasies about other persons); or *to the extent* that such activity is not perverted, it is because the doll fills in as a *substitute* for something that is preferred but not available. A unitary model can avoid these judgments. In a unitary model, there is no conceptual difference between sexual activities between two people and an "encounter" between a person and the doll, as long as the doll is capable of producing the pleasurable sensations its user demands of it. A unitary model does not distinguish activity with a person from activity with the doll by using the categories "sexual" and "perversion." It does allow that persons will have contingent preferences for contact with a person or with a doll, but insists that these preferences require explanation that goes beyond a mere binary definition of sexual desire or sexual activity.

Nagel's use of the word *intercourse,* in his phrase "intercourse with . . . inanimate objects" (17), to talk about masturbation engaged in by the shoe fetishist, illustrates how his use of a binary model has colored his view of the sexual. If we take paired, genital intercourse as logically primary or paradigmatic, then even the rubbing of the penis on or in a shoe will be seen as intercourse. We will try to make it fit a binary model, even though a shoe is not a person. On the other side, employing a unitary model will lead us to see paired intercourse as masturbatory, an idea we discussed earlier. For if the rubbing of skin for the sake of the pleasure it produces is central to the sexual, and that is what masturbation is, then the insertion of the penis into the vagina will be seen as just a case of the rubbing of skin for the sake of the pleasure it yields, that is, as masturbatory. Of course, paired coitus *can* also be, depending on context, personality, and so forth, an instance of other things: a way to satisfy a desire for contact with another body (Goldman), a route to expanding one's consciousness to include an awareness of the self as sexual object (Nagel), a means of communication (Solomon), a technique of reproduction (Finnis), or a way of fostering our metaphysical pretensions (Scruton). A unitary model in no way limits other interpretations of single, particular sexual acts. It is this logical openness that makes the unitary model attractive and worth exploring.

Guilt

A familiar platitude says, "there is not one shred of evidence that masturbation is harmful. . . . The only harm that can result from masturbation is if the individual is plagued with feelings of guilt."[26] Thus, in reply to the oft-heard advice that we should not masturbate because doing so will make us anxious or depressed or induce feelings of guilt, it is just as frequently mentioned that we run the risk of experiencing anxiety or guilt in the first place only because philosophy, medicine, theology, and popular opinion treat masturbation in a disparaging way. To some extent this rejoinder is true, but to repeat it, and repeat it again, might no longer be convincing. Maybe we have gone too far in reaction against views critical of masturbation; maybe it is the right time, historically, for a swing back to traditional intuitions, if not thermoelectrocautery and cutting off our offending hand. There are other reasons for moral criticism of fantasy and masturbation, some of which have come from feminists, especially those who have continued to press the question of pornography: if pornography is morally objectionable by being seriously degrading to women, making heterosexual men feel guilty for masturbating with such horrible stuff might be legitimate.[27] For, after all, maybe Rousseau was right that to engage in sexual fantasizing is little different from rape.[28]

Notes

1. *The Confessions* (New York: Penguin, 1979), bk. 3, 109.
2. Here's one example of the mainstreaming of (light) sadomasochism. A woman wrote this letter to Irma Kurtz's "Agony Column" in *Cosmopolitan* (Janu-

ary 1997, 34): "I'm thirty-four, successful, smart, independent . . . and *obsessed* by the bizarre fantasy of being spanked by a lover. What's *wrong* with me?" Kurtz replies: "Nothing's bizarre about your fantasy or wrong with you. . . . For some women *and* men, simply thinking about tushy slapping is extremely arousing. . . . When erotic fantasies become reality, they sometimes lose their power, but I see no harm in giving this one a try. . . . Next time you and a beau are getting intimate, why not confess you've been a naughty girl? Then climb over his knee . . . and savor your punishment." See also Daphne Merkin's spanking confessional, "Unlikely Obsession: Confronting a Taboo," *The New Yorker* (February 26 and March 4, 1996), 98–115. For discussions and defenses of more intense, serious, and potentially harmful (psychologically or physically) types of sadomasochism, see Samois, ed., *Coming to Power,* 2nd edition (Boston, Mass.: Alyson Publications, 1982); Thomas Weinberg, ed., *S&M: Studies in Dominance & Submission* (Amherst, N.Y.: Prometheus, 1995); and, especially, the writings of Pat Califia: "Feminism and Sadomasochism," in (among many other anthologies) Stevi Jackson and Sue Scott, eds., *Feminism and Sexuality: A Reader* (New York: Columbia University Press, 1996), 230–37; *Public Sex: The Culture of Radical Sex* (Pittsburgh, Pa.: Cleis Press, 1994; and *Macho Sluts* (Los Angeles, Calif.: Alyson Books, 1988).

3. Sexual activity between humans and animals (bestiality) may be more of a black sheep. For a brief essay that brings this sexual practice out of the closet, see Peter Singer, "Heavy Petting," which can be downloaded from the Internet site <http://www.nerve.com/Opinions/Singer/heavyPetting/main.asp>.

4. Some male clients of female prostitutes purchase "hand jobs" instead of either fellatio or coitus. For discussion of the men's motives, see Carole Pateman, *The Sexual Contract* (Stanford, Calif.: Stanford University Press, 1988), 199; and my *Sexual Investigations* (New York: New York University Press, 1996), 87.

5. About problems in defining "sex" for lesbians, see Marilyn Frye, "Lesbian 'Sex'," in her *Willful Virgin: Essays in Feminism 1976–1992* (Freedom, Calif.: Crossing Press, 1992), 109–19.

6. Philip Roth, *Portnoy's Complaint* (New York: Random House, 1969), 88.

7. Immanuel Kant, *Lectures on Ethics,* trans. Louis Infield (Indianapolis, Ind.: Hackett, 1989), 163 (in this volume, 199–200).

8. *Lectures on Ethics,* 166–67 (in this volume, 202–3).

9. This is the interpretation offered by Robert Baker and Frederick Elliston. They write, "If a fusion of one and the other truly exists, . . . the very possibility of using an *other* as a means no longer exists" ("Introduction" to Robert Baker and Frederick Elliston, eds., *Philosophy and Sex* [Buffalo, N.Y.: Prometheus, 1975, 1984], 1st edition, 18; 2nd edition, 26–27).

10. Exactly how Kant justifies marital sexual activity is a bit of a mystery. For discussion, see my "Sexual Use and What to Do about It: Internalist and Externalist Sexual Ethics," in this volume, 225–58.

11. The answer to Barbara Herman's question, "sex would then be what?" if Kant were right that (in her words) "we become parts of a new self that has two bodies," would be "solitary masturbation" ("Could it Be Worth Thinking about Kant on Sex and Marriage?" in Louise M. Antony and Charlotte Witt, eds., *A Mind of One's Own* [Boulder, Colo.: Westview, 1993], 49–67, at 61). If marital sexual activity, via a union of two persons into one, is masturbation, then Mary Ann Gardell's understanding of Kantian marriage, that "marriage transforms an oth-

erwise manipulative masturbatory relationship into one that is essentially altruistic in character," must be modified ("Sexual Ethics: Some Perspectives from the History of Philosophy," in Earl E. Shelp, ed., *Sexuality and Medicine*, vol. 2: *Ethical Viewpoints in Transition* [Dordrecht, Hol.: Reidel, 1987], 3–15, at 11). More accurately, a Kantian marriage transforms two-person masturbation into one-person masturbation.

12. Herman, "Could It Be Worth Thinking," 66, n. 22.

13. *Lectures on Ethics,* 170 (in this volume, 204).

14. A notable contrast is Russell Vannoy's humanist treatment of masturbation in *Sex without Love: A Philosophical Exploration* (Buffalo, N.Y.: Prometheus, 1980), 111–17.

15. "Plain Sex," *Philosophy and Public Affairs* 6 (1977): 267–87 (reprinted in this volume, 39–55).

16. "Sexual Perversion," *Journal of Philosophy* 66 (1969): 5–17 (reprinted in this volume, 9–20).

17. "Sexual Paradigms," *Journal of Philosophy* 71 (1974): 336–45 (reprinted in this volume, 21–29); and "Sex and Perversion," in Baker and Elliston, *Philosophy and Sex,* 1st edition, 268–87. (References to the former essay are preceded by *SP;* references to the latter by *SAP.*)

18. See Goldman, "Plain Sex," this volume, 46–47; and, especially, Hugh Wilder, "The Language of Sex and the Sex of Language," in Alan Soble, ed., *Sex, Love, and Friendship* (Amsterdam, Hol.: Editions Rodopi, 1997), 23–31.

19. *Refusing to Be a Man* (Portland, Oreg.: Breitenbush Books, 1989), 39.

20. *Anarchy, State, and Utopia* (New York: Basic Books, 1974), 32.

21. In John Finnis and Martha Nussbaum, "Is Homosexual Conduct Wrong? A Philosophical Exchange," *The New Republic* (November 15, 1993), 12–13 (reprinted in this volume, 97–100).

22. Finnis, "Law, Morality, and 'Sexual Orientation,' " *Notre Dame Law Review* 69, 5 (1994): 1049–76, at 1068.

23. An exception to the formal marriage requirement is advanced halfheartedly by Vincent Punzo, whose sexual views are otherwise nearly identical to those of Finnis and Kant. See his *Reflective Naturalism* (New York: Macmillan, 1969), chap. 6.

24. *Sexual Desire: A Moral Philosophy of the Erotic* (New York: Free Press, 1986), 130.

25. On the implications of this comment by Nagel, see Arnold Davidson, "Conceptual History and Conceptions of Perversion," in Robert Baker, Kathleen Wininger, and Frederick Elliston, eds., *Philosophy and Sex,* 3rd edition (Amherst, N.Y.: Prometheus, 1998), 476–86, at 479–80.

26. James Haynes, "Masturbation," in Vern Bullough and Bonnie Bullough, eds., *Human Sexuality: An Encyclopedia* (New York: Garland, 1994), 381–85, at 384.

27. My most recent and extended argument that feminists overstate their case against pornography is presented in *Pornography, Sex, and Feminism* (Amherst, N.Y.: Prometheus, 2002).

28. My thanks to Martha Cornog, Tim Perper, Edward Johnson, and Norton Nelkin.

PART 2

HOMOSEXUALITY

Chapter 8

IS HOMOSEXUAL CONDUCT WRONG?
A PHILOSOPHICAL EXCHANGE

John Finnis and Martha C. Nussbaum

John Finnis

The underlying thought is on the following lines. In masturbating, as in being masturbated or sodomized, one's body is treated as instrumental for the securing of the experiential satisfaction of the conscious self. Thus one disintegrates oneself in two ways, (1) by treating one's body as a mere instrument of the consciously operating self, and (2) by making one's choosing self the quasi-slave of the experiencing self which is demanding gratification. The worthlessness of the gratification, and the disintegration of oneself, are both the result of the fact that, in these sorts of behavior, one's conduct is not the actualizing and experiencing of a real common good. Marriage, with its double blessing—procreation and friendship—is a real common good. Moreover, it is a common good that can be both actualized and experienced in the orgasmic union of the reproductive organs of a man and a woman united in commitment to that good. Conjugal sexual activity, and—as Plato and Aristotle and Plutarch and Kant all argue—*only* conjugal activity is free from the shamefulness of instrumentalization that is found in masturbating and in being masturbated or sodomized.

© 1993, *The New Republic*. Reprinted with permission from *The New Republic,* 15 November 1993, pp. 12–13. This material was extracted from legal depositions filed in *Romer v. Evans* (the 1993 "Colorado Amendment 2" case).

At the very heart of the reflections of Plato, Xenophon, Aristotle, Musonius Rufus, and Plutarch on the homoerotic culture around them is the very deliberate and careful judgment that homosexual *conduct* (and indeed all extramarital sexual gratification) is radically incapable of participating in, or actualizing, the common good of friendship. Friends who engage in such conduct are following a natural impulse and doubtless often wish their genital conduct to be an intimate expression of their mutual affection. But they are deceiving themselves. The attempt to express affection by orgasmic nonmarital sex is the pursuit of an illusion. The orgasmic union of the reproductive organs of husband and wife really unites them biologically (and their biological reality is part of, not merely an instrument of, their *personal* reality); that orgasmic union therefore can actualize and allow them to experience their real common good—their marriage with the two goods, children and friendship, which are the parts of its wholeness as an intelligible common good. But the common good of friends who are not and cannot be married (man and man, man and boy, woman and woman) has nothing to do with their having children by each other, and their reproductive organs cannot make them a biological (and therefore a personal) unit. So their genital acts together cannot do what they may hope and imagine.

In giving their considered judgment that homosexual conduct cannot actualize the good of friendship, Plato and the many philosophers who followed him intimate an answer to the questions why it should be considered shameful to use, or allow another to use, one's body to give pleasure, and why this use of one's body differs from one's bodily participation in countless other activities (e.g., games) in which one takes and/or gets pleasure. Their response is that pleasure is indeed a good, when it is the experienced aspect of one's participation in some intelligible good, such as a task going well, or a game or a dance or a meal or a reunion. Of course, the activation of sexual organs with a view to the pleasures of orgasm is sometimes spoken of as if it were a game. But it differs from real games in that its point is not the exercise of skill; rather, this activation of reproductive organs is focused upon the body precisely as a source of pleasure for one's consciousness. So this is a "use of the body" in a strongly different sense of "use." The body now is functioning not in the way one, as a bodily person, acts to instantiate some other intelligible good, but precisely as providing a service to one's consciousness, to satisfy one's desire for satisfaction.

This disintegrity is much more obvious when masturbation is solitary. Friends are tempted to think that pleasuring each other by some forms of mutual masturbation could be an instantiation or actualization or promotion of their friendship. But that line of thought overlooks the fact that if their friendship is not marital . . . activation of their reproductive organs cannot be, in reality, an instantiation or actualization of their friendship's common good. In reality, whatever the generous hopes and dreams with which the loving partners surround their use of their genitals, *that use* cannot express more than is expressed if two strangers engage in genital activity to give each other orgasm, or a prostitute pleasures a client, or a man pleasures himself. Hence, Plato's judgment, at the decisive moment of the *Gorgias,* that there is no important distinction in essential moral worthlessness between solitary masturbation, being sodomized as a prostitute and being sodomized for the pleasure of it. . . .

Societies such as classical Athens and contemporary England (and virtually every other) draw a distinction between behavior found merely (perhaps extremely) offensive (such as eating excrement) and behavior to be repudiated as destructive of human character and relationships. Copulation of humans with animals is repudiated because it treats human sexual activity and satisfaction as something appropriately sought in a manner that, like the coupling of animals, is divorced from the expressing of an intelligible common good—and so treats human bodily life, in one of its intense activities, as merely animal. The deliberate genital coupling of persons of the same sex is repudiated for a very similar reason. It is not simply that it is sterile and disposes the participants to an abdication of responsibility for the future of humankind. Nor is it simply that it cannot *really* actualize the mutual devotion that some homosexual persons hope to manifest and experience by it; nor merely that it harms the personalities of its participants by its disintegrative manipulation of different parts of their one personal reality. It is also that it treats human sexual capacities in a way that is deeply hostile to the self-understanding of those members of the community who are willing to commit themselves to real marriage [even one that happens to be sterile] in the understanding that its sexual joys are not mere instruments or accompaniments to, or mere compensation for, the accomplishments of marriage's responsibilities, but rather are the *actualizing and experiencing* of the intelligent commitment to share in those responsibilities. . . .

This pattern of judgment, both widespread and sound, concludes as follows. Homosexual orientation—the deliberate willingness to promote and engage in homosexual acts—is a standing denial of the intrinsic aptness of sexual intercourse to actualize and give expression to the exclusiveness and open-ended commitment of marriage as something good in itself. All who accept that homosexual acts can be a humanly appropriate use of sexual capacities must, if consistent, regard sexual capacities, organs, and acts as instruments to be put to whatever suits the purposes of the individual "self" who has them. Such an acceptance is commonly (and in my opinion rightly) judged to be an active threat to the stability of existing and future marriages; it makes nonsense, for example, of the view that adultery is per se (and not merely because it may involve deception), and in an important way, inconsistent with conjugal love. A political community that judges that the stability and educative generosity of family life is of fundamental importance to the community's present and future can rightly judge that it has a compelling interest in denying that homosexual conduct is a valid, humanly acceptable choice and form of life, and in doing whatever it properly can, as a community with uniquely wide but still subsidiary functions, to discourage such conduct.

Martha C. Nussbaum

Finnis's arguments against homosexuality set themselves in a tradition of "natural law" argumentation that derives from ancient Greek traditions. The term "law of nature" was first used by Plato in his *Gorgias*. The approach is further developed by Aristotle and, above all, by the Greek and Roman Stoics, who are usually considered to be the founders of natural law argumentation in the modern legal tradition, through their influence on Roman law. This being so, it is worth looking to see whether those traditions did in fact use "natural law" arguments to rule homosexual conduct morally or legally substandard.

Plato's dialogues contain several extremely moving celebrations of male–male love, and judge this form of love to be, on the whole, superior to male–female love because of its potential for spirituality and friendship. The *Symposium* contains a series of speeches, each expressing conventional views about this subject that Plato depicts in an appealing light. The speech by Phaedrus points to the military advantages derived by including homosexual couples in a fighting force: Because of their intense love, each will fight better, wishing to show himself in the best light before his lover. The speech of Pausanias criticizes males who seek physical pleasure alone in their homosexual relationships, and praises those who seek in sex deeper spiritual communication. Pausanias mentions that tyrants will sometimes promulgate the view that same-sex relations are shameful in order to discourage the kind of community of dedication to political liberty that such relations foster. The speech of Aristophanes holds that all human beings are divided halves of formerly whole beings, and that sexual desire is the pursuit of one's lost other half; he points out that the superior people in any society are those whose lost "other half" is of the same sex—especially the male–male pairs—since these are likely to be the strongest and most warlike and civically minded people. Finally, Socrates' speech recounts a process of religious-mystical education in which male–male love plays a central guiding role and is a primary source of insight and inspiration into the nature of the good and beautiful.

Plato's *Phaedrus* contains a closely related praise of the intellectual, political, and spiritual benefits of a life centered around male–male love. Plato says that the highest form of human life is one in which a male pursues "the love of a young man along with philosophy," and is transported by passionate desire. He describes the experience of falling in love with another male in moving terms, and defends relationships that are mutual and reciprocal over relationships that are one-sided. He depicts his pairs of lovers as spending their life together in the pursuit of intellectual and spiritual activities, combined with political participation. (Although no marriages for these lovers are mentioned, it was the view of the time that this form of life does not prevent its participants from having a wife at home, whom they saw only rarely and for procreative purposes.)

Aristotle speaks far less about sexual love than does Plato, but it is evident that he too finds in male–male relationships the potential for the highest form of friendship, a friendship based on mutual well-wishing and mutual awareness of good character and good aims. He does not find this potential in male–female relationships, since he holds that females are incapable of good character. Like Pausanias in Plato's *Symposium*, Aristotle is critical of relationships that are superficial and concerned only with bodily pleasure; but he finds in male–male relationships—including many that begin in this way—the potential for much richer developments.

The ideal city of the Greek Stoics was built around the idea of pairs of male lovers whose bonds gave the city rich sources of motivation for virtue. Although the Stoics wished their "wise man" to eliminate most passions from his life, they encouraged him to foster a type of erotic love that they defined as "the attempt to form a friendship inspired by the perceived beauty of young men in their prime." They held that this love, unlike other passions, was supportive of virtue and philosophical activity.

Furthermore, Finnis's argument . . . against homosexuality is a bad moral argument by any standard, secular or theological. First of all, it assumes that the purpose of a homosexual act is always or usually casual bodily pleasure and the instrumental use of another person for one's own gratification. But this is a false premise, easily disproved by the long historical tradition I have described and by the contemporary lives of real men and women. Finnis offers no evidence for this premise, or for the equally false idea that procreative relations cannot be selfish and manipulative. Second, having argued that a relationship is better if it seeks not casual pleasure but the creation of a community, he then assumes without argument that the only sort of community a sexual relationship can create is a "procreative community." This is, of course, plainly false. A sexual relationship may create, quite apart from the possibility of procreation, a community of love and friendship, which no religious tradition would deny to be important human goods. Indeed, in many moral traditions, including those of Plato and Aristotle, the procreative community is ranked beneath other communities created by sex, since it is thought that the procreative community will probably not be based on the best sort of friendship and the deepest spiritual concerns. That may not be true in a culture that values women more highly than ancient Greek culture did; but the possibility of love and friendship between individuals of the same sex has not been removed by these historical changes.

Chapter 9

AGAINST HOMOSEXUAL LIBERATION

Michael E. Levin

The intrinsic maladaptiveness of homosexuality means that its production is not the aim of any gene, including those homosexuality
expresses, and therefore not a normal state even of homosexuals. The ultimate goal of any gene is replication, and expressions that frustrate this
function are dysfunctional. Sickle-cell anemia, Tay-Sachs disease among
Jews, schizophrenia, and, evidently, homosexuality are genetic abnor-
malities that have tagged along with traits that are or recently were adaptive. A gene expressed as homosexuality, should one be found, would not
make homosexuality any less intrinsically maladaptive, which leaves common sense right after all in thinking homosexuality abnormal.

A genetic basic for homosexuality would, however, leave the liberationists with two dilemmas. One concerns the quite real possibility that
both ethnocentrism and dislike of homosexuals will also turn out to have
a genetic basis and not be due to those liberationist whipping-boys, capitalism and patriarchy. After all, xenophobia, the ability to detect individuals genetically unlike oneself combined with a tendency to aggress
against them, would keep resources from unrelated genes. Selection for
xenophobia is certainly consistent with mankind's history of intergroup
conflict. Similarly, evidence for the genetic predisposition of men to
dominate women may soon be undeniable. One imagines the liberationist greeting such discoveries with insistence that what is genetic is not

---

Reprinted (slightly abridged), with the permission of Michael E. Levin, from pp. 124–45
of his contribution to Laurence M. Thomas and Michael E. Levin, *Sexual Orientation and
Human Rights* (Rowman and Littlefield, 1999), pp. 79–158.

necessarily normal, and encouragement for all of us to try to overcome an unfortunate biological heritage. But he can't at the same time hold that a gene for a trait automatically makes it natural and agreeable. He can't have it one way about xenophobia and male dominance, another way about homosexuality; it may prove interesting to see which way he goes.

A second dilemma will be raised by the again real possibility of a reliable intrauterine genetic test for potential homosexuality. Liberationists want homosexuality accepted, but they are also inclined to regard abortion rights as absolute, so they will have to defend the right of women to abort potential homosexuals. This dilemma was the subject of the drama *The Twilight of the Golds*. After some agonizing, [Simon] LeVay comes down against restricting abortion. But 41 percent of the respondents in a poll of readers of the homosexual magazine *The Advocate* reported believing that while women generally have the right to choose, it should be denied in this case.[1] A more hysterical article in *The Village Voice* described refusal to nurture homosexual embryos as "genocide,"[2] which implies that refusal to nurture an embryo is killing. (One wonders what the author thinks of late-term abortion.) . . .

Conservatives who abominate homosexuality but also oppose legal abortion would face the mirror-image problem, although I suspect most would quickly side against abortion.

Some Implications of Homosexual Abnormality

One consequence of the abnormality of homosexuality is a profound difference between homosexuals and other "victims." There are many ethnic and racial groups, and many people dislike members of groups other than their own, but none of these groups is unnatural and not even their enemies, whatever other unfaltering beliefs they may hold, think of them this way. Some whites dislike blacks, some blacks dislike whites, but nobody supposes that being black or white is akin to a disease. Susan Sontag did once call the white race "the cancer of mankind," but this was (I hope) hyperbole;[3] nobody really thinks of whites, or blacks, or Croatians, as outside the natural biological order. But homosexuals are. This distinguishes the antipathy toward this group from any sort of ethnic hostility; dislike of homosexuals is powered by—well-founded—intuitions of deviance. The ideal of all men living together in brotherhood, at least in many of its versions, presumes that the same human clay will be found in every group if you dig deeply enough. Whether this is actually so and, if it is, whether it can sustain universal harmony, are to my mind very open questions; but where homosexuality is concerned the question is closed. Homosexuals are not to heterosexuals as blacks are to whites or Croatians to Serbs. Homosexuality is deviant, and the "common human clay" argument, whatever its merits for multiculturalism, does not extend to multisexualism.

When advocating civil rights, liberationists maintain that sexual preference has no predictive value, just as race and sex have none, so discrimination on its basis is irrational (and should therefore be illegal). Evidence of a biological basis for homosexuality suggests otherwise. Common sense recognizes the importance of an individual's sex drive as an organizing principle of his personality, of his attitude toward himself, toward members of his own and the opposite sex, his family, and the next generation. Since innate differences in sexuality correlate with personality differences between men and women, it is reasonable to expect similar correlations for homosexuals and heterosexuals. Liberationists themselves are of two minds about a "homosexual personality." While denying it in the civil rights context, as I have said, they stress homosexual creativity, a sensibility geared to emotionality and sentimenality, and a waspish, "campy" sense of humor[4] when seeking to establish homosexuals as a distinguishable group. One may paper over this inconsistency by attributing the homosexual style to oppression, but so doing still admits the style exists, just as attributing race and sex differences in personality to "oppression" concedes their existence. A biological basis for homosexuality only eliminates persecution as its sole cause.

The biological evidence represents inversion as part of a syndrome of traits clustered about the greater femininity of homosexual men and the greater masculinity of lesbians. Some features of this syndrome, such as the greater law-abidingness, creativity, verbal ability, and imaginativeness of male homosexuals can be viewed as positive. But even if the homosexual personality was entirely positive, it is easy to understand that it disturbs many people. Human beings have evidently evolved different strategies for dealing with members of the two sexes. Males see other males as rivals whose presence tends to elicit dominance-seeking (or retreat), while they see females as potential mates whose presence elicits display. It is disconcerting to encounter someone whose male appearance elicits one response-readiness but whose quasi-female manner elicits another. I suspect that some of the unease occasioned by homosexuals results from signal conflict.

A much more disturbing aspect of the homosexual personality, however, is a penchant for extreme promiscuity. Here I refer primarily to male homosexuals, who appear far more promiscuous than lesbians (a difference that complicates the picture of homosexuals as psychologically intermediate between male and female). Bell and Weinberg's study,[5] the most thorough to date and the more convincing because of its authors' explicit wish to vindicate homosexuality, found that 28 percent of the homosexuals surveyed reported having more than fifty sex partners annually; 43 percent reported having had more than 500 sexual partners in their lifetime, and 26 percent reported having had more than 1,000. These are numbers to dumbfound the most dedicated heterosexual womanizer. A majority of male homosexuals reported choosing strangers for sex partners most of the time and having no affection for a majority of their sex partners. Nearly half reported spending, on average, less than two hours with a partner. This capacity to detach sexual urgency from emotion, this purity of lust, is foreign to heterosexuals. Don Juan must first make his target's acquaintance, at least feign some interest if he hopes to arouse her, and he will typically not leave her side immediately after coitus.

Given this sexual hyperactivity, an association between homosexuality and sexually transmitted diseases is inevitable. Bell and Weinberg report—this is prior to AIDS—that two-thirds of the men surveyed claim to have contracted a venereal disease at some time. The AIDS epidemic for its part is too familiar a story to need retelling.

A preoccupation with sex seems bound to carry personality correlates, some at variance with ordinary heterosexual standards of decency, not to say employability. An essay by one of the "young men with 'no excuse'," published as the cover story of the *New York Times Magazine*—and therefore presumably representative of a major strand in homosexual thought—conveys something of this antinomianism:

> At this point, let's face it, we're the least innocent of "victims"—we have no excuse, the barrage of safe sex information, the free condoms, blah blah blah . . . [sic]. Well, rubbers break. (Use two or three). Maybe oral sex without ejaculation isn't as safe as you thought. Maybe the antibodies take more than six months to show up in your bloodstream, so your negative test is no guarantee. The answer? Celibacy, of course. Masturbation, maybe, but be sure to wear rubber gloves. Fantasy. But we, the second wave, we obviously aren't sublimating very well. Maybe the image of death, a dark, sexy man in black is something we find exciting. . . . There are days when we don't even remember that it's there, we're so wrapped up in the real tragedy, which is not in our dying, but in our living: applying for ridiculous jobs, filling out forms, selling books to buy food, stealing vitamins. Shoplifting is hard work; so is applying for food stamps, and every pathetic moron of a boss with a part-time temporary position licking out toilet bowls wants a résumé, two work interviews, work experience and a college degree. It's really getting us down. We are sad so often.[6]

It is hard to imagine more loathsome sentiments or a more repellent individual.

It is perfectly rational for an employer to want to avoid such personalities and rational for him to believe that hiring homosexuals creates a greater risk of being saddled with one. Or consider a landlord disinclined to rent to homosexuals because of his reasonable and correct belief that homosexuals are much more promiscuous than heterosexuals. He may fear, again reasonably, that promiscuous tenants attract strangers who will threaten security and be heedless of his property. He may worry that homosexuals, ever on the prowl, will keep late hours annoying to other tenants, who themselves prefer heterosexual neighbors. The landlord may consider homosexuals unclean, another reasonable concern given the data about venereal disease. Homosexuality is a valid, information-rich proxy. Laws against "arbitrary" discrimination, even if they survived Mill's principle, would permit discrimination based on sexual preference. . . .

Homosexual tendencies also bear on the military. Liberals understand that armed forces are needed to meet external threats, a vital function that subordinates any right to serve[7] to military efficiency. This being so, homosexuals have no place in the military if they weaken morale, and there are good reasons to think they do. First, the physical aggressiveness necessary for fighting is associated with the male personality. Women have never demonstrated the physical or psychological ability to endure sustained combat,[8] and since homosexuals do not display the full male personality, putting them among men who do is likely to be disruptive. Second, the young, highly aggressive male who makes the paradigm soldier characteristically prides himself on his virility; he likes to brag about his athletic and, above all, sexual exploits. He will feel uncomfortable with homosexuals, and placing an open homosexual among a group of young men of this sort spells trouble. Third, combat units depend upon the sort of male bonding that also unites athletic teams. Once again, homosexual males do not display the requisite personality—one of the "sex-atypical" behaviors psychologists use to predict homosexuality among children is dislike of team sports—and introducing "sensitivity training" to counter the friction caused by mixing open homosexuals with heterosexuals makes as much sense as adding extra lubricants to an engine into which one has dumped sand. Some homosexuals may have served in the armed forces without incident in the past, when the prospect of penalties kept them discreet, but a legal right to serve openly would undo these restraints. Remember, liberationists reject a "Don't ask/Don't tell" policy of anonymity as incompatible with homosexuals' right to "be themselves," and want homosexuals in the military to bear no heavier burdens than heterosexuals. This means that if a heterosexual recruit is allowed to openly brag about his sexual conquests or describe the anatomical charms of a local female, a homosexual recruit must be allowed equal openness about his interest in men, including those he bunks with. It is hard to image such a system running smoothly.

On Homosexual Promiscuity

Liberationists explain the promiscuity of homosexuals by the forbidden nature of their love. Taboo desires naturally result in furtive, sordid encounters, they say; were homosexuality accepted and homosexual marriage permitted, homosexuals would be as faithful as heterosexuals. But this explanation has worn thin. This intelligentsia and the media have been pro-homosexual and anti-anti-homosexual for three decades. Can you recall the last homosexual portrayed unsympathetically in the movies or on TV? The love that dare not speak its name is bellowing into megaphones, kissing in public, holding hands in front of presidents.[9] Yet there is no evidence that, apart from the impact of AIDS, homosexual promiscuity has abated.

Two explanations of this promiscuity not based on social learning come to mind. One is that homosexual sex is less emotionally fulfilling than heterosexual sex. The natural rewards of reproductive behavior are not found in substitutes, so homosexuals are forever seeking an unattainable satisfaction. (Reasons for suspecting this become clearer in the next section.) A second, complementary, hypothesis is that homosexual promiscuity represents the male sex drive freed from accommodation to females. Men are generally more promiscuous than women, for biological reasons. It is in the male's genetic interest to desire numerous sexual partners, since he is physically able to sire thousands of offspring. A woman, capable of bearing only a few time-consuming, metabolically costly offspring, and thus at great risk whenever she copulates, wants a mate who, after sowing his seed, will remain to provide resources as the seed develops into an adult. Darwinian sexual selection has shaped a compromise male strategy of willingness to settle for a single mate, experienced phenomenologically as falling in love, plus a residual yearning for variety. Homosexual males, by contrast, need not accommodate female reticence. It is questionable, in my view, whether they ever experience the emotion of love, as opposed to lust, infatuation, and other drives also familiar to heterosexuals.

The model of the male homosexual sex drive as a hypertrophic heterosexual one explains more than an exaggerated desire for variety. Men are easily aroused by physical features such as large breasts, while women respond to aspects of personality. One of the most striking features of publications for a male homosexual readership is their constant references to "bubble butts," hunky muscles, penis size, and related anatomical matters. Preoccupation with youthfulness has survived any number of "gay pride" marches. The standard explanation for the sex difference in cuing stimuli among heterosexuals is that males track observable signs of youth, strongly associated with fertility, whereas women track indicators of power and status. Once again, in effect, male homosexual tastes reflect what the male sex drive would be in a world where women were as eager as men for anonymous sex.

LeVay is right to ask why homosexuals are so disliked, and one hypothesis to explore is that heterosexual antipathy toward homosexuals is partly an evolved response. The negativity of this response, especially on the part of male heterosexuals, is at first puzzling, since more homosexual males means less competition for females. One would think a heterosexual would welcome homosexuals. On the other hand, homosexuals mean fewer potential mates for himself and his offspring. The main genetic basis for animus probably lies elsewhere, however, perhaps as a hedge against the huge opportunity cost of fathering a homosexual, a genetic dead-end on whom a father risks spending years that might have been invested elsewhere. A further factor is the association of homosexual promiscuity with disease and, because of anal penetration, feces, aversion to both of which enhances fitness.

It is reasonable to conclude that evolutionary factors produced the homosexual sex drive and that the homosexual personality therefore has a biological dimension. These same considerations suggest that aversion to homosexuals is more than an inexplicable "phobia."

Normalcy, Fitness, Happiness

Attentive readers will have noticed that "normal" has so far not been linked to value. We cannot yet say there is anything good about normality or bad about abnormality. We have agreed that there is something formerly and perhaps currently maladaptive about abnormality, but what's so great about adaptiveness? Some traits helpful to our ancestors—one thinks of high levels of aggression—have become downright dangerous. The linkage problem has become pressing in the [prior]... sections, where the assessment of homosexuality was begun.

The full evaluative force of "normal" cannot be saved, as the world's undoubted connotations of propriety and conformity to a Grand Plan are no part of a naturalist worldview. Erstwhile maladaptiveness is neither wicked nor sinful: to that extent the objection to natural teleology is sustained. Erstwhile adaptiveness nonetheless remains relevant to human concerns, and, more specifically, to liberationist demands. The nexus is the eudaimonia—or positive hedonic tone, or happiness, or sense of reward—that accompanies adaptive behavior. Adaptive actions are more enjoyable than their rivals and in that sense "better."

The behaviorist's version of enjoyment is reinforcement, the process by which a stimulus strengthens any behavior that produces it. The taste of sugar reinforces you if sugar in coffee makes you more likely to drink it. Some stimuli—packets labeled "sugar"—reinforce because of learned associations, whereas others—the taste of sugar—reinforce unconditionally. Broadening "reinforcer" to include the unique objective causes of preferred stimuli, as when we say people like sugar (the cause of that sweet taste),[10] some behaviors are themselves reinforcing. Just as some activities are undertaken because of their correlates—nobody adds sugar to coffee unless he expects to like the results—many, including sex, are done for their own sakes and strengthen any other behaviors that facilitate their performance. They are unconditionally self-reinforcing.

Psychological hedonists believe that there is but one desirable internal state, pleasure, produced by all other so-called reinforcers, and that behaviors ostensibly pursued for their own sakes are really pursued because they produce this state. Critics of psychological hedonism dismiss such an all-purpose reinforcer and its affiliated theory of action, objecting that (a) activities we did not already enjoy for themselves would give no pleasure, (b) activities as experientially dissimilar as surfing and solving acrostics are all called "pleasant," and (c) some actions (e.g., for babies, sucking the nipple) are desired before being experienced, hence before even a prewired association with pleasure could be noticed.[11] An attractive compromise is that "pleasure" names the experience of being reinforced.[12] Fortunately, all three theories can be stretched to make room for unconditioned reinforcement, so speculation about its evolutionary role is not hostage to any one of them.

Nature, wanting its creatures to repeat certain behaviors, insures they do so by making these behaviors pleasant. And the question of what behaviors nature has made pleasant, or (dispensing with metaphor) what is adaptive for organisms to find self-reinforcing, practically answers itself. There will be selection for enjoyment of *adaptive* behavior. An adaptive action enhances the fitness of organisms emitting it, so the more adaptively an organism acts, the more copies of its genes it leaves. Likewise, a gene is fit insofar as it programs adaptive behavior, since the more adaptive the behavior it programs, the more readily it replicates. As pleasurable behavior is, all else equal, emitted more frequently than its alternatives, genes that make adaptive behavior pleasurable thereby ensure its more frequent repetition and are more fit. Enjoyment of what enhances fitness enhances fitness further, spreading genes that program it. This is why, although we can't read a lion's mind, we are sure meat tastes good to him. Eating meat (once) help(ed)s lions reproduce, giving a lion gene that programmed carnivorousness an advantage. A gene that made carnivorousness self-reinforcing had a greater advantage still, so that is the gene today's lions are apt to carry. The two aspects of behavioral drives are telescoped in the word "appetite," which implies both an urge to do something and pleasure in the doing.[13]

That enjoyable behaviors once enhanced fitness but may do so no longer explains why people overeat despite the patent maladaptiveness of gluttony. High-energy food was once so hard to get that eating until satiation was adaptive, hence enjoyable, and we, to our distress, have inherited the genes that make it so. Our eating habits have simply not been maladaptive long enough to be deselected,[14] although evolutionary theory predicts that they will eventually be replaced by enjoyment of more salubrious diets should food remain as plentiful as it now is in the West. So too, innate mating patterns may change now that medicine has made it unnecessary for a woman to have ten children for two to survive—a circumstance, together with the danger of overpopulation, sometimes cited as a (rather fanciful) defense of homosexuality. However, until mankind's innate endowments do change, we will come equipped with the feelings that are adaptive for hunter-gatherers in small communities. One cannot make unnatural behaviors (xenophilia or homosexuality) natural by pointing to their advantages in the twentieth century; we will have to wait for our genes to get the news. People as currently designed cannot help experiencing and reacting to these behaviors as if they were maladaptive.

The reinforcing quality of adaptive behavior may shed light on the phenomenology of homosexual promiscuity. That homosexuals seem ever to itch for something new can be seen as a result of homosexual sex lacking the natural rewards of heterosexual sex. This does not mean homosexual sex is self-punishing, or that it insures unhappiness in some absolute sense, but it does mean that homosexuals are less likely to find their sex lives, and their lives as a whole, as satisfying as heterosexuals find theirs. There may well be happy, faithful homosexual male couples,[15] but they are relatively rare; the average male homosexual live-in relationship lasts less than three years.[16] The fact that homosexual advocacy literature goes out of its way to mention long-time homosexual couples underlines their relative rarity; it would hardly surprise or impress the reader to learn that several of his acquaintances have lived faithfully with their wives for decades. The link between normalcy and happiness explains this discrepancy.

Homosexual Domesticity

I have taken pains to insist that the abnormality of homosexuality does not make it evil or warrant criminalizing private homosexual acts, although the association of abnormality with unhappiness is a good reason to discourage homosexuality, to the extent that it can be discouraged, in informal ways. But certain legal consequences do follow. Insofar as the state has a duty to consider the well-being of children—that is, insofar as people may and should consider the welfare of offspring not their own—it must sometimes classify by sexual preference. An "ERA for homosexuals" is out of the question.

. . . [T]he young of a species do best when raised normally, namely in the way(s) in which their ancestors were. Human children in particular presumably do best when reared as children were when mankind was evolving in the Pleistocene (with breast milk, not formula). There was selection for rearing by biological mothers with substantial input from fathers because feral children, children without access to milk, and children without male protection tended to die before reproducing. Since rearing by Mom and Dad optimized junior's genetic fitness (and therefore Mom and Dad's), it was also optimally adaptive for infants to develop adaptively when so reared.

"Optimal" applied to upbringing colloquially means "most apt to yield happy children who become happy, productive adults," whereas in the evolutionary tone of voice it means "most apt to yield grandchildren," but by now we know the two notions converge. Happiness is the subjective accompaniment of fitness. Not only is it fitness-enhancing for children to develop adaptive traits in the normal two-parent environment, it is fitness-enhancing for them to like that environment. Any infants not reinforced by, hence less responsive to, the normal upbringing they received in normal environments were less fit than their rivals, so we, more likely to have descended from those rivals, carry those rival response tendencies. Certainly, psychologists and common sense recognize bonds of affection between father and mother as necessary for children's emotional development. There are all sorts of critical periods, developmental sequences, and parent-child interactions designed to be triggered under normal circumstances. Since these developmental milestones exist because they yield reproductively fit adults, passing through them is also psychologically rewarding. It would be sheer luck for these rewarding experiences to be triggered in other ways.

No rearing environment could be farther from normal than caretaking by homosexuals. Human beings were never raised by homosexual pairs before the last third of this century, so adaptive responses to such an upbringing cannot have been selected in. Neither was there selection for maladaptive reactions to such rearing—Nature's inventiveness cannot match the liberationist imagination—but children are almost certainly born disposed to react more positively to normal parents than to homosexual "parents." . . . [L]esbian pairs might well provide a rearing environment closer to normal than male homosexuals would, but it would still not be one for which human infants are prepared. It would be a remarkable coincidence were homosexual foster parents apt to provide cuing stimuli for development milestones. Hence, absent indisputable evidence to the contrary, homosexual rearing must be presumed to be biologically and emotionally far inferior to heterosexual rearing.

Parentage much closer to normal than that provided by homosexual pairs is recognized as highly suboptimal. Psychologists constantly warn of the difficulties besetting children of divorce, or those raised without fathers. The crime rate among illegitimate males is many times that of males born in wedlock (although race is a confounding variable); sons of divorce entering adolescence are especially prone to academic difficulties, and daughters of divorce are prone to promiscuity by the end of it.[17] It seems obvious, then, that children raised by homosexuals are much more likely to be troubled than children raised by heterosexuals. In addition to lacking a normal emotional matrix and a masculine figure, adoptees of homosexuals face the ridicule of their normally raised peers. Children notice the deviant, although liberationists of the Koppelman school would no doubt take this as a reason to ban teasing as "hate speech" and have the state teach children the value of homosexual parenthood. One should view with skepticism any claim that rearing by homosexuals is harmless, since the phenomenon is too rare for adequate samples to exist, too new for longitudinal studies, and the conclusion too exquisitely politically correct for its propagation to be trusted.

The topic of adoption by homosexuals naturally leads to the larger issue of homosexual marriage. Speaking generally, the institution of marriage confers certain rights on the partners involved; the question is which of these legal rights homosexuals now lack and which of those they should have.

The principle . . . that the state may act only to prevent harm is universally understood to apply only to adults. No one is Millian about children. You may without incurring legal liability walk away from a friend at a busy intersection miles from home, but you may not leave your five-year-old there. Other people—the state—may punish a parent that negligent. The most familiar reason for letting the state intercede on children's behalf in cases such as this is that children are not fully rational. Five-year-olds do not genuinely consent to take walks, nor are they as able as adults to avoid danger when alone. Then too, we think of parents as *doing* something to a child by bringing it into the world, indeed that they have made its situation more precarious. A child's baseline is the safety of Limbo, whereas it becomes helpless on entering Reality. Since (in this way of thinking) parents harm a baby by exposing it to a risky world, others may insist they take affirmative steps to guard it against those risks. A final reason the state is allowed to intercede to protect children is that everyone wants society to continue and thus cares about the rearing of the next generation. This concern may be innate: The members of the small communities in which mankind evolved typically carried a few of everyone else's genes, so a desire to ensure society's future enhanced inclusive fitness.

Only the first consideration legitimately entitles strangers to force parents to care for their children, but the other two probably make such intervention inevitable. At any rate, no Western society has ever regarded child-rearing as a purely private matter over which parents alone have a legitimate say. Most of the constraints imposed on biological parents do not of course apply to homosexuals, but the state also regulates adoption in what it presumes is the adoptees' interest, and this does have bearing. The presumption that rearing by homosexuals is much worse for children than rearing by heterosexuals warrants a state ban on homosexual adoption. No adoption agency would allow a heterosexual couple to adopt if the half-life of its relationship was as short as three years. Since adoption is (or was until recently) a prerogative of married couples, denying homosexuals the right to marry denies them the legal right to adopt. But this is no reason to recognize homosexual marriage, since, for the reasons just explained, adoption is a legal right that homosexuals may and indeed should be denied.

The complaint that a maladaptiveness argument also counsels against adoption by single men and women will leave unmoved anyone doubtful about adoption by singles, but anyway there is the usual difference: The rearing environment provided by single heterosexuals, especially females, to some extent approximates the normal, and may elicit from children some programmed adaptive responses and their experiential accompaniments. The environment provided by homosexuals is incomparably less normal.

. . . [L]egal symbolism (on the assumption that it should count at all) favors exclusively heterosexual marriage. I have just argued that the state should withhold adoption rights from homosexuals. With regard to two of marriage's primary functions, then—expressing state approval of an important personal relationship, and regulating child-rearing—homosexual marriage is undesirable. There are no grounds for forbidding lesbian couples to acquire (illegitimate) children via artificial insemination unless this procedure is also denied to unmarried heterosexual women, and a liberal would have trouble justifying the latter restriction. But rather than being a reason to let lesbians marry, it is a reason for sperm donors and doctors to refuse to impregnate lesbians.

A third legal effect of matrimony, imposition of special duties on the partners, is also no reason to let homosexuals marry. For homosexuals demanding the right to assume the contractual burdens of marriage, this right is theirs already. Homosexuals can subject themselves to the same obligations created by marriage via private contracts that the courts should uphold. In California, for instance, a divorced couple splits their property. Homosexuals in California desirous of a similar commitment can sign legal instruments guaranteeing a property split should they go their separate ways. Homosexuals can now bequeath their property to lovers. Everyone should have the legal right to bind himself in such ways, but marriage is not necessary.

The fourth major effect of marriage under current law is a lowering of taxes. This marriage break does not literally reward families, since all taxation is burdensome; rather, the burden on married couples is reduced to make it less difficult for them to create the next generation and to prompt the unmarried to change their status. Still, higher taxes for the unmarried, which includes all "out" homosexuals, is wrong on Millian grounds, since unmarried homosexuals are being burdened more heavily than married heterosexuals despite having done nothing wrong. If, moreover, encouraging fertility is not a proper government function, a distinction in tax law between married heterosexuals and homosexuals is arbitrary. However, unmarried heterosexuals can lodge identical complaints. They have done nothing to warrant a heavier state-imposed tax burden, and, if fertility is not state business, discriminating against them is also arbitrary. Lower taxes for "married" homosexuals would discriminate against unmarried heterosexuals, and discriminating in favor of married heterosexuals and homosexuals against unmarried heterosexuals is as unjust as discriminating in favor of married heterosexuals against unmarried homosexuals and heterosexuals. Indeed, equity would allow unmarried same-sex heterosexuals to "marry" each other to lower *their* taxes. There is thus no reason to confer on homosexuals a tax status equal to that of married heterosexuals but more favorable than that of unmarried heterosexuals, and with that the last argument for homosexual marriage collapses.

Not only does the case for homosexual marriage fail, homosexual promiscuity constitutes a powerful case against it. Fidelity has been essential to marriage for as long as the institution has existed, the whole point of the marital vow being renunciation of the quest for sex elsewhere. In this country adultery was automatic grounds for dissolving a marriage before the advent of "no-fault" divorce; elsewhere, female infidelity has been punished much more harshly. The compulsive promiscuity of homosexuals thus makes "homosexual marriage" an oxymoron, a joke, or an abuse of language. Andrew Sullivan pleads that same-sex unions will be more stable than heterosexual ones because homosexuals "understand the need for extramarital outlets." As James Q. Wilson has written in reply, "we are now referring to two different kinds of arrangements."[18]

The liberationist may rightly ask what is in a name. Assuming that partners in marriage must by definition intend to be faithful, just call homosexual unions with outlets for promiscuity something else, say "flarriage." The issue now becomes whether the state should recognize homosexual flarriage along with (necessarily heterosexual) marriage. But most of the arguments against homosexual "marriage," now verbally transposed, remain in force. Adoption by flarried couples is bad for children. Statutory recognition of flarriage would insult married couples. Homosexuals wishing to assume the legal burdens of flarriage can do so by private contract. A tax break for married and flarried couples discriminate against unmarried, unflarried heterosexuals to just the extent a tax break for marrieds discriminates against flarrieds. There is thus no reason to, and good reason not to, legalize flarriage.

A thoroughly laissez-faire approach to personal relations that excluded government from all cohabitation arrangements would partially resolve the marriage dispute. Adoption by homosexuals would remain forbidden, but otherwise the state would avoid discriminating against some lifestyles by declining to bless any, leaving marriage a wholly religious ceremony without civil ramifications. A willing minister is all it would take to join any two individuals. While liberals might support this compromise, consistency would force most liberationists to oppose it, since they favor extensive state intervention in private spheres (such as employment and housing) more peripheral to the aims of government than the perpetuation of society. And, realistically, it is hard to imagine any modern human society leaving all aspects of mating in private hands.

Homosexual Values: "Sex . . . The Essence of Our Lives"

Having examined a range of legal-ethical issues, it is time to look at the broader cultural transformation sought by more ambitious liberationists. Abstractly put, liberationists wish homosexual sexuality to be just as acceptable as heterosexual sexuality. In operational terms, liberationists seek the day when introducing one man's boyfriend will raise eyebrows no higher than introducing another man's wife—when "coming out" is impossible because society no longer classifies sexual desires by their objects. Opposed to this hope is the traditionalist conviction that human society turns on the natural family unit and is threatened by values inimical to it.

To get a sense of the values that "mainstreaming" homosexuality would inject into society's veins, I consulted a number of homosexual websites[19] and periodicals targeted to a homosexual readership, including *The Advocate, Out, Curve (The Lesbian Magazine), XY* (the "Pride" issue), *Naked Genre, HX* and *Q* (a smaller "regional" newspaper for the Pittsburgh homosexual community). *Out* and *The Advocate* in particular are slick, well edited, and aimed at an affluent, college-educated demographic. To judge by these outlets, homosexuals are interested in penises, partying, "pride" (incongruously, one would think: one website advertises "Festival, Events and Shopping—Experience a Month of

Pride"), and above al sex, sex, sex. If these publications and websites accurately reflect the homosexual milieu, concern with sex therein is ubiquitous. Ads in *HX* call attention to "hot clubs for hot men," where you can "dance your ass off." A party organization throws a "pervert pride" party to raise money to send a team to the Gay Games; it advertises "novelty love booths" and the "Clitclub float," advising all who attend to "rubber up." The 1996–1997 catalogue of Haworth, a highly professional publisher with academic aspirations for an up-market homosexual audience, lists the following books (among many similar ones): *Sailors and Sexual Identity* ("describes homoerotic initiation rites, . . . the eroticism of tattooing, and the rivalry between sailors and Marines which persists even when they get together in bed"), *Barrack Buddies and Soldier Lovers* ("challenges assumptions and stereotypes. . . . These revealing interviews with 16 GIs, all in their twenties, share the stories of gay life and sex in the armed forces"), *Lie Down with Panthers* ("a uniquely candid memoir about the sex and romance in [*sic*] an old gay man after the death of his lover"), *Gays, Lesbians and Consumer Behavior* ("We're here, we're queer, and we're going shopping"), *Growing Up Gay in the South* ("not," the reader is assured, "just a simple compilation of 'coming out' stories"), and the self-explanatory *Men Who Beat Men Who Love Them*. Perhaps the most indicative item is *The Golden Boy*, a memoir described by *INCHES* magazine as "a gay wish book of another era." According to its blurb, "[The author's] good looks offered him immediate entry into exclusive clubs and onto the sexual fast track with actors, male models, and other members of the 'Clique.' . . . For 200 pages, the reader is brought back to the era [1970–1980 in New York City] that for many older readers is just a memory, and for younger readers a time they never knew—when to be a 'Golden Boy' was to be a prince, and sex was only fun and games." Most ironically, perhaps, *Q* juxtaposes a predictable essay denouncing the "stereotyping" of homosexuals as sex-mad with a listing by the paper's movie reviewer of current leading men he would most like to [have intercourse with].

This single-mindedness is often disguised and sanitized. The late homosexual artist Keith Haring, for instance, became known for his outlines of crawling babies and dancers radiating energy lines. A recent retrospective at the Whitney, however, featured his drawings of anal intercourse, anal penetration of dogs, a masturbating Mickey Mouse, a masturbating Pinocchio, and flying saucers beaming rays on erect penises. Whether this is the work of genius or crude degeneracy, it is saturated with sex.

Selection of citations by an unsympathetic outsider can be dismissed as biased, and anyway piling on the anecdotes never amounts to proof. More telling are the murmurs of disquiet from homosexuals themselves. One columnist[20] meditates on "demystifying the dick size complex," al though his ultimate point is that you will never meet anyone "cute" or "hot" if "they only send you a picture of their dick." One correspondent to *The Advocate* wonders "what our (my) purpose is, besides trying to look good without a shirt on the dance floor." Another remarks, to my mind most tellingly, "For years we have asked the straight world to ignore the sex in homosexuality, while our fiction, art, plays, and films promote it as the essence of our lives." When the mayor of New York proposed zoning ordinances to decrease the number of pornography vendors, Manhattan Borough President Ruth Messinger, a recognized champion of homosexuals, protested that these shops were an "integral part" of homosexual neighborhoods like Greenwich Village. Indeed, liberationist steps to domesticate homosexual habits underscore the salience of sex. A state-funded AIDS education program in Vermont, for instance,[21] includes a class on dating, which emphasizes not having sex on the first date and practicing get-acquainted lines more staid than an invitation to step into the back room.

Granted, heterosexuals too have their pornography. But a typical publication aimed at a typical heterosexual readership—a newsmagazine or daily newspaper—contains no pictures of couples having intercourse or discussions of genitalia. There are websites for heterosexuals that are *not* about sex. No heterosexual institution corresponds to the gay bar. Singles bars—the seeming heterosexual counterpart—are less central to heterosexual life than gay bars are to homosexual life. While men may frequent them mainly in the hope of finding sex partners, female habitués are mainly looking for Mr. Right; above all, there are no facilities for sex on the premises, as there are in many homosexual venues.[22] It must also be granted that heterosexual males, particularly unmarried ones, fantasize a good deal about quick, anonymous sex with beautiful, willing women. However, the hope of such encounters is not the premise for most heterosexual social events. Sex is part, but not the essence, of heterosexual lives: the average heterosexual's existence does not revolve around it to remotely the extent that the average homosexual's seems to. There are plenty of books by open heterosexuals about heterosexual sex, but many more about other subjects, including most of the world's narrative, dramatic, scientific, and philosophical literature. Anthony Trollope lived openly with a woman (his wife), yet wrote novels on topics other than sex. The *Principia Mathematica* of Bertrand Russell (a notorious heterosexual womanizer) and Alfred North Whitehead (another "out" heterosexual) runs over two thousand pages yet never mentions anything long, hard, or throbbing. Rembrandt never tried to hide his taste for women, and produced many images of his son Titus, but seems to have been uninterested in heterosexual pornography.

The notion of "gay pride" deserves an aside. Because pride usually rests on an achievement or some outstanding personal quality, what homosexuals qua homosexuals are supposed to be proud of is quite unclear. If it is the accomplishments of some homosexuals throughout history, as in "Rudolf Nureyev was gay, and so am I,"[23] the typical heterosexual has more to be proud of: Aristotle, Einstein, and Bach were also straight. More than this, sameness of sexual orientation is far too tenuous a connection to sustain vicarious bragging. Actually, to judge by the tone of utterance, the slogan "I'm gay and I'm proud" is meant to express pride in homosexuality per se. But how is the sheer capacity to be aroused by members of one's own sex an excellence? Should heterosexuals be proud of their arousability by women? I suspect liberationists have confused a contrary with a contradictory here. Liberationists wish to convince homosexuals not to feel shame, a reasonable sentiment best expressed as "I'm gay and I accept myself." Going to the opposite extreme as enthusiasts will, they instead encourage nonsensical boasting.

Aesthetic distaste is not the only reason to deplore homosexual preoccupation with sex and attendant fixations on youth and appearance. These concerns indicate time preferences too high to sustain civilization—not merely the high-tech world of the modern West, but any tolerable social order. It takes long-term horizons to build a world like the one we know. Resources must be accumulated, goods produced, and investments allowed to ripen, all of which require deferral of gratification. Whenever a hunter patiently sharpens a spear to bring down larger game than he could attack with a stick, he forgoes present consumption. This exchange of the present for a lightly discounted future comes naturally to heterosexuals, imposed on them as it is by the fact of children. A father saving for a daughter's dowry or her college education, resisting momentary temptations to squander money for the sake of his family, sets aside resources for payoffs that may not ripen until after his death. Heterosexuals must take an interest in what things will be like a generation or two hence, since that is the world their descendants (carrying their genes) will inhabit; homosexuals, without issue, feel no pressure to share this interest. Relatively long-term horizons seem intrinsic to heterosexuality itself; homosexuality is more present-oriented.[24]

Freud's theory that the price of civilization is repressed libido and neurosis has given sublimation a bad name. Liberationists periodically seize on his theory to bolster alternatives to ordinary sexual morality, whether free love (marriage is a prison; Samoans can teach us how to relax) or, in the present instance, homophilia. In this connection psychoanalytic diagnoses are deployed to intimidate traditionalists: any foe of any sexual revolution must be "sick"—uptight, frigid, envious, or a secret self-hating homosexual.[25] In fact, Freud, at least as popularly interpreted, was wrong. There is no evidence whatever that law and technology (the indicia of civilization) correlate with neurosis. Indeed, since social institutions are summations over individual preferences, bourgeois sexual arrangements would long since have been discarded if they genuinely frustrated the mass of humanity. Nor did Freud appreciate that, since community-wide cooperative channeling of sexual energy into nonsexual tasks tends to enhance the inclusive fitness of community members, there has almost certainly been selection for willingness to sublimate. Far from seething with frustration that life is not one extended orgy, the average heterosexual would be less happy if it were. The joy of sexual anarchy is not a good that is, regretfully, outweighed by the advantages of order; given the opportunity by some cosmic intervener to act on homosexual time preferences, heterosexuals, including heterosexual men, would probably find them uncongenial and recur to the old ways. In the midst of an endless roundelay of copulation, men as well as women would find themselves falling in love, experiencing jealousy, desiring exclusivity, and inventing marriage.

This return to a biological orientation brings up perhaps the strongest objection to cultural transformation, namely its sheer impossibility. Self-sacrificing heterosexuals cannot help but scorn the homosexual imperative to follow lust wherever it leads. Thriving in a social milieu that depends upon some confinement of the sex drive, they will tend to praise impulses that fall inside permitted parameters and condemn impulses lying outside. Not only would it be impossible for a successful society to be as preoccupied with sex as male homosexuals are, it is impossible for a society even to *try* to be. Of biological necessity, any enduring population will be overwhelmingly heterosexual. Of sociological necessity, a society's norms will reflect the preferences of its median members. The norms of any society are therefore inevitably oriented around marriage, the family, and the mutual affection of men and women. These norms accept sex as necessary and pleasurable, reject it as life-defining. There is no point discussing whether heterosexuals should welcome homosexuals as warmly as they do other heterosexuals. They won't. Even as egalitarian fantasies go, uncritical acceptance of homosexuality is a pipe dream.

Nonrational Preferences

But suppose most of what I have said so far is false. Suppose that homosexuals are not promiscuous, sex obsessed, prone to venereal disease, that homosexual time horizons are consistent with civilization, that sexual orientation is useless as a proxy for traits relevant to association—that, sexual object choice aside, homosexuals are just like heterosexuals. Suppose that "homophobes" know or suspect this and beneath their rationales simply dislike homosexuals.

It might then seem to follow that civil rights, along with broader efforts to accommodate the culture to homosexuals, are in order. Certainly moral philosophers generally assume that preferences must be reasonable to be worthy of recognition when preferences are transformed into individual duties and public policy. Utilitarians are thus instructed to ignore the preferences of child molesters (and, according to Ronald Dworkin,[26] of "racists") in seeking to maximize happiness. Pure, unreasoned, ground-floor dislike of homosexuals, as we are now assuming "homophobia" to be, would likewise be unworthy, leaving the case for civil rights and cultural transformation easy to make. Why leave anyone free to indulge indefensible desires?

In fact, however, visceral, unreasoned preferences deserve as much deference as any others. To see why, it is necessary first to distinguish *ir*rational preferences from merely *non*rational ones. A rational preference may be defined as one commanded by reason, and an irrational one as forbidden by reason, perhaps because reason commands a contrary. Nonrational preferences, by contrast, are neither commanded nor forbidden by reason, neither rational nor irrational. Irrational preferences are obviously to be avoided, but on reflection there is no similar imperative to avoid or disdain the nonrational. Nonrationality does not deserve the opprobrious connotations of irrationality.

There are two standard theories of how reason can issue commands, both of which tend to count unconditioned preferences as nonrational. The first holds that preferences can be as intrinsically rational or irrational as cognitive states. Spinoza says that "he who lives in accordance with reason" will assist his neighbor. But even those who maintain that some desires either follow from or contravene reason in this sense admit that not all do. Reason is mute about a desire to chew gum, or unconditioned tastes such as fondness for sugar. So far as I can see, feelings about homosexuals also fall into this third category. Dislike of homosexuals is not inherently against reason.

Most philosophers today, however, reject this rationalist theory of preferences in favor of Hume's, that actions, choices, and preferences can be rational or irrational only in the derivative sense of aiding or impeding the satisfaction of more deeply entrenched preferences.[27] It is instrumentally rational for me to wear a topcoat in a blizzard because I wish to remain healthy. An impulse to gambol naked in the snow is irrational because heeding it would result in illness, which I don't want. However, a preference serving no end beyond itself, hence not instrumentally rational, need not threaten any other ends, hence need not be instrumentally irrational. Under most circumstances the desire to chew gum, for instance, is instrumentally nonrational. So is an unconditioned aversion to certain smells. This aversion presumably evolved because it was adaptive, the smells in questions being associated with decaying matter and other threats to fitness, but that history is not *my* reason for avoiding them. I simply dislike them. "Homophobia" appears to fall into this last category. A desire to avoid homosexuals is unlikely to further, or frustrate, any larger goals.[28] Despite liberationist assurances that mainstreaming homosexuals will be "good for everybody," dislike of homosexuals is not instrumentally irrational.

Unconditioned preferences, not pursued because of learned association with other reinforces, can be instrumentally rational only by accident. For all that they are not irrational, as we have just seen, and deserve the respect shown instrumentally rationally preferences. They deserve respect because every instrumentally rational preference is ultimately justified by an unconditioned one, on pain of a familiar regress: Means are justified by their ends, so were there no ends justified other than as further means, no means, hence no preferences whatever, would be justified. I want an umbrella in a downpour because I want to stay dry, and I want to stay dry to avoid feeling feverish subsequently. Why do I want to avoid feeling feverish? No reason. I just do. From my point of view that is the end of it. Pushing the issue back to my health or continued existence changes nothing. There is no way to justify a desire to live in terms of other desires. (Nor, says the Humean, can a desire be validated by pure reason.) If these absolute ends are not worth pursuing, neither is any means to them. Absolute ends are the subbasement, the last stop on the dialectical elevator down to the foundations.

Instrumentally nonrational desires give life purpose. They are what people *really* want, the telos of their actions. Imagine a philosopher-tyrant permitting only those actions for which intrinsic or instrumental reasons can be offered. He allows jogging for fitness, but not for the fun of it. Those seeking health to prolong life may buy medicine, but those who merely like feelings of vitality may not. Foul smells can be avoided when associated with germs but must be endured otherwise. Intercourse for pleasure is outlawed. You the citizen are allowed to seek the company of anyone likely to help you and to avoid anyone who might be harmful or obstructive, but you may not associate with someone simply because you find his company agreeable, or avoid him simply because he rubs you the wrong way. Life in such a regime would be a nightmare.

Apart perhaps from acting from duty, every step take in life is directed toward the satisfaction of unconditioned preferences. This is so thoroughly understood at an intuitive level that no special barriers exist to acting on such preferences, *even when others are affected.* The noisome employee, who earlier showed that treatment of others may be based on involuntary traits, also shows that treatment of others may be based on nonrational preferences. His boss, coworkers, and customers cannot justify their dislike of his aroma; reason does not dictate this dislike, and while avoidance of disease is its evolutionary function, evolution is not something they think about. Yet we ordinarily suppose revulsion toward body odor entitles one to turn away from it, even when avoidance means stigmatizing its source. In point of nonrationality and unconditionedness, there is no difference between gut aversion to someone's smell and gut aversion to his sexual practices. If we are allowed to avoid one, we are allowed to avoid the other.

This conclusion may seem odd because the pursuit of a preference is often thought to be only as rational as the preference itself, which implies that pursuing a nonrational preference is itself nonrational. This is an error. You may be unable to say why you want something, and there may be no reason for (as opposed to cause of) your wanting it, but given that you *do* want it, you have every reason you need to pursue it. The alternative, again, is a regress leading to nihilism. This same error lies behind current philosophical challenges to such everyday practices and values as carnivorousness, animal experimentation, and favoring one's own children over strangers in foreign lands. The targeted practice is first shown to rely on a distinction derived from "sentiment," not "reason." On this basis the practice itself and the institutions surrounding it are then judged arbitrary. It is noted, for instance, that nothing distinguishes your child from complete strangers except how you happen to feel about him. This is supposed to show you the groundlessness of spending money on your child that you could send to Oxfam. (A slippery slope may be greased: You'd help an unrelated child starving right in front of you, starving ten feet from you, starving behind a gauzy curtain . . . so you ought to help children starving in foreign lands.) But if caring more about your own children is not enough to justify your treating them better than you treat strangers, nothing justifies treating human beings in foreign lands better than animals, or animals better than plants, or plants better than rocks, for reason can vouchsafe none of these distinctions either: they all rest on "sentiment." (Nor can reason select any point on the slippery slope to dig in its heels.)

In general: refusal to pursue *X* rather than *Y* unless there is some reason to prefer *X* to *Y* leads to the cessation of all action. In particular: equating dislike of homosexuals with dislike of rotten smells does not derogate action based on either. Individuals are and should be free to avoid people with offensive smells, and individuals who dislike homosexuals should be free to avoid them.

Traditionalists are said to find homosexuality "immoral," and no doubt many talk as if they do think this. But I am not sure this is what they have in mind. Traditionalists *deplore* homosexuality, and like most people they utilize the language of disapprobation that is handiest, namely, moral disapprobation, to express themselves. But what they really mean is that homosexuality is disgusting, nauseating, closely connected with fecal matter. One need not show that anal intercourse is immoral to be warranted in wanting to be as far away from it as possible.

Notes

1. "The Advocate Poll: The Gay Gene," *The Advocate,* June 24, 1997, 8.

2. Mark Schoofs, "Gene-ocide," *The Village Voice,* June 25, 1997, 40–43.

3. Some feminists also seem to view men as pathological monstrosities.

4. A homosexual mystery parody is entitled "The Nancy Boys at Mincing Manor."

5. A. Bell and M. Weinberg, *Homosexualities* (New York: Simon and Schuster, 1978).

6. S. Beachy, "20+, HIV+," *New York Times Magazine,* April 17, 1994, 52–53.

7. It is hard to construe a right to serve when military service has always been seen as an onerous duty.

8. See my *Feminism and Freedom* (New Brunswick, N.J.: Transaction, 1987), ch. 11, for data on male-female differences in tests of upper body strength relevant to military occupational specialties. Anyone who thinks women fight as well as men should be willing to field a 100 percent female army. The current placement of women in the military will merely determine how many women a fighting force can sustain before crumbling.

9. Lesbians Ellen DeGeneres and Anne Heche, at a White House ceremony, June 1997.

10. W.V.O. Quine (*Word and Object* [Cambridge, Mass.: MIT Press, 1960], ch. 2) limits a word's objective semantics to the sensory stimuli that control it. The doubtful consequence of this restriction that nouns lack objective reference can be averted by letting "stimulus" include objects that produce sensory states.

11. But if these actions are ends in themselves, how did we know a priori that we would enjoy them?

12. So there is common experiential element in "pleasant" episodes, yet ends-in-themselves remain plural.

13. Once again there are delicate philosophical questions about the distinguishability of drive-satisfying behavior from experiences of satisfaction.

14. Compare Brian Skyrms on the objection that there has been no selection for adaptive social behavior because rich families now have fewer children than poor ones: "Does the objection imagine yuppie Homoerectus driving BMWs on the savannah? Through most of evolutionary time, payoff in real goods means the difference between nutrition and starvation, and it correlates very well with Darwinian fitness" (*Evolution of the Social Contract* [New York: Cambridge University Press, 1996], 118–19, n.18).

15. Although reports of them tend to be exaggerated. The poet W. H. Auden and his companion were advertised as one such couple, but disclosures of infidelity and recrimination came out after Auden's death.

16. Robert Knight and Daniel Garcia, *Homosexual Parenting: Bad for Children, Bad for Society* (Washington, D.C.: Family Research Council, 1997).

17. I imagine the average liberationist would struggle to keep an errant son in school and become positively Victorian at the prospect of a promiscuous teenaged daughter.

18. "Against Homosexual Marriage," *Commentary,* March 1996, 39.

19. Among them, "Boy Oh Boy," "Well Hung Net," and "Click for Dick." In *Political Tolerance* [Thousand Oaks, Ca.: Sage, 1998], Robert Weissberg surveys

esoteric homosexual publications in greater depth. Saturation with sex is evident from Weissberg's survey as well.

20. Eriq Chang, *XX,* July 1997, 186.

21. See A. Cockburn, "A Better Wank," *NYPress,* July 9, 1997, 18.

22. Gay bars are best compared to brothels without the commercial element.

23. Liberationists have rather loose criteria for detecting homosexuality among historical figures.

24. Did the selection forces that created gay genes also influence time preferences? Do object-choice genes, assuming they exist, pleiotropically express themselves in rate of time discounting?

25. A stock villain in this literature is the lustful, hypocritical Bible-thumper.

26. *Taking Rights Seriously* (Cambridge, Mass.: Harvard University Press, 1977).

27. This is not quite right. *A*'s leading to highly valued *B* does not rationalize a desire for *A* unless the subject believes this connection holds. Unclarities persist: while this belief may be necessary, is it sufficient, or must it also be justified?

28. Dislike of homosexuals when one's superior is a homosexual may be instrumentally irrational.

Chapter 10

A CHRISTIAN HOMOSEXUALITY?

Edward Vacek, S.J.

The contemporary debates over homosexuality are heated up like a blast furnace. Ever since 1969 when homosexuals began to assert gay pride, the solid iron ore of traditional sexual preferences has turned into a churning, molten mass. The first, faltering moves "out of the closet" have prompted "Save Our Children" campaigns and Protestant ordinations of homosexuals. Unfortunately, like a blast furnace, the issue has generated for most people immense heat and little light.

One of the first steps toward the light is a confession of some basic ignorance. The central unknown is why some people (somewhere between 5 and 10 percent of the population) are exclusively homosexual. Some evidence suggests that homosexuality is biologically based. There is greater evidence that it results from early childhood experiences, though no one is sure what factor or factors lead to it. There is some scant evidence that it can be learned in adolescence, either when one is frustrated at heterosexual activity or is initiated into homosexual activity by someone more experienced. The best answer at present is that we do not know why people are homosexual.

Recently I asked thirty-five of my students whether they thought that being a homosexual was more like having a withered arm or like being left-handed. The point of this comparison should be clear. Most of us think that there is something biologically askew with having a deformed arm; but few of us think that left-handers have something wrong with

Reprinted with permission from *Commonweal* (5 December 1980), pp. 681–84. © 1980 Commonweal Foundation. For subscriptions, call toll-free 1-888-495-6755.

their biological make-up. The world would not be greatly altered if the
majority of people were left-handed. The world, however, would be a
worse place if the vast majority had withered arms.

Much to my surprise, all but two of my students thought homosexuality was like being left-handed. These students are training to be future
ministers, and I was consoled at the compassion and understanding they
will probably show to homosexuals they will meet. And yet, I still had to
ask myself, Are they correct?

Homosexual *orientation* must be distinguished from homosexual *activity*. Those who are homosexual may remain single or celibate; and they
can, at least physically, engage in heterosexual acts. Many, in fact, are
married. The orientation is not externally visible. It is experienced internally as an enduring, romantic, and sexual attraction to members of
the same sex.

Sexual orientation is not a habit like smoking. Hence one is not
morally responsible for having the orientation. One is responsible for
what one does with this orientation, just as heterosexuals are responsible
for how they express their own orientation.

Few people are totally homosexual or heterosexual. Children, adolescents, and even some heterosexual adults quite commonly go through
homosexual phases. Good counselors usually encourage them not to
make too much of a passing dalliance. Similarly, some homosexuals occasionally experience heterosexual attraction. So we are speaking of a
dominant or prevailing pattern of attraction toward one sex or the other.

How do homosexuals experience themselves and their activity? Put
simply, some are quite happy with their condition, some confused, and
some quite unhappy. To those who are at peace with their homosexuality it seems an affront to demand that they change themselves. They ask
heterosexuals to imagine wanting to extinguish one of the great sources
of *their* identity, namely, the heterosexual feelings that form so much of
the way a heterosexual relates to the world.

To those who are confused, gay alliances recommend that they accent
the heterosexual aspect of themselves as long as they can, if only as a way
of avoiding societal defamation.

Those who are unhappy with their orientation are often encouraged to
change. The problem is, most will be unable to do so. The change is
"morally impossible" because many homosexuals do not have the time or
money to enter a therapy where there are no "sure-fire cures." The *most*
optimistic of therapists report only a 60 percent "cure rate," and this cure
is reached only by those homosexuals most strongly motivated to change.

Conversions in orientation due to special graces may occur, but many
claims of these graced reorientations have been shown to be misleading
or false. Frequently the change is from active homosexuality to a dor-
mant, celibate homosexuality. In other cases, the "conversion" is only

short-lived. In the words of a recent Vatican Declaration, many are "incurable."

It should be clear in what follows that no one recommends the kind of activity that would be condemned if it were performed in a heterosexual context. No argument for homosexual relations should be construed as an argument for promiscuity, prostitution, mate swapping, infidelity, and the like. Homosexuals must exhibit the same personalist virtues as heterosexuals. The major question is whether they should be bound to act as heterosexuals.

Now to the question, Is a homosexual orientation and consequent homosexual activity merely a different life-style, or is there something inherently wrong with it? There are at least three ways to get at an answer to this question: Scripture; authority; and human reason. Roman Catholics have traditionally tried to bring all three to bear on perplexing moral issues.

Scripture does not offer much comfort to those who engage in homosexual acts. Although homosexuality holds a very minor place in Scripture and is not mentioned by Jesus or the prophets, some terribly severe judgments are made against it. Leviticus (18:22; 20:13) tells us that active homosexuals should be put to death, a practice renewed in the form of burning at the stake during the late Middle Ages. Paul tells us that they belong to the class of idolators (Rom. 1:18–32), and that they shall never enter the kingdom of heaven (1 Cor. 6:9–10). It is hard to imagine penalties worse than loss of physical and eternal life.

The basis for these judgments is set out in the early chapters of Genesis. In order to image himself, God made both man and woman. Together, the two sexes mirror God. In order to overcome Adam's loneliness, God created a woman, not another man.

There are two approaches to the Scriptures that Roman Catholics should not take. The first is a fundamentalist attitude that protests, I take everything in the Bible "just as it is written." The Catholic tradition has always seen the need for an on-going interpretation and reinterpretation of the Scriptures. That process began in the Scriptures themselves; and it continues today. The promise of the on-going presence of the Spirit is at the same time a command to interpret the Scriptures. The second erroneous approach is to ignore the Scriptures, a tack that is also not acceptable for it would deprive us of the originating inspiration of our historical faith.

A third approach is to evaluate the scriptural texts even as they judge us. We often discover upon study that they mean something other than what we have always assumed. For example, many scholars think that the sin of Sodom was not primarily homosexuality, but inhospitality, gang rape, and even attempted sexual congress with angels. Some scholars argue that what Scripture really condemns is the promiscuity that so much homosexuality involved. Still other scholars note that the sacred authors were unaware that some people are homosexual in orientation. That is, the scriptural condemnations assume a conscious choice by a heterosexual to exchange a heterosexual partner for a homosexual one. We can make no such assumption today.

Another facet of this third approach is to note the possible cultural relativity of the scriptural judgments. The Scriptures legislate on a whole range of sexual behaviors that we do not consider to be sinful. For a son to see his father naked was tantamount to a crime. For husband and wife to have sexual intercourse during the seven days of her menstrual period meant punishment. Polygamy was permitted, even required. Celibacy was abnormal; bishops were to have only one wife, and so on.

However one interprets these texts, it seems safe to say that our sexual ethic is at least partially different from the one (or, rather, the several) proposed in Scripture. The question returns, Are homosexual acts wrong? Has the evolution of culture meant only that people should not be put to death for such acts, just as we no longer stone people caught in adultery? We still judge adultery to be wrong, though we have changed the punishment. Or does it mean that we "enlightened" moderns now see that at least certain cases of homosexual acts are as sinless as the touching of menstrual fluids, an act that once made a person ritually unclean?

In sum, when reading Scripture we see that some typically cited texts do not treat of homosexuality; others do, and do so in a very direct fashion. But are these texts literally valid for us, or are they culturally bound?

Church tradition and ecclesiastical authority have continuously rejected homosexual activity. The first objection raised against homosexual activity was that it was "against nature." This unnaturalness frequently meant that men were acting like women. Women have rather regularly been seen, even by such luminaries as Thomas Aquinas, as naturally inferior to men. Therefore part of the degradation involved in homosexuality was seen to be not so much a degradation of human nature, but a degradation of a man to the level of a woman. Therefore, too, lesbianism has seldom been proscribed in our scripture or our tradition. Male homosexuality, on the other hand, was commonly thought to be a more serious sin than rape, prostitution, or fornication, all of which are "natural."

Homosexuality was also judged sinful because it is not open to procreation. The early Christian tradition showed an uneasiness with sexual passion, and procreation was in many cases thought to be the sole justification for marriage and sexual relations. Hence homosexuality was roundly condemned for being sterile. Only in the late nineteenth century did "expression of interpersonal love" come to be recognized in church teaching as a reason for sexual intercourse.

Within the past five years, church authorities have again taken strong stands against homosexual activity. Yet, at the same time, they have spoken clearly on the human rights of those who have a homosexual orientation. Their message would seem to be that it is all right to be a homosexual, as long as one does not express this orientation genitally.

As with scriptural passages, one can take a fundamentalist attitude or a "who-cares!" attitude toward church tradition and authority on the issue of homosexuality. Neither of these is acceptable. The latter position is untenable for a person who wants to be a member of the church. The former position fails to reckon with some of the dubious reasons given for opposition to homosexuality. Bad reasons, of course, do not invalidate a conclusion; but neither do they make it right. There are a number of significant questions about the church's past attitude toward sexuality that make one wonder whether it too has been culture-bound and ought to be transcended.

My own approach tries to discover the relevant biological, psychological, rational, and religious values. It then tries to weigh these values and make a judgment within an ethics of proportionality. In examining homosexuality, I find myself confronted by Jesus's demand (Lk. 12:57) "Why can you not judge for yourselves what is the right course?" Stated briefly, my judgment is this. Homosexual actions are biologically deficient, but they may be psychologically healthy, the best available exercise of one's interpersonal freedom, and may even be a form of authentic Christian spirituality. Let us look at each of these four levels of human existence.

Homosexual couples cannot do, biologically, what heterosexual couples can do, namely, bear children. The significance of that fact should be neither overestimated nor underestimated. I want to argue that to the extent that any sexual activity is closed to children, to that extent it is deficient. It represents a failure to carry out one of the most basic and fulfilling tasks of the human race, namely, to propagate the race.

Homosexual activity also contravenes the complementary aptness of the male and female sexual systems for one another. Again this biological deficiency should be neither overestimated nor ignored. Thus the human race has discouraged homosexuality because stable heterosexual unions are so utterly vital to its survival interests and because of its sense of biological fittingness. We must not ignore these factors.

Secondly, homosexual relations may be psychologically healthy. Various psychological tests show that—apart from the one characteristic of "adequate heterosexual development"—homosexuals are about as healthy as anyone else. Homosexuals take encouragement from such tests because one would expect that, since they have suffered intense discrimination, they would score significantly lower than their heterosexual counterparts. They do not.

Thirdly, persons who are homosexuals are able to function and grow at least as well as heterosexuals. They are able to be creative, put in a hard day's work, act as citizens, help their neighbor, much like hetero-sexuals. Somewhat surprisingly, they "make love" more humanely, largely because they are better able empathetically to feel what their partner is feeling. With regard to human psyche and mind, human persons are so richly complex that they can often compensate (which need not mean overcompensate) for whatever deficiencies they have on the biological, psychological, or mental levels. We all know, for example, people who have lost a leg and are still great workers and extraordinary human beings. Homosexual activity, however deficient, does not keep homosexuals from human greatness.

Finally, homosexuals can develop a form of authentic Christian spirituality. Their spirituality is, of course, basically like that of heterosexuals. They believe and enact in their lives the Incarnation, Cross, and Resurrection. They live or try to live, consciously dependent on the power of the Spirit. But just as grace, mind, and psyche penetrate their sexual orientation, so also this orientation affects their psyche, mind, and spirit. Whatever is distinctive about their human existence due to their homosexual orientation offers a new possibility for life in the spirit, a possibility that heterosexuals do not have. A number of articles and books have been written to explore this possibility.

"The harvest of the Spirit," Paul tells us (Gal. 5:22–23), is "love, joy, peace, patience, kindness, goodness, fidelity, gentleness, and self-control." Some homosexuals exhibit these qualities as strikingly as any heterosexual. To be sure, we human beings are so complex that we can manifest all these virtues and still be sinful in some aspect of our lives. But abundant evidence of these virtues in many active homosexuals leads one to presume that they are Spirit-filled.

Now, to apply an ethic of proportionality. The God we serve and co-operate with wants to conserve and enhance creation, bringing all things to their greatest possible fullness. A sexual act that helps to continue the human race is good. But the homosexual act is not open to generation, and so to that extent it is deficient. On the other hand, engaging in heterosexual activity can alienate genuinely homosexual persons from themselves at the level of their psyche, mind, and spirit. What they gain at the level of propagation, they lose in authenticity at the other levels of their being. Thus, the disproportionate evil of insisting that homosexual persons, if they are going to have sexual relations at all, must have them with persons of the opposite sex, must be assessed.

Should the significant numbers who are homosexual remain permanently single or celibate? Is this a cross they are given by God, to be carried all their adult life? As a personal vocation from God, it might well be that they are called to genital non-activity. The desire never to act contrary to certain explicit statements of our Scriptures and tradition may itself constitute such a vocation for some.

Apart from this personal vocation, it seems a violation of humanness automatically to deprive homosexuals of the values that Christians have found in sexuality. Such values include pleasure, romantic feelings, companionship, mutual support, sexual outlet, ecstasy, intimacy, and interpersonal communication. It seems to compound "unnaturalness" to insist that persons not heterosexually inclined must simply, without further consideration, be sexually inactive. One biological deficiency then turns all too easily into biological, psychological, rational, and spiritual alienation. A homosexual orientation would become synonymous with fate. It is not clear to me that every Christian homosexual is fated to such restrictions on his or her human expressiveness. Put perhaps too simply, if there are positive values in a committed, loving sexual relation, then very strong reasons have to be given why anyone including homosexuals should be denied those positive values. The biological deficiencies do not seem in themselves serious enough in our time to justify that denial.

The unknown and the unsuspected usually cause us to be uncomfortable. This is especially so when it deals with our sexual identity. Every one of us spends decades if not a lifetime trying to accept and become comfortable with those "deep dark urges," as they have been called, that pop up to disturb our equilibrium at the most unexpected times. This uncertainty has generated an intense hostility towards homosexuals, far out of proportion to whatever "sin" there may be in homosexual activity and far from the loving response one would expect from Spirit-filled Christians.

The American bishops have made it very clear that all persons deserve great respect, whatever their sexual orientation. No one, merely because of his or her sexual orientation, should be denied housing, jobs, or public office. Since homosexual children generally are reared in heterosexual families, and since, in the studies made thus far, children reared in homosexual environments are as likely to be heterosexual as any other, there seems to be no solid foundation for discrimination.

Finally, since homosexual persons are presently highly discriminated against, they should be especially favored by all Christians. A recent book title asks, "Is the homosexual my neighbor?" Christians who are deeply alive to the parable of the Good Samaritan can only answer yes to that question. Even if someday it becomes crystal clear that homosexual persons should not "make love" to one another, it will always be Christianly clear that we should love our homosexual sisters and brothers.

Chapter 11

HOMOSEXUALITY: THE NATURE AND HARM ARGUMENTS

John Corvino

Tommy and Jim are a homosexual couple I know. Tommy is an accountant; Jim is a botany professor. They are in their early forties and have been together fourteen years, the last five of which they've lived in a Victorian house that they've lovingly restored. Though their relationship has had its challenges, each has made sacrifices for the sake of the other's happiness and the relationship's long-term success.

I assume that Tommy and Jim have sex with each other (although I've never bothered to ask). Furthermore, I suspect that they probably *should* have sex with each other. For one thing, sex is pleasurable. But it is also much more than that: a sexual relationship can unite two people in a way that virtually nothing else can. It can be an avenue of growth, communication, and lasting interpersonal fulfillment. These are reasons most heterosexual couples have sex even if they don't want children, don't want children yet, or don't want additional children. And if these reasons are good enough for most heterosexual couples, then they should be good enough for Tommy and Jim.

Of course, having a reason to do something does not preclude there being an even better reason for not doing it. Tommy might have a good

---

This article is an abbreviated version of "Why Shouldn't Tommy and Jim Have Sex? A Defense of Homosexuality," which appears in John Corvino, ed., *Same Sex: Debating the Ethics, Science, and Culture of Homosexuality* (Rowman & Littlefield, 1997), pp. 3-16. The longer version includes a section on biblical arguments against homosexuality.

reason for drinking orange juice (it's tasty and nutritious) but an even better reason for not doing so (he's allergic). The point is that one would need a pretty good reason for denying a sexual relationship to Tommy and Jim, given the intense benefits widely associated with such relationships. The question I shall consider in this paper is thus quite simple: Why shouldn't Tommy and Jim have sex?[1]

I. Homosexuality Is Unnatural

Many contend that homosexual sex is "unnatural." But what does that mean? Many things that people value—clothing, houses, medicine, and government, for example—are unnatural in some sense. On the other hand, many things that people detest—disease, suffering, and death, for example—are natural in some sense (after all, they occur "in nature"). If the unnaturalness charge is to be more than empty rhetorical flourish, those who levy it must specify what they mean. Borrowing from Burton Leiser, I will examine several possibilities.[2]

(1) *What is unusual or abnormal is unnatural.* One meaning of "unnatural" refers to that which deviates from the norm, that is, from what most people do. Obviously, most people engage in heterosexual relationships. But does it follow that it is wrong to engage in homosexual relationships? Relatively few people read Sanskrit, pilot ships, play the mandolin, breed goats, or write with both hands, yet none of these activities is immoral simply because it is unusual. As the Ramsey Colloquium, a group of Jewish and Christian scholars who oppose homosexuality, write, "The statistical frequency of an act does not determine its moral status."[3] So while homosexuality might be "unnatural" in the sense of being unusual, that fact is morally irrelevant.

(2) *What is not practiced by other animals is unnatural.* Some people argue, "Even animals know better than to behave homosexually; homosexuality must be wrong." This argument is doubly flawed. First, it rests on a false premise. Numerous studies—including Anne Perkins's study of "gay" sheep and George and Molly Hunt's study of "lesbian" seagulls—have shown that some animals do form homosexual pair-bonds.[4] Second, even if that premise were true, it would not prove that homosexuality is immoral. After all, animals don't cook their food, brush their teeth, attend college, or drive cars; human beings do all these things without moral censure. Indeed, the idea that animals could provide us with our standards, especially our sexual standards, is simply amusing.

(3) *What does not proceed from innate desires is unnatural.* Recent studies suggesting a biological basis for homosexuality have resulted in two popular positions. One side says, "Homosexual people are born that way;

therefore it's natural (and thus good) for them to form homosexual relationships." The other side retorts, "No, homosexuality is a lifestyle choice, therefore it's unnatural (and thus wrong)." Both sides seem to assume a connection between the cause or origin of homosexual orientation, on the one hand, and the moral value of homosexual activity, on the other. And insofar as they share that assumption, both sides are wrong.

Consider first the pro-homosexual side: "They are born that way; therefore it's natural and good." This inference assumes that all innate desires are good ones (that is, that they should be acted upon). But that assumption is clearly false. Research suggests that some people are born with a predisposition towards violence, but such people have no more right to strangle their neighbors than anyone else. So while some people may be born with homosexual tendencies, it doesn't follow that they ought to act on them.

Nor does it follow that they ought *not* to act on them, even if the tendencies are not innate. I probably do not have any innate tendency to write with my left hand (since I, like everyone else in my family, have always been right-handed), but it doesn't follow that it would be immoral for me to do so. So simply asserting that homosexuality is a "lifestyle choice" will not show that it is an immoral lifestyle choice.

Do people "choose" to be homosexual? People certainly don't seem to choose their sexual *feelings*, at least not in any direct or obvious way. (Do you? Think about it.) Rather, they find certain people attractive and certain activities arousing, whether they "decide" to or not. Indeed, most people at some point in their lives wish that they could control their feelings more (for example, in situations of unrequited love) and find it frustrating that they cannot. What they *can* control to a considerable degree is how and when they act upon those feelings. In that sense, both homosexuality and heterosexuality involve "lifestyle choices." But in either case, determining the cause or origin of the feelings will not determine whether it is moral to act upon them.

(4) *What violates an organ's principal purpose is unnatural.* Perhaps when people claim that homosexual sex is unnatural they mean that it cannot result in procreation. The idea behind the argument is that human organs have various "natural" purposes: eyes are for seeing, ears are for hearing, genitals are for procreating. According to this argument, it is immoral to use an organ in a way that violates its particular purpose.

Many of our organs, however, have multiple purposes. Tommy can use his mouth for talking, eating, breathing, licking stamps, chewing gum, kissing women, or kissing Jim, and it seems rather arbitrary to claim that all but the last use are "natural."[5] (And if we say that some of the other uses are "unnatural, but not immoral," we have failed to specify a morally relevant sense of the term "natural.")

Just because people can and do use their sexual organs to procreate, it does not follow that they should not use them for other purposes. Sexual organs seem very well suited for expressing love, for giving and receiving pleasure, and for celebrating, replenishing, and enhancing a relationship, even when procreation is not a factor. Unless opponents of homosexuality are prepared to condemn heterosexual couples who use contraception or individuals who masturbate, they must abandon this version of the unnaturalness argument. Indeed, even the Roman Catholic Church, which forbids contraception and masturbation, approves of sex for sterile couples and of sex during pregnancy, neither of which can lead to procreation. The Church concedes here that intimacy and pleasure are morally legitimate purposes for sex, even in cases where procreation is impossible. But since homosexual sex can achieve these purposes as well, it is inconsistent for the Church to condemn it on the grounds that it is not procreative.

One might object that sterile heterosexual couples do not *intentionally* turn away from procreation, whereas homosexual couples do. But this distinction doesn't hold. It is no more possible for Tommy to procreate with a woman whose uterus has been removed than it is for him to procreate with Jim. By having sex with either one, he is intentionally engaging in a nonprocreative sexual act.

Yet one might press the objection further: Tommy and the woman *could* produce children if the woman were fertile. Whereas homosexual relationships are essentially infertile, heterosexual relationships are only incidentally so. But what does that prove? Granted, it might require less of a miracle for a woman without a uterus to become pregnant than for Jim to become pregnant, but it would require a miracle nonetheless. Thus it seems that the real difference here is not that one couple is fertile and the other not, nor that one couple "could" be fertile (with the help of a miracle) and the other not, but rather that one couple is male–female and the other male–male. In other words, sex between Tommy and Jim is wrong because it's male–male—that is, because it's homosexual. But that, of course, is no argument at all.[6]

(5) *What is disgusting or offensive is unnatural.* It often seems that when people call homosexuality "unnatural" they really just mean that it's disgusting. But plenty of morally neutral activities—handling snakes, eating snails, performing autopsies, cleaning toilets, and so on—disgust people. Indeed, for centuries most people found interracial relationships disgusting, yet that feeling, which has by no means disappeared, hardly proves that such relationships are wrong. In sum, the charge that homosexuality is unnatural, at least in its most common forms, is longer on rhetorical flourish than on philosophical cogency.

II. Homosexuality Is Harmful

One might argue, instead, that homosexuality is harmful. The Ramsey Colloquium, for instance, argues that homosexuality leads to the breakdown of the family and, ultimately, of human society, and points to the "alarming rates of sexual promiscuity, depression, and suicide and the ominous presence of AIDS within the homosexual subculture."[7] Thomas Schmidt marshals copious statistics to show that homosexual activity undermines physical and psychological health.[8] Such charges, if correct, would seem to provide strong evidence against homosexuality. But are the charges correct? And do they prove what they purport to prove?

One obvious (and obviously problematic) way to answer the first question is to ask people like Tommy and Jim. It would appear that no one is in a better position to judge the homosexual "lifestyle" than those who live it. Yet it is unlikely that critics would trust their testimony. Indeed, the more that homosexual people try to explain their lives, the more critics accuse them of deceitfully promoting an agenda. (It's like trying to prove that you're not crazy. The more you object, the more people think, "That's exactly what a crazy person would say.")

One might instead turn to statistics. An obvious problem with this tack is that both sides of the debate bring forth extensive statistics and "expert" testimony, leaving the average observer confused. There is a more subtle problem as well. Because of widespread antigay sentiment, many homosexual people will not acknowledge their feelings to themselves, much less to researchers.[9] I have known a number of gay men who did not "come out" until their 40s and 50s, and no amount of professional competence on the part of interviewers would have been likely to open their closets sooner. Such problems compound the usual difficulties of finding representative population samples for statistical study.

Yet even if the statistical claims of gay-rights opponents were true, would they prove what they purport to prove? I think not, for the following reasons. First, as any good statistician realizes, correlation does not equal cause. Even if homosexual people were more likely to commit suicide, be promiscuous, or contract AIDS than the general population, it would not follow that their homosexuality causes them to do these things. An alternative and very plausible explanation is that these phenomena, like the disproportionately high crime rates among blacks, are at least partly a function of society's treatment of the group in question. Suppose you were told from a very early age that the romantic feelings that you experienced were sick, unnatural, and disgusting. Suppose further that expressing these feelings put you at risk of social ostracism or, worse yet, physical violence. Is it not plausible that you would, for instance, be more inclined to depression than you would be without such obstacles? And that such depression could, in its extreme forms, lead to suicide or other self-destructive behaviors? (It is indeed remarkable that in the face of such obstacles couples like Tommy and Jim continue to flourish.)

A similar explanation can be given for the alleged promiscuity of homosexuals.[10] The denial of legal marriage, the pressure to remain in the closet, and the overt hostility toward homosexual relationships are all more conducive to transient, clandestine encounters than they are to long-term unions. As a result, that which is challenging enough for heterosexual couples—settling down and building a life together—becomes far more challenging for homosexual couples.

Indeed, there is an interesting tension in the critics' position here. Opponents of homosexuality commonly claim that "marriage and the family . . . are fragile institutions in need of careful and continuing support." [11]And they point to the increasing prevalence of divorce and premarital sex among heterosexuals as evidence that such support is declining. Yet they refuse to concede that the complete absence of similar support for homosexual relationships might explain many of the alleged problems of homosexuals. The critics can't have it both ways: If heterosexual marriages are in trouble despite the various social, economic, and legal incentives for keeping them together, society should be little surprised that homosexual relationships—which not only lack such supports but face overt attack—are difficult to maintain.

One might object that if social ostracism were the main cause of homosexual people's problems, then homosexual people in more "tolerant" cities like New York and San Francisco should exhibit fewer such problems than their small-town counterparts; yet statistics do not seem to bear this out. This objection underestimates the extent of antigay sentiment in our society. By the time many gay and lesbian people move to urban centers, much damage has already been done to their psyches. Moreover, the visibility of homosexuality in urban centers makes homosexual people there more vulnerable to attack (and thus more likely to exhibit certain difficulties). Finally, note that urbanites *in general* (not just homosexual urbanites) tend to exhibit higher rates of promiscuity, depression, and sexually transmitted disease than the rest of the population.

But what about AIDS? Opponents of homosexuality sometimes claim that even if homosexual sex is not, strictly speaking, immoral, it is still a bad idea, since it puts people at risk for AIDS and other sexually transmitted diseases. But that claim is misleading. Note that it is infinitely more risky for Tommy to have sex with a woman who is HIV-positive than with Jim, who is HIV-negative. The reason is simple: it's not homosexuality that's harmful, it's the virus, and the virus may be carried by both heterosexual and homosexual people.

Now it may be the case that in a given population a homosexual male is statistically more likely to carry the virus than a heterosexual female, and thus, from a purely statistical standpoint, male homosexual sex is more risky than heterosexual sex (in cases where the partner's HIV status is unknown). But surely opponents of homosexuality need something stronger than this statistical claim. For if it is wrong for men to have sex with men because their doing so puts them at a higher AIDS risk than heterosexual sex, then it is also wrong for women to have sex with men because their doing so puts them at a higher AIDS risk than homosexual sex (lesbians as a group have the lowest incidence of AIDS). Purely from the standpoint of AIDS risk, women ought to prefer lesbian sex.

If this response seems silly, it is because there is obviously more to choosing a romantic or sexual partner than determining AIDS risk. And a major part of the decision, one that opponents of homosexuality consistently overlook, is considering whether one can have a mutually fulfilling relationship with the partner. For many people like Tommy and Jim, such fulfillment, which most heterosexuals recognize to be an important component of human flourishing, is only possible with members of the same sex.

Of course, the foregoing argument hinges on the claim that homosexual sex can only cause harm indirectly. Some would object that there are certain activities (anal sex, for instance) that for anatomical reasons are intrinsically harmful. But an argument against anal intercourse is by no means tantamount to an argument against homosexuality: neither all nor only homosexuals engage in anal sex. There are plenty of other things for both gay men and lesbians to do in bed. Indeed, for women, it appears that the most common forms of homosexual activity may be *less* risky than penile–vaginal intercourse, since the latter has been linked to cervical cancer.[12]

In sum, there is nothing *inherently* risky about sex between persons of the same gender. It is only risky under certain conditions: for instance, if they exchange diseased bodily fluids or if they engage in certain "rough" forms of sex that could cause tearing of delicate tissue. Heterosexual sex is equally risky under such conditions. Thus, even if statistical claims like those of Schmidt and the Ramsey Colloquium were true, they would not prove that homosexuality is immoral. At best they would prove that homosexual people, like everyone else, ought to take great care when deciding to become sexually active.

Of course, there's more to a flourishing life than avoiding harm. One might argue that even if Tommy and Jim are not harming each other by their relationship, they are still failing to achieve the higher level of fulfillment possible in a heterosexual relationship, which is rooted in the complementarity of male and female. But this argument just ignores the facts. Tommy and Jim are homosexual *precisely because* they find relationships with men (and in particular, with each other) more fulfilling than relationships with women. Even evangelicals (who have long advocated "faith healing" for homosexuals) are beginning to acknowledge that the choice for most homosexual people is not between homosexual relationships and heterosexual relationships, but rather between homosexual relationships and celibacy.[13] What the critics need to show, therefore, is that no matter how loving, committed, mutual, generous, and fulfilling the relationship may be, Tommy and Jim would flourish more if they were celibate. This is a formidable (indeed, probably impossible) task.

Thus far I have focused on the allegation that homosexuality harms those who engage in it. But what about the allegation that homosexuality harms other, nonconsenting parties? Here I will briefly consider two claims: that homosexuality threatens children and that it threatens society.

Those who argue that homosexuality threatens children may mean one of two things. First, they may mean that homosexual people are child molesters. Statistically, the vast majority of reported cases of child sexual abuse involve young girls and their fathers, stepfathers, or other familiar (and presumably heterosexual) adult males.[14] But opponents of homosexuality argue that when one adjusts for relative percentage in the population, homosexual males appear more likely than heterosexual males to be child molesters. As I argued above, the problems with obtaining reliable statistics on homosexuality render such calculations difficult. Fortunately, they are also unnecessary.

Child abuse is a terrible thing. But when a heterosexual male molests a child (or rapes a woman, or commits assault), the act does not reflect upon all heterosexuals. Similarly, when a homosexual male molests a child, there is no reason why that act should reflect upon all homosexuals. Sex with adults of the same sex is one thing; sex with *children* of the same sex is quite another. Conflating the two not only slanders innocent people, it also misdirects resources intended to protect children. Furthermore, many men convicted of molesting young boys are sexually attracted to adult women and report no attraction to adult men.[15] To call such men "homosexual" or even "bisexual" is probably to stretch such terms too far.[16]

Alternatively, those who charge that homosexuality threatens children might mean that the increasing visibility of homosexual relationships makes children more likely to become homosexual. The argument for this view is patently circular. One cannot prove that doing X is bad by arguing that it causes people to do X, which is bad. One must first establish independently that X is bad. That said, there is not a shred of evidence to demonstrate that exposure to homosexuality leads children to become homosexual.

But doesn't homosexuality threaten society? A Roman Catholic priest once put the argument to me as follows: "Of course homosexuality is bad for society. If everyone were homosexual, there would be no society."

Perhaps it is true that if everyone were homosexual, there would be no society. But if everyone were a celibate priest, society would collapse just as surely, and my priest-friend didn't seem to think that he was doing anything wrong simply by failing to procreate. Jeremy Bentham made the point somewhat more acerbically roughly two hundred years ago: "If then merely out of regard to population it were right that [homosexuals] should be burnt alive, monks ought to be roasted alive by a slow fire."[17]

From the fact that the continuation of society requires procreation, it does not follow that *everyone* must procreate. Moreover, even if such an obligation existed, it would not preclude homosexuality. At best it would preclude *exclusive* homosexuality: Homosexual people who occasionally have heterosexual sex can procreate just fine. And given artificial insemination, even those who are exclusively homosexual can procreate. In short, the priest's claim—if everyone were homosexual, there would be no society—is false, and even if it were true, it would not establish that homosexuality is immoral.

The Ramsey Colloquium commits a similar fallacy.[18] Noting (correctly) that heterosexual marriage promotes the continuation of human life, they then infer that homosexuality is immoral because it fails to accomplish the same.[19] But from the fact that procreation is good it does not follow that childlessness is bad, a point that the members of the Colloquium, several of whom are Roman Catholic priests, should readily concede.

I have argued that Tommy and Jim's sexual relationship harms neither them nor society. On the contrary, it benefits both. It benefits them because it makes them happier, not merely in a short-term, hedonistic sense, but in a long-term, "big picture" sort of way. And in turn it benefits society, since it makes Tommy and Jim more stable, more productive, and more generous than they would otherwise be. In short, their relationship, including its sexual component, provides the same kinds of benefits that infertile heterosexual relationships provide (and perhaps other benefits as well). Nor should we fear that accepting their relationship and others like it will cause people to flee in droves from the institution of heterosexual marriage. After all, as Thomas Williams points out, the usual response to a gay person is not "How come he gets to be gay and I don't?"[20]

III. Conclusion

As a last resort, opponents of homosexuality typically change the subject: "But what about incest, polygamy, and bestiality? If we accept Tommy and Jim's sexual relationship, why shouldn't we accept those as well?" Opponents of interracial marriage used a similar slippery-slope argument thirty years ago when the Supreme Court struck down antimiscegenation laws.[21] It was a bad argument then and it is a bad argument now.

Just because there are no good reasons to oppose interracial or homosexual relationships, it does not follow that there are no good reasons to oppose incestuous, polygamous, or bestial relationships. One might argue, for instance, that incestuous relationships threaten delicate familial bonds, that polygamous relationships result in unhealthy jealousies (and sexism), or that bestial relationships (do I need to say it?) aren't really "relationships" at all, at least not in the sense we've been discussing. Perhaps even better arguments could be offered (given much more space than I have here). The point is that there is no logical connection between homosexuality, on the one hand, and incest, polygamy, and bestiality, on the other.

Why, then, do critics continue to push this objection? Perhaps it's because accepting homosexuality requires them to give up one of their favorite arguments: "It's wrong because we've always been taught that it's wrong." This argument—call it the argument from tradition—has an obvious appeal: People reasonably favor "tried and true" ideas over unfamiliar ones, and they recognize the foolishness of trying to invent morality from scratch. But the argument from tradition is also a dangerous argument, as any honest look at history will reveal.

To recognize Tommy and Jim's relationship as good is to admit that our moral traditions are imperfect. Condemning people out of habit is easy. Overcoming deep-seated prejudice takes courage.[22]

Notes

1. Although my central example in the paper is a gay male couple, much of what I say will apply *mutatis mutandis* to lesbians as well, since many of the same arguments are used against them. This is not to say that gay male sexuality and lesbian sexuality are largely similar or that discussions of the former will cover all that needs to be said about the latter. Furthermore, the fact that I focus on a long-term couple should not be taken to imply any judgment about homosexual activity outside of such unions. If the argument of this paper is successful, then the evaluation of homosexual activity outside of committed unions should be largely (if not entirely) similar to the evaluation of heterosexual activity outside of committed unions.

2. Burton M. Leiser, *Liberty, Justice, and Morals: Contemporary Value Conflicts* (New York: Macmillan, 1986), pp. 51–57.

3. The Ramsey Colloquium, "The Homosexual Movement," *First Things*, March 1994, pp. 15–20.

4. For an overview of some of these studies, see Simon LeVay's *Queer Science* (Cambridge, Mass.: M.I.T. Press, 1996), chap. 10.

5. I have borrowed some items in this list from Richard Mohr's pioneering work *Gays/Justice* (New York: Columbia University Press, 1988), p. 36.

6. For a fuller explication of this type of natural law argument, see John Finnis, "Law, Morality, and 'Sexual Orientation,'" *Notre Dame Law Review* 69:5

(1994): 1049–76; revised, shortened, and reprinted in John Corvino, ed., *Same Sex: Debating the Ethics, Science, and Culture of Homosexuality* (Lanham, Md.: Rowman & Littlefield, 1997). For a cogent and well-developed response, see Andrew Koppelman, "A Reply to the New Natural Lawyers," in the same volume.

7. The Ramsey Colloquium, p. 19.

8. Thomas Schmidt, *Straight and Narrow? Compassion and Clarity in the Homosexuality Debate* (Downer's Grove, Ill.: InterVarsity Press, 1995), chap. 6, "The Price of Love."

9. Both the American Psychological Association and the American Public Health Association have conceded this point. "Reliable data on the incidence of homosexual orientation are difficult to obtain due to the criminal penalties and social stigma attached to homosexual behavior and the consequent difficulty of obtaining representative samples of people to study." See *Amici Curiae* brief in *Bowers v. Hardwick*, Supreme Court No. 85–140 (October Term 1985).

10. It is worth noting that allegations of promiscuity are probably exaggerated. Note that the study most commonly cited to prove homosexual male promiscuity, the Bell and Weinberg study, took place in 1978, in an urban center (San Francisco), at the height of the sexual revolution—hardly a broad sample. (See Alan P. Bell and Martin S. Weinberg, *Homosexualities* [New York: Simon and Schuster, 1978].) The far more recent and extensive University of Chicago study agreed that homosexual and bisexual people "have higher average numbers of partners than the rest of the sexually active people in the study," but concluded that the differences in the mean number of partners "do not appear very large" (Edward O. Laumann, et al., *The Social Organization of Sexuality: Sexual Practices in the United States* [Chicago: University of Chicago Press, 1994], pp. 314, 316). I am grateful to Andrew Koppelman for drawing my attention to the Chicago study.

11. The Ramsey Colloquium, p. 19.

12. See S. R. Johnson, E. M. Smith, and S. M. Guenther, "Comparison of Gynecological Health Care Problems Between Lesbian and Bisexual Women," *Journal of Reproductive Medicine* 32 (1987): 805–11.

13. See for example Stanton L. Jones, "The Loving Opposition," *Christianity Today* 37:8 (July 19, 1993).

14. See Danya Glaser and Stephen Frosh, *Child Sexual Abuse,* 2nd ed. (Houndmills, Eng.: Macmillan, 1993), pp. 13–17, and Kathleen Coulbourn Faller, *Understanding Child Sexual Maltreatment* (Newbury Park, Calif.: Sage, 1990), pp. 16–20.

15. See Frank G. Bolton, Jr., Larry A. Morris, and Ann E. MacEachron, *Males at Risk: The Other Side of Child Sexual Abuse* (Newbury Park, Calif.: Sage, 1989), p. 61.

16. Part of the problem here arises from the grossly simplistic categorization of people into two or, at best, three sexual orientations: heterosexual, homosexual, and bisexual. Clearly, there is great variety within (and beyond) these categories. See Frederick Suppe, "Explaining Homosexuality: Philosophical Issues, and Who Cares Anyhow?" in Timothy F. Murphy, ed., *Gay Ethics: Controversies in Outing, Civil Rights, and Sexual Science* (New York: Haworth Press, 1994), especially pp. 234–38.

17. "An Essay on 'Paederasty,'" in Robert Baker and Frederick Elliston, eds., *The Philosophy of Sex* (Buffalo, N.Y.: Prometheus, 1984), pp. 360–61. Bentham uses the word "paederast" where we would use the term "homosexual"; the latter term was not coined until 1869, and the term "heterosexual" was coined a few

years after that. Today, "pederasty" refers to sex between men and boys, a different phenomenon from the one Bentham was addressing.

18. The Ramsey Colloquium, pp. 17–18.

19. The argument is a classic example of the fallacy of denying the antecedent: If X promotes procreation, then X is good; X does not promote procreation; therefore, X is not good. Compare: If X is president, then X lives in the White House; Chelsea Clinton is not president, therefore Chelsea Clinton does not live in the White House.

20. Actually, Williams makes the point with regard to celibacy, while making an analogy between celibacy and homosexuality. See Thomas Williams, "A Reply to the Ramsey Colloquium," in *Same Sex*.

21. *Loving v. Virginia*, 1967.

22. This paper grew out of a lecture, "What's (Morally) Wrong with Homosexuality?" which I first delivered at the University of Texas in 1992 and have since delivered at numerous other universities around the country. I am grateful to countless audience members, students, colleagues, and friends for helpful dialogue over the years. I would especially like to thank the following individuals for detailed comments on recent drafts of the paper: Edwin B. Allaire, Daniel Bonevac, David Bradshaw, David Cleaves, Mary Beth Mader, Richard D. Mohr, Jonathan Rauch, Robert Schuessler, Alan Soble, James P. Sterba, and Thomas Williams. I dedicate this paper to my partner, Carlos Casillas.

Chapter 12

DEFENDING MARRIAGE

Cheshire Calhoun

On 21 September 1996, President Clinton signed into law the Defense of Marriage Act (DOMA). That Act did two things. It amended the Full Faith and Credit Clause so that states that do not already expressly prohibit same-sex marriages would not be required to honor same-sex marriages performed in other states. Second, it 'defended' marriage by defining marriage for federal purposes as involving one man and one woman.

The immediate impetus behind the Defense of Marriage Act was the Hawaii Supreme Court's ruling in *Baehr v. Lewin* that a same-sex marriage bar would be deemed an unconstitutional form of sex discrimination unless the state could demonstrate a compelling interest served by prohibiting same-sex marriage. Although the Hawaii case received a great deal of notoriety, court suits for the right of gays and lesbians to marry are not new. They date from the 1970s. Previous suits, however, invariably stumbled on courts' insistence that marriage is by definition between a man and a woman. If same-sex marriage is definitionally impossible, then gays and lesbians are not being denied a fundamental right to marry when same-sex unions are not legally recognized. In addition, the 1986 Supreme Court ruling in *Bowers v. Hardwick*, affirming the constitutionality of anti-sodomy laws, have made arguments for same sex-marriage even more difficult. Courts have assumed that sodomy is the act that de-

fines the class 'homosexual'. And if it is constitutional to prohibit
sodomy, it must similarly be constitutional to impose additional restrictions on members of this class—such as prohibiting same-sex marriage.
Thus, equal protection arguments that marriage bars discriminate
against gays and lesbians have been unsuccessful. What distinguished the
Hawaii case was the court's unwillingness to use definitional arguments
to rule out same-sex marriage and its willingness to consider a different
equal protection argument, namely, that same-sex marriage bars discriminate on the basis of sex.

Although it might seem that the Hawaii Supreme Court was moving in
an obviously correct direction, while Congress, in passing the Defense of
Marriage Act, was not, the topic of same-sex marriage rights has in fact
been controversial among lesbians and gays. Because the right to same-sex
marriage is so controversial, that right is not, at first blush, a promising candidate for the center of lesbian and gay politics. However, I intend to argue
that that is exactly where the right to same-sex marriage belongs. . . . Before
we can fully assess any particular critique of same-sex marriage, we need to
know whether the marriage bar is simply one restriction among many that
gays and lesbians face or whether it plays an especially central role in sustaining lesbian and gay oppression. If the latter is true, then much stronger
arguments will be needed for not pursuing the right to marry within a lesbian and gay politics. In this chapter, I intend to argue that same-sex marriage bars do play an especially central role in displacing gays and lesbians
to the outside of civil society. In particular, being fit for marriage is intimately bound up with our cultural conception of what it means to be a citizen. This is because marriage is culturally conceived as playing a uniquely
foundational role in sustaining civil society. As a result, only those who are
fit to enter marital and family life deserve full civic status. Bars on same-sex
marriage encode and enforce the view that lesbians and gays are inessential citizens because they are unable to participate in the foundational social institution. Marriage bars thus play a critical role in displacing gays and
lesbians.

At first glance, it might seem that formal considerations of justice alone
provide a sufficient reason for endorsing same-sex marriage rights. Consider that, under American jurisprudence, the right to marry is generally
assumed to be part of a more basic right to privacy. Appealing to tradition, particularly religious tradition, seems an inadequate basis in a liberal society for limiting same-sex couples' right to privacy. Historically,
such appeals have been used to justify not only same-sex marriage bars,
but also bars to interracial marriage. And just as anti-miscegenation laws
constitute a form of racial discrimination, so too same-sex marriage bars
seem to constitute a form of sexual orientation discrimination. Thus,
on grounds of formal equality alone, one might reject bars on same-sex
marriage.

In addition, the most obvious reasons in favor of same-sex marriage rights are practical. Marriage gives access to set of material benefits—dental and health insurance, income tax breaks, and spousal social security and pension benefits. Marriage also provides spouses with legal protection against third parties' (e.g. grandparents and sperm donors) claims to child custody and visitation rights as well as rights to give proxy consent and to inherit. Marriage also facilitates partnerships by giving spouses immigration preference and a right to conjugal visits. Here too, formal considerations of justice suggest that it is wrong to deny same-sex couples the rights and benefits of marriage that heterosexual couples enjoy.

However, gay and lesbian opponents of same-sex marriage rights are, I think, correct *not* to accept these sorts of arguments as sufficient and to insist that some persuasive positive moral argument is necessary. In particular, they are right not to accept considerations of formal equality as sufficient reasons to give political priority to securing marriage rights. The problem with arguments appealing to formal equality is that they are aimed narrowly at answering the question of *who* should have marriage rights given that some do. They do not fully answer equally important questions about whether *anyone* should have this right or about *how important* this right is. Claudia Card helpfully brings out this point in her article against same-sex marriage.[1] She invites us to imagine a world in which white men are permitted to own slaves, but white women are not. On grounds of formal equality, one might argue that it is unjust to deprive white women of a right that white men have. Yet the right to own slaves is not a right anyone should have. What is needed in the case of marriage, then, is a positive moral argument for the value of *any one* having a right to marry. In addition, we need a positive moral argument for *how important* that right is if it is a legitimate right. By themselves, arguments appealing to formal equality do not tell us this. There may in fact be moral reasons for not giving political priority to securing this right. Some have argued that distributing benefits, such as health insurance, through marriage is itself unjust. Others have argued that marriage has historically been oppressive to women and that to seek same-sex marriage rights amounts to endorsing a sexist institution. Yet others have argued that gay men and lesbians should resist normalizing institutions like marriage and should instead continue creating multiple new forms of intimate and familial arrangements. Finally, even if seeking same-sex marriage rights were entirely unobjectionable, it might still be true that other political goals, such as securing coverage under anti-discrimination laws, might intervene more directly in the system of heterosexual domination and thus deserve higher priority.

Thus, because we need to know why formal equality with respect to marriage rights is worth pursuing and how much priority those rights should be given, we need to ask what positive moral arguments there might be. Examining the positive moral argument for marriage rights matters for a second reason as well. The moral significance of extending rights is to a large extent a function of the sorts of arguments that get culturally circulated in the process of extending rights. Take, for example, anti-discrimination laws protecting women. While the laws themselves contributed to greater equality, the culturally circulated arguments against sex discrimination have arguably had a greater impact. They have helped to produce a cultural world in which critical reflection on gender roles, on the assumption that biology is destiny, and on power relations between women and men regularly takes place. Quite different arguments supporting anti-discrimination laws *could* have gained cultural prominence. In 1792, Mary Wollstonecraft, for example, argued for women's right to education on the grounds that better education would better fit women for their roles as children's educators and their husband's companion.[2] And she argued for women's employment opportunities so that women would be able to support their families in the event of their husband's death. Culturally contextualized within these sorts of arguments, anti-discrimination laws would not have had the same moral significance. They would be viewed as supporting a system of separate gender roles for men and women rather than as constituting a challenge to that system.

It is especially because it matters *which* arguments get culturally circulated that I think the positive arguments for same-sex marriage rights warrant careful scrutiny. In what follows, I will focus on three different arguments. The first argument links marriage rights to a normative ideal of long-term, monogamous, sexually faithful intimacy and defends marriage rights on the basis of the value of that ideal. The second argument presses the connection between homophobia and sexism, stressing the way that securing same-sex marriage rights might reduce sexism. This is the sort of argument that the Hawaii Supreme Court relied on. The third argument, and the one I intend to defend, links the denial of marriage rights to the cultural construction of gay men and lesbians as outsiders to the family who are *for that reason* defective citizens. In pursuing this third line of argument I will have a good deal to say about the House and Senate arguments supporting the Defense of Marriage Act.

I. Marriage as Normative Ideal

One positive moral argument for same-sex marriage begins by recognizing that the legal institution of marriage is founded on an antecedent moral conception of marriage. On the moral conception of marriage, marriage is about the emotional and spiritual unity of two persons. Such unity requires monogamy, long-term commitment, and sexual fidelity. It is both a unity of companionship and an economic unity of mutual support. On natural law accounts, marital unity is partly expressed through procreation and child rearing; on more secular accounts, the stability of a relationship based on long-term commitment simply provides the ideal environment for child rearing. Understood morally, marriage is not simply one among many intimate relationships that people can voluntarily enter into. It is *the* normative ideal for how sexuality, companionship, affective, personal economics, and child rearing should be organized.

This moral conception of marriage provides the justification for state regulation of marriage. The state grants the legal right to marry, protects marital privacy, provides unique material benefits to marital couples, and regulates the dissolution of marriages because marriage is a basic personal and social good. Although state neutrality may require permitting other forms of intimate relationship, the state also has an obligation to promote valued ways of living. As Senator Byrd observed in the DOMA debates, '. . . humanity has discovered that the permanent relationship between man and woman is a keystone to the stability, strength, and health of human society'.[3] Promoting marriage is the point of giving state sanction to marriages.

In *The Case for Same-Sex Marriage,* William Eskridge Jr. uses this sort of argument to defend same sex-marriage rights. In his view, 'the dominant goal of marriage is and should be *unitive,* the spiritual and personal union of the committed couple'.[4] Such unity requires long-term commitment, monogamy, and sexual fidelity. Eskridge argues for the value of long-term commitment in part by suggesting that commitment adds depth to a relationship,[5] and in part by drawing on a communitarian view of the self as a relational self whose identity is constituted and sustained by ties to others.[6] Contemporary life, he claims, is increasingly hostile to the possibility of sustaining stable relations and a stable sense of self. The plurality of roles we now occupy, our geographical mobility and, often, our lack of stable employment all militate against a stable sense of self. In addition, liberal culture encourages us to think in terms of a 'marketplace of intimacies' where both entering and exiting relationships is a matter purely of individual choice. The result is that our identities are fluid, unstable, and fractured. Taking such fluidity and instability to be a bad thing, Eskridge concludes that some relationships should be viewed as unchosen, or at least not easily revisable once entered into. Marital relations and parent-child relations are cases in point. Because a stable sense of self is such an important good to the individual, using the law to protect marital and parenting relationships both from external intervention and internal dissolution is warranted.

Additional reasons for the importance of both long-time commitment and sexual fidelity might be drawn from the sort of argument given by cultural conservatives.[7] Cultural conservatives charge liberalism with breeding an excessive emphasis on personal choice, self-expression, and lifestyle experimentation. The consequence is that we now live in a 'sex-riddled, divorce-prone' culture that militates against the development of such personal and civic virtues as self-sacrifice, self-discipline, planning for the future, concern for others, responsible conduct, and loyalty.[8] Promoting, and to some extent coercively enforcing, the normative ideal of sexual fidelity and long-term commitment is designed to counteract this trend and to provide individuals with a context for cultivating and expressing the virtues of loyalty, self-discipline, self-sacrifice, and self-transcendence. This, it is assumed, will be good both for individuals and for society. Thus the answer to the question: 'Why should anyone have the right to marry?' is that committed, monogamous, sexually faithful relationships contribute to personal and social flourishing.

On this type of viewpoint, one of the most important features of legal marriage is the costliness of dissolving a marriage. That costliness means that entering a marriage involves a higher level of personal commitment than, say, entering a domestic partnership. It also means that, once married, couples have an additional incentive to stay married. Eskridge hypothesizes that such incentives are especially important for gay men who are more likely than lesbians to be sexually promiscuous and thus to have difficulty sustaining committed relationships.

There is a good deal to object to in this argument for same-sex marriage. Let me begin with coercion. Under present no-fault divorce laws, the coercive pressures exerted on couples to marry and stay married are limited to the tax penalties imposed on couples who choose not to get legally married, and, once married, the costliness of divorce proceedings. However, any argument that appeals to the value of promoting *long-term* marriage clearly justifies toughening divorce laws, a move that is already underfoot in some states. Even if there is something to be said for committed relationships, it is hard to see how using the law to keep couples together could be justified. As Karen Struening has pointed out, basing state policy on the value of commitment elevates marital and familial stability to the status of the sole, or overriding good.[9] The values of personal and marital happiness, emotional and sexual intimacy, avoiding abusive or inegalitarian intimacies, and revising identities constituted through relationships all take a backseat to the overriding goal of stability. One might, however, wonder why stability provides a good reason to preserve either an identity or a relationship that has nothing else to recommend it. In addition, feminists have special cause for con-

cern about what pressuring couples to stay together might mean for heterosexual women. Now that many women have the economic resources
to leave unhappy marriages, they may find their way barred by restrictive
divorce laws.[10] And, as Claudia Card has pointed out, because marriage
includes the right to cohabit with one's spouse, it is more difficult for a
married person to protect herself from battery and rape by a spouse
since the spouse is entitled to reside where she does.[11] Placing obstacles
to divorce exacerbates this vulnerability.

Equally troubling is the fact that coercion would be exerted in the
name not just of commitment, but of a substantive moral conception of
how people ought to organize their sexual, economic, parenting, and affectionate lives from which law and social practice have been retreating.
Most states have eliminated fault-based divorce and criminal penalties
for adultery and do not enforce criminal statutes against cohabitation.
The divorce rate runs at about 50 per cent. More people are cohabiting
and marrying later. And parenting takes a variety of forms, from single-
parenting, to joint custody, to parenting within divorce-extended families. It is, however, just this diminishing heterosexual compliance with
the normative ideal of long-term, sexually faithful, two-parent families
that has motivated a variety of suggestions for bolstering compliance.
They have included restigmatizing divorce, toughening divorce laws
for couples with children, punitive welfare policies for poor women
who have children out of wedlock, and a return to some form of gender-
structured marriage.[12] What is especially worrisome about this first argument for same-sex marriage rights, then, is its natural place within a
larger cultural conversation about the benefits of returning to a particular normative ideal of marriage and parenting. It is a return that requires
using law and social policy to dissuade individuals from pursuing a plurality of conceptions of how intimate relationships ought to be organized.

Because this argument for same-sex marriage rights depends on the
view that the state ought to promote one normative ideal for intimacies,
it plays directly into queer theorists' and lesbian feminists' worst fears
about what advocating same-sex marriage might mean. Queer theorists
worry that pursuing marriage rights is assimilationist, because it rests on
the view that it would be better for gay and lesbian relationships to be as
much like traditional heterosexual intimate relationships as possible. To
pursue marriage rights is to reject the value of pursuing possibly more
liberating, if less conventional, sexual, affectional, care-taking, and economic intimate arrangements. Feminists worry that pursuing marriage
rights will have the effect of endorsing gender-structured heterosexual
marriage, since the pursuit of marriage rights rests on an uncritical endorsement of traditional marriage.

Directed against the legal right to same-sex marriage, *no matter how defended,* these fears are, I think, misplaced. To claim that same-sex mar-

riage would necessarily assimilate gays and lesbians to mainstream culture ignores the fact that many heterosexuals (who, of course, do have the right to marry) have been anything but assimilationists. Evolution in both marriage law and marital and parenting practices has been a result of heterosexuals' *resistance* to the legal and social conception of traditional marriage. And it is precisely heterosexual noncompliance that gives force to Representative Barr's remark during the DOMA debates that '[t]he flames of hedonism, the flames of narcissism, the flames of self-centered morality are licking at the very foundations of our society: the family unit'.[13] If having the right to marry has not prevented heterosexuals from challenging legal and social conceptions of marriage, there is no reason to suppose that gays and lesbians will cease thinking critically about marital norms once granted a right to marry.

However, when extending marriage rights gets tied to the public policy goal of promoting one normative ideal for intimacy, queer theorists' objection is well placed. Marriage rights, so construed, ought not to have priority in a gay and lesbian political agenda. To endorse the goal of promoting one moral conception of marriage would, one might think, amount to deprioritizing securing legal rights—for example, the right to give proxy consent or the right to immigration preference—to those who are functioning as family members even if their families diverge from a conventional picture of family. But it is precisely legal rights for unconventional family arrangements that gays and lesbians may need most. Freed from conventional assumptions about what families and intimate relationships should look like, gays and lesbians have pursued alternative constructions of family involving extended networks of friends rather than biological kin. They have also pursued multiple parenting arrangements that sometimes involve more than the allotted two parents, because lesbian couples and gay couples may set up parenting arrangements with each other or with former spouses.[14] In short, to tie same-sex marriage rights to state promotion of one normative conception of marriage and family is to abandon the goal of critically rethinking which rights and benefits should be distributed to whom given a plurality of intimate and familial forms.

Similarly, the lesbian feminist argument that to pursue same-sex marriage is to endorse patriarchal gender-structured marriage is a bad argument when targeted at any possible defense of same-sex marriage. It ignores the fact that heterosexuals have resisted the gender-structuring of marriage, producing substantial changes in marital law that have included eliminating legal enforcement of separate husband-wife roles, fault-based divorce, long-term alimony, shared domicile requirements, and the like.[15] It also, oddly, ignores the fact that same-sex couples cannot replicate male-female power relations within marriage; and even if they do replicate gender structured marriage, it will be a gender structure decoupled from sexual difference. So it is hard to see how same-sex marriages could reinforce patriarchal marriage.

However, when extending marriage rights gets tied to the public policy goal of promoting one normative ideal for intimacy, the objection has some merit. What gets put into cultural circulation is a particular style of thinking about marriage. It is a style that resists any thorough-going departure from the most traditional normative ideal of marriage and family. It is a style that links marital-familial arrangements so tightly to the public good that state neutrality with respect to conceptions of the intimate good cannot go all the way down. And it is a style whose terms—procommitment, profamily, anti-promiscuity—are easily invoked to support moral norms and social policies that constrain women's reproductive, sexual, and relational liberty.

One last objection. To my mind, the greatest defect in arguments that defend same-sex marriage by appealing to a moral conception of marriage is that they ignore the connection between marriage bars and the system of heterosexual domination. On this view, a marriage bar simply denies gays and lesbians incentives to form and remain in long-term, monogamous, sexually faithful partnerships. Placing marriage rights on a gay and lesbian political agenda, however, requires a different sort of argument. In particular, we need a reason for supposing that denying same-sex marriage rights is integral to sustaining heterosexual domination. Arguments showing the connection between the denial of marriage rights and gender discrimination claim to do just that.

II. Gender-based Arguments

A substantial body of largely legal literature is devoted to the claim that the marriage bar originates from a system of male dominance. Thus eliminating the bar challenges that system.[16] Arguments that connect same-sex marriage bars to male dominance are what I will call 'gender-based' arguments. According to gender-based arguments for same-sex marriage, cultural hostility to same-sex marriage derives from the fact that same-sex marriages are gender-free. A marriage between two women or two men cannot easily be organized around husband and wife roles. Blumstein and Schwartz's frequently cited study of American couples showed that gay and lesbian relationships do indeed tend to be more egalitarian than heterosexual ones.[17] This deviance from conventional marital gender norms by women, who happen to be lesbian, and men, who happen to be gay, presumably signifies the potential for similar gender deviance by all women and men, including those who happen to be heterosexual. This, it is claimed, explains the cultural hostility to same-sex marriage. To legalize same-sex marriage would be tantamount to declaring that gendered husband and wife roles are inessential to marriage—not only for lesbians and gays, but for heterosexuals as well. To sanction same-sex marriage legally would be to invite heterosexuals to model their own marriages on the already more egalitarian models adopted by lesbians and gay men.

Thus, as Cass Sunstein puts it, same-sex marriage bars are, like anti-miscegenation laws, rooted in the assumption that there are 'only two kinds.'[18] Just as bars to interracial marriage were rooted in the idea that there are two distinct races whose differences must be preserved, so same-sex marriage bars are rooted in the idea that there are two distinct genders whose differences must be preserved. Just as the ideology of racial difference is the linchpin of white supremacy, so the ideology of gender difference is the linchpin of male supremacy. Thus, prohibiting same-sex marriage is a form of sex discrimination. That prohibition is simply a specific expression of a general intolerance to the blurring of gender difference anywhere, by anyone, including by heterosexuals in heterosexual marriages. The positive moral argument for same-sex marriage, then, is that same-sex marriage would make gender difference irrelevant within *all* marriages. It would thus contribute to the larger goal of producing a gender-just society.

Forging a link between same-sex marriage bars and sex discrimination was central to *Baehr v. Lewin*. Given that many states have laws prohibiting sex discrimination, but not sexual orientation discrimination, this particular argument for same-sex marriage rights seems most promising from a purely pragmatic point of view.

One particular advantage of arguing for same-sex marriage by showing that such rights would promote gender equality is that one need not make any substantive normative assumptions about the value of traditional marriage over other intimate relationships. Nor need one assume that the rights and benefits now distributed to married couples should not be distributed to others as well. Nor need one assume that the definition of marriage (e.g. as necessarily monogamous) and aims of marriage law (e.g. to coerce couples to stay together) are fixed and incontestable. This is an important point. Too often it is assumed that demanding the right to marry is equivalent to endorsing the traditional moral conception of marriage that was central to the first argument for marriage rights that we considered. Too often it is also assumed that anyone demanding the right to marry must also support the present system of marital rights and benefits. This is not true. A person can want, for example, a right to equal opportunity within the present labor structure and still be highly critical of the labor system for being undemocratic and organized around categories of gender, race, and intellectual versus manual labor. Similarly, a person can want the right to marry and still be highly critical of, say, the lack of freedom of choice of marriage contract and the lack of state neutrality with respect to competing conceptions of the intimate and familial good. Only arguments for marriage rights that are based on the idea that the state should promote one form of intimacy equate the quest for marriage rights with endorsing one, typically traditional, moral conception of marriage.

However, the gender-based argument for same-sex marriage is not without its own defects. First, it provides a better reason for *heterosexuals* to make same-sex marriage a political priority than it does for gays and lesbians to do so. After all, the primary beneficiaries, on this view, would be heterosexual couples, particularly heterosexual women. Lesbians and gay men, it is assumed, are *already* not complying with gender norms and have *already* reconstructed their partnerships around more egalitarian ideals. It is heterosexuals who persist in imagining that gendered husband and wife roles are essential to marriage and who are deprived of a legally legitimated alternative model—to be provided by married lesbians and gays—for restructuring their own marriages.[19]

More importantly, the thesis that the principal aim of barring same-sex marriage is to enforce separate gender roles is simply not adequately supported by the full range of evidence. Typically, arguments for this thesis begin by observing that social animus is visited upon lesbians and gays because of their gender deviance.[20] Gay men are culturally stereotyped as having excessively feminine personalities, vocations, avocational interests, dress, and demeanor. Gay men also violate sexual gender norms by being willing to occupy the passive, penetrated role in sex. In adopting inferior female positions, particularly in sex, gay men debase themselves and fail to do their bit in sustaining male dominance. Similarly, lesbians are culturally stereotyped as having excessively masculine personalities, vocations, avocational interests, dress, and demeanor. They also violate sexual gender norms by refusing to occupy the passive, penetrated sexual role in relation to men. In making themselves sexually unavailable to men, lesbians insubordinately repudiate male right of sexual access to women. In short, by not complying with their assigned gender roles, gays and lesbians threaten the system of male dominance. For this, both are subjected to penalties ranging from discriminatory employment policies, to physical violence, to same-sex marriage bars. The idea that cultural aversion to homosexuality and lesbianism is connected to sexist conceptions of proper male and female behavior is supported by studies showing that people who have the most conservative gender role attitudes are also most homophobic.[21]

This evidence does indeed suggest that the point of same-sex marriage bars is to compel men to behave as men and women to behave as women. The problem is that arguments attributing same-sex marriage bars exclusively to sexism omit two important pieces of evidence. The omitted evidence suggests that sexism is not the primary, let alone sole, factor motivating same-sex marriage bars. Consider first the fact that lesbians and gays are not the only gender deviants. Heterosexual men and heterosexual women may also fail to conform to traditional gender roles. Heterosexual women, in particular, have had good reason to rebel against both feminine gender norms and the gender structure of traditional marriage. Were compelling men to behave as men and women to behave as women the primary rationale behind same-sex marriage bars, one would expect to see this same rationale at work in the legal regulation of heterosexual marriage. But this simply is not the case. Heterosexual marriages have largely been *de*-gendered under the law. All of the nineteenth- and early twentieth-century laws have been eliminated that made married women legally dead on the assumption that man and wife are one and that that one is the husband. The law no longer compels married women to adopt their husband's name, to share his domicile wherever he choose it to be, to provide domestic services, and to submit to marital rape. The elimination of long-term alimony and the introduction of alimony for needy ex-husbands both resulted from abandoning the assumption that only husbands are economic providers within marriage. Repeated court refusal to employ sex-based classifications in family law has meant that all that is left of gender in marriage law are the constructs 'husband' and 'wife', evacuated of substantive content.[22] In addition, anti-discrimination laws which forbid formal and informal enforcement of gender differences in the workplace, education, access to housing, loans, and the like contribute to de-gendering the public sphere. In short, the law has taken a largely permissive attitude toward *heterosexual* gender deviance by refusing to enforce gender roles inside and outside of marriage. Thus, the claim that the law aims to enforce gender conformity by barring same-sex marriage is, at the very least, an overstatement. Whether the law takes a permissive or coercive approach to gender deviant intimate relationships appears to be a function of *whose* intimate relationships are at issue. Only specifically lesbian and gay intimate relations are subjected to legal control. This fact needs to be explained. Arguments that attribute same-sex marriage bars entirely to sexism fail to do this.

Second, those who argue that the principal aim of barring same-sex marriage is to enforce separate gender roles ignore evidence that in fact same-sex relations are not culturally interpreted as posing either a general threat to maintaining distinct gender roles for heterosexual men and women or a specific threat to preserving gender-structured heterosexual marriages. The only way that lesbian and gay behavior could threaten a system of gender roles and gender-structured marriage would be if their sexual orientation were irrelevant to their sex-gender categorization. That is, in order to imagine that lesbian gender insubordination represents a potential in *all* women, one would have to assume that there is no essential difference between lesbians and heterosexual women. Both are equally women. As a result, what some women (who just happen to prefer sex with women) do might readily be adopted by other women (who just happen to prefer sex with men). But this picture misrepresents how our culture thinks about sexual orientation. From the early twentieth century to the present day, sexual orientation has been culturally interpreted as marking an *essential* difference between heterosexual women and lesbians and between heterosexual men and gays. Recall that at the turn of the century, sexologists accommodated the existence of lesbians and gay men by pluralizing sex-gender categories beyond the original two. Both gay men and lesbians were described as a third sex. Moreover, lesbian and gay difference from heterosexual men and women has persistently been interpreted as an immutable difference. Early sexologists claimed that true inversion was a congenital condition; Freudians traced homosexuality and lesbianism to early childhood experiences that made conversion to heterosexuality extremely difficult if not impossible; and contemporary scientific theories have attempted to locate a genetic origin for homosexuality and lesbianism. That is, lesbians and gay men have, for the past hundred years, been constructed as a kind of naturally fixed third sex for whom gender deviance is a uniquely constitutive and unavoidable part of their nature.

Because sexual orientation marks an essential difference between real men and women—who are also heterosexual—and those who by nature or early psychological development are not really men and women, lesbian and gay behavior does not signal a potential in heterosexual women and men. Quite the contrary, because lesbians and gays are members of a supposedly naturally gender-deviant third sex, their behavior will of course differ from real (heterosexual) women's and men's behavior. Lesbian's and gays' essential difference makes them incapable of significantly threatening either heterosexual gender roles or the gender structure of heterosexual marriage. Of course, since the end of the nineteenth century, it has been part of our cultural view that lesbians and gays might seduce and convert those who are not 'really' gay or lesbian.[23] However, such worries leave in place a basic assumption that heterosexuals can generally be relied on to conform to gender norms. That includes conformity to gender-structured heterosexual marriage.

In sum, looking at both the differential treatment of heterosexuals versus lesbians and gays within the marriage law and the social construction of lesbians and gays as an essentially different type of person who is neither man nor woman suggests that same-sex marriage bars are not simply an expression of legal sexism. It also suggests that there is insufficient reason to suppose that removing same-sex marriage bars will have much of any impact on our gender expectations for heterosexual behavior inside and outside of marriage. It is possible, however, to construct a second gender-based argument that preserves the connection between same-sex marriage bars and sex discrimination, while at the same time avoiding the problematic assumption that lesbian and gay gender deviance signals a potential in all men and all women. I turn now to this second possibility.

This argument might begin by recognizing that gays and lesbians are culturally constructed as beings for whom gender nonconformity is endemic. Hostility to this third sex derives from the view that the only normal, natural, healthy kinds of people are real women, who at least by nature have the capacity to conform to gender norms, and real men, who at least by nature have the capacity to conform to gender norms. Heterosexuals may not comply with gender norms, and that is a bad thing. But it is far worse to have on the social scene a whole category of persons who are not even naturally fit for gender norms.

Obviously, it is the gender ideology attached to our system of male dominance that makes being lesbian or gay so stigmatizing. Thus, even if lesbians and gays, as members of a third sex, are singled out for special mistreatment and legal regulation not visited upon gender-deviant heterosexuals, and thus even if we can meaningfully talk about the distinctive political relations between heterosexuals and nonheterosexuals (not just the political relations between men and women), it remains true that the special opprobrium felt toward lesbianism and homosexuality is ultimately rooted in gender ideology. Same-sex marriage bars may not be, precisely, sex discrimination, since they are not aimed at controlling all women. They are, nevertheless, of a piece with policies that discriminate on the basis of sex.

There is a good deal to be said for this second argument. It accounts for the special animus motivating mistreatment of gays and lesbians. Members of a third sex are not simply *noncompliant* with gender norms. They are distinctively *unfit* for incorporation in a society governed by gender norms. As a result, this argument explains why gays and lesbians would have a special political interest in challenging legal regulations that target them. In addition, this argument also accounts for the intimate connection between gay and lesbian subordination and male dominance.

Even so, I think this is the wrong argument for same-sex marriage rights—or at least it is seriously incomplete. All gender-based arguments start from an assumption that merits questioning. They assume that the fundamental inequality at stake in all gay rights issues is the inequality between men and women. On these arguments, male dominance alone accounts for both the oppression of women and the oppression of gays and lesbians. As a result, the possibility is never entertained that heterosexual domination might be a separate axis of oppression; not is the possibility entertained that in maintaining same-sex marriage bars, in

maintaining the liberty to discriminate against lesbians and gays in housing and employment, in controlling the normative content of school
curricula and publicly funded artistic and scholarly endeavors, and in
limiting gay and lesbian access to children, what is at stake is preserving
heterosexuals' privileged socio-political status. That gender ideology factors into gay and lesbian oppression does not entail that it is the only factor. Gender ideology, as Andrew Koppelman has recently argued, also
factored into anti-miscegenation laws that were aimed particularly at
protecting white women from black male sexuality.[24] But the primary
factor remained the system of white-supremacy. If we are going to construct a positive moral argument for same-sex marriage rights, caution
needs to be taken not to overlook systems of inequality that may play a
more constitutive role in gay and lesbian oppression than male dominance does.

A central problem with gender-based arguments is that they under-
describe the ideological construction of 'gay' and 'lesbian' as stigmatized social identities. Recall that both gender-based accounts assume
that gay and lesbian gender deviance fully explains the stigmatizing of
these identities. Now, it is true that cross-genderization was the defining
feature of the third sex at the beginning of the twentieth century. It is
also true that hostility to gender blurring continues to sustain part of the
stigma attached to being gay or lesbian. This is manifested in, for example, fear that heterosexual soldiers will be subject to feminizing sexual
advances from gay soldiers as well as fear that gay or lesbian parents will
raise children who are themselves defectively gendered. However, gender deviance does not fully exhaust the content of what it culturally
means to be gay or lesbian. Equally important in the cultural construction of gay and lesbian identities is the idea that gay and lesbian sexuality is dangerously uncontrolled, predatory, insatiable, narcissistic, and
self-indulgent. . . . [T]his aspect of gay and lesbian identity came to particular culture prominence during the 1930s through 1960s—the era of
both the sex crime panics and the formal exclusion of 'sex perverts'
from all governmental service. Imagined to possess an excessive and unregulated sexuality, both gays and lesbians were claimed to pose a threat
to heterosexual adults and to children, who might be either molested or
seduced. This stigmatizing conception motivates policies barring gays
and lesbians from adoption, foster parenting, employment as teachers,
day care workers, and scout leaders, and also motivates some custody denials. In addition, because of their sexual insatiability, gays and lesbians
were viewed as psychologically unable to maintain stable relationships.
The idea that homosexuality is connected to undisciplined, self-indulgent
sexual desire has recently been re-emphasized by natural law legal theorists who suggest that homosexual sex resembles solitary masturbation.[25]
One natural law theorist argues that homosexuality should not be pro-

moted in the public realm because the public realm is 'the milieu in which and by which all citizens are encouraged and helped, or discouraged and undermined, in their own resistance to being lured by temptation into falling way from their own aspirations to be people of integrated good character, and to be autonomous, self-controlled persons rather than slaves to impulse and sensual gratification.'[26]

Linking both the images of the gender deviant and the sex pervert is the culturally elaborated view that gays and lesbians are multiply unfit for marriage and family. Not only are they unfit for assuming gendered familial roles and producing properly gendered children, they are incapable of sustaining long-term stable relationships, pose a sexual threat to their own and others' children, and risk reproducing their own defects in a second generation.

. . . [B]eginning in the 1980s, the stigmatizing conception of gays and lesbians as unfit for family life and as anti-family has begun to take on a life of its own, partially detached from its original roots in fears of gender deviance and sexual perversion. The increasing visibility of successful gay and lesbian families as well as the publicizing of empirical studies challenging, for example, the ideas that gays and lesbians constitute the majority of child molesters and that they are more likely to produce gay and lesbian children, have made it increasingly difficult to sustain the claim that gays and lesbians are unfit for family life. What remains an open possibility is to characterize gay and lesbians families as 'pretended family relationships'. That is, what remains an open possibility is the bald assertion that heterosexuality itself is the sole distinguishing feature of real versus pretended families.[27]

In sum, gender-based accounts of hostility to homosexuality and lesbianism take up only one theme in an historically complex construction of lesbian and gay identity. As a result, such accounts lack sufficient explanatory scope. They fail, for example, to explain why hostility to homosexuality and lesbianism crystallizes around marital and familial issues in the way that it does. Moreover, they fail to explain adequately the content of contemporary anti-gay discourse. If the gender-based account were correct, the House and Senate debates surrounding the Defense of Marriage Act should have focused on gays' and lesbians' unsuitability for fulfilling husband and wife roles, the possibility of producing gender- or sex-deviant children, and unnaturalness of men marrying men or women marrying women, and the importance of traditional gender-structured marriage. The DOMA debates, however, are strikingly *devoid* of any gender content. Instead, proponents of DOMA studiously—one might say deafly—refused to answer charges that heterosexuals were themselves posing the biggest threat to marriage through divorce, abandonment, spouse abuse, promiscuity, alcohol abuse, lack of marital commitment, watching Sunday football, and having children out of wedlock. Rather than contrasting the *behavior* of heterosexuals to homosexuals, DOMA proponents insisted on a single definitional point: Real marriage requires one man and one woman.

I turn now to the Defence of Marriage Act debates and what I think the positive moral argument for same-sex marriage should be.

III. DOMA's Defense of Heterosexual Status

Same-sex marriage bars are indeed predicated on the assumption that there are just 'two kinds'. But the relevant two kinds are not men and women. They are heterosexuals and nonheterosexuals. Same-sex marriage bars, sodomy laws, bars to adoption or foster parenting, and court denial of child custody are all predicated on stereotypes of nonheterosexuals' different relation to gender, sexual self-control, and the family. Specifically, they presuppose views about gays' and lesbians' gender deviance, lack of sexual self-control, and unfitness for family life. They thus assume that heterosexuals and nonheterosexuals are different kinds of people who should therefore be treated differently under the law. Anti-gay policies, however, differ in kind from racist or sexist policies. . . . [T]he aim of racist and sexist policies is to keep racial minorities and women *in their place*. Anti-gay policies, by contrast, aim to *displace* gays and lesbians from civil society by refusing to recognize that lesbians and gay men belong to either the public or the private sphere.

The same-sex marriage bar works in a particularly powerful way to displace gays and lesbians because we, as a culture, assume that married couples play a unique role in sustaining civil society. Within both specifically legal reasoning and broader cultural discourse, marriage and the family are typically construed as the bedrock on which social and political life is built. As Senator Faircloth put it during the DOMA debates: 'Marriage forms families, and families form societies. Strong families form strong societies. Fractured families form fractured societies. So all of us have an interest in seeing that strong families are formed in the first place.'[28] Proponents of DOMA repeatedly emphasized the foundational status of marriage in civil society: 'Marriage is the foundation of our society; families are built on it and values are passed through it.'[29] Marriage is 'the keystone in the arch of civilization.'[30] 'The time-honored and unique institution of marriage between one man and one woman is a fundamental pillar of our society and its values'.[31] '[T]hroughout the annals of human experience, in dozens of civilizations and cultures of varying value systems, humanity has discovered that the permanent relationship between man and woman is a keystone to the stability, strength, and health of human society—a relationship worthy of legal recognition and judicial protection.'[32] And '. . . governments have recognized the traditional family as the foundation of prosperity and happiness, and in democratic societies, as the foundation of freedom'.[33]

The central concept of marriage being forwarded here is as a prepolitical institution. Although states may create the legal package of rights and benefits that attach to marriage and may set age, sex, biological relationship and other restrictions on who may marry, the state does not create the institution of marriage itself. 'There is no moment in recorded history when the traditional family was not recognized and sanctioned by a civilized society—it is the oldest institution that exists.'[34] In addition, while the state may choose to recognize and provide legal protections for a variety of voluntary relationships (e.g. domestic partnerships or labor unions), the state does not *choose* to recognize marriages. Since the very possibility of civil society depends on people entering marriages and forming families, the state *must* recognize marriages.

This conception of marriage as the prepolitical foundation of society has an important implication. It means that if a social group can lay claim to being inherently qualified or fit to enter into marriage and found a family, it can also claim a distinctive political status. To be inherently qualified for entering marriage is not like being inherently qualified for this or that cooperative endeavor that societies may or may not set up (as men, for example, have in the past claimed to be inherently qualified for being doctors, miners, and preachers). It is instead to be qualified for sustaining the foundation of civil society itself. Conversely, if a particular social group is deemed *un*fit to enter marriage and found a family, that group can then be denied this distinctive political status. Because they are incapable, as a group, of providing the necessary foundation for civil society, they are, ultimately, inessential citizens. At best, they are dependent citizens. Whatever social contribution they might make to civil society depends on the antecedent marital and familial labor of others.

For proponents of DOMA, the central debate was about *who* could lay claim to the political status that derives from being deemed qualified for marriage and the family.[35] The aim of proponents was to reaffirm, by constructing a federal definition of marriage, that only heterosexuals have this status.

Anxiety about what would happen to their own status if same-sex marriage were legally recognized ran very close to the surface. Many comments echoed Attorney General Bowers' assertion in this brief for *Bowers v. Hardwick* that '[h]omosexual sodomy is anathema of the basic units of our society—marriage and the family. To decriminalize or artificially withdraw the public's expression of its disdain for this conduct does not uplift sodomy, but rather demotes these sacred institutions to merely alternative lifestyles'.[36] Representative Smith, for example, asserted that '[s]ame-sex "marriages" demean the fundamental institution of marriage. They legitimize unnatural and immoral behavior. And they trivialize marriage as a mere "lifestyle choice". The institution of marriage sets a necessary and high standard. Anything that lowers this standard, as same-sex "marriages" do, inevitably belittles marriage'.[37] Others echoed this sentiment. '[I]t is vital that we protect marriage against attempts to redefine it in a way that causes the family to lose its special meaning'.[38] 'Should the law express its neutrality between homosexual and heterosexual relationships? Should the law elevate homosexual unions to the same status as the heterosexual relationships on which the traditional family is based, a status which has been reserved from time immemorial for the union between a man and a woman?'[39] 'Allowing for gay marriages would be the final straw, it would devalue the love between a man and a woman and weaken us as a Nation'.[40]

But exactly why would same-sex marriages devalue heterosexual love, belittle marriage, and render it a mere lifestyle choice? The obvious answer is that homosexuality is immoral. To recognize same-sex marriages legally would place the sacred institution of marriage in the disreputable company of immoral, unnatural unions, thus cheapening its status. This was surely part of the thinking. But it is not the whole story. For if concern about giving the same state seal of approval to immoral same-sex unions as to honorable heterosexual marriages were the primary concern, then one would expect proponents of DOMA to also be adamantly opposed to any legal protection of same sex unions. Yet Representative Lipinski, who thought that allowing gay marriages would be the final straw devaluating love between man and woman also observed that 'gays can legally achieve the same ends as marriage through draft wills, medical powers of attorney, and contractual agreements in the event that the relationship should end.'[41] Other proponents affirmed the importance of guaranteeing the right to privacy[42] and pointed out that the law protects a variety of unions outside of marriage law (presumably potentially including same sex-ones).[43] These types of remarks suggest that the immorality of homosexuality was not the only issue.

The central concern instead seemed to be that recognizing same-sex unions as marriages would demote marriage from a naturally defined pre-political institution to a state-defined contract. Senators Gramm and Byrd clearly express this concern. According to Gramm, '[h]uman beings have always given traditional marriage a special sanction. Not that there cannot be contracts among individuals, but there is something unique about the traditional family in terms of what it does for our society and the foundation it provides. . . .'[44] Byrd articulated a similar distinction:

> Obviously, human beings enter into a variety of relationships. Business partnerships, friendships, alliances for mutual benefits, and team member-

ships all depend upon emotional unions of one degree or another. For that
reason, a number of these relationships have found standing under the
laws of innumerable nations.

However, in no case, has anyone suggested that these relationships deserve the special recognition or the designation commonly understood as
'marriage'.[45]

Reading between the lines, the underlying view seems to be this: Free,
self-defining, sociable citizens may choose to enter a variety of voluntary
relationships with each other. In deciding what legal protections might
be in order for these relationships, a liberal political society that values
freedom of association and the right to the pursuit of happiness must
adopt a position of neutrality. Rather than giving priority to some of
these relationships on moral grounds, the state instead assumes that citizens may reasonably choose any of these relationships on the basis of
their own conception of the good. Thus, such voluntary associations
might reasonably be dubbed 'lifestyle choices'. To call them 'lifestyle
choices' is not to say that they are in fact morally equivalent. One might
think that sodomy is immoral or that same-sex unions are immoral, but
nevertheless think the state should adopt a neutral position, refraining
from criminalizing sodomy and offering legal protection for same-sex
unions under domestic partnership laws. To say that a particular form of
relationship is a 'lifestyle choice', then, is simply to say that it falls within
the category of relationships with respect to which state neutrality is appropriate.

What proponents of DOMA took pains to emphasize was that marriage falls in a different category. Marriage is not one among many voluntary associations that citizens might choose to enter. Nor is it one
among many relationships whose nature free, self-defining persons
might determine for themselves. Marriage constitutes the prepolitical
foundation of society. To say that marriage is prepolitical is to say both
that societies depend for their functioning on marriages and that the essential nature of marriage is fixed independently of liberal society—by
God, or by human nature, or by the prerequisites for civilization. Consequently, state neutrality with respect to the definition of marriage involves a category mistake. State neutrality would involve treating a
prepolitical institution as though it were a political institution, that is, as
though it were an institution that must be compatible with multiple conceptions of the good. Since, on this view, it is not in fact a political institution, the appropriate legal treatment of marriage is instead to *insulate*
marriage against revision according to liberal political principles. This is
what DOMA does. Representative Seastrand summarized the point in
her remark that '[a]s special interest pressure increasingly demands a
tolerant and fluid definition of marriage, we progressively attempt to re-

define marriage to fit social trends. . . . This bill will fortify marriage against the storm of revisionism'.[46]

In my view, then, what makes same-sex marriage rights so important is that marriage bars do not represent merely one among many ways that the state may discriminate against gays and lesbians by enacting laws based on stereotypes of lesbians' and gay men's gender deviance, undisciplined sexual desire, and unfitness for family life. They do, of course, rest on an underlying ideological construction of lesbians and gay men as unfit for stable relationships and child rearing. But marriage bars attach something else to that unfitness. That something else is political status—both the individual's political status as a citizen and the political status of particular kinds of relationships. Specifically, marriage bars enact the view that heterosexual love, marriage, and family have a uniquely prepolitical, foundational status in civil society. As a result, heterosexuals can claim for their own relationships not just moral superiority, but a uniquely privileged status beyond the reach of liberal political values. Marriage bars also enact the view that because only heterosexuals are fit to participate in this foundational marital institution, only heterosexuals are entitled to lay claim to a unique citizenship status. Heterosexuals are not *just* free, rational, self-defining persons. They are also naturally fit to participate in the one institution that all societies, liberal or otherwise, must presuppose. Thus they may lay claim to a citizenship status that *exceeds* what individuals are entitled to on the basis of being free, rational, self-defining persons. In addition to the rights of free association, including intimate association, to which all citizens are entitled, the special rights and privileges attached to marriage are set aside for heterosexuals only. And not only this.

Heterosexuals may also claim for themselves special entitlement to control future generations' ongoing commitment to heterosexuality and heterosexual marriage. Although children were infrequently mentioned in the DOMA debates, when they were, the primary concern was that the next generation might cease to think that heterosexual marriage and being heterosexual matters. Senator Coats, for example, proclaimed that '[t]he institution of marriage is our most valuable cultural inheritance. It is our duty—perhaps our first duty—to pass it intact to the future'.[47] Others insisted that '[w]e should not be forced to send a message to our children that undermines the definition of marriage as the union of one man and one woman'.[48]

> Should Congress tell the children of America that it is a matter of indifference whether they establish families with a partner of the opposite sex or cohabit with someone of the same sex? Should this Congress tell the children of America that we as a society believe there is no moral difference be-

tween homosexual relationships and heterosexual relationships? Should this Congress tell the children of America that in the eyes of the law the parties to a homosexual union are entitled to all the rights and privileges that have always been reserved for a man and a woman united in marriage?[49]

Here are large political prizes. They explain both why it is reasonable to consider lesbian and gay subordination an axis of subordination separate from gender oppression and why same-sex marriage rights belong high up on a gay and lesbian political agenda. One of the major stumbling blocks to constructing a positive moral argument for same-sex marriage rights on the grounds that marriage bars are motivated by a desire to maintain a *sexual orientation* caste system analogous to racial and gender caste systems has been that it is not immediately obvious what heterosexuals might stand to gain from such a caste system. By contrast, it is far more obvious what men (and indeed some women) stand to gain from a gender caste system and what whites stand to gain from a racial caste system. What I have tried to argue here is that the gain takes the form of a unique citizenship status that grounds heterosexuals' claims to special state solitude for their private lives, a partial insulation of their legal privileges from liberal principles, and special entitlement to influence the evaluative commitments of future generations.

Conclusion

The political significance of having a right to marry is, I have argued, a function of the fact that marriage itself is culturally taken to be a prepolitical institution. The bar to same-sex marriage thus plays such a central role in lesbian and gay subordination only because we, as a culture, assume that marriage is not like other voluntary associations that the state might choose to facilitate. We assume that marriages and families are essential to the functioning of any society in a way that other voluntary associations are not. Giving gays and lesbians the right to marry might, consequently, disrupt gay and lesbian oppression in one of two possible ways. On the one hand, we might continue to construe marriage as a prepolitical institution that plays a crucial role in society. Same-sex marriage rights would, in essence, affirm gays' and lesbians' fitness to participate in this foundational institution. On the other hand, we might reject the idea that marriage and family differ in any politically significant way from other voluntary associations. Same-sex marriage rights would, on this second view, disrupt gay and lesbian subordination not by incorporating them into a special, foundational institution, but by denying that marriage and family had any special political importance in the first place. Because marriage is similar to other voluntary associations, there is no good reason for the state to impose stricter regulations on marriage than on other voluntary associations. Thus there is no good reason to continue insisting that only a man and a woman may marry.

Both options are worth considering. If we take the first option, then we are agreeing, in part, with proponents of DOMA. Marriage, even if not heterosexual marriage, is unlike other possible voluntary intimate arrangements. That is, even if we have reason to think that marriages might take a wider array of forms than are presently recognized—for example, same-sex marriages, polygamous marriages, marriages where children have multiple mothers and fathers—we might still draw a distinction between associations called 'marriage' and other voluntary associations. And we might regard the arrangements labeled 'marriages' as prepolitical, foundational, and meriting special legal treatment. It is important to see here that it is possible to think that some forms of intimate and care-taking associations are critical to societies, in a way that other voluntary associations are not, and yet deny that traditional, heterosexual, two-parent families are the *only* intimate associations that fit this bill. However, any attempt to pick out which intimate associations are foundational would require that we endorse *some* (even if highly expanded) normative ideal for how persons should organize their intimate, affectional, personal economic, reproductive, sexual, and child rearing lives. The political task would be to determine which forms of (heterosexual, nonheterosexual, monogamous, polygamous, etc.) intimacy would be dignified with the label 'marriage' and the status of being regarded as foundational to civil society. In this case, the bid for same-sex marriage rights would amount to a demand to be deemed fit to participate in the foundational social institution and thus an essential citizen not dependent on the marital and familial work of others.

On the other hand, if we take the second option, we would reject the idea altogether that there are any prepolitical, foundational forms of intimacies. We might argue that civil societies depend only in the most general way on its citizens having the capacities for and interest in casting their personal lot with others and sharing, in voluntary private arrangements, sex, affection, reproduction, economic support, and care for the young, the inform and the elderly. But no one form or set of forms for doing so is foundational to civil society. Nor need all of these activities be consolidated within one relationship, as we standardly consolidate them within couples and couple-based families.[50] Parenting, the provision of emotional and economic support to an adult, and sex might take place in the context of different relationships rather than the same one. Nor need all of these activities be best undertaken through private arrangements, as we have up to this point typically thought to be true of

the care of children and the provision of sex. Much more extensive public child support arrangements and the legal commercialization of sex
might replace much of the traditional function of marriage and family.
That is, we might envision a fully liberal society in which no private relationships are insulated from liberal principles. Whatever legal protection and support were provided for individuals' private intimate
relations and the production of future generations would be predicated
on the assumption that persons might choose a plurality of intimate
arrangements in accord with their own conceptions of the good. In this
case, the bid for same-sex marriage rights would amount to a demand
to be deemed equal citizens within a fully liberal society that is simply
committed to facilitating voluntary associations between people of
whatever form people might choose. This would amount, in essence, to
following a recommendation that Ruthann Robson has recently made
that the legal categories of 'marriage' and 'family' be completely abolished. In that case, the state would interact with all citizens purely as individuals rather than as members (or nonmembers) of a particular
intimate relationship.[51]

Which is the better option? To many, the obviously correct option is
the second one. *Of course* the state should be neutral with respect to conceptions of the good. *Of course* it is always a bad thing for the state to promote any normative ideal of intimate relations. While I agree, I also find
the choice of option two more difficult to make. Recall that at the beginning I said that I thought it was important *which* arguments get culturally circulated, not just *that* gays and lesbians get the right to marry.
Liberal political reasoning that stresses state neutrality works best in societies that are *already* egalitarian, and where state neutrality serves to
maintain equality. In inegalitarian societies, state neutrality often con-
strains interventions in the ideological status quo. For example, state
neutrality on whether it would be a good or bad thing for adult men to
have access to pornographic materials makes it more difficulty to intervene in the sexual objectification of women. Defending same-sex marriage on grounds of state neutrality with respect to individuals' voluntary
associations requires only that same-sex marriages be legally permitted
regardless of how they are morally viewed. Genuine equality for gays and
lesbians, however, requires more than merely coming to be tolerated. It
requires that we, as a culture, give up the belief that gays and lesbians are
unfit to participate in normatively ideal forms of marriage, parenting,
and family. Only the first option permits us to put into cultural circulation legal arguments that directly challenge the ideology sustaining gays'
and lesbians' social inequality.

I intend to leave open this question of whether we should continue
treating marriage and the family as a prepolitical institution meriting
special legal protections. As a matter of social fact, we do assign marriage

and the family special social significance. What is most important to see is the effect that excluding gays and lesbians from marital and familial status has on maintaining a system of gay and lesbian subordination. . . .

Notes

1. Claudia Card, 'Against Marriage and Motherhood,' *Hypatia* 11 (1996):1–23.

2. Mary Wollstonecraft, *A Vindication of the Rights of Woman* (New York: Norton, 1967).

3. *Congressional Record*, 104th Cong., 2nd sess., 1996, 142, pt S10109.

4. William N. Eskridge, Jr., *The Case for Same-Sex Marriage: From Sexual Liberty to Civilized Commitment* (New York: Free Press, 1996), 91.

5. Ibid. 72.

6. William N. Eskridge, Jr., 'Beyond Lesbian and Gay "Families We Choose,"' in *Sex, Preference, and Family,* ed. David M. Estlund and Martha C. Nussbaum (New York: Oxford University Press, 1996), 277–89.

7. Karen Struening, 'Feminist Challenges to the New Familialism: Lifestyle Experimentation and the Freedom of Association', *Hypatia* 11 (1996): 135–54.

8. Stephen Macedo, 'Sexuality and Liberty: Making Room for Nature and Tradition?' in *Sex, Preference, and Family,* 86–101. Karen Struening surveys the main themes of cultural conservatives with respect to the family, focusing particularly on William Galston. See 'Feminist Challenges to the New Familialism'.

9. Karen Struening, 'Feminist Challenges to the New Familialism'.

10. That the US has the highest divorce rate has recently been attributed to the fact that US women have the greatest economic independence.

11. Card, 'Against Marriage and Motherhood'.

12. Struening, 'Feminist Challenges to the New Familialism'.

13. *Congressional Record,* 104th Cong., 2nd sess., 1996, 142, pt H7482.

14. See Nancy D. Polikoff, 'This Child Does Have Two Mothers', *Georgetown Law Journal* 78 (1990): 459–575.

15. Of course, not all of these changes have been salutary for women, since the beneficial consequences of eliminating the formal gender structure of marriage depends in large part on the *actual* degendering of marital practices as well as gender equity in the paid workforce.

16. See Sylvia Law, 'Homosexuality and the Social Meaning of Gender', *Wisconsin Law Review* 1988: 187–235; Cass R. Sunstein, 'Homosexuality and the Constitution', in *Sex, Preference, and Family,* 208–26; Andrew Koppelman, 'The Miscegenation Analogy: Sodomy Law as Sex Discrimination', *Yale Law Journal* 98 (1988): 145–64; 'Why Discrimination Against Lesbians and Gay Men is Sex Discrimination', *NYU Law Review* 69 (1994): 197–287; Nan D. Hunter, 'Marriage, Law, and Gender: A Feminist Inquiry', in *Sex Wars: Sexual Dissent and Political Culture,* Lisa Duggan and Nan D. Hunter, eds. (New York: Routledge, 1995), 107–22.

17. Philip Blumstein and Pepper Schwartz, *American Couples: Money, Work, Sex* (New York: Morrow, 1983).

18. Sunstein, 'Homosexuality and the Constitution', in *Sex, Preference, and Family,* 208–26.

19. Susan Moller Okin uses this role model argument in 'Sexual Orientation and Gender: Dichotomizing Differences', in *Sex, Preference, and Family*, 44–59.

20. For classic statements of this argument, see Andrew Koppelman, 'Why Discrimination Against Lesbians and Gay Men is Sex Discrimination', and Sylvia A. Law, 'Homosexuality and the Social Meaning of Gender'.

21. Koppelman cites a variety of studies supporting this claim in 'Why Discrimination Against Lesbians and Gay Men is Sex Discrimination'.

22. Koppelman.

23. Nineteenth-century sexologists distinguished between congenital and situational inverts. Judge Richard A. Posner has recently recast this distinction as one between preference homosexuals and opportunistic homosexuals ('The Economic Approach to Homosexuality', in *Sex, Preference, and Family*, 173–91). The concern about conversion has motivated, in the last decade, a series of what Nan Hunger aptly labels 'no promo homo' legislative initiatives. See 'Identity, Speech, and Equality', *Virginia Law Review* 79 (1993): 1695–719.

24. Koppelman, 'Why Discrimination Against Lesbians and Gay Men is Sex Discrimination', 224–34.

25. John Finnis, 'Law, Morality, and "Sexual Orientation"', *Notre Dame Journal of Law, Ethics and Public Policy* 9 (1995): 11–39, 25. See also Patrick Lee and Robert George, 'What Sex Can Be: Self-Alienation, Illusion, or One-Flesh Union', *The American Journal of Jurisprudence*, 42 (1997): 135–57, 138.

26. John Finnis, 15.

27. In 'Law, Morality, and "Sexual Orientation"', John Finnis comes very close to this view, since the only reason why same-sex couples lack access to 'the marital good' and why their sex is no better than masturbation is that same-sex sex fails to unite biologically the reproductive organs of the couple in acts of a reproductive kind.

28. *Congressional Record,* 104th Cong., 2nd sess., 1996, 142, pt S10117.

29. Representative Lipinski of Illinois speaking for the Defense of Marriage Act (DOMA) to the House floor, H.R. 3396, 104th Cong., 2nd sess., *Congressional Record* (12 July 1996), 142, pt H7495.

30. William J. Bennett, 'Not a Very Good Idea', qtd. in *Washington Post,* 21 May 1996, in the *Congressional Record,* 104th Cong., 2nd sess., 142, pt H7495.

31. Representative Ensign of Nevada speaking for DOMA to the House floor. Ibid. pt H7493.

32. Senator Byrd of West Virginia speaking for DOMA to the Senate floor, H.R. 3396, *Congressional Record,* 104th Cong., 2nd sess., 1996, 142, pt S10109.

33. Senator Gramm of Texas speaking for DOMA to the Senate floor. Ibid., pt S10106.

34. Senator Gramm, Ibid., pt S10105.

35. Opponents clearly took the debate to be about something else, namely, about why, in practice, real families are not flourishing. Completely bypassing proponents' point, opponents instead focused on the misbehavior of heterosexual family members as well as inadequate health, education and day care, unemployment, the absence of a livable minimum wage, inability to afford single family homes, and loss of pensions, and insufficient Medicare payments.

36. Qtd in Sylvia Law, 'Homosexuality and the Social Meaning of Gender', 219.

37. *Congressional Record,* 104th Cong., 2nd sess., 1996, 142, pt H7494.

38. Representative Weldon of Florida speaking for DOMA to the House floor, H.R. 3396. Ibid. H7493.

39. Representative Canady of Florida speaking for DOMA to the House floor. Ibid. H7491.

40. Representative Lipinski. Ibid. H7495.

41. Ibid. H7495.

42. Senator Burns of Montana speaking for DOMA to the House floor, H.R. 3396, 104th Cong., 2nd sess., *Congressional Record* (10 Sept. 1996), 142, pt S10117.

43. Senator Byrd. Ibid., pt S10109.

44. Senator Gramm. Ibid., pt S10106.

45. Senator Byrd. Ibid., pt S10109.

46. Representative Seastrand of California speaking for DOMA to the House floor, H.R. 3396, 104th Cong., 2nd sess., *Congressional Record* (12 July 1996), 142, pt H7485.

47. *Congressional Record,* 104th Cong., 2nd sess., 1996, 142, pt S10114.

48. Representative Delay of Texas speaking for DOMA to the House floor, H.R. 3396, 104th Cong., 2nd sess., *Congressional Record* (12 July 1996), 142, pt 7487.

49. Representative Canady. Ibid. pt 7491.

50. Will Kymlicka has argued for fully contractual intimate arrangements in 'Rethinking the Family', *Philosophy and Public Affairs* 20 (1991): 77–97.

51. See both 'States of Marriage' and 'Resisting the Family: Repositioning Lesbians,' in Ruthann Robson's *Sappho Goes to Law School* (New York: Routledge, 1998).

PART 3
ABORTION

Chapter 13

ABORTION AND THE SEXUAL AGENDA: A CASE FOR PROLIFE FEMINISM

Sidney Callahan

The abortion debate continues. In the latest and perhaps most crucial development, prolife feminists are contesting prochoice feminist claims that abortion rights are prerequisites for women's full development and social equality. The outcome of this debate may be decisive for the culture as a whole. Prolife feminists, like myself, argue on good feminist principles that women can never achieve the fulfillment of feminist goals in a society permissive toward abortion.

These new arguments over abortion take place within liberal political circles. This round of intense intra-feminist conflict has spiraled beyond earlier right-versus-left abortion debates, which focused on "tragic choices," medical judgments, and legal compromises. Feminist theorists of the prochoice position now put forth the demand for unrestricted abortion rights as a *moral imperative* and insist upon women's right to complete reproductive freedom. They morally justify the present situation and current abortion practices. Thus it is all the more important that prolife feminists articulate their different feminist perspective.

These opposing arguments can best be seen when presented in turn. Perhaps the most highly developed feminist arguments for the morality and legality of abortion can be found in Beverly Wildung Harrison's *Our Right to Choose* (Beacon Press, 1983) and Rosalind Pollack Petchesky's *Abortion and Woman's Choice* (Longman, 1984). Obviously it is difficult to

Reprinted with permission from *Commonweal* (25 April 1986), pp. 232–38. © 1986 Commonweal Foundation. For subscriptions, call toll-free 1-888-495-6755.

do justice to these complex arguments, which draw on diverse strands of philosophy and social theory and are often interwoven in prochoice feminists' own version of a "seamless garment." Yet the fundamental feminist case for the morality of abortion, encompassing the views of Harrison and Petchesky, can be analyzed in terms of four central moral claims: (1) the moral right to control one's own body; (2) the moral necessity of autonomy and choice in personal responsibility; (3) the moral claim for the contingent value of fetal life; (4) the moral right of women to true social equality.

1. The moral right to control one's own body. Prochoice feminism argues that a woman choosing an abortion is exercising a basic right of bodily integrity granted in our common law tradition. If she does not choose to be physically involved in the demands of a pregnancy and birth, she should not be compelled to be so against her will. Just because it is *her* body which is involved, a woman should have the right to terminate any pregnancy, which at this point in medical history is tantamount to terminating fetal life. No one can be forced to donate an organ or submit to other invasive physical procedures for however good a cause. Thus no woman should be subjected to "compulsory pregnancy." And it should be noted that in pregnancy much more than a passive biological process is at stake.

From one perspective, the fetus is, as Petchesky says, a "biological parasite" taking resources from the woman's body. During pregnancy, a woman's whole life and energies will be actively involved in the nine-month process. Gestation and childbirth involve physical and psychological risks. After childbirth a woman will either be a mother who must undertake a twenty-year responsibility for child rearing, or face giving up her child for adoption or institutionalization. Since hers is the body, hers the risk, hers the burden, it is only just that she alone should be free to decide on pregnancy or abortion.

This moral claim to abortion, according to the prochoice feminists, is especially valid in an individualistic society in which women cannot count on medical care or social support in pregnancy, childbirth, or child rearing. A moral abortion decision is never made in a social vacuum, but in the real life society which exists here and now.

2. The moral necessity of autonomy and choice in personal responsibility. Beyond the claim for individual *bodily* integrity, the prochoice feminists claim that to be a full adult *morally,* a woman must be able to make responsible life commitments. To plan, choose, and exercise personal responsibility, one must have control of reproduction. A woman must be able to make yes-or-no decisions about a specific pregnancy, according to her present situation, resources, prior commitments, and life plan. Only with such reproductive freedom can a woman have the moral autonomy necessary to make mature commitments, in the area of family, work, or education.

Contraception provides a measure of personal control, but contraceptive failure or other chance events can too easily result in involuntary pregnancy. Only free access to abortion can provide the necessary guarantee. The chance biological process of an involuntary pregnancy should not be allowed to override all the other personal commitments and responsibilities a woman has: to others, to family, to work, to education, to her future development, health, or well-being. Without reproductive freedom, women's personal moral agency and human consciousness are subjected to biology and chance.

3. *The moral claim for the contingent value of fetal life.* Prochoice feminist exponents like Harrison and Petchesky claim that the value of fetal life is contingent upon the woman's free consent and subjective acceptance. The fetus must be invested with maternal valuing in order to become human. This process of "humanization" through personal consciousness and "sociality" can only be bestowed by the woman in whose body and psychosocial system a new life must mature. The meaning and value of fetal life are constructed by the woman; without this personal conferral there only exists a biological, physiological process. Thus fetal interests or fetal rights can never outweigh the woman's prior interest and rights. If a woman does not consent to invest her pregnancy with meaning or value, then the merely biological process can be freely terminated. Prior to her own free choice and conscious investment, a woman cannot be described as a "mother" nor can a "child" be said to exist.

Moreover, in cases of voluntary pregnancy, a woman can withdraw consent if fetal genetic defects or some other problem emerges at any time before birth. Late abortion should thus be granted without legal restrictions. Even the minimal qualifications and limitations on women embedded in *Roe v. Wade* are unacceptable—repressive remnants of patriarchal unwillingness to give power to women.

4. *The moral right of women to full social equality.* Women have a moral right to full social equality. They should not be restricted or subordinated because of their sex. But this morally required equality cannot be realized without abortion's certain control of reproduction. Female social equality depends upon being able to compete and participate as freely as males can in the structures of educational and economic life. If a woman cannot control when and how she will be pregnant or rear children, she is at a distinct disadvantage, especially in our male-dominated world.

Psychological equality and well-being is also at stake. Women must enjoy the basic right of a person to the free exercise of heterosexual intercourse and full sexual expression, separated from procreation. No less than males, women should be able to be sexually active without the constantly inhibiting fear of pregnancy. Abortion is necessary for women's sexual fulfillment and the growth of uninhibited feminine self-confidence and ownership of their sexual powers.

But true sexual and reproductive freedom means freedom to procreate as well as to inhibit fertility. Prochoice feminists are also worried that women's freedom to reproduce will be curtailed through the abuse of sterilization and needless hysterectomies. Besides the punitive tendencies of a male-dominated health-care system, especially in response to repeated abortions or welfare pregnancies, there are other economic and social pressures inhibiting reproduction. Genuine reproductive freedom implies that day care, medical care, and financial support would be provided mothers, while fathers would take their full share in the burdens and delights of raising children.

Many prochoice feminists identify feminist ideals with communitarian, ecologically sensitive approaches to reshaping society. Following theorists like Sara Ruddick and Carol Gilligan, they link abortion rights with the growth of "maternal thinking" in our heretofore patriarchal society. Maternal thinking is loosely defined as a responsible commitment to the loving nurture of specific human beings as they actually exist in socially embedded interpersonal contexts. It is a moral perspective very different from the abstract, competitive, isolated, and principled rigidity so characteristic of patriarchy.

How does a prolife feminist respond to these arguments? Prolife feminists grant the good intentions of their prochoice counterparts but protest that the prochoice position is flawed, morally inadequate, and inconsistent with feminism's basic demands for justice. Prolife feminists champion a more encompassing moral ideal. They recognize the claims of fetal life and offer a different perspective on what is good for women. The feminist vision is expanded and refocused.

1. From the moral right to control one's own body to a more inclusive ideal of justice. The moral right to control one's own body does apply to cases of organ transplants, mastectomies, contraception, and sterilization; but it is not a conceptualization adequate for abortion. The abortion dilemma is caused by the fact that 266 days following a conception in one body, another body will emerge. One's own body no longer exists as a single unit but is engendering another organism's life. This dynamic passage from conception to birth is genetically ordered and universally found in the human species. Pregnancy is not like the growth of cancer or infestation by a biological parasite; it is the way every human being enters the world. Strained philosophical analogies fail to apply: having a baby is not like rescuing a drowning person, being hooked up to a famous violinist's artificial life-support system, donating organs for transplant—or anything else.

As embryology and fetology advance, it becomes clear that human development is a continuum. Just as astronomers are studying the first three minutes in the genesis of the universe, so the first moments, days, and weeks at the beginning of human life are the subject of increasing scientific attention. While neonatology pushes the definition of viability ever earlier, ultrasound and fetology expand the concept of the patient *in utero*. Within such a continuous growth process, it is hard to defend logically any demarcation point after conception as the point at which an immature form of human life is so different from the day before or the day after, that it can be morally or legally discounted as a nonperson. Even the moment of birth can hardly differentiate a nine-month fetus from a newborn. It is not surprising that those who countenance late abortions are logically led to endorse selective infanticide.

The same legal tradition which in our society guarantees the right to control one's own body firmly recognizes the wrongfulness of harming other bodies, however immature, dependent, different looking, or powerless. The handicapped, the retarded, and newborns are legally protected from deliberate harm. Prolife feminists reject the suppositions that would except the unborn from this protection.

After all, debates similar to those about the fetus were once conducted about feminine personhood. Just as women, or blacks, were considered too different, too underdeveloped, too "biological," to have souls or to possess legal rights, so the fetus is now seen as "merely" biological life, subsidiary to a person. A woman was once viewed as incorporated into the "one flesh" of her husband's person; she too was a form of bodily property. In all patriarchal unjust systems, lesser orders of human life are granted rights only when wanted, chosen, or invested with value by the powerful.

Fortunately, in the course of civilization there has been a gradual realization that justice demands the powerless and dependent be protected against the uses of power wielded unilaterally. No human can be treated as a means to an end without consent. The fetus is an immature, dependent form of human life which only needs time and protection to develop. Surely, immaturity and dependence are not crimes.

In an effort to think about the essential requirements of a just society, philosophers like John Rawls recommend imagining yourself in an "original position," in which your position in the society to be created is hidden by a "veil of ignorance." You will have to weigh the possibility that any inequalities inherent in that society's practices may rebound upon you in the worst, as well as in the best, conceivable way. This thought experiment helps ensure justice for all.

Beverly Harrison argues that in such an envisioning of society everyone would institute abortion rights in order to guarantee that if one turned out to be a woman one would have reproductive freedom. But surely in the original position and behind the "veil of ignorance," you would have to contemplate the possibility of being the particular fetus to be aborted. Since everyone has passed through the fetal stage of development, it is false to refuse to imagine oneself in this state when thinking about a potential world in which justice would govern. Would it be

just that an embryonic life—in half the cases, of course, a female life—
be sacrificed to the right of a woman's control over her own body? A
woman may be pregnant without consent and experience a great many
penalties, but a fetus killed without consent pays the ultimate penalty.

It does not matter (*The Silent Scream* notwithstanding) whether the fetus being killed is fully conscious or feels pain. We do not sanction killing
the innocent if it can be done painlessly or without the victim's awareness. Consciousness becomes important to the abortion debate because
it is used as a criterion for the "personhood" so often seen as the prerequisite for legal protection. Yet certain philosophers set the standard of
personhood so high that half the human race could not meet the criteria
during most of their waking hours (let alone their sleeping ones). Sen-
tience, self-consciousness, rational decision-making, social participation?
Surely no infant, or child under two, could qualify. Either our idea of person must be expanded or another criterion, such as human life itself, be
employed to protect the weak in a just society. Prolife feminists who defend the fetus empathetically identify with an immature state of growth
passed through by themselves, their children, and everyone now alive.

It also seems a travesty of just procedures that a pregnant woman now,
in effect, acts as sole judge of her own case, under the most stressful conditions. Yes, one can acknowledge that the pregnant woman will be subject to the potential burdens arising from a pregnancy, but it has never
been thought right to have an interested party, especially the more powerful party, decide his or her own case when there may be a conflict of
interest. If one considers the matter as a case of a powerful versus a powerless, silenced claimant, the prochoice feminist argument can rightly
be inverted: since hers is the body, hers the risk, and hers the greater
burden, then how in fairness can a woman be the sole judge of the fetal
right to life?

Human ambivalence, a bias toward self-interest, and emotional stress
have always been recognized as endangering judgment. Freud declared
that love and hate are so entwined that if instant thoughts could kill, we
would all be dead in the bosom of our families. In the case of a woman's
involuntary pregnancy, a complex, long-term solution requiring effort
and energy has to compete with the immediate solution offered by a
morning's visit to an abortion clinic. On the simple, perceptual plane,
with imagination and thinking curtailed, the speed, ease, and privacy of
abortion, combined with the small size of the embryo, tend to make
early abortions seem less morally serious—even though speed, size, technical ease, and the private nature of an act have no moral standing.

As the most recent immigrants from nonpersonhood, feminists have
traditionally fought for justice for themselves and the world. Women
rally to feminism as a new and better way to live. Rejecting male aggres-

sion and destruction, feminists seek alternative, peaceful, ecologically sensitive means to resolve conflicts while respecting human potentiality. It is a chilling inconsistency to see prochoice feminists demanding continued access to assembly-line, technological methods of fetal killing— the vacuum aspirator, prostaglandins, and dilation and evacuation. It is a betrayal of feminism, which has built the struggle for justice on the bedrock of women's empathy. After all, "maternal thinking" receives its name from a mother's unconditional acceptance and nurture of dependent, immature life. It is difficult to develop concern for women, children, the poor and the dispossessed—and to care about peace—and at the same time ignore fetal life.

   2. *From the necessity of autonomy and choice in personal responsibility to an expanded sense of responsibility.* A distorted idea of morality over-emphasizes individual autonomy and active choice. Morality has often been viewed too exclusively as a matter of human agency and decisive action. In moral behavior persons must explicitly choose and aggressively exert their wills to intervene in the natural and social environments. The human will dominates the body, overcomes the given, breaks out of the material limits of nature. Thus if one does not choose to be pregnant or cannot rear a child, who must be given up for adoption, then better to abort the pregnancy. Willing, planning, choosing one's moral commitments through the contracting of one's individual resources becomes the premier model of moral responsibility.

   But morality also consists of the good and worthy acceptance of the unexpected events that life presents. Responsiveness and response-ability to things unchosen are also instances of the highest human moral capacity. Morality is not confined to contracted agreements of isolated individuals. Yes, one is obligated by explicit contracts freely initiated, but human beings are also obligated by implicit compacts and involuntary relationships in which persons simply find themselves. To be embedded in a family, a neighborhood, a social system, brings moral obligations which were never entered into with informed consent.

   Parent–child relationships are one instance of implicit moral obligations arising by virtue of our being part of the interdependent human community. A woman, involuntarily pregnant, has a moral obligation to the now-existing dependent fetus whether she explicitly consented to its existence or not. No prolife feminist would dispute the forceful observations of prochoice feminists about the extreme difficulties that bearing an unwanted child in our society can entail. But the stronger force of the fetal claim presses a woman to accept these burdens; the fetus possesses rights arising from its extreme need and the interdependency and unity of humankind. The woman's moral obligation arises both from her status as a human being embedded in the interdependent human community and her unique lifegiving female reproductive power. To

follow the prochoice feminist ideology of insistent individualistic autonomy and control is to betray a fundamental basis of the moral life.

*3. From the moral claim of the contingent value of fetal life to the moral claim
for the intrinsic value of human life.* The feminist prochoice position which
claims that the value of the fetus is contingent upon the pregnant
woman's bestowal—or willed, conscious "construction"—of human-
hood is seriously flawed. The inadequacies of this position flow from the
erroneous premises (1) that human value and rights can be granted by
individual will; (2) that the individual woman's consciousness can exist
and operate in an *a priori* isolated fashion; and (3) that "mere" biological, genetic human life has little meaning. Prolife feminism takes a very
different stance toward life and nature.

Human life from the beginning to the end of development *has* intrinsic value, which does not depend on meeting the selective criteria or
tests set up by powerful others. A fundamental humanist assumption is
at stake here. Either we are going to value embodied human life and humanity as a good thing, or take some variant of the nihilist position that
assumes human life is just one more random occurrence in the universe
such that each instance of human life must explicitly be justified to prove
itself worthy to continue. When faced with a new life, or an involuntary
pregnancy, there is a world of difference in whether one first asks, "Why
continue?" or "Why not?" Where is the burden of proof going to rest?
The concept of "compulsory pregnancy" is as distorted as labeling life
"compulsory aging."

In a sound moral tradition, human rights arise from human needs,
and it is the very nature of a right, or valid claim upon another, that it
cannot be denied, conditionally delayed, or rescinded by more powerful
others at their behest. It seems fallacious to hold that in the case of the
fetus it is the pregnant woman alone who gives or removes its right to life
and human status solely through her subjective conscious investment or
"humanization." Surely no pregnant woman (or any other individual
member of the species) has created her own human nature by an indi-
vidually willed act of consciousness, nor for that matter been able to
guarantee her own human rights. An individual woman and the unique
individual embryonic life within her can only exist because of their participation in the genetic inheritance of the human species as a whole. Biological life should never be discounted. Membership in the species, or
collective human family, is the basis for human solidarity, equality, and
natural human rights.

*4. The moral right of women to full social equality from a prolife feminist per-
spective.* Prolife feminists and prochoice feminists are totally agreed on
the moral right of women to the full social equality so far denied them.
The disagreement between them concerns the definition of the desired
goal and the best means to get there. Permissive abortion laws do not

bring women reproductive freedom, social equality, sexual fulfillment, or full personal development.

Pragmatic failures of a prochoice feminist position combined with a lack of moral vision are, in fact, causing disaffection among young women. Middle-aged prochoice feminists blamed the "big chill" on the general conservative backlash. But they should look rather to their own elitist acceptance of male models of sex and to the sad picture they present of women's lives. Pitting women against their own offspring is not only morally offensive, it is psychologically and politically destructive. Women will never climb to equality and social empowerment over mounds of dead fetuses, numbering now in the millions. As long as most women choose to bear children, they stand to gain from the same constellation of attitudes and institutions that will also protect the fetus in the woman's womb—and they stand to lose from the cultural assumptions that support permissive abortion. Despite temporary conflicts of interest, feminine and fetal liberation are ultimately one and the same cause.

Women's rights and liberation are pragmatically linked to fetal rights because to obtain true equality, women need (1) more social support and changes in the structure of society, and (2) increased self-confidence, self-expectations, and self-esteem. Society in general, and men in particular, have to provide women more support in rearing the next generation, or our devastating feminization of poverty will continue. But if a woman claims the right to decide by herself whether the fetus becomes a child or not, what does this do to paternal and communal responsibility? Why should men share responsibility for child support or child rearing if they cannot share in what is asserted to be the woman's sole decision? Furthermore, if explicit intentions and consciously accepted contracts are necessary for moral obligations, why should men be held responsible for what *they* do not voluntarily choose to happen? By prochoice reasoning, a man who does not want to have a child, or whose contraceptive fails, can be exempted from the responsibilities of fatherhood and child support. Traditionally, many men have been laggards in assuming parental responsibility and support for their children; ironically, ready abortion, often advocated as a response to male dereliction, legitimizes male irresponsibility and paves the way for even more male detachment and lack of commitment.

For that matter, why should the state provide a system of day care or child support, or require workplaces to accommodate women's maternity and the needs of child rearing? Permissive abortion, granted in the name of women's privacy and reproductive freedom, ratifies the view that pregnancies and children are a woman's private individual responsibility. More and more frequently, we hear some version of this old rationalization: if she refuses to get rid of it, it's her problem. A child becomes a product of the individual woman's freely chosen investment, a form of private property resulting from her own cost-benefit calculation. The larger community is relieved of moral responsibility.

With legal abortion freely available, a clear cultural message is given: conception and pregnancy are no longer serious moral matters. With abortion as an acceptable alternative, contraception is not as responsibly used; women take risks, often at the urging of male sexual partners. Repeat abortions increase, with all their psychological and medical repercussions. With more abortion there is more abortion. Behavior shapes thought as well as the other way round. One tends to justify morally what one has done; what becomes commonplace and institutionalized seems harmless. Habituation is a powerful psychological force. Psychologically it is also true that whatever is avoided becomes more threatening; in phobias it is the retreat from anxiety-producing events which reinforces future avoidance. Women begin to see themselves as too weak to cope with involuntary pregnancies. Finally, through the potency of social pressure and the force of inertia, it becomes more and more difficult, in fact almost unthinkable, *not* to use abortion to solve problem pregnancies. Abortion becomes no longer a choice but a "necessity."

But "necessity," beyond the organic failure and death of the body, is a dynamic social construction open to interpretation. The thrust of present feminist prochoice arguments can only increase the justifiable indications for "necessary" abortion; every unwanted fetal handicap becomes more and more unacceptable. Repeatedly assured that in the name of reproductive freedom, women have a right to specify which pregnancies and which children they will accept, women justify sex selection, and abort unwanted females. Female infanticide, after all, is probably as old a custom as the human species possesses. Indeed, all kinds of selection of the fit and the favored for the good of the family and the tribe have always existed. Selective extinction is no new program.

There are far better goals for feminists to pursue. Prolife feminists seek to expand and deepen the more communitarian, maternal elements of feminism—and move society from its male-dominated course. First and foremost, women have to insist upon a different, woman-centered approach to sex and reproduction. While Margaret Mead stressed the "womb envy" of males in other societies, it has been more or less repressed in our own. In our male-dominated world, what men don't do, doesn't count. Pregnancy, childbirth, and nursing have been characterized as passive, debilitating, animallike. The disease model of pregnancy and birth has been entrenched. This female disease or impairment, with its attendant "female troubles," naturally handicaps women in the "real" world of hunting, war, and the corporate fast track. Many prochoice feminists, deliberately childless, adopt the male perspective when they cite the "basic injustice that women have to bear the babies," instead of seeing the injustice in the fact that men cannot. Women's biologically unique capacity and privilege has been denied, despised, and suppressed under male domination; unfortunately, many women have fallen for the phallic fallacy.

Childbirth often appears in prochoice literature as a painful, traumatic, life-threatening experience. Yet giving birth is accurately seen as an arduous but normal exercise of life-giving power, a violent and ecstatic peak experience, which men can never know. Ironically, some prochoice men and women think and talk of pregnancy and childbirth with the same repugnance that ancient ascetics displayed toward orgasms and sexual intercourse. The similarity may not be accidental. The obstetrician Niles Newton, herself a mother, has written of the extended threefold sexuality of women, who can experience orgasm, birth, and nursing as passionate pleasure-giving experiences. All of these are involuntary processes of the female body. Only orgasm, which males share, has been glorified as an involuntary function that is nature's great gift; the involuntary feminine processes of childbirth and nursing have been seen as bondage to biology.

Fully accepting our bodies as ourselves, what should women want? I think women will only flourish when there is a feminization of sexuality, very different from the current cultural trend toward masculinizing female sexuality. Women can never have the self-confidence and self-esteem they need to achieve feminist goals in society until a more holistic, feminine model of sexuality becomes the dominant cultural ethos. To say this affirms the view that men and women differ in the domain of sexual functioning, although they are more alike than different in other personality characteristics and competencies. For those of us committed to achieving sexual equality in the culture, it may be hard to accept the fact that sexual differences make it imperative to talk of distinct male and female models of sexuality. But if one wants to change sexual roles, one has to recognize preexisting conditions. A great deal of evidence is accumulating which points to biological pressures for different male and female sexual functioning.

Males always and everywhere have been more physically aggressive and more likely to fuse sexuality with aggression and dominance. Females may be more variable in their sexuality, but since Masters and Johnson, we know that women have a greater capacity than men for repeated orgasm and a more tenuous path to arousal and orgasmic release. Most obviously, women also have a far greater sociobiological investment in the act of human reproduction. On the whole, women as compared to men possess a sexuality which is more complex, more intense, more extended in time, involving higher investment, risks, and psychosocial involvement.

* * *

Considering the differences in sexual functioning, it is not surprising that men and women in the same culture have often constructed different sexual ideals. In Western culture, since the nineteenth century at least, most women have espoused a version of sexual functioning in which sex acts are embedded within deep emotional bonds and secure long-term commitments. Within these committed "pair bonds" males assume parental obligations. In the idealized Victorian version of the Christian sexual ethic, culturally endorsed and maintained by women, the double standard was not countenanced. Men and women did not need to marry to be whole persons, but if they did engage in sexual functioning, they were to be equally chaste, faithful, responsible, loving, and parentally concerned. Many of the most influential women in the nineteenth-century women's movement preached and lived this sexual ethic, often by the side of exemplary feminist men. While the ideal has never been universally obtained, a culturally dominant demand for monogamy, self-control, and emotionally bonded and committed sex works well for women in every stage of their sexual life cycles. When love, chastity, fidelity, and commitment for better or worse are the ascendant cultural prerequisites for sexual functioning, young girls and women expect protection from rape and seduction, adult women justifiably demand male support in child rearing, and older women are more protected from abandonment as their biological attractions wane.

Of course, these feminine sexual ideals always coexisted in competition with another view. A more male-oriented model of erotic or amative sexuality endorses sexual permissiveness without long-term commitment or reproductive focus. Erotic sexuality emphasizes pleasure, play, passion, individual self-expression, and romantic games of courtship and conquest. It is assumed that a variety of partners and sexual experiences are necessary to stimulate romantic passion. This erotic model of the sexual life has often worked satisfactorily for men, both heterosexual and gay, and for certain cultural elites. But for the average woman, it is quite destructive. Women can only play the erotic game successfully when, like the "*Cosmopolitan* woman," they are young, physically attractive, economically powerful, and fulfilled enough in a career to be willing to sacrifice family life. Abortion is also required. As our society increasingly endorses this male-oriented, permissive view of sexuality, it is all too ready to give women abortion on demand. Abortion helps a woman's body be more like a man's. It has been observed that *Roe v. Wade* removed the last defense women possessed against male sexual demands.

Unfortunately, the modern feminist movement made a mistaken move at a critical juncture. Rightly rebelling against patriarchy, unequal education, restricted work opportunities, and women's downtrodden political status, feminists also rejected the nineteenth-century feminine sexual ethic. Amative, erotic, permissive sexuality (along with abortion rights) became symbolically identified with other struggles for social equality in education, work, and politics. This feminist mistake also turned off many potential recruits among women who could not deny the positive dimensions of their own traditional feminine roles, nor their allegiance to the older feminine sexual ethic of love and fidelity.

An ironic situation then arose in which many prochoice feminists preach their own double standard. In the world of work and career, women are urged to grow up, to display mature self-discipline and self-control; they are told to persevere in long-term commitments, to cope with unexpected obstacles by learning to tough out the inevitable sufferings and setbacks entailed in life and work. But this mature ethic of commitment and self-discipline, recommended as the only way to progress in the world of work and personal achievement, is discounted in the domain of sexuality.

In prochoice feminism, a permissive, erotic view of sexuality is assumed to be the only option. Sexual intercourse with a variety of partners is seen as "inevitable" from a young age and as a positive growth experience to be managed by access to contraception and abortion. Unfortunately, the pervasive cultural conviction that adolescents, or their elders, cannot exercise sexual self-control undermines the responsible use of contraception. When a pregnancy occurs, the first abortion is viewed in some prochoice circles as a *rite de passage*. Responsibly choosing an abortion supposedly ensures that a young woman will take charge of her own life, make her own decisions, and carefully practice contraception. But the social dynamics of a permissive, erotic model of sexuality, coupled with permissive laws, work toward repeat abortions. Instead of being empowered by their abortion choices, young women having abortions are confronting the debilitating reality of *not* bringing a baby into the world; *not* being able to count on a committed male partner; *not* accounting oneself strong enough, or the master of enough resources, to avoid killing the fetus. Young women are hardly going to develop the self-esteem, self-discipline, and self-confidence necessary to confront a male-dominated society through abortion.

The male-oriented sexual orientation has been harmful to women and children. It has helped bring us epidemics of venereal disease, infertility, pornography, sexual abuse, adolescent pregnancy, divorce, displaced older women, and abortion. Will these signals of something amiss stimulate prochoice feminists to rethink what kind of sex ideal really serves women's best interests? While the erotic model cannot encompass commitment, the committed model can—happily—encompass and encourage romance, passion, and playfulness. In fact, within the security of long-term commitments, women may be more likely to experience sexual pleasure and fulfillment.

* * *

The prolife feminist position is not a return to the old feminine mystique. That espousal of "the eternal feminine" erred by viewing sexuality as so sacred that it cannot be humanly shaped at all. Woman's *whole* nature was supposed to be opposite to man's, necessitating complementary and radically different social roles. Followed to its logical conclusion, such a view presumes that reproductive and sexual experience is necessary for human fulfillment. But as the early feminists insisted, no woman has to marry or engage in sexual intercourse to be fulfilled, nor does a woman have to give birth and raise children to be complete, nor must she stay home and function as an earth mother. But female sexuality does need to be deeply respected as a unique potential and trust. Since most contraceptives and sterilization procedures really do involve only the woman's body rather than destroying new life, they can be an acceptable and responsible moral option.

With sterilization available to accelerate the inevitable natural ending of fertility and childbearing, a woman confronts only a limited number of years in which she exercises her reproductive trust and may have to respond to an unplanned pregnancy. Responsible use of contraception can lower the probabilities even more. Yet abortion is not decreasing. The reason is the current permissive attitude embodied in the law, not the "hard cases" which constitute 3 percent of today's abortions. Since attitudes, the law, and behavior interact, prolife feminists conclude that unless there is an enforced limitation of abortion, which currently confirms the sexual and social status quo, alternatives will never be developed. For women to get what they need in order to combine childbearing, education, and careers, society has to recognize that female bodies come with wombs. Women and their reproductive power, and the children women have, must be supported in new ways. Another and different round of feminist consciousness raising is needed in which all of women's potential is accorded respect. This time, instead of humbly buying entrée by conforming to male lifestyles, women will demand that society accommodate itself to them.

New feminist efforts to rethink the meaning of sexuality, femininity, and reproduction are all the more vital as new techniques for artificial reproduction, surrogate motherhood, and the like present a whole new set of dilemmas. In the long run, the very long run, the abortion debate may be merely the opening round in a series of far-reaching struggles over the role of human sexuality and the ethics of reproduction. Significant changes in the culture, both positive and negative in outcome, may begin as local storms of controversy. We may be at one of those vaguely realized thresholds when we had best come to full attention. What kind of people are we going to be? Prolife feminists pursue a vision for their sisters, daughters, and granddaughters. Will their great-granddaughters be grateful?

Chapter 14

ABORTION: IS A WOMAN A PERSON?

Ellen Willis

If propaganda is as central to politics as I think, the opponents of legal
abortion have been winning a psychological victory as important as
their tangible gains. Two years ago, abortion was almost always discussed
in feminist terms—as a political issue affecting the condition of women.
Since then, the grounds of the debate have shifted drastically; more and
more, the right-to-life movement has succeeded in getting the public
and the media to see abortion as an abstract moral issue having solely to
do with the rights of fetuses. Though every poll shows that most Ameri-
cans favor legal abortion, it is evident that many are confused and dis-
armed, if not convinced, by the antiabortionists' absolutist fervor. No
one likes to be accused of advocating murder. Yet the "pro-life" position
is based on a crucial fallacy—that the question of fetal rights can be isolated from the question of women's rights.

Recently, Garry Wills wrote a piece suggesting that liberals who defended the snail-darter's right to life and opposed the killing in Vietnam
should condemn abortion as murder. I found this notion breathtaking
in its illogic. Environmentalists were protesting not the "murder" of individual snail-darters but the practice of wiping out entire species of organisms to gain a short-term economic benefit; most people who

Ellen Willis, "Abortion: Is a Woman a Person?" from *Beginning to See the Light,* © 1992 by
Wesleyan University Press. Reprinted by permission of Wesleyan University Press and Ellen
Willis. This essay began as two columns written for *The Village Voice* (March and April 1979);
they were first combined as "Abortion: Is a Woman a Person?" in *Beginning to See the Light*
(New York: Knopf, 1981), pp. 205–11.

opposed our involvement in Vietnam did so because they believed the United States was waging an aggressive, unjust, and/or futile war. There was no inconsistency in holding such positions and defending abortion on the grounds that women's welfare should take precedence over fetal life. To claim that three very different issues, each with its own complicated social and political context, all came down to a simple matter of preserving life was to say that all killing was alike and equally indefensible regardless of circumstance. (Why, I wondered, had Wills left out the destruction of hapless bacteria by penicillin?) But aside from the general mushiness of the argument, I was struck by one peculiar fact: Wills had written an entire article about abortion without mentioning women, feminism, sex, or pregnancy.

Since the feminist argument for abortion rights still carries a good deal of moral and political weight, part of the antiabortionists' strategy has been to make an end run around it. Although the mainstream of the right-to-life movement is openly opposed to women's liberation, it has chosen to make its stand on the abstract "pro-life" argument. That emphasis has been reinforced by the movement's tiny left wing, which opposes abortion on pacifist grounds and includes women who call themselves "feminists for life." A minority among pacifists as well as right-to-lifers, this group nevertheless serves the crucial function of making opposition to abortion respectable among liberals, leftists, and moderates disinclined to sympathize with a right-wing crusade. Unlike most right-to-lifers, who are vulnerable to charges that their reverence for life does not apply to convicted criminals or Vietnamese peasants, antiabortion leftists are in a position to appeal to social conscience—to make analogies, however facile, between abortion and napalm. They disclaim any opposition to women's rights, insisting rather that the end cannot justify the means—murder is murder.

Well, isn't there a genuine moral issue here? If abortion *is* murder, how can a woman have the right to it? Feminists are often accused of evading this question, but in fact an evasion is built into the question itself. Most people understand "Is abortion murder?" to mean "Is the fetus a person?" But fetal personhood is ultimately as inarguable as the existence of God; either you believe in it or you don't. Putting the debate on this plane inevitably leads to the nonconclusion that it is a matter of one person's conscience against another's. From there, the discussion generally moves on to broader issues: whether laws defining the fetus as a person violate the separation of church and state; or conversely, whether people who believe an act is murder have not only the right but the obligation to prevent it. Unfortunately, amid all this lofty philosophizing, the concrete, human reality of the pregnant woman's dilemma gets lost, and with it an essential ingredient of the moral question.

Murder, as commonly defined, is killing that is unjustified, willful, and malicious. Most people would agree, for example, that killing in defense of one's life or safety is not murder. And most would accept a concept of self-defense that includes the right to fight a defensive war or revolution in behalf of one's independence or freedom from oppression. Even pacifists make moral distinctions between defensive violence, however deplorable, and murder; no thoughtful pacifist would equate Hitler's murder of the Jews with the Warsaw Ghetto rebels' killing of Nazi troops. The point is that it's impossible to judge whether an act is murder simply by looking at the act, without considering its context. Which is to say that it makes no sense to discuss whether abortion is murder without considering why women have abortions and what it means to force women to bear children they don't want.

We live in a society that defines child rearing as the mother's job; a society in which most women are denied access to work that pays enough to support a family, child-care facilities they can afford, or any relief from the constant, daily burdens of motherhood; a society that forces mothers into dependence on marriage or welfare and often into permanent poverty; a society that is actively hostile to women's ambitions for a better life. Under these conditions the unwillingly pregnant woman faces a terrifying loss of control over her fate. Even if she chooses to give up the baby, unwanted pregnancy is in itself a serious trauma. There is no way a pregnant woman can passively let the fetus live; she must create and nurture it with her own body, in a symbiosis that is often difficult, sometimes dangerous, always uniquely intimate. However gratifying pregnancy may be to a woman who desires it, for the unwilling it is literally an invasion—the closest analogy is to the difference between lovemaking and rape. Nor is there such a thing as foolproof contraception. Clearly, abortion is by normal standards an act of self-defense.

Whenever I make this case to a right-to-lifer, the exchange that follows is always substantially the same:

RTL: If a woman chooses to have sex, she should be willing to take the consequences. We must all be responsible for our actions.

EW: Men have sex, without having to "take the consequences."

RTL: You can't help that—it's biology.

EW: You don't think a woman has as much right as a man to enjoy sex? Without living in fear that one slip will transform her life?

RTL: She has no right to selfish pleasure at the expense of the unborn.

It would seem, then, that the nitty-gritty issue in the abortion debate is not life but sex. If the fetus is sacrosanct, it follows that women must be continually vulnerable to the invasion of their bodies and loss of their freedom and independence—unless they are willing to resort to the only perfectly reliable contraceptive, abstinence. This is precisely the "solution" right-to-lifers suggest, usually with a touch of glee; as Representative Elwood Rudd once put it, "If a woman has a right to control her own body, let her exercise control before she gets pregnant." A common ploy is to compare fucking to overeating or overdrinking, the idea being that pregnancy is a just punishment, like obesity or cirrhosis.

In 1979 it is depressing to have to insist that sex is not an unnecessary, morally dubious self-indulgence but a basic human need, no less for women than for men. Of course, for heterosexual women giving up sex also means doing without the love and companionship of a mate. (Presumably, married women who have had all the children they want are supposed to divorce their husbands or convince them that celibacy is the only moral alternative.) "Freedom" bought at such a cost is hardly freedom at all and certainly not equality—no one tells men that if they aspire to some measure of control over their lives, they are welcome to neuter themselves and become social isolates. The don't-have-sex argument is really another version of the familiar antifeminist dictum that autonomy and femaleness—that is, female sexuality—are incompatible; if you choose the first, you lose the second. But to pose this choice is not only inhumane; it is as deeply disingenuous as "Let them eat cake." No one, least of all the anti-abortion movement, expects or wants significant numbers of women to give up sex and marriage. Nor are most right-to-lifers willing to allow abortion for rape victims. When all the cant about "responsibility" is stripped away, what the right-to-life position comes down to is, if the effect of prohibiting abortion is to keep women slaves to their biology, so be it.

In their zeal to preserve fetal life at all costs, antiabortionists are ready to grant fetuses more legal protection than people. If a man attacks me and I kill him, I can plead self-defense without having to prove that I was in danger of being killed rather than injured, raped, or kidnapped. But in the annual congressional battle over what if any exceptions to make to the Medicaid abortion ban, the House of Representatives has bitterly opposed the funding of abortions for any reason but to save the pregnant woman's life. Some right-to-lifers argue that even the danger of death does not justify abortion; others have suggested "safeguards" like requiring two or more doctors to certify that the woman's life is at least 50 percent threatened. Antiabortionists are forever worrying that any exception to a total ban on abortion will be used as a "loophole": better that any number of women should ruin their health or even die than that one woman should get away with not having a child "merely" because she doesn't want one. Clearly this mentality does not reflect equal concern for all life. Rather, antiabortionists value the lives of fetuses above the lives and welfare of women, because at bottom they do not concede women the right to an active human existence that transcends their reproductive function. Years ago, in an interview with Paul Krassner in *The Realist,* Ken Kesey declared himself against abortion. When Krassner asked if his objection applied to victims of rape, Kesey replied—I may not be remembering the exact words, but I will never forget the substance—"Just because another man planted the seed, that's no reason to destroy the crop."[1] To this day I have not heard a more eloquent or chilling metaphor for the essential premise of the right-to-life movement: that a woman's excuse for being is her womb. It is an outrageous irony that antiabortionists are managing to pass off this profoundly immoral idea as a noble moral cause.

The conservatives who dominate the right-to-life movement have no real problem with the antifeminism inherent in their stand; their evasion of the issue is a matter of public relations. But the politics of antiabortion leftists are a study in self-contradiction: in attacking what they see as the violence of abortion, they condone and encourage violence against women. Forced childbearing does violence to a woman's body and spirit, and it contributes to other kinds of violence: deaths from illegal abortion; the systematic oppression of mothers and women in general; the poverty, neglect, and battering of unwanted children; sterilization abuse.

Radicals supposedly believe in attacking a problem at its roots. Yet surely it is obvious that restrictive laws do not keep women from seeking abortions; they just create an illicit, dangerous industry. The only way to drastically reduce the number of abortions is to invent safer, more reliable contraceptives, ensure universal access to all birth control methods, eliminate sexual ignorance and guilt, and change the social and economic conditions that make motherhood a trap. Anyone who is truly committed to fostering life should be fighting for women's liberation instead of harassing and disrupting abortion clinics (hardly a nonviolent tactic, since it threatens the safety of patients). The "feminists for life" do talk a lot about ending the oppression that drives so many women to abortion; in practice, however, they are devoting all their energy to increasing it.

Despite its numerical insignificance, the antiabortion left epitomizes the hypocrisy of the right-to-life crusade. Its need to wrap misogyny in the rhetoric of social conscience and even feminism is actually a perverse tribute to the women's movement; it is no longer acceptable to declare openly that women deserve to suffer for the sin of Eve. I suppose that's progress—not that it does the victims of the Hyde Amendment much good.

Note

1. A reader later sent me a copy of the Kesey interview. The correct quotation is "You don't plow under the corn because the seed was planted with a neighbor's shovel."

PART 4

KANT AND SEX

Chapter 15

DUTIES TOWARDS THE BODY IN RESPECT OF SEXUAL IMPULSE

Immanuel Kant

Amongst our inclinations there is one which is directed towards other human beings. They themselves, and not their work and services, are its Objects of enjoyment. It is true that man has no inclination to enjoy the flesh of another—except, perhaps, in the vengeance of war, and then it is hardly a desire—but none the less there does exist an inclination which we may call an appetite for enjoying another human being. We refer to sexual impulse. Man can, of course, use another human being as an instrument for his service; he can use his hands, his feet, and even all his powers; he can use him for his own purposes with the other's consent. But there is no way in which a human being can be made an Object of indulgence for another except through sexual impulse. This is in the nature of a sense, which we can call the sixth sense; it is an appetite for another human being. We say that a man loves someone when he has an inclination towards another person. If by this love we mean true human love, then it admits of no distinction between types of persons, or between young and old. But a love that springs merely from sexual impulse cannot be love at all, but only appetite. Human love is good-will, affection, promoting the happiness of others and finding joy in their happiness. But it is clear that, when a person loves another purely from

Reprinted, from Immanual Kant, *Lectures on Ethics,* trans. Louis Infield (Methuen, 1930), pp. 162–71, with the permission of Taylor and Francis Books, Ltd., and Routledge.

sexual desire, none of these factors enter into the love. Far from there being any concern for the happiness of the loved one, the lover, in order to satisfy his desire and still his appetite, may even plunge the loved one into the depths of misery. Sexual love makes of the loved person an Object of appetite; as soon as that appetite has been stilled, the person is cast aside as one casts away a lemon which has been sucked dry. Sexual love can, of course, be combined with human love and so carry with it the characteristics of the latter, but taken by itself and for itself, it is nothing more than appetite. Taken by itself it is a degradation of human nature; for as soon as a person becomes an Object of appetite for another, all motives of moral relationship cease to function, because as an Object of appetite for another a person becomes a thing and can be treated and used as such by every one. This is the only case in which a human being is designed by nature as the Object of another's enjoyment. Sexual desire is at the root of it; and that is why we are ashamed of it, and why all strict moralists, and those who had pretensions to be regarded as saints, sought to suppress and extirpate it. It is true that without it a man would be incomplete; he would rightly believe that he lacked the necessary organs, and this would make him imperfect as a human being; none the less men made pretence on this question and sought to suppress these inclinations because they degraded mankind.

Because sexuality is not an inclination which one human being has for another as such, but is an inclination for the sex of another, it is a principle of the degradation of human nature, in that it gives rise to the preference of one sex to the other, and to the dishonouring of that sex through the satisfaction of desire. The desire which a man has for a woman is not directed towards her because she is a human being, but because she is a woman; that she is a human being is of no concern to the man; only her sex is the object of his desires. Human nature is thus subordinated. Hence it comes that all men and women do their best to make not their human nature but their sex more alluring and direct their activities and lusts entirely towards sex. Human nature is thereby sacrificed to sex. If then a man wishes to satisfy his desire, and a woman hers, they stimulate each other's desire; their inclinations meet, but their object is not human nature but sex, and each of them dishonours the human nature of the other. They make of humanity an instrument for the satisfaction of their lusts and inclinations, and dishonour it by placing it on a level with animal nature. Sexuality, therefore, exposes mankind to the danger of equality with the beasts. But as man has this desire from nature, the question arises how far he can properly make use of it without injury to his manhood. How far may persons allow one of the opposite sex to satisfy his or her desire upon them? Can they sell themselves, or let themselves out on hire, or by some other contract allow use to be made of their sexual faculties? Philosophers generally point out the harm done by this inclination and the ruin it brings to the body or to the commonwealth, and they believe that, except for the harm it does, there would be nothing contemptible in such conduct in itself. But if this were so, and if giving vent to this desire was not in itself abominable and did not involve immorality, then any one who could avoid being harmed by them could make whatever use he wanted of his sexual propensities. For the prohibitions of prudence are never unconditional; and the conduct would in itself be unobjectionable, and would only be harmful under certain conditions. But in point of fact, there is in the conduct itself something which is contemptible and contrary to the dictates of morality. It follows, therefore, that there must be certain conditions under which alone the use of the *facultates sexuales* would be in keeping with morality. There must be a basis for restraining our freedom in the use we make of our inclinations so that they conform to the principles of morality. We shall endeavour to discover these conditions and this basis. Man cannot dispose over himself because he is not a thing; he is not his own property; to say that he is would be self-contradictory; for in so far as he is a person he is a Subject in whom the ownership of things can be vested, and if he were his own property, he would be a thing over which he could have ownership. But a person cannot be a property and so cannot be a thing which can be owned, for it is impossible to be a person and a thing, the proprietor and the property.

Accordingly, a man is not at his own disposal. He is not entitled to sell a limb, not even one of his teeth. But to allow one's person for profit to be used by another for the satisfaction of sexual desire, to make of oneself an Object of demand, is to dispose over oneself as over a thing and to make of oneself a thing on which another satisfies his appetite, just as he satisfies his hunger upon a steak. But since the inclination is directed towards one's sex and not towards one's humanity, it is clear that one thus partially sacrifices one's humanity and thereby runs a moral risk. Human beings are, therefore, not entitled to offer themselves, for profit, as things for the use of others in the satisfaction of their sexual propensities. In so doing they would run the risk of having their person used by all and sundry as an instrument for the satisfaction of inclination. This way of satisfying sexuality is *vaga libido,* in which one satisfies the inclinations of others for gain. It is possible for either sex. To let one's person out on hire and to surrender it to another for the satisfaction of his sexual desire in return for money is the depth of infamy. The underlying moral principle is that man is not his own property and cannot do with his body what he will. The body is part of the self; in its togetherness with the self it constitutes the person; a man cannot make of his person a thing, and this is exactly what happens in *vaga libido.* This manner of satisfying sexual desire is, therefore, not permitted by the rules of morality. But what of the second method, namely *concubinatus?* Is this also inad-

missible? In this case both persons satisfy their desire mutually and there
is no idea of gain, but they serve each other only for the satisfaction of
sexuality. There appears to be nothing unsuitable in this arrangement,
but there is nevertheless one consideration which rules it out. Concubinage consists in one person surrendering to another only for the satisfaction of their sexual desire whilst retaining freedom and rights in
other personal respects affecting welfare and happiness. But the person
who so surrenders is used as a thing; the desire is still directed only towards sex and not towards the person as a human being. But it is obvious
that to surrender part of oneself is to surrender the whole, because a human being is a unity. It is not possible to have the disposal of a part only
of a person without having at the same time a right of disposal over the
whole person, for each part of a person is integrally bound up with the
whole. But concubinage does not give me a right of disposal over the
whole person but only over a part, namely the *organa sexualia*. It presupposes a contract. This contract deals only with the enjoyment of a part of
the person and not with the entire circumstances of the person. Concubinage is certainly a contract, but it is one-sided; the rights of the two parties are not equal. But if in concubinage I enjoy a part of a person, I
thereby enjoy the whole person; yet by the terms of the arrangement I
have not the rights over the whole person, but only over a part; I, therefore, make the person into a thing. For that reason this method of satisfying sexual desire is also not permitted by the rules of morality. The sole
condition on which we are free to make use of our sexual desire depends
upon the right to dispose over the person as a whole—over the welfare
and happiness and generally over all the circumstances of that person. If
I have the right over the whole person, I have also the right over the part
and so I have the right to use that person's *organa sexualia* for the satisfaction of sexual desire. But how am I to obtain these rights over the
whole person? Only by giving that person the same rights over the whole
of myself. This happens only in marriage. Matrimony is an agreement
between two persons by which they grant each other equal reciprocal
rights, each of them undertaking to surrender the whole of their person
to the other with a complete right of disposal over it. We can now apprehend by reason how a *commercium sexuale* is possible without degrading humanity and breaking the moral laws. Matrimony is the only
condition in which use can be made of one's sexuality. If one devotes
one's person to another, one devotes not only sex but the whole person;
the two cannot be separated. If, then, one yields one's person, body and
soul, for good and ill and in every respect, so that the other has complete
rights over it, and if the other does not similarly yield himself in return
and does not extend in return the same rights and privileges, the
arrangement is one-sided. But if I yield myself completely to another and
obtain the person of the other in return, I win myself back; I have given

myself up as the property of another, but in turn I take that other as my property, and so win myself back again in winning the person whose property I have become. In this way the two persons become a unity of will. Whatever good or ill, joy or sorrow befall either of them, the other will share in it. Thus sexuality leads to a union of human beings, and in that union alone its exercise is possible. This condition of the use of sexuality, which is only fulfilled in marriage, is a moral condition. But let us pursue this aspect further and examine the case of a man who takes two wives. In such a case each wife would have but half a man, although she would be giving herself wholly and ought in consequence to be entitled to the whole man. To sum up: *vaga libido* is ruled out on moral grounds; the same applies to concubinage; there only remains matrimony, and in matrimony polygamy is ruled out also for moral reasons; we, therefore, reach the conclusion that the only feasible arrangement is that of monogamous marriage. Only under that condition can I indulge my *facultas sexualis*. We cannot here pursue the subject further.

But one other question arises, that of incest. Incest consists in intercourse between the sexes in a form which, by reason of consanguinity, must be ruled out; but are there moral grounds on which incest, in all forms of sexual intercourse, must be ruled out? They are grounds which apply conditionally, except in one case, in which they have absolute validity. The sole case in which the moral grounds against incest apply absolutely is that of intercourse between parents and children. Between parents and children there must be a respect which should continue throughout life, and this rules out of court any question of equality. Moreover, in sexual intercourse each person submits to the other in the highest degree, whereas between parents and their children subjection is one-sided; the children must admit to the parents only; there can, therefore, be no equal union. This is the only case in which incest is absolutely forbidden by nature. In other cases incest forbids itself, but is not incest in the order of nature. The state prohibits incest, but at the beginning there must have been intermarriage between brothers and sisters. At the same time nature has implanted in our breasts a natural opposition to incest. She intended us to combine with other races and so to prevent too great a sameness in one society. Too close a connection, too intimate an acquaintance produces sexual indifference and repugnance. But this propensity must be restrained by modesty; otherwise it becomes commonplace, reduces the object of the desire to the commonplace and results in indifference. Sexual desire is very fastidious; nature has given it strength, but it must be restrained by modesty. It is on that account that savages, who go about stark-naked, are cold towards each other; for that reason, too, a person whom we have known from youth evokes no desire within us, but a strange person attracts us much more strongly. Thus nature has herself provided restraints upon any desire between brother and sister.

Crimina Carnis

Crimina carnis are contrary to self-regarding duty because they are against the ends of humanity. They consist in abuse of one's sexuality. Every form of sexual indulgence, except in marriage, is a misuse of sexuality, and so a *crimen carnis*. All *crimina carnis* are either *secundum naturam* or *contra naturam*. *Crimina carnis secundum naturam* are contrary to sound reason; *crimina carnis contra naturam* are contrary to our animal nature. Among the former we reckon *vaga libido*, which is the opposite of matrimony and of which there are two kinds: *scortatio* and *concubinatus*. *Concubinatus* is indeed a *pactum*, but a *pactum inaequale*, in which the rights are not reciprocal. In this pact the woman surrenders her sex completely to the man, but the man does not completely surrender his sex to the woman. The second *crimen carnis secundum naturam* is *adulterium*. Adultery cannot take place except in marriage; it signifies a breach of marriage. Just as the engagement to marry is the most serious and the most inviolable engagement between two persons and binds them for life, so also is adultery the greatest breach of faith that there can be, because it is disloyalty to an engagement than which there can be none more important. For this reason adultery is cause for divorce. Another cause is incompatibility and inability to be at one, whereby unity and concord of will between the two persons is impossible. Next comes the question whether incest is incest *per se,* or whether it is by the civil law that it is made a *crimen carnis,* natural or unnatural. The question might be answered either by natural instinct or by reason. From the point of view of natural instinct incest is a *crimen carnis secundum naturam,* for it is after all a union of the sexes; it is not *contra naturam animalium,* because animals do not differentiate in this respect in their practices. But on the judgment of the understanding incest is *contra naturam.*

Uses of sexuality which are contrary to natural instinct and to animal nature are *crimina carnis contra naturam*. First amongst them we have onanism. This is abuse of the sexual faculty without any object, the exercise of the faculty in the complete absence of any object of sexuality. The practice is contrary to the ends of humanity and even opposed to animal nature. By it man sets aside his person and degrades himself below the level of animals. A second *crimen carnis contra naturam* is intercourse between *sexus homogenii,* in which the object of sexual impulse is a human being but there is homogeneity instead of heterogeneity of sex, as when a woman satisfies her desire on a woman, or a man on a man. This practice too is contrary to the ends of humanity; for the end of humanity in respect of sexuality is to preserve the species without debasing the person; but in this instance the species is not being preserved (as it can be by a *crimen carnis secundum naturam*), but the person is set aside, the self is degraded below the level of the animals, and humanity is dishonoured. The third *crimen carnis contra naturam* occurs when the object of the desire is in fact of the opposite sex but is not human. Such is sodomy, or intercourse with animals. This, too, is contrary to the ends of humanity and against our natural instinct. It degrades mankind below the level of animals, for no animal turns in this way from its own species. All *crimina carnis contra naturam* degrade human nature to a level below that of animal nature and make man unworthy of his humanity. He no longer deserves to be a person. From the point of view of duties towards himself such conduct is the most disgraceful and the most degrading of which man is capable. Suicide is the most dreadful, but it is not as dishonourable and base as the *crimina carnis contra naturam*. It is the most abominable conduct of which man can be guilty. So abominable are these *crimina carnis contra naturam* that they are unmentionable, for the very mention of them is nauseating, as is not the case with suicide. We all fight shy of mentioning these vices; teachers refrain from mentioning them, even when their intention is unobjectionable and they only wish to warn their charges against them. But as they are of frequent occurrence, we are in a dilemma: are we to name them in order that people should know and prevent their frequent occurrence, or are we to keep them dark in order that people should not learn of them and so not have the opportunity of transgressing? Frequent mention would familiarize people with them and the vices might as a result cease to disgust us and come to appear more tolerable. Hence our modesty in not referring to them. On the other hand, if we mention them only circumspectly and with disinclination, our aversion from them is still apparent. There is also another reason for our modesty. Each sex is ashamed of the vices of which its members are capable. Human beings feel, therefore, ashamed to mention those things of which it is shameful for humanity to be capable. These vices make us ashamed that we are human beings and, therefore, capable of them, for an animal is incapable of all such *crimina carnis contra naturam*.

Chapter 16

SEXUAL MORALITY AND THE CONCEPT OF USING ANOTHER PERSON

Thomas A. Mappes

The central tenet of *conventional* sexual morality is that nonmarital sex is immoral. A somewhat less restrictive sexual ethic holds that *sex without love* is immoral. If neither of these positions is philosophically defensible, and I would contend that neither is, it does not follow that there are no substantive moral restrictions on human sexual interaction. *Any* human interaction, including sexual interaction, may be judged morally objectionable to the extent that it transgresses a justified moral rule or principle. The way to construct a detailed account of sexual morality, it would seem, is simply to work out the implications of relevant moral rules or principles in the area of human sexual interaction.

As one important step in the direction of such an account, I will attempt to work out the implications of an especially relevant moral principle, the principle that it is wrong for one person to use another person. However ambiguous the expression "using another person" may seem to be, there is a determinate and clearly specifiable sense according to which using another person is morally objectionable. Once this morally significant sense of "using another person" is identified and explicated, the concept of using another person can play an important role in the articulation of a defensible account of sexual morality.

Reprinted with the permission of the author from *Social Ethics: Morality and Social Policy,* 3rd edition (McGraw-Hill, 1987), pp. 248–62, edited by Thomas A. Mappes and Jane S. Zembaty. © 1985, Thomas A. Mappes.

I. The Morally Significant Sense of "Using Another Person"

Historically, the concept of using another person is associated with the ethical system of Immanuel Kant. According to a fundamental Kantian principle, it is morally wrong for A to use B *merely as a means* (to achieve A's ends). Kant's principle does not rule out A using B as a means, only A using B *merely* as a means, that is, in a way incompatible with respect for B as a person. In the ordinary course of life, it is surely unavoidable (and morally unproblematic) that each of us in numerous ways uses others as a means to achieve our various ends. A college teacher uses students as a means to achieve his or her livelihood. A college student uses instructors as a means of gaining knowledge and skills. Such human interactions, presumably based on the voluntary participation of the respective parties, are quite compatible with the idea of respect for persons. But respect for persons entails that each of us recognize the rightful authority of other persons (as rational beings) to conduct their individual lives as they see fit. We may legitimately recruit others to participate in the satisfaction of our personal ends, but they are used merely as a means whenever we undermine the voluntary or informed character of their consent to interact with us in some desired way. A coerces B at knife point to hand over $200. A uses B merely as means. If A had requested of B a gift of $200, leaving B free to determine whether or not to make the gift, A would have proceeded in a manner compatible with respect for B as a person. C deceptively rolls back the odometer of a car and thereby manipulates D's decision to buy the car. C uses D merely as a means.

On the basis of these considerations, I would suggest that the morally significant sense of "using another person" is best understood by reference to the notion of *voluntary informed consent*. More specifically, A immorally uses B if and only if A intentionally acts in a way that violates the requirement that B's involvement with A's ends be based on B's voluntary informed consent. If this account is correct, using another person (in the morally significant sense) can arise in at least two important ways: via *coercion*, which is antithetical to voluntary consent, and via *deception*, which undermines the informed character of voluntary consent.

The notion of voluntary informed consent is very prominent in the literature of biomedical ethics and is systematically related to the much emphasized notion of (patient) autonomy. We find in the famous words of Supreme Court Justice Cardozo a ringing affirmation of patient autonomy. "Every human being of adult years and sound mind has a right to determine what shall be done with his own body." Because respect for individual autonomy is an essential part of the respect for persons, if medical professionals (and biomedical researchers) are to interact with their patients (and research subjects) in an acceptable way, they must respect individual autonomy. That is, they must respect the self-determination of the patient/subject, the individual's right to determine what shall be done with his or her body. This means that they must not act in a way that violates the requirement of voluntary informed consent. Medical procedures must not be performed without the consent of competent patients; research on human subjects must not be carried out without the consent of the subjects involved. Moreover, consent must be voluntary; coercion undermines individual autonomy. Consent must also be informed; lying or withholding relevant information undercuts rational decision making and thereby undermines individual autonomy.

To further illuminate the concept of using that has been proposed, I will consider in greater detail the matter of research involving human subjects. In the sphere of researcher-subject interaction, just as in the sphere of human sexual interaction, there is ample opportunity for immorally using another person. If a researcher is engaged in a study that involves human subjects, we may presume that the "end" of the researcher is the successful completion of the study. (The researcher may desire this particular end for any number of reasons: the speculative understanding it will provide, the technology it will make possible, the eventual benefit of humankind, increased status in the scientific community, a raise in pay, etc.) The work, let us presume, strictly requires the use (employment) of human research subjects. The researcher, however, immorally uses other people only if he or she intentionally acts in a way that violates the requirement that the participation of research subjects be based on their voluntary informed consent.

Let us assume that in a particular case participation as a research subject involves some rather significant risks. Accordingly, the researcher finds that potential subjects are reluctant to volunteer. At this point, if an unscrupulous researcher is willing to resort to the immoral using of other people (to achieve his or her own ends), two manifest options are available—deception and coercion. By way of deception, the researcher might choose to lie about the risks involved. For example, potential subjects could be explicitly told that there are no significant risks associated with research participation. On the other hand, the researcher could simply withhold a full disclosure of risks. Whether pumped full of false information or simply deprived of relevant information, the potential subject is intentionally deceived in such a way as to be led to a decision that furthers the researcher's ends. In manipulating the decision making process of the potential subject in this way, the researcher is guilty of immorally using another person.

To explain how an unscrupulous researcher might immorally use another person via coercion, it is helpful to distinguish two basic forms of coercion.[1] "Occurrent" coercion involves the use of physical force. "Dispositional" coercion involves the threat of harm. If I am forcibly thrown out of my office by an intruder, I am the victim of occurrent coercion. If, on the other hand, I leave my office because an intruder has threatened to shoot me if I do not leave, I am the victim of dispositional coercion. The victim of occurrence coercion literally has no choice in what happens. The victim of dispositional coercion, in contrast, does intentionally choose a certain course of action. However, one's choice, in the face of the threat of harm, is less than fully voluntary.

It is perhaps unlikely that even an unscrupulous researcher would resort to any very explicit measure of coercion. Deception, it seems, is less risky. Still, it is well known that Nazi medical experimenters ruthlessly employed coercion. By way of occurrence coercion, the Nazis literally forced great numbers of concentration camp victims to participate in experiments that entailed their own death or dismemberment. And if some concentration camp victims "volunteered" to participate in Nazi research to avoid even more unspeakable horrors, clearly we must consider them victims of dispositional coercion. The Nazi researchers, employing coercion, immorally used other human beings with a vengeance.

II. Deception and Sexual Morality

To this point, I have been concerned to identify and explicate the morally significant sense of "using another person." On the view proposed, A immorally uses B if and only if A intentionally acts in a way that violates the requirement that B's involvement with A's ends be based on B's voluntary informed consent. I will now apply this account to the area of human sexual interaction and explore its implications. For economy of expression in what follows, "using" (and its cognates) is to be understood as referring only to the morally significant sense.

If we presume a state of affairs in which A desires some form of sexual interaction with B, we can say that this desired form of sexual interaction with B is A's end. Thus A sexually *uses* B if and only if A intentionally acts in a way that violates the requirement that B's sexual interaction with A be based on B's voluntary informed consent. It seems clear then that A may sexually use B in at least two distinctive ways, (1) via coercion and (2) via deception. However, before proceeding to discuss deception and then the more problematic case of coercion, one important point must be made. In emphasizing the centrality of coercion and deception as mechanisms for the sexual using of another person, I have in mind sexual interaction with a fully competent adult partner. We should also want to say, I think, that sexual interaction with a child inescapably involves the sexual using of another person. Even if a child "consents" to sexual interaction, he or she is, strictly speaking, incapable of *informed* consent. It's a matter of being *incompetent* to give consent. Similarly, to the extent that a mentally retarded person is rightly considered incompetent, sexual interaction with such a person amounts to the sexual using of that person, unless someone empowered to give "proxy consent" has done so. (In certain circumstances, sexual involvement might be in the best interests of a mentally retarded person.) We can also visualize the case of an otherwise fully competent adult temporarily disordered by drugs or alcohol. To the extent that such a person is rightly regarded as temporarily incompetent, winning his or her "consent" to sexual interaction could culminate in the sexual using of that person.

There are a host of clear cases in which one person sexually uses another precisely because the former employs deception in a way that undermines the informed character of the latter's consent to sexual interaction. Consider the example. One person, A, has decided, as a matter of personal prudence based on past experience, not to become sexually involved outside the confines of a loving relationship. Another person, B, strongly desires a sexual relationship with A but does not love A. B, aware of A's unwillingness to engage in sex without love, professes love for A, thereby hoping to win A's consent to a sexual relationship. B's ploy is successful; A consents. When the smoke clears and A becomes aware of B's deception, it would be both appropriate and natural for A to complain, "I've been used."

In the same vein, here are some other examples. (1) Mr. A is aware that Ms. B will consent to sexual involvement only on the understanding that in time the two will be married. Mr. A has no intention of marrying Ms. B but says that he will. (2) Ms. C has herpes and is well aware that Mr. D will never consent to sex if he knows of her condition. When asked by Mr. D, Ms. C denies that she has herpes. (3) Mr. E knows that Ms. F will not consent to sexual intercourse in the absence of responsible birth control measures. Mr. E tells Ms. F that he has had a vasectomy, which is not the case. (4) Ms. G knows that Mr. H would not consent to sexual involvement with a married woman. Ms. G is married but tells Mr. H that she is single. (5) Ms. I is well aware that Ms. J is interested in a stable lesbian relationship and will not consent to become sexually involved with someone who is bisexual. Ms. I tells Ms. J that she is exclusively homosexual, whereas the truth is that she is bisexual.

If one person's consent to sex is predicated on false beliefs that have been intentionally and deceptively inculcated by one's sexual partner in an effort to win the former's consent, the resulting sexual interaction involves one person sexually using another. In each of the above cases, one person explicitly *lies* to another. False information is intentionally conveyed to win consent to sexual interaction, and the end result is the sexual using of another person.

As noted earlier, however, lying is not the only form of deception. Under certain circumstances, the simple withholding of information can be considered a form of deception. Accordingly, it is possible to sexually use another person not only by (deceptively) lying about relevant facts but also by (deceptively) not disclosing relevant facts. If A has good reason to believe that B would refuse to consent to sexual interaction should B become aware of certain factual information, and if A withholds disclosure of this information in order to enhance the possibility of gaining B's consent, then, if B does consent, A sexually uses B via deception. One example will suffice. Suppose that Mr. A meets Ms. B in a singles bar. Mr. A realizes immediately that Ms. B is the sister of Ms. C, a woman that Mr. A has been sexually involved with for a long time. Mr. A, knowing that it is very unlikely that Ms. B will consent to sexual interaction if she becomes aware of Mr. A's involvement with her sister, decides not to disclose this information. If Ms. B eventually consents to sexual interaction, since her consent is the product of Mr. A's deception, it is rightly thought that she has been sexually used by him.

III. Coercion and Sexual Morality

We have considered the case of deception. The present task is to consider the more difficult case of coercion. Whereas deception functions to undermine the *informed* character of voluntary consent (to sexual interaction), coercion either obliterates consent entirely (the case of occurrent coercion) or undermines the voluntariness of consent (the case of dispositional coercion).

Forcible rape is the most conspicuous, and most brutal, way of sexually using another person via coercion.[2] Forcible rape may involve either occurrent coercion or dispositional coercion. A man who rapes a woman by the employment of sheer physical force, by simply overpowering her, employs occurrent coercion. There is literally no sexual *interaction* in such a case; only the rapist performs an action. In no sense does the woman consent to or participate in sexual activity. She has no choice in what takes place, or rather, physical force results in her choice being simply beside the point. The employment of occurrent coercion for the purpose of rape "objectifies" the victim in the strongest sense of that term. She is treated like a physical object. One does not interact with physical objects; one acts upon them. In a perfectly ordinary (not the morally significant) sense of the term, we "use" physical objects. But when the victim of rape is treated as if she were a physical object, there we have one of the most vivid examples of the immoral using of another person.

Frequently, forcible rape involves not occurrent coercion (or not *only* occurrent coercion) but dispositional coercion.[3] In dispositional coercion, the relevant factor is not physical force but the threat of harm. The rapist threatens his victim with immediate and serious bodily harm. For example, a man threatens to kill or beat a woman if she resists his sexual demands. She "consents," that is, she submits to his demands. He may demand only passive participation (simply not struggling against him) or he may demand some measure of active participation. Rape that employs dispositional coercion is surely just as wrong as rape that employs occurrent coercion, but there is a notable difference in the mechanism by which the rapist uses his victim in the two cases. With occurrent coercion, the victim's consent is entirely bypassed. With dispositional coercion, the victim's consent is not bypassed. It is coerced. Dispositional coercion undermines the *voluntariness* of consent. The rapist, by employing the threat of immediate and serious bodily harm, may succeed in bending the victim's will. He may gain the victim's "consent." But he uses another person precisely because consent is coerced.

The relevance of occurrent coercion is limited to the case of forcible rape. Dispositional coercion, a notion that also plays an indispensable role in an overall account of forcible rape, now becomes our central concern. Although the threat of immediate and serious bodily harm stands out as the most brutal way of coercing consent to sexual interaction, we must not neglect the employment of other kinds of threats to this same end. There are numerous ways in which one person can effectively harm, and thus effectively threaten, another. Accordingly, for example, consent to sexual interaction might be coerced by threatening to damage someone's reputation. If a person consents to sexual interaction to avoid a threatened harm, then that person has been sexually used (via dispositional coercion). In the face of a threat, of course, it remains possible that a person will refuse to comply with another's sexual demands. It is probably best to describe this sort of situation as a case not of coercion, which entails the *successful* use of threats to gain compliance, but of *attempted* coercion. Of course, the moral fault of an individual emerges with the *attempt* to coerce. A person who attempts murder is morally blameworthy even if the attempt fails. The same is true for someone who fails in an effort to coerce consent to sexual interaction.

Consider now each of the following cases:

Case 1   Mr. Supervisor makes a series of increasingly less subtle sexual overtures to Ms. Employee. These advances are consistently and firmly rejected by Ms. Employee. Eventually, Mr. Supervisor makes it clear that the granting of "sexual favors" is a condition of her continued employment.

Case 2   Ms. Debtor borrowed a substantial sum of money from Mr. Creditor, on the understanding that she would pay it back within one year. In the meantime, Ms. Debtor has become sexually attracted to Mr. Creditor, but he does not share her interest. At the end of the one-year period, Mr. Creditor asks Ms. Debtor to return the money. She says she will be happy to return the money so long as he consents to sexual interaction with her.

Case 3   Mr. Theatregoer has two tickets to the most talked-about play of the season. He is introduced to a woman whom he finds sexually attractive and who shares his interest in the theater. In the course of their conversation, she expresses disappointment that the play everyone is talking about is sold out; she would love to see it. At this point, Mr. Theatregoer suggests that she be his guest at the theater. "Oh, by the way," he says, "I always expect sex from my dates."

Case 4   Ms. Jetsetter is planning a trip to Europe. She has been trying for some time to develop a sexual relationship with a man who has shown little interest in her. She knows, however, that he has always wanted to go to Europe and that it is only lack of money that has deterred him. Ms. Jetsetter proposes that he come along as her traveling companion, all expenses paid, on the express understanding that sex is part of the arrangement.

Cases 1 and 2 involve attempts to sexually use another person whereas cases 3 and 4 do not. To see why this is so, it is essential to introduce a distinction between two kinds of proposals, viz., the distinction between *threats* and *offers*.[4] The logical form of a threat differs from the logical form of an offer in the following way. Threat: "If you *do not* do what I am proposing you do, I will bring about an *undesirable consequence* for you." Offer: "If you *do* what I am proposing you do, I will bring about a *desirable consequence* for you." The person who makes a threat attempts to gain compliance by attaching an undesirable consequence to the alternative of noncompliance. This person attempts to *coerce* consent. The person who makes an offer attempts to gain compliance by attaching a desirable consequence to the alternative of compliance. This person attempts not to coerce but to *induce* consent.

Since threats are morally problematic in a way that offers are not, it is not uncommon for threats to be advanced in the language of offers. Threats are represented as if they were offers. An armed assailant might say, "I'm going to make you an *offer*. If you give me your money, I will allow you to go on living." Though this proposal on the surface has the logical form of an offer, it is in reality a threat. The underlying sense of the proposal is this: "If you do not give me your money, I will kill you." If, in a given case, it is initially unclear whether a certain proposal is to count as a threat or an offer, ask the following question. Does the proposal in question have the effect of making a person *worse off upon non-compliance?* The recipient of an offer, upon noncompliance, *is not worse off* than he or she was before the offer. In contrast, the recipient of a threat, upon noncompliance, *is worse off* than he or she was before the threat. Since the "offer" of our armed assailant has the effect, upon noncompliance, of rendering its recipient worse off (relative to the preproposal situation of the recipient), the recipient is faced with a threat, not an offer.

The most obvious way for a coercer to attach an undesirable consequence to the path of noncompliance is by threatening to render the victim of coercion materially worse off than he or she has heretofore been. Thus a person is threatened with loss of life, bodily injury, damage to property, damage to reputation, etc. It is important to realize, however, that a person can also be effectively coerced by being threatened with the withholding of something (in some cases, what we would call a "benefit") to which the person is entitled. Suppose that A is mired in quicksand and is slowly but surely approaching death. When B happens along, A cries out to B for assistance. All B need do is throw A a rope. B is quite willing to accommodate A, "provided you pay me $100,000 over the next ten years." Is B making A an offer? Hardly! B, we must presume, stands under a moral obligation to come to the aid of a person in serious distress, at least when such assistance entails no significant risk, sacrifice of time, etc. A is entitled to B's assistance. Thus, in reality, B attaches an undesirable consequence to A's noncompliance with the proposal that A pay B $100,000. A is undoubtedly better off that B has happened along, but A is not rendered better off *by B's proposal*. Before B's proposal, A legitimately expected assistance from B, "no strings attached." In attaching a very unwelcome string, B's proposal effectively renders A worse off. What B proposes, then, is not an offer of assistance. Rather, B threatens A with the withholding of something (assistance) that A is entitled to have from B.

Since threats have the effect of rendering a person worse off upon noncompliance, it is ordinarily the case that a person does not welcome (indeed, despises) them. Offers, on the other hand, are ordinarily welcome to a person. Since an offer provides no penalty for noncompliance with a proposal but only an inducement for compliance, there is *in principle* only potential advantage in being confronted with an offer. In real life, of course, there are numerous reasons why a person may be less than enthusiastic about being presented with an offer. Enduring the presentation of trivial offers does not warrant the necessary time and energy expenditures. Offers can be both annoying and offensive; certainly this is true of some sexual offers. A person might also be unsettled by an offer that confronts him or her with a difficult decision. All this, however, is compatible with the fact that an offer is fundamentally welcome to a rational person in the sense that the *content* of an offer necessarily widens the field of opportunity and thus provides, in principle, only potential advantage.

With the distinction between threats and offers clearly in view, it now becomes clear why cases 1 and 2 do indeed involve attempts to sexually use another person whereas cases 3 and 4 do not. Cases 1 and 2 embody threats, whereas cases 3 and 4 embody offers. In case 1, Mr. Supervisor proposes sexual interaction with Ms. Employee and, in an effort to gain compliance, threatens her with the loss of her job. Mr. Supervisor thereby attaches an undesirable consequence to one of Ms. Employee's alternatives, the path of noncompliance. Typical of the threat situation, Mr. Supervisor's proposal has the effect of rendering Ms. Employee worse off upon noncompliance. Mr. Supervisor is attempting via (dispositional) coercion to sexually use Ms. Employee. The situation in case 2 is similar. Ms. Debtor, as *she* might be inclined to say, "offers" to pay Mr. Creditor the money she owes him *if* he consents to sexual interaction with her. In reality, Mrs. Debtor is threatening Mr. Creditor, attempting to coerce his consent to sexual interaction, attempting to sexually use him. Though Mr. Creditor is not now in possession of the money Ms. Debtor owes him, he is *entitled* to receive it from her at this time. She threatens to deprive him of something to which he is entitled. Clearly, her proposal has the effect of rendering him worse off upon noncompliance. Before her proposal, he had the legitimate expectation, "no strings attached," of receiving the money in question.

Cases 3 and 4 embody offers; neither involves an attempt to sexually use another person. Mr. Theatregoer simply provides an inducement for the woman he has just met to accept his proposal of sexual interaction. He offers her the opportunity to see the play that everyone is talking about. In attaching a desirable consequence to the alternative of compliance, Mr. Theatregoer in no way threatens or attempts to coerce his potential companion. Typical of the offer situation, his proposal does not have the effect of rendering her worse off upon noncompliance. She now has a new opportunity; if she chooses to forgo this opportunity, she is no worse off. The situation in case 4 is similar. Ms. Jetsetter provides an inducement for a man that she is interested in to accept her proposal of sexual involvement. She offers him the opportunity to see Europe, without expense, as her traveling companion. Before Ms. Jetsetter's proposal, he had no prospect of a European trip. If he chooses to reject her proposal, he is no worse off than he has heretofore been. Ms. Jetsetter's proposal embodies an offer, not a threat. She cannot be accused of attempting to sexually use her potential traveling companion.

Consider now two further cases, 5 and 6, each of which develops in the following way. Professor Highstatus, a man of high academic accomplishment, is sexually attracted to a student in one of his classes. He is very anxious to secure her consent to sexual interaction. Ms. Student, confused and unsettled by his sexual advances, has begun to practice "avoidance behavior." To the extent that it is possible, she goes out of her way to avoid him.

Case 5 Professor Highstatus tells Ms. Student that, though her work is such as to entitle her to a grade of B in the class, she will be assigned a D unless she consents to sexual interaction.

Case 6   Professor Highstatus tells Ms. Student that, though her work is such as to entitle her to a grade of B, she will be assigned an A if she consents to sexual interaction.

It is clear that case 5 involves an attempt to sexually use another person. Case 6, however, at least at face value, does not. In case 5, Professor Highstatus *threatens* to deprive Ms. Student of the grade she deserves. In case 6, he *offers* to assign her a grade that is higher than she deserves. In case 5, Ms. Student would be worse off upon noncompliance with Professor Highstatus' proposal. In case 6, she would not be worse off upon noncompliance with his proposal. In saying that case 6 does not involve an attempt to sexually use another person, it is not being asserted that Professor Highstatus is acting in a morally legitimate fashion. In offering a student a higher grade than she deserves, he is guilty of abusing his institutional authority. He is under an obligation to assign the grades that students earn, as defined by the relevant course standards. In case 6, Professor Highstatus is undoubtedly acting in a morally reprehensible way, but in contrast to case 5, where it is fair to say that he both abuses his institutional authority *and* attempts to sexually use another person, we can plausibly say that in case 6 his moral failure is limited to abuse of his institutional authority.

There remains, however, a suspicion that case 6 might after all embody an attempt to sexually use another person. There is no question that the literal content of what Professor Highstatus conveys to Ms. Student has the logical form of an offer and not a threat. Still, is it not the case that Ms. Student may very well feel threatened? Professor Highstatus, in an effort to secure consent to sexual interaction, has announced that he will assign Ms. Student a higher grader than she deserves. Can she really turn him down without substantial risk? Is he not likely to retaliate? If she spurns him, will he not lower her grade or otherwise make it harder for her to succeed in her academic program? He does, after all, have power over her. Will he use it to her detriment? Surely he is not above abusing his institutional authority to achieve his ends; this much is abundantly clear from his willingness to assign a grade higher than a student deserves.

Is Professor Highstatus naive to the threat that Ms. Student may find implicit in the situation? Perhaps. In such a case, if Ms. Student reluctantly consents to sexual interaction, we may be inclined to say that he has *unwittingly* used her. More likely, Professor Highstatus is well aware of the way in which Ms. Student will perceive his proposal. He knows that threats need not be verbally expressed. Indeed, it may even be the case that he consciously exploits his underground reputation. "Everyone knows what happens to the women who reject Profession Highstatus's little offers." To the extent, then, that Professor Highstatus intends to convey a threat in case 6, he is attempting via coercion to sexually use another person.

Many researchers "have pointed out the fact that the possibility of sanctions for noncooperation is implicit in all sexual advances across authority lines, as between teacher and student."[5] I do not think that this consideration should lead us to the conclusion that a person with an academic appointment is obliged in all circumstances to refrain from attempting to initiate sexual involvement with one of his or her students. Still, since even "good faith" sexual advances may be ambiguous in the eyes of a student, it is an interesting question what precautions an instructor must take to avoid unwittingly coercing a student to consent to sexual interaction.

Much of what has been said about the professor/student relationship is an academic setting can be applied as well to the supervisor/subordinate relationship in an employment setting. A manager who functions within an organizational structure is required to evaluate fairly his or her subordinates according to relevant corporate or institutional standards. An unscrupulous manager, willing to abuse his or her institutional authority in an effort to win the consent of a subordinate to sexual interaction, can advance threats and/or offers related to the managerial task of employee evaluation. An employee whose job performance is entirely satisfactory can be threatened with an unsatisfactory performance rating, perhaps leading to termination. An employee whose job performance is excellent can be threatened with an unfair evaluation, designed to bar the employee from recognition, merit pay, consideration for promotion, etc. Such threats, when made in an effort to coerce employee consent to sexual interaction, clearly embody the attempt to sexually use another person. On the other hand, the manager who (abusing his or her institutional authority) offers to provide an employee with an inflated evaluation as an inducement for consent to sexual interaction does not, at face value, attempt to sexually use another person. Of course, all of the qualifications introduced in the discussion of case 6 above are applicable here as well.

IV. The Idea of a Coercive Offer

In section III, I have sketched an overall account of sexually using another person *via coercion*. In this section, I will consider the need for modifications or extensions of the suggested account. As before, certain case studies will serve as points of departure.

Case 7 Ms. Starlet, a glamorous, wealthy, and highly successful model, wants nothing more than to become a movie superstar. Mr.

Moviemogul, a famous producer, is very taken with Ms. Starlet's beauty. He invites her to come to his office for a screen test. After the screen test, Mr. Moviemogul tells Ms. Starlet that he is prepared to make her a star, on the condition that she agree to sexual involvement with him. Ms. Starlet finds Mr. Moviemogul personally repugnant; she is not at all sexually attracted to him. With great reluctance, she agrees to his proposal.

Has Mr. Moviemogul sexually used Ms. Starlet? No. He has made her an offer that she has accepted, however reluctantly. The situation would be quite different if it were plausible to believe that she was, before acceptance of his proposal, *entitled* to his efforts to make her a star. Then we could read case 7 as amounting to his threatening to deprive her of something to which she was entitled. But what conceivable grounds could be found for the claim that Mr. Moviemogul, before Ms. Starlet's acceptance of his proposal, is under an obligation to make her a star? He does not threaten her; he makes her an offer. Even if there are other good grounds for morally condemning his action, it is a mistake to think that he is guilty of coercing consent.

But some would assert that Mr. Moviemogul's offer, on the grounds that it confronts Ms. Starlet with an overwhelming inducement, is simply an example of a *coercive offer*. The more general claim at issue is that offers are coercive precisely inasmuch as they are extremely enticing or seductive. Though there is an important reality associated with the notion of a coercive offer, a reality that must shortly be confronted, we ought not embrace the view that an offer is coercive merely because it is extremely enticing or seductive. Virginia Held is a leading proponent of the view under attack here. She writes:

> A person unable to spurn an offer may act as unwillingly as a person unable to resist a threat. Consider the distinction between rape and seduction. In one case constraint and threat are operative, in the other inducement and offer. If the degree of inducement is set high enough in the case of seduction, there may seem to be little difference in the extent of coercion involved. In both cases, persons may act against their own wills.[6]

Certainly a rape victim who acquiesces at knife point is forced to act *against her will*. Does Ms. Starlet, however, act against her will? We have said that she consents "with great reluctance" to sexual involvement, but she does not act against her will. She *wants* very much to be a movie star. I might want very much to be thin. She regrets having to become sexually involved with Mr. Moviemogul as a means of achieving what she wants. I might regret very much having to go on a diet to lose weight. If we say that Ms. Starlet acts against her will in case 7, then we must say that I am acting against my will in embracing "with great reluctance" the diet I despise.

A more important line of argument against Held's view can be advanced on the basis of the widely accepted notion that there is a moral presumption against coercion. Held herself embraces this notion and very effectively clarifies it:

> ... although coercion is not always wrong (quite obviously: one coerces the small child not to run across the highway, or the murderer to drop his weapon), there is a presumption against it. . . . This has the standing of a fundamental moral principle. . . .
>
> What can be concluded at the moral level is that we have a *prima facie* obligation not to employ coercion.[7] [all italics hers]

But it would seem that acceptance of the moral presumption against coercion is not compatible with the view that offers become coercive precisely inasmuch as they become extremely enticing or seductive. Suppose you are my neighbor and regularly spend your Saturday afternoon on the golf course. Suppose also that you are a skilled gardener. I am anxious to convince you to do some gardening work for me and it must be done this Saturday. I offer you $100, $200, $300, . . . in an effort to make it worth your while to sacrifice your recreation and undertake my gardening. At some point, my proposal becomes very enticing. If my proposal were becoming coercive, surely our moral sense would be aroused.

Though it is surely not true that the extremely enticing character of an offer is sufficient to make it coercive, we need not reach the conclusion that no sense can be made out of the notion of a coercive offer. Indeed, there is an important social reality that the notion of a coercive offer appears to capture, and insight into this reality can be gained by simply taking note of the sort of case that most draws us to the language of "coercive offer." Is it not a case in which the recipient of an offer is in circumstances of genuine need, and acceptance of the offer seems to present the only realistic possibility for alleviating the need? Assuming that this sort of case is the heart of the matter, it seems that we cannot avoid introducing some sort of distinction between *genuine needs* and *mere wants*. Though the philosophical difficulties involved in drawing this distinction are not insignificant, I nevertheless claim that we will not achieve any clarity about the notion of a coercive offer, at least in this context, except in reference to it. Whatever puzzlement we may feel with regard to the host of borderline cases that can be advanced, it is nevertheless true, for example, that I *genuinely need* food and that I *merely want* a backyard tennis court. In the same spirit, I think it can be acknowledged by all that Ms. Starlet, though she *wants* very much to be a star, does not in any relevant sense *need* to be a star. Accordingly, there is little plausibility in thinking that Mr. Moviemogul makes her a coercive offer. The following case, in contrast, can more plausibly be thought to embody a coercive offer.

Case 8 Mr. Troubled is a young widower who is raising his three children. He lives in a small town and believes that it is important for him to stay there so that his children continue to have the emotional support of other family members. But economic times are tough. Mr. Troubled has been laid off from his job and has not been able to find another. His unemployment benefits have ceased and his relatives are in no position to help him financially. If he is unable to come up with the money for his mortgage payments, he will lose his rather modest house. Ms. Opportunistic lives in the same town. Since shortly after the death of Mr. Troubled's wife, she has consistently made sexual overtures in his direction. Mr. Troubled, for his part, does not care for Ms. Opportunistic and has made it clear to her that he is not interested in sexual involvement with her. She, however, is well aware of his present difficulties. To win his consent to a sexual affair, Ms. Opportunistic offers to make mortgage payments for Mr. Troubled on a continuing basis.

Is Ms. Opportunistic attempting to sexually use Mr. Troubled? The correct answer is yes, even though we must first accept the conclusion that her proposal embodies an offer and not a threat. If Ms. Opportunistic were threatening Mr. Troubled, her proposal would have the effect of rendering him worse off upon noncompliance. But this is not the case. If he rejects her proposal, his situation will not worsen; he will simply remain, as before, in circumstances of extreme need. It might be objected at this point that Ms. Opportunistic does in fact threaten Mr. Troubled. She threatens to deprive him of something to which he is entitled, namely, the alleviation of a genuine need. But this approach is defensible only if, before acceptance of her proposal, he is entitled to have his needs alleviated *by her*. And whatever Mr. Troubled and his children are entitled to from their society as a whole—they are perhaps slipping through the "social safety net"—it cannot be plausibly maintained that Mr. Troubled is entitled to have his mortgage payments made *by Ms. Opportunistic*.

Yet, though she does not threaten him, she is attempting to sexually use him. How can this conclusion be reconciled with our overall account of sexually using another person? First of all, I want to suggest that nothing hangs on whether or not we decide to call Ms. Opportunistic's offer "coercive." More important than the label "coercive offer" is an appreciation of the social reality that inclines us to consider the label appropriate. The label most forcefully asserts itself when we reflect on what Mr. Troubled is likely to say after accepting the offer. "I really had no choice." "I didn't want to accept her offer but what could I do? I have my children to think about." Both Mr. Troubled and Ms. Starlet (in our previous case) *reluctantly* consented to sexual interaction, but I think it can be agreed that Ms. Starlet had a choice in a way that Mr. Troubled did not. Mr. Troubled's choice was *severely constrained by his needs*, whereas Ms. Starlet's was not. As for Ms. Opportunistic, it seems that we might describe her approach as in some sense exploiting or taking advantage of Mr. Troubled's desperate situation. It is not so much, as we would say in the case of threats, that she coerces him or his consent, but rather that she achieves her aim of winning consent by taking advantage of the fact that he is already "under coercion," that is, his choice is severely constrained by his need. If we choose to describe what has taken place as a "coercive offer," we should remember that Mr. Troubled is "coerced" (constrained) by his own need or perhaps by preexisting factors in his situation rather than by Ms. Opportunistic or her offer.

Since it is not quite right to say that Ms. Opportunistic is attempting to coerce Mr. Troubled, even if we are prepared to embrace the label "coercive offer," we cannot simply say, as we would say in the case of threats, that she is attempting to sexually use him *via coercion*. The proper account of the way in which Ms. Opportunistic attempts to sexually use Mr. Troubled is somewhat different. Let us say simply that she attempts to sexually use him *by taking advantage of his desperate situation*. The sense behind this distinctive way of sexually using someone is that a person's choice situation can sometimes be subject to such severe prior constraints that the possibility of *voluntary* consent to sexual interaction is precluded. A advances an offer calculated to gain B's reluctant consent to sexual interaction by confronting B, who has no apparent way of alleviating a genuine need, with an opportunity to do so, but makes this opportunity contingent upon consent to sexual interaction. In such a case, should we not say simply that B's need, when coupled with a lack of viable alternatives, results in B being incapable of *voluntarily* accepting A's offer? Thus A, in making an offer which B "cannot refuse," although not coercing B, nevertheless does intentionally act in a way that violates the requirement that B's sexual interaction with A be based upon B's voluntary informed consent. Thus A sexually uses B.

The central claim of this paper is that A sexually uses B if and only if A intentionally acts in a way that violates the requirement that B's sexual interaction with A be based on B's voluntary informed consent. Clearly, deception and coercion are important mechanisms whereby sexual using takes place. But consideration of case 8 has led us to the identification of yet another mechanism. In summary, then, limiting attention to cases of sexual interaction with a fully competent adult partner, A can sexually use B not only (1) by deceiving B or (2) by coercing B but also (3) by taking advantage of B's desperate situation.

NOTES

1. I follow here an account of coercion developed by Michael D. Bayles in "A Concept of Coercion," in J. Roland Pennock and John W. Chapman, eds., *Coercion: Nomos XIV* (Chicago: Aldine-Atherton, 1972), pp. 16–29.

2. Statutory rape, sexual relations with a person under the legal age of consent, can also be construed as the sexual using of another person. In contrast to forcible rape, however, statutory rape need not involve coercion. The victim of statutory rape may freely "consent" to sexual interaction but, at least in the eyes of the law, is deemed incompetent to consent.

3. A man wrestles a woman to the ground. She is the victim of occurrent coercion. He threatens to beat her unless she submits to his sexual demands. Now she becomes the victim of dispositional coercion.

4. My account of this distinction largely derives from Robert Nozick, "Coercion," in Sidney Morgenbesser, Patrick Suppes, and Morton White, eds., *Philosophy, Science, and Method* (New York: St. Martin's Press, 1969), pp. 440–72, and from Michael D. Bayles, "Coercive Offers and Public Benefits," *The Personalist* 55, no. 2 (Spring 1974), 139–44.

5. The National Advisory Council on Women's Educational Programs, *Sexual Harassment: A Report on the Sexual Harassment of Students* (August 1980), p. 12.

6. Virginia Held, "Coercion and Coercive Offers," in *Coercion: Nomos XIV*, p. 58.

7. *Ibid.*, pp. 61, 62.

Chapter 17

SEXUAL USE AND WHAT TO DO ABOUT IT: INTERNALIST AND EXTERNALIST SEXUAL ETHICS

Alan Soble

I begin (in section 1) by describing the hideous nature of sexuality, that in virtue of which sexual desire and activity are morally suspicious, or at least what we have been told about the moral foulness of sex by, in particular, Immanuel Kant.[1] A problem arises because acting on one's sexual desire, given Kant's metaphysics of sex, apparently conflicts with the Categorical Imperative, especially its Second Formulation (section 2). I then propose a typology of possible solutions to this problem and critically discuss recent philosophical ethics of sex that fall into the typology's various categories (sections 3 and 4). I conclude (sections 5 and 6) with remarks about Kant's own solution to this sex problem.

1. The Nature of Sex

On Kant's view, a person who sexually desires another person objectifies that other, both before and during sexual activity.[2] This can occur in several ways. Certain types of manipulation and deception (primping, padding, making an overly good first impression) seem required prior

---

Reprinted, revised, from *Essays in Philosophy* 2, 2 (June 2001), with the permission of the editor, Michael Goodman. The Internet journal *Essays in Philosophy* can be accessed at the Website <www.humboldt.edu/~essays/>.

to engaging in sex, or are so common as to appear part of the nature of human sexual interaction.[3] The other's body, his or her lips, thighs, buttocks, and toes, are desired as the arousing parts they are, distinct from the person. As Kant says (about the genitals, apparently),

> sexuality is not an inclination which one human being has for another as such, but is an inclination for the sex of another. . . . [O]nly her sex is the object of his desires. . . . [A]ll men and women do their best to make not their human nature but their sex more alluring.[4]

Further, both the body and the compliant actions of the other person are tools (a means) that one uses for one's own sexual pleasure, and to that extent the other person is a fungible, functional thing. Sexual activity itself is a strange activity, not only by manifesting uncontrollable arousal and involuntary movements of the body, but also with its yearning to master, dominate, and even consume the other's body. During the sexual act, then, a person both loses control of himself and loses regard for the humanity of the other. Sexual desire is a threat to the other's personhood, but the one who is under the spell of sexual desire also loses hold of his or her own personhood. The person who desires another depends on the whims of that other for satisfaction and becomes as a result a jellyfish, vulnerable to the other's demands and manipulations.[5] Merely being sexually aroused by another person can be experienced as coercive; similarly, a person who proposes an irresistible sexual offer may be exploiting another who has been made weak by sexual desire.[6] Moreover, a person who willingly complies with another person's request for a sexual encounter voluntarily makes an object of himself or herself. As Kant puts it, "For the natural use that one sex makes of the other's sexual organs is *enjoyment,* for which one gives oneself up to the other. In this act a human being makes himself into a thing."[7] And, for Kant, because those engaged in sexual activity make themselves into objects merely for the sake of sexual pleasure, both persons reduce themselves to animals. When

> a man wishes to satisfy his desire, and a woman hers, they stimulate each other's desire; their inclinations meet, but their object is not human nature but sex, and each of them dishonours the human nature of the other. They make of humanity an instrument for the satisfaction of their lusts and inclinations, and dishonour it by placing it on a level with animal nature.[8]

Finally, the power of the sexual urge makes it dangerous.[9] Sexual desire is inelastic, relentless, the passion most likely to challenge reason and make us succumb to *akrasia,* compelling us to seek satisfaction even when doing so involves the risks of dark-alley gropings, microbiologically filthy acts, slinking around the White House, or getting married impetuously. Sexually motivated behavior easily destroys our self-respect.

The sexual impulse or inclination, then, is morally dubious and, to boot, a royal pain. Kant made this point in more general terms, claiming that humans would be delighted to be free of such promptings:

> Inclinations . . . , as sources of needs, are so far from having an absolute value to make them desirable for their own sake that it must rather be the universal wish of every rational being to be wholly free from them.[10]

I am not sure I believe all these claims about the nature of sexuality, but that is irrelevant for my purpose, since many philosophers, with good reason, have taken them seriously. In some moods I might reply to Kant by muttering a Woody Allen type of joke: "Is sex an autonomy-killing, mind-numbing, subhuman passion? Yes, but only when it's good." In this essay, however, I want to examine how sexual acts could be moral, if this description is right.

2. Sex and the Second Formulation

Michael Ruse has explained in a direct way how a moral problem arises in acting on sexual desire:

> The starting point to sex is the sheer desire of a person for the body of another. One wants to feel the skin, to smell the hair, to see the eyes—one wants to bring one's own genitals into contact with those of the other. . . . This gets dangerously close to treating the other as a means to the fulfillment of one's own sexual desire—as an object, rather than as an end.[11]

We should add, to make Ruse's observation more comprehensively Kantian, that the desire to be touched, to be thrilled by the touch of the other, to be the object of someone else's desire, is just as much "the starting point" that raises the moral problem.

Because this sex problem arises from the intersection of a Kantian view of the nature of sexuality and Kantian ethics, let us review the Second Formulation: "Act in such a way that you always treat humanity, whether in your own person or in the person of any other, never simply as a means, but always at the same time as an end." Or "man . . . *exists* as an end in himself, *not merely as a means* for arbitrary use by this or that will: he must in all his actions, whether they are directed to himself or to other rational beings, always be viewed *at the same time as an end*."[12] So the question arises: How can sexual desire be expressed and satisfied without merely using the other or treating the other as an object, and without treating the self as an object? How can sexual activity be planned and carried out while "at the same time" treating the other and the self as persons, while treating their "humanity" as an end, while confirming their autonomy and rationality? Of course, the Second Formulation directs us not to treat ourselves and others *merely* as means or objects. It is permissible to treat another and ourselves as a means as long as we are also treated as persons or our humanity is treated as an end. How can this be done?

A person providing free and informed consent to an action or to interactions with other person is, in general for Kant, a necessary but not sufficient condition for satisfying the Second Formulation. In addition, for Kant, treating someone as a person at least includes taking on the other's ends as if they were one's own ends. Thus Kant writes in the *Groundwork*, "the ends of a subject who is an end in himself must, if this conception is to have its *full* effect in me, be also, as far as possible, *my* ends."[13] And I must take on the other's ends for their own sake, not because that is an effective way to advance my own goals in using the other. It is further required, when I treat another as a means, that the other can take on my ends, my purpose, in so using him or her as a means. Kant likely expressed this condition in the *Groundwork:* "the man who has a mind to make a false promise to others will see at once that he is intending to make use of another man *merely as a means* to an end he does not share. For the man whom I seek to use for my own purposes by such a promise cannot possibly agree with my way of behaving to him, and so cannot himself share the end of [my] action."[14] Given Kant's metaphysics of sexuality, can *all* these requirements of the Second Formulation of the Categorical Imperative be satisfied in *any* sexual interaction? That is the Kantian sex problem.

But it should be noted that even though, in general, Kant advances these two conditions in addition to free and informed consent—I must take on your ends, and you must be able to take on my ends—Kant apparently relaxes his standard for some situations, allowing one person to use another just with the free and informed consent of the used person, as long as one allows the used person to *retain* personhood or one does not *interfere* with his or her retaining personhood. This weaker variation of how to satisfy the Second Formulation may be important in Kant's account of the morality of work-for-hire and of sexual relations, as I discuss below.[15]

I now proceed to display a conceptual typology of various solutions to the Kantian sex problem, and discuss critically whether, or to what extent, solutions that occupy different logical locations in the typology conform with the Second Formulation. There are five types of solutions: behavioral internalist, psychological internalist, thin externalist, thick minimalist externalist, and thick extended externalist. I define and discuss examples of each type in that order.

3. Internalist Solutions to the Sex Problem

Internalist solutions to the sex problem advise us to modify the character of sexual activity so that persons engaged in it satisfy the Second Formulation. For internalists, restraints on how sexual acts are carried out, or restraints on the natural expression of the impulse, must be present. Consent, then, is necessary for the morality of sexual acts, but not sufficient. Note that one might fix a sexual act internally so that qua sexual act the act is unobjectionable, but it still might be wrong for other reasons; for example, it might be adulterous. There are two internalisms: *behavioral* internalism, according to which the physical components of sexual acts make the moral difference, and *psychological* internalism, according to which certain attitudes must be present during sexual activity.

Behavioral Internalism

Alan Goldman defines "sexual desire" as the "desire for contact with another person's body and for the pleasure which such contact produces. . . . The desire for another's body is . . . the desire for the pleasure that physical contact brings."[16] Since sexual desire is a desire for one's own self-interested pleasure, it is understandable that Goldman senses a Kantian problem with sexual activity. Thus Goldman writes that sexual activities "invariably involve at different stages the manipulation of one's partner for one's own pleasure" and thereby, he notes, seem to violate the Second Formulation—which, on Goldman's truncated rendition, "holds that one ought not to treat another as a means to such private ends."[17] The sex problem is one that Goldman must deal with from a Kantian perspective, because he firmly rejects a utilitarian view of sexual morality. But Goldman reminds us that from a Kantian perspective, "using other individuals for personal benefit," in sex or in other interactions, is "immoral only when [the acts] are one-sided, when the benefits are not mutual."[18] As a solution to the sex problem, then, Goldman proposes that

> Even in an act which by its nature "objectifies" the other, one recognizes a partner as a subject with demands and desires by yielding to those desires, by allowing oneself to be a sexual object as well, by giving pleasure or ensuring that the pleasures of the act are mutual.[19]

This sexual moral principle—make sure that you provide sexual pleasure to your partner—seems plausible enough. And because, for Goldman, consent is a necessary condition but not sufficient for the morality of a sexual act (one must go beyond consent, attempting to ensure that the other experiences sexual pleasure), and if providing sexual pleasure for your partner is a way to make the other person's ends your own ends, Goldman's proposal seems at least in spirit consistent with the Second Formulation.[20]

But let us ask: *Why* might one sexually please the other? (Pleasing the other person can be done, as Goldman recognizes, by actively doing something to or for the other, or by allowing the other person to treat us as an object, so that they do things to us as we passively acquiesce.) One answer is suggested by a form of sexual egoism or hedonism: pleasing the other is *necessary for or contributes to one's own pleasure.* How so? By inducing the other, through either the other's sexual arousal or gratitude, to act to furnish pleasure to oneself. Or because sexually pleasing the other satisfies one's desire to exert power or influence over the other. Or because in providing pleasure to the other we get pleasure by witnessing the effects of our exertions.[21] Or by inducing the other to hold us in an esteem that may heighten our arousal. ("You are *so* good," the other moans.) Or because while giving pleasure to the other person we identify with his or her arousal and pleasure, which identification increases our own arousal and pleasure.[22] Or because pleasing the other alleviates or prevents guilt feelings, or doing so makes us feel good that we have kept a promise. I am sure readers can supplement this list of self-serving reasons for providing sexual pleasure to the other person.

Another answer is that providing pleasure to the other can *and should* be done just for the sake of pleasing the other, just because you know the other person has sexual needs and desires and has hopes for their satisfaction. The sexual satisfaction of the other is, or is to be taken as, an end in itself, as something valuable in its own right, not as something that has instrumental value. It follows, as a corollary, that in some circumstances you must be willing and ready to please the other person sexually when doing so does not contribute to your own satisfaction or even runs counter to it. (The last scenario is the kind of case Kant likes to focus on in the *Groundwork,* cases that single out the motive of benevolence or duty from motives based on inclination.)

By the way, according to the Marquis de Sade, sexual desire is absolutely egoistic; it is concerned only with its own satisfaction, not caring a whit about the pleasure of the other. This Kantian claim is compatible, in principle, with one's getting sexual pleasure by providing sexual pleasure to the other, when providing that pleasure is a mechanism for increasing one's own pleasure. Sade, however, does not take the thesis in that direction. Instead, Sade asserts that the pleasure of the other is an impediment to or a distraction from one's own sexual pleasure, that allowing the other to pursue his or her pleasure at the same time is to undermine one's own pleasure.[23] I think we can acknowledge some truth here: when both persons attempt to satisfy their own sexual desire at the same time, their frantic grabbings sometimes result in sexually incongruous bodies and movements. The sexual satisfaction of one person often requires the passive acquiescence of the other, an abandonment to what the first one wants and how he or she wants it—in Goldman's language, one must sometimes allow the other to treat oneself as an object. Romantically perfect sexual events are hard to come by.

To return to Goldman's proposal: I have categorized Goldman as a behavioral internalist because all he insists on, in order to make sexual activity morally permissible from a Kantian perspective, is the *behavior* of providing pleasure for the other person. Goldman never claims that providing pleasure be done with a benevolent *motive* or purity of purpose. But this feature of his proposal is exactly why it fails, in its *own* terms. If providing pleasure to the other is just a mechanism for attaining or improving one's own pleasure, providing pleasure to the other *continues to treat the other merely as a means.* Since giving pleasure to the other is instrumental in obtaining my pleasure, giving pleasure has not at all succeeded in internally *fixing* the nature of the sexual act. Providing pleasure can be a genuine internalist solution, by changing the nature of the sexual act, only if providing pleasure is an unconditional giving; otherwise objectification, instrumentality, and use remain.

Goldman's proposal thus fails to accommodate his own Kantian commitments. When Kant claims that we must treat the other as a person by taking on his or her ends as our own—by providing sexual pleasure, if that is his or her end—Kant does not mean that as a hypothetical, as if taking on the other's ends were a mechanism for getting the other person to allow us to treat him or her as a means.[24] We must not take on the other's ends as our own simply because doing so is useful for us in generating our own pleasure or achieving our own sexual goals. Attitude, for Kant, is also morally important, not only behavior, even if that behavior has the desired and beneficial effects for the other person. Sharing the ends of the other person means viewing those ends as valuable in their own right. Further, for Kant, we may take on the ends of the other as our own only if the other's ends are themselves morally permissible: I may "make the other's ends my ends provided only that these are not immoral."[25] Given the objectification and use involved in sexual activity, as conceded by Goldman, the moral permissibility of the end of seeking sexual pleasure by means of another person has not yet been established for *either* party. We are not to make the other's ends our own ends if the other's ends are not, in themselves, already morally permissible, and whether the sexual ends of the other person *are* permissible is precisely the question at issue. Thus, to be told by Goldman that it is morally permissible for one person to objectify another in sexual activity if the other also objectifies the first, with the first's allowance, does not answer the question. Goldman's internalist solution attempts to change the nature of the sexual act, from what it is essentially to what it might be were we to embrace *slightly* better bedroom behavior—by avoiding raw selfishness. But this really doesn't go far enough to fix or change the nature of sexual activity, if all that is required is that both parties must add the giving of pleasure to an act that is by its nature, and remains, self-centered. Finally (and *perhaps* most important; see Kant's Solution, below), Goldman ignores, in Kant's statement of the Second Formulation, that we must also respect the humanity *in one's own person*. To make oneself voluntarily an object for the sake of the other person's sexual pleasure, as Goldman recommends, only multiplies the use, and does not eliminate it, and so apparently violates that prescription.

Goldman has, in effect, changed the problem from one of sexual objectification and use to one of distributive justice.[26] Sex is morally permissible, on his view, if the pleasure is mutual; the way to make sexual activity moral is to make it nonmorally good for both participants. Use and objectification remain, but they are permissible, on his view, because the objectification is reciprocal and the act is mutually beneficial. Even though in one sense Goldman makes sexual activity moral by making it *more* nonmorally good, for the *other* party, he also makes sexual activity moral by making it *less* nonmorally good, for the *self,* since one's sexual urgings must be restrained. What goes morally wrong in sexual activity, for Goldman, is that only one person might experience pleasure (or lopsidedly) and only one might bear the burden of providing it. This is what Goldman means, I think, by saying that "one-sided" sexual activity is immoral. The benefits of receiving pleasure, and the burdens of the restraint of seeking pleasure and of providing it to the other, must be passed around to everyone involved in the encounter. This is accomplished, for Goldman, by an equal or reciprocal distribution of being used as an object.

Suppose, instead, that both parties are expected to inject *unconditional* giving into an act that is essentially self-centered. Then both parties must buckle down more formidably, in order to restrain their impulses for their own pleasure and to provide pleasure to the other. But if altruistic giving were easy, given our natures, there would be less reason for thinking, to begin with, that sexual desire tends to use the other person in a self-centered way. To the extent that the sexual impulse is self-interested, as Goldman's definitions make clear, it is implausible that sexual urges could be controlled by a moral command to provide pleasure unconditionally. The point is not only that a duty to provide pleasure unconditionally threatens the nonmoral goodness of sexual acts, that it reduces the sexual excitement and satisfaction of both persons. The point is, further, that fulfilling such a duty, if we assume Goldman's account of sexual desire, may be unlikely.[27] Kant might have seen this point, for his own solution to the sex problem was not that persons engaged in sexual activity should unconditionally provide sexual pleasure for each other.

Psychological Internalism

We have seen that if Goldman is to be able to fix the sexual act internally, to change its nature, he needs to insist not merely on our performing behaviors that produce pleasure for the other, but on our producing pleasure for a certain reason. In this way, we move from behavioral to psychological internalism, which claims that sexual acts must be accompanied and restrained by certain attitudes, the presence of which ensure the satisfaction of the Second Formulation.

At one point in her essay "Defining Wrong and Defining Rape," Jean Hampton lays out a view that is similar to Goldman's, in which the occurrence of mutual pleasure alone solves the sex problem:

> when sex is as much about pleasing another as it is about pleasing oneself, it certainly doesn't involve using another as a means and actually incorporates the idea of respect and concern for another's needs.[28]

Providing sexual pleasure to the other person, then, seems to satisfy Kant's Second Formulation. But Hampton goes beyond Goldman in attempting to understand the depth or significance of the sexual experience:

> one's humanity is perhaps never more engaged than in the sexual act. But it is not only present in the experience; more important, it is "at stake" in the sense that each partner puts him/herself in a position where the behavior of the other can either confirm it or threaten it, celebrate it or abuse it.[29]

This point is surely Kantian: sex is metaphysically and psychologically dangerous.[30] Hampton continues:

> If this is right, then I do not see how, for most normal human beings, sexual passion is heightened if one's sexual partner behaves in a way that one finds personally humiliating or that induces in one shame or self-hatred or that makes one feel like a "thing." . . . Whatever sexual passion is, such emotions seem antithetical to it, and such emotions are markers of the disrespect that destroys the morality of the experience. . . . [W]hat makes a sexual act morally right is also what provides the groundwork for the experience of emotions and pleasures that make for "good sex."[31]
>
> If the wrongness of the act is a function of its diminishing nature, then that wrongness can be present even if, ex ante, each party consented to the sex. So . . . consent is *never by itself* that which makes a sexual act morally right. . . . Lovemaking is a set of experiences . . . which includes attitudes and behaviors that are different in kind from the attitudes and behaviors involved in morally wrongful sex.[32]

Hampton's thesis, then, as I understand it, is that sexual activity must be accompanied by certain humanity-affirming attitudes or emotions that manifest themselves in the sexual activity itself. Attitudes and emotions that repudiate humanity, that are disrespectful, are morally wrong and (because) destructive of mutual pleasure.[33] Hampton's psychological internalism seems fairly consistent with Kant's Second Formulation: for Hampton, consent may be a necessary condition, but it is not sufficient for behaving morally or respectfully toward another person sexually; giving pleasure to the other person, taking on their sexual ends, is required; and *why* the persons produce pleasure for each other is morally relevant. But Kant would still object to Hampton's view, even though he might well admit that she is on the right track. The willingness to provide, selflessly, sexual pleasure for the other, for Kant, does not erase the fundamentally objectifying nature of sexual activity. And the nonmarital (even if humanity-affirming) sexual activity that is in principle justifiable by Hampton's criterion would be rejected by Kant as immoral.

It seems to follow from Hampton's view that casual sex, in which both parties are just out to satisfy their own randiness, is morally wrong, along with prostitution, since these sexual acts are not likely to be, in some robust sense, humanity-affirming. And sadomasochistic sexual acts would seem to be morally wrong, on her view, because they likely involve what Hampton sees as humanity-denying attitudes. Yet casual sex and prostitution, as objectifying and instrumental as they can be, and sadomasochistic sexual acts, as humiliating to one's partner as they can be, still often produce tremendous sexual excitement and pleasure—contrary to what Hampton implies. For this reason I perceive a problem in Hampton's position. She believes, as does Goldman, that morally permissible sex involves mutual sexual pleasing, that the morality of sexual activity then depends on its nonmoral goodness, and, further, that disrespectful attitudes destroy this mutual pleasure or nonmoral goodness. But is the expression of disrespectful attitudes morally wrong exactly because these attitudes destroy the other's sexual pleasure or, instead, just because they are disrespectful? This question is important regarding Hampton's assessment of sadomasochism. For if her argument is that disrespectful attitudes that occur during sexual encounters are morally wrong exactly because they are disrespectful, then sadomasochistic sexual activities are morally wrong even if they do, contra Hampton's intuition, produce pleasure for the participants. (If so, Hampton may be what I later call an "externalist.") But if her argument is that disrespectful attitudes are wrong because or when they destroy the mutuality of the pleasure, or the pleasure of the experience for the other person, then sadomasochism does not turn out to be morally wrong. (And, in this case, Hampton remains an "internalist.")

Perhaps Hampton means that sexual activity is morally permissible only when it is *both* mutually pleasure-producing *and* incorporates humanity-affirming attitudes. This dual test for the morality of sexual encounters prohibits casual sex between strangers, prostitution, and sadomasochistic sexuality, no matter how sexually satisfying these activities are. In Hampton's essay, however, I could find no clear criterion of "humanity-affirming" behavior and attitudes other than "provides mutual pleasure." This is exactly why Hampton has trouble denying the permissibility of sadomasochism. Consider what the lesbian sadomasochist Pat Califia has said about sadomasochism: "The things that seem beautiful, inspiring, and life-affirming to me seem ugly, hateful, and ludicrous to most other people."[34] As far as I can tell, Califia means "provides sexual pleasure" by "life-affirming." If so, no disagreement in principle exists between Hampton and Califia, if Hampton means "provides pleasure" by "humanity-affirming." What Hampton does not take seriously, indeed what she rejects, is Califia's observation that brutal behaviors and humiliating attitudes that occur or are expressed during sexual activity can, even for "normal" people, make for mutually exciting and pleasurable sex.

4. Externalist Solutions to the Sex Problem

According to *externalism,* morality requires that we place restraints on when sexual acts are engaged in, with whom sexual activity occurs, or on the conditions under which sexual activities are performed. Properly setting the background context in which sexual acts occur enables the persons to satisfy the Second Formulation. One distinction among externalisms is that between *minimalist* externalism, which claims that morality requires that only the context of the sexual activity be set, and the sexual acts may be whatever they turn out to be, and *extended* externalism, which claims that setting the context will also affect the character of the sexual acts. Another distinction among externalisms is that between *thin* externalism, according to which free and informed consent is both necessary and sufficient for the moral permissibility of sexual acts (with a trivial ceteris paribus clause), and *thick* externalism, which claims that something beyond consent is required for the morality of sexual activity.

Thin Externalism

I begin my discussion of externalism by examining a theory of sexual morality proposed by Thomas Mappes, who argues that only weak contextual constraints are required for satisfying Kantian worries about sexual activity.[35] According to Mappes, the giving of free and informed consent by the persons involved in a sexual encounter is both a necessary condition and sufficient for the morality of their sexual activity, for making permissible the sexual use of one person by another person.[36] Consent is not sufficient for the morality of sexual acts *simpliciter,* because even though a sexual act might be a morally permissible qua sexual act, it still might be, for example, adulterous. Mappes's position is a thin minimalist externalism. Indeed, thin externalism, defined as making consent both necessary and sufficient, must also be minimalist. This criterion of the morality of sexual activity is contentless, or fully procedural: it does not evaluate the form or the nature of the sexual act (for example, what body parts are involved, or in what manner the sexual acts are carried out), but only the antecedent and concurrent conditions or context in which the sexual acts take place. In principle, the acts engaged in need not even produce (mutual) sexual pleasure for the consenting participants, an implication that differs from Goldman's behavioral internalism.[37]

Mappes, while developing his theory of sexual ethics, begins by repeating a point made frequently about Kantian ethics:

> According to a fundamental Kantian principle, it is morally wrong for A to use B *merely as a means* (to achieve A's ends). Kant's principle does not rule out A using B as a means, only A using B *merely* as a means, that is, in a way incompatible with respect for B as a person.

Then Mappes lays out his central thesis:

> A immorally uses B if and only if A intentionally acts in a way that violates the requirement that B's involvement with A's ends be based on B's voluntary informed consent.[38]

For Mappes, the presence of free and informed consent—there is no deception and no coercive force or threats—satisfies the Second Formulation, since each person's providing consent ensures that the persons involved in sexual activity with each other are not *merely* or *wrongfully* using each other as means. Mappes intends that this principle be applied to any activity, whether sexual or otherwise; he believes, along with Goldman, that sexual activity should be governed by moral principles that apply in general to human behavior.[39]

Having advanced this interpretation of what it takes to satisfy the Second Formulation in sexual matters, Mappes spends almost all his essay discussing various situations that might, or might not, involve violating the free and informed consent criterion taken as stating a necessary condition for the morality of sexual activity. Mappes discusses what sorts of actions count as deceptive, coercive (by force or threat), or exploitative, in which case sexual activity made possible by such maneuvers would be morally wrong. Some of these cases are intriguing, as anyone familiar with the literature on the meaning and application of the free and informed consent criterion in the area of medical ethics knows. But, putting aside for now the important question of the sufficiency of consent, not everyone agrees that in sexual (or other) contexts free and informed consent is absolutely necessary. Jeffrie Murphy, for one, has raised some doubts:

> "Have sex with me or I will find another girlfriend" strikes me (assuming normal circumstances) as a morally permissible threat, and "Have sex with me and I will marry you" strikes me (assuming the offer is genuine) as a morally permissible offer. . . . We negotiate our way through most of life with schemes of threats and offers . . . and I see no reason why the realm of sexuality should be utterly insulated from this very normal way of being human.[40]

Both "Have sex with me or I will find another girlfriend" and "Marry me or I will never sleep with you again (or at all)" seem to be coercive yet permissible threats,[41] but sexual activity obtained by the employment of these coercions involves immoral use, on Mappes's criterion. Further, it is not difficult to imagine circumstances in which deception in sexual contexts is not morally wrong (even if we ignore the universal and innocuous practice of deceptive physical primping: the use of cosmetics and suggestive clothing).[42] Mappes claims that my *withholding* information from you, information that I believe would influence your decision as to whether to have sexual relations with me, is deception that makes any subsequent sexual activity between us morally wrong.[43] But if I withhold the fact that I have an extraordinarily large or minuscule penis, and withholding that fact about my sexual anatomy plays a role in your eventually agreeing to engage in sex with me, it is not obviously true that my obtaining sex through this particular deception-by-omission is morally wrong. I suspect that what such cases tend to show is that we cannot rely comprehensively on a consent criterion to answer all (or perhaps any) of our pressing questions about sexual morality.[44] Does the other person have a *right* to know the size of my penis while deliberating whether to have sex with me? What types of coercive threat do we have a *right* to employ in trying to achieve our goals? These significant questions cannot be answered by a free and informed consent criterion; they also suggest that reading the Second Formulation such that consent by itself can satisfy the Second Formulation is questionable.

Indeed, Mappes provides little reason for countenancing his unKantian notion that the presence of free and informed consent is a sufficient condition for the satisfaction of the Second Formulation, for not treating another person merely as a means or not wrongfully using him or her. He does write that "respect for persons entails that each of us recognize the rightful authority of other persons (as rational beings) to conduct their individual lives as they see fit,"[45] which suggests the following kind of argument: allowing the other's consent to control when the other may be used for my sexual or other ends is to respect that person by taking his or her autonomy, his or her ability to reason and make choices, seriously, while not to allow the other to make the decision about when to be used for my sexual or other ends is disrespectfully paternalistic. If the other's consent is acknowledged to be sufficient, that shows that I respect his or her choice of ends, sexual or otherwise; or that even if I do not respect his or her particular choice of ends, at least I thereby show respect for his or her ends-making capacity or for his or her being a self-determining agent. And taking the other's consent as a sufficient condition can be a way of taking on his or her sexual or other ends as my own ends, as well as his or her taking on my sexual or other ends in my proposing to use him or her. According to such an argument, perhaps the best way to read Kant's Second Formulation is as a pronouncement of moral libertarianism—or a quasi libertarianism that also, as Mappes does, pays careful moral attention to and scrutinizes situations that are ripe for exploitation.[46]

Even if the argument makes some Kantian sense, Mappes's sexual principle seems to miss the point. The Kantian problem about sexuality is not, or is not only, that one person might make false promises, engage in deception, or employ force or threats against another person in order to gain sex. The problem of the objectification and use of both the self and the other arises for Kant even in those cases, or especially in those cases, in which both persons give perfectly free and informed consent. Thin externalism does not get to the heart of *this* problem. Perhaps no liberal philosophy that borders on moral libertarianism could even sense it as a problem; at any rate, no minimalist externalism could. The only sexual objectification that Mappes considers in his essay is that which arises with coercion, most dramatically in rape.[47] Nothing in his essay deals with what Kant and other philosophers discern as the intrinsically objectifying nature of sexuality itself. As Goldman does, Mappes assimilates sexual activity to all other human activities, all of which should be governed by the same moral principles. Whether Mappes's proposal works will depend, then, in part on whether sex is not so different from other joint human activities that free and informed consent is not too weak a criterion in this area of life.

It is an interesting question why free and informed consent does not, for Kant, solve the sex problem. It seems so obvious, to many today, that Mappes's consent criterion solves the sex problem that we wonder what Kant was up to in his metaphysical critique of sexuality. Kant's rejection of Mappes's solution suggests that Kant perceived deeper problems in sexual desire and activity than Mappes and Goldman acknowledge. In the *Lectures on Ethics*, Kant apparently accepts a Mappesian consent criterion regarding work-for-hire, but rejects it for sexual activity:

> Man [may], of course, use another human being as an instrument for his services; he [may] use his hands, his feet, and even all his powers; he [may] use him for his own purposes with the other's consent. But there is no way in which a human being can be made an Object of indulgence for another except through sexual impulse.[48]

For Kant, it seems that using another person in a work-for-hire situation is permissible, just with free and informed consent, as long as one does not undermine or deny the worker's humanity in any other way. But Kant finds something problematic about sexual interaction that does not exist during, say, a tennis game between two people (or in a work-for-hire situation), while Mappes sees no moral difference between playing tennis with someone and playing with their genitals, as long as free and informed consent is present. This disagreement between those philosophers who view sexual activity as something or as somehow special, and those philosophers who lump all human interactions together, requires further philosophical thought.[49]

Thick Externalism

Let us see if thick externalism, according to which more stringent contextual constraints in addition to free and informed consent are required for the morality of sexual activity, offers anything more substantial in coming to grips with the Kantian sex problem. My central example is Martha Nussbaum's essay "Objectification," in which Nussbaum submits that the Kantian sex problem is solved if sexual activity is confined to the context of an abiding, mutually respectful, and mutually regarding relationship. However, Nussbaum advances both a thick minimalist externalism and a thick extended externalism. Thus, in her long and complex essay, we can find at least two theses: (1) a background context of an abiding, mutually respectful and regarding relationship makes noxious objectification during sexual activity morally *permissible;* and (2) a background context of an abiding, mutually respectful and regarding relationship turns what might have been noxious objectification into something *good* or even "wonderful," a valuable type of objectification in which autonomy is happily abandoned—a thesis she derives from her reading of D. H. Lawrence.

Thick Minimalist Externalism

In several passages of Nussbaum's essay, she proposes a thick minimalist externalism, according to which sexual objectification is morally permissible in the context of an abiding, mutually respectful relationship. To start, consider this modest statement of her general thesis:

If I am lying around with my lover on the bed, and use his stomach as a pillow, there seems to be nothing at all baneful about this [instrumental objectification], provided that I do so with his consent . . . and without causing him pain, provided, as well, that I do so in the context of a relationship in which he is generally treated as more than a pillow. This suggests that what is problematic is not instrumentalization per se but treating someone *primarily* or *merely* as an instrument [for example, as a pillow]. The overall context of the relationship thus becomes fundamental.[50]

We can modify this passage so that Nussbaum's general point about permissible instrumental objectification-in-context can be applied more directly to the sex problem:

If I am lying around with my lover on the bed, and use his penis for my sexual satisfaction, there seems to be nothing at all baneful about this instrumental objectification, provided that I do so with his consent . . . and without causing him pain, provided, as well, that I do so in the context of a relationship in which he is generally treated as more than a penis. This suggests that what is problematic is not instrumentalization per se but treating someone *primarily* or *merely* as an instrument [for example, as a penis]. The overall context of the relationship thus becomes fundamental.

Other passages in Nussbaum's essay also express her thick minimalist externalism: "where there is a loss in subjectivity in the moment of lovemaking, this can be and frequently is accompanied by an intense concern for the subjectivity of the partner *at other moments*."[51] Again: "When there is a loss of autonomy in sex, the context . . . can be . . . one in which, on the whole, autonomy is respected and promoted"[52] And "denial of autonomy and denial of subjectivity are objectionable if they persist throughout an adult relationship, but *as phases* in a relationship characterized by mutual regard they can be all right, or even quite wonderful."[53]

One of Nussbaum's theses, then, is that a loss of autonomy, subjectivity, and individuality in sex, and the reduction of a person to his or her sexual body or its parts, in which the person is or becomes a tool or object, are morally acceptable if they occur within the background context of a psychologically healthy and morally sound relationship, an abiding relationship in which one's personhood—one's autonomy, subjectivity, and individuality—is generally respected and acknowledged. This solution to the sex problem seems plausible. It confirms the common (even if sexually conservative) intuition that one difference between morally permissible sexual acts and those that are wrongful because they are merely mutual use is the difference between sexual acts that occur in the context of a loving or caring relationship and those that occur in the absence of love, mutual care, or concern. Further, it appeals to our willingness to tolerate, exculpate, or even bless (as the partners' own private business) whatever nastiness that occurs in bed between two people *as long as* the rest, and the larger segment, of their relationship is morally sound. The lovers may sometimes engage in objectifying sexual games, by role-playing boss and secretary, client and prostitute, or teacher and student (phases of their relationship in which autonomy, subjectivity, and individuality might be sacrificed), since *outside* these occasional sexual games, they do display respect and regard for each other and abidingly support each other's humanity.

But this solution to the sex problem is inconsistent with Kant's Second Formulation, for that moral principle requires that a person be treated as an end *at the same time* he or she is being treated as a means.[54] On Nussbaum's thick minimalist externalism, small, sexually vulgar chunks of a couple's relationship, small pieces of noxious sexual objectification, are morally permissible in virtue of the larger or more frequent heavenly chunks of mutual respect that make up their relationship. But it is not, in general, right (except, perhaps, for some utilitarians) that my treating you badly today is either *justified* or *excusable* if I treated you admirably the whole day yesterday and will treat you more superbly tomorrow and the next day. As Nussbaum acknowledges, Kant insists that we ought not to treat someone *merely* as means, instrumentally, or as an object, but by that qualification Kant does not mean that treating someone as a means, instrumentally, or as an object at *some* particular time is morally permissible as long as he or she is treated with respect as a full person at *other* particular times.[55] That Nussbaum's thick minimalist externalist solution to Kant's sex problem violates the Second Formulation in this way is not the fault of the details of her account of the proper background context; the problem arises whether the background context is postulated to be one of abiding mutual respect and regard, or love, or marriage, or something else. Any version of thick minimalist externalism violates Kant's prescription that someone who is treated as a means must be treated *at the same time* as an end. Thick minimalist externalism, in any version, fails at least because, unlike behavioral or psychological internalism, it makes no attempt to improve or fix the nature of sexual activity itself. It leaves sexual activity exactly as it was or would be, as essentially objectifying or instrumental, although it claims that even when having this character, it is morally permissible.

Thick Extended Externalism

Thick extended externalism tries to have it both ways: to justify sexual activity when it occurs within the proper context *and* to fix the nature of the sexual acts that occur in that context. So Nussbaum's second proposal would seem to stand a better chance of conforming with the Second Formulation. In explaining the thesis that sexual objectification can be a wonderful or good thing in the proper context, Nussbaum says that in Lawrence's *Lady Chatterley's Lover,*

> both parties put aside their individuality and become identified with their bodily organs. They see one another in terms of those organs. And yet Kant's suggestion that in all such focusing on parts there is denial of humanity seems quite wrong. . . . The intense focusing of attention on the bodily parts seems an *addition,* rather than a subtraction.[56]

Nussbaum means that being reduced to one's body or its parts is an addition to one's personhood, not a subtraction from it, *as long as* the background context of an abiding, mutually respectful and regarding relationship exists, as she assumes it did between Constance Chatterley and Oliver Mellors. Nussbaum is claiming that sexual objectification, the reduction of a person to his or her flesh, and the loss of individuality and autonomy in sexual activity,[57] can be a wonderful or good aspect of life and sexuality. Being reduced to one's flesh, to one's genitals, supplements, or is an expansion or extension of, one's humanity, as long as it happens in a psychologically healthy and morally sound relationship.[58]

Nussbaum goes so far in this reasoning as to make the astonishing assertion that "In Lawrence, being treated as a cunt is a permission to expand the sphere of one's activity and fulfillment."[59] In the ablutionary context of an abiding relationship of mutual regard and respect, it is permissible and good for persons to descend fully to the level of their bodies, to become "cock" and "cunt," to become identified with their genitals, because in the rest of the relationship they are treated as *whole* persons. Or, more precisely, the addition of the objectification of being sexually reduced to their flesh *makes* their personhoods whole (it is, as Nussbaum writes, not a "subtraction"), as if without such a descent into their flesh they would remain partial, incomplete persons. This is suggested when Nussbaum writes, "Lawrence shows how a kind of sexual objectification . . . , how the very surrender of autonomy in a certain sort of sex act can free energies that can be used to make the self *whole and full.*"[60] I suppose it is a metaphysical truth of some sort that to be whole and full (to be all that I can be, as the U.S. Army, following J. S. Mill, used to promise in its television advertisements), I must realize all my potential. But some of this potential, it is not unreasonable to think, should not be realized, just because it would be immoral or perversely and stupidly imprudent to do so. Shall I, a professor of philosophy, fulfill my humanity by standing on street corners in the French Quarter and try homosexual tricking? Recall Kant: I may take on the other's ends only if those ends are themselves moral. Similarly, I may supplement or try to attain the fullness of my humanity only in ways that are moral. And whether adding to my personhood the identification of myself with my genitals is moral is precisely the question at issue. Merely because reducing myself to my genitals is an "expansion" of myself and of my "sphere of . . . activity" does little to justify it.

In any event, one implication of Nussbaum's requirement of a background context of an abiding, mutually respectful relationship worries me, whether this background context is part of a thick minimalist or a thick extended externalism: casual sex turns out to be morally wrong. In the sexual activity that transpires between strangers or between those who do not have much or any mutual regard for each other, sexual objectification and instrumentalization make those sexual acts wrong, because there is no background context of the requisite sort that would either justify the sexual objectification or transform it into something good. Casual sex is a descent to the level of the genitals with nothing for the persons to hang on to, nothing that would allow them to pull themselves back up to personhood when their sexual encounter is over. (This is, in effect, what Kant claims about prostitution and concubinage.)[61] Nussbaum explicitly states this sexually conservative trend in her thought and does not seem to consider it a weakness or defect of her account. Sounding like Kant, she writes:

> For in the absence of any narrative history with the person, how can desire attend to anything else but the incidental, and how can one do more than use the body of the other as a tool of one's own states? . . . Can one really treat someone with . . . respect and concern . . . if one has sex with him in the anonymous spirit? . . . [T]he instrumental treatment of human beings, the treatment of human beings as tools of the purposes of another, is always morally problematic; if it does not take place in a larger context of regard for humanity, it is a central form of the morally objectionable.[62]

Now, it is one thing to point out that Nussbaum's thick externalism is inimical to casual sex, or sex in the "anonymous spirit," for many would agree with her. Yet there is another point to be made. If noxious sexual objectification is permissible or made into something good only in the context of an abiding, mutually respectful relationship, then it is morally impermissible to engage in sexual activity while getting a relationship *under way.* The two persons may not engage in sexual activity early in their acquaintance, before they know whether they will come to have such an abiding and respectful relationship, because the sexual objectification of that premature sex could not be redeemed or cleansed—the requisite background context is missing. But, as some of us know, engaging in sexual activity, even when the persons do not know each other very well, often reveals to them important information about whether to pursue a relationship, whether to attempt to ascend to the abiding level.

This is another aspect of Nussbaum's conservative turn: the persons must *first* have that abiding, mutually respectful relationship before engaging in sexual activity.[63] It would be unconvincing to argue, in response, that sexual objectification in the early stages of their relationship is morally permissible, after all, because that sexual activity might contribute to the formation of an abiding, mutually respectful and regarding relationship that does succeed, later, in eliminating or cleansing the sexual objectification of the couple's sexual activity. That argument simply repeats in another form the dubious claim that morally bad phases or segments of a relationship are justified or excused in virtue of the larger or more frequent morally good segments of that relationship.

Let me close my discussion of Nussbaum's proposals by examining what she writes about sadomasochism. In response to her own question, "Can sadomasochistic sexual acts ever have a simply Lawrentian character, rather than a more sinister character?" Nussbaum replies:

> There seems to be no . . . reason why the answer . . . cannot be "yes." I have no very clear intuitions on this point, . . . but it would seem that some narrative depictions of sadomasochistic activity do plausibly attribute to its consensual form a kind of Lawrentian character in which the willingness to be vulnerable to the infliction of pain . . . manifests a more complete trust and receptivity than could be found in other sexual acts. Pat Califia's . . . short story ["Jessie"] is one example of such a portrayal.[64]

This is unconvincing (it also sounds more like a Hamptonian psychological internalism than a thick externalism). Califia describes in this lesbian sadomasochistic short story a first sexual encounter between two *strangers*, women, who meet at a party, an encounter about which neither knows in advance whether it will lead to a narrative history or an abiding relationship between them. In the sexual encounter described by Califia, there is no background context of an abiding, let alone mutually respectful and regarding, relationship. This means that the nature of their sexual activity *as sadomasochism* is irrelevant; the main point is that each woman, as a stranger to the other, must, on Nussbaum's own account, be merely using each other in the "anonymous spirit." Something Califia writes in "Jessie" makes a mockery of Nussbaum's proposal:

> I hardly know you—I don't know if you play piano, I don't know what kind of business it is you run, I don't know your shoe size—but I know you better than anyone else in the world.[65]

If Nussbaum wants to justify sadomasochistic sexual acts, she must say that, *in the context of an abiding, mutually regarding and respectful relationship,* either sadomasochistic sexuality is permissible, no matter how humiliating or brutal the acts are to the participants (thick minimalist externalism); or sadomasochistic sexuality is permissible because, in this background context, it can be a good or wonderful thing, an expansion of the couple's humanity (thick expanded externalism). In either case, appealing to Califia's "Jessie" is of no help at all.

5. Kant's Solution

To satisfy (or provoke) the reader's curiosity about Kant, and to stimulate further research on the topic, I conclude by making some preliminary remarks about Kant's own solution to the sex problem. These remarks must be preliminary, because this topic requires a separate, lengthy essay in its own right.[66]

Kant argues in both the earlier *Lectures on Ethics* and the later *Metaphysics of Morals* that sexual activity is morally permissible only within the context of a heterosexual, lifelong, and monogamous marriage, a contractual marriage formalized in law. Hence Kant advances a thick externalism. (I will soon suggest that his externalism is also minimalist.) Kant barely argues in these texts, or argues weakly, that marriage must be lifelong and heterosexual.[67] But Kant's argument that the only permissible sexual activity is married sexual activity is distinctive and presented forcefully. In the *Metaphysics of Morals*, for example, Kant writes:

> There is only one condition under which this is possible: that while one person is acquired by the other *as if it were a thing,* the one who is acquired acquires the other in turn; for in this way each reclaims itself and restores its personality. But acquiring a member of a human being [i.e., access to or possession of the other's genitals and associated sexual capacities] is at the same time acquiring the whole person, since a person is an absolute unity. Hence it is not only admissible for the sexes to surrender and to accept each other for enjoyment under the condition of marriage, but it is possible for them to do so *only* under this condition.[68]

Kant's idea seems to be that sexual activity, with its essential sexual objectification, is morally permissible only in marriage, because only in marriage can each of the persons engage in sexual activity *without losing* their own personality—their personhood or humanity. In a marriage of a Kantian type, each person is "acquired" by the other person (along with his or her genitals and sexual capacities) as if he or she were an object, and hence, by being acquired, loses his or her humanity (autonomy, individuality). But because the acquisition in marriage is reciprocal, each person *regains* his or her personhood (and hence does not lose it, after all). When I "surrender" myself to you, and you thereby acquire me, but you also "surrender" yourself to me, and I thereby acquire you, which "you" includes the "me" that you have acquired, we each surrender but then re-acquire ourselves. (I think this means that the "I do"s of the marriage ceremony must be said simultaneously, not consecutively.)

There are many puzzles in Kant's solution.[69] One is that Kant does not explicitly state in laying out his solution that through such a reciprocal surrender and acquisition the persons in some robust sense treat each other as persons or acknowledge each other's humanity as an end, in bed or otherwise. That is, after laying out his relentless criticism of sexual desire and activity, Kant never poses the question, "How might two people, married or not, treat themselves and each other as persons during sexual activity?" Kant is notorious for being stingy with examples, but why here? In fact, in only one place that I could find, a mere footnote in the *Metaphysics of Morals,* does Kant use the language of the Second Formulation to speak about marriage:

> [I]f I say "my wife," this signifies a special, namely a rightful, relation of the possessor to an object as a *thing* (even though the object is also a person). Possession (*physical* possession), however, is the condition of being able to *manage* . . . something as a thing, even if this must, in another respect, be treated at the same time as a person.[70]

But neither in the footnote nor in the text does Kant explain what "in another respect" being treated as a person amounts to. The language of the Second Formulation is plainly here, in the footnote, including the crucial "at the same time," but not its substance. Further, in the text, Kant refrains from using the language of the Second Formulation:

> What is one's own here does not . . . mean what is one's own in the sense of property in the person of another (for a human being cannot have property in himself, much less in another person), but means what is one's own in the sense of usufruct . . . to make direct use of a person *as of* a thing, as a means to my end, but still *without infringing* upon his personality.[71]

Kant is asserting, I think, that it is permissible in *some* contexts to use another person as a means or treat the other as an object, merely with the other's free and informed consent, as long as one does not violate the humanity of the other in some other way, as long as one allows him or her otherwise to retain intact his or her personhood. The reciprocal surrender and acquisition of Kantian marriage, which involves a contractual free and informed agreement to exchange selves, *prevents* this (possibly extra) denial or loss of personhood. But this principle is far removed from the Second Formulation as Kant usually articulates and understands it.

Kant, I now submit, advances an externalism that is minimalist: the objectification and instrumentality that attach to sexuality remain even in marital sexual activity. Hence not even Kant abides by the "at the same time" requirement of the Second Formulation in his solution to the sex problem. Nussbaum, for one, seems to recognize Kant's minimalism when she writes, "sexual desire, according to his analysis, drives out every possibility of respect. This is so even in marriage."[72] Raymond Belliotti, by contrast, finds thick extended externalism in Kant:

> Kant suggests that two people can efface the wrongful commodification inherent in sex and thereby redeem their own humanity only by mutually exchanging "rights to their whole person." The *implication* is that a deep, abiding relationship of the requisite sort ensures that sexual activity is not separated from personal interaction which honors individual dignity.[73]

But the "implication" is something Belliotti illicitly reads into Kant's texts. Nowhere does Kant say that in marriage, which is for him a contractual relationship characterized by mutual acquisition of persons as if they were objects (hardly a "deep, abiding relationship"), sexual activity "honors individual dignity." Belliotti reads Kant as if Kant were Nussbaum. When Kant asserts in the *Metaphysics of Morals* that sexual activity is permissible only in marriage, he speaks about the *acquisition* or *possession* of the other person by each spouse, and never mentions love, altruism, or benevolence. For similar reasons, Robert Baker and Frederick Elliston's view must be rejected. They claim that, according to Kant, "marriage transubstantiates immoral sexual intercourse into morally permissible human copulation by transforming a manipulative masturbatory relationship into one of altruistic unity."[74] But Kant never says anything about "altruism" in his account of marriage or of sexual activity in marriage; nowhere, for example, does he claim that the persons come to treat each other as ends and respect their humanity in sexual activity by unconditionally providing sexual pleasure to each other. Indeed, Kant writes in the *Metaphysics of Morals* that "benevolence . . . deter[s] one from carnal enjoyment."[75] Further, both these readings of Kant are insensitive to the sharp contrast between Kant's glowing account of male friendship, in both the *Lectures on Ethics* and the *Metaphysics of Morals,* as a morally exemplary and fulfilling balance of love and respect, and Kant's dry account of heterosexual marriage, which makes marriage look like a continuation, or culmination, of the battle of the sexes. Kant never says about marriage, for example, anything close to this: "Friendship . . . is the union of two persons through equal mutual love and respect. . . . [E]ach participat[es] and shar[es] sympathetically in the other's well-being through the morally good will that unites them."[76]

Of course, the virtue of Belliotti's reading, and that of Baker and Elliston, is that if sexual activity can indeed be imbued with Kantian respect or "altruism," then the "at the same time" requirement of the Second Formulation is satisfied. But there is good evidence that Kant's own view is minimalist. For example, when Kant writes in the *Lectures on Ethics* that

> If . . . a man wishes to satisfy his desire, and a woman hers, they stimulate each other's desire; their inclinations meet, but their object is not human nature but sex, and each of them dishonours the human nature of the other. They make of humanity an instrument for the satisfaction of their lusts and inclinations, and dishonour it by placing it on a level with animal nature.[77]

he intends this description to apply to sexual activity even in marriage, and not only to casual sex, prostitution, or concubinage. This point is confirmed by Kant's letter to C. G. Schütz, who had written to Kant to complain about Kant's similar treatment of sexuality in the later *Metaphysics of Morals*. To this objection offered by Schütz, "You cannot really believe that a man makes an object of a woman just by engaging in marital cohabitation with her, and vice versa," Kant concisely replies: "[I]f the cohabitation is assumed to be *marital*, that is, *lawful*, . . . the authorization is already contained in the concept."[78] Note that Kant does not deny that objectification still occurs in marital sex; he simply says it is permissible, or authorized. Schütz makes the point another way: "[M]arried people do not become *res fungibiles* just by sleeping together," to which Kant replies: "An enjoyment of this sort involves at once the thought of this person as merely *functional,* and that in fact is what the reciprocal use of each other's sexual organs by two people *is.*"[79] "Is," that is, even in marriage.

Further, that marriage is designed and defined by Kant to be only about sexuality, about having access to the other person's sexual capacities and sexual body parts—for enjoyment or pleasure, not necessarily for reproduction—also suggests that his solution is minimalist. Consider Kant's definition of marriage in the *Metaphysics of Morals:* "Sexual union in accordance with principle is *marriage* (*matrimonium*), that is, the union of two persons of different sexes for lifelong possession of each other's sexual attributes."[80] There is no suggestion in this definition of marriage that Belliottian human, individual dignity will make its way into marital sexual activity (quite the contrary). Howard Williams tartly comments, about Kant's notion of marriage, that "sex, for Kant, seems simply to be a form of mutual exploitation for which one must pay the price of marriage. He represents sex as a commodity which ought only to be bought and sold for life in the marriage contract."[81] If sexual activity in marriage is, for Kant, a commodity, it has hardly been cleansed of its essentially objectionable qualities. Kant's view of marriage has much in common with

St. Paul's (see 1 Corinthians 7), in which each person has power over the body of the other spouse, and each spouse has a "conjugal debt" to engage in sexual activity with the other nearly on demand.[82] That marriage is defined by Kant to be only about access to sex is what is astounding, even incomprehensible, to the contemporary mind, and may explain why modern philosophers are quick to attribute to Kant more congenial solutions to the sex problem.

Finally, a commonly neglected aspect of the Second Formulation, that one must *also* treat the humanity in one's own person as an end, is important in understanding Kant's solution to the sex problem. Duties to self are important for Kant, a fact overlooked by those philosophers (for example, Mappes and Goldman) who emphasize the treat-the-other-as-an-end part of the Second Formulation. Notice the prominence of Kant's discussion of the duties to self in the *Lectures on Ethics*. They are elaborately discussed early in the text, well before Kant discusses moral duties to others, and in the *Lectures* Kant launches into his treatment of sexuality immediately after he concludes his account of duties to self in general and before he, finally, gets around to duties to others. Allen Wood is one of the few commentators on Kant who, I think, gets this right:

> [Kant] thinks sexual intercourse is "a degradation of humanity" because it is an act in which "people *make themselves* into an object of enjoyment, and hence into a thing" (VE 27:346). He regards sex as permissible only within marriage, and even there it is in itself "a merely animal union" (MS 6:425).[83]

Kant does make it clear that a duty to treat the humanity in one's own person as an end is his primary concern in restricting sexual activity to marriage:

> [T]here ar[ises] from one's duty to oneself, that is, to the humanity in one's own person, a right (*ius personale*) of both sexes to acquire each other as persons *in the manner of things* by marriage.[84]

For Kant, then, the crux of the argument about sex and marriage does not turn on a duty to avoid sexually objectifying the other, but to avoid the sexual objectification of the self. It would be an ironic reading of Kant to say that he claims that *my right to use you* in sexual activity in marriage arises from *my duty to myself*. What Kant is saying, without irony, is that as a result of the duty toward myself, I cannot enter into sexual relations with you unless I preserve my personhood; you, likewise, cannot enter into sexual relations with me unless you are able to preserve your own personhood. Each of us can accomplish that goal only by mutual surrender and acquisition, by the exchange of rights to our persons and to our genitals and sexual capacities that constitutes marriage. It is not the right to use you sexually that is my goal, although I do gain that right. My goal is to preserve my own personhood in the face of the essentially objectifying nature of sexuality. But preserving my own personhood, as admirable as that might be, is not the same thing as treating you with dignity (or altruism) during marital sexual activity or in marriage generally. Kant has still done nothing to accomplish that—nor, if I am right, was that his intention.

6. Metaphilosophical Finale

Howard Williams has made a shrewd observation about Kant's solution to the sex problem:

> [A]n important premiss of Kant's argument is that sexual relations necessarily involve treating oneself and one's partner as things. . . . [T]o demonstrate convincingly that marriage is the only ethically desirable context for sex, Kant ought to start from better premisses than these.[85]

Let me explain what is interesting here. Bernard Baumrin argues that if we want to justify sexual activity *at all*, we should start our philosophizing by conceding the worst: "I begin . . . by admitting the most damaging facts . . . that any theory of sexual morality must countenance," viz., that "human sexual interaction is essentially manipulative—physically, psychologically, emotionally, and even intellectually."[86] Starting with premises about sexuality any less ugly or more optimistic would make justifying sexual activity too easy. Williams's point is that if we want to justify the specific claim that sex is permissible *only in marriage,* starting with Kantian premises about the nature of sex makes *that* task too easy. If sex is in its essence wholesome, or if, as in Mappes and Goldman, sexual activity does not significantly differ from other activities that involve human interaction, then it becomes easier both to justify sexual activity and to justify sex outside of marriage. Those, including many Christian philosophers and theologians, who assume the worst about sexuality to begin with, gain an advantage in defending the view that sexuality must be restricted to matrimony.[87] This tactic is copied in a milder way by Nussbaum and Hampton, who reject casual sex. The convincing intellectual trick would be to assume the *best* about sex, that it is by its nature wholesome, and then argue, *anyway,* that it should be restricted to lifelong, monogamous matrimony and that casual sex is morally wrong.[88] Perhaps the liberals Baumrin and Goldman are trying to pull off the reverse trick, in that they admit the worst about sexuality and still come out with a permissive sexual morality. But in admitting the worst, how do they avoid concluding, with Kant, that sexual activity is permissible only in the restrictive conditions of marriage? Perhaps they succeed, or think they do, only by reading the Second Formulation in a very narrow or an easily satisfied way.[89]

Notes

1. Immanuel Kant's views on sexuality are presented mainly in his *Lectures on Ethics* [ca. 1780], trans. Louis Infield (Indianapolis, Ind.: Hackett, 1963), 162–71, and in *The Metaphysics of Morals* [1797], trans. Mary Gregor (Cambridge: Cambridge University Press, 1996), 61–64, 126–28, 178–80. There is also much on sex, gender, and marriage in his *Anthropology from a Pragmatic Point of View*, trans. Mary J. Gregor (The Hague: Martinus Nijhoff, 1974). The sex section from the *Lectures on Ethics* is reprinted in this volume, 199–205.

2. For more on the Kantian view of the nature of sex, see my discussion of metaphysical sexual pessimism in "The Fundamentals of the Philosophy of Sex," in this volume, xxi–xxiv.

3. See Bernard Baumrin, "Sexual Immorality Delineated," in Robert Baker and Frederick Elliston, eds., *Philosophy and Sex*, 2nd edition (Buffalo, N.Y.: Prometheus, 1984), 300–11, at 300–302.

4. Kant, *Lectures on Ethics*, 164; in this volume, 200.

5. "In desire you are compromised in the eyes of the object of desire, since you have displayed that you have designs which are vulnerable to his intentions" (Roger Scruton, *Sexual Desire: A Moral Philosophy of the Erotic* [New York: Free Press, 1986], 82).

6. See Virginia Held, "Coercion and Coercive Offers," in J. Roland Pennock and John W. Chapman, eds., *Coercion: Nomos VIX* (Chicago, Ill.: Aldine, 1972), 49–62, at 58: "A person unable to spurn an offer may act as unwillingly as a person unable to resist a threat. Consider the distinction between rape and seduction. In one case constraint and threat are operative, in the other inducement and offer. If the degree of inducement is set high enough in the case of seduction, there may seem to be little difference in the extent of coercion involved. In both cases, persons may act against their own wills." I think we do recognize that a sexual offer may be a powerful, even overwhelming, inducement. Whether a person is able to resist depends at least on his or her nature (desires, needs) and what is being offered.

7. Kant, *Metaphysics of Morals*, 62.

8. Kant, *Lectures*, 164; in this volume, 200. Kant also suggests that sexuality can reduce humans *below* the level of animals; animals in their instinctual innocence do not and cannot use each other sexually. See Kant, *Lectures*, 122–23: "In the case of animals inclinations are already determined by subjectively compelling factors; in their case . . . disorderliness is impossible. But if man gives free rein to his inclinations, he sinks lower than an animal because he then lives in a state of disorder which does not exist among animals."

9. For Adam Smith, "the passion by which nature unites the two sexes . . . [is] the most furious of the passions" (*The Theory of Moral Sentiments* [New York: Au-

gustus M. Kelley, 1966], part 1, sect. 2, chap. 1, page 33).

10. Kant, *Groundwork of the Metaphysic of Morals,* trans. H. J. Paton (New York: Harper Torchbooks, 1964), 95–96 (AK 4:428). Marcia W. Baron, in *Kantian Ethics Almost without Apology* (Ithaca, N.Y.: Cornell University Press, 1995), 199–204, and H. J. Paton, well before her, in *The Categorical Imperative: A Study in Kant's Moral Philosophy* (New York: Harper and Row, 1967), 55–57, point out that in his later works Kant retracts or softens this judgment. Baron's discussion is more complete and especially enlightening.

11. Michael Ruse, *Homosexuality: A Philosophical Inquiry* (Oxford: Basil Blackwell, 1988), 185.

12. Kant, *Groundwork,* 96 (429); 95 (428).

13. Kant, *Groundwork,* 98 (430); see also *Metaphysics,* 199.

14. Kant, *Groundwork,* 97 (429). See Christine Korsgaard, "Creating the Kingdom of Ends: Reciprocity and Responsibility in Personal Relations," *Philosophical Perspectives* 6, *Ethics* (1992), 305–32 at 309: "respect gets its most positive and characteristic expression at precisely the moments when we must act together. . . . If my end requires your act for its achievement, then I must let you make it your end too. . . . Thus I must make your ends and reasons mine, and I must choose [my ends] in such a way that they can be yours."

15. C. E. Harris Jr., seems to have this weaker version of the Second Formulation in mind when he claims that we are permitted to use another person in our transactions or interactions with him or her (e.g., a post office worker, doctor, professor) as long as, beyond using these persons for our purposes, we "do nothing to negate [their] status as a moral being," "do not deny him his status as a person," or "do not obstruct [their] humanity." Harris applies this principle to casual sex: as long as "neither person is overriding the freedom of the other or diminishing the ability of the other to be an effective goal-pursuing agent," it is permissible (*Applying Moral Theories,* 4th edition [Belmont, Calif.: Wadsworth, 2002], 153–54, 164).

16. Alan Goldman, "Plain Sex," in this volume, 39–55, at 40.

17. Goldman, "Plain Sex," in this volume, 51. Kant would have said "subjective," "discretionary," or "arbitrary" ends, instead of Goldman's "private" ends, but he would be making the same point.

18. Goldman, "Plain Sex," in this volume, 51.

19. Goldman, "Plain Sex," in this volume, 51.

20. David Archard's position is similar to Goldman's. See his *Sexual Consent* (Boulder, Colo.: Westview, 1998), 41 (italics added):

> If Harry has sex with Sue solely for the purpose of deriving sexual gratification from the encounter and with no concern for what Sue might get out of it, if Harry pursues this end single-mindedly and never allows himself to think of how it might be for Sue, then Harry treats Sue merely as a means to his ends. If, *by contrast,* Harry derives pleasure from his sex with Sue but also strives to attend to Sue's pleasure and conducts the encounter in a way that is sensitive to her needs, then Harry does not treat Sue merely as a means.
>
> That the sexual relationship between Sue and Harry is consensual does not mean that neither one of them is treating the other merely as a means.

21. See Hobbes: "the delight men take in delighting, is not sensual, but a pleasure or joy of the mind consisting in the imagination of the power they have so much to please" ("Human Nature, or the Fundamental Elements of Policy," in *The English Works of Thomas Hobbes*, vol. IV, ed. Sir William Molesworth [Germany: Scientia Verlag Aalen, 1966], chap. 9, sect. 15, page 48).

22. See Thomas Nagel, "Sexual Perversion," in this volume, 13–15.

23. De Sade, *Justine, Philosophy in the Bedroom, and Other Writings,* trans. Richard Seaver and Austryn Wainhouse (New York: Grove Press, 1965), in *Philosophy in the Bedroom,* 343–44.

24. The conditionality of giving pleasure is inherent in Baumrin's approach: "the crucial element in creating specifically sexual rights and duties is the desire to use another as a means for a certain kind of end and the willingness to offer oneself to that person as an inducement" ("Sexual Immorality Delineated," 304). One person in effect says to the other: "I wish to use you as an instrument for my sexual purposes and therefore undertake to make myself the instrument of your sexual purposes to the extent that you accept my proposal" (303–304; italics omitted).

25. Kant, *Metaphysics,* 199.

26. See my discussion, "Orgasmic Justice," in *Sexual Investigations* (New York: New York University Press, 1996), 53–57.

27. Requiring that persons inject unconditional giving into sexual activity is incompatible with the letter and spirit of Goldman's "Plain Sex," which is in part devoted to undermining restrictive in favor of permissive sexual ethics. Casual sex in which there are no commitments, consensual sex between perfect strangers, and prostitution, which liberal sexual ethics usually permit, would seem to be the least likely situations in which to find altruistic sexual giving, although it is not impossible.

28. Jean Hampton, "Defining Wrong and Defining Rape," in Keith Burgess-Jackson, ed., *A Most Detestable Crime: New Philosophical Essays on Rape* (New York: Oxford University Press, 1999), 118–56, at 147.

29. Hampton, "Defining Wrong and Defining Rape," 147.

30. It is interesting that Hampton makes this Kantian point about the dangerous nature of sex, because she also criticizes what she takes to be Kant's overly pessimistic metaphysics of sex; see "Defining Wrong and Defining Rape," 146–47. For a stronger rejection of Kant's metaphysics of sex, see Irving Singer, "The Morality of Sex: Contra Kant," in this volume, 259–72.

31. Hampton, "Defining Wrong and Defining Rape," 147–48.

32. Hampton, "Defining Wrong and Defining Rape," 150.

33. A similar view is advanced by Alan Donagan, in *The Theory of Morality* (Chicago: University of Chicago Press, 1977), who praises "life-affirming and nonexploitative" sexuality. By contrast, "sexual acts which are life-denying in their imaginative significance, or are exploitative, are impermissible." He rejects, specifically, sadomasochism, prostitution, and casual sex (107; italics omitted).

34. Pat Califia, "Introduction," *Macho Sluts* (Los Angeles, Calif.: Alyson Books, 1988), 9.

35. Thomas A. Mappes, "Sexual Morality and the Concept of Using Another Person," in this volume, 207–33. Mappes's Kantian theory of sexual ethics can be understood as a solution to the Kantian sex problem, for he concedes that "the

domain of sexual interaction seems to offer ample opportunity for 'using' another person" (from Mappes's introductory essay to Chapter 4, "Sexual Morality," in Thomas A. Mappes and Jane S. Zembaty, eds., *Social Ethics: Morality and Social Policy*, 6th edition [New York: McGraw-Hill, 2002], 157–64, at 160; or see the 4th edition, 1992, 192; or the 5th, 1997, 153).

36. For another Kantian consent view, see Raymond Belliotti, "A Philosophical Analysis of Sexual Ethics," *Journal of Social Philosophy* 10, 3 (1979): 8–11.

37. I interpret Baumrin's theory of sexual ethics as an amalgam of Mappes's thin externalism and Goldman's behavioral internalism. For Baumrin, consent is both necessary and sufficient for the morality of sexual activity, as in Mappes; but Baumrin also thinks that each person consents, in particular, to be the instrument for the sexual satisfaction of the other, as in Goldman ("Sexual Immorality Delineated," 304).

38. Mappes, "Sexual Morality and the Concept of Using Another Person," in this volume, 208.

39. Goldman, "Plain Sex," in this volume, 49–51.

40. Jeffrie Murphy, "Some Ruminations on Women, Violence, and the Criminal Law," in Jules Coleman and Allen Buchanan, eds., *In Harm's Way: Essays in Honor of Joel Feinberg* (Cambridge: Cambridge University Press, 1994), 209–30, at 218.

41. Alan Wertheimer argues that "Have sexual relations with me or I will dissolve our dating relationship" is *not* "a coercive proposal" (although it *might* still be wrong); see his "Consent and Sexual Relations," in this volume, 341–66, at 354–55.

42. I found this interesting passage in Rex Stout's Nero Wolfe mystery novel, *Before Midnight* (New York: Bantam, 1955): "a bill which . . . had been introduced into the English Parliament in 1770 . . . ran[:] All women of whatever age, rank, profession, or degree, whether virgins, maids, or widows, that shall, from and after this Act, impose upon, seduce, and betray into matrimony, any of His Majesty's subjects, by the scents, paints, cosmetic washes, artificial teeth, false hair, Spanish wool, iron stays, hoops, high heeled shoes, bolstered hips, shall incur the penalty of the law in force against witchcraft and like misdemeanors and the marriage, upon conviction, shall stand null and void" (54; italics omitted). Stout doesn't say whether the bill passed.

43. Mappes, "Sexual Morality and the Concept of Using Another Person," in this volume, 211–12.

44. This is the thrust of Alan Wertheimer's "Consent and Sexual Relations," in this volume, 341–66."

45. Mappes, "Sexual Morality and the Concept of Using Another Person," in this volume, 208.

46. Mappes's free and informed consent test seems to imply that prostitution is permissible if the prostitute is not exploited, taken advantage of in virtue of her economic needs. Baumrin's consent view seems to imply that prostitution is permissible, because either party may "discharge" the other's duty of providing sexual satisfaction ("Sexual Immorality Delineated," 303; see also 305). But the implications of Goldman's position for prostitution are unclear. He does not advance a mere free and informed consent test, but lays it down that each person must make a sexual object of himself or herself for the sake of the pleasure of

the other, or must provide sexual pleasure to the other so that their activity is mutually pleasurable. That seems to condemn prostitution, unless the client provides pleasure for the prostitute, or unless the prostitute's pleasure in receiving money makes their encounter "mutual."

47. Mappes, "Sexual Morality and the Concept of Using Another Person," in this volume, 212.

48. Kant, *Lectures*, 163; in this volume, 199. In several places I replaced "can" in Infield's translation with "may"; Kant's point is moral, not about natural or conceptual possibility.

49. The "New Natural Law" philosophers (as well as the old ones) emphasize the difference that *only* in (hetero)sexuality can a new life be generated by a procreative sexual act. For example, see John Finnis's contribution to "Is Homosexual Conduct Wrong? A Philosophical Exchange," in this volume, 97–100; and his "Law, Morality, and 'Sexual Orientation'," *Notre Dame Law Review* 69, 5 (1994): 1049–76, at 1066f.

50. Martha Nussbaum, "Objectification," in this volume, 381–419, at 394. In a slightly revised version of "Objectification," which appears in Nussbaum's *Sex and Social Justice* (New York: Oxford University Press, 1999), 213–39, she changed "without causing him pain" to "without causing him unwanted pain" (223).

51. Nussbaum, "Objectification," in this volume, 401 (italics added).

52. Nussbaum, "Objectification," in this volume, 401.

53. Nussbaum, "Objectification," in this volume, 411 (italics added).

54. "The words 'at the same time' . . . must not be overlooked: they are absolutely essential to Kant's statement" of the Second Formulation (Paton, *The Categorical Imperative*, 165).

55. There is a similar problem of Kant exegesis in Baumrin's "Sexual Immorality Delineated." He claims that what is morally wrong, for Kant, is treating a person in *every* respect as a means. What is permissible, for Baumrin (or Baumrin's Kant), then, is treating a person as a means as long as the person is treated in (at least and perhaps only) *one* respect *not* as a means (300). What this means and whether it is compatible with the Second Formulation are unclear. Note that Baumrin's rendition of the Second Formulation (he quotes the translation of Lewis White Beck) does not include the phrase "at the same time" (310, n. 1).

56. Nussbaum, "Objectification," in this volume, 400–401 (italics added).

57. Nussbaum could cite Scott Tucker: "one reason so many of us like sex so much is because we can selectively entrust ourselves to annihilation, and rise with new life from our graves and beds. . . . Of course, not all sex is like this; not all sex should be; plenty of sex is companionable, habitual, and self-possessed" ("Gender, Fucking, and Utopia: An Essay in Response to John Stoltenberg's *Refusing to Be a Man*," *Social Text*, no. 27 [1990]: 3–34, at 30).

58. By contrast, for Roger Scruton, the reduction of a person to flesh, as occurs (for example) in masturbation, is obscene; "masturbation involves a concentration on the body and its curious pleasures" (*Sexual Desire*, 319). See also 139: in obscenity and perversion, "we suffer that dangerous shift of attention which is the mark of original sin—the shift from the embodied person to the dominating and dissolving body."

59. Nussbaum, "Objectification," in this volume, 405. It is interesting to consider that "though cunt was a standard term until the 16th century, it then be-

came regarded as so vulgar as to be taboo through the 20th century. . . . Only when the word began to be used by writers such a D. H. Lawrence and James Joyce did the taboo begin to crumble" (Alan Richter, *Dictionary of Sexual Slang* [New York: John Wiley, 1993], 59). Maybe Lawrence et al. killed the taboo surrounding the *use* of the word *cunt,* but they did little to destroy its sharp negative connotations, as when we call a woman (or a man), disparagingly, a "cunt," or when we say that a man (or a woman) treats a woman as a "cunt."

60. Nussbaum, "Objectification," in this volume, 402 (italics added).

61. Kant, *Lectures,* 165–66; in this volume, 201–2.

62. Nussbaum, "Objectification," in this volume, 409, 409–10, 411. I am not able to explore here the tension between Nussbaum's rejecting sexuality in the "anonymous spirit" and her legal and moral defense of prostitution, as presented in "'Whether from Reason or Prejudice.' Taking Money for Bodily Services," *Sex and Social Justice,* 276–98. See my discussion of Nussbaum in *Pornography, Sex, and Feminism* (Amherst, N.Y.: Prometheus, 2002), 72–78, 163–74.

63. Contrast, on the value of premarital sex for women, the essay by the conservative feminist Sidney Callahan ("Abortion and the Sexual Agenda: A Case for Prolife Feminism") and the essay by the liberal feminist Ellen Willis ("Abortion: Is a Woman a Person?"), in this volume, 177–90 and 191–95.

64. Nussbaum, "Objectification," in this volume, 509. Nussbaum mistakenly calls Califia's short story "Jenny."

65. Califia, "Jessie," in *Macho Sluts,* 28–62, at 60. This was said by the top, Jessie, to her bottom, Liz, the morning after their sexual encounter.

66. Some important accounts of Kant on sexuality are provided by Vincent M. Cooke, "Kant, Teleology, and Sexual Ethics," *International Philosophical Quarterly* 31, 1 (1991): 3–13; Onora O'Neill, "Between Consenting Adults," in her *Constructions of Reason: Explorations of Kant's Practical Philosophy* (Cambridge: Cambridge University Press, 1989), 105–25; Susan Meld Shell, *The Embodiment of Reason: Kant on Spirit, Generation, and Community* (Chicago: University of Chicago Press, 1996) and *The Rights of Reason: A Study of Kant's Philosophy and Politics* (Toronto: University of Toronto Press, 1980); Irving Singer, *The Nature of Love,* vol. 2: *Courtly and Romantic* (Chicago: University of Chicago Press, 1984); Keith Ward, *The Development of Kant's View of Ethics* (Oxford: Basil Blackwell, 1972); and others referred to in the notes below. (What follows in this essay is an addition to the version published in *Essays in Philosophy,* and makes it more "whole.")

67. Kant's philosophical objections to homosexuality and, a fortiori, to homosexual marriage, are examined critically in my "Kant and Sexual Perversion," *The Monist* 86:1 (2003), forthcoming.

68. Kant, *Metaphysics,* 62. See *Lectures,* 167; in this volume, 202–3.

69. On problems with the notion of a metaphysical "union" of two-into-one, and the implications of such a union for the fate of individual autonomy and genuine benevolence, see my "Union, Autonomy, and Concern," in Roger Lamb, ed., *Love Analyzed* (Belmont, Calif.: Westview Press, 1997), 65–92. The ideas I would like to develop are that a Kantian marriage union destroys the autonomy that lies at the heart of Kantian humanity or personhood and that it also, thereby, logically prevents the spouses from being genuinely benevolent to each other, as required by the Second Formulation.

70. Kant, *Metaphysics,* 126*n.*

71. Kant, *Metaphysics,* 127; italics added.

72. Nussbaum, "Objectification," in this volume, 415, n. 30.

73. Raymond Belliotti, *Good Sex: Perspectives on Sexual Ethics* (Lawrence: University Press of Kansas, 1993), 100; italics added.

74. Robert Baker and Frederick Elliston, "Introduction," *Philosophy and Sex,* 1st edition (Buffalo, N.Y.: Prometheus, 1975), 8–9; 2nd edition (Buffalo, N.Y.: Prometheus, 1984), 17–18. Or see the "Introduction" in Robert B. Baker, Kathleen J. Wininger, and Frederick A. Elliston, eds., *Philosophy and Sex,* 3rd edition (Amherst, N.Y.: Prometheus, 1998), 23.

75. Kant, *Metaphysics,* 180. In her earlier translation of the *Metaphysics,* Gregor rendered this line "benevolence . . . stop[s] short of carnal enjoyment" (*The Doctrine of Virtue: Part II of the Metaphysic of Morals* [New York: Harper Torchbooks, 1964], 90).

76. Kant, *Metaphysics,* 215. There are maybe two lines in the *Lectures* that might be construed as supporting a "love" or "altruism" reading of Kant's solution to the sex problem. These lines might explain why Robert Trevas, Arthur Zucker, and Donald Borchert (*Philosophy of Sex and Love: A Reader* [Upper Saddle River, N.J.: Prentice-Hall, 1997], 129) claim that, *for Kant,*

> If . . . we give our whole selves to each other, we become committed to concern for each other's total well-being and overall happiness. Indeed, we find ourselves treating each other as "ends" and not simply as "means."

But on the basis of Kant's slender statement that in marriage one person obtains "the right to dispose over the [other] person as a whole—over the welfare and happiness and generally over all the circumstances of that person" (*Lectures,* 166–67; in this volume, 202), we cannot conclude that Kant meant that in exchanging their selves the spouses thereby become concerned for each other's well-being or treat each other as ends. Similarly, in the statement "one devotes one's person to another, one devotes not only sex but the whole person; the two cannot be separated. . . . [O]ne yields one's person, body and soul, for good and ill in every respect, so that the other has complete rights over it" (*Lectures,* 167; in this volume, 202), Kant does not say that love or altruism overcomes mere use. Any hint of altruism in the "devotes" that occurs in this passage is erased by the closing "so that the other has complete rights over it," which reasserts the acquisition or possession of Kantian marriage. Even if Kant thought that marriage should include love, this does not mean that he thought that the love in marriage is that which makes sexual activity permissible; nor does it mean that he thought that love in marriage fixed the nature of the sexual act, from something objectifying to something not objectifying.

77. Kant, *Lectures,* 164; in this volume, 200.

78. Kant, *Philosophical Correspondence: 1759–99,* trans. Arnulf Zweig (Chicago: University of Chicago Press, 1967), letter dated July 10, 1797, page 235.

79. Kant, *Philosophical Correspondence,* 235–36; italics added to "is."

80. Kant, *Metaphysics,* 62.

81. Howard Williams, *Kant's Political Philosophy* (New York: St. Martin's Press, 1983), 117.

82. For some hints of Kant's debt to Paul, see *Metaphysics,* 179–80.

83. Allen Wood, *Kant's Ethical Thought* (Cambridge: Cambridge University

Press, 1999), 2; italics added. Here is the line in the *Metaphysics* to which Wood refers ("MS 6:425") at the end: "even the permitted bodily union of the sexes in marriage . . . [is] a union which is in itself merely an animal union" (179). This line is more evidence that Kant's solution is minimalist.

84. Kant, *Metaphysics*, 64.

85. Williams, *Kant's Political Philosophy*, 117.

86. Baumrin, "Sexual Immorality Delineated," 301, 300.

87. Mary Geach (a daughter of Peter Geach and Elizabeth Anscombe), for example, claims, in the manner of Augustine and Jerome, that Christianity "encourages men and women to recognize the whoredom in their own souls. It is a decline from Christianity to see oneself as better than a prostitute if one is . . . given to masturbatory fantasies, or if one defiles ones [*sic*] marriage with contraception." Geach, not surprisingly, limits sexual activity to marriage ("Marriage: Arguing to a First Principle in Sexual Ethics," in Luke Gormally, ed., *Moral Truth and Moral Tradition: Essays in Honour of Peter Geach and Elizabeth Anscombe* [Dublin: Four Courts Press, 1994], 177–93, at 178).

88. But what wholesome definition of the sexual impulse could there be, that would soften the sex problem—that sexual desire essentially wants only to please the other for the other's sake? That metaphysical optimism would be a convenient account of the nature of human sexuality, in which eros is already by its nature perfectly moral and would not need marriage, or anything else (not even consent?), to improve or restrain it. Maybe, then, a nasty metaphysical account of sexuality is *required* if one wants to argue that only in marriage is sexual activity morally permissible.

89. An early, short, and rough version of this essay ("Kant on Sex") was presented at a meeting of The Society for the Philosophy of Sex and Love, held with the Central Division meetings of the American Philosophical Association, New Orleans, May 8, 1999. I thank, for their assistance, Laura D. Kaplan, who was in the audience during the presentation, and Natalie Brender, the commentator on my paper. Another version of this essay ("Sexual Use") was presented at Washburn University (Topeka, Kansas) as the Keynote Lecture of the 54th Mountain-Plains Philosophy Conference, October 13, 2000. I thank the audience for its questions and, especially, Russell Jacobs and the other organizers of the Conference for their kind invitation and generous hospitality. I am also grateful for Edward Johnson's many useful suggestions at various stages in the essay's history.

Chapter 18

THE MORALITY OF SEX: CONTRA KANT

Irving Singer

Philosophers who think that sex is just an instinctual and appetitive faculty oriented toward selfish gratification or reproductive need will always find its ethical status problematic. Under many circumstances, the satisfaction of both the instinct and the appetites related to it can be good or bad, right or wrong, ethically better or worse. Human sexuality is subject to this ambivalence of valuation in a way that does not apply to the sexuality of what are called "lower" species. We do not condemn these other animals because of the beastiality, or even cruelty, of their sexual responses. But we generally believe that sex in human beings should be held to a higher standard that supervenes upon biological urges and is equally ingrained in our nature.

However defined, this standard proclaims an ethical or metaphysical imperative that transcends the merely physical. At least, that is how the mainstream of Western philosophy and religion has conceived of our sexuality. What lingers, as an open problem, is the possibility that by its very being sex always and invariably thwarts any such moral aspiration. "Sexual love" would then be a contradiction in terms. Kant sought to resolve that problem in his philosophy of sex.

The traditional view of love and compassion treated them as significantly different from sexuality. It placed them in a separate category,

This essay is extracted from Irving Singer's book *Explorations in Love and Sex* (Lanham, Md.: Rowman & Littlefield, 2001), 1–20. Reprinted with permission of Irving Singer and Rowman and Littlefield.

one that classifies these affective dispositions as inherently ethical in some, if not all, of their modalities. Just as Luther claimed that human nature precludes the ability to love but still remains accessible to God's love as it joins people in a spiritual unity over and above their mortal finitude, so too did Kant argue that sexuality, even as a part of what is called sexual love, can be condoned only when it exists in the context of a normative state that transforms it into something superior to itself. Kant thought this occurs through the normativity of marital oneness. The contractual mandates of monogamous matrimony, he believed, are capable of making sexuality truly moral as well as truly human.

Attacking the beliefs of Kant as well as Luther, Schopenhauer repudiates their glorification of marriage and of married love in ways that duplicate his assaults on other idealistic notions about interpersonal intimacy. The only kind of love that Schopenhauer deems moral emanates from compassion. His term for this is *Mitleidshaft,* which is usually translated as either *compassionate love* or *loving-kindness.* Though Kant and Schopenhauer are sometimes similar in their views about sex, they differ radically in their ideas about compassion. Schopenhauer takes it to be not only ethical in itself but also the foundation of ethics as a whole. He describes compassion as an affective attachment that imbues moral action, a sense of identity often felt (though also often absent) in our relations with other living creatures. But that puts it in the realm of what Kant called "the heteronomous," which is to say a response that does not devolve from rational principles.

Kant excludes the heteronomous from his definition of morality. What is merely felt, he says, need not be ethical in itself or in its consequences; duty requires obedience to necessary and universal dictates of reason; and so, even a commendable sentiment of benevolence or compassion does not provide an adequate explanation of moral conduct. At that point, Kant and Schopenhauer are worlds apart.

The following questions need to be asked in relation to these matters: How does Kant's moral theory intersect with his ideas about the nature of sex, love, and compassion? Does Schopenhauer correctly perceive the total burden of Kant's ethical philosophy, and does he himself give an acceptable analysis of compassion? How are both philosophers liable to criticism that will enable us to get beyond each of them? And can we thereby attain an outlook, preferable to theirs, that might possibly reveal how either sex or love or compassion may be authentically moral? Approaching these problems as I do, I amplify my attempts in previous writings to show that the different types of affect are internally related to each other. I made that claim in *Sex: A Philosophical Primer.*[1] In *Explorations in Love and Sex,* the book from which this essay is taken, I try to see whether a critical reading of Kant and Schopenhauer can further this speculation on my part.

To carry out our inquiry fully, we would have to examine Kant's ideas about respect, beneficence, and the kingdom of ends, as well as sex and marriage. Since Kant believed in the goodness of compassionate love and what he nominates as "human love," these views must also be studied in connection with his ethical theory. Here I concentrate on Kant's philosophy of sex.

* * *

In his *Lectures on Ethics,* delivered between 1775 and 1780, Kant raises basic questions about the possible morality of what is usually called sexual love. He begins by stating that the notion would seem to be self-contradictory. Human love, Kant argues, is concerned with the welfare of the loved one. It is a state in which people recognize their mutual equality as human beings, each an end in him- or herself, each an autonomous totality, each a person rather than a thing, and therefore someone who must not be used merely for the sake of anyone's selfish desire. Kant defines human love or affection as "the love that wishes well, is amicably disposed, promotes the happiness of others and rejoices in it." But it is wholly clear, he then remarks, that "those who merely have sexual inclination love the person from none of the foregoing motives. . . . In loving from sexual inclination, they make the other into an object of their appetite. . . . The sexual impulse . . . taken in and by itself, is nothing more than appetite."[2]

This entails that sex is not only different from human love, but also in conflict with it. And while human love is moral insofar as it expresses a goodwill and a concern about another person's well-being, sexual love cannot be moral. In itself, in its basic structure, it is necessarily immoral, as any attempt to reduce a person to a thing would have to be. Moreover, Kant asserts, sexuality is "the only case in which a human being [in his or her totality] is designed by nature as the Object of another's enjoyment."[3]

In saying this, Kant maintains that sexuality is a means of *enjoying* another person. But he scarcely clarifies his concept of enjoyment. He primarily wishes to establish that far from being just an interest in a bit of flesh or region within another's body, sexual desire seeks to render a man or woman into an object of one's selfish gratification, as if he or she were, as a totality, nothing but a thing.

Kant concludes that in itself sexuality is always a degradation of one's nature. It is not a uniting of human beings but rather a device that reduces them to what he calls their purely genital aspect. "The desire of a man for a woman is not directed to her as a human being; on the contrary, the woman's humanity is of no concern to him, and the only object of his desire is her sex."[4]

From this alone, it follows that sexuality must be immoral. Since love is goodwill, a humane and benevolent concern about another's welfare, no such thing as ethical sexual love would seem to be a possibility. Kant holds something much more extreme than the commonplace belief that *by* itself, apart from other interests people have, unadulterated sex cannot be moral. He makes the stronger claim that *in* itself sexuality is immoral and debasing to all participants. Still he insists upon the importance of combining sexual desire with human love. To demonstrate how this miraculous feat may occur, he presents a theory of marriage that is as extravagant and idealistic as anything that the nineteenth-century Romantics were later to imagine.

* * *

Before examining Kant's solution, we should consider the way he formulated the issue about sexual love in the first place. When Kant declares that through sexuality one enjoys another person, he introduces three different ideas: first, that sexual desire is the only desire that directs itself toward the totality of a human being; second, that, even as an effort to enjoy someone, sexual desire is not a means of delighting in him or her; and third, that sexual desire is appetitive in a manner that is comparable to appetites like hunger or thirst. As a generalization about the nature of sexuality, each of these statements is false, although the second one includes a proposition that is both true and significant.

It is false to say that by its nature sexuality is appetitive, if in saying this we imply—as Kant does—that on all occasions, inevitably and uniformly, it seeks to appropriate other persons for the benefit of one's own organic needs. Hunger and thirst are appetites of that sort. We reach into the refrigerator and devour a chicken for no reason other than our wanting to gratify our desire for nourishment or gustatory pleasure. We do not care about the chicken as an end that has, or rather once had, vital interests of its own. If we had had that concern, the chicken might never have ended up in the refrigerator.

At times sexual desire is undoubtedly appetitive in that sense. Men and women are not infrequently motivated by physiological forces that cause them to hunger for anyone or anything that will satisfy their hormonal sex drive. But though this is a part, and often a major part, of human sexuality, it does not characterize all of sex or exclude components of a different type. Kant makes a fundamental mistake in not recognizing this.

We need not linger here on the extent to which human sexuality is appetitive. On numerous occasions it may even differ only slightly from hunger and thirst. What really matters is whether it always resembles them, and whether the degree and frequency of resemblance are sufficient for us to treat it as a comparable mode of appropriation and self-gratification. Kant's underlying presupposition about the character of this resemblance is what I wish to repudiate.

In many, perhaps most, instances, sexual appetite reveals an attitude toward its object that has no counterpart in hunger or thirst. The person one desires is usually seen to have human characteristics that are like our own, or at least complementary to them. Normally we do not yearn for the enjoyment of another's genitalia, but rather for direct, albeit physical, intimacy with that other person. If people were sexless and had no genitalia, we might not have erotic or libidinal feelings in relation to them. All the same, our sexual feelings are ordinarily directed toward more than just their genitals, or any other portion of their body. To this extent, the appetitiveness of human sexuality is unlike the appetitiveness of hunger and thirst. A craving for roast chicken is the strongly felt activation of alimentary processes that are capable of quieting stomach pangs once the food has been ingested. Sex is not like that. Even when it is highly goal-oriented, it generally lusts after a someone, whether in imagination or actuality, who is the man or woman that arouses mental and physical excitation in us. Our attention may become fixated upon a particular erotogenic zone; but the carnality of the other person is rarely desired for itself alone.

As Kant errs in thinking that sexuality is merely appropriative, so too is he mistaken when he claims that it, and only it, addresses itself to the totality of other persons. For one thing, are we sure we know what such an attitude would be like? How might one describe the entirety of a person we desire? Does it comprise all of that individual's past and future attributes, or is it only what he or she is at the moment? And if the latter, where do we draw the line between relevant and irrelevant properties of this man or woman? Can Kant possibly mean that sexual desire includes an interest in the veins and inner organs that operate within someone's body, or the welter of perceptions, sensations, thoughts, fears, hopes, and varied feelings that throng within his or her consciousness and overall personality? In our effort to enjoy another human being as a totality, what exactly are we trying to enjoy? And why believe that sex is the means, the only means, by which this enjoyment can occur?

While I find these questions somewhat unmanageable, and most likely unanswerable, I realize that people can have a vaguely panoramic attachment to someone who is experienced not as a composite of different attributes but as a complete and whole individual. A man who is attracted by a woman's physical appearance may be responding to more than just her embodiment of sexual beauty. His impulse might be focused upon her particular features because they belong to *her*, as the person whose intimate presence he desires. And perhaps that is why Kant thought that sexual feeling is a yearning to enjoy the totality of another. But he never tells us what this means, and anyhow it runs counter to his belief that sex is an appetite like hunger or thirst. Though these can be directed toward parts of an object as well as its totality, they are not means of enjoying it *as* a totality. On the other hand, when sex is appetitive in the way that hunger and thirst are, which happens in solitary masturbation or limiting situations where people exist for each other as little more than sexual outlets, enjoying a person in his or her totality does not seem to be what is going on.

Nevertheless, Kant is right, I believe, insofar as he implies that sex is a means of enjoying persons. As we variably enjoy listening to music, or watching a tennis match, or having a lively conversation, or taking a walk in springtime, so too can we enjoy persons in responses that are distinctively sexual. Interpersonal enjoyment of any sort is not the same as taking delight in or wishing well. The latter are more selfless than enjoyment, especially sexual enjoyment, since they are exclusively concerned about what is good for the other. At the same time, enjoying a person is not equivalent to using him or her for one's own personal benefit, or for just the satisfying of one's hedonic needs. To enjoy another person is to feel comfort and renewed well-being in associating with this man or woman, and sometimes a sense of oneness with him or her. Through a bond that we welcome as a good thing, we draw sustenance from the other without diminishing either of us. Our ability to enjoy each other augments the being of us both. It is an enrichment in which we partake jointly.

Suggestive though it may be, Kant's notion of sex as an attempt to enjoy another person is tainted by his belief that only in sex do we seek such enjoyment. That is not the case. We enjoy people across a vast gamut of affective experiences. The search for interpersonal enjoyment plays a major role in relations of nonsexual love, of friendliness as well as friendship, or of any affirmative response to a person's beauty, charm, cheerfulness, elegance, wit, intelligence, moral character, and artful self-presentation. As a means of uniting with someone, sexual desire—in its most common occurrence—is the longing by a human being to establish vibrant contact through enjoyment of the body and living presence of some other person. Moreover, a man or woman we desire sexually can also represent, or symbolize, or serve as surrogate for, various people who have had importance in our past experience, and within the many stages of our developmental growth.

The traits or bodily features that are sexually enjoyable need not be related to anything genital. A man can desire a woman because she is gracious in her movements, has a mellifluous voice and lovely eyes, perhaps, or because she is intellectually brilliant but also mysterious. Not much, if any, of this may be traceable to the physiology of reproductive instincts; yet it all pertains to the person that woman is or appears to be. It reveals what a man may wish to enjoy, though not necessarily to appropriate, by means of sexual closeness to her. Like most of the other ways that people can be enjoyed, doing so through sexuality is interwoven with everything else that matters to human beings. It is operative in accordance with their individual system of values.

As I have suggested, and as Kant also mentions, enjoying a person is not the same as delighting in that person. This is a confusion that Diderot makes in formulating his concept of *jouissance* (enjoyment), which Kant may have been thinking about.[5] But here again, Kant's seminal idea remains undeveloped. To delight in someone is to feel joy in what he or she is and does, apart from whatever we ourselves enjoy or desire. The feeling of delight is an expression of aesthetic, and often moral, approbation. It readily mingles with dispassionate, though receptive, acceptance of the person who has elicited our joyful response. While we may delight in people we enjoy, provided the enjoyment is sufficiently inclusive of what is good for them, we can enjoy a person without delighting in him or her.

Enjoying is also different from liking. To like a person is to like some of the attributes that constitute what he or she is. But however greatly we may enjoy a person because of properties we like in him or her, it is not the same as enjoying either the properties or the totality of that person. Enjoying people is similar to enjoying good health or the commendation of those whose opinion means something to us. It is life-enhancing, and therefore more conducive to mutual happiness than merely liking someone. Had Kant recognized this, he might not have assumed that sexual enjoyment is inherently inimical to delighting in the welfare and respect that its chosen object deserves insofar as it is a person and not a thing.

Kant fails to understand the kind of enjoyment and delight that sexual acuity may create because he thinks sexuality inevitably treats the other person as an object of selfish appetite. And if it did entail, necessarily and as a matter of definition, acting toward people as if they were things—just instrumentalities for satisfying one's own desire—Kant would be right to see a moral antithesis between sex and human love. As he says, love (at least the love of persons) involves goodwill and a benevolent disposition toward its recipient as an end in him- or herself. Love not only delights in, but also fosters, another's search for consummation without rendering that person into something we use simply for our own purposes.

By denying that sexuality violates the conditions needed for human love to exist, we can explain the possible affiliation between sex and love more easily than Kant does. Sexual love, the conjunction and genuine harmonization of sex and love, occurs on some, even many, occasions of sexual desire, though certainly not on all of them. There is thus no antinomy to be overcome and no reason to believe that in itself sexuality is basically immoral.

* * *

The approach that I am following is coherent with statements about sexual love that Hume enunciates in *A Treatise of Human Nature*. He there suggests that "the amorous passion, or love betwixt the sexes" is composed of three elements: "the pleasing sensation arising from beauty; the bodily appetite for generation; and a generous kindness or good-will."[6] Though Hume points out that lust, the bodily appetite, can sometimes conflict with the good intent of generous kindness, he maintains that in sexual love the three components are "inseparable." This alone assures the potential morality of sex. When love occurs, even one "who is enflamed by lust, feels at least a momentary kindness towards the object of it, and at the same time fancies her more beautiful than ordinary; as there are many, who begin with kindness and esteem for the wit and merit of the person, and advance from that to the other passions."[7]

Hume credits the sense of beauty with making the amorous state into a humane and ethical condition. He says that it unites lust with kindness, and therefore sex with love. It alters the nature of the two other elements and produces sexual love when it "diffuses" through them both. Kant knew Hume's work and could have availed himself of its benign and wholesome implications. They seem to have had no effect upon him.

* * *

Deriving from his presuppositions about sex, Kant's solution in terms of marriage is equally dubious. Seeking a viable relationship within which human beings might relate to one another sexually without their being treated as things because of their sexuality, Kant infers that only monogamous matrimony can meet these requirements. No other arrangement is moral.

Kant finds prostitution and free love immoral because, by their very nature, they preclude what is needed for there to be morality in sex. Prostitution implies that a person is renting out his or her body for sexual purposes as if it were property to be disposed of like any other. But our body is so intimately related to our personality, Kant asserts, that such employment means treating another, and/or oneself, as if he or she were not a person but only a thing. Even where carnal pleasures are freely exchanged, Kant believes that the ingredient desires remain geared to the using of someone as a thing to be possessed. He insists that unmarried lovers who engage in sexual behavior cannot truly respect the humanity in each other.

At times Kant reaches similar conclusions on the grounds that having sex for its own sake involves treating another or oneself as a thing because an activity of this sort, seeking only the gratification of our desires, opposes "the natural law." That adheres to the biological purpose for which sex exists, and Kant says it transcends "mere animal pleasure."[8] To lend some credibility to his belief, he would have to demonstrate that the pursuit of sexual pleasures in and for themselves is not only "unnatural" in human beings but also such as to prevent the participants from being treated as persons. Kant gives no such demonstration, and I do not see how he could make a convincing argument along those lines.

Kant's assertions in this regard may seem odd, indeed outrageous, to us two hundred years later. Do they not ignore the fact that liberated sex, but also prostitution, can include authentic concern about the other person? And are we willing to assume that autonomy belonging to personhood is threatened by either commercialized or freely bestowed sexuality apart from marriage? Are we not morally free to use our body as we wish, provided that no one is thereby harmed? If a man sells his plasma to a blood bank, or contributes it as a gratuity, is he treating his body and therefore himself as merely a thing? Most people nowadays would answer in the negative. And should we not say the same about sex? In an obvious sense, sex is a more personal deployment of one's body than the giving of blood, but why consider that pertinent to the matter at hand?

Kant recommends marriage as the sole moral agency of sex because he thinks that only marriage enables people to give each other the respect that human beings deserve, while also gratifying their instinctual needs. How then is sexuality compatible with respect as he defines it, and how does respect transform the immorality of mere sex into the morality of human love ideally present in matrimony?

According to Kant, only if we have a right over another person can we have a right to use that person's sexuality for our own selfish benefit. But we cannot legitimately acquire such rights unless we agree that the other person shall have the same rights over us. This comes into being through the contractual institution that is marriage. Only in marriage does this occur, Kant argues, for only then do we exchange the crucial rights in a situation that unites our autonomous wills. Spousal unity is the sole circumstance he envisages in which people exchange equal and reciprocal rights to their entire person. Being more thoroughly interpersonal than any other, the marital commitment provides a couple with total and mutual access to each other's body. Since husband and wife possess identical rights to the total being of each other, their relationship conduces to no reduction of personhood, no disrespect, no misuse of the humanity in either of them.

The consummation of sexuality in legal and functional matrimony is moral, Kant concludes, because the surrendering of rights through marriage does not entail any ultimate loss: "If I yield myself completely to another and obtain the person of the other in return, I win myself back; I have given myself up as the property of another, but in turn I take that other as my property, and so win myself back again in winning the person whose property I have become."[9]

Kant does not venture into the question of what constitutes a happy or desirable marriage. Like everyone else, he knows that successful matrimony largely depends upon psychological attunement between the spouses and their capacity to please each other. He is not inspecting the elements and criteria of a fully commendable marriage. Nor is he considering the fact that marriages very often turn out to be disastrous, which he himself emphasizes in his anthropological writings. As a moralist, he concerns himself only with the ability of the marital bond to make sexual love both human and ethical.

What would otherwise be immoral because it reduces persons to things is thus subsumed within a moral relationship predicated upon reciprocal rights. For sexual love to be a confluence of human love and sexuality it must enact an interest in the welfare of the other person. But only marriage can do that, since only it provides an exchange of reciprocal rights which overcomes the underlying selfishness in sex. Consequently, marriage, and nothing else, makes possible the kind of sexual love that Kant considers worthy of a human being. "In this way," he informs us, "the two persons become a unity of will. Whatever good or ill, joy or sorrow befall either of them, the other will share in it."[10]

* * *

That Kant should end up with a description of sexual or married love as a union of wills comes as no surprise. A similar conception was long since built into the wedding service of Western religions. It issues from the biblical portrayal of husband and wife as "one flesh," which John Milton interpreted as meaning "one heart, one soul" and Shakespeare called the "marriage of true minds." Like Milton and Shakespeare, Kant knows that a union of wills implies friendship between those who participate in it. The ideal of friendship itself he depicts as a oneness similar to marriage insofar as each friend surrenders his happiness to the other's keeping but then is completely recompensed because the friend is doing likewise.

In several books I have criticized the notion that human beings can merge or fuse or have a union of wills in this fashion. I argued at length that love demands a different type of unity—an acceptance of another person and a sharing of oneself, but not a fusion of identities.[11] The concept of merging became a major factor in Romantic theories of love in the nineteenth and early twentieth century. Kantian philosophy was foundational to much of the thought about love that developed then.[12]

What rubs most against the current grain is Kant's assurance that a union of wills results from the marital contract itself. His reasoning would seem to be impaled upon an equivocation. Though he is referring to a bond in which the spouses share in the good or ill, the joy or sorrow, of each other, he gives us no grounds for thinking that this must result from marriage as he defines it. The marital relation may establish a giving of equal and reciprocal rights to one's person. But it does not follow that such reciprocity alone leads to an authentic union of wills, or to any comparable sharing of goods, evils, joys, and sorrows. Though the sharing and the relevant oneness can occur, Kant makes hardly any attempt to show how they might be essential components of the married state. Consequently, it is not only his view of marriage that is suspect but also his belief that the humanization and morality of sexual love is possible only in the context of marriage.

In Kant's defense, one could take him as meaning that moral sexual love presupposes a reciprocation of goodwill, which cannot exist unless rights of access are jointly exchanged, and that this requires a legal—therefore ethical—union of the sort that (monogamous) marriage is. Kant would then be interpreted as affirming only that marriage is a necessary condition for the morality of sexual love, but not a sufficient condition. In other words, there would have to be further conditions as well in order for human love to occur between the sexually active spouses. This more moderate approach is not, however, what Kant intends. He proposes the stronger, less tenable, conception because he wants to argue that *in itself*, as the institution that it is, marriage joins people in an ethical as well as sexual unity. But that begs the question. Kant does nothing to support any such assumption, though even the lesser claim—in terms of marriage as a necessary condition—needs substantiation on its own.

Finally, we should note how Kant articulates the notion of granting equal and reciprocal rights. He speaks of each member of the marriage "undertaking to surrender" the whole of his or her person, both being willing to "yield [themselves] completely." He holds that the rights at stake are not suitably exchanged unless husband and wife sacrifice their interests and themselves in a total submission to each other. But must self-abnegation of this sort, however mutual and freely undertaken, be part of our definition of the marital bond? Is this self-sacrificial attitude a prerequisite for the creation of a moral relationship between spouses who have sex with each other? Is it a worthy, or even feasible, means of uniting them as beings whose autonomy must be respected?

My own intuitions tell me that the answer to these questions is "Surely not." Marriage and the advent of sexual love as something ethical presuppose a mutual giving of rights, but not of the calculated and legalistic kind that Kant invokes. For one thing, there is no way that we could determine whether all the rights a spouse bestows are truly and identically restored. What, in fact, would this mean? If the wife gives her husband the right to caress her shoulders, which he likes to do, must he give her the right to caress his, which he does not like? In mutual married love, as in mutual love as a whole, there has to be an equalization of rights inasmuch as each person must be concerned about the well-being of the other. But this is quite different from the idea of exchanging rights in a manner that somehow returns to oneself whatever one has given up. Long before Kant, that concept appeared in the writings on love by Marsilio Ficino. It is as fanciful in Kant as it was in Ficino.[13]

Kant depicts marriage as a joint subservience in which each occasion of surrender or renunciation is finally justified by the restitution the other person makes through his or her correlative surrender and renunciation. But then, one may reply, as Nietzsche does, that it is through self-fulfillment, rather than self-submission, that spousal ties can serve as a moral and jointly beneficial bond. Without mentioning Kant, Nietzsche has his doctrine of marital union in mind when he ridicules those who extol an "equal will to renunciation." As he puts it: "If both partners felt impelled by love to renounce themselves, we should then get—I do not know what; perhaps an empty space?"[14]

The emptinesses in Kant's conception of marriage and its dependence upon a contractual exchange of rights may well be irremediable. His idea of human love as goodwill and an interest in the welfare of the beloved is defensible as far as it goes. But it does not go far enough to explain what love is like, either in sexuality or in other social relations. While much that is admirable in romanticism stems from Kant's philosophy, a better account of how sexuality can be an ethical possibility exceeds the cramped parameters that he imposes.

*　*　*

Until recently, technical philosophers tended to ignore Kant's writings about sex and marriage. His contractarian approach is reborn, however, in an article by Bernard H. Baumrin entitled "Sexual Immorality Delineated." Like Kant, Baumrin begins with the assertion that "human sexual interaction is essentially manipulative."[15] From this, Baumrin concludes: first, that it is a mistake to think that sexual intimacy is what he calls "a romance between feelings, where feelings have been elevated to a sacrosanct position," and second, that sex avoids being necessarily immoral only when each participant acknowledges that his or her desire to manipulate initiates not only a corresponding right to manipulate in the other but also a duty to submit to such manipulation.[16] Against Baumrin, as against Kant, one can respond that it is erroneous to think of sex as *essentially* manipulative. If that were the case, sexuality would have to be considered selfish on each and every occasion, whether or not it becomes moral through contractual devices that create rights and duties.

We avoid this baleful paradox by characterizing interpersonal sex as neither selfish nor manipulative in its very nature, but rather as part of our reaching out for connection and communication with other human beings. Sexual love, and therefore sexual morality, differs from rectitude in business or administration inasmuch as it provides an attunement between people and their responses to each other without any formalistic adjudication of personal desires. Contracts exist as a means of controlling our self-oriented motivation, and one might conceivably think that this applies to sex as it does to other pursuits. But since sexuality is to some degree a vehicle of our yearning for persons who matter to us and with whom we want to make sensory contact, it belongs to a different region of moral discourse.

In part, at least, sex is indeed a "romance between feelings," even though this aspect of it may sometimes be minimal or such as to present itself in a crude, distorted, or abusive fashion. Sexual feelings—whether they be *libidinal* or *erotic* or *romantic* in my use of those terms—are not sacrosanct, but they are too subtle and too pervasive as manifestations of our humanity to be encompassed by contractarian interpretations. The promises we make, the expectations we arouse, the invitations we extend, the behavior we engage in are all social acts, and as such they can be subject to the mandates of a contract. But the feelings expressed by these acts are aesthetic phenomena that have a goodness and a badness all their own. Their "romance" is the narrative of our immediate experience as we live it from moment to moment. That is why fictional works of art are supremely adept at conveying the nature and the affective meaning of sexuality as well as love.

Once we free ourselves from the notion that sex is always and ineluctably manipulative, once we recognize that frequently it is a gratifying search for someone we do not wish to manipulate and may even want to strengthen as an autonomous person, there can be no valid reason to think that its ethical potentiality resides within the dictates of a contract. The character and justifiability of either married or sexual love must depend upon other considerations.[17]

Notes

1. *Sex: A Philosophical Primer* (Lanham, Md.: Rowman & Littlefield, 2001).

2. Immanuel Kant, *Lectures on Ethics*, ed. Peter Heath and J. B. Schneewind, trans. Peter Heath (Cambridge: Cambridge University Press, 1997), 155–56.

3. Immanuel Kant, *Lectures on Ethics*, trans. Louis Infield (New York: Harper & Row, 1963), 163 (in this volume, 200).

4. Kant, *Lectures on Ethics*, trans. Heath, 156.

5. For Diderot on *jouissance*, see my book *The Nature of Love: Courtly and Romantic* (Chicago.: University of Chicago Press, 1984), 313–14.

6. David Hume, *A Treatise of Human Nature* (Oxford: Clarendon, 1888), 394.

7. Hume, *A Treatise of Human Nature*, 395.

8. On this, see Roger J. Sullivan, *Immanuel Kant's Moral Theory* (Cambridge:

Cambridge University Press, 1989), 202.

   9. Kant, *Lectures on Ethics,* trans. Infield, 167 (in this volume, 202–3).

   10. Kant, *Lectures on Ethics,* trans. Infield, 167 (in this volume, 203).

   11. See in particular *The Nature of Love: The Modern World* (Chicago: University of Chicago Press, 1987), passim; and *The Pursuit of Love* (Baltimore: Johns Hopkins University Press, 1994), 23–30.

   12. On this development, see *The Nature of Love: Courtly and Romantic,* 376–431.

   13. On Ficino's concept, see *The Nature of Love: Courtly and Romantic,* 174–75.

   14. Friedrich Nietzsche, *The Gay Science,* trans. Walter Kaufmann (New York: Vintage, 1974), 319.

   15. Bernard Baumrin, "Sexual Immorality Delineated," in *Philosophy and Sex,* 1st edition, Robert Baker and Frederick Elliston, eds. (Buffalo, N.Y.: Prometheus, 1975), 116.

   16. Baumrin, "Sexual Immorality Delineated," 122.

   17. For further discussion of material in this chapter, see Alan Soble, *The Philosophy of Sex and Love: An Introduction* (St. Paul, Minn.: Paragon, 1998), 50–61; also his "Kant on Sex," included in the program for the May 8, 1999, meeting of the Society for the Philosophy of Sex and Love, together with a reply by Natalie Brender entitled "Revisiting Kant on Sex." See also Allen W. Wood, *Kant's Ethical Thought* (Cambridge: Cambridge University Press, 1999), 256–82; Barbara Herman, "Could It Be Worth Thinking about Kant on Sex and Marriage?" in *A Mind of One's Own: Feminist Essays on Reason and Objectivity,* Louise M. Antony and Charlotte Witt, eds. (Boulder, Colo.: Westview, 1993), 49–67; Christine M. Korsgaard, *Creating the Kingdom of Ends* (Cambridge: Cambridge University Press, 1996), 190–95; Rae Langton, "Love and Solipsism," in *Love Analyzed,* Roger Lamb, ed. (Boulder, Colo.: Westview, 1997), particularly 126–40, and her companion essay, "Sexual Solipsism," *Philosophical Topics* 23: 2 (1995): 149–87; and Timothy J. Madigan, "The Discarded Lemon: Kant, Prostitution and Respect for Persons," *Philosophy Now,* no. 21 (Summer/Autumn, 1998): 14–16.

PART 5

RAPE AND HARASSMENT

Chapter 19

IS *THIS* SEXUAL HARASSMENT?

Robin Warshaw

S exual harassment? Not you. You're the new breed of male, sensitive to the age-old gender stereotypes women have had to battle as they gain the equality and respect rightfully theirs in a male-dominated business world. As far as you're concerned, bartering promotions for sexual favors is inappropriate office conduct of the worst sort—the kind of behavior that not only demeans co-workers but also tarnishes your own character and diminishes managerial effectiveness.

No. In this matter your conscience is as shiny and clean as Sir Galahad's shield.

So throughout the long media blizzard precipitated by Anita Hill, Clarence Thomas and the Senate judiciary peanut gallery, you sat snug and cozy, hands warming by the fire of your own morally appropriate behavior. But when the storm subsided, you may have found a new America waiting to challenge your conduct.

It is an America in which women, overcoming their fear of reprisal and disbelief, are bringing their grievances to court in record numbers. In the first half of 1992 alone, reports of harassment made to the Equal Employment Opportunity Commission increased more than 50 percent over the previous year.

It is also an America that is finally ready to take these grievances seriously. And while you may applaud this trend that's finally packing

---

Reprinted from *Exec* (Summer 1993), pp. 62–65, by permission of Robin Warshaw. © 1993, Robin Warshaw.

muscle onto what was formerly a pleasant but ineffective civil rights sentiment, the bottom line is that you may get caught in the crossfire.

The problem faced by men in this new environment is twofold: First, while most media-worthy cases of sexual harassment involve spectacularly colorful instances of inappropriate behavior, the majority of unheralded arguments currently being heard in the nation's courts don't fit so neatly into the public's perceptions of right and wrong. Harassment sometimes is in the eye of the beholder, and what may be one man's clumsy attempt at friendship or even honest romance may be one woman's sheer hell.

Complicating the whole matter are the hazy boundaries of the law. Except in cases of actual assault, there's still no steadfast uniformity regarding the type of behavior the courts and mediating agencies should judge to be harassing.

The following cases have all been culled from legal battles and disputes brought before public hearing examiners. Each has been chosen because it explores in some fashion the gray areas that lie just outside the realm of obviously inoffensive and threatening behavior. As you read them, ask yourself: Are the women involved simply too sensitive? Or are these in fact bona fide cases of harassment? Before you read the verdict, make your own judgment and see whether your behavioral gyroscope is guiding you straight and true—or wobbling dangerously.

CASE #1:
Is Sex Between Consenting Adults Harassment?

The Securities and Exchange Commission office was a sociable place to work—sociable, that is, if you were one of several employees, including supervisors, having romantic affairs with each other, holding frequent parties and leaving the office during the day to go drinking.

But one female attorney who did not participate in the carousing found her co-workers' behavior repulsive. She claimed she was harassed by the environment in which she had to work. Moreover, she said, women who had affairs with male supervisors were rewarded with bonuses and promotions. The woman conceded that no one had pressured her for sex or denied her any promotions because she wasn't one of the crowd.

Was she being too touchy?

The decision: Although the woman wasn't harassed on a quid pro quo (give something to get something) basis, a judge ruled that the "pervasive" behavior in the SEC office had created an offensive work environment. She was awarded back pay, a promotion and her choice of two jobs. The SEC also agreed to an outside review of its personnel practices.

The expert analysis: "That's a hostile work environment—no question about it," says Thomas A. McGinn, a human-resources consultant in Charlottesville, Virginia, and co-author (with Nancy Dodd McCann) of *Harassed: 100 Women Define Inappropriate Behavior in the Workplace* (Business One Irwin).

Socializing at work has its limits, and those limits certainly were crossed in the Roman Empire–type revels at that SEC office. Federal guidelines warn specifically that an employer who gives benefits to anyone in exchange for sex may be held liable for discriminating against other workers. But any affairs within an office—even among peers—can raise the potential for unequal treatment of nonparticipants.

CASE #2:
That's Entertainment?

Few things are as boring as most corporate meetings. In an attempt to liven up the presentations, an oil company brought a barely clad woman on a motorcycle to a regional meeting, according to a sexual-harassment complaint filed by a female supervisor for the company.

Moreover, she charged, when the corporation held a sales meeting at a restaurant, the entertainment was provided by strippers. And at a slide show held for employees, one slide featured the female supervisor's clothed rear end.

Was the woman harassed?

The decision: The federal judge presiding over this case noted that the incidents were without question inappropriate but weren't "sufficiently severe or pervasive to constitute a hostile environment." That noted, he found that no harassment had taken place.

The expert analysis: Surely there are other ways to entertain and inform employees, suggests Anthony M. Micolo, a human-resources representative with Eastman Kodak in New York City. As for the incidents in the case: "I would probably feel myself, as a man, uncomfortable with this stuff," he says.

More to the point is that while a "hostile environment" charge often needs more than one or two incidents to substantiate it, other judges might find episodes such as the preceding sufficient to establish a pervasive climate of harassment. Micolo points out that corporations need to consider what conduct will be deemed acceptable. "Above and beyond sales goals and operational goals, there have to be people goals," he says. "You have to view the work environment as one that's productive to employees, not oppressive to them."

CASE #3:
Just a Friendly Ride

A midwinter snowstorm hit so hard that one Virginia corporation sent its workers home early. A female word-processing technician needed a ride, which was readily offered by a male engineer for whom she had done some work. He assured her that his four-wheel drive vehicle would have no trouble navigating the storm.

Indeed, it didn't. When they arrived, he entered her apartment. He says he only kissed her. She says he tried to kiss and fondle her, despite her protestations. When she complained to their employer, the man was reprimanded and warned he would be fired if he committed another such act.

Was he simply a clumsy guy looking for companionship or a threatening menace?

What happened: The woman's lawyers showed in court that the corporation had received previous complaints from other women about the man's behavior. After a ruling determined that the company had a legal responsibility to prevent the incident, the employer made an out-of-court settlement.

The expert analysis: According to Louise Fitzgerald, a psychologist and researcher on sexual harassment at the University of Illinois at Champaign, such a scenario is common but not innocuous. "This is unwanted sexual attention of a predatory nature and is a violation of someone's right to bodily integrity." In research Fitzgerald conducted among working women, 15 percent had been victims at work of undesired attempts at touching, fondling, grabbing or kissing.

CASE #4:
The Chummy Boss

The new secretary thought it strange that her boss walked her to her car every night, but she believed it was to offer security. She couldn't explain why he walked her to the bathroom, hovered over her desk, left her personal notes about her appearance or bought her gifts. She complained about this to her friends, but not to management.

She hoped that by letting her boss know she was happily married, the unwanted attention would stop. Instead, when she was hospitalized for back surgery, he called frequently, visited, sent notes and brought flowers. When she returned to work, he tried to give her back rubs whenever he noticed her stretching. She told him to stop. Finally, she spoke to a supervisor, who told her to talk to her boss again. Ultimately, she quit the job after her boss accused her of having an affair with a male co-worker and threatened to withhold a promised raise if it was true.

Was the boss anything more than an annoying pest?

What happened: A local human-relations commission ruled in the woman's favor and the company offered a $6,700 settlement. She declined the settlement and went to court.

Then a federal judge asserted that no harassment had taken place. He ruled that the boss's conduct "would not have interfered with a reasonable person's work performance or created an intimidating, hostile or offensive working environment." He added that the woman's protests to her boss "were not delivered with any sense of urgency, sincerity or force." Legal experts say such cases will now more often be decided by juries, with verdicts increasingly likely to favor complainants.

The expert analysis: Some argue that in order to dispel any hint of sexual harassment in an office, all friendly interactions would have to stop. However, Jonathan A. Segal, a management attorney in Philadelphia who advises companies on sexual harassment issues, disputes that dour view. "An occasional compliment is not harassment," he says, "but an excessive interest in an employee's private life is."

Segal spends most of his time providing employers with preventive education on how to avoid situations such as the one above. "Any thorough training program would make clear that what this individual did was wrong," he says. Moreover, he adds, complaints should never be handled by the individuals charged with harassment.

CASE #5:
The Writing on the Wall

A woman learned that obscene cartoons about her had been posted in the men's room of her office building. The graffiti sketches depicted various sex acts and mentioned her name.

The lewd illustrations remained on display in the public bathroom for a week, even after the company's chief executive had seen them. It was only after he learned the woman was upset about the cartoons that they were removed.

Was the office worker sexually harassed or was she just the target of crude, yet childish, pranksters?

What happened: The court sided with the woman, determining that the cartoons were "highly offensive to a woman who seeks to deal with her fellow employees and clients with professional dignity." The employer agreed to pay her full salary and psychiatric bills until she found new employment.

In a similar case, a federal judge in Jacksonville, Florida, determined that pinup calendars and posters of women's genitals that were displayed at a shipyard were a "visual assault on the sensibilities of female workers," constituted sexual harassment and kept women out of jobs there.

The expert analysis: Where certain men might feel flattered or amused to have their names attached to sexually explicit cartoons, most women would likely feel shame and humiliation. Joan Lester, director of the Equity Institute, an Emeryville, California, consultancy in multicultural issues, points out that for a woman to be chosen for such treatment is "chilling and intimidating." It's also potentially dangerous: "The cartoons could be an incitement to sexual violence." For the targeted woman, that fear—coupled with the ridicule—could quickly destroy her work world.

It would have been far better if a male co-worker had taken the pictures down immediately, but such allies for women are often rare in work settings. "There's the fear [for a male co-worker] of breaking rank, that his masculinity will be questioned," says Lester. The situation was worsened by the company president's knowledge of the drawings. "It shows he didn't have an understanding of the human consequences and the legal issues," Lester adds.

CASE #6:
What Is Reasonable

Two office employees, female and male, worked at desks just a few yards away from each other. One day they went to lunch together.

When the man later asked the woman out for yet another lunch (and perhaps a drink), she turned him down. After that rebuff, he began sending her love letters, including one that was three pages long and single-spaced. The woman became increasingly frightened about the unwanted attention and filed a sexual harassment complaint.

Was the man just doing some harmless, old-fashioned courting?

What happened: The woman's case was dismissed at first by a judge who called the man's behavior "trivial," but an appellate court, in a precedent-setting decision, found that sexual harassment should be viewed as a "reasonable woman" might experience it and remanded it back to the lower court. More and more future cases will be decided using this "reasonable woman" standard.

The expert analysis: In a society in which sexual assault is not uncommon, such persistent, unwelcome advances from a man are frightening. "Physical size and physical well-being have a lot to do with it," says San Francisco labor attorney Cliff Palefsky, who represents plaintiffs in sexual harassment cases. That's why, Palefsky explains, if a man is subjected to excessive staring by a woman, he might think, "So what?" But when the situation is reversed, "it's enough to give a woman the creeps." Most men, he adds, have never experienced such scary intrusiveness.

Because of men's and women's disparate views, the evaluation of sexual harassment charges is now moving away from the legal tradition of using a "reasonable man's" (or "reasonable person's") interpretation of an incident to judgments based on how a "reasonable woman" might view an event. Palefsky says the concept has received quick acceptance. "This isn't paternalistic protection for women," he says. "It's a reality. There's such a huge difference in perspective."

Chapter 20

SEXUAL HARASSMENT IN THE LAW: THE DEMARCATION PROBLEM

Mane Hajdin

1. Introduction

This paper presupposes that the law about sexual harassment in the work place,[1] if it is to be acceptable, ought to provide a workable criterion of demarcation between sexual harassment and those forms of sexual interaction between people who work together that do not constitute sexual harassment. It also presupposes that the law ought to do so without leaving the latter class empty or almost empty, and without becoming a vehicle of legal moralism (for example, the fact that a certain act involves adultery should not in itself constitute a reason for classifying it as an act of sexual harassment). I do *not* presuppose that the demarcation ought to be sharp: it can be as fuzzy as similar legal demarcations usually are.

I believe that the overwhelming majority of people, including the overwhelming majority of those who strongly support the present sexual harassment law, can accept these presuppositions, and that it is therefore safe to take them as one's starting point. Most people also believe that the present sexual harassment law in fact satisfies the conditions that I have presupposed. The aim of this paper is to show that it does not,

Sections 1–6 of this essay are an abridged reprint of "Sexual Harassment in the Law: The Demarcation Problem," *Journal of Social Philosophy* 25:3 (1994), pp. 102–22; sections 7–8 are an abridged reprint of "Sexual Harassment and Negligence," *Journal of Social Philosophy* 28:1 (1997), pp. 37–53. Reprinted by permission of Mane Hajdin and the *Journal of Social Philosophy*.

to examine why it does not, and to explore how it might be modified so that it does.

2. Consent

However, before we start that examination of the law itself, it will be instructive to look briefly at the way the problem of demarcation is treated in some nonlegal writings on the topic.

One widely quoted book on sexual harassment, for example, raises the question of demarcation by acknowledging that

> Sexual give-and-take—the friendly verbal interaction between colleagues, the acknowledged attraction between coworkers, the accepted physical gesturing of male and female—is a healthy behavior in which individuals of various ages and stations choose to engage.
> . . . The humor and affection in sexual give-and-take may be a way to reduce sexual tensions. It may relieve the monotony of routine work. It may even be preliminary courtship, a kind of testing before proceeding with a more serious relationship.[2]

This book offers the following as the solution: " 'Choice' is the critical concept. . . . Whatever the intent, sexual give-and-take is based on mutual *consent* of equals. This is obviously not the case in sexual harassment."[3]

Relying on the word "consent" to mark the boundary between sexual harassment and other forms of sexual interaction[4] appears natural both because of the widespread use of the phrase "consenting adults" in connection with other sex-related matters and because the word "consent" usually marks the boundary between rape and sexual intercourse that is not rape, and analogies between sexual harassment and rape readily suggest themselves. Another popular book on the topic thus says that "sexual harassment is not synonymous with all sexual activity any more than rape is synonymous with intercourse."[5]

The actual law explicitly[6] rejects the presence of consent as the criterion of demarcation, but the idea that the presence of consent *could* be the criterion is nevertheless a tempting one. Showing, within this section, why that idea is misguided will facilitate our discussion of the actual law, in the sections that follow.

People, in general, have no difficulty understanding the requirement that one should seek the consent of one's intended partner before engaging in sexual intercourse. It is notorious that cases occasionally arise in which one's general understanding of that requirement may be difficult to apply, but such cases are exceptional. In the overwhelming majority of cases, people know how to go about complying with this requirement, and find it relatively easy to pursue their sexual interests without violating it.

There is also no deep difficulty about understanding how the requirement of consent applies not only to sexual intercourse itself, but also to many other forms of physical contact aimed at sexual satisfaction.

The law about sexual harassment, however, applies not only to activities of this kind, but also to acts such as "requests for sexual favors" and "sexual advances." Those who think about sexual harassment in terms of consent seem to believe that this is simply an *extension* of the range of activities to which the requirement of consent applies and that the requirement can still be understood by analogy with the requirement of consent for sexual intercourse.

This is not so. The analogy breaks down because requests for sexual favors and sexual advances *are* precisely the acts of seeking consent for sexual interaction. To say that one should seek consent for these acts is to say that one should seek consent for seeking consent for sexual interaction. Thinking about sexual harassment in this way thus introduces *iterated* requirements of consent, which is something that is absent from the straightforward requirement of consent that is embodied in the law about rape.

This is not in itself an argument against looking at sexual harassment in terms of consent. *Sometimes* it makes perfect sense to say that one should not even seek consent for something unless one is in the appropriate relationship with the person whose consent one intends to seek, and that one can be in such a relationship only as a result of having sought and obtained consent to be in it. In the matter at hand, for example, it makes sense to say that one should never straightforwardly ask for someone's consent to sexual intercourse, unless that person has already consented to be in a certain kind of personal relationship in which consent for sexual intercourse may be sought. Whatever one might think about the wisdom of making this into a legal rule, one cannot claim that the fact that this rule involves iterated requirements of consent in any way impairs its intelligibility, or that it would make it unduly difficult to comply with it. In fact, most people have always followed some such rule as a matter of social convention anyway.

One could easily think of other examples, in which there are three, four, and perhaps many more iterated requirements of consent, and in which that still does not cause any serious problem. There is, however, a serious problem when we have *infinitely* many iterated requirements of consent, and this is precisely what we end up having if we think about sexual harassment in terms of consent. An act of seeking consent for sexual interaction of any kind can, namely, always be aptly described as a sexual advance itself, and this is what generates the infinite regress. If there were a requirement that one seek consent for every sexual advance one intends to make, then one could comply with that requirement only by making another, prior, sexual advance. But given that the requirement applies to all advances, it applies to that prior advance too: in order to legitimize it, one has to make another, still earlier sexual advance. The requirement, however, applies to *it* as well and so on, *ad infinitum*.

The requirement that one seek consent prior to engaging in any form of behavior that is currently within the scope of the sexual harassment law would therefore be in principle impossible to comply with, except by never engaging in *any* form of sexual interaction with the people one works with.

Every relationship of sexual nature, as a matter of logic, begins with a first step, and that first step is, again as a matter of logic, bound to be non-consensual. To prohibit all non-consensual sexual interaction is thus to prohibit the first step of every relationship of sexual nature, and to prohibit the first step of something is to prohibit the whole of it. The prohibition of all non-consensual sexual interaction would therefore amount to a prohibition of *all* sexual interaction.

3. Unwelcomeness

Having thus disposed of the suggestion that the term "consent" could play a role in providing the criterion of demarcation, we should now examine whether the criteria that the law actually uses fare any better. According to the Supreme Court, "the gravamen of any sexual harassment claim is that the alleged sexual advances were 'unwelcome'."[7] The term "unwelcome" comes from the well-known federal EEOC Guidelines on Sexual Harassment, where it is used in a way that appears to provide a criterion of demarcation.

We can all probably think of clear-cut cases of unwelcome sexual advances and clear-cut cases of welcome sexual advances, and it therefore seems unquestionable that the word "unwelcome" marks a genuine distinction here. This, however, is not enough, because if the rules about sexual harassment are to be legitimate legal rules, they have to be capable not only of being applied by various observers after the fact, but also of playing a role in guiding potential harassers before they act.

In order to comply with a rule that prohibits unwelcome sexual advances, one has to find out, of each sexual advance that one considers making, whether it would be unwelcome or not. Given that people's preferences in sexual matters tend to vary greatly from one individual to another, and that they usually do not advertise them, readily available information about a given person typically does not provide sufficient ground for concluding whether that person would, under the given circumstances, welcome a sexual advance from such-and-such other person or not. Broad generalizations, such as the generalization that a married person is less likely to welcome an advance than an unmarried one, are far too broad to entail anything useful about individual cases. This means that, in a typical case, the only way to find out whether the sexual advance one is contemplating would be welcome is to ask whether it would be welcome. But asking whether something would be welcome is very similar to seeking consent for it. Therefore although the consent-based and welcomeness-based demarcation may look different from the viewpoint of an after-the-fact observer, they are very similar from the viewpoint of a person who is trying to comply with the prohibition of sexual harassment. This similarity makes a welcomeness-based attempt at the demarcation liable to the same argument that was used in the preceding section.

Asking whether a sexual advance would be welcome need not, of course, take the form of a straightforward verbal inquiry: our culture provides numerous nonverbal and roundabout verbal ways of accomplishing the same purpose. But in whatever way it may be carried out, it remains true that this prior inquiry itself constitutes a sexual advance. The prohibition of unwelcome sexual advances therefore applies to it as well: the only way to comply is to find out whether it would be unwelcome, and one can find that out only if one undertakes another, still earlier, inquiry, which inquiry, in turn, is going to constitute yet another sexual advance, and so forth. The same infinite regress gets generated again.

Someone may try to respond to this argument by claiming that an *inquiry* as to whether X would be (un)welcome is, in general, *less likely* to be unwelcome than X itself. On that basis, one could argue that the likelihood of unwelcomeness keeps diminishing as we follow the regress, and that after a certain *finite* number of steps it becomes so low as not to create any practical difficulty. Therefore, he could claim, for most ends and purposes, the regress need not be regarded as infinite, after all.

This counterargument is however mistaken: the likelihood of unwelcomeness does *not* diminish along the regress. An inquiry as to whether X would be unwelcome, other things being equal, has *exactly* the same likelihood of being unwelcome as X itself. This is because whenever X itself would be unwelcome, an inquiry as to whether X would be (un)welcome is bound to be unwelcome too. If I would not welcome X, then I have no reason whatsoever to welcome an inquiry about it (viewed as such) and at least some reasons not to welcome it, namely that answering it requires expenditure of my time and energy (not to mention that it might be disruptive).

For some values of X, I may have further reasons for not welcoming any inquiries as to whether X would be welcome, but we do not need to discuss these, because the reason based on expenditure of time and energy is sufficient to establish the connection between the unwelcomeness of X and the unwelcomeness of inquiries about it, for all values of

$X.$[8] We therefore have to conclude that the word "unwelcome" does generate the same kind of infinite regress as the word "consent."

To make this point still clearer, I should emphasize that the "logic" of the word "unwelcome" is different from that of some other words for negative attitudes, such as "repugnant" and "outrageous." The appeal that the above objection to my infinite regress argument may, at first sight, have is probably due to not appreciating that difference.

From the fact that I would find X repugnant it does not, in general, follow that I would find an inquiry about it repugnant. This is because the *intensity* of my negative attitude towards the inquiry is often lower than the intensity of my negative attitude towards X, and it is thus possible that it would fall below the threshold for application of the word "repugnant." The crucial difference between "repugnant" and "unwelcome" is that "repugnant" is not simply a word for a negative attitude, but a word for a negative attitude above a certain threshold of intensity, while the meaning of "unwelcome" does not involve the intensity of the attitude. As long as the attitude *is* negative, rather than positive, the word "unwelcome" is appropriate, no matter how low the intensity of that negative attitude might be. It is quite possible that, as we follow the regress that my argument presents, the intensity of the negative attitude is diminishing, but the likelihood of the applicability of the word "unwelcome" to describe that attitude is not thereby diminishing, because the meaning of that word is indifferent to intensity. If one attempted to create such a regress with the word "repugnant," the intensity threshold that is built into the meaning of *that* word could prevent the regress from becoming infinite. There is no such threshold to stop the regress with the word "unwelcome."

4. Offensiveness

The argument that I have just presented shows that the word "unwelcome" is incapable of playing any useful role in providing the criterion of demarcation. This, however, does not constitute a complete argument against the present law, because the law, following the EEOC Guidelines, does not treat the unwelcomeness of a sexual advance as a sufficient condition for its being an instance of sexual harassment: the criterion of unwelcomeness is supposed to work together with a number of other criteria.

The relevant part of the Guidelines reads:

> Unwelcome sexual advances, requests for sexual favors, and other verbal or physical conduct of a sexual nature constitute sexual harassment when (1) submission to such conduct is made either explicitly or implicitly a term or condition of an individual's employment, (2) submission to or rejection of

such conduct by an individual is used as the basis for employment decisions affecting such individual, or (3) such conduct has the purpose or effect of unreasonably interfering with an individual's work performance or creating an intimidating, hostile, or offensive working environment.

As can be seen, this formulation has the structure of a complex disjunction. The rate of incidence and the intuitive moral gravity of the behavior described vary considerably from one disjunct to another.

Because of its complexity, one cannot tell, just by glancing at it, whether this formulation is capable of providing the criterion of demarcation. However, for my purposes, it might not be necessary to examine all elements of the formulation. In order to prove that a disjunctively structured criterion of demarcation is defective, it is enough to show that one of its disjuncts "leaks." Showing that there is no workable criterion of demarcation between the conduct covered by *one* disjunct that purports to spell out *a* sufficient condition for sexual harassment and sexual interaction that does not constitute sexual harassment is, therefore, sufficient to prove that the Guidelines, as a whole, do not provide the criterion of demarcation we are looking for.

According to the quoted part of the EEOC Guidelines, a sufficient reason for regarding something as sexual harassment is that it is an instance of

unwelcome sexual advances or other verbal conduct of a sexual nature which has the effect of creating an offensive working environment.

Suppose one wishes to avoid engaging in this kind of conduct. How does one go about that?

Given that we have already seen that the word "unwelcome" is not doing any useful job here, the only thing that remains to be done is to try to predict whether the conduct that one is contemplating will actually have the effect of "creating an offensive working environment" for the person (or persons) in question. Now, again, given that people tend to differ greatly[9] in what they find offensive in sexual matters, this is often very difficult to predict on the basis of the readily available information about the person.[10] The only way to arrive at such a prediction seems to be to ask the person. But to do that is to engage in "sexual advances or other verbal conduct" that may well turn out to contribute to creating "an offensive working environment." So we seem to have the regress again.

However, the argument I used above cannot be transposed here completely. This is because the word "offensive" seems to be, in the relevant respect, more similar to the word "repugnant" than to "unwelcome." It is quite possible to make inquiries as to whether X is offensive in a way that will not be offensive even to those who find X itself offensive. For example, the question "Do you find it offensive if someone tells sexual jokes in your presence?" (asked in a serious tone of voice) is unlikely to be offensive even to those who find actual sexual jokes offensive.

Such cautious inquiries may indeed stop the infinite regress, but they give rise to another problem. They purchase their relative inoffensiveness at the price of imprecision. If I put to someone the above question about sexual jokes, that person may well answer "no," having in mind some mildly off-color jokes, and then nevertheless feel offended by a particularly gross joke that I proceed to tell. If the person is more thoughtful, the answer may end up being true but unhelpful: "it all depends on the joke." In order to get the information one needs, one has to make one's inquiry more specific. But the more specific, precise, or unambiguous such an inquiry is, the more similar to its subject matter it becomes. This similarity entails increased likelihood of offensiveness. If one makes the inquiry about jokes more specific by asking, "Do you find it offensive if, in your presence, people tell sexual jokes that contain the following features: . . . ?," one reduces the probability of misunderstanding, but also creates the risk that the listing of the features of sexual jokes that one has in mind will itself be offensive to one's interlocutor. An increase in the precision of such inquiries thus goes together with an increase in the likelihood of their being offensive. The limiting case would be to ask something like, "Do you find it offensive if, in your presence, people tell jokes like this one: '. . .'?," which is bound to trigger the same reaction as if the joke had been straightforwardly told.

If one is to be reasonably certain that one's preliminary inquiry, as to whether one's contemplated course of behavior would be offensive, will not itself be offensive, one has to formulate it in vague general terms, which means that it becomes unlikely to accomplish its purpose. If one is to ensure that it does accomplish its purpose, one has to make it specific, unambiguous, precise, but in sexual matters such a specific, unambiguous, precise inquiry is almost as likely to cause offense as the behavior that it is about. Because of this dilemma, compliance with the requirement presented by the EEOC Guidelines is *impossible*, except by abstaining from *all* sexual advances and other verbal conduct of a sexual nature.

5. Pervasiveness

There is, however, an important objection that can be raised against my argument. The Supreme Court has held that sexual harassment of the kind I have been considering is actionable only if it is "sufficiently *severe or pervasive*'to alter the conditions of [the victim's] employment and create an abusive working environment'."[11] This means that (except for *severe* incidents) a single act is not sufficient to give rise to liability: viable action has to be based on "incidents, comments, or conduct that occurred with some frequency."[12] Someone may try to argue that, when the requirement of pervasiveness is taken into account, the law about sexual harassment turns out to be much less absurd than my argument has made it appear.

In order to see why the requirement of pervasiveness does not detract from the argument I have presented, we need to remind ourselves of the fact that the mechanism by means of which the harassment law is intended to prevent harassment has two stages. With certain exceptions, the law does *not* directly require individual potential harassers to abstain from harassment. Rather, the law requires *employers* to *see to it* that there is no harassment in their businesses. Employers normally comply with that requirement by enacting and enforcing internal regulations that require individual potential harassers to abstain from harassment.

Now, the threshold of pervasiveness belongs to the first stage: it is a condition of employers' legal liability. If A's harassment of B crosses the threshold of pervasiveness, then their employer becomes legally liable for having allowed this to happen. This means that the employer cannot afford to wait until the threshold is crossed. In order to avoid liability, the employer has to have in place mechanisms that will make it possible to interfere with A's conduct *before* it gets to the threshold. The regulations of the employer's business therefore have to make internally actionable any conduct that *contributes* to creating an offensive working environment, even if that conduct is, on its own, neither severe nor pervasive.

That the employer has to prohibit its individual employees from engaging in any such acts becomes particularly vivid in the light of the Fifth Circuit decision in *Waltman v. International Paper Co.*[13] According to that decision it is not necessary that the threshold be crossed by the cumulative effect of the acts of one harasser or a group of harassers acting in concert. The threshold may, instead, be crossed by the cumulative effect on one person of the acts of different harassers who are acting independently of each other. Thus, if A_1 performs one and only one act that is offensive to B, and A_2 then independently performs another, but again only one, act that is offensive to B, and $A_3 \ldots A_n$ each independently performs one act offensive to B, the threshold may be crossed and the employer liable. Given that A_1, A_2, . . . , A_n are *ex hypothesi* acting independently of each other, the employer can prevent this from occurring only if each individual act of A_1, A_2, . . . , A_n is prohibited by its regulations.

From the viewpoint of individual potential harassers, the operation of sexual harassment law therefore, in spite of the severe-or-pervasive test, amounts to a prohibition of *all* offensive acts of a sexual nature. This prohibition is subject to my argument according to which it, in turn, amounts to a prohibition of all conduct of a sexual nature.

6. Reasonableness

Up to this point, I have been treating the criterion of demarcation set out in the EEOC Guidelines as a *subjective* standard, which is what it, on its face, appears to be. Courts, however, often make the standard partially objective by introducing into their deliberations the perspective of a *reasonable person*[14] or, more recently, of a *reasonable woman*.[15]

The presence of the notion of reasonableness in the case law on sexual harassment, however, does not significantly affect the arguments of the preceding sections. Central to these arguments was the simple observation that people differ greatly in what they find unwelcome and offensive in sexual matters. That observation remains true even if one restricts one's attention to reasonable people. For most examples of conduct of a sexual nature, one can find some reasonable people who would find it unwelcome and offensive, *and* other reasonable people who would not. Some reasonable people find deeply offensive the same sexual jokes that other, equally reasonable, people find highly entertaining. Some reasonable people would be offended by the same sexual advances that other reasonable people would be happy to receive.

The same is true if one focuses on reasonable women. The kinds of sexual advances that offend some reasonable women make other women, who satisfy all the usual criteria of reasonableness, happy. Some reasonable women find offensive the same sexual jokes that other reasonable women find entertaining. The question as to whether a reasonable woman would be offended by such-and-such sexual joke is thus analogous to the question whether a reasonable woman would like anchovies on her pizza. The only answer that can be given to such questions is: "Some reasonable women would, some would not."

Because of such huge differences among reasonable people, and among reasonable women, when it comes to sexuality, invoking the notion of reasonableness is of no help in solving the demarcation problem.

7. Deliberate Insults vs. *Bona Fide* Sexual Advances

What the preceding sections show is that the sexual harassment law is incapable of providing a workable criterion of demarcation between sexual harassment and other forms of sexual interaction, without leaving the latter class empty or almost empty. The prohibition of sexual harassment thus amounts to a prohibition of all sexual interaction between people who work together. The argument was not that the law makes the demarcation at the wrong place, or that it makes a demarcation that is fuzzy, but rather that it makes no real demarcation at all.

The root of the demarcation problem is that defining sexual harassment in terms of the unwelcomeness and offensiveness of the conduct to its recipient jumbles together two very different kinds of conduct: deliberate insults of a sexual nature and *bona fide* sexual advances that happen to end up offending their recipients.

The aim of a deliberate insult of a sexual nature is to give some kind of satisfaction to the person who is making it *at the expense* of the person insulted. In other words, its aim is to increase the well-being of the person making it by decreasing the well-being of the person subjected to it. And not only are deliberate insults intended to produce the decrease in the well-being of the persons to whom they are directed, but they almost always do in fact produce it.

A *bona fide* sexual advance is, on the other hand, aimed at increasing the well-being of the person making it without decreasing the well-being of the person to whom it is directed. In making a sexual advance, one normally hopes that it will lead to interaction that will be satisfying not only to oneself but also to the other person. In technical terminology, this important difference between sexual advances and deliberate insults can be expressed by saying that *bona fide* sexual advances are aimed at producing a Pareto improvement (at least so far as the people directly involved are concerned), while deliberate insults most definitely are not.

Needless to say, sexual advances do not always produce the hoped-for Pareto improvements. All too often a sexual advance ends up being directed to a person who is in fact disinclined, sometimes quite strongly disinclined, to pursue sexual interaction of the kind that is being proposed, with the person who is proposing it. Instead of leading to a mutually fulfilling experience, a sexual advance may thus result in making the person to whom it is directed feel offended, humiliated, annoyed, uncomfortable, or otherwise displeased. This *is* a serious problem for everyone concerned, but it is a problem that is rather different from the problem posed by deliberate insults of a sexual nature.

Moreover, although sexual advances do not always produce the results that those who make them hope for, it is important not to forget that they sometimes do. Sometimes, sexual advances do lead to mutually fulfilling sexual interaction that brings a great deal of happiness to those involved. The kind of fulfillment and happiness that mutually satisfying sexual relationships bring cannot be achieved except by someone making some steps toward its being achieved—steps that can always be characterized as sexual advances. In other words, sexual advances sometimes do lead to Pareto improvements, and the Pareto improvements to which they lead cannot be realized without sexual advances being made. This makes sexual advances very different from deliberate insults of a sexual nature, which practically never lead to any Pareto improvements. Indeed, deliberate insults of a sexual nature typically lead to a net decrease in total well-being, because the decrease in the well-being of the person insulted is typically greater than the increase in the well-being of the person making the insult. This difference is supremely relevant to determining how the problems caused by these kinds of conduct should be dealt with, and yet it often ends up being swept under the carpet in discussions of sexual harassment.

In the literature on sexual harassment one frequently finds the idea that "sexual harassment has always been primarily about power, only rarely about sex, and never about romance."[16] As one writer has elaborated it:

> Sexual harassment has nothing whatsoever to do with libido and lust. It has everything to do with exploiting, objectifying, and dominating women. It is a manifestation of the extreme loathing so many men bear toward women.[17]

These claims are fairly plausible as an analysis of what goes on in deliberate insults of a sexual nature, but it is difficult to see how the claim that sexual harassment is about power and not sex is supposed to apply to *bona fide* sexual advances that turned out to have bad effects on the person receiving them. Consider, for example, the case of Sterling Gray writing a note to co-worker Kerry Ellison, in which he said

> I cried over you last night and I'm totally drained today. . . . Thank you for talking with me. I could not stand to feel your hatred for another day.[18]

This note did make Ms. Ellison "shocked and frightened"[19] and a federal court of appeals held that writing such notes may constitute sexual harassment. But to say that in writing these words Mr. Gray was somehow asserting his power over Ms. Ellison stretches the meaning of the word "power" beyond recognition. It is also difficult to see how this note could be interpreted as an expression of Mr. Gray's "extreme loathing" either toward women in general or toward Ms. Ellison in particular.

Many of those who write about sexual harassment proceed as if the whole problem posed by the conduct that is currently so classified amounted to a straightforward clash of interests. They seem to assume that on one side is the interest that harassers have in pursuing harassment, and that on the other side is the interest that the potential victims have in not being subjected to harassment. On that assumption, if harassment takes place, it is the interests of the harassers that are satisfied; if it does not take place, it is the interests of those who otherwise would have been its victims that are satisfied. To those who view sexual harassment in that way it appears that the main issue we are facing in deciding what kinds of laws we should have about it is whether we should have the laws that support the interests of harassers in harassing, or the laws that support the interests of potential victims in not being harassed. Once that is taken to be the main issue, the answer seems obvious: of course we should support the interests of potential victims and not of the harassers. This way of framing the issue leads those who accept it to advocate the laws that will restrict behavior classified as sexual harassment as much as possible.

This model fits well the harassment that consists in deliberate insults of a sexual nature. The problem posed by such insults can be treated as amounting to the clash between the interest that those who are inclined to make such insults have in the satisfaction that they get out of making them and the interest that the potential victims have in not being insulted.

The reliance on this model, however, seriously distorts the problem posed by *bona fide* sexual advances that, contrary to what those who are making them are hoping for, turn out to be offensive to those to whom they are directed. That problem does not amount to such a straightforward clash of interests. To be sure, those who may be subjected to such advances do have an interest in not being subjected to them. But those who make the advances that turn out to be offensive do not have any interest in making *them*. What they want is to make advances that will be accepted, not advances that will be offensive. The outcome of a *bona fide* advance that turned out to be offensive is not only against the interests of the recipient of the advance, but also against the interests of the maker of the advance. The advances that turn out to be offensive are usually a source of at least some embarrassment to those who make them. Moreover, such advances are undesirable even from the viewpoint of those advance-makers who are sufficiently thick-skinned not to suffer such embarrassment, because they constitute a waste of their time and energy. Given that what happens in such advances is against the interests of both parties, the problem posed by it cannot be regarded as a matter of straightforward clash between the interests of the two parties involved.

If the outcomes of such advances are against the interests of those who make them, why do they make them? The answer is that, in making them, they are driven by the interest that they have in making successful advances, advances that will be accepted and lead to some kind of fulfillment and happiness. It is in the nature of the kind of cases we are looking at that the makers of offensive advances, at the moment when they are making them, do not know that they are making unsuccessful advances; they are hoping that their advances will turn out to be successful. And when a sexual advance is successful, that is, when it leads to a fulfilling sexual relationship, its outcome is not only in the interests of the maker of the advance, but also in the interests of its recipient.

We thus have, on one side, offensive sexual advances, which are against the interests of both parties and, on the other side, successful sexual advances, leading to mutually satisfying sexual relationships, which are in the interests of both parties. When these two kinds of cases are considered separately, in neither of them do we have any clash of interests. The problem that we have here does not arise out of anything that could be seen by considering the two kinds of cases separately, but out of the fact that the two kinds of cases are inextricably bound together. What binds them together is the ignorance of the makers of advances as to whether their advances are going to turn out to be successful or unwelcome, offensive, and so forth. Successful advances and offensive advances do not result from decisions of different kinds; they both result from decisions of one and the same kind, namely the decisions to make sexual advances, of which one hopes that they will turn out to be successful, but which may turn out to be offensive. Because both kinds of advances result from decisions of the same kind, it is impossible to have laws, or rules of any other sort, that would regulate successful and offensive advances separately. Any rule that by its wording purports to be about advances of only one of the two kinds will still, inevitably, end up regulating the other kind as well.

Even if we focus only on the potential makers and recipients of sexual advances and set aside any interests of third parties, we need to take into account at least four sets of interests in order to understand the workings of any rule that tries to regulate such advances. These four sets of interests are:

(1) the interests of potential makers of sexual advances in making advances that will lead to mutually satisfying sexual relationships;

(2) the interests of potential makers of sexual advances in not making advances that will turn out to be unwelcome, offensive, and so forth, to their recipients;

(3) the interests of potential recipients of sexual advances in receiving advances that will lead to mutually satisfying sexual relationships; and

(4) the interests of potential recipients of sexual advances in not receiving advances that will be unwelcome, offensive, and so forth, to them.

Makers of *bona fide* sexual advances have interests of both the first and the second kind. Those who have interests of the third kind normally also have interests of the fourth kind. Given that one and the same person is often both a potential maker and potential recipient of sexual advances, it is often the case that one and the same person has interests of all four kinds.

There are also quite a few people who are not, at a given moment, interested in establishing any new sexual relationships, and who thus have interests of the fourth kind without having interests of any of the other three kinds. But although an individual may have interests of the fourth kind only, at a typical contemporary work place the interests of all four kinds are likely to be represented in some way.

Much of the literature about sexual harassment is written as if the interests of the fourth kind were somehow decisive, as if they were obviously more worthy of legal protection than the interests of the other kinds. This bias is probably a result of the distorting influence of trying to deal with *bona fide* sexual advances that went wrong by using the same model that is used for dealing with deliberate insults of a sexual nature. It needs to be emphasized that this bias in favor of the interests of the fourth kind is unfair not only to the makers of sexual advances, but also to all the potential recipients of sexual advances who have interests of the third kind. Unless one believes that sexual relationships are somehow intrinsically suspect, it is not clear why the interests of the fourth kind should be more important than the interests of the third kind.

The absurdity of treating the interests of the fourth kind as decisive becomes even more obvious if we compare sexual advances to other activities that involve a similar pattern of interests. For example, although we do think that the interests of potential victims of traffic accidents deserve legal protection, we do not think that they are the only interests relevant to our deciding what kind of legal rules to have about motor traffic. If we thought that these interests were decisive, we would have to prohibit completely motor traffic, because that is the only way to ensure that no one will ever suffer a traffic accident. The reason why no one would support such a prohibition is that motor traffic is something that brings considerable benefits to both motorists and non-motorists. In determining what kind of legal regime to have about motor traffic we take into account both the interests that people have in not being victims of accidents and the interests that they (both motorists and non-motorists) have in the benefits that the existence of motor traffic brings (together with other interests they may have in its being cheap, quick, and readily available).

8. How We Might Try to Solve the Demarcation Problem

In determining what kind of legal rules should govern a particular kind of activity, we normally take into account both the interests that people have in the benefits that the activity brings when it goes well and the interests they have in avoiding the consequences that appear when it does not. We base our decisions on comparing the expected social utility of a practice (the magnitude of the benefits multiplied by the probability of their occurrence) with the expected social disutility or the expected social cost (the magnitude of the harms multiplied by the probability of their occurrence). We are thus not tempted to prohibit all motor traffic, since it is far more probable that an individual car trip will be successful than that it will result in an accident. But we do prohibit particular kinds of driving that significantly increase the probability of accidents, such as driving at very high speeds or under the influence of alcohol.

What rules about sexual harassment would emerge if we took into account all the relevant interests, the same way we do in all other areas of life? One thing that we immediately notice is that, in most everyday circumstances, the probability that a given sexual advance someone is considering making will be unsuccessful is quite high, far higher than, say, the probability that a given car trip will end in an accident. However, we need to also take into account the fact that, although the probability of a given advance being successful might not be all that high, the magnitude of the benefit that is achieved when it is successful is high indeed. For most people, successful personal relationships that have a sexual component are a source of more intense happiness and sense of fulfillment than anything else.

In comparison with the benefits that result from successful sexual advances, the harms that result from unsuccessful, unwelcome, sexual advances are usually minor. Having to turn down a sexual advance is annoying, but in most cases it is not anything more than mildly annoying. Much of the literature on sexual harassment emphasizes that unwelcome sexual advances sometimes cause very serious harm to their recipients. That this is so is undoubtedly true, and that is a fact that needs to be taken into account in any deliberations as to what kind of rules there should be about sexual harassment. The literature, however, tends to obscure the fact that it is only *sometimes* that unwelcome sexual advances cause such serious harm and that receiving an unwanted sexual advance and turning it down is usually not a deeply traumatic experience.

When we apply to these facts the patterns of reasoning that we use in other areas of life, we are forced to conclude that sexual advances are often worthwhile and ought to be legally permitted. The fact that the magnitude of the benefits (to both parties taken together) of a successful sexual advance is typically much greater than the magnitude of the harms (to both parties taken together) of an unsuccessful sexual advance entails that sexual advances are typically worthwhile, even when they are not particularly likely to be successful. For example, in most situations it is quite plausible to say that, taking into account the interests of both parties, a sexual advance that has only 10 percent probability of being successful is still worthwhile, because the benefits that will obtain if it is successful are more than ten times greater than the harms that will result if it is unsuccessful.

This pattern of reasoning also enables us, at least in principle, to isolate the kinds of sexual advances that are not worthwhile. A crude sexual advance may still have some probability of being successful and bringing happiness to the people concerned but, in assessing whether it is worthwhile, we need to also take into account that it has considerable probability of causing serious harm (and not just mere annoyance). For at least some crude or aggressive advances we will have to conclude that the magnitude of the harm, multiplied by its probability, is so great that the advances in question are not worthwhile, and that it may be desirable to have rules that prohibit them.

Moreover, in determining whether sexual advances of a particular kind would be worthwhile we need to compare the making of such advances not only with not making any advances, but also with making other kinds of advances that can be made under the circumstances. Suppose, for example, that under certain circumstances one kind of a sexual advance has 10 percent probability of being successful, 88 percent probability of being unsuccessful and causing mild annoyance, and 2 percent probability of causing serious offense. Considered on its own, such an advance may well seem worthwhile. Suppose, however, that there is a different kind of advance that one can make under these circumstances that also has 10 percent chance of being successful, but only 1 percent probability of causing serious offense (and 89 percent probability of causing mild annoyance), and that is not any more burdensome to make than the first kind. Surely, if we knew all that, we would want to encourage people to make advances of the latter kind: the risk of harm is decreased without anything else being affected. Or suppose that there is a third kind of advance that can be made under the same circumstances, one that would increase the probability of success from 10 percent to 11 percent, but that would at the same time increase the probability of offense to 20 percent. In that case the relevant question to ask would not be whether the 11 percent probability of success outweighs the 20 percent probability of offense (together with 69 percent probability of mild annoyance), but rather whether the *additional* 1 percent probability of success justifies the *additional* 19 percent probability of offense. If the answer to that question is "no," as it may well be (that depends on the precise intensity of the offense), then we may want to discourage people from making advances of this third type and encourage them to make the advances that are less risky instead. This is exactly analogous to the reasoning that leads us to impose speed limits on motor traffic. We ask ourselves whether any extra benefits that would be gained by people driving at a high rather than moderate speed are worth the extra risk of accidents; if it turns out they are not, we impose the speed limit that prohibits driving at high speed.

The pattern of reasoning about sexual advances that has just been sketched is also analogous to the reasoning expressed, within the context of torts, in the celebrated Learned Hand's formula. According to that formula, the duty that the law of torts imposes on a potential tortfeasor is the duty to undertake every precaution against causing injuries that satisfies the condition that the burden of undertaking it is less than the gravity of the injury that is at stake, multiplied by the probability of its occurrence[20] (or, more precisely, by the reduction in the probability that would be achieved by the precautions). There is, according to the formula, no duty to undertake any precautions that would be more burdensome than that. Those who omit to undertake the precautions required by the formula are liable for any damages that do occur, but those who have undertaken such precautions have secured themselves against liability.

Making a crude, aggressive, sexual advance, which is fairly likely to offend, when a more polite, less likely to offend, advance could have been made, is analogous to omitting to take precautions that could have been made. Just as Learned Hand's formula imposes on potential tortfeasors the duty to take precautions that are not excessively burdensome, the way of thinking about sexual advances that has been sketched above would lead to the duty to opt for polite rather than crude sexual advances whenever doing so is not excessively burdensome. The burden may, in the case of sexual advances, include the reduction of the probability of success, and whether it is excessive would depend, as in Learned Hand's formula, on whether it exceeds the magnitude of the harm multiplied by the reduction in the probability of its occurrence that would result from opting for the polite advance. Just like Learned Hand's formula, this way of thinking would, however, not lead to any duty regarding sexual advances that would be too burdensome. It would not, for example, lead to the duty to abstain from sexual advances altogether simply because people might be offended by them, which is what the present law about sexual harassment amounts to.

A rule that would say that sexual advances are prohibited if they are not worthwhile in the sense that has been explained above, and that they are permitted if they are, would thus be a considerable improvement over the rules embodied in the present law about sexual harassment. Saying that *bona fide* sexual advances that are not worthwhile in that sense constitute sexual harassment (together with *quid pro quo* harassment, deliberate insults of a sexual nature and similar acts), but that worthwhile sexual advances do not, fits fairly well the ordinary meaning of the word "harassment": a body of law that would be centered around such a rule could thus be quite naturally called the law about sexual harassment, in spite of being rather different from the present sexual harassment law.

Such a rule would, unlike the present sexual harassment law, remain neutral among the four kinds of interests that are at stake in sexual advances: it would take them all into account, without treating some of them as more worthy of protection than others. Such neutrality among specific interests that are at stake is precisely what we generally expect from the legal system.

Notes

1. This paper is *worded* as a paper about sexual harassment in the work place, but its argument *mutatis mutandis* applies to sexual harassment in higher education as well.

2. Billie Wright Dziech and Linda Weiner, *The Lecherous Professor: Sexual Harassment on Campus* (Boston: Beacon Press, 1984), 25.

3. *Ibid.*, italics added.

4. Throughout this paper, the phrase "sexual interaction" should be understood as an abbreviation for "sexual interaction between people who work together."

5. Lin Farley, *Sexual Shakedown: The Sexual Harassment of Women on the Job* (New York: Warner Books, 1978), 188.

6. " 'Voluntariness' in the sense of consent is not a defense to such a claim" (*Meritor Savings Bank v. Vinson*, 477 U.S. 57, 69 [1986]).

7. *Meritor Savings Bank v. Vinson*, 477 U.S. 57, 68 (1986).

8. The above reasoning is of course concerned with inquiries as to whether X would be (un)welcome only *as such:* an inquiry that is unwelcome as such may well turn out to be welcome because of some special circumstances.

9. Notice that the only thing that the language of the quoted part of the Guidelines makes relevant is whether the conduct *actually* has the required kind of effect on the *plaintiff;* it is irrelevant that it might have different effects on others. Cf. *Morgan v. Hertz Corp.,* 542 F. Supp. 123, 128 (1981), where the court noted that some of the women at Hertz who were exposed to the same conduct as the plaintiffs "did not mind, or even participated in the comments and remarks," but dismissed that as irrelevant.

10. For example, married people who have strict views about adultery may be offended by *any* sexual advance directed at them, no matter how it is formulated, because they regard it as implying that they are immoral, while some married people are longing for affairs. Yet, the two may be indistinguishable in terms of the general information that is likely to be available to those who work with them.

11. *Meritor Savings Bank v. Vinson*, 477 U.S. 57, 67 (1986), italics added, quoting *Henson v. City of Dundee*, 682 F.2d 897, 904 (1982).

12. *Rabidue v. Osceola Refining Co.*, 805 F.2d 611, 620 (1986).

13. 875 F.2d 468 (1989).

14. "To accord appropriate protection to both plaintiffs and defendants in a hostile and/or abusive work environment sexual harassment case, the trier of fact, when judging the totality of the circumstances impacting upon the asserted abusive and hostile environment placed in issue by the plaintiff's charges, must adopt the perspective of a reasonable person's reaction to a similar environment under essentially like or similar circumstances" (*Rabidue v. Osceola Refining Co.*, 805 F.2d 611, 620 [1986]).

15. The case of *Ellison v. Brady* (924 F.2d 872 [1991]) has achieved notoriety for having "introduced" the reasonable woman standard, although it can be found in the somewhat earlier case *Andrews v. City of Philadelphia,* 895 F.2d 1469, 1482–1483 (1990).

16. Louise F. Fitzgerald, "Science v. Myth: The Failure of Reason in the Clarence Thomas Hearings," *Southern California Law Review* 65 (1992): 1399–1410, at 1399.

17. Kerry Segrave, *The Sexual Harassment of Women in the Workplace, 1600 to 1993* (Jefferson, N.C.: McFarland, 1994), 2.

18. *Ellison v. Brady,* 924 F.2d 872, 874 (1991).

19. *Ibid.*

20. *United States v. Carroll Towing Co.,* 159 F.2d 169, 173 (1947).

Chapter 21

HOW BAD IS RAPE?

H. E. Baber

R ape is bad. This is uncontroversial.[1] It is one of the many wrongs committed against women. But *how* bad is rape, more particularly, how bad is it vis-à-vis other gender-based offenses? I shall argue that while rape is very bad indeed, the work that most women employed outside the home are compelled to do is more seriously harmful insofar as doing such work damages the most fundamental interests of the victim, what Joel Feinberg calls "welfare interests," whereas rape typically does not.[2]

It may be suggested that the very question of which of these evils is the more serious is misconceived insofar as the harms they induce are so different in character as to be incommensurable. Nevertheless, for practical purposes we are often obliged to weigh interests in diverse goods against one another and to compare harms which are very different in nature. Feinberg's account of how we may assess the relative seriousness of various harms, in *Harm to Others* and elsewhere, provides a rational basis for such comparisons and for my consideration of the relative seriousness of rape and work. In addition, my comparison of these harms brings to light a lacuna in Feinberg's discussion which I propose to fill by providing an account of the way in which the duration of a harmed state contributes to its seriousness.

Reprinted from *Hypatia* 2:2 (1987), pp. 125–38, with the permission of H. E. Baber.
© 1987, H. E. Baber.

Why Rape Is Bad

Rape is bad because it constitutes a serious harm to the victim. To harm a person is to thwart, set back or otherwise interfere with his interests. Understood in this sense, "harm" is not synonymous with "hurt." We typically have an interest in avoiding chronic, distracting physical pain and psychic anguish insofar as we require a certain degree of physical and emotional well-being to pursue our projects, hence hurts are often harmful (e.g., root canal work). Arguably, there are also harms which are not hurtful. Our interests extend to states of affairs beyond immediate experience. I have an interest, for example, in my reputation so that if I am slandered I am harmed even if I am altogether unaware of what is being said about me. Names can never hurt me but they can, even without my knowledge, harm me insofar as I have an interest in others' thinking well of me. Harms are thus to be understood in terms of the interests or stakes that persons have in states of affairs.

Virtually everyone has an interest in avoiding involuntary contact with others, particularly unwanted contacts which are intimate or invasive. Being raped violates this interest, hence, quite apart from any further consequences it may have for the victim or for others, it constitutes a harm. In addition, people have an interest in not being used as mere means for the benefit of others, an interest which is violated by rape. Finally, all persons can be presumed to have an interest in going about their business free of restriction and interference. Rape, like other crimes of violence, thwarts this interest. Since rape sets back some of the victim's most important interests, the victim of rape is in a harmed condition.

Furthermore, the condition of being raped is a *harmful* condition as well as a *harmed* condition insofar as it has a tendency to generate further harms—anxiety, feelings of degradation and other psychological states which may interfere with the victim's pursuit of other projects. In these respects rape is no different from other violent crimes. The victim of assault or robbery is violated and this in and of itself constitutes a harm. In addition, being assaulted or robbed is harmful insofar as victims of assault and robbery tend to suffer from fears and psychological traumas as a result of their experience which may interfere with their pursuit of other projects.

Now there is a tendency to exaggerate the *harmfulness* of rape, that is, to make much of the incapacitating psychological traumas that some victims suffer as a result of being raped. One motive for such claims is the recognition that the harm of rape *per se* is often underestimated and hence that, in some quarters, rape is not taken as seriously as it ought to be taken. Rape has not been treated in the same way as other crimes of violence. A person, whether male or female, who is mugged is not asked to produce witnesses, to provide evidence of his good character or display bodily injuries as evidence of his unwillingness to surrender his wallet to his assailant. In the past, however, the burden of proof has been placed wrongfully on the victims of rape to show their respectability and their unwillingness, the assumption being that (heterosexual) rape is merely a sexual act rather than an act of violence and that sex acts can be presumed to be desired by the participants unless there is strong evidence to the contrary. This is not so. Writers who stress the traumas rape victims suffer cite the deleterious consequences of rape in response to such assumptions.

It is, however, quite unnecessary to exaggerate the harmfulness of rape to explain its seriousness. Women are not merely sexual resources whose wants and interests can be ignored—and women do not secretly want to be raped. Like men, women have an important interest in not being used or interfered with, hence being raped is a harm. Even if it did not hurt the victim physically or psychologically or tend to bring about any *further* harms it would still be a harm in and of itself. A person who is assaulted or robbed does not need to produce evidence of the psychological trauma he suffers as a consequence in order to persuade others that he has been harmed. We recognize that, quite apart from the consequences, the act of assault or robbery is itself a harm. The same should be true of rape. If we recognize rape for what it is, a violent crime against the person, we shall not take past sexual activity as evidence that the victim has not "really" been raped any more than we should take a history of habitual charitable contributions as evidence that the victim of mugging has not "really" been robbed, neither shall we feel compelled to stress the psychological consequences of rape to persuade ourselves that rape is in and of itself a harm.

If this is made clear, there is no compelling reason to harp on the suffering of rape victims. Furthermore, arguably, on balance, it may be undesirable to do so. First, making much of the traumas rape victims allegedly suffer tends to reinforce the pervasive sexist assumption that women are cowards who break under stress and are incapable of dealing with physical danger or violence. Secondly, it would seem that conceiving of such traumas as normal, expected consequences of rape does a disservice to victims who might otherwise be considerably less traumatized by their experiences.

The Relative Seriousness of Harms

Everyone agrees that rape is bad. The disagreement is over how bad. This raises a more general question, namely that of ranking harms with regard to their relative seriousness.

Given our understanding of harm as the thwarting of a being's interests and our assumption that a person's interests extend beyond immediate experience, it will not do to rank harms strictly according to the amount of disutility they generate for the victim or the extent to which they decrease his utility. A person is harmed when his interests are impeded regardless of whether he suffers as a consequence. Persons have an interest in liberty, for example, and are harmed when deprived of liberty even if they do not *feel* frustrated as a consequence. The advice of stoics has a hollow ring; projects for "adjusting" people to severely restrictive conditions strike most of us as unacceptable precisely because we recognize that even if self-cultivation or conditioning can prevent us from being hurt or feeling frustrated by the thwarting of our most fundamental interests, such practices cannot prevent us from being harmed.

Intuitively, the seriousness of a harm is determined by the importance of the interest which is violated within the network of the victim's interests.

> Some interests are more important than others in the sense that harm to them is likely to lead to greater damage to the whole economy of personal (or as the case may be, community) interests than harm to the lesser interest will do, just as harm to one's heart or brain will do more damage to one's bodily health than an "equal degree" of harm to less vital organs. Thus, the interest of a standard person in X may be more important than his interest in Y in that it is, in an analogous sense, more "vital" in his whole interest network than is his interest in Y. A person's welfare interests tend to be his most vital ones, and also to be equally vital. (Feinberg, 204–5)

A person's "welfare interests" are those which are typically most vital in a personal system of interests, e.g., interests in minimally decent health and the absence of chronic distracting pain, a tolerable environment, economic sufficiency, emotional stability, the absence of intolerable stress and minimal political liberty—all those things which are required for the "standard person" to pursue any further projects effectively.

> These are interests in conditions that are generalized means to a great variety of possible goals and whose joint realization, in the absence of very special circumstances, is necessary for the achievement of more ultimate aims. . . . When they are blocked or damaged, a person is very seriously harmed indeed, for in that case his more ultimate aspirations are defeated too; whereas setbacks to a higher goal do not to the same degree inflict damage on the whole network of his interests. (Feinberg, 37)

Three points should be noted here. First, we decide which interests are to count as welfare interests by reflecting upon the needs and capacities of the "standard person." Some people indeed are more capable than the standard person—and we have all heard their inspirational stories *ad nauseam.* The standard person, however, cannot be expected to produce saleable paintings with a brush held in his mouth if paralyzed nor can the standard person be expected to overcome grinding poverty and gross discrimination to achieve brilliant success at the very pinnacle of the corporate ladder.

Secondly, welfare interests are interests in having minimally tolerable amounts of good things, just enough to enable their possessor to pursue his ulterior interests. Empirical questions may be raised as to what sort of environment is "tolerable" to the standard person, what degree of political liberty he needs to pursue his goals and how much material security he requires. Nevertheless a person who lives under conditions of extreme political oppression, who ever fears the midnight visit of the secret police, or one who spends most of his time and energy scratching to maintain the minimal material conditions for survival is effectively blocked from pursuing other ends.

Now persons have an interest in having more of goods such as health, money and political liberty than they require for the pursuit of their ulterior interests since such surplus goods are a cushion against unforeseen reverses. In hard times, a middle class family may have to cut its entertainment and clothing budget—a working class family, however, may be reduced to chill penury while the truly poor are forced out onto the street. Nevertheless the interest in having money, health and the like in excess of the tolerable minimum is not itself a *welfare* interest.

Finally it should be noted that "welfare interests, taken together, make a chain that is no stronger than its weakest link." There are few, if any, tradeoffs possible among welfare interests: an excess of one good cannot compensate for the lack of a minimally tolerable level of another. "All the money in the world won't help you if you have a fatal disease, and great physical strength will not compensate for destitution or imprisonment" (Feinberg, 57)—nor, one might add, will fringe benefits, company picnics, impressive titles or even high pay compensate for dull, demeaning work in an all but intolerable environment.

The greatest harms which can come to persons are those which affect their most vital interests. To maim or cripple a person is to do him a great harm insofar as one's interest in physical health is a very vital interest, indeed, a welfare interest. Stealing a sum of money from a rich man is less harmful than stealing the same sum of money from a pauper insofar as depriving a person of his means of survival sets back a welfare interest whereas depleting his excess funds does not.

Now in light of these considerations it should be apparent, first, that rape is a serious harm but, secondly, that it is not among the most serious harms that can befall a person. It is a serious offense because everyone has an interest in liberty construed in the broadest sense not merely as freedom from state regulation but as freedom to go about one's business without interference. Whenever a person's projects are impeded, whether by a public agency or a private individual, he is, to that extent, harmed. Rape interferes with a person's freedom to pursue his own projects and is, to that extent, a harm. It does not, however, render a person altogether incapable of pursuing his ulterior interests. Having a certain minimally tolerable amount of liberty is a welfare interest without which a person cannot pursue any further projects. While rape diminishes one's liberty, it does not diminish it to such an extent that the victim is precluded from pursuing other projects which are in his interest.

No doubt most rape victims, like victims of violent crime generally, are traumatized. Some rape victims indeed may be so severely traumatized that they incur long-term, severe psychological injury and are rendered incapable of pursuing other projects. For the standard person, however, for whom sexuality is a peripheral matter on which relatively little hinges,[3] being raped, though it constitutes a serious assault on the person, does not violate a welfare interest. There is no evidence to suggest that most rape victims are permanently incapacitated by their experiences nor that in the long run their lives are much poorer than they otherwise would have been. Again, this is not to minimize the harm of rape: rape is a grave harm, nevertheless some harms are graver still and, in the long run, more harmful.

Times, Interests, Harms

What can be worse than rape? A number of tragic scenarios come to mind:

(1) A person is killed in the bloom of youth, when he has innumerable projects and plans for the future. Intuitively death is always a bad thing, though it is disputed whether it is a harm, but clearly untimely death is a grave harm insofar as it dooms the victim's interest in pursuing a great many projects.

(2) A person is severely maimed or crippled. The interests of a person who is mentally or physically incapacitated are thwarted as the range of options available to him in his impaired state is severely limited.

(3) A person is destitute, deprived of food, clothing and shelter. Here one thinks of the victims of famine in Africa or street people reduced to sleeping in doorways in our otherwise affluent cities. Persons in such circumstances have not the resources to pursue their ulterior interests.

(4)   A person is enslaved. He is treated as a mere tool for the pursuit of his master's projects and deprived of the time and resources to pursue his own.

Each of these misfortunes is worse than rape. And the list could be continued.

Notice that all of the harmed conditions described are not merely painful or traumatic but chronic rather than episodic. They occupy large chunks of persons' histories—or, in the case of untimely death, actually obliterate large segments of their *projected* histories. To this extent such harmed conditions interfere more with the pursuit of other projects which are conducive to persons' well-being than does rape.

Now it is not entirely clear from Feinberg's discussion how the temporal extent of harms figure into calculations of their relative seriousness. Feinberg (45ff.) suggests that transitory hurts, whether physical or mental, do not harm the interests of the standard person, for whom the absence of pain is not a focal aim, whereas chronic, distracting pain and emotional instability set back persons' most vital interests insofar as they preclude them from pursuing their goals and projects.

Nevertheless, intense pain, however transitory, may be all-encompassing and completely distracting for the extent of its duration. It is not entirely clear from Feinberg's discussion, however, why, given his account of interests and harms, we should not be forced to conclude that some transitory hurts are harms not because they violate an interest in not being hurt but because they preclude the victim from pursuing other interests, albeit for a very short time. Indeed, it is not clear why we should not be compelled to regard some very transitory pains, traumas, and inconveniences as set-backs to welfare interests. If we agree that being imprisoned for a number of years impedes a welfare interest insofar as it precludes the prisoner from pursuing his ulterior interests while imprisoned, why should we not say that being locked in the bathroom for twenty minutes is a harm of equal, if not greater magnitude, though of shorter duration? After all, while locked in the bathroom, I am, if anything, in a worse position to pursue my ulterior interests than I should be if I were in prison.

Intuitively, however, the duration of a harmed state figures importantly in assessments of its seriousness. Being locked in the bathroom for twenty minutes is not, we think, a great harm of short duration—it is simply a trivial harm insofar as it makes no significant difference to the victim's total life plan. Being imprisoned for several years, on the contrary, does make an important difference to the victim's biography: all other things being equal it precludes him from realizing a great number of aims that he should otherwise have accomplished. All is not as it was after the prisoner has served his sentence. After his release, the prisoner has much less time to accomplish his ends. A large chunk of his life has been blanked out and most likely his total life history will be poorer for it.

Imprisonment impedes a welfare interest insofar as it deprives the prisoner of the minimal amount of liberty requisite for the pursuit of a great many of his ulterior interests. Furthermore, the deprivation of liberty imposed upon the prisoner, like other harms to welfare interests, cannot be truly compensated by an abundance of other goods. Even the lavish banquets and luxurious accommodations imagined by self-proclaimed advocates of law and order who deplore the "soft treatment" of offenders could not compensate for the restriction of individual liberty imposed upon prisoners. Furthermore, benefits conferred *after* the prisoner's release cannot truly compensate him either. A person who has been falsely imprisoned may be "compensated" after a fashion with a monetary settlement but we all recognize that this does not really set things right: he has, after all, lost that many years off of his life and as a consequence he will *never* achieve a great many things that he would otherwise have achieved.

We might capture our intuitions about the role that the duration of harmed states plays in determining their seriousness in the following way: Typically, people's focal aims are, as it were, timeless. Some people, indeed, may have the ambition to accomplish certain feats at certain times of their lives, e.g., to make a million by age thirty, but in most cases the objects of our desires are not temporally tagged and timing is not, in the strict sense, essential to their realization. I can no longer make-a-million-by-age-thirty though I still can make a million. Of course I would prefer to have the million sooner than later. If, however, my aim is merely to make a million at some time or other I can afford to sit tight. Though the circumstances that prevail at some times may be more conducive to the achievement of my goal than those which prevail at other times, it is not essential to the realization of my ambition that it occur at any special time. My aim is not essentially time-bound.

Because most of persons' focal aims are not time-bound, persons by and large can afford to sit tight. Barring the occasional Man from Porlock, our interests are not seriously set back by transitory pains or other relatively short-lived distractions. A momentary twinge may prevent me from starting to write my paper at 12:05. No matter: I shall start it at 12:06, and the delay is unlikely to have any significant effect on my total opus. My interest is in producing a certain body of work during my lifetime and this interest is sufficiently robust to withstand a good many temporary set-backs. Nevertheless, while most people's interests are relatively robust, insofar as they are not time-bound, they are not impregnable. Long-term or chronic distractions can seriously impede even those interests which are not time-bound. If I suffer from chronic, distracting pain or emotional instability for a number of years I may *never* write my paper or realize many of my other ambitions. Art is long but life, alas, is short.

Now when it comes to assessing the relative seriousness of various harms we consider them with respect to their tendency to interfere with our typically "timeless" aims. The most serious harms are those which interfere with the greatest number of interests for the longest time, those which are most likely to prevent us from ever achieving our goals. The greatest harms, those which damage welfare interests, therefore, bring about harmed states which are chronic rather than episodic.

Working Is Worse Than Being Raped

On this account being obliged to work is, for many people, a very serious harm indeed insofar as work is chronic: it occupies a large part of the worker's waking life for a long time. For the fortunate few, work in and of itself contributes to the worker's well-being. For many workers, however, work provides few satisfactions. For the least fortunate, whose jobs are dull, routine and regimented, work provides no satisfactions whatsoever and the time devoted to work prevents them from pursuing any other projects which might be conducive to their well-being.

As a matter of fact, women figure disproportionately though not exclusively in this group. Discrimination is not only unfair—and this in itself constitutes a harm—it is harmful insofar as many women as a result of discriminatory employment practices are compelled to take very unpleasant, underpaid, dead-end jobs and, as a consequence, to spend a substantial part of their waking lives at tedious, regimented, mind-killing toil. A great many men have equally appalling jobs. I suggest, however, that anyone, whether male or female, who spends a good deal of time at such work is in a more seriously harmed state than one who is raped. Women however have an additional grievance insofar as such jobs fall disproportionately to them as a consequence of unfair employment practices.

A few hours or even a week of typing statistics or operating a switchboard, however unpleasant, may not be seriously harmful. For most women in the workforce, however, such unpleasantness occupies a substantial part of their waking hours for years. Currently most women can look forward to spending the greater part of their adult lives typing, hash-slinging, cashiering or assembling small fiddly mechanisms. To be compelled to do such work is to be harmed in the most serious way. Doing such work impedes a welfare interest: it deprives the worker of the minimal degree of freedom requisite for the pursuit of a number of other interests. As with other such deprivations, the harm done cannot be undone by other benefits. Sexists may suggest that women in such positions gain satisfaction from selfless service to their employers and families and some self-proclaimed feminists may suggest that the satisfaction of financial independence makes up for the drudgery. This is, however, plainly false. The amount of time workers must spend at their jobs deprives them of the freedom necessary to the effective pursuit of their other projects. For this there can be no true compensation.

Rape, like all crimes against the person, is bad in part because it deprives the victim of some degree of freedom; being compelled to work is worse in this regard insofar as it chronically deprives the victim of the minimal amount of freedom requisite to the pursuit of other important interests which are conducive to his well-being.

Work is worse than rape in other respects as well. The pink-collar worker, like the rape victim, is used as a mere means to the ends of others, but arguably, in being used the worker is violated in a more intimate, more detrimental way than the rape victim. Rape is an emotionally charged issue insofar as it has become a symbol of all the ways in which women are violated and exploited, but rape *per se* merely violates the victim's sexual integrity. The work that most women do, however, violates their integrity as intellectual beings. The routine clerical work which falls almost exclusively to women precludes the worker's thinking about other matters: she is fettered intellectually for the greater part of her day. Such work occupies the mind just enough to dominate the worker's inner life but not enough to be of any interest. One does not have to buy questionable Cartesian doctrines about the nature of the self to recognize that persons have a greater stake in their mental and emotional lives than they do in their sexuality. Recognizing this, it seems reasonable to suggest that being "raped" intellectually violates a more vital interest than being raped sexually.

Now there are indeed certain disanalogies between the harms of rape and pink-collar work. First, arguably, persons have a right not to be raped but they do not have a right to avoid unpleasant work. Secondly, while rapists clearly harm their victims it is not so clear that employers, particularly if they have not engaged in unfair hiring practices, harm their employees. Thirdly, it may be suggested that the rape victim is *forced* into a compromising position whereas the pink-collar worker is not. Finally, it will be suggested that the work most women do is not so grim as I have suggested. None of these suggestions, however, seriously damages my case.

First, I have not argued that being compelled to do unpleasant work is a *wrong* but only that it is a *harm*, and a grave one. To be harmed is not necessarily to be wronged, nor do persons have a right absolute not to be harmed in any way. It may be, in some cases, that the advancement of the interests of others outweighs the harm that comes to the victim so that, on balance, the harm to the victim does not constitute an injustice or a wrong. As consumers, all of us, men and women alike, have an interest in retaining women as a source of cheap clerical and service work. It may be that, on balance, this outweighs the interest of women as potential workers in not being exploited—though I doubt it. If this is so, then the exploitation of women in these positions is not a wrong. It is, nevertheless, a harm.

Secondly, on Feinberg's account, natural disasters—and not merely persons who omit to aid victims—cause great harm. More generally, to be in a harmed state is not necessarily to be harmed by some moral agent. To suggest that workers are seriously harmed by the work they do is not to say that their employers are harming them. Indeed, it seems that most supervisors, managers and owners of businesses are rather like carriers of harmful diseases: they are causally responsible for persons' coming to harm, but we should not want to say that they *harm* anyone.

Thirdly, most women in the pink-collar sector are compelled to work: the myth that most women enter the workforce to get out of the house and make pin money has long been exploded. Now intuitions about what constitutes coercion differ radically. Some suggest, for example, that a woman who cannot display bruises or wounds as evidence of a desperate struggle has not really been forced to have sex with her assailant. I, however, go with the commonsensical meaning of coercion, without pretending to know the analysis. On this account a woman with a knife to her throat is forced to engage in sexual intercourse and a woman with no other adequate means of support for herself and her family is forced to work. An exceptional person indeed may pull herself up by the bootstraps; the standard person, however, cannot.

Fourthly, a growing sociological literature on women in the workforce, observation, and personal experience all suggest that the work most women do is every bit as harmful as I have suggested. A "phenomenology" of womenswork is beyond the scope of this paper, and beyond my competence as an analytic philosopher. Even if I should succeed in conveying the dull misery of the working day, the stress at other times, knowing that another day of work is getting closer, and beyond this, the knowledge that there is no way out, it would not be entirely to the point. As Feinberg notes, except for Epicureans, for whom the absence of pain is a focal aim, neither physical pain nor psychic anguish is in and of itself a harm: they are harms only insofar as they impede the agent's interests. It is not the misery of working *per se* but the extent to which most work precludes one's pursuit of other ends which makes work the grave harm that it is. Even if many workers avoid the hurt, all endure the harm insofar as their interests are impeded and their lives are impoverished.

Finally, I recognize that many men are forced to do demeaning, dull, often dangerous work. Again, this is hardly a criticism of my case. I grant that men are harmed in the most serious way by being forced into such drudgery. My suggestion is merely that a person, whether male or female, who spends a good deal of time doing such work is in a more seriously harmed state than one who is raped. Rape is bad, indeed, very bad. But being a keypunch operator is worse.

I recognize that this conclusion will be met with considerable hostility. Beyond the harm that rapists inflict upon their victims, rape is a powerful symbol of the oppression women suffer and thus naturally arouses the wrath and indignation of virtually all women who are aware of their situation. Still, to the vast numbers of single parents who are unable to provide a minimally decent standard of living for their families on the wages paid for "women's work," to all women who do pink-collar work, and to all who recognize that they are in danger of being compelled to take such work—and virtually all of us are in danger—the shift of emphasis by some feminist organizations from activities geared to end sex discrimination in employment to a range of other projects is extremely irritating.

Why Rape Is Considered the Supreme Evil—a Postscript

In light of the fact (which should be apparent to all reasonable people) that spending the better part of one's waking hours over a period of years at boring, regimented work is worse than being the victim of violent crime, one wonders why it is so often assumed that rape is the supreme evil. Two conjectures come to mind.

First, it is generally assumed that women are largely incapable of dealing with danger or physical violence. Since rape is a crime against women primarily, given this assumption, it would follow that most rape victims would be more traumatized than victims of other violent crimes. This is an insult to women: it is incumbent upon us to show that we are as macho as anyone!

Secondly, women are traditionally viewed primarily in connection with concerns which center around their sexuality—in terms of their roles as lovers, wives and mothers. Because women are seen in this way, it is commonly assumed that they have a greater stake in matters concerning sexuality in the broadest sense than do men. So, for example, all issues concerning reproduction are thought of as "women's issues" despite the recognition by all but the most primitive peoples that men play an essential role in the reproductive process. Indeed, it is often assumed that women have more of a stake in sexual matters than they do in any other concerns.

Given these assumptions it would follow that any violation of sexual integrity would be extremely harmful to women. Arguably if rape is considered among the gravest of harms it is largely because women are regarded as beings whose welfare is tied up most intimately with sexual concerns and relationships, persons to whom other matters, such as intellectual stimulation and professional achievement, are relatively peripheral.

Most women take strong exception to being regarded as "sex objects." What is often thought to be objectionable about this role is the suggestion of passivity, the implication that one is an *object* which is used for sexual purposes rather than a *subject* of sexual experience. But there is something even more objectionable about the idea of being a "sex object," namely the suggestion that one is primarily a sexual being, a person whose most important interests are connected to the genital area and the reproductive system and with roles that are tied up with one's sexuality.

I suggest that the primary reason why rape is regarded as one of the most serious harms that can befall a woman is precisely because women are regarded as sex objects, beings who have little of value beyond their sexuality. Further I suggest that women who would regard being raped as the supreme violation and humiliation are implicitly buying into this view.

If these are indeed the reasons why rape is seen as supremely harmful to women, as I suggest they are, then it follows that the suggestion that rape is the worst harm that can befall a woman is a consequence of sexist assumptions about the character and interests of women. Rape, like all other crimes of violence, constitutes a serious harm to the victim. Nevertheless, I have suggested that to consider it the most serious of all harms is no less sexist than to consider it no harm at all.

Notes

1. Everyone agrees that rape is bad. The controversy concerns the criteria for counting an act as an instance of rape in the first place, including the relevance of the victim's prior sexual conduct, and the trustworthiness of victims' testimony. The recent reopening of the Dotson case, for example, represents a threat to feminist gains insofar as it tends to undermine the credibility of victims—not because it suggests that rape is less serious than is commonly supposed.

The core meaning of "rape" is "forcible or fraudulent sexual intercourse especially imposed on women" (*The Little Oxford Dictionary*); but, given the elaborate and confusing rules of sexual etiquette that have traditionally figured in human courtship rituals, it has not always been clear what constituted fraud or coercion in these matters. In particular, it has been assumed that female coyness is simply part of the courtship ritual so that women who acquiesce to the sexual demands of acquaintances under protest are merely playing the game and thus have not in fact been forced into anything. That is to say it is assumed that under such conditions the sexual act is *not an instance of rape at all,* hence that a woman who claims she has been raped in such circumstances is disingenuous and may be assumed to have malicious motives.

It is to these assumptions that women should object—not to my suggestion that rape is a less serious harm than has commonly been thought. What sexists underestimate is not the seriousness of rape but rather the frequency with which it occurs.

2. See especially chapters 1 and 5 in Joel Feinberg, *Harm to Others* (Oxford, Eng.: Oxford Univ. Press, 1984).

3. My argument rests on the assumption that very little hangs on sexuality issues, that persons' focal aims, and hence their interests, have to do primarily with matters which are quite separate and not much affected by sexual activities, whether voluntary or involuntary. In spite of popular acceptance of Freudian doctrines, this does seem to be the case.

In a society where people's most important aims were tied up with sexual activities, things would be different and rape would be even more serious than it is among us. Imagine, for example, a society in which women were excluded entirely from the workforce and marriage was their only economic option so that a woman's sexuality, like the cowboy's horse, was her only means of livelihood; imagine that in this society sexual purity were highly valued (at least for women) and a woman who was known to be "damaged goods" for whatever reason, was as a result rendered unmarriageable and subjected to constant humiliation by her relatives and society at large. In such circumstances rape would indeed violate a welfare interest and would be among the most serious of crimes, rather like horsetheft in the Old West. There are no doubt societies in which this is the case. It is not, however, the case among us.

Again, some people may regard their sexual integrity as so intimately wrapped up with their self-concept that they would be violated in the most profound way if forced to have sexual intercourse against their will. There are no doubt persons for whom this is the case. It is not, however, the case for the standard person.

Admittedly, this is an empirical conjecture. But we do recognize that it is the case for the standard male person, and the assumption that women are different seems to be a manifestation of the sexist assumption that women are primarily sexual beings.

Chapter 22

THE HARMS OF CONSENSUAL SEX

Robin West

Are consensual, non-coercive, non-criminal, and even non-tortious, heterosexual transactions ever harmful to women? I want to argue briefly that many (not all) consensual sexual transactions are, and that accordingly we should open a dialogue about what those harms might be. Then I want to suggest some reasons those harms may be difficult to discern, even by the women sustaining them, and lastly two ways in which the logic of feminist legal theory and practice itself might undermine their recognition.

Let me assume what many women who are or have been heterosexually active surely know to be true from their own experience, and that is that some women occasionally, and many women quite frequently, consent to sex even when they do not desire the sex itself, and accordingly have a good deal of sex that, although consensual, is in no way pleasurable. Why might a woman consent to sex she does not desire? There are, of course, many reasons. A woman might consent to sex she does not want because she or her children are dependent upon her male partner for economic sustenance, and she must accordingly remain in his good graces. A woman might consent to sex she does not want because she rightly fears that if she does not her partner will be put into a foul humor, and she simply decides that tolerating the undesired sex is less burdensome than tolerating the foul humor. A woman might consent to sex

---

Reprinted, with the permission of Robin West and The American Philosophical Association, from *The American Philosophical Association Newsletters* 94:2 (1995), pp. 52–55.

she does not want because she has been taught and has come to believe that it is her lot in life to do so, and that she has no reasonable expectation of attaining her own pleasure through sex. A woman might consent to sex she does not want because she rightly fears that her refusal to do so will lead to an outburst of violence behavior some time following— only if the violence or overt threat of violence is *very* close to the sexual act will this arguably constitute a rape. A woman may consent to sex she does not desire because she *does* desire a friendly man's protection against the very real threat of non-consensual violence rape by other more dangerous men, and she correctly perceives, or intuits, that to gain the friendly man's protection, she needs to give him, in exchange for that protection, the means to his own sexual pleasure. A woman, particularly a young woman or teenager, may consent to sex she does not want because of peer expectations that she be sexually active, or because she cannot bring herself to hurt her partner's pride, or because she is uncomfortable with the prospect of the argument that might ensue, should she refuse.

These transactions may well be rational—indeed in some sense they all are. The women involved all trade sex for something they value more than they value what they have given up. But that doesn't mean that they are not harmed. Women who engage in unpleasurable, undesired, but consensual sex may sustain real injuries to their sense of selfhood, in at least four distinct ways. First, they may sustain injuries to their capacities for self-assertion: the "psychic connection," so to speak, between pleasure, desire, motivation, and action is weakened or severed. *Acting* on the basis of our own felt pleasures and pains is an important component of forging our own way in the world—of "asserting" our "selves." Consenting to *un*pleasurable sex—acting in spite of displeasure—threatens that means of self-assertion. Second, women who consent to undesired sex many injure their sense of self-*possession*. When we consent to undesired penetration of our physical bodies we have in a quite literal way constituted ourselves as what I have elsewhere called "giving selves"—selves who cannot be violated, because they have been defined as (and define themselves as) being "for others." Our bodies to that extent no longer belong to ourselves. Third, when women consent to undesired and unpleasuarable sex because of their felt or actual dependency upon a partner's affection or economic status, they injure their sense of autonomy: they have thereby neglected to take whatever steps would be requisite to achieving the self-sustenance necessary to their independence. And fourth, to the extent that these unpleasurable and undesired sexual acts are followed by contrary to fact claims that they enjoyed the whole thing—what might be called "hedonic lies"—women who engage in them do considerable damage to their sense of integrity.

These harms—particularly if multiplied over years or indeed over an entire adulthood—may be quite profound, and they certainly may be serious enough to outweigh the momentary or day-to-day benefits garnered by each individual transaction. Most debilitating, though, is their circular, self-reinforcing character: the more thorough the harm—the deeper the injury to self-assertiveness, self-possession, autonomy and integrity—the greater the likelihood that the woman involved will indeed *not* experience these harms as harmful, or as painful. A woman utterly lacking in self-assertiveness, self-possession, a sense of autonomy, or integrity will not experience the activities in which she engages that reinforce or constitute those qualities *as harmful,* because she, to that degree, lacks a self-asserting, self-possessed self who *could* experience those activities as a threat to her selfhood. But the fact that she does not experience these activities as harms certainly does not mean that they are not harmful. Indeed, that they are not felt as harmful is a consequence of the harm they have already caused. This phenomenon, of course, renders the "rationality" of these transactions tremendously and even tragically misleading. Although these women may be making rational calculations in the context of the particular decision facing them, they are, by making those calculations, sustaining deeper and to some degree unfelt harms that undermine the very qualities that constitute the capacity for rationality being exercised.

Let me quickly suggest some reasons that these harms go so frequently unnoticed—or are simply not taken seriously—and then suggest in slightly more detail some ways that feminist legal theory and practice may have undermined their recognition. The first reason is cultural. There is a deep-seated U.S. cultural tendency to equate the legal with the good, or harmless: we are, for better or worse, an anti-moralistic, anti-authoritarian, and anti-communitarian people. When combined with the sexual revolution of the 1960s, this provides a powerful cultural explanation for our tendency to shy away from a sustained critique of the harms of consensual sex. Any suggestion that legal transactions to which individuals freely consent may be harmful, and hence *bad,* will invariably be met with skepticism—*particularly* where those transactions are sexual in nature. This tendency is even further underscored by more contemporary postmodern skeptical responses to claims asserting the pernicious consequences of false consciousness.

Second, at least our legal-academic discourses, and no doubt academic political discourses as well, have been deeply transformed by the "exchange theory of value," according to which, if I exchange A for B voluntarily, then I simply must be better off after the exchange than before, having, after all, agreed to it. If these exchanges *are* the source of value, then it is of course impossible to ground a *value* judgment that some voluntary exchanges are harmful. Although stated baldly this theory of value surely has more critics than believers, it nevertheless in some way perfectly captures the modern zeitgeist. It is certainly, for example, the starting and ending point of normative analysis for many, and perhaps most, law students. Obviously, given an exchange theory of value, the harms caused by consensual sexual transactions simply fade away into definitional oblivion.

Third, the exchange theory of value is underscored, rather than significantly challenged, by the continuing significance of liberal theory and ideology in academic life. To the degree that liberalism still rules the day, we continue to valorize individual choice against virtually anything with which it might seem to be in conflict, from communitarian dialogue to political critique, and continue to perceive these challenges to individual primacy as somehow on a par with threats posed by totalitarian statist regimes.

Fourth, and perhaps most obvious, the considerable harms women sustain from consensual but undesired sex must be downplayed if the considerable pleasure men reap from heterosexual transactions is morally justified—*whatever* the relevant moral theory. Men do have a psycho-sexual stake in insisting that voluntariness alone ought be sufficient to ward off serious moral or political inquiry into the value of consensual sexual transactions.

Let me comment in a bit more detail on a further reason why these harms seem to be underacknowledged, and that has to do with the logic of feminist legal theory, and the efforts of feminist practitioners, in the area of rape law reform. My claim is that the theoretical conceptualizations of sex, rape, force, and violence that underscore both liberal and radical legal feminism undermine the effort to articulate the harms that might be caused by consensual sexuality. I will begin with liberal feminism and then turn to radical feminism.

First, and entirely to their credit, liberal feminist rape law reformers have been on the forefront of efforts to stiffen enforcement of the existing criminal sanction against rape, and to extend that sanction to include non-consensual sex which presently is not cognizable legally as rape but surely should be. This effort is to be applauded, but it has the *almost* inevitable consequence of valorizing, celebrating, or, to use the critical term, "legitimating" consensual sexual transactions. If rape is bad *because* it is non-consensual—which is increasingly the dominant liberal-feminist position on the badness of rape—then it seems to follow that *consensual* sex must be good because it is consensual. But appearances can be misleading, and this one certainly is. That non-consensual transactions—rape, theft, slavery—are bad because non-consensual does *not* imply the value, worth or goodness of their consensual counterparts—sex, property, or work. It only follows that consensual sex, property, or work are not bad in the ways that non-consensual transactions are bad; they surely may be bad for some other reason. We need to explore, in the case of sex (as well as property and work), what those other reasons might be. Non-consensuality does not exhaust the types of harm we inflict on each other in social interactions, nor does consensuality exhaust the list of benefits.

That the liberal-feminist argument for extending the criminal sanction against rape to include non-consensual sex *seems* to imply the positive value of consensual sex is no doubt in part simply a reflection of the powers of the forces enumerated above—the cultural, economic, and liberal valorization of individualism against communal and authoritarian controls. Liberal feminists can obviously not be faulted for that phenomenon. What I want to caution against is simply the ever present temptation to *trade* on those cultural and academic forces in putting forward arguments for reform of rape law. We need not trumpet the glories of consensual sex *in order to* make out a case for strengthening the criminal sanction against coercive sex. Coercion, violence, and the fear under which women live because of the threat of rape are sufficient evils to sustain the case for strengthening and extending the criminal law against those harms. We need not and should not supplement the argument with the unnecessary and unwarranted celebration of consensual sex—which, whatever the harms caused by coercion, does indeed carry its own harms.

Ironically, radical feminist rhetoric—which *is* aimed at highlighting the damage and harm done to women by ordinary, "normal" heterosexual transactions—*also* indirectly burdens the attempt to articulate the harms done to women by consensual heterosexual transactions, although it does so in a very different way. Consider the claim, implicit in a good deal of radical feminist writing, explicit in some, that "all sex is rape," and compare it for a moment with the rhetorical Marxist claim that "all property is theft." Both claims are intended to push the reader or listener to a reexamination of the ordinary, and both do so by blurring the distinction between consent and coercion. Both seem to share the underlying premise that that which is coerced—and perhaps *only* that which is coerced—is bad, or as a strategic matter, is going to be perceived as bad. Both want us to re-examine the value of that which we normally think of as good or at least unproblematic because of its apparent consensuality—heterosexual transactions in the first case, property transactions in the second—and both do so by putting into doubt the reality of that apparent consensuality.

But there is a very real difference in the historical context and hence the practical consequences of these two rhetorical claims. More specifically, there are two pernicious, or at least counter-productive, consequences of the feminist claim which are not shared, at least to the same degree, by the Marxist. First, and as any number of liberal feminists have noted, the radical feminist equation of sex and rape runs the risk of undermining parallel feminist efforts in a way not shared by the Marxist equation of property and theft. Marxists are for the most part not engaged in the project of attempting to extend the existing laws against *theft* so as to embrace non-consensual market transactions that are currently not covered by the laws against larceny and embezzlement. Feminists, however, *are* engaged in a parallel effort to extend the existing laws against rape to include all non-consensual sex, and as a result, the radical feminist equation of rape and sex is indeed undermining. The claim that all sex is in effect non-consensual runs the real risk of "trivializing," or at least confusing, the feminist effort at rape reform so as to include all truly non-consensual sexual transactions.

There is, though, a second cost to the radical feminist rhetorical claim, which I hope these comments have by now made clear. The radical feminist equation of rape and sex, no less than the liberal rape reform movement, gets its rhetorical force by trading on the liberal, normative-economic, and cultural assumptions that whatever is coercive is bad, and whatever is non-coercive is morally non-problematic. It has the effect, then, of further burdening the articulation of harms caused by consensual sex by forcing the characterization of those harms into a sort of "descriptive funnel" of non-consensuality. It requires us to say, in other words, that consensual sex is harmful, if it is, only because or to the extent that it shares in the attributes of non-consensual sex. But this might not be true—the harms caused by consensual sex might be just as important, just as serious, but nevertheless *different* from the harms caused by non-consensual sex. If so, then women are disserved, rather than served, by the equation of rape and sex, even were that equation to have the rhetorical effect its espousers clearly desire.

Liberal feminist rape reform efforts and radical feminist theory both, then, in different ways, undermine the effort to articulate the distinctive harms of consensual sex; the first by indirectly celebrating the value of consensual sex, and the latter by at least rhetorically denying the existence of the category. Both, then, in different ways, underscore the legitimation of consensual sex effectuated by non-feminist cultural and academic forces. My conclusion is simply that feminists could counter these trends in part by focusing attention on the harms caused women by consensual sexuality. Minimally, a thorough-going philosophical treatment of these issues might clear up some of the confusions on both sides of the "rape/sex" divide, and on the many sides of what have now come to be called the intra-feminist "sex wars," which continue to drain so much of our time and energy.

Chapter 23

ANTIOCH'S "SEXUAL OFFENSE POLICY": A PHILOSOPHICAL EXPLORATION

Alan Soble

She: For the last time, do you love me or don't you?
He: I DON'T!
She: Quit stalling, I want a *direct* answer.
 —Jane Russell and Fred Astaire[1]

"When in Doubt, Ask"

Consider this seemingly innocuous moral judgment issued by philosopher Raymond Belliotti:

"teasing" without the intention to fulfill that which the other can reasonably be expected to think was offered is immoral since it involves the non-fulfillment of that which the other could reasonably be expected as having been agreed upon.[2]

This might be right in the abstract; provocative and lingering flirtatious glances sometimes can reasonably be taken as an invitation to engage in sex; hence brazenly flirting and not fulfilling its meaning, or never intending to fulfill its meaning, is, like failing to honor other promises or invitations, ceteris paribus a moral defect—even if not a mortal sin.[3] Abstractions

Reprinted, revised, from *Journal of Social Philosophy* 28, 1 (1997): 22–36, with the permission of the journal. © 1997 *Journal of Social Philosophy*.

aside, however, how are we to grasp "can *reasonably* be taken as"? A woman's innocent, inquisitive glance might be taken as a sexual invitation by an awfully optimistic fellow, and he and his peers might judge his perception "reasonable." This is why Catharine MacKinnon says that to use

> reasonable belief as a standard without asking, on a substantive social basis, to whom the belief is reasonable and why—meaning, what conditions make it reasonable—is one-sided: male-sided.[4]

Similarly, a man's innocent, inquisitive glance might be taken as a sexual leer by an anxiously sensitive woman, and she and her peers might judge this perception "reasonable."

But Belliotti writes as if all were well with the slippery concept of "reasonable":

> Although sexual contracts are not as formal or explicit as corporation agreements the rule of thumb should be the concept of reasonable expectation. If a woman smiles at me and agrees to have a drink I cannot reasonably assume . . . that she has agreed to spend the weekend with me.[5]

I suppose not. But why not? We do not now have in our culture a convention, a practice like the display of colored hankies, in which a smile before an accepted drink has that meaning. But nothing intrinsic to the action prevents its having, in the proper circumstances, that very meaning. And an optimistic fellow might say that the *special* sort of smile she, or another he, gave him constituted a sexual invitation. Belliotti continues his example:

> On the other hand if she did agree to share a room and bed with me for the weekend I could reasonably assume that she had agreed to have sexual intercourse.

This is not true for many American couples as they travel through foreign lands together. Or maybe in accepting the invitation to share a room or sleeping car she agreed only to snuggle. Cues indicating the presence and kind of sexual interest are fluid; at one time in the recent past, a woman's inviting a man to her apartment or room carried more sexual meaning than it does now—even if that meaning still lingers on college campuses and elsewhere.[6] To forestall such objections, Belliotti offers these instructions:

> If there is any doubt concerning whether or not someone has agreed to perform a certain sexual act with another, I would suggest that the doubting party simply ask the other and make the contract more explicit. . . . [W]hen in doubt assume nothing until a more explicit overture has been made.[7]

What could be more commonsensical than this? But it is wrong. The man who thinks it reasonable in a given situation to assume that the woman has agreed to have sex will not have any doubt and so will have no motive to ask more explicitly what she wants. His failure to doubt, or his failure to imagine the bare possibility of doubting, whether the other has consented to engage in sex is brought about by the same factors that determine, for him, the reasonableness of his belief in her consent. It is silly to suggest "*when* in doubt, ask," because the problem is that not enough doubt arises in the first place, that is, the brief look is taken too readily as reasonable or conclusive evidence of a sexual invitation. A man touches the arm of a woman who briefly glanced at him; she pulls away abruptly; but he is not caused to have doubts about her interest. Even if he does not take her resistance as further evidence of her desire, the reasonableness, for him, of his belief that her earlier glance was intentionally sexual is enough to prevent doubt from taking root when it should—immediately.

" 'No' Means 'No' "

According to Susan Estrich, a man who engages in sex with a woman on the basis of an unreasonable belief in her consent should be charged with rape; only a genuinely reasonable belief in her consent should exculpate an accused rapist. Estrich (perhaps utilizing MacKinnon's point) wants it to be legally impossible for a man accused of rape to plead that he believed that the woman consented, when that belief was unreasonable, even though *he* thought it was reasonable. Estrich realizes that "reasonable belief" is a difficult notion. Still, she heroically proposes that "the reasonable man in the 1980s should be the one who understands that a woman's word is deserving of respect, whether she is a perfect stranger or his own wife." The reasonable man "is the one who . . . understands that 'no means no'."[8] The man pawing the arm of the woman who pulls abruptly away—the physical equivalent of "no"—had better immediately doubt the quality of his belief in her sexual interest. At the psychological level, this man might not doubt that she is sexually interested in him; Estrich's normative proposal is that he is to be held liable anyway, because he *should* be doubtful. Beyond this crude sort of case, I think Estrich means that, for the reasonable man, a woman's qualified locution ("Please, not tonight, I think I'd rather not"; "I don't know, I just don't feel like it") is not an invitation to continue trying, but means "no." The woman's wish is expressed softly because she is tactful or frightened or because this is the language of women's culture that she has learned to speak. For the reasonable man, her "I'm not sure I want

to" is either a tactful "no" or a request to back off while she autono-
mously makes up her own mind.

As congenial as Estrich's proposal is, she muddies the water with a tan-
talizing piece of logic:

> Many feminists would argue that so long as women are powerless relative to
> men, viewing a "yes" as a sign of true consent is misguided. . . . [M]any
> women who say yes to men they know, whether on dates or on the job,
> would say no if they could. I have no doubt that women's silence sometimes
> is the product not of passion and desire but of pressure and fear. Yet if yes
> may often mean no, at least from a woman's perspective, it does not seem
> so much to ask men, and the law, to respect the courage of the woman who
> does say no and to take her at her word.[9]

Estrich's reasoning seems to be: if something as antithetical to "no" as
"yes" can mean "no," then surely something as consistent with "no," "no"
itself, means "no." This argument has a curious consequence. If "yes"
can mean "no," at least from a woman's *own* perspective (the woman
who consents for financial reasons but whose heart and desire are not
wrapped up in the act; a woman who agrees, but only after a barrage of
pleading),[10] then it will be difficult to deny that "no" spoken by some
women can mean "maybe" or even "yes." From the perspective of some
women, "no" can mean "try harder to convince me" or "show me how
manly you are." Charlene Muehlenhard and Lisa Hollabaugh have reported that some women occasionally say "no" but do not mean it; 39.3
percent of the 610 college women they surveyed at Texas A&M University indicated that they had offered "token resistance" to sex "even
though [they] had every intention to and [were] willing to engage in
sexual intercourse."[11] Susan Rae Peterson partially explains these findings: "typical sexual involvement includes some resistance on the part of
women . . . because they have been taught to do so, or they do not want
to appear 'easy' or 'cheap'."[12]

Men cannot always tell when a woman's resistance is real or token, serious or playful; men are, moreover, often insensitive, even callous, as to
what a woman does intend to communicate; and, after all, Muehlenhard
and Hollabaugh's figure is only 39 percent and not 99 percent. For these
reasons, as well as her own, Estrich's proposal is a wise suggestion. Men,
and the courts, should always assume, in order to be cognitively, morally,
and legally safe, that a woman's "no" means "no"—*even in those cases when
it does or might not.* A man who takes "no" as "no" even when he suspects
that a woman is testing his masculinity with token resistance is advised by
Estrich to risk suffering a loss of sexual pleasure and a possible blow to
his ego, in order to secure the greater good, for both him and her, of
avoiding rape.

But if men are *always* to assume that "no" means "no," even though there is a nontrivial chance that it means "keep trying" or "yes," then Estrich, to be consistent, should permit men to assume that a woman's "yes" *always* means "yes"—even though, on her view, a woman's "yes" sometimes means "no."[13] If, instead, Estrich wants men to sort out when a woman's "yes" really means "yes" and when it does not, in order that he be able to decide whether to take the "yes" at its face value and proceed with sex, she should propose some workable procedure for men to follow. Yet her description of the reasonable man mentions only what his response to "no" should be, and not what his response to "yes" should be. Encouraging women to abandon the token resistance maneuver, to give up saying "no" when they mean "maybe" or "yes," is helpful. But it will not take theorists of sex, or men in the presence of an apparently consenting woman, very far in deciphering when "yes" means "no."[14]

The Antioch Policy

I propose that we understand Antioch University's "Sexual Offense Policy" as addressing the issues raised in our discussion of Belliotti and Estrich. The policy's central provisions are these:[15]

A1. "Consent must be obtained verbally before there is any sexual contact or conduct."

A2. "[O]btaining consent is an ongoing process in any sexual interaction."

A3. "If the level of sexual intimacy increases during an interaction . . . the people involved need to express their clear verbal consent before moving to that new level."

A4. "The request for consent must be specific to each act."

A5. "If you have had a particular level of sexual intimacy before with someone, you must still ask each and every time."

A6. "If someone has initially consented but then stops consenting during a sexual interaction, she/he should communicate withdrawal verbally and/or through physical resistance. The other individual(s) must stop immediately."

A7. "Don't ever make any assumptions about consent."

In an ethnically, religiously, economically, socially, and sexually diverse population, there might be no common and comprehensive understanding of what various bits of behavior mean in terms of expressing interest in or consenting to sex. In the absence of rigid conventions or a homogeneous community, a glance, either brief or prolonged, is too indefinite to be relied on to transmit information; an invitation to come to one's room, or sharing a room, or a bed, on a trip might or might not have some settled meaning; clothing and cosmetics in a pluralistic culture are equivocal. (Young men, more so than young women, take tight jeans and the absence of a bra under a top to signal an interest in sex.) [16] Because physical movements and cues of various kinds can be interpreted in widely different ways, sexual activity entered into or carried out on the basis of this sort of (mis)information is liable to violate someone's rights or otherwise be indecent or offensive. Antioch therefore insists that consent to sexual activity be verbal (A1) instead of merely behavioral.[17] Following this rule will minimize miscommunication and the harms it causes and will encourage persons to treat each other with Kantian respect as autonomous, or self-determining, agents.

Further, bodily movements or behaviors of a sexual sort that occur in the early stages of a sexual encounter can also be ambiguous and do not necessarily indicate a willingness to increase the intensity of, or to prolong, the encounter (hence A2, A3). Verbal communication is supposed to prevent misunderstandings rooted in indefinite body language; we should not assume consent to continue the encounter on the basis of expressions of desire (lubrication, groans) or failures to resist an embrace. None of these bodily phenomena—reacting with sexual arousal to a touch; not moving away when intimately touched—necessarily means that the touched person welcomes the touch or wants it to continue. There are times when one's body responds with pleasure to a touch but one's mind disagrees with the body's judgment; Antioch's insistence on verbal consent after discussion and deliberation is meant to give the mind decisive and autonomous power. Similarly, the request for, and the consent to, sexual contact must be not only *verbally explicit,* but also *specific* for any sexual act that might occur (A4). Consenting to and then sharing a kiss does not imply consent to any other sexual act; the bodily movements that accompany the sexual arousal created by the kiss do not signal permission to proceed to some other sexual activity not yet discussed (A3, A4).

One provision of the Antioch policy (A7) is a rebuttal of Belliotti's advice, that "when in doubt, ask." Antioch demands, more strictly than this, that the potential sexual partners entertain *universal* doubt and therefore *always* ask. Doubt about the other's consent must be categorical rather than hypothetical: not Belliotti's "when in doubt, assume nothing," but a Cartesian "doubt!" and "assume nothing!" To be on the cognitive, moral, and legal safe side, to avoid mistakes about desire or intention, always assume "no" unless a clear, verbal, explicit "yes" is forthcoming (A1, A3, A4). If this rule is followed, men no longer have to worry about distinguishing a woman's mildly seductive behavior from her "incomplete rejection strategy,"[18] about which men and boys are often confused; in the absence of an explicit "yes" on her part, he is, as demanded by Estrich, respectfully to assume "no." There's still the question of how a man is to know, when obvious consent-negating factors are lacking (for example, she's had too much alcohol), whether a woman's "yes" truly means "yes." Antioch's solution is to rely on explicit, probing verbal communication that must occur not only before but also during a sexual encounter (A3, A5). The constant dialogue, the "ongoing process" (A2) of getting consent in what Lois Pineau calls "communicative sexuality,"[19] is meant to provide the man with an opportunity to assess whether the woman's "yes" means "yes," to give her the opportunity to say a definite even if tactful "no," and to clear up confusions created by her earlier or current silence or passive acquiescence. At the same time, there is to be no constant badgering—especially not under the rubric of "communicative sexuality"—of a woman by a man in response to her "no." A man's querying whether a woman's "no" really means "no" is to disrespect her "no" and fails to acknowledge her autonomy. It is also to embark on a course that might constitute verbal coercion.[20]

It is illuminating to look at the Antioch policy from the perspective of the sadomasochistic subculture, in particular its use of "safe words." A set of safe words is a language, a common understanding, a convention jointly created in advance (hence a Cartesian foundation) of sex by the partners, to be used during a sexual encounter as a way to say "yes," "more," or "no," or to convey details about wants and dislikes, without spoiling the erotic mood. Thus the use of safe words attempts to achieve some of the goals of Antioch's policy without the cumbersome apparatus of explicit verbal consent at each level of sexual interaction (A3, A4). And a tactful and ingenious safe word can gently accomplish an Antiochian withdrawal of consent to sex (A6). But there is a major difference between sadomasochism and Antiochian sex: a sadomasochistic pair wants the activities to proceed smoothly, spontaneously, realistically, so one party grants to the other the right to carry on as he or she wishes, subject to the veto or modifications of safe words, which are to be used sparingly, only when necessary, as a last resort; the couple therefore eschews Antiochian constant dialogue. In dispensing with the incessant chatter of ongoing consent to higher levels of sexual interaction (A2, A3), the sadomasochistic pair violates another provision (A7): consent is assumed throughout the encounter in virtue of the early granting of rights. No such prior consent to sex into an indefinite future is admissible by Antioch.[21]

Pleasure

Does Antioch's policy make sex less exciting? Does it force a couple to slow down, to savor each finger and tooth, when they would rather be overwhelmed by passion? Sarah Crichton criticizes the Antioch policy on the grounds that "it criminalizes the delicious unexpectedness of sex— a hand suddenly moves to here, a mouth to there."[22] But this consideration is not decisive. One goal of the policy is to decrease the possibility that a person will unexpectedly experience (that is, without being warned by being asked) something unpleasant that he or she does not want to experience: a mouth sucking on the wrong toe, a finger too rudely rammed in the rectum. The risk of undergoing unwanted acts or sensations is especially great with strangers, and it is in such a context that the requirement that consent be obtained specifically for each act makes the most sense. Sometimes we do not want the unexpected but only the expected, the particular sensations we know, trust, and yearn for. So there is in the Antioch policy a tradeoff: we lose the pleasure, if any, of the unexpected, but we also avoid the unpleasantness of the unexpected. This is why Crichton's point is not decisive. Perhaps for the young, or for those people more generally who do not yet know what they like sexually, verbal consent to specifically described touches or acts might make less sense. But in this case, too, there are reasons to insist, for the sake of caution, on such consent.

Julia Reidhead also attempts to rebut the objection that Antioch's policy begets dull sex.[23] She claims that the policy gives the partners a chance to be creative with language, to play linguistically with a request to touch the breast or "kiss the hollow of your neck" and to "reinvent [sex] privately." But Antioch thinks that sexual language needs to be less, rather than more, private; more specific, not less.[24] Hence Reidhead's praise for Antioch's policy misses its point: common linguistic understandings cannot be assumed in a heterogeneous population. To encourage the creative, poetic use of language in framing sexual requests to proceed to a new level of sex is to provoke the misunderstandings the policy was designed to prevent. Thus, when Reidhead queries, "What woman or man on Antioch's campus, or elsewhere, wouldn't welcome . . . 'May I kiss the hollow of your neck'," Reidhead's homogenizing "or elsewhere" betrays an insensitivity to the cultural and social differences and their linguistic and behavioral concomitants that Antioch is trying to overcome.

Reidhead defends Antioch also by arguing that vocalizing creatively about sex before we do it is a fine way to mix the pleasures of language with the pleasures of the body. Indeed, the pleasures of talk are themselves sensual and sexual: "Antioch's subtle and imaginative mandate is an erotic windfall: an opportunity for undergraduates to discover that wordplay and foreplay can be happily entwined." Reidhead is right that talking about sex can be sexy and arousing, but wrong that this fact is consistent with the Antioch policy and one of its advantages. This cutesy reading of communication as itself sex almost throws Antioch's procedure into a vicious regress: if no sexual activity is permissible without prior consent (A1), and consent must be verbal or spoken, then if a request for sexual activity is constructed to be a sexually arousing locution, it would amount to a sexual act and hence would be impermissible unless it, in turn, had already received specific consent (A1, A4). So *Y*'s consent to nonverbal sexual activity must be preceded by *X*'s verbal request for that activity *and* by *X*'s verbal request to utter that sexual or sexually arousing verbal request. Further, to try to get consent for the sexual act of kissing the neck by talking sensually about kissing the neck is to employ the pleasure elicited by one sexual act to bring about the occurrence of another sexual act. But obtaining consent for a sexual act by causing even mild sexual pleasure with a seductive request is to interfere with calm and rational deliberation—as much as a shot or two of whiskey would. This is why Antioch insists (A3) that between any two sexual levels there must be a pause, a sexual gap, that makes space for three things: a thoughtful, verbal act of request, deliberations about whether or not to proceed, and then either consent or denial. A well-timed hiatus respected by both parties provides an obstacle to misreadings; the demands of Augustinian bodily perturbations are to be checked while the mind (re)considers.

Body Talk

But the body should not be dismissed altogether. When two people in love embrace tightly, eyes glued to each other's eyes, bodies in contact pulsating with pleasure, they often do know (*how*, is the mystery) without explicit verbalization, from the way they touch each other and respond to these touches, that each wants and at least implicitly, if not explicitly, consents to the sex that is about to occur. Other cases of successful communication—in and out of sexual contexts—are explicit and specific without being verbal. So even if the truth of the particular claim that the mouth can say "no" while the body exclaims an overriding "yes" is debatable or doubtful, the general idea, that the body sometimes does speak a clear language, seems fine. Maybe this is why Antioch, even though it requires a verbal "yes" for proceeding with sex (A1), allows a *nonverbal* "no" to be sufficient for *withdrawing* consent (A6). Nonverbal behavior can have a clear meaning after all. Certain voluntary actions, even some impulsive, reflex-like, bodily movements, do mean "no," and about these there should be no mistake, in the same Estrichian way that about the meaning of the simple verbal "no" there should be no mistake. But if such bodily motions can be assumed or demanded to be understood in a pluralistic community—*pulling away when touched means "no"*— then some voluntary behaviors and involuntary bodily movements must reliably signal "yes."

According to the policy, a verbal "yes" replaces any possible bodily movement or behavior as the one and only reliable sign that proceeding with sexual activity is permissible. If I ask, "may I kiss you?" I may not proceed on the basis of your bodily reply, for example, your pushing your mouth out at me, or your groaning and opening your mouth invitingly, because even though it seems obvious to me what these behaviors mean ("yes"), I might be making an interpretive mistake: I see your open mouth as presented "invitingly" because I have with undue optimism deceived myself into thinking that is what you mean. So I must wait for the words, "yes, you may kiss me,"[25] about which such interpretive unclarity is not supposed to arise (else the problem Antioch set for itself is unsolvable). The verbal "yes," *after* communicative probing, is Antioch's Cartesian foundation. But can the ambiguities of the verbal be cleared up by language itself? How much communicative probing is *enough*? This question creates a hermeneutic circle that threatens to trap Antioch's policy. Her "yes," repeated several times under the third-degree interrogation that comprises communicative sex, can always be probed more for genuineness, if I wanted to *really* make sure. But, losing patience, she shows her "yes" to be genuine when she grabs me or plants a kiss on my lips. The body reasserts itself.

My continuing to probe her "yes" over and over again, to make sure that her heart and desire are wrapped up in the act to which she is apparently consenting (must I ask her whether she realizes that her agreement might have been engineered for my benefit by "compulsory heterosexuality"?), is a kind of paternalism. The robust respect that Antioch's policy fosters for a woman's "no" is offset by the weaker respect it fosters for her "yes." Hence conceiving of the Antioch policy not as attempting to foster respect for the autonomy of the other, but as simply attempting to prevent acquaintance rape (that is, harmful actions), is more accurate. At best, the relationship between Antioch's policy and the autonomy of potential sexual partners is unclear. One Antioch student, Suzy Martin, defends the policy by saying that "It made me aware I *have* a voice. I didn't know that before."[26] Coming in the mid-90s from a college-age woman, the kind of person we expect to know better, this remark is astonishing. In effect, she admits that what Antioch is doing for her, at such an advanced age, is what her parents and earlier schooling should have done long ago, to teach her that she has a voice. Thus Antioch is employing an anti-autonomy principle in its treatment of young adults—in loco parentis—that my college generation had fought to eliminate.

Consent

The policy lays it down that previous sexual encounters between two people do not relax or change the rules to be followed during their later encounters (A5); the casual sex of one-night stands and that of ongoing relationships are governed by the same rules or standards. Nor does a person's sexual biography (for example, reputation) count for anything. No historical facts allow "assumptions about consent" (A7). Indeed, in requiring consent at each different level of a single sexual encounter, Antioch applies the same principle of the irrelevance of history to each sub-act within that encounter. Earlier consent to one sub-act within a single encounter creates no presumption that one may proceed, without repeating the procedure of obtaining explicit and specific consent, to later sub-acts in the same encounter, in the same way that a sexual encounter on Friday night does not mean that consent can be assumed for a sexual encounter on the following Saturday night. The history of the relationship, let alone the history of the evening, counts for nothing.[27] The Antioch policy, then, implies that one cannot consent in advance to a whole night of sex, but only to a single atomistic act, one small part of an encounter. Similarly, in denying the relevance of the historical, Antioch makes both a Pauline and a Kantian marriage contract impossible.[28] In such marriages, one consents at the very beginning, in advance, to a whole series of sexual acts that might make up the rest of one's sexual life; consent to sex is presumed continuously after the exchange of vows and rings; each spouse owns the body and sexual powers of the other; and marital rape is conceptually impossible, replaced by a notion of fulfilling the "marriage debt." In rejecting the possibility of such an arrangement, even if voluntary and contractual, Antioch cuts back on a traditional power of consent: its ability to apply to an indefinite, open future. For Antioch, consent is short-lived; it dies an easy death, and must always be replaced by a new generation of consents.

Antioch also cuts back on the power of consent by making it not binding: one can withdraw consent at any time during any act or sub-act (A6). Nothing in the policy indicates that the right to withdraw is limited by the sexual satisfaction or other expectations of one's partner. Any such qualification would also run counter to the policy's spirit. This is a difference between Antioch's policy and Belliotti's libertarianism, according to which breaking a sexual promise is at least a prima facie moral fault. It is also contrary to the indissolubility of Pauline marriage. But that Antioch would be indulgent about withdrawing consent makes sense, given Antioch's distrust of the historical. Consenting is an act that occupies a discrete location in place and time; it is a historical event, and that it has occurred is a historical fact; thus consent is itself precisely the kind of thing whose weight Antioch discounts. Consenting to a sexual act does not entail, for Antioch, that one ought to perform the act, and not even that one has a prima facie duty to do so; the act need not take place because the only justification for it to occur is the act of consenting that has already receded into the past and has become a mere piece of impotent history. When consent into the future, today for tomorrow, is ruled out, so too is consent into the future, now for ten seconds from now. Then how could consent have the power to legitimize any subsequent sexual act? An air of paradox surrounds the policy: it makes consent the centerpiece of valid sexual conduct, yet its concept of consent is emaciated. Of course, as Carole Pateman says, "unless refusal of consent or withdrawal of consent are real possibilities, we can no longer speak of 'consent' in any genuine sense."[29] But that withdrawing consent must be possible does not entail that we have carte blanche permission to do so. My guess is that Belliotti is right, that withdrawing consent to an act to which one has consented is prima facie wrong. The logical possibility that consent is binding in this way is necessary for taking consent seriously in the first place as a legitimizer of sexual activity.

Still, if X has promised a sexual act to Y, but withdraws consent and so reneges, it does *not* follow from Belliotti's libertarianism that Y has a right to compel X into compliance.[30] Nor does it follow from the terms of Pauline or Kantian marriage, in which the spouses consent to a lifetime of sexual acts. Neither the fact that each person has a duty, the marriage debt, to provide sexual pleasure for the other whenever the other wants it, nor the fact that in such a marriage the one initial act of consent makes rape conceptually impossible, imply that a spurned spouse may rightfully force himself or herself upon the other. Pauline marriage is, in principle, egalitarian; the wife owns the husband and his ability to perform sexually as much as he owns her capacity to provide pleasure. In patriarchal practice, however, the man expects sexual access to his wife in exchange for economic support, and even if rape is conceptually impossible he might still extract or enforce the marriage debt: "if she shows unwillingness or lack of inclination to engage with him in sexual intercourse, he may wish to remind her of the nature of the bargain they struck. The act of rape may serve conveniently as a communicative vehicle for reminding her."[31] But neither violence nor abuse are legitimated by the *principles* of Pauline marriage; perhaps their possibility explains why Paul admonishes the spouses to show "due benevolence" to each other (1 Corinthians 7:3).[32]

Finally, Antioch's policy also does not permit "metaconsent," or consent about (the necessity of) consent. Consent, in principle, should be able to alter the background presumption, in the relationship between two people, *from* "assume 'no' unless you hear an explicit 'yes' " *to* "assume 'yes' unless you hear an explicit 'no'," or *from* "don't you dare try without an explicit go-ahead" *to* "feel free to try but be prepared for a 'no'." This power of consent is abolished by Antioch's making history irrelevant; consent to prior sexual acts creates no presumption in favor of "yes" tonight (A5). Further, to give consent into the future allows one's partner to make a prohibited assumption (A7). There is no provision in the policy that empowers a couple to jettison the policy by free and mutual consent; here is another way Antioch's policy does not foster autonomy. In Pauline marriage, by contrast, one act of consent, the marriage vow, has the power to change presumptions from "no" to an ongoing "yes." Such is the power of consent for Paul, that it both applies to the future and is binding: we make our bed and then lie in it. Antioch's notion of consent has freed us from such stodgy concerns.[33]

Notes

1. This is the epigraph to chap. 9 of Susan Haack's *Evidence and Inquiry* (Oxford: Blackwell, 1993), 182. Professor Haack thanks David Stove for supplying it.

2. Raymond Belliotti, "A Philosophical Analysis of Sexual Ethics," *Journal of Social Philosophy* 10, 3 (1979): 8–11, at 11.

3. According to John Sabini and Maury Silver ("Flirtation and Ambiguity," chap. 6 of their *Moralities of Everyday Life* [New York: Oxford University Press, 1982], 107–23, at 116, *n.* 11), "Flirtation . . . offers no commitment and gives no right to claim abuse. To claim you were teased is to claim [that the other] went beyond flirting to committing. Of course, the disappointed one may be inclined to see a tease in a flirt." That is indeed the problem.

4. MacKinnon, *Toward a Feminist Theory of the State* (Cambridge, Mass.: Harvard University Press, 1989), 183; see 181.

5. Belliotti, "A Philosophical Analysis of Sexual Ethics," 9.

6. See T. Perper and D. Weis, "Proceptive and Rejective Strategies of U.S. and Canadian College Women," *Journal of Sex Research* 23, 4 (1987): 455–80, at 462.

7. Belliotti repeats the "when in doubt, ask" advice in his essay "Sex" (in Peter Singer, ed., *A Companion to Ethics* [Oxford: Blackwell, 1991], 315–26, at 325) and in his treatise *Good Sex: Perspectives on Sexual Ethics* (Lawrence: University Press of Kansas, 1993), 106–107. See my book note on *Good Sex*, in *Ethics* 105, 2 (1995): 447–48.

8. Susan Estrich, *Real Rape* (Cambridge, Mass.: Harvard University Press, 1987), 97–98.

9. Estrich, *Real Rape*, 102.

10. These examples are like Robin West's (who might not approve of my use of them), in "The Harms of Consensual Sex," *American Philosophical Association Newsletters* 92, 2 (1995): 52–55, at 53; in this volume, 317–22, at 317–18. I am not sure that the examples capture what Estrich's brief remark, that some women who say "yes" would say "no" *if they could*, means. She makes the point, elsewhere, this way: "many women who say 'yes' are not in fact choosing freely but are submitting because they feel a lack of power to say 'no'" ("Rape," in Patricia Smith, ed., *Feminist Jurisprudence* [New York: Oxford University Press, 1993], 158–87, at

177).

11. Muehlenhard and Hollabaugh, "Do Women Sometimes Say No When They Mean Yes? The Prevalence and Correlates of Token Resistance to Sex," *Journal of Personality and Social Psychology* 54, 5 (1988): 872–79.

12. Susan Rae Peterson, "Coercion and Rape: The State as a Male Protection Racket," in Mary Vetterling-Braggin, Frederick A. Elliston, and Jane English, eds., *Feminism and Philosophy* (Totowa, N.J.: Littlefield, Adams, 1977), 360–71, at 365. See also Muehlenhard and Hollabaugh ("Do Women Sometimes Say No When They Mean Yes?") on the wide variety of reasons women have for carrying out this sometimes "rational" strategy (875, 878).

Rae Langton suggests that men's failure to take a woman's "no" as "no" is an effect of pornography on men ("Speech Acts and Unspeakable Acts," *Philosophy and Public Affairs* 22, 4 [1993]: 293–330, at 324–25). This thesis is surprising, because in most pornography women are portrayed as active seekers of sexual activity, as eschewing the traditional games, and not as reluctant participants. Consistent with men's fantasies, women's favorite word in pornography, it seems, is *yes* or an equivalent. Still, Langton supposes that because women as portrayed in pornography rarely say "no," men who learn "the rules of the [sexual] game" from pornography do not learn to recognize refusals for what they are. But do men learn about sex (only, mostly, or at all) from pornography? Do men really (and stupidly) take the fact that women rarely say "no" in pornography to mean that the real women in their presence do not mean "no" when they do say it? Beatrice Faust proposes an alternative way, more plausible than Langton's, in which pornography might have an effect:

> Many nonviolent rapes are simply results of scrambled signals between the sexes. Pornography is relevant to this category of rape, since it reinforces the belief that women respond to sex exactly as men do. (*Women, Sex, and Pornography* [New York: Macmillan, 1980], 132.)

Women in pornography energetically seek sexual encounters and respond to the sexual advances of others without hesitation; they are portrayed as being as much interested in sex for its own sake, as eager to consent, and as easily aroused as men are (or as men think men are). Men who believe that women are as quick-triggered as men are might have difficulty comprehending a woman's unwillingness to proceed directly from a long kiss to more intimate sexual touches; a man, being already aroused and wanting to proceed, might assume that she is just as aroused and hence also wants to proceed—despite her pauses or silence. But men, especially when young, likely assimilate the sexuality of women to their own not in virtue of pornographic portrayals of sexually assertive women, but out of simple sexual inexperience.

Indeed, boys discover that "no" does not always mean "no" when they are young (i.e., pre-pornographically). Boys detect the maneuver in girls who say "no" but soon show they do not mean it; these girls say "no" only because they have been pushed by their mothers to say "no," even though pushed by their mothers, without complete success, to mean it. Muehlenhard and Hollabaugh's research shows that the phenomenon extends beyond grade school into college and strongly suggests that mechanisms other than pornography are at work. If we are worried, as we should be, about where college-age men get the idea, or have it reinforced, that a woman's "no" does not always mean "no," we might want to consider the effects of Muehlenhard's publication itself, which let a popular cat out of the scholarly bag. Men can read "39.3%" in print in a refereed, respected journal, which must be a more persuasive documentation of women's artifice than the fantasy world of pornography. Robin Warshaw and Andrea Parrot ("The Contribution of Sex-Role Socialization to Acquaintance Rape," in Andrea Parrot and Laurie Bechhofer, eds., *Acquaintance Rape: The Hidden Crime* [New York: John Wiley, 1991], 73–82) claim that "men's social training tells them . . . that women who say 'no' don't really mean it" (75) and "men are socialized to believe . . . that women do not mean 'no' when they say 'no' " (80). But if men discover that "no" does not always mean "no" *firsthand,* from women who say "no" but do not mean it, it is a conceptual disaster to point an accusing causal finger at "socialization" or "social training."

13. Carole Pateman turns this around: "if 'no,' when uttered by a woman, is to be reinterpreted as 'yes,' then . . . why should a woman's 'yes' be more privileged, be any the less open to invalidation" ("Women and Consent," *Political Theory* 8, 2 [1980]: 149–68, at 162)—that is, if men do not take "no" as "no," they have no right to take "yes" as "yes."

14. Stephen Schulhofer ("The Gender Question in Criminal Law," in Jeffrie G. Murphy, ed., *Punishment and Rehabilitation,* 3rd edition [Belmont, Calif.: Wadsworth, 1995], 274–311, at 308–309) discusses some cases in which "yes" does not mean "yes": the man obtains a woman's consent through fraud or deception. Estrich does not seem to have this sort of case in mind. Maybe she agrees with MacKinnon's point about the indistinguishability in patriarchy of rape and consensual sex, or with her rhetorical skepticism: "What is it reasonable for a man to believe concerning a woman's desire for sex when heterosexuality is compulsory?" (MacKinnon, *Toward a Feminist Theory of the State,* 183). "Nothing" is the implied answer; he may never assume that "yes" means "yes."

15. I quote from a copy of the policy and its introduction sent to me in 1994 by the Office of the President, Antioch University. The numbering of the provisions is my own. The policy was intended to be gender-neutral and sexual orientation-neutral, allowing the possibility of gay or lesbian acquaintance rape and a woman's raping a man.

16. Jacqueline D. Goodchilds and Gail L. Zellman, "Sexual Signaling and Sexual Aggression in Adolescent Relationships," in Neil M. Malamuth and Edward Donnerstein, eds., *Pornography and Sexual Aggression* (Orlando, Fla.: Academic Press, 1984), 233–43, at 236. In any event, "males have a more sexualized view of the world than females, attributing more sexual meaning to a wide range of behaviors" (239).

17. At least seven times in the policy and its introduction, it is stated that consent to sexual activity must be verbal. Only once does the policy depart from this formula: "the person with whom sexual contact/conduct is initiated is responsible to express verbally and/or physically her/his willingness or lack of willingness." Because the bulk of the policy insists that consent be verbal, I discount this one awkward and *possibly* contradictory sentence.

The policy also says, "If sexual contact . . . is *not* mutually and simultaneously initiated, then the person who initiates sexual contact . . . is responsible for getting the verbal consent of the other individuals(s) involved" (italics added).

From the statement that when mutual and simultaneous initiation is absent, verbal consent is required, it does not follow (nor does the policy ever assert) that when mutual and simultaneous initiation is present, verbal consent can be dispensed with. To claim otherwise—that is, to deny on the basis of that sentence that the Antioch policy always requires verbal consent—is to commit an elementary logical fallacy. (I think this mistake is made by Eva Feder Kittay, "AH! My Foolish Heart: A Reply to Alan Soble's 'Antioch's "Sexual Offense Policy": A Philosophical Exploration'," *Journal of Social Philosophy* 28, 2 [1997]: 153–59, at 154. See also note 25, below.) At any rate, if we are to construe the Antioch policy as an interesting and novel approach to the problems we are discussing, we should not read it as asserting that "mutual and simultaneous initiation" cancels the need for verbal consent. The aroused and optimistic person who subjectively has no doubt that the other person is consenting, but is mistaken about that, is a version of the aroused and optimistic person who assumes that his initiation is reciprocated mutually and simultaneously by the other, but is similarly mistaken. Thus the good intentions of the Antioch policy would fall prey to the same psychological and moral delusions that undermine Belliotti's principle, "when in doubt, ask."

18. Perper and Weis, "Proceptive," 476.

19. For Pineau, a man "cannot know, except through the practice of communicative sexuality, whether his partner has any sexual reason for continuing the encounter"—or any other reason for doing so ("Date Rape: A Feminist Analysis," *Law and Philosophy* 8 [1989]: 217–43, at 239). The essays in Leslie Francis's anthology *Date Rape* (University Park: Penn State University Press, 1996) explore both the Antioch policy and Pineau's essay. See also, on Antioch's policy, Bruno Leone, ed., *Rape on Campus* (San Diego, Calif.: Greenhaven Press, 1995).

20. Is a man's badgering a woman for sex "coercion"? Charlene Muehlenhard and Jennifer Schrag think so: "We define verbal sexual coercion as a woman's consenting to unwanted sexual activity because of a man's verbal arguments, not including verbal threats of physical force" ("Nonviolent Sexual Coercion," in Parrot and Bechhofer, eds., *Acquaintance Rape*, 115–28, at 122). Muehlenhard and Schrag describe ways in which they think "women are coerced into having unwanted sexual intercourse," ways that are "more subtle" than being violently raped (115). Among the things listed that *coerce* women into unwanted sexual intercourse are "compulsory heterosexuality" (116–17), "status coercion" (119), "verbal sexual coercion" (122–23), and "discrimination against lesbians" (121). In agreement with Muehlenhard, Mary Koss uses the expression "sexually coercive men" to refer to those who obtain sex "after continual discussions and arguments" or by false avowals of love (Mary P. Koss and Kenneth E. Leonard, "Sexually Aggressive Men: Empirical Findings and Theoretical Implications," in Malamuth and Donnerstein, *Pornography and Sexual Aggression*, 213–232, at 216). For discussion, see Neil Gilbert, "Realities and Mythologies of Rape," *Society* (May/June 1992): 4–10, at 7; and Alan Wertheimer, "Consent and Sexual Relations," in this volume, 341–66.

21. Pineau proposes that consensual sadomasochism be admissible by law, if "the court has a right to require that there be a system of signals whereby each partner can convey to the other whether she has had enough" ("Date Rape," 242). The safe words of consensual sadomasochism apparently fulfill the re-

quirements of communicative sexuality (see her note 23).

22. Sarah Crichton, "Sexual Correctness: Has It Gone too Far?" in Susan J. Bunting, ed., *Human Sexuality 95/96* (Guilford, Conn.: Dushkin, 1995), 208–11, at 209.

23. Julia Reidhead, "Good Sex" [letter], *The New Yorker* (January 10, 1994), 8.

24. Antioch, however, does very little to make specific the "specific" of clause A4. Thus the policy is vulnerable to wisecracks. The scene is that *X* and *Y* are sitting on a couch, face-to-face.

X: May I kiss you?

Y: Of course. Go ahead.

[*Y* makes Y's mouth available; X slides X's tongue deeply into Y's oral cavity. Y pulls sharply away.]

Y: I didn't say you could *French* kiss me!

25. According to the Policy, "Consent must be clear and verbal (i.e., saying: yes, I want to kiss you also)."

26. Quoted by Jennifer Wolf, in "Sex By the Rules," *Glamour* (May 1994), 256–59, 290, at 258.

27. According to the Model Anti-Pornography Law drafted by Catharine MacKinnon and Andrea Dworkin (see "Symposium on Pornography: Appendix," *New England Law Review* 20, 4 [1984–85]: 759–77; sec. 3.1, 760), that a woman is or has been a prostitute outside of the making of an item of pornography means nothing in deciding whether she has been coerced into making this particular item of pornography. The historical fact of earlier or concurrent prostitution cannot be used as evidence by the defendant to show that her acts of prostitution in the making of this item of pornography were entered into by her free consent. The Model Law, in making history irrelevant, resembles the Antioch policy.

28. For St. Paul, see 1 Corinthians 7:4, "The wife hath not power of her own body, but the husband: and likewise also the husband hath not power of his own body, but the wife." And here is Immanuel Kant's definition of marriage: "Sexual union in accordance with principle is *marriage* (*matrimonium*), that is, the union of two persons of different sexes for lifelong possession of each other's sexual attributes" (*The Metaphysics of Morals* [1797], trans. Mary Gregor [Cambridge: Cambridge University Press, 1996], 62). For discussion of Kant on marriage, see my "Sexual Use and What to Do about It: Internalist and Externalist Sexual Ethics," in this volume, 225–58, especially section 5, 245–50.

29. Pateman, "Women and Consent," 150.

30. Some teenagers (of both sexes) think that male anger and even assault are justified by a girl's apparently reneging on a sexual deal; see Goodchilds and Zellman, "Sexual Signaling," 237, 241–42.

31. Carolyn Shafer and Marilyn Frye, "Rape and Respect," in Mary Vetterling-Braggin et al., *Feminism and Philosophy,* 333–46, at 342.

32. Pope Paul VI makes the same point: "It is in fact justly observed that a conjugal act imposed upon one's partner without regard for his or her condition

and lawful desires is not a true act of love, and therefore denies an exigency of right moral order in the relationships between husband and wife" ("Humanae Vitae," in Robert Baker and Frederick Elliston, eds., *Philosophy and Sex*, 2nd ed. [Buffalo, N.Y.: Prometheus, 1984], 167–83, at 173).

33. Assistance in carrying out the research for and the writing of this essay was provided by the University of New Orleans and its College of Liberal Arts, through the release time of a university research professor appointment, and by the Research Support Scheme of the Open Society Institute (grant 1520/706/94). The earliest version of this paper was presented as a seminar at the philosophy department of the Budapest Technical University, May 1994. (Travel to Budapest was made possible by grants from the International Research and Exchanges Board and the Hungarian Ministry of Culture and Education.) A later version was presented on February 24, 1995, as a "Current Research in Philosophy" colloquium at Tulane University; and one more version was read at the Eastern Division meetings of the American Philosophical Association, December 30, 1995. This version has in part been cannibalized from the end of the first chapter of my *Sexual Investigations* (New York: New York University Press, 1996), but also goes beyond it.

Chapter 24

CONSENT AND SEXUAL RELATIONS

Alan Wertheimer

I. INTRODUCTION

This article has two broad purposes. First, as a political philosopher who has been interested in the concepts of coercion and exploitation, I want to consider just what the analysis of the concept of consent can bring to the question, what sexually motivated behavior should be prohibited through the criminal law?[1] Put simply, I shall argue that conceptual analysis will be of little help. Second, and with somewhat fewer professional credentials, I shall offer some thoughts about the substantive question itself. Among other things, I will argue that it is a mistake to think that sexual crimes are about violence rather than sex and that we need to understand just why the violation of sexual autonomy is a serious wrong. I shall also argue that the principle that "no means no" does not tell us when "yes means yes," and that it is the latter question that poses the most interesting theoretical difficulties about coercion, misrepresentation, and competence. In addition, I shall make some brief remarks concerning two questions about consent and sexual relations that lie beyond the criminal law: What "consent compromising behaviors" should be regarded as indecent, although not criminal? When *should* someone consent to sexual relations within an enduring relationship?

© 1996, Cambridge University Press. Reprinted, with the permission of Alan Wertheimer and Cambridge University Press, from *Legal Theory* 2:2 (1996): 89–112.

[A word about notation. In what follows, A will represent a person who attacks B or makes a proposal to B, and it is B's consent that is at issue. A will always be male and B will always be female.]

II. CONSENT AND CONCEPTUAL ANALYSIS

A standard picture about this topic goes something like this. We start with the principle that the criminal law should prohibit behavior that seeks to obtain sexual relations without valid consent. To determine which specific behaviors should be prohibited by the criminal law, we must engage in a detailed philosophical analysis of the concept of consent (and related concepts). If such an analysis can yield the criteria of valid consent, we are then in a better position to identify the behaviors that should be prohibited.

I believe that this picture is mistaken. My central point in this section is that the questions (and their facsimiles)—What is consent? What is valid or meaningful consent?—are less important than they first seem. The concept of consent provides a useful template to organize many of the moral issues in which we are interested, but it cannot do much more than that. The question as to what behavior should be prohibited through the criminal law will be settled by moral argument informed by empirical investigation. Any attempt to resolve that question through an inquiry into the "essence" of consent or the conditions under which we can use the word "consent" will prove to be of only limited help.

A. Consent as Morally Transformative

Let us begin by noting that we are not interested in consent as a free-standing concept. Rather, we are interested in consent because consent is *morally transformative;* that is, it changes the moral relationship between A and B and between them and others.[2] B's consent may *legitimate* an action by A that would not be legitimate without B's consent, as when B's consent to surgery transforms A's act from a battery to a permissible medical procedure. B's consent to a transaction with A provides a reason for others not to interfere with that transaction, as when B's consent to let A put a tattoo on her arm gives C a reason to let them be. And B's consent may give rise to an *obligation.* If B consents to do X for A, B acquires an obligation to do X for A.

To say that B's consent is morally transformative is not to say that B's consent is either necessary or sufficient to change an "all things considered" moral judgment about A's or B's action. It may be legitimate for A to perform surgery on a delusional B without B's consent. It may be wrong for A to perform surgery on B with B's consent if the procedure is not medically indicated.[3] Similarly, we may think that exchanging money for sexual relations is wrong even if the prostitute consents to the exchange. But this does not show that the prostitute's consent is not morally transformative. After all, the prostitute's consent to sexual relations with A eliminates one very important reason for regarding A's behavior as wrong, namely, that A had sexual relations with B without her consent. B's consent is morally transformative because it provides a reason, although not a conclusive reason, for thinking that A's behavior is legitimate.

B. The Logic of Consent Arguments

To put the point of the previous section schematically, we are interested in the following sort of argument.

Major Premise: If B consents to A's doing X to B, then it is legitimate for A to do X to B.

Minor Premise: B has (has not) consented to A's doing X to B.

Conclusion: It is (is not) legitimate for A to do X to B.

Given the major premise, it seems that we must determine when the *minor premise* is true if we are going to know when the conclusion is warranted. For that reason, we may be tempted to think that an analysis of the concept of consent will identify the *criteria* or necessary and sufficient conditions of valid consent, and that empirical investigation can then (in principle) determine if those criteria are met. If the criteria are met, then the minor premise is true and the conclusion follows. If not, then the minor premise is false and the conclusion does not follow.

If things were only so simple. It is a mistake to think that we will be able to make much progress toward resolving the substantive moral and legal issues in which we are interested by philosophical resources internal to the concept of consent. In the final analysis, we are always going to have to ask: Given the facts that relate to issues of consent, how should we think about the moral and legal status of a transaction or relationship? In that sense, I am squarely in the camp that maintains that the concept of consent is fundamentally normative.

In suggesting that consent is essentially normative, I do not deny that it is possible to produce a morally neutral account of consent that would allow us to say when B consents by reference to specific empirical criteria. I do maintain that if we were to operate with a morally neutral account of consent, we would then have to go on to ask whether B's consent legitimates A's action, and that we will be unable to answer that question without introducing substantive moral arguments. A morally neutral account of consent would do little work in our moral argument. If we want consent to do more work in our moral argument, we must build some of our substantive moral principles into the account of consent that we deploy. We could say that B "really" consents only when B's consent token is morally transformative. In the final analysis, it does not matter much whether we adopt a thin, morally neutral, account of consent or a thick, morally laden, account of consent. Either way, the point remains that we will not be able to go from a morally neutral or empirical account of consent to moral or legal conclusions without introducing substantive moral arguments.

C. The Fallacy of Equivocation

Precisely because we can pack a lot or a little into our account of consent, it is all too easy for a "consent argument" to commit the fallacy of equivocation, in which the meaning of consent assumed by the major premise is not identical to the meaning of consent in the minor premise, and, thus, the conclusion does not follow even though both the major premise and minor premise may be true (given different meanings of consent). Consider a classic problem of political philosophy: Do citizens have a general (prima facie) obligation to obey the law? A standard argument goes like this:

   Major Premise: One is obligated to obey the laws if one consents to do so.

   Minor Premise (Version 1): One who remains in his society rather than leaves thereby gives his consent to that society (Plato).[4]

   Minor Premise (Version 2): One who benefits from living in a society gives his consent to that society (Locke).[5]

   Conclusion: One who does not leave his society or benefits from living in a society has an obligation to obey its laws.

Are either versions of the minor premise true? The problem is this: There may be a linguistically plausible sense in which one who accepts the benefits of one's government has consented to that government or in which one who remains in one's society has consented to remain in that society. But, even if that were so, that will not resolve the problem of political obligation. We will have to determine if the type or strength of consent that figures in the major premise has been met in the minor premise. And it may not. Thus, we could agree with Plato that there is a sense in which one who does not leave his society gives his consent, while also agreeing with Hume that it is not the sort of *free* consent that would justify the ascription of a strong obligation to obey the law.[6] We can make a similar point about Locke's view.

The danger of equivocation arises with respect to two other concepts that will figure in our analysis: coercion and harm. Let us assume that one who is coerced into consenting does not give valid or morally transformative consent. When is consent coerced? Consider Harry Frankfurt's example:

> The courts may refuse to admit in evidence, on the grounds that it was coerced, a confession which the police have obtained from a prisoner by threatening to beat him. But the prisoner's accomplices, who are compromised by his confession, are less likely to agree that he was genuinely coerced into confession.[7]

Was the prisoner's confession coerced? There is no reason to think that there must be a single acceptable answer to this question. The answer to this question will depend on the sort of moral transformation that consent is meant to trigger. The sort of pressure to which the prisoner was subject may be sufficient to deprive his confession of legal validity. At the same time, and if there is anything like honor among thieves, the very same pressures may not be sufficient to excuse his betrayal of his accomplices. It will do no good to ask what appears to be a conceptual and empirical question: Was his confession coerced or not? Rather, we need to answer two moral questions: What sorts of pressures on prisoners to confess are sufficient to bar the introduction of the confession as evidence? What sorts of pressures on prisoners are sufficient to excuse the ascription of blame by those to whom the prisoner has obligations of silence?

A similar point can be made about the concept of harm. Suppose we start from the Millian principle that the state can justifiably prohibit only conduct that causes harm to others. The following questions arise: Does the psychic distress caused by offensive speech count as harmful? Does trespass that causes no physical damage to one's property constitute a harm? Does a peeping Tom harm his target? Does he harm his target if she is unaware of his voyeurism? Clearly there is a sense in which psychic distress caused by offensive speech is harmful. As a matter of empirical psychology, it is simply untrue that "sticks and stones will break your bones, but names will never hurt you." And there is clearly a sense in which one has *not* been harmed by trespass that causes no physical damage, or by the peeping Tom, particularly if the target is unaware of his voyeurism. But these observations will not tell us which activities can be legitimately prohibited by the state under the Millian principle.[8]

Once again, we have two choices. We could opt for a morally neutral or neurological account of harm, but then we will have to go on to ask whether harm so defined should or should not be prohibited, and whether some acts excluded by that definition can be legitimately prohibited. On the other hand, we could opt for a moralized account of harm, say, one in which one is harmed if one's rights are violated. On this view, we can maintain that the psychic distress caused by offensive speech does not count as a harm because it does not violate one's rights, whereas trespassing and voyeurism do count as harm because they violate one's rights to property and privacy. From this perspective, sexual offenses may cause a particularly serious harm because they violate an important right of the subject, not (solely) because they are physically or psychologically more damaging than nonsexual violence (although that may also be true).

III. A (BRIEF) THEORY OF CONSENT

With these anti-essentialist ruminations behind us, I shall sketch an account of consent in two stages. First, I shall consider the ontology of consent, the phenomena to which the template of consent calls our attention. Second, I shall consider what I shall call the "principles of consent," the conditions under which these phenomena are morally transformative.

A. The Ontology of Consent

First, morally transformative consent always involves a verbal or nonverbal action, some token of consent. Consent is performative rather than attitudinal. It might be objected that there is a plausible understanding of the *word* consent, in which mental agreement is sufficient to establish consent. I do not want to quibble over words. If one wants to insist that mental agreement is sufficient to establish consent, then I shall say that B's mental agreement to allow A to do X does not *authorize* or *legitimate* A's doing X in the absence of B's communication. If B has decided to accept A's business proposal and was about to communicate that decision to A when their call was disconnected, it would not be legitimate for A to proceed as if B had agreed. Similarly, that B actually desires sexual relations with A does not authorize A to have sexual relations with A if B has said "no."

Second, and to cover well-trod ground, B's consent token can be explicit or tacit, verbal or nonverbal. B gives verbal explicit agreement to A's proposal when B says "yes" or some equivalent. B may give nonverbal but explicit consent to A's proposal that they have sexual relations if B smiles and leads A into her bedroom. One gives tacit consent when silence or inaction is understood to constitute agreement. Thus if my department chair says, "Unless I hear from you, I'll assume that you can advise students at orientation," my silence is an indication that I am available. In general, it is of no fundamental importance whether consent is explicit or tacit, if it is understood that silence or inaction indicates consent, if there is a genuine opportunity for B to dissent, and if B's dissent will have moral force.

And that brings me to the third consideration. Consent will be valid or morally transformative only when certain conditions are met or, perhaps more helpfully, only in the absence of certain background defects. Those conditions will include, among other things, that B is competent to give consent, the absence of coercion, and also perhaps the absence of misrepresentation and concealment of important information. We could say that one who signs a contract at the point of a gun has not consented at all, or that her consent isn't sufficiently free to give rise to an obligation. Either way, her consent token will not be morally transformative.

B. The Principles of Consent

To put the argument in somewhat different terms, we do not start from the assumption that B's consent is morally transformative, in which case the question for philosophical analysis becomes whether B has or has not consented to A's action. Rather, the determination as to when consent is morally transformative is an *output* of moral theorizing rather than an *input*. Let us call the principles that define when a consent token is morally transformative the *principles of consent*.

The principles of consent may vary from context to context. To see this, consider four cases: (1) A physician tells his patient that she has breast cancer and that she should immediately undergo a mastectomy. He does not explain the risks of the procedure or other options. Because the patient trusts her physician, she signs a consent form. (2) A patient's leg is gangrenous and she must choose between amputation and death. She understands the alternatives, and, because she does not want to die, she signs the consent form. (3) A dance studio gets an elderly woman to contract to pay $20,000 for dance lessons by "a constant and continuous barrage of flattery, false praise, excessive compliments, and panegyric encomiums."[9] (4) A psychotherapist proposes that he and the patient have sexual relations. Because the patient has become sexually attracted to the psychotherapist, she enthusiastically agrees.

We might think that the woman's consent in (1) is not valid because the principles of consent for medical procedures require that the physician explain the risks and alternatives. In this case, valid or morally transformative consent must be *informed* consent. Yet, the principles of consent may also entail that the consent given in (2) is valid even though the patient reasonably believed that she had no choice but to agree, say, because the very real constraints on her decision were not the result of *illegitimate* pressures on her decision-making process. By contrast, the principles of consent might hold that the consent given in (3) is not valid or morally transformative because the dance studio acted illegitimately in procuring the woman's consent, even though she had more "choice" than in (2). And the principles of consent might hold that the consent given in (4) does not render it legitimate for the psychotherapist to have sexual relations with his patient, because he has a fiduciary obligation to refrain from sexual relations with his patient. Period.[10]

These are just intuitions. How do we determine the correct principles of consent for one context or another? At one level, the answer to these questions will ultimately turn on what is the best account of morality in general or the sorts of moral considerations relevant to this sort of problem. Somehow, I think we are unlikely to resolve that here. Suppose that the best account of the principles of consent reflect a commitment to impartiality, and that this commitment will be cashed out along consequentialist or contractarian lines. If we adopt a consequentialist outlook, we will want to examine the costs and benefits of different principles of consent and will adopt those principles that generate the best consequences all things considered. From a contractarian perspective, we can think of the principles of consent as the outcome of a choice made under conditions of impartiality, perhaps as modeled by a Rawlsian veil of ignorance, although here, too, we will want to consider the costs and benefits of different principles (which is not to say that a contractarian will consider them in the way in which a consequentialist would). But the crucial and present point is that from either perspective, the point of moral theorizing is not to determine when one consents, *per se*. The task is to determine the principles for morally transformative consent.

IV. CRIMINAL OFFENSES

In this section, I want to bring the previous analysis to bear on the central question of this symposium: What sexually motivated behaviors should be regarded as criminal offenses? In considering this question, I shall bracket several related issues. First, I have nothing to say about the history of the law of rape. Second, I shall have little to say about problems of proof that arise because sexual offenses involve behavior that is frequently consensual, and because we operate in a legal context in which we are especially concerned to avoid the conviction of the innocent.

Third, I shall not be concerned with questions as to the best interpretations of existing statutes. The question here is not, for example, whether Rusk was guilty under an existing statute if he caused his victim to fear being stranded in an unknown part of the city unless she engaged in sexual acts with him, but whether legislation should be designed so as to regard such behavior as a criminal offense.[11] Finally, I shall have little to say about questions of culpability, the sorts of issues raised in the (in)famous case of Regina v. Morgan, in which several men claimed to believe that the wife of a friend consented to sexual relations with them even though she strongly objected at the time.[12] I am concerned with the question as to what conduct should be criminal, and not the conditions under which one might be justifiably excused from liability for such conduct.

A. Criminal Elements

In considering the question so posed, it will be useful to disaggregate some of the ways in which sexually motivated behavior might be seriously wrong.

First, a sexual offense involves a nonconsensual touching or bodily contact, that is, the elements of a standard battery. Nonconsensual touchings need not be violent or painful or involve the penetration of a bodily orifice.

Second, a sexual offense may involve a violent assault or battery, that is, physical contact that involves overpowering restraint of movement or physical pain or harm to the victim's body that lasts beyond the duration of the incident.

Third, a sexual offense may involve *threats* of violence. The perpetrator puts the victim in fear of harm to her life or body, and then uses that fear to obtain sexual relations. As the victim in *Rusk* put it, "If I do want you want, will you let me go?"

Fourth, sexual offenses may often involve harm or the fear of harms that *flow from* penetration as distinguished from the penetration itself, for example, unwanted pregnancy and sexually transmitted diseases.

Fifth, and of greatest relevance to this article, is the moral and psychological harm associated with the fact that a sexual offense involves unwanted and nonconsensual penetration, that it "violates the interest in exclusive control of one's body for sexual purposes."[13]

B. Seriousness

The seriousness of a sexual offense may vary with the way in which these elements are combined. We can distinguish at least five sorts of sexual offense. Although reasonable people may disagree about the precise ranking, one view of their relative seriousness, in descending order of seriousness, looks like this: (1) sexually motivated assault with penetration and where violence is actually used to inflict harm or overcome resistance; (2) sexually motivated assault with penetration where violence is threatened but not used; (3) sexually motivated assault (where violence is used or threatened) where penetration does not occur ("attempted rape"); (4) penetration of the victim in the face of the victim's refusal to have sexual relations or her inability to consent to sexual relations, but without the use or threat of violence; (5) sexual battery or sexual harassment, where the victim is touched without her consent, but where penetration does not occur.

Before going further, let me make several points about this list. First, this list makes no distinction between cases in which the penetrator and victim are strangers and those in which they are acquaintances (or married). Second, this ordering does not draw a fundamental distinction between the *use* and *threat* of violence, an important departure from the traditional law of rape, in which actual violence and resistance to that violence were sometimes required. It is clearly a mistake to minimize the importance of threats. Consider a case in which A says something like this (perhaps using cruder language):

> You and I are going to play a game. We are going to have sex and I want you to act like you want it and are enjoying it. If you play the game, you won't be hurt. Indeed, I will do everything I know how to do to make the sex as pleasurable as possible. Otherwise, I will kill you with this gun.

Because B regards A's threat as credible, B goes along with A's game. This example indicates that the mere utterance of a phrase that would constitute valid consent if uttered in the absence of such threats ("Please do it!") does not constitute any kind of valid consent in the presence of such threats.[14]

For the purposes of this article, the most interesting questions concern cases (3) and (4). A sexual offense may involve assault without what Dripps calls the "expropriation" of the victim's body (as in (3)) and may involve expropriation without the use or threat of violence (as in (4)). It might be argued that (4) is a more serious offense than (3) because nonconsensual sexual penetration is a greater harm than the use or threat of violence that does not result in penetration. If this is a plausible view, even if not the most widely held or correct view, we need to ask why nonconsensual penetration is such a serious wrong. Second, if it should be criminal to have sexual relations with someone who has refused sexual relations, if "no means no," we still need to ask when "yes means yes." We have already described a case in which a consent token ("Please do it!") does *not* mean yes. Other cases are more difficult.

C. Is Sex Special?

A currently fashionable view maintains that rape is about violence not sex. That view might be resisted in two ways. It might be argued that rape is about sex because sex itself is about violence (or domination).[15] I have little to say about that view, expect to note that even if there is a violent dimension to "ordinary" sex, there is still a distinction between the violence intrinsic to ordinary sex and the violence peculiar to what we have traditionally regarded as sexual crimes.

But I want to suggest that, for both empirical and moral reasons, it is crucial to see that sexual offense is at least partly about sex. First, there is considerable evidence that nonconsensual sexual relations are "a substitute for consensual sexual intercourse rather than a manifestation of male hostility toward women or a method of establishing or maintaining male domination."[16] Second, we cannot explain why the use or threat of violence to accomplish sexual penetration is more traumatic and a graver wrong than the use or threat of violence *per se*, except on the assumption that invasion of one's sexual being is a special sort of violation. Third, if women experience *non*violent but nonconsensual sex as a serious violation, this, too, can be explained only in the view that violation of a woman's sexual being is special. Consider, for example, the case in which A has sexual relations with an unconscious B. Some of the elements associated with a violent sexual assault would be lacking. There would be no fear, no overpowering of the will or experience of being coerced, and no experience of pain. Yet, even if B never discovers that A had sexual relations with her while she was unconscious, we might well think that B has been harmed or violated by A.[17]

The view that nonconsensual but nonviolent sex is a serious violation has been previously defended by several authors. Stephen Schulhofer argues that it should be a criminal offense to violate a person's sexual autonomy.[18] On Donald Dripps's "commodity" theory of sexual crime, the "expropriation" of another persons's body for purposes of sexual gratification violates that person's interest in exclusive control over her body for sexual purposes.[19] Joan McGregor connects nonconsensual sexual relations to the invasion of privacy and the control of information about ourselves. She argues that nonconsensual sexual relations can be understood as violating an individual's right to control the "borders" of her relations with others.[20]

For present purposes, there is not much difference among these views. Although Dripps uses the avowedly "unromantic" language of commodity and expropriation, whereas Schulhofer and McGregor use the more philosophically respectable language of autonomy and control, these views are virtually extensionally equivalent.[21] They all maintain that is should be a criminal offense for A to engage in sexual penetration of B if B objects, whether or not A uses or threatens physical harm. It is true that Dripps would criminalize only the disregard of another's refusal to engage in sexual acts (except in cases in which the victim is unable to refuse) whereas Schulhofer and McGregor require a verbal or nonverbal yes. But this is of little practical import. If the law clearly states that B need only say "no" to render A liable to a criminal offense, then B's passivity will not be misunderstood.

Let us assume that this general view is correct. But why is it correct? Jeffrie Murphy suggests that it is not self-evident why the nonconsensual "penetration of a bodily orifice" is such a grave offense. He maintains that there is nothing that makes sexual assault "objectively" more serious than non-sexual assault, that the importance attached to penetration "is essentially cultural," and that if we did not "surround sexuality with complex symbolic and moral baggage," then nonconsensual sex would not be viewed as a particularly grave wrong.[22]

Murphy's science is probably wrong. A woman's abhorrence of nonconsensual sex may be at least partially hard-wired. Evolutionary psychologists have argued that because reproductive opportunities for women are relatively scarce, it is genetically costly for a woman to have sex with a man whose attributes she could not choose and who shows "no evident inclination to stick around and help provide for the offspring."[23] Thus, evolution would favor those women who were most disposed to abhor such sexual encounters. This is not to deny that there is great individual and cultural variability in the way in which people experience nonconsensual sexual relations. It is only to say that there is no reason to assume that culture is writing on a blank slate.

Yet, for our purposes, it does not really matter whether the best explanation for a woman's aversion to nonconsensual penetration is cultural or biological. The important question for moral and legal theory is whether the seriousness of a violation should be understood as *experience-dependent* or (at least partially) *experience-independent*. Although Murphy contrasts a "cultural" explanation of the wrongness of sexual crime with an "objective" explanation, what would an "objective" explanation look like? Murphy thinks that we need to explain why the penetration of an orifice is objectively more harmful than a punch in the nose. Fair enough. But then we also need to explain why physical injury is "objectively" worse than harm to our property or reputations or feelings or character. If the objective seriousness of harm is experience-*dependent*, there is nothing inherently special about physical injury, which Murphy takes to be the paradigm case of objective harm. After all, we could experience insults to our reputations as worse than physical injury and harm to our souls or character as a fate worse than death. On the other hand, if an objective account of harm is experience-*independent*, we would also need to explain why violations of sexuality are more serious than a punch in the nose. But here, once again, sexual harm is on a par with physical harm, for we would need to explain why harm to one's body is objectively more harmful than harm to one's property or reputation or soul.

I cannot produce an adequate account of the objective seriousness of sexual offense in this article (and not just for lack of space), although the truth about that matter will affect the criminal penalties we are prepared to apply.[24] Although I am inclined to think that the character of this harm is at least partially experience-independent (that is, it would be a serious wrong even if it is not experienced that way), it should be noted that, even if it is experience-dependent, the criminal law is not designed to respond to the harm to the individual victim. Suppose, for example, that A rapes B, who, unbeknownst to A, actually embodies the alleged male fantasy: B wants to be raped. If the wrongness of a crime depends on the harm to the particular victim, then we might regard the rape of B as a lesser wrong. But, while the harm to a specific victim may affect the compensation owed to the victim in a civil action, the criminal law concerns harms to society and can be triggered even when there is no harm to a specific victim, as in an attempted crime in which no one is hurt. Similarly, even if the rape of a prostitute is a less serious offense because it does not involve the forcible taking of something that she regards as a "sacred and mysterious aspect of her self-identity," but merely the theft of a commodity that she normally trades for monetary gain, it does not follow that the criminal law should treat this rape as a less serious wrong.[25]

D. Defective Consent: When Does Yes Mean Yes?

Let us assume that the criminal law regards the disregard of a "no" (or the absence of a verbal or nonverbal "yes") as a basis for criminal liability. As we have seen, that would not resolve all of the problems. We have already seen that when B says "yes" in response to a threat of violence, her consent has no morally transformative power. The question arises, however, as to what other consent-eliciting behavior should be criminal. In this section, I want to focus on three ways in which B's consent token might be considered defective: (1) coercion; (2) misrepresentation or concealment; and (3) incompetence.

1. Coercion

Let us say that A coerces B to consent to engage in a sexual act when (a) A threatens to make B worse off if she does not perform that act *and* (b) it is reasonable to expect B to succumb to the threat rather than suffer the consequences.

It can be ambiguous as to whether condition (a) is met for two reasons. First, it can be ambiguous as to whether A threatens B at all. We do not say that a panhandler threatens B if he says, "Do you have any money to spare?" But does a large and tough-looking A threaten B when he says "I would appreciate it if you would give me your wallet," but issues no threat as to what he will do if B refuses? We are inclined to think that some nonverbal behaviors are reasonably understood as proposing to make B worse off if B refuses, and that it is also reasonable to expect A to understand this.

Let us assume that there is no misunderstanding as to the likely consequences of refusal. It can be ambiguous as to whether condition (a) is met because we must ask, "Worse off than what?" I have argued elsewhere that the crucial element in coercive proposals is that A proposes to make B worse off than she has a *right* to be vis-à-vis A or that A proposes to violate B's right, and not (as it might seem) that A proposes to make B worse off than her status quo.[26] Whereas the gunman's proposal—"Sign this contract or I will shoot you"—proposes to make B worse off than both her status quo baseline and her right-defined baseline, those baselines can diverge. If a drowning B has a right to be rescued by A, then A's proposal to rescue B only if she pays him $10,000 is a coercive proposal on this view because A proposes to make B worse off than her right-defined baseline, even though he proposes to make her better off than her status quo-defined baseline. On the other hand, A's proposal is not coercive on this view if A proposes to make B worse off than her status quo-defined baseline, but not worse off than her right-defined baseline ("Plead guilty to a lesser offense or I will prosecute you on the charge of which we both know you are guilty").

Consider six cases:

1. A says to B, "Have sex with me or I won't return your car keys and you will be left stranded in a dangerous area."

2. A says, "Have sexual relations with me or I will dissolve our dating relationship."

3. A, a professor, says, "Have sexual relations with me or I will give you a grade two grades lower than you deserve."

4. A, a professor, says, "Have sexual relations with me and I will give you a grade two grades higher than you deserve."

5. A, who owes B money, says, "Have sexual relations with me and I will repay the money that I owe you. Otherwise, ciao."

6. A, a jailer, says, "Have sexual relations with me and I will arrange your escape; otherwise you and I know that you will be executed by the state."[27]

On my view, A makes a coercive proposal in cases (1), (3), and (5), but not in cases (2), (4), and (6). In cases (1), (3), and (5), A proposes to make B worse off than she has a right to be if she refuses—to have her car keys returned, to receive the grade she deserves, to have her loan repaid. By contrast, in cases (2), (4), and (6), A does not propose to make B worse off than she has a right to be if she refuses. B has no right that A continue their dating relationship or a right to a higher grade than she deserves or not to be executed by the state (bracketing general objections to capital punishment).

To anticipate objections, I do not deny that it is wrong for A to make his proposal in (4) and (6) or (sometimes) in (2). A jailer violates his obligation to society if he helps a prisoner escape and commits an additional wrong if he trades that favor for sexual services. It is wrong for a professor to use his control over grades to obtain sexual favors. He violates his responsibility to his institution and to other students. Moreover, and perhaps unlike (6), A's proposal in (4) may entice B into accepting an arrangement that she will subsequently regret. In general, it is often wrong for A to make a "seductive offer" to B, that is, where A has reason to believe that it is likely that B will mistakenly perceive the (short-term) benefits of accepting the offer as greater than the (long-term) costs.

In any case, do not say that A's proposals are coercive in (4) and (6) simply because, like (3), they create a choice situation in which B decides that having sexual relations with A is the lesser of two evils. After all, we could imagine that B, not A, initiates the proposals in (4) and (6) or is delighted to receive them, and it would be strange to maintain that B is coerced by a proposal that she initiates or is delighted to receive.

Now, consider (2) once again. B may regard the consequences of refusing A's proposal as devastating, as worse, for example, than receiving a lower grade than she deserves. It is also true that B's situation will be worse than her status quo if she refuses. Still, B cannot reasonably claim that she is the victim of "status coercion" or, more importantly, that her consent is not morally transformative.[28] And this is because A does not propose to violate B's rights if she refuses, for B has no *right* that A continue his relationship with B on her preferred terms.

The general point exemplified by (2) is that people make many decisions that they would not make if more attractive options were available to them. If I were independently wealthy, I might not choose to teach political philosophy for a living. If I were not at risk for losing my teeth, I would not consent to painful dental work. But it does not follow that I have been coerced into teaching or agreeing to have dental work performed. In principle, sex is no different. If B were wealthier or more attractive or more famous, she might not have to agree to have sexual relations with A in order to keep him in the relationship. Things being what they are, however, B might well decide that what she wants to do—all things considered—is to have sexual relations with A. It may be regrettable that people bargain with their sexuality, but there is no reason to regard bargaining *within the framework of one's rights* as compromising consent, at least in any way that should be recognized by the criminal law.

Let us now consider condition (b), which states that A coerces B only when it is reasonable to expect B to succumb to A's (admittedly coercive) threat rather than suffer the consequences or pursue a different course of action. Suppose that A proposes to tickle B's feet if she does not have sexual relations with him. I believe that A has made a coercive proposal to B, because A proposes to make B worse off than both her status quo baseline and her right-defined baseline. Still, if B decides to have sexual relations to avoid being tickled, I doubt that we would want to charge A with a criminal offense (unless, perhaps, A believed that B had an extreme aversion to being tickled). Here, we expect B to endure the consequences of A's coercive proposal rather than succumb to it.

Now, recall case (5). In my view, A has made a coercive proposal because A has proposed to violate B's right to be repaid if B refuses. But we might also say that B should sue A for breach of contract, and that we should not regard A's proposal as so compromising B's consent (because she has other legal options) that is should render A subject to a criminal charge.[29] We might disagree about this case. There are resources internal to the notion of coerced consent that allow us to go the other way. But it is moral argument, and not conceptual analysis, that will determine whether this is the sort of sexually motivated behavior that should be punished through the criminal law.

2. Fraud and Concealment

Suppose that A does not threaten B or propose to violate B's rights if she refuses to have sexual relations with A, but that B agrees to sexual relations with A only because B has certain beliefs about A that result from things that A has or has not said.

Consider:

7. A falsely declares that A loves B.

8. A falsely declares that he intends to marry B.

9. A falsely declares that he intends to dissolve the relationship if B does not consent (unlike (2), A is bluffing).

10. A fails to disclose that he has a sexually transmitted disease.

11. A fails to disclose that he has been having sexual relations with B's sister.

Has B given "valid" consent in these cases? We know that A has misrepresented or concealed important information in all of these cases. That is not at issue. The question is whether we should regard A's conduct as criminal.

There are several possibilities. If we were to extend the principle of *caveat emptor* to sexual relations, then there is arguably no problem in any of these cases. On the other hand, if we were to extend principles of criminal fraud or anything like the well-known medical principle of informed consent to the arena of sexual relations, then we could conclude that many representations that are now part and parcel of courtship should be illegal. I do not have anything close to a firm view about this matter. I think it entirely possible that, from either a contractualist or consequentialist perspective, we would choose a legal regime in which we treat the failure to disclose information about sexuality transmitted diseases as criminal, but that we would not want to treat misrepresentation or failure to disclose information about one's feelings or marital intentions or other relationships as criminal offenses.[30] But that is only a guess. For now, I want only to stress that the question as to whether A should be criminally liable in any of these cases will be resolved by moral argument as to what parties who engage in sexual relations owe each other by way of intentional falsehood and disclosure of information, and not by an analysis of the concept of consent.

3. Competence

B can give valid or "morally transformative" consent to sexual relations with A only if B is sufficiently competent to do so. It is uncontroversial that B cannot consent to sexual relations with A if she is unconscious.[31] It is also relatively uncontroversial that B cannot give valid or morally transformative consent if she does not possess the appropriate mental capacities, say, because B is below an appropriate age or severely retarded.

The most interesting *theoretical* questions about competence arise with respect to (otherwise) competent adults who consent to sexual relations because they are under the influence of voluntarily consumed alcohol or some other judgment-distorting substance. Consider two possible positions about this issue. It might be argued that if a competent adult allows herself to become intoxicated, her initial competence flows through to any decisions she makes while less than fully competent. In a second view, A should be liable for a criminal offense if he engages in sexual relations with B when B's first indication of consent is given while intoxicated, even if B is responsible for having put herself in that position.[32]

I do not have a firm view as to what position we should adopt about this matter. But we should not say that A should not be held liable just because B has acted imprudently, or even wrongly, in allowing herself to become intoxicated. Although B's behavior may put her on the moral hook, it does not take A off the moral hook. Although B acts imprudently if she leaves her keys in an unlocked car, A still commits a theft if he takes it. We could adopt a similar view about sexual relations with an intoxicated B.

E. Benefits and Costs

I have argued that the principle that society should make it criminal for individuals to engage in sexual acts without the consent of the other party is highly indeterminate, that we must decide under what conditions consent is morally transformative. Suppose that we were to consider a choice between what I shall call a *permissive legal regime* (LR_p), under which A commits a sexual crime only when he uses violence or the threat of violence against B, and a *rigorous legal regime* (LR_R), say, one in which it is a criminal offense (1) to engage in sexual acts without the express consent of the other party, (2) to obtain that consent by proposing to violate a legal right of the other party, (3) to misrepresent or fail to disclose information about sexually transmitted diseases, (4) to engage in a sexual act with a party whose consent was first given when severely intoxicated, and so on. It is not important to define the precise contours of these two legal regimes. The point is that we are considering a choice between a (relatively) permissive and a (relatively) rigorous regime.

Which regime should we choose? I have suggested that we could model the choice along consequentialist lines, where we would calculate the costs and benefits associated with different sets of rules, or we could model the choice along contractualist lines, in which people would choose from behind a Rawlsian veil of ignorance. Suppose that we adopt the Rawlsian approach. To make progress on this issue, we must relax the veil. The contractors must know what life would be like for people under different sets of laws and norms, including the full range of information about the trade-offs between the costs and benefits of the two regimes. Here, as elsewhere, the contractors would know that there is no free and equal lunch. At the same time, the veil would be sufficiently thick to deprive them of information regarding their personal characteristics. They would not know whether they were male or female, a potential perpetrator or victim, or, say, their attitude toward sexual relations. They would not know whether *their* sexual lives would go better under one set of rules or another. I don't think we can say with any confidence what rules would be chosen under any of these models, but we might be able to say something about the sorts of benefits and costs they would have to consider.

On the assumption that LR_R would actually affect behavior in the desired direction, it would provide greater protection to the sexual autonomy of women and would promote an environment in which men come to consider "a woman's consent to sex significant enough to merit [their] reasoned attention and respect."[33] These are clear benefits. But there would be costs. Some of these costs would be endogenous to the legal system. LR_R may consume legal resources that would be better spent elsewhere. It may result in the prosecution or conviction of more innocent persons. LR_R may also generate some negative effects on the general structure of sexual and social relations. It may cause a decline in spontaneity and excitement in sexual relations. In addition, just as some persons enjoy the process of haggling over consumer transactions, some may enjoy the game of sexual negotiation, the haggling, bluffing, and concealment that have been a standard fixture of courtship. After all, whether coyness is biologically hard-wired or culturally driven, many women have long thought that it is better to (first) consent to sex after an initial indication of reluctance, lest they be viewed as too "easy" or "loose."[34] So B may suffer if A is too respectful of her initial reluctance. Finally, it is distinctly possible that some persons choose to become intoxicated precisely to render themselves less inhibited—the reverse of a standard Ulysses situation in which one acts *ex ante* to inhibit one's actions *ex post*.[35] So, if A were to comply with LR_R by refusing to have sexual relations with an intoxicated B, A would prevent B from doing precisely what B wanted to do.

Of course, to say that there is no free lunch does not mean that lunch isn't worth buying: The gains may be worth the costs. Whether that is so will depend, in part, on the way in which we aggregate the gains and costs. From a contractarian perspective, it is distinctly possible that we should give some priority to the interests of the worse off, that is, the potential victims of sexual offenses, rather than simply try to maximize the sum total of preference satisfaction or happiness or whatever. The weight of that priority will depend on the gravity of that violation, an issue that has not been settled. But I do not think we should be indifferent to numbers. If LR_R would work to the detriment of many and help but a few, that would make a difference. Still, here as elsewhere, we should be prepared to trade off considerable positive benefits to some persons in order to provide greater protection to those who would otherwise be harmed.

V. DECENT SEXUAL RELATIONS

Even if we were to expand the range of sexually motivated behaviors subject to criminal sanctions, the criminal law is a blunt instrument to be used relatively sparingly. There remains the question of what sort of behaviors should be regarded as indecent or seriously wrong. Is it seriously wrong for A to obtain B's consent to sexual relations by threatening to end a dating relationship? Is it less wrong if A is *warning* but not *threatening* B, that is, if A is not trying to manipulate B's behavior but is stating the truth, that he would not want to continue the relationship without sexual relations? Is it seriously wrong for A to falsely declare love in order to secure B's consent to sexual relations or to secure her consent while she is intoxicated?

I have no intention of trying to answer these questions in this article. I do want to make a few remarks about the issues they present. First, there is no reason to think that the justified legal demands on our behavior are coextensive with the moral demands on our behavior. Just as we may have a (morally justified) legal right to engage in behavior that is morally wrong (for example, to give a lecture that the Holocaust is a hoax), we may have a morally justified legal right to produce another's consent to sexual acts in ways that are seriously wrong. Second, just as we might regard the principles of consent for the criminal law as the output of moral theorizing, we can regard the principles of consent for acting decently as the output of moral theorizing, although there would be a different mixture of benefits and costs. Third, this is not an issue without practical consequences. When millions of students are enrolled in sex education courses, it is a genuine question as to what principles we should teach them.

I think it fair to say that, at present, there is no consensus as to what constitutes immoral behavior in this arena. I believe that many people view the pursuit of sexual gratification in dating relationships along the lines of a "capitalist" model, in which all parties are entitled to try to press for the best deal they can get. On a standard (predominantly male) view of dating relationships, it is legitimate for A to seek B's consent to sexual relations, even if A believes B will come to regret that decision. Moreover, just as it is thought legitimate to misrepresent one's reservation price in a business negotiation (there is no assumption that one is speaking the truth when one says, "I won't pay more than $15,000 for that car"), one is entitled to misrepresent one's feelings or intentions. By contrast, in a fiduciary relationship, such as between physicians and patients, A has an obligation to act in the interests of his client rather than his own interests. A should not seek B's consent to a transaction if A believes it is not in B's interest to consent to that transaction.

It would probably be a mistake to apply a strong fiduciary model to sexual relations among competent adults. It might be argued that a paternalistic attitude toward another's sexual life would be rightly rejected as failing to respect the autonomy of the parties "to act freely on their own unconstrained conception of what their bodies and their sexual capacities are for."[36] This is all well and good as far as it goes, but it begs the question of how to understand autonomy, the pressures that it is reasonable for one to bring to bear on another's decision and whether one fails to respect another's autonomy when one fails to tell the truth and nothing but the truth about one's feelings, intentions, and other relationships. It may well turn out that some hybrid of these two models best captures A's moral responsibilities. Unlike the capitalist model, A must give considerable weight to B's interests, as well as his own. Unlike the fiduciary model, B's decision as to what serves her interests is in the driver's seat.

VI. WHEN SHOULD ONE CONSENT TO SEXUAL RELATIONS?

In this section, I want to open up a question that is frequently discussed among parties in enduring relationships but rarely mentioned in the academic literature: How should a couple deal with an asymmetrical desire for sexual relations? Let us assume that A desires sexual relations more frequently than B. Let us also assume that A and B agree that it is not permissible for A to have sexual relations with B when B does not consent. Their question—indeed, it is B's question—is whether she should consent to sexual relations when, other things being equal, she would prefer not to consent. In particular, they want to know if they could reasonably view the frequency of sexual relations or the distribution of satisfaction with their sexual lives as a matter to be governed by a principle of distributive justice. If, as Susan Moller Okin has argued, justice applies to some intrafamilial issues, such as the control of economic resources and the distribution of household labor, does justice also apply to sex?[37]

It might be thought that it is wrong to think that B should ever consent to sexual relations when she does not want sex. But this simply begs the question, for people's "wants" are complex and multifaceted. Consider the problem that has come to be known as the "battle of the sexes." In one version of the problem, A and B both prefer to go to the movies together than to go alone, but each prefers to go to different types of movies. Their problem is to determine what movie they should see.[38] Although the "battle of the sexes" is usually used to exemplify a bargaining problem, I want to use the example to make a point about the character of one's "wants." For we can well imagine that A may not "want" to see B's preferred movie, other things being equal. Still, given that B really wants to see the movie and given that they most recently went to the movie that A preferred, A may genuinely want to see the movie that B prefers—all things considered.

It might be objected that "I want to do what you want to do" is fine for movies, but not sex. In this view, there are some "not wants" that are legitimate candidates for "all things considered wants," but the lack of a desire for sexual relations is not among them. In one variant of this view, sexual relations are radically different from other activities in which partners engage together because it would be self-defeating for partners to think that they are having sexual relations on this basis. A can enjoy the movie that he sees with B, although he knows that B would (otherwise) prefer to see something else, but A would not get satisfaction from sexual relations with B if A knows that B wants to have sexual relations only to satisfy or placate A's desire for sexual relations.

With some trepidation, I want to suggest that to think of sexual relations between partners in an enduring relationship as radically different from all other activities in which they engage "wildly misdescribes" their experience.[39] Sexual relations among such partners are simply not always viewed as sacred or endowed with greater mystery. But my point is not solely negative or deflationary. After all, to say that the most desirable form of sexual relations occurs within a loving relationship is also to say that sexual relations are a way of expressing affection and commitment, and not simply to express or satisfy erotic desire. It is, for example, entirely plausible that parties who have been fighting might engage in sexual relations as a way of demonstrating to themselves that the disagreement is relatively minor in the context of their relationship, that their love for each other is unshaken. In general, I see no reason to tightly constrain what counts as legitimate reasons to want to engage in sexual relations—all things considered.

But what about distributive justice? Assume that A and B both understand that it is frustrating for A to forgo sexual relations when B does not desire sexual relations, whereas it is erotically unsatisfying for B to engage in sexual relations when she does not desire sexual relations—not awful or abhorrent, just unsatisfying. On some occasions, A would rather have sex than go to sleep, whereas B's utility function is the reverse. Given this situation, there are three possibilities: (1) A can absorb the burden of the asymmetry by forgoing sexual relations when B is not otherwise motivated to have sex; (2) B can absorb the burden of the asymmetry by consenting to sexual relations whenever A desires to do so; or (3) A and B can share the burden of the asymmetry by agreeing that they will have sexual relations less often than A would (otherwise) prefer and more often than B would (otherwise) prefer. And B is trying to decide if she should choose (3). Note, once again, that the question is not whether B should consent to sexual relations that she does not want. Rather, she is trying to decide if she should want to have sexual relations—all things considered—when the things to be considered involve a commitment to fairness.

It might be objected that even if we do not tightly constrain the reasons that might legitimately motivate B to "want" to have sex with A, sexual relations lie beyond reasons based on justice or fairness. It might be maintained that a concern with fairness or justice arises only when interests conflict. As Hume remarked, justice has no place among married people who are "unacquainted with the *mine* and *thine*, which are so necessary and yet cause such disturbance in human society."[40] From this perspective, a conscious preoccupation with fairness in a marriage can be a symptom that the parties have failed to achieve the identity of interests that characterize a good marriage and may (causally) inhibit the formation of a maximally intimate relationship.[41] Love precludes a concern with justice, what Hume described as "the cautious, jealous virtue."[42]

I want to make several replies to this line of argument. First, and least important, there is obviously a limit to the identity of interests it is logically possible to achieve. If each party has an overall want to do what the other has a primary want to do, they will achieve an altruistic draw ("I want to do what you want to do." "But I want to do what you want to do."). And if each has an overall want to do what the other has an overall want to do, there will be no wants for the overall wants to get hold of.

Second, if we think that a good marriage is characterized by an identity of interests, this still leaves open the question as to how married partners should respond to the asymmetry of desire for sexual relations. Just as A might say, "I wouldn't want to have sexual relations if B doesn't want to," B might say, "If A wants to have sexual relations, then I want to have sexual relations." So if we reject the argument from distributive justice because it assumes that the interests of the parties conflict, there is no reason to think that the parties will settle on (1) rather than (2) or (3).

Third, I think it both unrealistic and undesirable to expect that the desires or interests of persons in the most successful intimate relationships will fully coincide. It is relatively, although not absolutely, easy for married partners not to distinguish between "mine" and "thine" with respect to property. It is much more difficult to achieve a communal view with respect to activities. Do loving spouses not care at all how many diapers they change? To which movies they go? Where they locate? Are they no longer loving if they do care? Indeed, it is not clear that it is even desirable for people to strive for a relationship in which their interests are so completely merged. It might be thought that a good marriage represents a "union" of autonomous individuals who do and should have goals and aspirations that are independent of their relationship.

From this perspective, a couple's concern with fairness simply reflects the fact that their desires are not identical, that they do not see why this fact should be denied or regretted, and that they want to resolve these differences in a fair way. As Susan Moller Okin puts it (albeit in a different context), "Why should we suppose that harmonious affection, indeed deep and long-lasting love, cannot co-exist with ongoing standards of justice?"[43] Indeed, I would go further. It might be argued that it is not merely that love can coexist with justice, but that to love another person is to want to be fair to them, or, more precisely, to want *not* to be *unfair* to them, for to love someone is typically to want to be *more* than fair to them, to be generous.

I have not actually argued that the distribution of satisfaction with one's sexual life in a enduring relationship is an appropriate topic for distributive justice. Although I have argued against several objections to the view that sexual relations are beyond the scope of justice, it is possible that other arguments would work. Moreover, even if the distribution of satisfaction with one's sexual life is an appropriate topic for a principle of justice, I make no suggestions here as to what the substance of a theory of justice in sexual relations would look like. It is entirely possible that such a theory would dictate that the parties choose something like (1) rather than (3) (I take it that (2) is a nonstarter). I only want to suggest that the topic may belong on the table.

Notes

1. *See* A. Wertheimer, COERCION (1987) and EXPLOITATION (1996).

2. I borrow this phrase from Heidi Hurd's remarks at the conference at the University of San Diego Law School, which gave rise to this symposium.

3. For example, it may be wrong for a physician to accede to a beggar's request to have his leg amputated so that he can enhance his success as a beggar.

4. "You have never left the city, even to see a festival, nor for any other reason except military service; you have never gone to stay in any other city, as people do; you have had no desire to know another city or other laws; we and our city satisfied you. So decisively did you choose us and agree to be a citizen under us." Plato, CRITO (G.M.A. Grube trans. 1975).

5. " . . . every man that hath any possession or enjoyment of any part of the dominions of any government doth thereby give his tacit consent, and is as far forth obliged to obedience to the laws of that government, during such enjoyment, whether this his possession be of land to him and his heirs for ever, or a lodging only for a week; or whether it be barely travelling freely on the highway . . . " Locke, SECOND TREATISE OF GOVERNMENT Ch. 8 (1690).

6. "Can we seriously say, that a poor person or artisan has a free choice to leave his country, when he knows no foreign language or manners, and lives, from day to day, by the small wages which he acquires? We may as well assert that a man, by remaining in a vessel, freely consents to the dominion of the master; though he was carried on board while asleep, and must leap into the ocean and perish, the moment he leaves her." Hume, OF THE ORIGINAL CONTRACT (1777).

7. Frankfurt, *Coercion and Moral Responsibility* in ESSAYS ON FREEDOM OF ACTION (T. Honderich ed., 1973) at 65.

8. As Jeremy Waldron has put it, "[T]he question is . . . not what 'harm' re-

ally means, but what reasons of principle there are for preferring one conception to another . . . the question is not simply which is the better conception of harm, but which conception answers more adequately to the purposes for which the concept is deployed." LIBERAL RIGHTS 119–20 (1993). For a somewhat different view, see Schauer, *The Phenomenology of Speech and Harm,* 103 ETHICS 635 (1993).

9. Vokes v. Arthur Murray, Inc., 212 So. 2d 906 (1968) at 907.

10. *See* Ch. 6, *Sexual Exploitation in Psychotherapy,* in Wertheimer, EXPLOITATION (1996).

11. *See* State v. Rusk, 289 Md. 130, 424. A. 2d 720 (1981). The defendant had also intimidated the prosecutrix by taking the keys to her car, disregarded her statement that she did not want to have sexual relations with him, and was said to have "lightly choked" her.

12. Director of Public Prosecutions v. Morgan (1975), 2 All E.R. 347.

13. D. Dripps, *Beyond Rape: An Essay on the Difference Between the Presence of Force and the Absence of Consent,* 92 COLUM. L. REV. 1780 (1992) at 1797.

14. Indeed, it might be thought that this case is, in one way, more serious than those in which force is used to overcome the victim's resistance, namely, that it requires the victim to act inauthentically.

15. *See* C. MacKinnon, FEMINISM UNMODIFIED 5–6 (1987).

16. *See* R. Posner, SEX AND REASON 384 (1992).

17. For a discussion of nonexperiential harm, see J. Feinberg, HARM TO OTHERS Ch. 2 (1984).

18. S.J. Schulhofer, *Taking Sexual Autonomy Seriously: Rape Law and Beyond,* 11 LAW & PHIL. 35 (1992) at 70.

19. Dripps, *supra* n. 13 at 1796.

20. Dripps, *Force, Consent, and the Reasonable Woman,* in IN HARM'S WAY (J.L. Coleman and A. Buchanan eds., 1994) at 235. McGregor says that she borrows the notion of "border crossings" from Robert Nozick's ANARCHY, STATE AND UTOPIA (1974).

21. I think it no objection to the commodity (or any other) view of the law of sexual crimes that it "wildly misdescribes" the victim's experience. R. West, *Legitimating the Illegitimate: A Comment on* Beyond Rape, 93 COLUM. L. REV. 1442 (1993) at 1448. The question is whether a view provides a coherent framework for protecting the rights or interests that we believe ought to be protected. Indeed, it is an advantage of a "property" theory that it provides a basis for critiquing the traditional law of rape. That A takes B's property without B's consent is sufficient to show that A steals B's property. Force or resistance is not required.

22. *See* J. Murphy, *Some Ruminations on Women, Violence, and the Criminal Law* in IN HARM'S WAY (J. Coleman and A. Buchanan eds., 1994) at 214.

23. R. Wright, *Feminists, Meet Mr. Darwin,* THE NEW REPUBLIC, November 28, 1994, at 37. The evolutionary logic of nonconsensual sex is different for men. It is physically difficult to accomplish, and "the worst likely outcome for the man (in genetic terms) is that pregnancy would not ensue . . . hardly a major Darwinian disaster."

24. This is obviously true on a retributive theory of punishment, in which the level of punishment is related to the seriousness of the offense. But it is also true on a utilitarian theory, for the more serious the harm to the victim, the greater

"expense" (in punishment) it makes sense to employ to deter such harms.

25. Murphy, *supra* n. 22 at 216.

26. Wertheimer, COERCION (1987).

27. This is derived from a case introduced by Schulhofer, *supra* n. 18.

28. C.L. Muelenhard and J.L. Schrag, *Nonviolent Sexual Coercion* in ACQUAINTANCE RAPE (A. Parrot and L. Bechhofer eds., 1991) at 119.

29. Don Dripps has suggested to me that case (5) is a variant on prostitution. In the standard case of prostitution, A proposes to pay B with A's money. In this case, A proposes to pay B with B's money.

30. As Stephen Schulhofer says, because there are "few pervasively shared intuitions" with regard to what constitutes serious misrepresentation as distinct from puffing or "story telling," the decisions as to "whether to believe, whether to rely and whether to assume the risk of deception . . . are often seen as matters to be left to the individual." *Supra* n. 18 at 92.

31. It is less clear—and informal intuition (and pumping of friends) has done little to help—whether women would regard sexual relations while unconscious as worse than or nor as bad as forcible sexual relations. One might think that it is worse to consciously experience an assault on one's bodily and sexual integrity, but it might also be thought that it is better to know what is happening to oneself than not to know.

32. I say "first" indication, because B could consent while sober to what she subsequently consents to while intoxicated.

33. S. Estrich, REAL RAPE (1987) at 98.

34. See the discussion of coyness in R. Wright, THE MORAL ANIMAL (1994).

35. "Here are the keys to my car; don't let met drive home if I'm drunk." *See, e.g.,* T. Schelling, *The Intimate Contest for Self-Command,* in CHOICE AND CONSEQUENCE Ch. 3 (1984).

36. Schulhofer, *supra* n. 18 at 70.

37. Okin, JUSTICE, GENDER, AND THE FAMILY (1989).

38. *See* B. Barry, THEORIES OF JUSTICE 116–17 (1989).

39. With apologies to Robin West.

40. Hume, A TREATISE OF HUMAN NATURE, bk. III, sec. II.

41. I thank Pat Neal and Bob Taylor for pressing me on this point.

42. Hume, AN ENQUIRY CONCERNING THE PRINCIPLES OF MORALS, sec. III, pt. I, par. 3.

43. Okin, *supra* n. 37 at 32.

PART 6

PORNOGRAPHY AND PROSTITUTION

Chapter 25

TALK DIRTY TO ME

Sallie Tisdale

Once or twice a month I visit my neighborhood adult store, to rent a movie or buy a magazine. I am often the only woman there, and I never see another woman alone. Some days there may be only a single clerk and a few customers; at other times I see a dozen men or more: heavyset working men, young men, businessmen. In their midst I often feel a little strange, and sometimes scared. To enter I have to pass the flashing lights, the neon sign, the silvered windows, and go through the blank, reflecting door.

It takes a certain pluck simply to enter. I can't visit on days when I am frail or timid. I open the door feeling eyes on me, hearing voices, and the eyes are my mother's eyes, and, worse, my father's. The voices are the voices of my priest, my lover, my friends. They watch the little girl and chide her, a naïf no more.

I don't make eye contact. Neither do the men. I drift from one section of the store to the other, going about my business. I like this particular store because it is large and well-lit; there are no dark corners in which to hide or be surprised. The men give me sidelong glances as I pass by, and then drop their eyes back to the box in their hands. Pornography, at its roots, is about watching; but no one here openly watches. This is a place of librarian silences. As I move from shelf to shelf, male customers gather at the fringes of where I stand. I think they would like to know which movies I will choose.

© Sallie Tisdale. Reprinted, with the permission of Sallie Tisdale, from *Harper's Magazine* (February 1992), pp. 37–46.

In the large front room with the clerks are glass counters filled with vibrators, promising unguents, candy bowls filled with condoms. On the wall behind the counter where you ask for help are giant dildos, rubber vaginas, rubber faces with slit eyes, all mouth. Here are the more mainstream films, with high production values and name stars. Near the door are the straight movies, the standard hard core you can find these days in most urban video-rental stores. Here is the large and growing amateur section: suburban porn. Here is a small section of straight Japanese movies, a section of gay male films, and the so-called lesbian films, directed toward the male viewer: *Dildo Party* and *Pussy Licker.*

The first time I came here alone I dressed in baggy jeans and a pullover sweater, and tied my long hair up in a bun. After a while I was approached by a fat man with a pale, damp face and thinning hair.

"Excuse me," he said. "I'm not trying to come on to you or anything, but I can't help noticing you're, you know, female."

I could only nod.

"And I wonder," he continued, almost breathless, "if you like this stuff"—and he pointed at a nearby picture of a blonde woman in red lingerie. "You see, my girlfriend, she broke up with me, and I'd bought her all this stuff—you know, sex clothes—and she didn't like it." He paused. "I mean, it's out in the back of my truck right now. If you just want to come outside you can have it."

I turned my back in polite refusal, and left before it could grow completely dark outside. He didn't follow; I've never been approached there again.

Another day, when I asked for my movies by number, I didn't want the clerk to glance at the titles, and I tried to distract him with a question. I asked if any women still work here. He was young, effeminate, with a wispy mustache and loose, shoulder-length hair, and he apologized when he said no.

"Even though we're all guys now, we try to be real sensitive," he said, pulling my requests off the shelf without a glance. "If anyone gives you a hard time, let us know. You let us know right away, and we'll take care of it." He handed me my choices in a white plastic bag.

"Have a nice day."

Later. I am home, with my movies. I drink a glass of wine, my lover eats from a silver bowl of popcorn he put beside us on the couch. We are watching a stylish film with expensive sets and a pulsing soundtrack. The beautiful actresses wear sunglasses in every scene, and the wordless scenes shift every few minutes. Now there are two women together; now two women and an adoring man, a tool of the spike-heeled women. A few scenes later there is only one woman, blonde, with a luxuriant body. She reaches one hand slowly down between her legs and pulls a diamond necklace from between her vaginal lips, jewel by jewel. She slides it up her abdomen, across her breast, to her throat, and into her mouth.

Some of my women friends have never seen or read pornography—by which I mean expressions of explicit sex. That I don't find strange; it's a world of women which sometimes seems not to be about women at all. What is odd to me is that I know women who say they never think about it, that they are indifferent, that such scenes and stories seem meant for other people altogether. They find my interest rather curious, I suppose. And a little awkward.

The images of pornography are many and varied; some are fragmented and idealized. Some are crude and unflattering. I like the dreamy, psychedelic quality of certain scenes; I like the surprises in others, and I like the arousal, the heat which can be born in my body without warning, in an instant. I have all the curiosity of the anthropologist and the frank hope of the voyeur. Pornography's texture is shamelessness; it maps the limits of my shame.

At times I find it harder to talk about pornography than my own sexual experience; what I like about pornography is as much a part of my sexuality as what I do, but it is more deeply psychological. What I *do* is the product of many factors, not all of them sexually motivated. But what I *imagine* doing is pure—pure in the sense that the images come wholly from within, from the soil of the subconscious. The land of fantasy is the land of the not-done and the wished-for. There are private lessons there, things for me to learn, all alone, about myself.

I feel bashful watching; that's one small surprise. I am self-conscious, prickly with the feeling of being caught in the act. I can feel that way with friends, with my lover of many years, and I can feel that way alone. Suddenly I need to shift position, avert my eyes. Another surprise, and a more important one: These images comfort me. Pornography reflects the obsessions of the age, which is my age. Sex awakens my unconscious; pornography gives it a face.

When I was ten or eleven my brother shared his stolen *Playboy* with me. The pneumatic figurines seemed magnificent and unreal. Certainly they seemed to have nothing at all to do with me or my future. I was a prodigious reader, and at an early age found scenes of sex and lasciviousness in many books: *The French Lieutenant's Woman,* which granted sex such power, and William Kotzwinkle's *Nightbook,* blunt and unpredictable.

I was not *taught,* specifically, much of anything about sex. I knew, but I knew nothing that counted. I felt arousal as any child will, as a biological state. And then came adolescence: real kisses, and dark, rough fumblings, a rut when all the rules disappeared. Heat so that I couldn't speak to say yes, or no, and a boy's triumphant fingers inside my panties was a glorious relief, and an awful guilt.

I entered sex the way a smart, post-Sixties teenager should, with fore-thought and contraception and care. My poor partner: "Is that all?" I said out loud when it was over. Is that really what all the fuss was about? But the books and magazines seemed a little more complicated to me af-ter that. I learned—but really just information. I had little enough un-derstanding of sex, and very little wisdom.

At the age of twenty, when I was, happily, several months' pregnant, the social work office where I was employed held a seminar on sexuality. We were determinedly liberal about the whole thing; I believe the point was to support clients in a variety of sexual choices. We were given a homework assignment on the first day, to make a collage that expressed our own sexuality. I returned the next morning and saw that my col-leagues, male and female both, had all made romantic visions of can-dlelight and sunsets. I was the youngest by several years, heavy-bellied, and I had brought a wild vision of masked men and women, naked tor-sos, skin everywhere, darkness, heat.

I knew I was struggling, distantly and through ignorance, with a deep shame. It was undirected, confusing; for years I had been most ashamed of the shame itself. Wasn't sex supposed to be free, easy? What was wrong with me, that I resisted? Why did I feel so afraid of the surrender, the sex-ual depths? And yet I was ashamed of what I desired: men and women both. I wanted vaguely to try . . . *things,* which no one spoke about; but surely people, somewhere, did. I was ashamed of all my urges, the small details within the larger act, the sudden sounds I made. I could hear that little voice: *Bad girl. Mustn't touch.*

I was a natural feminist; I knew the dialectic, the lingo. And all my se-crets seemed to wiggle free no matter what, expand into my unfeminist consciousness. I didn't even know the words for some of what I imag-ined, but I was sure of this: Liberated women didn't even *think* about what I wanted to do. My shame was more than a preoccupation with sex—everyone I knew was preoccupied with sex. It was more than being confused by the messy etiquette of the 1970s, more than wondering just how much shifting of partners I should do. It was shame for my own unasked-for appetites, which would not be still.

I was propelled toward the overt—toward pornography. I needed in-formation not about sex but about sexual parameters, the bounds of the normal. I needed reassurance, and blessing. I needed permission.

Several years ago, now in my late twenties, I began to watch what I at first called "dirty movies" and to read what were undoubtedly dirty books: *The Story of O* and *My Secret Life.* I went with the man I was living with, my arm in his and my eyes down, to a theater on a back street. It was very cold and dark inside the movie house, so that the other patrons were only dim shadows, rustling nearby. The movie was grainy, half-blurred, the sound muddy, the acting awful. At the same time I felt as though I'd crossed a line: There was a world of sexual material to see, and I was very curious to see it. Its sheer mass and variety reassured me. I couldn't imagine entering this world alone, though, not even for a quick foray into the screened-off section of the local video store, behind the sign reading OVER 18 ONLY. There were always men back there, and only men.

Watching, for the first time, a man penetrate another woman was like leaving my body all at once. I was outside my body, watching, because she on the screen above me *was* me; and then I was back in my body very much indeed. My lust was aroused as surely and uncontrollably by the sight of sex as hunger can be roused by the smell of food. I know how naive this sounds now, but I had never quite believed, until I saw it, that the sex in such films was *real*, that people fucked in front of cameras, eyes open. I found it a great shock: to see how different sex could be, how many different things it could mean.

Not all I felt was arousal. There are other reasons for a hurried blush. A woman going down on a man, sucking his cock as though starving for it, the man pulling away and shooting come across her face, the woman licking the come off her lips. I felt a heady mix of disgust and excitement, and confusion at that mix. Layers peeled off one after the other, because sometimes I disliked my own response. I resist it still, when something dark and forbidden emerges, when my body is provoked by what my mind reproves.

Inevitably, I came across something awful, something I really hated. The world of pornography is indiscriminate; boundaries get mixed up. Some stories are violent, reptilian, and for all their sexual content aren't about sex. I was reminded of a story I had found by accident, a long time ago, in a copy of my father's *True* magazine. I was forbidden to read *True*, for reasons unexplained. Before I was caught at it and the magazine taken away, I had found an illustration of a blood-splattered, nearly naked woman tied to a post in a dim basement, and had read up to the place in the text where the slow flaying of her legs had begun. It was gothic and horrible, and haunted me for years. Of course, I make my own definitions, everyone does; and to me that sort of thing has nothing to do with pornography. It *is* obscene, though, a word quite often applied to things that have nothing to do with sex. Pornography is sex, and sex is consensual, period. Without consent, the motions of sex become violence, and that alone defines it for me.

I realize this is not the opinion of conservative feminists such as the lawyer Catharine MacKinnon, who believes that violence, even murder, is the end point of all pornography. Certainly a lot of violent material has sexual overtones; the mistake is assuming that anything with sex in it is primarily about sex. The tendency to assume so says something about the person making the assumption. One important point about this

distinction is that the one kind of material is so much more readily available than the other: *True* and slasher films and tabloids are part of the
common culture. My father bought *True* at the corner tobacco store.
Scenes of nothing but mutual pleasure are the illicit ones.

I fall on a line of American women about midway between the actresses
whose films I rent and the housewife in Des Moines who has never seen
such a film at all. My female friends fall near me, to either side, but most
of them a little closer to Des Moines. The store I frequent for my books
and films reflects the same continuum: For all its blunt variety, that store
is clean, well-lit, friendly, and its variety of materials reflects a variety of
hoped-for customers. There are many places I will not go, storefronts and
movie houses that seem to me furtive and corrupt. Every society has its etiquette, its rules; so does the world of pornography.

I am deep into thinking about these rules; my cheeks are bright and
my palms damp, and the telephone rings. Without thinking I plunge my
caller into such thoughts. I chatter a few minutes into a heavy, shifting
silence, and then suddenly realize how ill-bred I must seem. Out here, in
the ordinary world, such things are not talked about at all. It's one definition of pornography: whatever we will not talk about.

I know I break a rule when I enter the adult store, whether my en-
trance is simply startling or genuinely unwelcome. The sweaty-lipped
man with lingerie wouldn't, couldn't approach me in a grocery store or
even a bar. Not like that, and perhaps not at all. Pornography degrades
the male vision of women in this way. When I stand among the shelves
there I am standing in a maze of female images, shelf after shelf of them,
hundreds of naked women smiling or with their eyes closed and mouths
open or gasping. I am just one more image in a broken mirror, with its
multiple reflections of women, none of them whole.

I am still afraid. These days I am most aware of that fear as a fear of
where I will and will not go, what I think of as *possible* for me. But, oh—
I'm curious. I can be so curious. A while ago I recruited two friends, one
man and one woman, and the three of us went to a peep show together
like a flying wedge, parting the crowds of nervy young men, them
jostling each other with elbows in the ribs, daring each other, *g'wan*. We
changed bills for quarters, leaned together in the dim hallways, elbowed
each other in the ribs—*g'wan*. There were endless film loops in booths
for singles, various movie channels from which to choose in booths for
two people, tissues provided, and a live show. One minute for twenty-five
cents, and the signs above each booth flashing on and off, on and off
again in the dark, from a green VACANT to a red IN USE and back again.

I pulled a door shut and disappeared into the musky dark; I could hear
muffled shouts from the young men in booths on either side. The panel
slid up on my first quarter to a brightly lit, mirrored room with three

women, all simulating masturbation. The one in the center was right in front of me, and she caught my eye and grinned at me, in black leather just like her. I think she sees few women in the booths, and many men.

Men—always the Man who is the standard-bearer for what is obscene and forbidden. That Man, the one I fear whether I mean to or not, in elevators and parking lots and on the street, is the man who will be inflamed by what he sees. I fear he will be *persuaded* by it, come to believe it, learn my fantasy and think I want him to make it come true. When I haven't the temerity to go through one of these veiled doors, it's because I am afraid of the men inside: afraid in a generic, unspoken way, afraid of Them.

Susan Sontag, exhaustively trying to prove that certain works of pornography qualify as "literature"—a proof almost laughably pointless, I think—notes its "singleness of intention" as a point against its inclusion. I am interested in literature, pornographic and otherwise, by my responses to any given piece; and my responses to pornography are layered and complex and multiple.

Some pieces bore me: They are cheesy or slow, badly written or mechanical. Others disturb me by the unhappiness I sense, as though the actors and actresses wished only to be somewhere else. There are days when I am saturated and feel weary of the whole idea. Sometimes I experience a kind of ennui, a *nausea* from all that grunting labor, the rankness of the flesh. I get depressed, for simple enough reasons. I rented a movie recently that opened with a scene of two naked women stroking each other. One of the women had enormous breasts, hard balloons filled with silicone riding high on her ribs and straining the skin. She looked mutilated, and the rest of the movie held no interest for me at all.

I wish for more craft, a more artful packaging. I tire of browsing stacks of boxes titled *Fucking Brunettes* and *Black Cocks and Black Cunts* and *Monumental Knockers*. The mainstream films, with their happy, athletic actors, can leave me a little cold. That's how I felt watching a comfortable film called *The Last Resort*. The plot, naturally, is simple: A woman with a broken heart accompanies her friends, a couple, to a resort. Over the next twenty-four hours she has vigorous sex with a waiter, a cook (he in nothing but a chef's hat and apron), a waitress, a waitress and a maintenance man together. The other guests cavort cheerfully, too. I found it all so earnest and wholesome. A friend and fellow connoisseur deplores these films where everyone has a "penis-deflatingly good time squirting sperm about with as much passion as a suburban gardener doing his lawn." These movies are too hygienic. They're not dirty enough.

And now women are making films for women viewers. The new films by and for lesbians can be nasty and hot. But the heterosexual films, heavy on relationships and light on the standard icons of hard core, seem ever so soft to me. (They're reminiscent of those social worker collages.) They're tasteful and discreet. I'm glad women have, so to speak,

seized the means of production. I'm glad women are making pornographic films, writing pornographic books, starting pornographic magazines; I'm happier still when the boundaries in which women create
expand. I don't believe there are limits to what women can imagine or
enjoy. I don't want limits, imposed from within or without, on what
women can see, or watch, or do.

Any amateur psychologist could have a field day explaining why I prefer low-brow, hard-core porn to feminine erotica. I've spent enough
time trying to explain things to myself: why I prefer *this* to *that*. There are
examples of pornography, films and stories both, that genuinely scare
me. They are no more bizarre or extreme than books or movies that may
simply excite or interest me, but the details affect me in certain specific
ways. The content touches me, just there, and I'm scared, for no reason
I can explain, or excited by a scene that repels me. It may be nothing
more than sound, a snap or thwack or murmur. And I want to keep
watching those films, reading those books; when I engage in my own
fears, I learn about them. I may someday master a few. When I happen
upon such scenes, I try to look directly. Seeing what I don't like can be
as therapeutic as seeing what I do.

Feminists against pornography (as distinct from other anti-pornography
camps) hold that our entire culture is pornographic. In a pornographic
world all our sexual constructions are obscene; sexual materials are necessarily oppressive, limited by the constraints of the culture. Even the act
of viewing becomes a male act—an act of subordinating the person
viewed. Under this construct, I'm a damaged woman, a heretic.

I take this personally, the effort to repress material I enjoy—to tell me
how wrong it is for me to enjoy it. Anti-pornography legislation is directed at me: as a user, as a writer. Catharine MacKinnon and Andrea
Dworkin—a feminist who has developed a new sexual orthodoxy in
which the male erection is itself oppressive—are the new censors. They
are themselves prurient, scurrying after sex in every corner. They look
down on me and shake a finger: *Bad girl. Mustn't touch.*

That branch of feminism tells me my very thoughts are bad. Pornography tells me the opposite: that *none* of my thoughts are bad, that anything goes. Both are extremes, of course, but the difference is profound.
The message of pornography, by its very existence, is that our sexual
selves are real.

Always, the censors are concerned with how men *act* and how women
are portrayed. Women cannot make free sexual choices in that world;
they are too oppressed to know that only oppression could lead them to
sell sex. And I, watching, am either too oppressed to know the harm that
my watching has done to my sisters, or—or else I have become the Man.
And it is the Man in me who watches and is aroused. (Shame.) What a

misogynistic worldview this is, this claim that women who make such choices cannot be making free choices at all—are not free to make a choice. Feminists against pornography have done a sad and awful thing: *They* have made women into objects.

I move from the front of the adult store I frequent to the back. Here is the leather underwear, dildos of all sizes, inflatable female dolls, shrink-wrapped fetish magazines. Here are movies with taboo themes—older movies with incest plots, newer ones featuring interracial sex, and grainy loops of nothing more than spanking, spanking, spanking. Here are the films of giant breasts, or all-anal sex, food fights, obese actresses, and much masturbation. This is niche marketing at its best.

In the far back, near the arcade booths, are the restraints, the gags and bridles, the whips and handcuffs, and blindfolds. Here are dildos of truly heroic proportions. The films here are largely European, and quite popular. A rapid desensitization takes me over back here, a kind of numbing sensory overload. Back here I can't help but look at the other customers; I find myself curious about which movies each of *them* will rent.

Women who have seen little pornography seem to assume that the images in most films are primarily, obsessively, ones of rape. I find the opposite theme in American films: that of an adolescent rut, both male and female. Its obsession is virility, endurance, lust. Women in modern films are often the initiators of sex; men in such films seem perfectly content for that to be so.

Power fantasies, on the other hand, are rather common for men and women both. I use the term "power" to describe a huge continuum of images: physical and psychological overpowering of many kinds, seduction and bondage and punishment, the extremes of physical control practiced by S&M enthusiasts. The word "rape" for such scenes is inappropriate; the fact of rape has nothing to do with sex, or pornography. Power takes a lot of forms, subtle, overt. Out of curiosity I rented a German film called *Discipline in Leather,* a film, I discovered, without sex, without nudity. Two men are variously bound, chained, laced, gagged, spanked, and ridden like horses by a Nordic woman. "Nein!" she shouts. "Nicht so schnell!" The men lick her boots, accept the bridle in cringing obeisance. I found it laughably solemn, a Nazi farce, and then I caught myself laughing. This is one of many similar films, and I never want to laugh at the desires of another. A lot of people take what I consider trifling or silly to be terribly important. I want never to forget the bell curve of human desire, or that few of us have much say about where on the curve we land. I've learned this from watching porn: By letting go of judgments I hold against myself, and my desires, I let go of judgments about the desires and the acts of others.

I recently saw a movie recommended by one of the clerks at the adult store, a send-up called *Wild Goose Chase.* In the midst of mild arousal, I found a scene played for laughs, about the loneliness taken for granted in the pornographic world. The actor is Joey Silvera, a good-looking man with blond hair and startling dark eyes. In this film he plays a detective; the detective has a torrid scene with his secretary, who then walks out on him. He holds his head in his hands. "I don't need her," he mumbles. "I got women. I got my *own* women!" He stands and crosses to a file cabinet. "I got plenty of women!" He pulls out a drawer and dumps it upside down, spilling porn magazines in a pile on the floor. He crawls over them, stroking the paper cunts, the breasts, the pictured thighs, moaning, kissing the immobile faces.

The fantasies of power are shame-driven, I think: When I envision my own binding, my submission, I am seeing myself free. Free of guilt, free of responsibility. So many women I've known have harbored these fantasies, and grown more guilty for having them. And so many of those women have been strong, powerful, self-assured. Perhaps, as one school of feminist thought says, we've simply "eroticized our oppression." I know I berated myself a long while for that very thing, and tried to make the fantasies go away. But doing so denies the fact of my experience, which includes oppression and dominance, fear and guilt, and a hunger for surrender. This is the real text of power fantasies: They are about release from all those things. A friend who admits such dreams herself gave me Pat Califia's collection of dominance stories, *Macho Sluts*. I opened at random and was rooted where I stood: The stories are completely nasty, well written, and they are smart. "I no longer thought about the future," one character says, spread-eagle and bound in front of mirrors during sex. "I did not exist, except as a response to her touch. There was nothing else, no other reality, and no whim of my own will moved me." Such dreams transcend mere sex and enter, unexpectedly, the world of relationship. I could not read such stories, watch such films, with anyone but a lover. I couldn't act them out except with the person whom I trusted most of all.

It was only last year when I stopped making my lover go with me to the adult store. I make myself go alone now, or not at all; if I believe this should be mine for the choosing, then I want to get it myself. Only alone will that act of choosing be a powerful act. So I went yesterday, on a Wednesday in the middle of the morning, and found a crowd of men. There was even a couple, the young woman with permed hair and a startled look, like a deer caught in headlights. She kept her hands jammed in the pockets of her raincoat, and wouldn't return my smile. There was an old man on crutches huddled over a counter, and a herd of clerks, playing bad, loud rock music. I was looking for a few specific titles, and a clerk directed me to the customers' computer, on a table in the amateur section. It's like the ones at the library, divided by title, category (fat girl, Oriental, spanking, hetero, and so on), or a particular star.

The big-bellied jovial clerk came over after a few minutes.

"That working for you?" he sang out. "I tell you, I don't know how the hell that works."

I tell him I'm looking for a movie popular several years ago, called *Talk Dirty to Me*.

"Hey, Jack," he yells. "We got *Talk Dirty to Me?*" In a few minutes four clerks huddle around me and the computer, watching me type in the title, offering little suggestions. From across the store I can still hear the helpful clerk. "Hey, Al," he's shouting. "Lady over there wants *Talk Dirty to Me*. We got that?"

I still blush; I stammer to say these things out loud. Sex has eternal charm that way—a perpetual, organic hold on my body. I am aroused right now, writing this. Are you, dear reader? Do you dream, too?

A friend called this story my "accommodation," as though I'd made peace with the material. I have never had to do that. I have always just been trying to make peace with my abyssal self, my underworld. Pornography helps; that's simple. I became sexual in a generation that has explored sex more thoroughly and perhaps less well than any before. I live with myself day to day in a sex-drenched culture, and that means living with my own sex. After exposing myself truly to myself, it's surprisingly easy to expose myself to another.

I want not to accommodate to pornography but to claim it. I want to be the agent of sex. I want to *own* sex, as though I had a right to these depictions, these ideas, as though they belonged to us all. The biggest surprise is this one: When I am watching—never mind what. I am suddenly restless, shifting, crossing my legs. And my perceptive lover smiles at me and says, "You like that, don't you? See—*everyone* does that."

Chapter 26

OBJECTIFICATION

Martha C. Nussbaum

It is true, and very much to the point, that women are objects, commodities, some deemed more expensive than others—but it is only by asserting one's humanness every time, in all situations, that one becomes someone as opposed to something. That, after all, is the core of our struggle.

Andrea Dworkin, *Woman Hating*

Sexual objectification is a familiar concept. Once a relatively technical term in feminist theory, associated in particular with the work of Catharine MacKinnon and Andrea Dworkin, the word "objectification" has by now passed into many people's daily lives. It is common to hear it used to criticize advertisements, films, and other representations, and also to express skepticism about the attitudes and intentions of one person to another, or of oneself to someone else. Generally it is used as a pejorative term, connoting a way of speaking, thinking, and acting that the speaker finds morally or socially objectionable, usually, though not always, in the sexual realm. Thus, Catharine MacKinnon writes of pornography, "Admiration of natural physical beauty becomes objectification. Harmlessness becomes harm."[1] The portrayal of women "dehumanized as sexual objects, things, or commodities" is, in fact, the first category of pornographic material made actionable under MacKinnon and Dworkin's proposed Minneapolis ordinance.[2] The same sort of pejora-

Nussbaum, Martha C., "Objectification," *Philosophy and Public Affairs* 24:4 (1995), pp. 249–91. Copyright © 1995 by Princeton University Press. Reprinted by permission of Princeton University Press.

tive use is very common in ordinary social discussions of people and events.

Feminist thought, moreover, has typically represented men's sexual objectification of women as not a trivial but a central problem in women's lives, and the opposition to it as at the very heart of feminist politics. For Catharine MacKinnon, "women's intimate experience of sexual objectification . . . is definitive of and synonymous with women's lives as gender female."[3] It is said to yield an existence in which women "can grasp self only as thing."[4] Moreover, this baneful experience is, in MacKinnon's view, unavoidable. In a most striking metaphor, she states that "All women live in sexual objectification the way fish live in water"— meaning by this, presumably, not only that objectification surrounds women, but also that they have become such that they derive their very nourishment and sustenance from it. But women are not fish, and for MacKinnon objectification is bad because it cuts women off from full self-expression and self-determination—from, in effect, their humanity.

But the term "objectification" can also be used, somewhat confusingly, in a more positive spirit. Indeed, one can find both of these apparently conflicting uses in the writings of some feminist authors: for example, legal theorist Cass Sunstein, who has been generally supportive of MacKinnon's critique of sexuality. Throughout his earlier writings on pornography, Sunstein speaks of the treatment of women as objects for the use and control of men as the central thing that is bad in pornographic representation.[5] On the other hand, in a mostly negative review of a recent book by Nadine Strossen defending pornography,[6] Sunstein writes the following:

> People's imaginations are unruly. . . . It may be possible to argue, as some people do, that objectification and a form of use are substantial parts of sexual life, or wonderful parts of sexual life, or ineradicable parts of sexual life. Within a context of equality, respect, and consent, objectification—not at all an easy concept to define—may not be so troublesome.[7]

To be sure, Sunstein expresses himself very cautiously, speaking only of an argument that might be made and not indicating his own support for such an argument. Nonetheless, to MacKinnon and Dworkin, who have typically represented opposition to objectification as at the heart of feminism, this paragraph might well seem puzzling. They might well wish to ask: What does Sunstein wish to defend? Why should "objectification and a form of use" ever be seen as "wonderful" or even as "ineradicable" parts of sexual life? Wouldn't it always be bad to use a "someone" as a "something"? And why should we suppose that it is at all possible to combine objectification with "equality, respect, and consent"? Isn't this precisely the combination we have shown to be impossible?

My hunch, which I shall pursue, is that such confusions can arise because we have not clarified the concept of objectification to ourselves, and that once we do so we will find out that it is not only a slippery, but also a multiple, concept. Indeed, I shall argue that there are at least seven distinct ways of behaving introduced by the term, none of which implies any of the others, though there are many complex connections among them. Under some specifications, objectification, I shall argue, is always morally problematic. Under other specifications, objectification has features that may be either good or bad, depending upon the overall context. (Sunstein was certainly right to emphasize the importance of context, and I shall dwell on that issue.) Some features of objectification, furthermore, I shall argue, may in fact in some circumstances, as Sunstein suggests, be either necessary or even wonderful features of sexual life. Seeing this will require, among other things, seeing how the allegedly impossible combination between (a form of) objectification and "equality, respect, and consent" might after all be possible.

I am going to begin with a series of examples, to which I shall return in what follows. All are examples of what might plausibly be called the objectification of one person by another, the seeing and/or treating of someone as an object. In all cases the objectified person is a sexual partner or would-be sexual partner, though the sexual context is not equally prominent in all of the cases. Deliberately, I have chosen examples from a wide variety of styles; and I have not restricted my sample to the male objectification of women, since we need to be able to ask how our judgments of the cases are influenced by larger issues of social context and social power.

(1.) His blood beat up in waves of desire. He wanted to come to her, to meet her. She was there, if he could reach her. The reality of her who was just beyond him absorbed him. Blind and destroyed, he pressed forward, nearer, nearer, to receive the consummation of himself, be received within the darkness which should swallow him and yield him up to himself. If he could come really within the blazing kernel of darkness, if really he could be destroyed, burnt away till he lit with her in one consummation, that were supreme, supreme.

D. H. Lawrence, *The Rainbow*

(2.) yes because he must have come 3 or 4 times with that tremendous big red brute of a thing he has I thought the vein or whatever the dickens they call it was going to burst though his nose is not so big after I took off all my things with the blinds down after my hours dressing and perfuming and combing it like iron or some kind of a thick crowbar standing all the time he must have eaten oysters I think a few dozen he was in great singing voice no I never in all my life felt anyone had one the size of that to make you feel full up he must have eaten a whole sheep after whats the idea making us like that with a big hole in the middle of us like a Stallion driving it up into you because thats all they want out of you with that determined vicious look in his eye I had to halfshut my eyes still he hasn't such a tremendous amount of spunk in him.

James Joyce, *Ulysses*

(3.)   She even has a sheet over her body, draped and folded into her contours. She doesn't move. She might be dead, Macrae thinks. . . . Suddenly a desire to violate tears through his body like an electric shock, six thousand volts of violence, sacrilege, the lust to desecrate, destroy. His thumbs unite between the crack of her ass, nails inwards, knuckle hard on knuckle, and plunge up to the palms into her. A submarine scream rises from the deep green of her dreaming, and she snaps towards waking, half-waking, half-dreaming with no sense of self . . . and a hard pain stabbing at her entrails. . . . Isabelle opens her eyes, still not knowing where or what or why, her face jammed up against the cracking plaster . . . as Macrae digs deeper dragging another scream from her viscera, and her jerking head cracks hard on the wall, . . . and her palms touch Macrae's hands, still clamped tight around her ass, kneading, working on it, with a violence born of desperation and desire, desire to have her so completely . . . that it seems as if he would tear the flesh from her to absorb it, crush it, melt it into his own hands. . . . And Isabelle . . . hears a voice calling out "don't stop; don't stop," a voice called from somewhere deep within her from ages past, ancestral voices from a time the world was young, "don't stop, don't stop." It's nearer now, this atavistic voice, and she realises with surprise that it is coming from her mouth, it is her lips that are moving, it is her voice.

"Laurence St. Clair," *Isabelle and Véronique: Four Months, Four Cities*

(4.)   Three pictures of actress Nicollette Sheridan playing at the Chris Evert Pro-Celebrity Tennis Classic, her skirt hiked up to reveal her black underpants. Caption: "Why We Love Tennis."

Playboy, April 1995

(5.)   At first I used to feel embarrassed about getting a hard-on in the shower. But at the Corry much deliberate excitative soaping of cocks went on, and a number of members had their routine erections there each day. My own, though less regular,

were, I think, hoped and looked out for. . . . This naked min-
gling, which formed a ritualistic heart to the life of the club,
produced its own improper incitements to ideal liaisons, and
polyandrous happenings which could not survive into the
world of jackets and ties, cycle-clips and duffel-coats. And how
difficult social distinctions are in the shower. How could I now
smile at my enormous African neighbour, who was responding
in elephantine manner to my own erection, and yet scowl at
the disastrous nearly-boy smirking under the next jet along?
  Alan Hollinghurst, *The Swimming-Pool Library*

(6.) She had passed her arm into his, and the other objects in the
room, the other pictures, the sofas, the chairs, the tables, the
cabinets, the 'important' pieces, supreme in their way, stood
out, round them, consciously, for recognition and applause.
Their eyes moved together from piece to piece, taking in the
whole nobleness—quite as if for him to measure the wisdom of
old ideas. The two noble persons seated, in conversation, at tea,
fell thus into the splendid effect and the general harmony: Mrs.
Verver and the Prince fairly 'placed' themselves, however unwittingly, as high expressions of the kind of human furniture
required, aesthetically, by such a scene. The fusion of their
presence with the decorative elements, their contribution to
the triumph of selection, was complete and admirable; though
to a lingering view, a view more penetrating than the occasion
really demanded, they also might have figured as concrete at-
testations of a rare power of purchase. There was much indeed
in the tone in which Adam Verver spoke again, and who shall
say where his thought stopped? '*Le compte y est*. You've got some
good things.'
  Henry James, *The Golden Bowl*[8]

Most of the works and authors are familiar. Hollinghurst's novel of gay
London before AIDS has been widely hailed as one of the most important
pieces of erotic writing in the 1980s. To those who are unfamiliar with
the *oeuvre* of Laurence St. Clair, it is probably sufficient to point out that
St. Clair is a pseudonym of James Hankinson, scholar in ancient Greek
philosophy and Professor of Philosophy at the University of Texas at
Austin, who wrote this novel for a standard hard-core pornographic series, and was later publicized as its author.

So: we have six examples of conduct that seems to deserve, in some
sense, the name of "objectification." In each case, a human being is regarded and/or treated as an object, in the context of a sexual relationship. Tom Brangwen sees his wife as a mysterious inhuman natural force,

a "blazing kernel of darkness." Molly reduces Blazes Boylan to his genital dimensions, regarding him as somewhat less human than the stallion
to which she jokingly compares him. Hankinson's hero Macrae treats
the sleeping Isabelle as a prehuman, preconscious being ripe for invasion and destruction, whose only quasi-human utterance is one that confirms her suitability for the infliction of pain. The *Playboy* caption
reduces the young actress, a skilled tennis player, to a body ripe for male
use: it says, in effect, she thinks she is displaying herself as a skilled athletic performer, but all the while she is actually displaying herself to *our*
gaze as a sexual object. Hollinghurst's hero represents himself as able to
see his fellow Londoners as equal interchangeable bodies or even body
parts, under the sexual gaze of the shower room, a gaze allegedly independent of warping considerations of class or rank. Maggie and Adam
contemplate their respective spouses as priceless antiques whom they
have collected and arranged.

In all such analyses of literary works, we need to distinguish the objectification of one character by another character from the objectification
of persons by a text taken as a whole. Both are of interest to me as examples of morally assessable human conduct, and, given the connections of
my analysis to the debate over pornography, I shall be concerned with the
morality of the conduct that consists in representing,[9] as well as with the
morality of represented conduct. Both sorts of conduct can be morally assessed, but they should be kept separate. Frequently it is difficult to do
this, but the attempt must be made, since important moral issues clearly
turn on the difference, and in dealing with literary examples we must
grapple with it. Fortunately, ethical criticism of literature has by now developed a rich set of distinctions to assist us. Especially helpful is Wayne
Booth's threefold distinction between (a) the *narrator* of a text (and/or
its other characters); (b) the *implied author,* that is, the sense of life embodied in the text taken as a whole; and (c) the *real-life author,* who has
many properties lacked by the implied author, and may lack some that
the implied author has.[10] Booth argues, and I agree, that the ethical criticism of the action represented in a text is one thing, and criticism of the
text as a whole another; to get to the second we need to focus on the *implied author,* asking ourselves what sort of interaction the text as a whole
promotes in us as readers, what sorts of desires and projects it awakens
and constructs. In this way, ethical criticism of texts can be both sensitive
to literary form and continuous with the ethical appraisal of persons.[11]

Here what we should probably say is that Brangwen's way of viewing his
wife is exemplary of attitudes that Lawrence advocates in his text taken as
a whole, and in other related texts; that Molly Bloom's attitude to Boylan
is far from being the only attitude to sexual relations that Joyce depicts,
even in his portrayal of Molly's imagining; that Hankinson's entire text
objectifies women in the manner of the passage cited, which is but the

first of a sequence of increasingly violent episodes that, strung together, constitute the whole of the "novel";[12] that *Playboy*'s typical approach to women's bodies and achievements is well captured in my example; that Henry James's novel, by contrast, awakens serious moral criticism of its protagonists by portraying them as objectifiers. Hollinghurst is the most puzzling example, and it remains to me quite unclear what attitude the text as a whole invites us to assume to its protagonist and his fantasies.

To give a suggestion of my reaction to the texts: I think that while none of them is without moral complexity, and none will be to everyone's taste, two examples of conduct in them, perhaps three, stand out as especially sinister. (The James characters are the ones of whom I would be most ready to use the term "evil.") At least one of the texts shows how objectification of a kind might be quite harmless and even pleasant; and at least one, perhaps more than one, shows what might lead someone to suggest that it could be a wonderful part of sexual life. Taken as a group, the examples invite us to distinguish different dimensions of objectification and to notice their independence from one another. When we do so, I shall argue, we discover that all types of objectification are not equally objectionable; that the evaluation of any of them requires a careful evaluation of context and circumstance; and that, once we have made the requisite distinctions, we will see how at least some of them might be compatible with consent and equality, and even be "wonderful" parts of sexual life.

1. Seven Ways to Treat a Person as a Thing

Now we need to begin the analysis. I suggest that in all cases of objectification what is at issue is a question of treating one thing as another: One is treating *as an object* what is really not an object, what is, in fact, a human being. The notion of humanity is involved in quite a Kantian way in the Dworkin quotation that is my epigraph, and I think that it is implicit in most critiques of objectification in the MacKinnon/Dworkin tradition. Beyond this, however, we need to ask what is involved in the idea of treating *as an object*. I suggest that at least the following seven notions are involved in that idea:

1. *Instrumentality:* The objectifier treats the object as a tool of his or her purposes.

2. *Denial of autonomy:* The objectifier treats the object as lacking in autonomy and self-determination.

3. *Inertness:* The objectifier treats the object as lacking in agency, and perhaps also in activity.

4. *Fungibility:* The objectifier treats the object as interchangeable (a) with other objects of the same type, and/or (b) with objects of other types.

5. *Violability:* The objectifier treats the object as lacking in boundary-integrity, as something that it is permissible to break up, smash, break into.

6. *Ownership:* The objectifier treats the object as something that is owned by another, can be bought or sold, etc.

7. *Denial of subjectivity:* The objectifier treats the object as something whose experience and feelings (if any) need not be taken into account.[13]

Each of these is a feature of our treatment of things, though of course we do not treat all things as objects in all of these ways. Treating things as objects is not objectification, since, as I have suggested, objectification entails making into a thing, treating *as* a thing, something that is really not a thing. Nonetheless, thinking for a bit about our familiar ways of treating things will help us to see that these seven features are commonly present, and distinct from one another. Most inanimate objects are standardly regarded as tools of our purposes, though some are regarded as worthy of respect for their beauty, or age, or naturalness. Most inanimate objects are treated as lacking autonomy, though at times we do regard some objects in nature, or even some machines, as having a life of their own. Many objects are inert and/or passive, though not by any means all. Many are fungible with other objects of a similar sort (one ballpoint pen with another), and also, at times, with objects of a different sort (a pen with a word processor), though many, of course, are not. Some objects are viewed as "violable"[14] or lacking in boundary-integrity, though certainly not all: We will allow a child to break and destroy relatively few things in the house. Many objects are owned, and are treated as such, though many again are not. (It is interesting that the unowned among the inanimate objects—parts of nature for the most part—are also likely to be the ones to which we especially often attribute a kind of autonomy and an intrinsic worth.) Finally, most objects are treated as entities whose experiences and feelings need not be taken into account, though at times we are urged to think differently about parts of the natural environment, whether with illicit anthropomorphizing or not I shall not determine here. In any case, we can see on the list a cluster of familiar attitudes to things, all of which seem to play a role in the feminist account of the objectification of persons. What objectification is, is to treat a human being in one or more of these ways.

Should we say that each is a sufficient condition for the objectification of persons? Or do we need some cluster of the features, in order to have a sufficient condition? I prefer not to answer this question, since I believe that use is too unclear. On the whole, it seems to me that "objectification" is a relatively loose cluster-term, for whose application we sometimes treat any one of these features as sufficient, though more often a plurality of features is present when the term is applied. Clearly there are other ways we standardly treat things—touching them, seeing them—that do not suggest objectification when we apply the same mode of treatment to persons, so we have some reason to think that these seven items are at least signposts of what many have found morally problematic. And there are some items on the list—especially denial of autonomy and denial of subjectivity—that attract our attention from the start because they seem to be modes of treatment we wouldn't bother discussing much in the case of mere things, where questions of autonomy and subjectivity do not arise; they seem most suited to the thinglike treatment of persons. This suggests that they may be of special interest to us in what follows, suggesting that we are going to be at least as interested in the treatment that is denied to persons as in the treatment that is accorded them.[15]

How are the features connected? It will be helpful to turn, first, to two examples from the thing-world: a ballpoint pen, and a Monet painting. The way in which a ballpoint pen is an object involves, it would seem, all the items on this list, with the possible exception of violability. That is, it might be thought inappropriate or at least wasteful to break up ballpoint pens, but I don't think that worry would rise to great moral heights. Certainly it seems that to treat the pen as a tool, as nonautonomous, as inert, as fungible (with other pens and at times with other instruments or machines), as owned, and as lacking in subjectivity—all this is exactly the standard and appropriate way to treat it. The painting, on the other hand, is certainly nonautonomous, owned, inert (though not passive), and lacking in subjectivity; it is definitely not fungible, either with other paintings or, except in the limited sense of being bought and sold, which doesn't imply thoroughgoing fungibility, with anything else either; its boundaries are precise, and there is a real question whether it is simply a tool for the purposes of those who use and enjoy it. What this tells us already is that objects come in many kinds. Some objects are precious objects, and these will usually lack fungibility and possess some boundary-integrity (inviolability).[16] Others are not so precious, and are both fungible and all right to break up.

The items on the list come apart in other ways as well. We see from the case of the painting that lack of autonomy does not necessarily imply instrumentality, though treating as instrumental may well imply treating as nonautonomous; the fact that most objects are inert should not conceal from us, for our later purposes, the fact that inertness is not a necessary condition of either lack of autonomy or instrumentality. Precisely what is useful about my word processor, what makes it such a good tool for my purposes, is that it is not inert. Nor does instrumentality entail lack of consideration for feelings and subjectivity—for one's purpose in using a tool may turn out to require concern for its experiences (as our pornographic examples will clearly show). As for violability, it is not entailed, it would seem, by any of the other six items. Even fungible items are not generally regarded as all right to break or smash, though the ones that are all right to smash are usually of the fungible sort, perhaps because it seems clear that they can be replaced by others of the kind.

Again, the fact that most objects are owned should not conceal from us the fact that ownership is not entailed by any of the other items on the list. Does it entail any of the others? Not fungibility, as is shown by the case of the painting. Not violability, not inertness, and probably not instrumentality, as our attitudes to household pets and even plants show us clearly. (We don't think they are just tools of our own purposes.) But probably ownership does entail lack of self-determination and autonomy; indeed it seems conceptually linked to that absence, though an item may certainly lack autonomy without being owned.

Finally, a thing may be treated as something whose experiences and feelings need not be taken into account without being treated as a mere tool, without being treated as fungible, without being seen as violable— all these are shown in the Monet painting case; also, without being seen as owned (the Grand Canyon, the Mojave Desert), and, it seems clear, without being seen as inert (my word processor). If one treats an object as something whose feelings and experiences need not be taken into account, is that consistent with treating as autonomous? I think very likely not. Again, it seems that there is a conceptual connection here.

In fact, what we are discovering is that autonomy is in a certain sense the most exigent of the notions on our list. It seems difficult if not impossible to imagine a case in which an inanimate object is treated as autonomous, though we can certainly imagine exceptions to all the others. And treating an item as autonomous seems to entail treating it as noninstrumental, as not simply inert, as not owned, and as not something whose feelings need not be taken into account. The only kind of objectification that seems clearly consistent with treating-as-autonomous, in fact, seems to be treating-as-fungible, and this in the limited sense of treating as fungible with other autonomous agents. This turns out to be highly pertinent to Hollinghurst, and to a well-developed ideology of gay male promiscuity, best exemplified, perhaps, in Richard Mohr's *Gay Ideas*, where fungibility-objectification is linked with democratic equality.[17] To this I shall return. Treating-as-violable, as lacking boundary-integrity, may well also be consistent with treating-as-autonomous, and it is a prominent claim of defenders of consensual sadomasochism, for example lesbian and gay writers Gayle Rubin and Richard Mohr, that this is so. Interestingly enough, the same claim has been defended by conservative political philosopher Roger Scruton, in an eloquent and surprising argument.[18] (In fact, Scruton's entire analysis has a great deal to offer the person who tries to think about this subject, and it is certainly the most interesting philosophical attempt as yet to work through the moral issues involved in our treatment of persons as sex partners.)

On the other hand, there is one way in which *instrumentality* seems to be the most morally exigent notion. We can think of many cases in which it is permissible to treat a person or thing as nonautonomous (the Monet painting, one's pets, one's small children), and yet inappropriate to treat the object merely or primarily as a tool of our own purposes. That, I have said, would be a bad attitude to the painting, even though the painting hardly displays autonomy. What is interesting is to see how few of the other forms of object-treatment are clearly ruled out by the decision not to treat a thing as instrumental. What more, in fact, is entailed by the decision to treat a thing as, to use the Kantian phrase, an end in itself? Not treating-as-autonomous, I have said; though this does not rule out the possibility that treating-as-autonomous would be a necessary feature of the noninstrumental treatment *of adult human beings*. Not treating as noninert, in the case of the painting; though again, it is at least arguable that noninstrumentality for adult humans entails recognition of agency and activity. Not treating as nonfungible, or at least not clearly so. I may view each one of many pieces of fine silver flatware as precious for its own sake, and yet view them as exchangeable one for another. Not treating as having subjectivity, or not generally (the painting again); though once again, it might turn out that to treat an adult human being as an end in him- or herself does entail recognition of subjectivity. And, finally, it seems quite unclear whether treating as an end in itself requires seeing as inviolable. That all seems to depend on the nature of the object. (Some experimental artworks, for example, invite breakage.) On the whole, though, there may be a conceptual connection between treating as an end in itself and treating as inviolable, in the sense that to break up or smash an object is usually to use it in accordance with one's own purposes in ways that negate the natural development and may even threaten the existence of the object.

I now pass over the fascinating issues of objectification raised by our treatment of plants and other animals, and move on to some cases involving the treatment of human beings by human beings. Let us for the moment avoid the sexual realm. And let us consider first of all the relationship between parent and child. The treatment of young children by their parents almost always involves a denial of autonomy; it involves some aspects of ownership, though not all. On the other hand, in almost all times and places it has been thought bad for parents to treat their children as lacking in bodily integrity—battery and sexual abuse, though common, are more or less universally deplored. Nor would it be at all common to find children treated as inert and lacking in activity. On the other hand, the extent to which children may be used as tools of their parents' purposes, as beings whose feelings need not be taken into account, and even as fungible,[19] has varied greatly across place and time. Modern American views of child rearing would view all three of these forms of objectification as serious moral wrongs; in other times and places, they have not been so regarded.

Let us now consider Marx's account of the objectlike treatment of workers under capitalism (abstracting from the question of its truth).[20] Absence of true autonomy is absolutely crucial to the analysis, as is also instrumentality and absence of concern for experiences and feelings (although Marx seems to grant that workers are still treated with some lingering awareness of their humanity, and are not regarded altogether as tools or even animals).[21] Workers are also treated as quite thoroughly fungible, both with other able-bodied workers and at times with machines. They are not, however, treated as inert: Their value to the capitalist producer consists precisely in their activity. Nor, whatever other flaws Marx finds with the system, does he think they are treated as physically violable. The physical safety of workers is at least nominally protected, though of course it is not all that well protected, and the gradual erosion of health through substandard living conditions may itself be regarded as a kind of slow bodily violation. Spiritual violation, on the other hand, lies at the heart of what Marx thinks is happening to workers, when they are deprived of control over the central means of their self-definition as humans. Finally, workers are not exactly owned, and are certainly morally different from slaves, but in a very profound sense the relationship is one of ownership—in the sense, namely, that what is most the worker's own, namely the product of his labor, is what is most taken away from him. MacKinnon has written that sexuality is to feminism what work is to Marxism: In each case something that is most oneself and one's own is what is seen by the theory to have been taken away.[22] We should remember this analogy, when we enter the sexual domain.

Now let us think of slavery. Slavery is defined as a form of ownership. This form of ownership entails a denial of autonomy, and it also entails the use of the slave as a mere tool of the purposes of the owner. (Aristotle defines the slave as "an animate tool.") This is true so far as the institution is concerned, and (as even Aristotle granted) is not negated by the fact that on occasion noninstrumental friendships may exist between slave and owner. (As Aristotle says, in that case the friendship is not with the slave *qua* slave, but with the slave *qua* human.[23]) Why so, given that I have noted that in the case of paintings, and house plants, and pets, treating-as-owned need not entail treating-as-instrumental? I believe that it is something about the type of ownership involved in slavery, and its relation to the humanity of the slave, that makes this connection. Once one treats a human being as a thing one may buy or sell, one is *ipso facto* treating that human being as a tool of one's own purposes. Perhaps this is because, as I have suggested, the noninstrumental treatment of adult human beings entails recognition of autonomy, as is not the case for paintings and plants; and ownership is by definition incompatible with autonomy.

On the other hand, slaves are certainly not treated as inert, far from it. Nor are they necessarily treated as fungible, in the sense that they may be specialized in their tasks. Yet the very toollike treatment inherent in the institution entails a certain sort of fungibility, in the sense that a person is reduced to a set of body parts performing a certain task, and under that understanding can be replaced by another similar body, or by a machine. Slaves are not necessarily regarded as violable; there may even be laws against the rape and/or bodily abuse of slaves. But it is easy to see how the thinglike treatment of persons inherent in the institution led, as it so often did, to the feeling that one had a right to use the body of that slave in whatever way one wished. Once one treats as a tool and denies autonomy, it is difficult to say why rape or battery would be wrong, except in the sense of rendering the tool a less efficient tool of one's purposes. Slaves, finally, are not always denied subjectivity; one may imagine them as beings mentally well suited to their lot; one may also think with a limited empathy about their pleasure or pain. On the other hand, once again, the very decision to treat a person as not an end in him- or herself, but as a mere tool, leads rather naturally to a failure of imagination. Once one makes that basic move it is very easy indeed to stop asking the questions morality usually dictates, such as, What is this person likely to feel if I do X? What does this person want, and how will my doing X affect her with respect to those wants? And so on.

This example prepares us for the MacKinnon/Dworkin analysis of sexuality, since it shows us how a certain sort of instrumental use of persons, negating the autonomy that is proper to them as persons, also leaves the human being so denuded of humanity, in the eyes of the objectifier, that he or she seems ripe for other abuses as well—for the refusal of imagination involved in the denial of subjectivity,[24] for the denial of individuality involved in fungibility, and even for bodily and spiritual violation and abuse, if that should appear to be what best suits the will and purposes of the objectifier. The lesson seems to be that there is something especially problematic about instrumentalizing human beings, something that involves denying what is fundamental to them as human beings, namely, the status of being ends in themselves. From this one denial, other forms of objectification that are not logically entailed by the first seem to follow.

Notice, however, that instrumentalization does not seem to be problematic in all contexts. If I am lying around with my lover on the bed, and use his stomach as a pillow,[25] there seems to be nothing at all baneful about this, provided that I do so with his consent (or, if he is asleep, with a reasonable belief that he would not mind), and without causing him pain, provided, as well, that I do so in the context of a relationship in which he is generally treated as more than a pillow.[26] This suggests that what is problematic is not instrumentalization per se, but treating someone *primarily* or *merely* as an instrument. The overall context of the relationship thus becomes fundamental, and I shall return to it.

II. Kant, Dworkin, and MacKinnon

We are now beginning to get a sense of the terrain of this concept, and to see how slippery, and how multiple, it is. We are also beginning to approach, I think, the core idea of MacKinnon's and Dworkin's analysis. As Barbara Herman has argued in a remarkable article,[27] this core notion is Kantian. Central to Kant's analysis of sexuality and marriage is the idea that sexual desire is a very powerful force that conduces to the thinglike treatment of persons, by which he meant, above all, the treatment of persons not as ends in themselves, but as means or tools for the satisfaction of one's own desires.[28] That kind of instrumentalizing of persons was very closely linked, in his view, to both a denial of autonomy—one wishes to dictate how the other person will behave, so as to secure one's own satisfaction—and also to a denial of subjectivity—one stops asking how the other person is thinking or feeling, bent on securing one's own satisfaction. It would appear that these three notions are the ones in which Kant is interested. Inertness, fungibility, ownership, and even violability don't seem to interest him, although one can easily see how the instrumentalization he describes might lead, here as in the case of the slave, to the view that the other body can be violated or abused, so long as that secures the agent's own pleasure. Certainly Dworkin, when she follows him, does make this connection, tracing the prevalence of sex abuse and sadistic violence to the initial act of denying autonomy and endlike status.[29]

Why does Kant think that sex does this? His argument is by no means clear, but we can try to elaborate it. The idea seems to be that sexual desire and pleasure cause very acute forms of sensation in a person's own body; that these sensations drive out, for a time, all other thoughts, including the thoughts of respect for humanity that are characteristic of the moral attitude to persons. Apparently he also thinks that they drive out every endlike consideration of the pleasure or experience of the sex partner, and cause attention to be riveted in on one's own bodily states. In that condition of mind, one cannot manage to see the other person as anything but a tool of one's own interests, a set of bodily parts that are useful tools for one's pleasure, and the powerful urge to secure one's own sexual satisfaction will ensure that instrumentalization (and therefore denial of autonomy and of subjectivity) continue until the sexual act has reached its conclusion. At the same time, the keen interest both parties have in sexual satisfaction will lead them to permit themselves to be treated in this thinglike way by one another, indeed, to volunteer eagerly to be dehumanized in order that they can dehumanize the other in turn.[30] Kant clearly believes this to be a feature of sexuality generally, not just of male sexuality, and he does not connect his analysis to any issues of social hierarchy or the asymmetrical social formation of erotic desire. He seems to think that in a typical sex act both parties eagerly desire both to be objectifiers and to be objects.

MacKinnon and Dworkin in a way follow Kant, but in a very important way depart from him. Like Kant, they start from the notion that all human beings are owed respect, and that this respect is incompatible with treating them as instruments, and also with denials of autonomy and subjectivity.[31] Unlike Kant, however, they do not believe that these denials are intrinsic to sexual desire itself. They do not have a great deal to say about how sexual desire can elude these problems, but the more overtly erotic parts of Dworkin's fiction suggest that it is possible to aim, in sex, at a mutually satisfying fused experience of pleasure in which both parties temporarily surrender autonomy in a good way (a way that enhances receptivity and sensitivity to the other) without instrumentalizing one another or becoming indifferent to one another's needs. Since she is clearly much influenced by Lawrence, I shall return to these issues when I discuss him later. Moreover, in her discussions of James Baldwin in *Intercourse*,[32] Dworkin makes it clear that she thinks that the lovemaking of gay men can right now, in our society, exemplify these good characteristics. The problem derives not from any obtuseness in sexual desire itself, but from the way in which we have been socialized erotically, in a society that is suffused with hierarchy and domination. Men learn to experience desire in connection with paradigm scenarios of domination and instrumentalization. (The fact that pornography is, for both MacKinnon and Dworkin, a primary source of these paradigm scenarios is what explains the importance of pornography in their thought.) Women learn to experience desire in connection with these same paradigm scenarios, which means that they learn to eroticize being dominated and being turned into objects. Thus objectification for MacKinnon and Dworkin is asymmetrical: on the one side the objectifier, on the other side, the volunteer for object-status. And this means that it is only the female for whom sex entails a forfeiture of humanity, being turned into something rather than someone. MacKinnon and Dworkin sometimes suggest that this objectification involves elements of inertness,[33] fungibility, and ownership;[34] but it seems to me clear that the central core of the concept, as they use it, is in fact that of instrumentality, connected in a Kantian way to denials of autonomy and subjectivity, and in a related way to the possibility of violation and abuse.[35]

Kant's solution to the problem of sexual objectification and use is marriage.[36] He argues that objectification can be rendered harmless only if sexual relations are restricted to a relationship that is structured institutionally in ways that promote and, at least legally if not morally, guarantee mutual respect and regard. If the two parties are bound to support one another in various ways, this ensures a certain kind of respect for personhood that will persist undestroyed by the ardors of lovemaking, though it is apparently Kant's view that this respect and "practical love" can never color or infuse the lovemaking itself.[37] Characteristically, Kant is not very much worried about the asymmetrical or hierarchical nature of marriage, or about its aspects of ownership and denial of autonomy. These aspects he sees as fitting and proper, and he never suggests that sexual objectification derives support from these institutional arrangements.

For Dworkin and MacKinnon, by contrast, hierarchy is at the root of the problem. The lack of respect that much lovemaking displays is not, as I have argued, a feature of sexuality in itself; it is created by asymmetrical structures of power. Marriage, with its historical connotations of ownership and nonautonomy, is one of the structures that makes sexuality go bad. We see this, for example, in Dworkin's *Mercy*, in which the mutually satisfying passionate sexual relationship between Andrea and the young revolutionary turns sour as soon as they are man and wife. Encouraged by the institution, he begins to need to assert his dominance sexually, and the relationship degenerates into a terrible saga of sadism and abuse. In this morality tale Dworkin illustrates her belief that institutions maim us despite our best intentions, causing the eroticization of forms of sexual conduct that dehumanize and brutalize. The remedy for this state of affairs, it is suggested, is no single institution, but rather the gradual undoing of all the institutional structures that lead men to eroticize power. Thus the critiques of sexual harassment, of domestic violence, and of pornography hang together as parts of a single program of Kantian moral/political reform.

Failure to sort out the different aspects of the concept of objectification leads at times to obscurity in MacKinnon's and Dworkin's critique. Consider, for example, the following passage from Dworkin's analysis of *The Story of O:*

> O is totally possessed. That means that she is an object, with no control over her own mobility, capable of no assertion of personality. Her body is *a* body, in the same way that a pencil is a pencil, a bucket is a bucket, or, as Gertrude

Stein pointedly said, a rose is a rose. It also means that O's energy, or power, as a woman, as Woman, is absorbed. . . . The rings through O's cunt with Sir Stephen's name and heraldry, and the brand on her ass, are permanent wedding rings rightly placed. They mark her as an owned object and in no way symbolize the passage into maturity and freedom. The same might be said of the conventional wedding ring.[38]

Here we have inertness, fungibility, and ownership, all treated as if they are more or less inevitable consequences of an initial denial of autonomy (mixed up, clearly, with instrumentalization). It may be true that the novel makes these connections, and that the particular way in which Sir Stephen possesses O is in fact incompatible with active agency, with qualitative individuality, or with nonownership. But it is important to insist that these are logically independent ideas. One may deny autonomy to a beloved child without these other consequences. So what we want to know is: How are they connected here? What should make us believe that a typical male way of relating to women as non-autonomous brings these other consequences in its train? (For it is clear, as the wedding-ring remark indicates, that for Dworkin *The Story of O* is a paradigm of a pattern of relationship prevalent in our culture.) If we are contemplating institutional and/or moral change, we need to understand these connections clearly, so that we will have a sense of where we might start.

What brings these different aspects of the concept together is, I believe, a certain characteristic mode of instrumentalization and use that is alleged to lie behind the male denial of autonomy to women. For Sir Stephen, O exists only as something to be used to gratify his own pleasure (and, as Dworkin perceptively points out, as a surrogate for the male René whom he loves, but will not approach physically). Apart from that, she is O, zero. So she is not like a beloved child, who may be denied autonomy but retain individuality and agency. She is just a set of bodily parts, in particular a cunt and an anus[39] to be entered and used, with nothing of salience over and above them, not even the individuality and agency of those parts. It is in this way, I believe, that Dworkin (and at times MacKinnon) makes the further step from the core concepts of instrumentalization and denial of autonomy to the other aspects of the concept of objectification. They believe that these connections are ubiquitous. This, they suggest, is the sum total of what women are under male domination. But once we have noticed that the connections are not as conceptually tight as they suggest, we are led to ask how pervasive in fact they are. And we are led to ask whether and to what extent women and men can combine these features in different ways in their lives, uncoupling passivity from instrumentality, for example, or fungibility from the denial of autonomy.

III. A Wonderful Part of Sexual Life?

Before returning to the passages, we must observe one fundamental point: In the matter of objectification, context is everything. MacKinnon and Dworkin grant this when they insist, correctly, that we assess male-female relations in the light of the larger social context and history of female subordination, and insist on differentiating the meaning of objectification in these contexts from its meaning in either male-male or female-female relations. But they rarely go further, looking at the histories and the psychologies of individuals. (In fact, in judging literary works they standardly refuse appeal to the work-as-a-whole test; even where narrative is concerned, context is held to be irrelevant.[40]) In a sense the fine details of context are of little interest to them, involved as they are in a political movement; on the other hand, such details are of considerable interest to us; for I shall argue that in many if not all cases, the difference between an objectionable and a benign use of objectification will be made by the overall context of the human relationship in question.

This can easily be seen if we consider a simple example. W, a woman, is going out of town for an important interview. M, an acquaintance, says to her, "You don't really need to go. You can just send them some pictures." If M is not a close friend of W, this is almost certain to be an offensively objectifying remark. It reduces W to her bodily (and facial) parts, suggesting, in the process, that her professional accomplishments and other personal attributes do not count. The remark certainly seems to slight W's autonomy; it treats her as an inert object, appropriately represented by a photograph; it may suggest some limited sort of fungibility. It may also, depending on the context, suggest instrumentalization: W is being treated as an object for the enjoyment of the male gaze. Suppose, now, M is W's lover, and he says this to her in bed. This changes things, but we really don't know how, because we don't know enough. We don't know what the interview is for (a modelling job? a professorship?). And we don't know enough about the people. If M standardly belittles her accomplishments, the remark is a good deal worse than the same remark made by a stranger, and more deeply suggestive of instrumentalization. If, on the other hand, there is a deeply understood mutual respect between them, and he is simply finding a way of telling her how attractive she is, and perhaps of telling her that he doesn't want her to leave town, then things become rather different. It may still be a risky thing to say, far more risky than the very same thing said by W to M, given the social history that colors all such relationships. Still, there is the sense that the remark is not reductive—that instead of taking away from W, the compliment to her appearance may have added something. (Much depends on tone of voice, gesture, sense of humor.) Consider, finally, the same remark made to W by a close friend. W knows that this friend respects her accomplishments, and has great confidence in his attitude toward her in all respects pertinent to friendship; but she wishes he would notice her body once in a while. In this case, the objectifying remark may come as a pleasant surprise to W, a joke embodying a welcome compliment. Though we still need to know more about what the interview is all about, and how it is related to W's capacities (and though we still should reflect about the fact that it is extremely unlikely, given the way our society currently is, that such a remark will ever be made by W to M), it may well seem to her as if the remark has added something without taking anything away. It is possible, of course, that W reacts this way because she has eroticized her own submission. Such claims, like all claims of false consciousness, are difficult to adjudicate. But it seems to me implausible that all such cases are of this sort. To these human complexities Dworkin and MacKinnon frequently seem to me insufficiently sensitive.

Let us now turn to the passages. Lawrence focuses, here as often, on the willing resignation of autonomy and, in a sense, of subjectivity. The power of sexuality is most authentically experienced, in his view, when the parties do put aside their conscious choice-making, and even their inner life of self-consciousness and articulate thought, and permit themselves to be, in a sense, objectlike, natural forces meeting one another with what he likes to call "blood knowledge." Thus Brangwen feels his blood surging up in a way that eclipses deliberation, that makes him "blind and destroyed." His wife at this moment does appear to him as a mysterious thinglike presence—in the striking metaphor, a "blazing kernel of darkness" (indicating that the illumination that comes from sexuality requires, first, the blinding of the intellect). This thinglike presence summons him—not, however, to instrumental use of it, but to a kind of surrender of his own personhood, a kind of yielding abnegation of self-containment and self-sufficiency. This sort of objectification has its roots, then, in a mutual denial of autonomy and subjective self-awareness. It has links with inertness, understood as passivity and receptivity, since both surrender agency before the power of the blood. It has links, as well, with fungibility: For in a certain sense Lydia's daily qualitative individuality does vanish before his desire, as she becomes an embodiment of something primal; and he puts aside his daily ways of self-definition, his own idiosyncrasies, before the dark presence that summons him. And that is also a link with violability: For in the sway of desire he no longer feels himself clearly individuated from her, he feels his boundaries become porous, he feels the longing to be "destroyed" as an individual, "burnt away."[41] Lawrence, like (and influenced by) Schopenhauer, sees a connection between the ascendancy of passion and the loss of definite boundaries, the loss of what Schopenhauer calls the *principium individuationis*.

All this is objectification. And whether or not one finds Lawrence's prose, or even his ideas, to one's taste, it seems undeniable that it captures some profound features of at least some sexual experiences. (As I have said, it is this very idea of sexuality that animates the fiction of Andrea Dworkin, and it is this wonderful possibility that she hates sexism for destroying.) If one were to attribute a sense to Sunstein's remark that objectification might be argued to be a wonderful part of sexual life, one might begin to do so along these lines. Indeed, one might go so far as to claim, with Schopenhauer, that it is a necessary feature of sexual life—though Lawrence seems to me to make a more plausible claim when he indicates that such resignation of control is not ubiquitous, and can in fact be relatively rare, especially in a culture very much given to self-conscious aloofness and the repression of feeling.

It is worth noting that Lawrentian objectification is frequently connected with a certain type of reduction of persons to their bodily parts, and the attribution of a certain sort of independent agency to the bodily parts. Consider this scene from *Lady Chatterley:*

"Let me see you!"

He dropped the shirt and stood still, looking towards her. The sun through the low window sent a beam that lit up his thighs and slim belly, and the erect phallus rising darkish and hot-looking from the little cloud of vivid gold-red hair. She was startled and afraid.

"How strange!" she said slowly. "How strange he stands there! So big! and so dark and cocksure! Is he like that?"

The man looked down the front of his slender white body, and laughed. Between the slim breasts the hair was dark, almost black. But at the root of the belly, where the phallus rose thick and arching, it was gold-red, vivid in a little cloud.

"So proud!" she murmured, uneasy, "And so lordly! Now I know why men are so overbearing. But he's lovely, really, like another being! A bit terrifying! But lovely really! And he comes to me—" She caught her lower lip between her teeth, in fear and excitement.

The man looked down in silence at his tense phallus, that did not change. . . . "Cunt, that's what tha'rt after. Tell lady Jane tha' wants cunt. John Thomas, an' th' cunt o' lady Jane!—"

"Oh, don't tease him," said Connie, crawling on her knees on the bed towards him and putting her arms round his white slender loins, and drawing him to her so that her hanging swinging breasts touched the top of the stirring erect phallus, and caught the drop of moisture. She held the man fast.

Here there is a sense in which both parties put aside their individuality and become identified with their bodily organs. They see one another in terms of those organs. And yet Kant's suggestion that in all such focusing on parts there is denial of humanity seems quite wrong. Even the suggestion that they are *reducing* one another to their bodily parts seems quite wrong, just as I think it seemed wrong in my simple photograph example. The intense focusing of attention on the bodily parts seems an addition, rather than a subtraction, and the scene of passion, which is fraught for Constance with a sense of terror, and the fear of being overborne by male power, is rendered benign and loving, is rendered in fact liberating, by this very objectification, in the manner in which Mellors undertakes it, combining humor with passion.

Why is Lawrentian objectification benign, if it is? We must point, above all, to the complete absence of instrumentalization, and to the closely connected fact that the objectification is symmetrical and mutual—and in both cases undertaken in a context of mutual respect and rough social equality.[42] The surrender of autonomy and even of agency and subjectivity are joyous, a kind of victorious achievement in the prison-house of English respectability. Such a surrender constitutes an escape from the prison of self-consciousness that, in Lawrence's quite plausible view, seals us off from one another and prevents true communication and true receptivity. In the willingness to permit another person to be this close, in a position where the dangers of being dominated and overborne are, as Constance knows, omnipresent, one sees, furthermore, enormous trust, trust that might be thought to be impossible in a relationship that did not include at least some sort of mutual respect and concern—although in Lawrence's depictions of a variety of more or less tortured male/female relationships we discover that this is complex. Where there is loss of autonomy in sex, the context is, or at least can be, one in which, on the whole, autonomy is respected and promoted; the success of the sexual relationship can have, as in Constance's case, wide implications for flourishing and freedom more generally. We do not need to find every single idea of Lawrence's about sexuality appealing in order to see in the scene something that is of genuine value. Again, where there is a loss in subjectivity in the moment of lovemaking, this can be and frequently is accompanied by an intense concern for the subjectivity of the partner at other moments, since the lover is intensely focused on the moods and wishes of that one person, whose states mean so much for his or her own. Brangwen's obsession with his wife's fluctuating moods shows this very clearly.

Finally, we see that the kind of apparent fungibility that is involved in identifying persons with parts of their bodies need not be dehumanizing at all, but can coexist with an intense regard for the person's individuality, which can even be expressed in a personalizing and individualizing of the bodily organs themselves, as in the exchange between Mellors and Constance. Giving a proper name to the genital organs of each is a way of signifying the special and individual way in which they desire one another, the nonfungible character of Mellors's sexual intentionality.[43] It is Mellors's way of telling Constance what she did not know before (and what MacKinnon and Dworkin seem at times not to know), that to be identified with her genital organs is not necessarily to be seen as dehumanized meat ripe for victimization and abuse, but can be a way of being seen more fully as the human individual she is. It is a reminder that the genital organs of people are not really fungible, but have their own individual character, and are in effect parts of the person, if one will really look at them closely without shame.[44]

We are now in a position to notice something quite interesting about Kant. He thinks that focusing on the genital organs entails the disregard of personhood—because he apparently believes that personhood and humanity, and, along with them, individuality, do not reside in the genital organs; the genital organs are just fungible nonhuman things, like so many tools. Lawrence says that is a response that itself dehumanizes us, by reducing to something animal what properly is a major part of the humanity in us, and the individuality as well. We have to learn to call our genital organs by proper names—that would be at least the beginning of a properly complete human regard for one another.

Thinking about Lawrence can make us question the account of the deformation of sexuality given by MacKinnon and Dworkin. For Lawrence suggests that the inequality and, in a sense, dehumanization of women in Britain—which he does frequently acknowledge, not least in *Lady Chatterley*—rests upon and derives strength from the denial of women's erotic potentiality, the insistence that women be seen as sexless things and not identified also with their genital organs. Like Audre Lorde among contemporary feminists,[45] Lawrence shows how a kind of sexual objectification—not, certainly, a commercial sort, and one that is profoundly opposed to the commercialization of sex[46]—can be a vehicle of autonomy and self-expression for women, how the very surrender of autonomy in a certain sort of sex act can free energies that can be used to make the self whole and full.[47] In effect, Mellor is the only character in that novel who sees Connie as an end in herself, and this noninstrumentalization, and the attendant promotion of her autonomy, is closely connected to his sexual interest.

MacKinnon and Dworkin would surely object that both Lawrence and Lorde are somewhat naive in their assumption that there is a domain of "natural" sexuality behind cultural constructions, that can be liberated in a sex act of the right sort. They would argue that this underestimates the depth to which sexual roles and desires are culturally shaped, and therefore infected by the ubiquitous distortions of gender roles. It is beyond the scope of this article to adjudicate this large controversy, but I can at least indicate the direction my reply would take. I believe that it is correct that Lawrence's romantic rhetoric of nature and blood knowledge probably is naive, underestimating the depth of socialization and, more generally, of cognitive awareness, in sexual life. Nor do I sympathize with Lawrence's idea that sexuality is better the freer it is of both culture and thought. On the other hand, I think that his larger case for the value of a certain type of resignation of control, and of both emotional and bodily receptivity, does not depend on these other theses, and that one can defend a kind of Lawrentian sexuality (as, indeed, Andrea Dworkin herself does, in the early chapters of *Mercy* and in her essays on Baldwin) without accepting them. Such a stance does involve the recognition that our culture is more heterogeneous, and allows us more space for negotiation and personal construction, than MacKinnon and Dworkin usually allow.[48]

We turn now to Molly Bloom. Molly regards Blazes Boylan as a collection of outsized bodily parts. She does so with humor and joy, though at the same time with certain reservations about the quality of Boylan's humanity. Her objectification of Boylan has little to do with either denial of his autonomy or instrumentalization and use—certainly not with inertness either, or ownership, or violability. It focuses on features of denial of subjectivity (she never in the entire monologue wonders about what he feels, as she so frequently does about Poldy), fungibility (he is just an especially large penis, "all right to spend time with as a joke," almost interchangeable with a stallion, or an inanimate dildolike crowbar). This is far from being a profound Lawrentian experience. It is a little unsatisfying, in its absence of depth, to Molly herself—whose ambiguous use of the word "spunk" to mean both "semen" and "character" shows us throughout the monologue her own confusion about the importance of this physical joy by comparison to her physically unsatisfying but loving relationship with Poldy. On the other hand, it seems that Molly's delight in the physical aspects of sex (which was found especially shocking by prudish attackers of the novel) is at least a part of what Lawrence and Audre Lorde want women to be free to experience, and it seems wrong to denigrate it because of its incompleteness. (Indeed, one might say that the theme of the novel as a whole is the acceptance of incompleteness, and what Joyce would most profoundly be opposed to would be a moralizing Lawrentian romantic denigration of Molly's pleasure on account of the fact that it was not especially earthshaking.[49]) So here we have quite a different way in which objectification may be a joyous part of sexual life—and maybe this sort of mythic focusing on body parts is even a regular or necessary feature of it, though Molly's comic exaggeration is not.

What is especially important to notice, for our purposes, is the way in which our reaction to Molly's objectification of Boylan is conditioned by context. Molly is socially and personally quite powerless, except through her powers of seduction. She is also aware that Boylan does not have an especially high regard for her—he is, like so many other men, using her

as a sex object—"because thats all they want out of you." There is a re-
taliatory self-protective character to her denial of subjectivity that makes
it seem right and just in a way that it might not be if it were Boylan thinking about Molly.

Hankinson's hard-core "novel" is both a typical example of the genre at-
tacked by MacKinnon and Dworkin and, in itself, quite an interesting
case in its pseudo-literary aspects. For if one holds this passage up next
to *The Rainbow,* as the customer of the Blue Moon Press is not very likely
to do, one notices the way in which Hankinson has borrowed from
Lawrence, and has incorporated into his narrative of violence and abuse
features of the Lawrentian "blood-knowledge" and denial of autonomy
that serve as legitimating devices for the violence that ensues. We said
that Lawrentian sexuality involves the surrender of individuation, and a
certain sort of porousness of boundaries that can border on violability.
Lawrence certainly depicts the willingness to be penetrated as a valuable
aspect of sexual receptivity. The questions then are, (a) can sadomasochistic sexual acts ever have a simply Lawrentian character, rather
than a more sinister character? and (b) is Hankinson's narrative a case
of that benign sort? (Here I shall not be able to say much about the characters and their conduct without focusing on the way in which the "implied author" has structured the narrative as a whole, since the "novel"
is exceedingly formulaic and lacking in complex characterization.)
    There seems to be no a priori reason why the answer to (a) cannot be
"yes." I have no very clear intuitions on this point, and here I'm going to
have to own to limits of experience and desire; but it would seem that
some narrative depictions of sadomasochistic activity do plausibly attribute to its consensual form a kind of Lawrentian character, in which
the willingness to be vulnerable to the infliction of pain, in some respects a sharper stimulus than pleasure, manifests a more complete trust
and receptivity than could be found in other sexual acts. Pat Califia's disturbing short story "Jenny" is one example of such a portrayal.[50] And
Hankinson certainly positions his narrative this way, suggesting that
there is a profound mutual desire that leads the two actors to seek an absence of individuation. The Lawrentian "atavistic voice" speaking from
within Isabelle asks for the continuation of violence, and Hankinson suggests that in asking this she is making contact with some depth in her being that lies beneath mere personality. All this is Lawrence, and
Schopenhauer, in Blue Moon Press clothing.
    What make the difference, clearly, are context and intention. For the
answer to (b) is clearly "no." Not only the character Macrae, but Hankinson's text as a whole, represent women as creatures whose autonomy
and subjectivity don't matter at all, insofar as they are not involved in the
gratification of male desire. The women, including whatever signs of hu-

manity they display, are just there to be used as sex objects for men in whatever way suits them. The eroticization of the woman's inertness, her lack of autonomy, her violability—and the assuaging fiction that this is what she has asked for, this is what nature has dictated for her—all these features, which make the example a textbook case of MacKinnon's views and a classic candidate under the Minneapolis and the Indianapolis version of the MacKinnon/Dworkin ordinance, also make it crucially unlike Lawrence, in which vulnerability and risk are mutually assumed and there is no malign or destructive intent.[51] In Lawrence, being treated as a cunt is a permission to expand the sphere of one's activity and fulfillment. In Hankinson, being treated like a cunt is being treated as something whose experiences don't matter at all. The entire novel, which is nothing but a succession of similar scenes, conceals the subjectivity of women from the reader's view, and constructs women as objects for male use and control. There is a ghastly way in which subjectivity does figure: For Macrae's desire is a desire "to violate . . . to desecrate, destroy." It is a desire that would not have been satisfied by intercourse with a corpse, or even an animal. What is made sexy here is precisely the act of turning a creature whom in one dim corner of one's mind one knows to be human into a thing, a something rather than a someone. And to be able to do that to a fellow human being is sexy because it is a dizzying experience of power.

J. S. Mill vividly described the distorted upbringing of men in England, who are taught every day that they are superior to one half of the human race, even though at the same time they see the fine achievements and character of women daily before their eyes. They learn that just in virtue of being male they are superior to the most exalted and talented woman, and they are corrupted by this awareness.[52] Consider in this light the education of Hankinson's reader, who learns (in the visceral way in which pornography leaves its impress, forming patterns of arousal and response[53]) that just in virtue of being male he is entitled to violate half of the human race, whose humanity is at the same time dimly presented to his vision. To the extent that he immerses himself in such works and regularly finds easy and uncomplicated satisfaction in connection with the images they construct, he is likely to form certain patterns of expectation regarding women—that they are for his pleasure, to be taken in this way. The work as a whole, which contains no episodes that are not of this kind, strongly encourages such projections.[54] Unlike MacKinnon and Dworkin, I do not favor any legal restrictions on such work, even the civil ordinance they propose, since I believe that any such proposal would jeopardize expressive interests that it is important to protect.[55] I also think that its availability has moral value, since we learn a lot about sexism from studying it. But I would certainly take it away from any young boy I know, I would protest against its inclusion on a

reading list or syllabus—except in the way I recommend our reading it
here[56]—and I would think that an ethical critique of it, which needs to
be given again and again, is indeed, as Andrea Dworkin says in my epigraph, "at the heart of struggle."

  Playboy is more polite, but ultimately similar. Here again I agree with
MacKinnon and Dworkin, who have repeatedly stressed the essential
similarity between the soft-core and the hard-core pornography indus-
tries. The message given by picture and caption is, "whatever else this
woman is and does, for us she is an object for sexual enjoyment." Once
again, the male reader is told, in effect, that he is the one with subjectivity and autonomy, and on the other side are things that look very sexy
and are displayed out there for his consumption, like delicious pieces of
fruit, existing only or primarily to satisfy his desire.[57] The message is
more benign, because, as a part of the *Playboy* "philosophy," women are
depicted as beings made for sexual pleasure, rather than for the infliction of pain, and their autonomy and subjectivity are given a nodding
sort of recognition. In a sense *Playboy* could be said to be part of the
movement for women's liberation, in the sense suggested by Lawrence
and Lorde. Insofar as women's full autonomy and self-expression are
hindered by the repression and denial of their sexual capacities, thus far
the cheery liberationist outlook of *Playboy* might be said to be feminist.

  However, the objectification in *Playboy* is in fact a profound betrayal
not only of the Kantian ideal of human regard but also, and perhaps especially, of the Lawrence/Lorde program. For *Playboy* depicts a thoroughgoing fungibility and commodification of sex partners, and, in the
process, severs sex from any deep connection with self-expression or
emotion. Lorde argues plausibly when she suggests that this dehumanization and commercialization of sex is but the modern face of an older
puritanism, and the apparent feminism of such publications is a mask
for a profoundly repressive attitude toward real female passion.[58] Indeed, Hankinson could argue that *Playboy* is worse than his novel, for his
novel at least connects sexuality to the depths of people's dreams and
wishes (both female and male) and thus avoids the reduction of bodies
to interchangeable commodities, whereas in *Playboy* sex is a commodity,
and women become very like cars, or suits, namely, expensive posses-
sions that mark one's status in the world of men.

  Who is objectified in *Playboy*? In the immediate context, it is the represented woman who is being objectified and, derivatively, the actress
whose photograph appears. But the characteristic *Playboy* generalizing
approach ("why we love tennis," or "women of the Ivy League")—as-
sisted in no small measure by the magazine's focus on photographs of
real women, rather than on paintings or fictions—strongly suggests that
real-life women relevantly similar to the tennis player can easily be cast
in the roles in which *Playboy* casts its chosen few. In that way it constructs

for the reader a fantasy objectification of a class of real women. Used as a masturbatory aid, it encourages the idea that an easy satisfaction can be had in this uncomplicated way, without the difficulties attendant on recognizing women's subjectivity and autonomy in a more full-blooded way.[59]

We can now observe one further feature of Lawrence that marks him as different from the pornographer. In Lawrence the men whose sexual behavior is approved are always remarkably unconcerned with worldly status and honor. The last thing they would think of would be to treat a woman as a prize possession, an object whose presence in their lives, and whose sexual interest in them, enhances their status in the world of men. (Indeed, that sort of status-centered attitude to women is connected by Lawrence with sexual impotence, in the character of Clifford Chatterley.) One cannot even imagine Mellors boasting in the locker room of the "hot number" he had the previous night, or regarding the tits and ass, or the sexual behavior, of Connie as items of display in the male world. What is most characteristic of Mellors (and of Tom Brangwen) is a profound indifference to the worldly signs of prestige; and this is a big part of the reason why both Connie Chatterley and the reader have confidence that his objectification of her is quite different from commodification (in my vocabulary, instrumentalization/ownership).

Playboy, by contrast, is just like a car magazine, only with people instead of cars to make things a little sexier—in the Hankinson way in which it is sexier to use a human being as a thing than simply to have a thing, since it manifests greater control, it shows that one can control what is of such a nature as to elude control. The magazine is all about the competition of men with other men, and its message is the availability of a readily renewable supply of more or less fungible women to men who have achieved a certain level of prestige and money—or rather, that fantasy women of this sort are available, through the magazine, to those who can fantasize that they have achieved this status. It is not in that sense very different from the ancient Greek idea that the victorious warrior would be rewarded with seven tripods, ten talents of gold, twenty cauldrons, twelve horses, and seven women.[60] Objectification means a certain sort of self-regarding display.

The one further thing that needs to be said about the picture is that in the *Playboy* world it is sexier, because more connected with status, to have a woman of achievement and talent than an unmarked woman, in the way that it is sexier to have a Mercedes than a Chevrolet, in the way that Agamemnon assures Achilles that the horses he is giving him are prize-winning racehorses and the women both beautiful and skilled in weaving. But a sleek woman is even more sexy than a sleek car, which cannot really be dominated since it is nothing but a thing. For what *Playboy* repeatedly says to its reader is, Whoever this woman is and whatever she has achieved, for you she is cunt, all her pretensions vanish before your sexual power. For some she is a tennis player—but you, in your mind, can dominate her and turn her into cunt. For some, Brown students are Brown students. For you, dear reader, they are *Women of the Ivy League* (an issue in preparation as I write, and the topic of intense controversy among my students[61]). No matter who you are, these women will (in masturbatory fantasy) moan with pleasure at your sexual power. This is the great appeal of *Playboy* in fact: It satisfies the desires of men to feel themselves special and powerful, by telling them that they too can possess the signs of exalted status that they think of as in real life reserved for such as Donald Trump. This, of course, Lawrence would see as the sterile status-seeking of Clifford Chatterley, in a modern guise.

Playboy, I conclude, is a bad influence on men[62]—hardly a surprising conclusion. I draw no legal implications from this judgment, but, as in the case of Hankinson, I think we should ponder this issue when we educate boys and young men, and meet the prevalence of that style of objectification with criticism—the most powerful form of which is, as Andrea Dworkin said, the assertion of one's own humanity at all times.

Hollinghurst is a case full of fascinating ambiguity. On its surface, this scene, like many in the novel, manifests the exuberant embrace of sexual fungibility that characterized parts of the male gay subculture in the pre-AIDS era. It seems like a very different sort of eroticizing of bodily parts from the sort that goes on in Hankinson and *Playboy,* more like Molly Bloom, in fact, in its delight in the size of organs, coupled with a cheerful nonexploitative attitude, albeit an emotionally superficial one, to the people behind the parts. Richard Mohr has written eloquently of this sort of promiscuous sexuality that it embodies a certain ideal of democracy, since couplings of the anonymous bathhouse sort neglect distinctions of class and rank. In a rather Whitmanesque burst of enthusiasm, he concludes that "Gay sexuality of the sort that I have been discussing both symbolizes and generates a kind of fundamental equality—the sort of fundamental equality that stands behind and is necessary for justifications of democracy."[63] The idea is that anonymous couplings establish that in an especially fundamental matter everyone really is equal to everyone else. Mohr makes it very clear that this can happen among men because they are already acknowledged socially as more than just bodies, because the social meaning of objectification among men is altogether different from its meaning between men and women. This being the case, promiscuous and anonymous sex can exemplify a norm of equality.

Mohr does seem to have gotten at something important about democracy, something about the moral role of the fungibility of bodies that is probably important in both the utilitarian and the Kantian liberal traditions. Certainly the fact that all citizens have similar bodies subject to similar accidents has played an important role in the thought of democratic theorists as diverse as Rousseau and Walt Whitman. Some such egalitarian idea animates Hollinghurst as well, at some moments. On the other hand, it is a little hard to know how the sexual scene at issue really is supposed to show the sort of equal regard for bodily need that underlies this democratic tradition. Notice how distinctions of class and rank are omnipresent, even in the prose that pushes them aside. The narrator is intensely conscious of racial differences, which he tends, here as elsewhere, to associate with stereotypes of genital organ size. Nor are the cycle-clips and duffel-coats that mark the lower-middle classes ever out of mind, even when they are out of sight—and the disdainful description of the small genitalia of the "smirking" neighbor strongly suggests the disdain of the "jacket and tie" for these signs of inferiority. We notice, in fact, that all the genitalia described are stereotypes, and none is personalized with the regard of Mellor for the "cunt of Lady Jane."

Now the question is, how is this connected with the emphasis on fungibility? Mohr would say, presumably, that there is no connection—that this narrator, an upper-class Englishman, has just not managed to enter fully enough into the democratic spirit of the bathhouse world. But the suspicion remains that there may after all be some connection between the spirit of fungibility and a focus on these superficial aspects of race and class and penis size, which do in a sense dehumanize, and turn people into potential instruments. For in the absence of any narrative history with the person, how can desire attend to anything else but the incidental, and how can one do more than use the body of the other as a tool of one's own states?[64] The photographs used by Mohr to illustrate his idea focus intently on hypermasculine characteristics of musculature and penis size, which presumably are not equally distributed among all citizens of this world, and indeed one imagines that the world so constructed is likely to be one in which morally irrelevant characteristics count for everything, rather than nothing, an extremely hierarchical world, rather than one without hierarchy. Maybe this just means that people are not after all treated as fungible, and that if they were to be more fully treated as fungible things would be well. But the worry is that in a setting which, in order to construct a kind of fungibility, denies all access to those features of personhood at the heart of the real democratic equality of persons, it is hard to see how things could turn out otherwise. This is not a knock-down argument showing that Mohr's Whitmanesque ideal is doomed to failure. The connection between fungibility and instrumentality is loose and causal, rather than conceptual. But it is a worry that would, I think, be shared by MacKinnon and Dworkin with Lorde and Lawrence: Can one really treat someone with the respect and concern that democracy requires if one has sex with him in the anonymous spirit of Hollinghurst's description?

We arrive, finally, at the end of *The Golden Bowl*. This is, to my mind, the most sinister passage on my list, if we focus on the conduct of the characters rather than the implied author, and the one that most clearly depicts a morally blameworthy instrumentalization of persons—though of course it is the business of the novel as a whole to question this behavior. Treating their respective spouses as fine antique furniture is, for Adam and Maggie, a way of denying them human status and asserting their right to the permanent use of those splendidly elegant bodies. This use involves denial of autonomy—Charlotte has to be sent off to the museum in America to be "buried," the Prince has to be turned into an elegant if flawed domestic object—and also denial of subjectivity. To appreciate them as antique furniture is to say, we don't have to ask ourselves whether they are in pain. We can just look at them and neglect the claims that they actively make. The *sposi* are rendered inert, morally and emotionally, and as in a sense, fungible—for from the outset Maggie has noted that to treat her husband as a work of art is to neglect his personal uniqueness.[65] In fact, we see every item on our list except physical violability—and emotional violation is amply attested.

The skeptical incursion of the narrator, with his "lingering view, a view more penetrating than the occasion demanded," points out that what we really see here is the "concrete attestatio[n]" of "a rare power of purchase."

This complicates our question—for it tells us that we should question the claim of Kant, Dworkin, and MacKinnon that the deformation of sexual desire is prior to, and causes, other forms of objectification of the sexual partner. It also seems possible that in many cases an antecedent deformation of attitudes to things and persons infiltrates and poisons desire.[67] I shall not be able to pursue this question further. I leave it on

This should tell us that the dehumanization and objectification of persons has many forms. It is not obvious that the "core" of such objectification is sexual, or that its primary vehicle is the specifically erotic education of men and women. Mill tells us that the entire education of men in his society teaches the lesson of domination and use; he does not put the blame at the door of the specifically sexual education. Here we are reminded that there can be morally sinister objectification without any particular connection to sex, or even to gender roles. Maggie and Adam learned their attitudes to persons by being rich collectors. Their attitude probably has consequences for sex, but it has its roots elsewhere, in an attitude to money and to other things that James associates with America. All things, in the rich American world, are regarded as having a price, as being essentially controllable and usable, if only one is wealthy enough. Nothing is an end in itself, because the only end is wealth.[66]

the table, in order to suggest the next chapter that would need to be written in any story of sexual objectification in our world.

To conclude, let me return to the seven forms of objectification and summarize the argument. It would appear that Kant, MacKinnon, and Dworkin are correct in one central insight: that the instrumental treatment of human beings, the treatment of human beings as tools of the purposes of another, is always morally problematic; if it does not take place in a larger context of regard for humanity, it is a central form of the morally objectionable. It is also a common feature of sexual life, especially, though not only, in connection with male treatment of women. As such, it is closely bound up with other forms of objectification, in particular with denial of autonomy, denial of subjectivity, and various forms of boundary-violation. In some forms, it is connected with fungibility and ownership or quasi-ownership: the notion of "commodification."

On the other hand, there seems to be no other item on the list that is always morally objectionable. Denial of autonomy and denial of subjectivity are objectionable if they persist throughout an adult relationship, but as phases in a relationship characterized by mutual regard they can be all right, or even quite wonderful in the way that Lawrence suggests. In a closely related way, it may at times be splendid to treat the other person as passive, or even inert. Emotional penetration of boundaries seems potentially a very valuable part of sexual life, and some forms of physical boundary-penetration also, though it is less clear which ones these are. Treating-as-fungible is suspect when the person so treated is from a group that has frequently been commodified and used as a tool, or a prize; between social equals these problems disappear, though it is not clear that others do not arise.

As for the aetiology of objectification, we have some reasons by now to doubt Kant's account, according to which the baneful form of use is inherent in sexual desire and activity themselves. We have some reason to endorse MacKinnon and Dworkin's account, according to which social hierarchy is at the root of the deformation of desire; but Lorde and Lawrence show us that the deformation is more complicated than this, working not only through pornography but also through puritanism and the repression of female erotic experience.[68] In that sense it may be plausible to claim, as Lawrence does, that a certain sort of objectifying attention to bodily parts is an important element in correcting the deformation and promoting genuine erotic equality. Finally, we should grant that we do not really know how central sexual desire is in all these problems of objectification and commodification, by comparison, for example, to economic norms and motives that powerfully construct desire in our culture.

There is no particular logical place to end what has been intended as an initial exploration of a concept whose full mapping will require many more investigations. So it may be fitting enough to end with the juxtaposition of two literary scenes involving what might well be called objectification. One is a vivid reminder, courtesy of James Hankinson, of what motivates the Kantian project of MacKinnon and Dworkin. The other is a passage in which Lawrence indicates the terms on which objectification, of a kind, can be a source of joy—mentioning a possibility that Kant, MacKinnon, and Dworkin, in different ways and for different reasons and with different degrees of firmness and universality, would appear to deny:

> She feels the sole of his foot on her waist, then waits for what seems like an eternity for him to bring the crop down onto her flesh, and when eventually the blow falls squarely across her buttocks and the pain courses through her, she feels a burning thrill of salvation as if the pain will cauterize her sins and make her whole again, and as Macrae bring the crop down on her again and again, she feels the sin falling from her, *agnus dei qui tollis peccata mundi,* and she finds in the mortifying a vision of the road to paradise lined with the grateful souls who have been saved from fire by fire, and she too is grateful to Macrae for beating her clean again.

> "But what do you believe in?" she insisted.
> "I believe in being warm hearted. I especially believe in being warm hearted in love, in fucking with a warm heart. . . ."
> She softly rubbed her cheek on his belly, and gathered his balls in her hand. . . .
> All the while he spoke he exquisitely stroked the rounded tail, till it seemed as if a slippery sort of fire came from it into his hands. . . .
> "An' if tha shits an' if tha pisses, I'm glad. I don't want a woman as couldna shit nor piss. . . ."
> With quiet fingers he threaded a few forget-me-not flowers in the fine brown fleece of the mount of Venus.[69]

Notes

1. Catharine MacKinnon, *Feminism Unmodified* (Cambridge, Mass.: Harvard University Press, 1987), p. 174.

2. See MacKinnon, *Feminism,* p. 262 n. 1. The Indianapolis ordinance struck down in *American Booksellers, Inc. v. Hudnut* (598 F. Supp. 1316 [S.D. Ind. 1984]) uses the related category: "women are presented as sexual objects for domination, conquest, violation, exploitation, possession, or use. . . ."

3. MacKinnon, *Toward a Feminist Theory of the State* (Cambridge, Mass.: Harvard University Press, 1989), p. 124.

4. Ibid.

5. Cass Sunstein, *The Partial Constitution* (Cambridge, Mass.: Harvard University Press, 1993), pp. 257–90; also "Neutrality in Constitutional Law (with Special Reference to Pornography, Abortion, and Surrogacy)," *Columbia Law Review* 92 (1992): 1–52.

6. *Defending Pornography: Free Speech, Sex, and the Fight for Women's Rights* (New York: Scribner, 1995).

7. Sunstein, review of Strossen, *The New Republic,* 9 January 1995.

8. Passages are taken from: D. H. Lawrence, *The Rainbow* (London: Penguin, 1989; first publication 1915), pp. 132–33; James Joyce, *Ulysses* (New York: Modern Library, 1961; first copyright 1914), p. 742; "Laurence St. Clair," *Isabelle and Véronique: Four Months, Four Cities* (New York: Blue Moon Books, Inc., 1989), pp. 2–4 (of 181 pages); Alan Hollinghurst, *The Swimming-Pool Library* (New York: Vintage, 1989; first published 1988), p. 20; Henry James, *The Golden Bowl* (New York: Penguin Books, 1985; first published 1904), p. 574.

9. On the artist's creative activity as an example of morally assessable conduct, see my discussion of Henry James in " 'Finally Aware and Richly Responsible': Literature and the Moral Imagination," in *Love's Knowledge* (New York: Oxford University Press, 1990).

10. See Booth, *The Company We Keep: An Ethics of Fiction* (Berkeley: University of California Press, 1988).

11. See Booth, *Company,* chap. 3. He uses Aristotle's account of friendship to ask about the ethical value of spending time in the company of texts of different sorts.

12. I want to emphasize that I speak only of the text, and make no claim about the motives and views of Hankinson himself, who may for all we know have had any number of different motives for writing in this genre. We should scrupulously observe Booth's distinction between the "implied author" and the "real-life author."

13. Each of these seven would ultimately need more refinement, in connection with debates about the proper analysis of the core notions. There are, for example, many theories of what autonomy and subjectivity are.

14. I put this in quotes because I am conscious that the word is not ideal; it is too anthropomorphic for things like ballpoint pens.

15. The same is true of "violability"—see n. 14 above—although if I had chosen a term such as "breakability" it would not be.

16. It is interesting to consider in this regard the legal doctrine of "moral rights" of the creators of artworks, which, in much of Europe and increasingly in the United States, protects creators against objectionable alterations in an artwork even after they have relinquished ownership. Technically speaking, these are rights of the artist, not of the artwork, and may be waived by the artist, though not, in a jointly produced work, by one artist without the consent of the others; but the resulting situation is one in which the work itself has, in effect, rights against being defaced or destroyed or in nonpermitted ways altered. For a good summary of the doctrine, see Martin A. Roeder, "The Doctrine of Moral Right: A Study in the Law of Artists, Authors and Creators," *Harvard Law Review* 53 (1940): 554–78; see also Peter H. Karlen, "Joint Ownership of Moral Rights," *Journal, Copyright Society of the U.S.A.* (1991): 242–75; for criticism of some recent U.S. state laws, see Thomas J. Davis, Jr., "Fine Art and Moral Rights: The Immoral Triumph of Emotionalism," *Hofstra Law Review* 17 (1989): 317 ff. I am grateful to William Landes for these references.

17. Richard D. Mohr, *Gay Ideas: Outing and Other Controversies* (Boston: Beacon Press, 1992), especially the essay " 'Knights, Young Men, Boys': Masculine Worlds and Democratic Values," pp. 129–218.

18. See Rubin, "Thinking Sex," in *The Lesbian and Gay Studies Reader,* ed. H. Abelove et al. (New York: Routledge, 1993); Mohr, " 'Knights, Young Men,'" cited above. See Scruton's *Sexual Desire: A Moral Philosophy of the Erotic* (New York: The Free Press, 1986).

19. In an interesting sense, the norm of unconditional love of children may lead love to disregard the particularizing qualities of the individual, and this may be seen as a good feature of parental love. See Gregory Vlastos, "The Individual as Object of Love in Plato," in *Platonic Studies* (Princeton: Princeton University Press, 1973).

20. For MacKinnon's account of the relation between this account and her feminist account of objectification, see *Feminist Theory,* p. 124; cf. also pp. 138–39. It is fairly clear from this discussion that the term "objectification" is intended by MacKinnon to correspond to Marx's language of "Versachlichung" or "Verdinglichung" in *Das Kapital,* and is closely connected with the notion of "Entaüsserung," closely linked by Marx to "Entfremdung," usually translated "alienation." MacKinnon explains Marx's argument that the "realization" of the self in private property is really a form of alienation of the self, and then says that in the case of property "alienation is the socially contingent distortion" of a process of realization, whereas in sexuality as currently realized, women's objectification just *is* alienation: ". . . from the point of view of the object, women have not authored objectifications, they have been them."

21. One might certainly wonder whether Marx has underestimated the distinction between the worker's situation, based on a contract in which there is at least some kind of consent, and the situation of the slave, which lacks any sort of consent. This tendency to equate relations that may be subtly distinct is closely related to MacKinnon and Dworkin's tendency to efface distinctions among different types of sexual relations.

22. *Feminism Unmodified* (Cambridge, Mass.: Harvard University Press, 1987), p. 48. See also *Feminist Theory,* pp. 124, 138–39. MacKinnon understands Marx to mean that the worker puts his selfhood into the "products and relationships" he creates, "becomes embodied in" these products. So read, Marx's idea is a version of Diotima's idea, in Plato's *Symposium,* that human beings seek to create items in which their identity may be extended and prolonged.

23. This is also the way in which I would regard the incentive of manumission as a reward for hard work: It is an incentive that is not exactly part of the institution, offered to the slave as human. Other incentives for hard work do not involve a recognition of autonomous agency and purpose.

24. Though, once again, we shall see that a certain sort of keen attention to subjective experience may be entailed by certain sorts of instrumental use of persons.

25. I owe this example to Lawrence Lessig.

26. One way of cashing this out further would be to ask to what extent my use of him as a pillow prevented him from either attaining or acting on important capacities with which he identifies his well-being. Am I preventing him from getting up to eat? From sleeping? From walking around? From reading a book? And so forth.

27. "Could It Be Worth Thinking About Kant on Sex and Marriage?" in Louise Antony and Charlotte Witt, eds., *A Mind of One's Own: Feminist Essays on Reason and Objectivity* (Boulder: Westview, 1993), pp. 49–67.

28. See *Lectures on Ethics*, esp. the following passage, quoted by Herman, p. 55: "Taken by itself [sexual love] is a degradation of human nature; for as soon as a person becomes an Object of appetite for another, all motives of moral relationship cease to function, because as an Object of appetite for another a person becomes a thing and can be treated and used as such by every one."

29. See *Intercourse* (New York: Free Press, 1987), pp.122–23: "There is a deep recognition in culture and in experience that intercourse is both the normal use of a woman, her human potentiality affirmed by it, and a violative abuse, her privacy irredeemably compromised, her selfhood changed in a way that is irrevocable, unrecoverable. . . . By definition, she [has] a lesser privacy, a lesser integrity of the body, a lesser sense of self, since her body can be physically occupied and in the occupation taken over."

30. Thus sex for Kant is not like a contractual relation in which one can use the other person as a means in an overall context of mutual respect: For sexual desire, according to his analysis, drives out every possibility of respect. This is so even in marriage (see below), although there the legal context ensures that at least in other parts of the relationship respect will be present.

31. See, for a very Kantian example, Dworkin's *Intercourse*, pp. 140–41: "It is especially in the acceptance of the object status that her humanity is hurt: it is . . . an implicit acceptance of less freedom, less privacy, less integrity. In becoming an object so that he can objectify her so that he can fuck her, she begins a political collaboration with his dominance; and then when he enters her, he confirms for himself and for her what she is: that she is something, not someone; certainly not someone equal."

32. Pp. 47–61.

33. See, for example, MacKinnon, *Feminist Theory*, p. 124: "Women have been the nature, the matter, the acted upon to be subdued by the acting subject seeking to embody himself in the social world"; and p. 198: "The acting that women are allowed is asking to be acted upon."

34. Both fungibility and ownership, for example, are implicit in MacKinnon's description of males as "consumers" and "women as things for sexual use" (ibid., pp. 138–39).

35. See the convincing discussion of MacKinnon's ideas in Sally Haslanger, "On Being Objective and Being Objectified," in *A Mind of One's Own*, pp. 85–125, esp. p. 111, where she argues that instrumentality is at the heart of MacKinnon's concept of objectification.

36. See Herman's excellent discussion, pp. 62–63: "The rules are not so much to restrain or oblige action as to construct moral regard. That is, they make the sexual interest in another person possible only where there is secure moral regard for that person's life, and they do this by making the acceptance of obligations with respect to that person's welfare a condition of sexual activity."

37. Compare MacKinnon, *Feminist Theory*, pp. 138–39: ". . . objectification itself, with self-determination ecstatically relinquished, is the apparent content of women's sexual desire and desirability."

38. Andrea Dworkin, *Woman Hating* (New York: E. P. Dutton, 1974), pp. 58, 62.

39. Dworkin points to the prevalence of anal penetration in the novel as evidence that O is a surrogate for René.

40. See, for example, MacKinnon, *Feminist Theory*, p. 202, objecting that the "as a whole" test legitimates publications such as *Playboy:* ". . . legitimate settings diminish the injury perceived to be done to the women whose trivialization and objectification it contextualizes. Besides, if a women is subjected, why should it matter that the work has other value? Perhaps what redeems a work's value among men enhances its injury to women."

41. In the particular case, this does not seem to be connected with a willingness to be broken or smashed, but one should see, I think, a close link between this sort of boundary-surrender and the boundary-surrender involved in at least some sadomasochistic relationships.

42. I mean here to say that a working-class man in England of that time is roughly comparable in social power to an upper-class woman. As for Brangwen and his wife, her higher-class origins and her property give her a rough parity with him.

43. This point is only slightly weakened by the fact that "John Thomas" is a traditional name for the penis, and is not original with Mellors. The entire exchange has a very personal character, and it is at any rate clear that this is the first time that Constance has heard the name, and that for her it is a fully proper name. The fact that the genital organ is given a personal proper name, and yet a name distinct from the name of the rest of Mellor is itself complexly related to my earlier point about loss of individuality: For it alludes to the fact that in allowing this part to take over, one does cease to be oneself.

What should one make of the fact that Constance's cunt is not given a proper name, but is simply called "the cunt of Lady Jane," with a joking allusion to the tension between sex and class? One could, of course, argue that Mellors is treating her genitals less personally than he treats his own; but then I think it would be a jarring note in the scene if he did simply invent a name for her cunt—presumably that is a game in which she ought to play a role, and she is too frightened at this point to play that game.

44. I think that this position is subtly different from the position developed in Scruton's *Sexual Desire*. Scruton holds that in a good sexual encounter the individual people encounter one another in one another's bodies, because they allow their respective bodies to be illuminated by their own personalities—"the body of the other becomes the other self, and is illuminated in the moment of arousal by the 'I' " (Scruton, letter of 1 April 1995). I feel that in Scruton's attitude to the body there is always a sense that just as it is, it is not a part of our personhood—it needs to be transfigured, and in a sense redeemed from mere animality, by a momentary and mysterious "illumination." The view I share with Lawrence holds, instead, that it was always, just as it is, a part of personhood, and doesn't need to be transfigured, or rather, that the only transfiguration it needs is shame-free attention and love. The difference comes out clearly in our respective attitudes to the bodies of animals—on which see my review of *Sexual Desire* in *The New York Review of Books*, December 18, 1986.

45. Audre Lorde, "The Uses of the Erotic," in *Sister Outsider* (Freedom, Calif.: Crossing Press, 1984), pp. 53–59.

46. See also Lorde, ibid., p. 54: "The erotic . . . has been made into the confused, the trivial . . . the plasticized sensation."

47. Ibid., p. 57: "For once we begin to feel deeply all the aspects of our lives,

we begin to demand from ourselves and from our life-pursuits that they feel in accordance with that joy which we know ourselves to be capable of."

48. In that sense, the proposal is in the spirit of the attitude to sexuality expressed in the writings of the late John J. Winkler, especially *The Constraints of Desire: The Anthropology of Sex and Gender in Greece* (New York: Routledge, 1990).

49. See my discussion in "The Transfiguration of Everyday Life," *Metaphilosophy* 25 (1994): 238–61.

50. "Jenny," in Pat Califia, *Macho Sluts: Lesbian Erotic Fiction* (Boston: Alyson, 1984). See also Roger Scruton, *Sexual Desire.*

51. Things are made more complex by the fact that the two Hankinson *characters* are in a sense quite Lawrentian—it is the implied author, not Macrae, who seems to be proceeding in bad faith, ascribing to the woman a subjectivity desirous of pain and humiliation. Why, then, do I move so quickly in the Hankinson case to a critique of the construction of the fiction as a whole, given that both cases are apparently equally fictional? The answer lies in the formulaic character of the Hankinson text, which invites us to see the characters as mere pretexts for the implied author's expression of a view about women's sexuality. It seems pointless to discuss their conduct independently of a discussion of the genre, and the author's participation in it.

52. Mill, *The Subjection of Women,* ed. Susan Okin (Indianapolis: Hackett, 1988), pp. 86–87: "Think what it is to a boy, to grow up to manhood in the belief that without any merit or any exertion of his own, though he may be the most frivolous and empty or the most ignorant and stolid of mankind, by the mere fact of being born a male he is by right the superior of all and every one of an entire half of the human race: including probably some whose real superiority to himself he has daily or hourly occasion to feel. . . . Is it imagined that all this does not pervert the whole manner of existence of the man, both as an individual and as a social being?"

53. For MacKinnon's accounts of this, see refs. in *Feminism Unmodified* and *Only Words.* See also Joshua Cohen, "Freedom, Equality, Pornography," in *Justice and Injustice in Legal Theory,* ed. Austin Sarat and Thomas Kearns (Ann Arbor: University of Michigan Press, 1996). Compare Mill's account of the way in which domination is "inoculated by one schoolboy upon another" (*Subjection,* ibid.), though with no explicit reference to specifically erotic education.

54. One might complain about the possible bad influence of the unrepresentative portrayal of women even in a narrative that contextualized the portrayal in a way inviting criticism or distancing; thus it is not obviously mistaken of MacKinnon and Dworkin to reject appeal to context in defense of objectionable passages. But their ideas about the construction of desire take on more power when the work as a whole encourages the belief that this is the way all male-female relations are, or can be. This point about the unrepresentative portrayal of women is logically independent of and has implications beyond the objectification issue: For one could, similarly, object to a work that, without objectifying women in any of the senses discussed here, portrayed all its female characters as stupid, or greedy, or unreliable.

55. My reasons are those given by Joshua Cohen in "Freedom, Equality, Pornography," presented at an APA Central Division session along with the present article, and forthcoming in *Justice and Injustice in Legal Theory,* ed. Sarat and Kearns.

56. It is an interesting question to what extent a critical context of reading can impede the formation of the patterns of desire constructed by the work as it addresses its implied reader. The ancient Greek Stoics, unlike Plato, wanted to keep tragic poetry around as a source of moral warning about the pain that would ensue from the overestimation of the "goods of fortune"—as Epictetus defined tragedy, "What happens when chance events befall fools." Rejecting Plato's banishment of the poets, they thought they could domesticate them by moral critique. Were they right? See Nussbaum, "Poetry and the Passions: Two Stoic Views," in J. Brunschwig and M. Nussbaum, eds., *Passions & Perceptions* (Cambridge: Cambridge University Press, 1993), pp. 97–149.

57. See the very good discussion in Alison Assiter, "Autonomy and Pornography," in *Feminist Perspectives in Philosophy*, ed. Morwenna Griffiths and Margaret Whitford (London: Macmillan, 1988), pp. 58–71, who argues that the person who frequently experiences satisfaction in connection with such limited relationships is less likely to seek out less distorting, more complicated relationships. Assiter's article contains a valuable parallel to Hegel's Master-Slave dialectic.

58. Lorde, "Uses of the Erotic," p. 54: "But pornography is a direct denial of the power of the erotic, for it represents the suppression of true feeling. Pornography emphasizes sensation without feeling."

59. See Assiter, "Autonomy and Pornography," pp. 66–69. One may accept this criticism of *Playboy* even if one is not convinced that its portrayal of women is sufficiently depersonalizing to count as objectification.

60. See Homer, *Iliad* IX.121–30; this is the offer Agamemnon makes to assuage the anger of Achilles.

61. The essence of the controversy was over the ethical question whether women should allow themselves to be hired as models, given that they would be cast in the role of representing Brown women generally, and given that Brown women generally didn't want to be represented in that way. Issues were also raised about whether the student newspaper should have run an ad for the recruitment, given that campus sentiment was against it; and students sponsored a forum to discuss the more general ethical and legal issues involved. Since the actual recruitment took place off campus, there was nothing else to say, and in fact Brown produced the largest number of applicant models of any Ivy League campus.

62. I am thinking of bad influence in Wayne Booth's way (*The Company We Keep*, see above), as a bad way of spending one's time thinking and desiring during the time one is reading. I make no claims in this article about causal connections between those times and other times, though I do find convincing Assiter's claim that the habit of having pleasure in connection with fantasies of this type is likely to lead one to seek out such undemanding relationships in life, rather than those involving a fuller recognition of women's subjectivity and autonomy.

63. *Gay Ideas*, p. 196.

64. I think that this is the point made by Roger Scruton in *Sexual Desire*, when he holds that a context of intimacy and mutual regard promote the sexual attention to individuality.

65. See Chap. I, Pt. i (Maggie to the Prince): "You're a rarity, an object of

beauty, an object of price. You're not perhaps absolutely unique, but you're so curious and eminent that there are very few others like you. . . . You're what they call a *morceau de musée*."

66. See the impressive Marxist reading of the novel in Ed Ahearn, *Marx and Modern Fiction* (New Haven: Yale University Press, 1989), pp. 76–99.

67. See Ahearn, *Marx,* p. 99: ". . . the celebration of the aesthetic and the misuse of persons, two forms of acquisition, are rooted in that original accumulation, the money of the amiable Adam Verver."

68. This double aetiology is suggested in some parts of Dworkin's *Intercourse,* especially "Dust/Dirt"; and in the episode in *Mercy* in which the Greek lover of Andrea abuses her after discovering that she has been having sex with other men.

69. I am grateful to many people for comments that have helped me revise the article, among them: Mary Becker, Joshua Cohen, Richard Craswell, David Estlund, Robert Goodin, John Hodges, Robert Kaster, William Landes, Lawrence Lessig, Charles Nussbaum, Rachel Nussbaum, Richard Posner, Roger Scruton, Cass Sunstein, Candace Vogler. Above all, I am grateful to the students in my Feminist Philosophy class at Brown University, who discussed the article with relentless critical scrutiny, and especially to: Kristi Abrams, Lara Bovilsky, Hayley Finn, Sarah Hirshman, James Maisels, Gabriel Roth, Danya Ruttenberg, Sarah Ruhl, and Dov Weinstein.

Chapter 27

PORNOGRAPHY AND THE
SOCIAL SCIENCES

Alan Soble

Augustine Brannigan and Sheldon Goldenberg have written a provocative essay about social scientific attempts to establish a connection between exposure to pornography and actions and attitudes harmful to women. Regarding laboratory experiments designed to demonstrate aggressive behavior after exposure to pornography, they argue that these laboratory results cannot be extrapolated to real life because the aggression found in laboratory experiments is neither the kind nor the amount of aggression that threaten women in real life, and because it should not be assumed that the responsiveness of laboratory subjects to pornography is the same as the responsiveness of ordinary consumers. Brannigan and Goldenberg offer similar arguments intended to undermine the significance of laboratory studies of the influence of pornography on attitudes. I will argue that these objections are not as powerful as Brannigan and Goldenberg make them out to be.

While demolishing, to their own satisfaction, some of the evidence

Reprinted with permission from *Social Epistemology* 2, no. 2 (1988): 135–44. This paper is a commentary on Augustine Brannigan and Sheldon Goldenberg, "Social Science Versus Jurisprudence in Wagner: the Study of Pornography, Harm, and the Law of Obscenity in Canada," *Social Epistemology* 2, no. 2 (1988), 107–16. Unless otherwise indicated, all quoted material is from this article. (See also their response, "Neither All the King's Horses Nor All the King's Men," *Social Epistemology* 3, no. 1 [1989]: 54–69.) I gratefully acknowledge the financial support of the National Endowment for the Humanities during the summer of 1985 and the conscientious typing of Jeannie Shapley.

suggesting that pornography contributes to violence against women, Brannigan and Goldenberg impugn the intellectual honesty not only of jurists who rely uncritically on the results of behavioral research, but also of the social scientists who provide those results. The conclusion that pornography contributes to harms against women is, according to Brannigan and Goldenberg, 'contrived'; it is arrived at by a selective and misleading interpretation of the data. Further, the experimental designs employed by some social scientists already assume to be true that which is supposed to be tested or discovered. Brannigan and Goldenberg claim that 'the current ideological opposition to pornography has come to dominant the interpretation of the . . . research in this area', and they call for a 'formal and impartial scientific reexamination' of the whole field of pornography research. I fear, however, that the demand for a 'formal and impartial scientific' assessment of the evidence is a demand that social science be value free, in which case the demand incorporates a naive view of the epistemological foundations of the social sciences.

1. The Causal Status of Pornography

I spent most of the summer of 1985 in Atlanta, Georgia, a city I was visiting for the first time. Since I had recently finished writing a book on pornography,[1] naturally I was curious about the state of porn in Atlanta, wondering how this blossoming Sun Belt metropolis compared with New York, Los Angeles, and other US porn centers. Walking through the downtown area, I found no adult book stores, and there were none listed in the Yellow Pages. I wandered into no hard-core porn movie theaters. Eventually, I came across maybe *six* stores in the entire city that stocked *Playboy, Penthouse,* and of course, *Players.* But I didn't see any sexually explicit material, *Hustler,* or SM/BD pornography. Why? In the early 1980s (a couple of lawyers told me) a zealous Baptist district attorney ran the porn business out of town. That was surprising enough. What was more surprising was the mid-summer announcement, in the local newspaper, that in 1984 Atlanta ranked #1 among cities in the country for rapes *per capita.*[2] Furthermore, Atlanta was #1 in rape both in 1980, when porn could still be found in the city, and in 1984, when there was no porn. And I thought it noteworthy that neither New York (#34) nor Los Angeles made it into the top 15 rape cities; and that Kansas City and Dallas did—hardly the porn connoisseur's choice for a place to go shopping.

I was surprised by this news because Robin Morgan's thesis that 'pornography is the theory, rape is the practice',[3] or, less flamboyantly, that the consumption of pornography by men increases their willingness to rape women, or that the use of pornography aggravates sexual hostility and aggression, seemed to be falsified by the Atlanta 'experiment'. But not exactly. *If* 'porn is the theory, rape is the practice' means that the consumption of pornography is *sufficient* for the occurrence of rape, then what I discovered in Atlanta is logically-speaking irrelevant. To refute the thesis understood in this sense, one should look for a city (or ten?) that has lots of porn but no rape. The Atlanta 'experiment', in which there is no porn but lots of rape, shows only that the presence of porn is *not necessary* for the occurrence of rape. Who, however, would have asserted otherwise? No one.[4] Recall that Brannigan and Goldenberg make heavy weather over the fact that in laboratory settings, at least, a movie of an eye operation, or even noise, has much the same effect on aggression as exposure to pornography. This observation is defused of its rhetorical punch when we acknowledge that no one ever claimed that pornography was *necessary* for rape.[5] Brannigan and Goldenberg argue that *if* the laboratory results are taken at face-value, and we want to reduce the frequency of rape, than we should be prepared to censor noise and surgical films. This conclusion is not the *reductio ad absurdum* that Brannigan and Goldenberg believe it to be. First, it is not obviously true that the right to make or be bombarded by noise overrides the right of women to be safe in their persons. Second, we could censor pornography but not noise on the grounds that in the attempt to reduce the frequency of rape we should focus on the more easily eliminable causal factors.

The claim that exposure to pornography is sufficient for the occurrence of rape is as false as the claim that it is necessary; no one asserts it, and that is not the intended meaning of Morgan's thesis or its variants. The fact that a man can buy some pornography, take it home, look at it, masturbate with it, and then go right to sleep and not commit a rape, shows that the most we could assert is that *given* the presence of factors *A, B,* and *C,* and/or the absence of factors *D, E,* and *F,* the additional factor of exposure to pornography will lead to rape or sexual aggression; i.e., that pornography may be sufficient 'relative' to other fixed factors. The failure to recognize that if pornography is a cause of rape or sexual aggression at all, it is a causal factor that operates only in the context of other factors, yields careless and avoidable errors in reasoning about the connection between pornography and sexual aggression. For example, imagine someone arguing that (1) lots of women buy or rent, and masturbate while watching, pornographic video tapes, (2) these women do not rape men (or other women), and *therefore,* (3) the consumption of pornography by men cannot be a factor leading *them* to commit rape. The argument is weak because there may be other social or psychological factors operating on men and not on women (and/or operating on women and not on men) which, when interacting with exposure to pornography, do lead to sexual aggression by men.

Similarly, the fact that women who go to bars in order to watch men dance in the nude, find the exhibition amusing and are not caused to become sexually aggressive, does not mean that men who go to bars in order to watch women dance in the nude are not encouraged to express sexual aggression.

This point is elementary, and Brannigan and Goldenberg implicitly recognize it when they say that the aggression found in laboratory studies 'is always an *interaction* effect and is *not* solely attributable to the film'. Yet Brannigan and Goldenberg ignore their own good advice and trade on exactly this sort of fallacy when presenting one of their major criticisms of behavioral research on pornography. They write:

> The metatheory has also been invoked to confine the design to studies of male-female aggression. In certain early experiments male aggression towards male . . . targets was higher than against female targets. Also, Zillman . . . found that aggression enhancement increased intra-female aggression. Does this mean that erotica causes men to bugger or assault other men? and women to rape other women? Since the metatheory presupposes that the lab aggression is a proxy for sexual aggression, male targets and female subjects are dropped from later studies, obviating such paradoxical extrapolations.[6]

The argument, it seems to me, is this. Some experimenters found that exposure to pornography in laboratory studies increased aggression in males against other males and in females against other females. But these facts are ignored by the experimenters, and later experimental designs do not involve tests for these effects, because for the experiments to acknowledge their existence is to admit that the laboratory studies of the influence of pornography on males cannot be employed to support the claim that in real life the consumption of pornography by males contributes to their sexual aggression. If the laboratory studies do show that in real life pornography leads men to be sexually aggressive toward women, then the laboratory studies also show that in real life pornography induces men to aggress sexually against men and encourages women to sexually assault women. (Call this conditional 'Q'.) But the experimenters do not want to draw that conclusion; after all, it is false that women aggress sexually against other women, and the conclusion is inconsistent with the experimenters' ideological opposition to pornography. Hence, to protect their ideological commitments, the experimenters conveniently forget the embarrassing facts they themselves discovered. Brannigan and Goldenberg are wrong to assume, however, that the conditional Q is true; at least, they have given us no reason to think it is true. In real life there may very well be other causal factors present (or absent), in addition to exposure to pornography, that permit pornography to induce male-female sexual aggression but put a clamp on some forms of male-male and female-

female aggression. Clearly, Brannigan and Goldenberg want to argue that because the female-female aggression in response to pornography in the laboratory cannot be extrapolated to the real world, neither can the male-female aggression. But this claim commits a version of the fallacy described above.

Brannigan and Goldenberg might object here that they assert only that *the experimenters* in question believe the conditional *Q*. Because the experimenters hold *Q*, *they* have reason to exclude female-female studies from later designs; the experimenters, not Brannigan and Goldenberg, commit the fallacy. I think, to the contrary, that Brannigan and Goldenberg themselves assert *Q*. The tone and wording of the quoted passage (and of the passage in my note 6) support this view. Indeed, the experimenters criticized by Brannigan and Goldenberg might have *rejected Q*; their doing so even suggests a quite different and not dishonest reason for their excluding female-female studies from later experimental designs: laboratory studies of female sexual responsivity and aggressiveness are less extrapolatable to real life than studies of males, because women in our society fall under a myriad of social and sexual regulations and prohibitions that men escape. Of course, the claims that women fall under more social regulations than men, and that these regulations operate on women in real life but do not reach into the laboratory setting, may be false. (There may be regulations on the aggressiveness of men that operate in real life and do not reach into the laboratory, or are suspended in that context.) But if believing that laboratory studies of male-female aggression can be more easily extrapolated to real life than studies of female-female aggression is the reason the experimenters dropped female-female studies, the experimenters are hardly the ideological villains Brannigan and Goldenberg make them out to be. Furthermore, Brannigan and Goldenberg and the experimenters they criticize now have something tangible to debate, viz. the truth of *Q* and its grounds; it is no longer convincing for Brannigan and Goldenberg to rely on the mere charge that the experimenters are dishonest.

In light of the fact that Morgan's thesis is not intended to mean that exposure to pornography is literally sufficient for the occurrence of rape, the Atlanta 'experiment' is, after all, logically relevant. The thesis urges the legal censorship of pornography, or some other technique for reducing its availability, *in order to* lower the frequency of rape, on the grounds that *given* other social and psychological factors the consumption of pornography contributes to rape. Understood in this way, the thesis implies that if the other factors are held constant, the frequency of rape will within limits vary directly with the availability or consumption of pornography. The thesis, then, is *prima facie* refuted by both the Danish 'experiment', in which an increase in the availability of pornography has not been matched by any increase in rape, and by the Atlanta 'experiment', in which a decrease in the availability of pornography has not been matched by a drop in the frequency of rape.

Why do I say 'prima facie' refuted? If Denmark and Atlanta are the only geographical areas in which the direct variation of rape with pornography fails, then these 'experiments' tell us nothing valuable about the pornography-rape connection. Finding one bona fide blade of grass that is blue surely proves that 'all blades of grass are green' is false. But because Morgan's thesis is that when *A, B,* and *C* are present and/or *D, E,* and *F* are absent, the frequency of rape follows the availability of pornography, a handful of counterexamples carries little weight. If the thesis is therefore difficult to refute, beyond a reasonable doubt, it is just as difficult to confirm. Even if we discovered a perfect correlation between the availability of pornography and the frequency of rape, *that* would hardly be enough evidence to allow us to conclude, beyond a reasonable doubt, that pornography was a causal factor in rape. As has been mentioned by many people already, a macroscopic correlation between the availability of pornography and the occurrence of rape, if one exists, is explainable by invoking a third phenomenon that independently causes both, in which case eliminating pornography will have no effect, contrary to the intention of Morgan's thesis, on the frequency of rape. The most obvious candidate for this phenomenon is 'the culture of male dominance' which simultaneously causes or allows a society to have pornography and encourages men to commit rape.[7] Even here we need to be careful: we must have a way of defining 'culture of male dominance' independently of the facts that such a society contains pornography and tolerates or encourages rape, otherwise the explanation will be circular. But 'exhibits a high frequency of rape' is one of the primary characteristics defining 'culture of male dominance'.

There are, of course, other problems. In Atlanta, I said, the availability of pornography declined between 1980 and 1984 while the frequency of rape remained high. But did the availability of pornography *really* decline? Should we count *Playboy, Penthouse,* and *Players* as genuinely pornographic, as a large bulk of that category? (*This* question explains why I wrote, above, that the blue specimen was a bona fide blade of grass.) Pornography, then, might not have declined much between 1980 and 1984. Is that *enough* pornography to account for the continuing rate of rape? Is it sexually explicit enough, or violent enough, to contribute to rape? Or perhaps all the hard-core pornography bought through 1980 was still in the possession of its Atlanta owners (or traded) and still at work in 1984. Or perhaps pornography was still available to Atlantans who went on shopping trips to South Carolina or Birmingham, or who ordered it through the mail from California. Or perhaps the effects of the pornography that existed before and during 1980 in Atlanta were persisting into 1984. Do totally nude female dancers count as a kind of pornographic genre? If so, Atlanta is hardly porn-free. It has no live or video peep-shows, but there are a half-dozen bars in center city, and several others in the outer regions, that offer nude entertainment. How many privately owned VCRs are there in Atlanta, and how many imported pornographic video tapes? Is this *enough* pornography to sustain the claim that Atlanta is *not* porn-free and the thesis that rape there is connected with the consumption of pornography?

Some of these questions are empirical, others are conceptual. All these questions must be answered before the Atlanta 'experiment' can be employed in the assessment of Morgan's thesis. Our question now is, Can the social sciences answer *these* questions? Can the social sciences confirm *or* refute, beyond a reasonable doubt, the thesis that the consumption of pornography is a significant causal factor in sexual aggression? Can the social sciences accurately fill in the *A, B, C, D, E,* and *F* of Morgan's thesis? Or demonstrate that there is nothing to fill in, or no point in doing so? One common answer goes like this: the social sciences, given the hard work, the cleverness, the patience, and the objectivity of its investigators, plus some good luck, can surely answer the empirical questions. In the process of testing hypotheses and interpreting the evidence, however, the investigators must make sure that their own values (including their ideological viewpoints, their political leanings, etc.) do not play any role, for that would prevent, as much as laziness would prevent, the social sciences from arriving at justified (or 'valid') empirical conclusions. Regarding the conceptual questions, operational definitions of some concepts are possible and partially solve the problem. Or perhaps in some cases it is especially obvious how a concept should be defined. At the very least, values should be excluded also from definitions; and as long as experimenters are up-front about their conceptual assumptions, their empirical claims can be objectively assessed. (*This* is what I'm going to count as grass; given that definition, here are the empirical facts.)

Brannigan and Goldenberg complain that the experimenters' ideological opposition to pornography has adversely affected not only the conclusions drawn when the experimenters interpret the data, but also the experimental designs employed to test hypotheses. Such research, then, is hardly trustworthy.[8] Brannigan and Goldenberg call for a 'formal and impartial scientific' assessment of the pornography-sexual aggression research. Both their complaint and their recommendation imply that Brannigan and Goldenberg presuppose the general picture of proper procedure in the social sciences that I have just outlined. Further evidence is provided by Brannigan's apparent espousal of the standard fact-value distinction:

> Public inquiries into obscenity tend to oscillate . . . between what is demo-
> cratic and political versus what is rational and scientific. Democratic forums
> sample public opinion and popular morality regarding sexual fiction and
> entertainment. Rationalist forums are preoccupied with the effects of
> pornography measured scientifically.[9]

The implication is that the democratic forum, and morality or values in
general, should not be permitted to interfere with the rational assessment of the scientific evidence or to play any other epistemological role
in the social sciences. On the question of how social scientists should approach conceptual matters, Brannigan and Goldenberg are less explicit.
Let's examine their handling of conceptual issues; doing so will illustrate
the logical fact that social science, contrary to the standard picture, cannot be the value-free enterprise Brannigan and Goldenberg want it to be.

2. Conceptual Analysis and Value Judgments

One of Brannigan and Goldenberg's major criticisms of the research investigating the effects of pornography on sexual aggression focuses on
an experimental design which, they argue, tells us nothing about real
life. Male subjects who are angered by a female confederate, and who are
then exposed to pornography, retaliate against the same confederate by
administering shocks in a bogus learning experiment. The problems
with using the fact, that previously angered males administer shocks to
females after being exposed to pornography, to defend Morgan's thesis
or its variants, are legion. The male subjects in the laboratory are not exposed to pornography in the way in which pornography is consumed in
real life by voluntary or confirmed users. Delivering electrical shocks to
a female in a learning experiment is a far cry from real life sexual aggression. The shocks are administered to exactly that person who had
earlier deliberately provoked the male subject. And so on. Of course the
experimenters bear the burden of proof; they must give us good reasons
for accepting the proposition that laboratory aggression is a reliable
proxy for real life sexual aggression. (Just as the biologist must not simply assume, but give us good reasons for thinking, that an *in vitro* nerve
preparation appreciably replicates the normal, intact functioning of the
tissue.) Perhaps the most that the experimenters are entitled to conclude is that if a man is unjustly provoked and angered by a woman, after which event he takes a brief look at some pornography, he will
punish that same woman for having angered him. If so, we are left wondering whether we have learned anything at all about the influence of
pornography on rape, sexual assault, wife-beating, and other aggressions
carried out against women.

But granting the victory to Brannigan and Goldenberg is premature. It seems quite perverse for them to complain that laboratory aggression in the form of the administration of electrical shocks in a bogus learning experiment cannot be considered a proxy for sexual aggression in real life. After all, for the experimenters to have given angered males the opportunity in the laboratory to carry out a real-life type of *sexual* aggression against the confederate female, would have been morally and pragmatically preposterous. When attempting to discover whether exposure to pornography contributes to the occurrence of sexual aggression against women, *some* nonsexual aggression or another must be studied in the laboratory. Surely Brannigan and Goldenberg are not about to assert that because laboratory studies are for moral or pragmatic reasons restricted to measuring nonsexual aggression, experimenters will *never* have a reliable proxy for real-life sexual aggression. To assert *that* would be to assert that social psychology is absolutely powerless to investigate Morgan's thesis, and would be to deny that a 'formal and impartial scientific' examination will eventually answer 'yes' *or* 'no' to the question of a pornography-sexual aggression link in real life.

There is a huge difference, or course, between the answers 'no' and 'not yet proven' (or, in the words of Brannigan and Goldenberg, 'far from well established') to the question 'Does exposure to pornography contribute to harms done to women?' The latter answer is compatible with 'maybe' and even with an eventual 'yes'. I just argued that Brannigan and Goldenberg believe that a 'no' answer can, in principle, be given eventually by social science; they have not criticized social science *per se* (they apparently think Milgram's social psychology has merit), but only the way it is carried out by some researchers. I suspect there is another reason Brannigan and Goldenberg must insist that a 'no' answer is eventually achievable. In order to claim persuasively that anti-pornography legislation is unnecessary, the answer 'no' is much more effective than 'not yet proven'. Because rape is one of the most horrible crimes, legislatures—without embarrassment, without having to apologize, and without violating Constitutional provisions (in the US, at least)—may assume that there is just enough evidence for a pornography-sexual aggression link (even though the thesis is 'not yet proven') and place the burden of proof on those who deny that exposure to pornography contributes to harms done to women. (Further, to assert that social science is *incapable* of answering the question is to give legislatures *carte blanche*.) To defend their own legislative goals, then, Brannigan and Goldenberg must suppose that a 'no' answer is achievable. But a 'no' answer presupposes that there *is* some laboratory nonsexual aggression that is a reliable proxy for real-life sexual aggression, and that experiments utilizing this measure will find no effect of exposure to pornography.

Regardless of exactly why Brannigan and Goldenberg believe that a 'no' answer is possible, a major weakness of their paper is that while criticizing other experimenters for not utilizing a reliable proxy, they are totally silent on the crucial question of what that proxy would be. To claim, as Brannigan and Goldenberg do, that the administration of electrical shocks during a bogus learning experiment is either not *at all* a proxy for sexual aggression in real life, or is an *inadequate* proxy, is to make a conceptual claim: that some types of laboratory aggression are *not similar enough* to real-life sexual aggression. But to assert this is to assert, implicitly, that one has *some* idea of what kind of laboratory aggression would be similar enough to real-life sexual aggression to count as a proxy. Yet, having entered the arena of conceptual dispute, Brannigan and Goldenberg's failure to propose a reliable proxy abandons the conceptual issue, rather than resolves it.

Note that Brannigan and Goldenberg also do not explain in any great detail *why* the administration of electrical shocks in bogus learning experiments is not an adequate proxy for real-life sexual aggression. Why are the studies defective, or why is pornography off the hook, if pornography only encourages men in real life to aggress against women in ways that are roughly similar in type to administering electrical shocks in a bogus learning experiment?—e.g., by being especially tough on women during driving examinations, or by grading their school examinations too critically, or even by passing a negative judgment on women's submissions to professional journals. After all, some of the experimenters criticized by Brannigan and Goldenberg claim that it is the *violence* in violent pornography, and not the pornographic dimension *per se*, that contributes to real-life aggression; if so, the laboratory aggression measured may be a quite adequate proxy.[10] Part of the problem is that Brannigan and Goldenberg understand the concept 'sexual aggression' rather narrowly, in terms of aggression carried out with and/or on sexual and quasi-sexual organs or in the process of a sexual act. But 'sexual aggression' can be conceived less narrowly as aggression carried out by a member of one sex (e.g., males) against a member of the other sex (e.g., females) *in virtue of* the fact that the object of aggression is a member of the other sex. Aggression motivated at least in part by the sexual difference is a kind of sexual aggression even if it does not include or is not constituted by a sexual act. Morgan, I take it, would be quite happy to have her thesis tested by employing this conception of sexual aggression. Brannigan and Goldenberg never tell us why their implicit notion of sexual aggression is the *right* one or *superior* to a broader definition. That perhaps Donnerstein *et al.* mean exactly what Brannigan and Goldenberg mean by 'sexual aggression' is irrelevant. If, unbeknownst to them, the broader notion of 'sexual aggression' helps Donnerstein *et al.* by making it more likely that their laboratory aggression is a decent proxy for real-life sexual aggression, that fact could be acknowledged by

Brannigan and Goldenberg in the interest of an 'impartial' assessment of the evidence.

As a result of overlooking the broader conception of sexual aggression, Brannigan and Goldenberg have also overlooked that there *are* real-life scenarios which are similar enough to the laboratory design they criticize. Suppose a man is angered by his wife (say, he comes home from work exhausted and she pesters him to take her out for dinner), and he mentally retreats from what he perceives to be unjustified nagging by flipping through a glossy sex magazine. The research implies that under these conditions the husband is likely to act aggressively toward his wife. Of course the husband cannot punish her by administering electric shocks—unless he keeps a cattle prod in the closet for such occasions—but perhaps he slaps her (harder or more often than he would have without looking at pornography), or screams at her, or even forces her into sexual activity. Clearly, this scenario is not a very pretty picture, and something is already very wrong with the marriage, or with him or her, that contributes to his aggression. But the laboratory experiments only claim to show that the presence of pornography may make things worse than they would have been. Even if the studies do not provide a convincing case for censorship (after all, if the husband drank a beer instead of flipping through a sex magazine, that might very well have had the same effect, and we are not ready to inaugurate a new Prohibition), they nonetheless might have some scientific validity in either explaining or predicting additional amounts of violence.

The way in which Morgan defines 'rape' does indeed make it much easier to confirm the thesis that exposure to pornography causally contributes to rape; one of her examples of a rape according to her broad definition is a situation in which a woman, under an ordinary sort of pressure from her husband (e.g., his pleading), agrees to have sex with him even though she prefers to watch television.[11] Despite the absurdity of this view, it has the virtue of alerting us to the point that all social science investigations into the connection between pornography and rape are unavoidably value-laden. Suppose we define 'rape' as it is commonly defined: x has raped y if x has had sexual contact with y in the absence of y's genuine consent. Then, whether a rape has occurred, or whether we should classify x's act as a rape, depends exquisitely on how we understand 'genuine consent'. And *that* is not a matter of empirical fact, but of values. Both confirmation *and* refutation of the thesis that exposure to pornography contributes to rape presuppose that we can define 'rape', and doing that presupposes in turn that we have made a value judgment as to when consent is and is not genuine. Underneath all social science research in this area, then, is a value judgment—an 'ideological' belief about the nature of consent.

Liberal and feminist values, we know, are different from conservative and nonfeminist values, and these different values influence the criteria to be used in classifying acts as rape. Here we have a case, typical of the social sciences, in which values operate not merely at the level of the interpretation or legal use of data, but at the deeper epistemological level of the composition—indeed, the existence—of data.[12] If we were to leave it up to the democratic forum to resolve the value dispute over 'genuine consent' (and, pray tell, where else to go?), Brannigan's neat dichotomy between popular morality and the rationality of science goes down the tubes. Take note that the values (the 'ideology') that Brannigan and Goldenberg wish to exclude at the level of interpretation are precisely the values operating within the evidential foundation. Therefore, even if Brannigan and Goldenberg are successful in eliminating the values at one level in the name of a 'formal and impartial' assessment *of* the evidence, those values will remain *in* the evidence to haunt them, utterly impervious to the demand for impartiality. I do not mean to suggest that ideology should rule supreme at the level of the interpretation and political use of the data; that sort of tomfoolery *is* eliminable. The point is that while it is correct to object to 'ideological opposition' interfering at the level of interpretation, it is *futile* and even self-defeating to object to 'ideological opposition' operating at the deeper epistemological level; either 'ideological opposition' *or* 'ideological approval' must, for logical reasons, inform the values that are necessarily present in the constitution of the evidence. At least we have a more accurate picture of social science and can continue to practice it, realizing openly that the values are there, rather than pretend they aren't there by promulgating a misleading picture of social science as value-free.

Notes

1. Soble, A. *Pornography. Marxism, Feminism, and the Future of Sexuality,* Yale University Press, New Haven (1986).

2. *The Atlanta Journal,* 21 July, 1985, p. 1B; 23 July, 1985, p. 8A.

3. Morgan, R. 'Theory and practice: pornography and rape', in L. Lederer (ed), *Take Back the Night,* Morrow, New York (1980), pp. 134–40. It may not be necessary to remark that Morgan means 'theory' and 'practice' in the standard sense, in which theory *precedes* practice and is accountable for it, rather than in the Marxist or Hegelian sense, in which theory *follows* practice and largely only rationalizes it (the Owl of Minerva, etc.).

4. Susan Brownmiller's history of rape amply documents that the occurrence of rape does not require the consumption of pornography—even as she argues that in the US today pornography contributes to the occurrence of rape. See Brownmiller, S. *Against Our Will: Men, Women, and Rape,* Simon and Schuster, New York (1975), pp. 390–95.

5. The social science experts quoted by the *Atlanta Journal* had no trouble

finding other explanations for the city's high rape rate: long, hot summers (like Los Angeles?); the large number of single persons and singles' bars (again, like LA?); and the city's 'culture of male dominance' (unlike *where*, exactly?).

6. Brannigan's accusation of intellectual dishonesty is more direct in his 'The politics of pornography research: some reflections on Meese and criminogenic obscenity' ([1986], p. 14, typescript): 'My thesis is that an *ideological* opposition to pornography has dominated the interpretation of the behavioural research . . . These experiments appear to be premised on the porn-rape-link metatheory. The heightened levels of aggression detected by psychologists in the lab are interpreted selectively in accord with this supposition. However, this requires the selective exclusion of some of the lab evidence. For example, in some Donnerstein studies males exposed to *explicit* erotica aggress more against other males than males exposed to *aggressive* pornography. Does this mean erotica makes men want to bugger or to beat up other men, while aggressive pornography does not? Some studies by Zillman focus on aggression between female subjects and female targets. Is this an indication of lesbian rape-proclivity among female porn consumers? Most of the experimentalists began to drop the same-gender targets in order to obviate the problem of extrapolating selectively to cross-gender situations in the real world. The resulting designs reinforce the notion that only females are 'victimized' and only by pornography-inflamed males, just as in the metatheory'.

7. Joel Feinberg has proposed that the culture of male dominance explains both the existence of men who commit rape and of *violent* pornography, in *Offense to Others*, Oxford University Press, New York (1985), pp. 152–53. Feinberg's microscopic hypothesis is less plausible. On his view, the culture of male dominance produces 'macho' men who both consume violent pornography and commit rape (hence the macroscopic correlation), and these men would commit rape even if they never took a look at violent pornography. I have doubts, however, that the 'macho' male buys pornography, violent or tame, and sits at home masturbating with it. Why not suppose, instead, that our culture of male dominance is not monolithic? It produces both 'macho' males who rape (but do not consume pornography) and less 'macho' or non-macho males who consume violent and tame pornography (but do not rape). This microscopic explanation, which also preserves the macroscopic correlation between pornography and rape, is suggested in my *Pornography* (1986), pp. 16–17, 81–85 (see note 1). Feinberg assumes that violent pornography appeals only or primarily to 'macho' males, who find welcome confirmation of their attitudes in this pornography, while I assume that violent pornography appeals only or primarily to 'regular' males—it allows them to fantasize a sexual world that they believe is beyond their power to create. 'Macho' males have no need to create that world by fantasy because they recognize no such limits to their power.

8. The experimenters criticized by Brannigan and Goldenberg can probably turn the tables, saying something like: 'Well, now, who's calling the kettle black? You protest *too* vigorously, in your many papers on the subject, that we have not shown *any* connection between pornography and sexual aggression. It is therefore abundantly clear that *you* have found a convenient and respectable avenue for voicing your own ideological approval of pornography'.

9. 'The politics of pornography research' (1986), p. 1, typescript (see note 6).

10. Similarly, the common feminist claim that rape is not a 'sexual' act but an act of violence suggests that *because* the laboratory aggression measured is *not* sexual, it is a perfectly good proxy for real-life aggression. But this feminist claim generates a problem: if pornography *is* 'sexual' and rape is *not* a sexual act, then ordinary nonviolent pornography is not the kind of item that could instigate rape. To solve this problem some feminists *deny* that even ordinary pornography is 'sexual'. See my *Pornography*, pp. 14–20 (see note 1).

11. Morgan (1980), p. 137 (see note 3).

12. For the long argument and other examples, see my 'The political epistemology of "masculine" and "feminine"', in M. Vetterling-Braggin (ed), *'Femininity', 'Masculinity', and 'Androgyny'*, Littlefield, Adams, Totowa, NJ (1982), pp. 99–127.

Chapter 28

SHOULD FEMINISTS OPPOSE PROSTITUTION?

Laurie Shrage

Because sexuality is a social construction, individuals as individuals are not free to experience *eros* just as they choose. Yet just as the extraction and appropriation of surplus value by the capitalist represents a choice available, if not to individuals, to society as a whole, so too sexuality and the forms taken by *eros* must be seen as at some level open to change.
Nancy Hartsock, *Money, Sex and Power*[1]

Introduction

Prostitution raises difficult issues for feminists. On the one hand, many feminists want to abolish discriminatory criminal statutes that are mostly used to harass and penalize prostitutes, and rarely to punish johns and pimps—laws which, for the most part, render prostitutes more vulnerable to exploitation by their male associates.[2] On the other hand, most feminists find the prostitute's work morally and politically objectionable. In their view, women who provide sexual services for a fee submit to sexual domination by men, and suffer degradation by being treated as sexual commodities.[3]

Reprinted from *Ethics* 99:2 (1989), pp. 347–61, with the permission of Laurie Shrage and the University of Chicago Press. © 1989 by The University of Chicago.

My concern, in this paper, is whether persons opposed to the social subordination of women should seek to discourage commercial sex. My goal is to marshal the moral arguments needed to sustain feminists' condemnation of the sex industry in our society. In reaching this goal, I reject accounts of commercial sex which posit cross-cultural and trans-historical causal mechanisms to explain the existence of prostitution or which assume that the activities we designate as "sex" have a universal meaning and purpose. By contrast, I analyze mercenary sex in terms of culturally specific beliefs and principles that organize its practice in contemporary American society. I try to show that the sex industry, like other institutions in our society, is structured by deeply ingrained attitudes and values which are oppressive to women. The point of my analysis is not to advocate an egalitarian reformation of commercial sex, nor to advocate its abolition through state regulation. Instead, I focus on another political alternative: that which must be done to subvert widely held beliefs that legitimate this institution in our society. Ultimately, I argue that nothing closely resembling prostitution, as we currently know it, will exist, once we have undermined these cultural convictions.

Why Prostitution Is Problematic

A number of recent papers on prostitution begin with the familiar observation that prostitution is one of the oldest professions.[4] Such 'observations' take for granted that 'prostitution' refers to a single trans-historical, transcultural activity. By contrast, my discussion of prostitution is limited to an activity that occurs in modern Western societies—a practice which involves the purchase of sexual services from women by men. Moreover, I am not interested in exploring the nature and extension of our moral concept "to prostitute oneself"; rather, I want to examine a specific activity we regard as prostitution in order to understand its social and political significance.

In formulating my analysis, I recognize that the term 'prostitute' is ambiguous: it is used to designate both persons who supply sex on a commercial basis and persons who contribute their talents and efforts to base purposes for some reward. While these extensions may overlap, their relationship is not a logically necessary one but is contingent upon complex moral and social principles. In this paper, I use the term 'prostitute' as shorthand for 'provider of commercial sexual services,' and correspondingly, I use the term 'prostitution' interchangeably with 'commercial sex.' By employing these terms in this fashion, I hope to appear consistent with colloquial English, and not to be taking for granted that a person who provides commercial sexual services "prostitutes" her- or himself.

Many analyses of prostitution aim to resolve the following issue: what would induce a woman to prostitute herself—to participate in an impersonal, commercial sexual transaction? These accounts seek the deeper psychological motives behind apparently voluntary acts of prostitution. Because our society regards female prostitution as a social, if not natural, aberration, such actions demand an explanation. Moreover, accepting fees for sex seems irrational and repugnant to many persons, even to the woman who does it, and so one wonders why she does it. My examination of prostitution does not focus on this question. While to do so may explain why a woman will choose prostitution from among various options, it does not explain how a woman's options have been constituted. In other words, although an answer to this question may help us understand why some women become sellers of sexual services rather than homemakers or engineers, it will not increase our understanding of why there is a demand for these services. Why, for example, can women not as easily achieve prosperity by selling child-care services? Finding out why there is a greater market for goods of one type than of another illuminates social forces and trends as much as, if not more than, finding out why individuals enter a particular market. Moreover, theorists who approach prostitution in this way do not assume that prostitution is "a problem about the women who are prostitutes, and our attitudes to them, [rather than] a problem about the men who demand to buy them."[5] This assumption, as Carole Pateman rightly points out, mars many other accounts.

However, I do not attempt to construct an account of the psychological, social, and economic forces that presumably cause men to demand commercial sex, or of the factors which cause a woman to market her sexual services. Instead, I first consider whether prostitution, in all cultural contexts, constitutes a degrading and undesirable form of sexuality. I argue that, although the commercial availability of sexuality is not in every existing or conceivable society oppressive to women, in our society this practice depends upon the general acceptance of principles which serve to marginalize women socially and politically. Because of the cultural context in which prostitution operates, it epitomizes and perpetuates pernicious patriarchal beliefs and values and, therefore, is both damaging to the women who sell sex and, as an organized social practice, to all women in our society.

Historical and Cross-cultural Perspectives

In describing Babylonian temple prostitution, Gerda Lerner reports: "For people who regarded fertility as sacred and essential to their own survival, the caring for the gods included, in some cases, offering them sexual services. Thus, a separate class of temple prostitutes developed. What seems to have happened was that sexual activity for and in behalf of the god[s] or goddesses was considered beneficial to the people and sacred."[6] Similarly, according to Emma Goldman, the Babylonians believed that "the generative activity of human beings possessed a mysterious and sacred influence in promoting the fertility of Nature."[7] When the rationale for the impersonal provision of sex is conceived in terms of the promotion of nature's fecundity, the social meaning this activity has may differ substantially from the social significance it has in our own society.

In fifteenth-century France, as described by Jacques Rossiaud, commercial sex appears likewise to have had an import that contrasts with its role in contemporary America. According to Rossiaud:

> By the age of thirty, most prostitutes had a real chance of becoming reintegrated into society. . . . Since public opinion did not view them with disgust, and since they were on good terms with priests and men of the law, it was not too difficult for them to find a position as servant or wife. To many city people, public prostitution represented a partial atonement for past misconduct. Many bachelors had compassion and sympathy for prostitutes, and finally, the local charitable foundations of the municipal authorities felt a charitable impulse to give special help to these repentant Magdalens and to open their way to marriage by dowering them. Marriage was definitely the most frequent end to the career of communal prostitutes who had roots in the town where they have publicly offered their bodies.[8]

The fact that prostitutes were regarded by medieval French society as eligible for marriage, and were desired by men for wives, suggests that the cultural principles which sustained commercial exchanges of sex in this society were quite different than those which shape our own sex industry. Consequently, the phenomenon of prostitution requires a distinct political analysis and moral assessment vis-à-vis fifteenth-century France. This historically specific approach is justified, in part, because commercial sexual transactions may have different consequences for individuals in an alien society than for individuals similarly placed in our own. Indeed, it is questionable whether, in two quite different cultural settings, we should regard a particular outward behavior—the impersonal provision of sexual services for fees or their equivalent—as the same practice, that is, as prostitution.

Another cross-cultural example may help to make the last point clear. Anthropologists have studied a group in New Guinea, called the Etoro, who believe that young male children need to ingest male fluid or semen in order to develop properly into adult males, much like we believe that young infants need their mother's milk, or some equivalent, to be properly nurtured. Furthermore, just as our belief underlies our practice of breast-feeding, the Etoro's belief underlies their practice of penis-feeding, where young male children fellate older males, often their relatives.[9] From the perspective of our society, the Etoro's practice involves behaviors which are highly stigmatized—incest, sex with children, and homosexuality. Yet, for an anthropologist who is attempting to interpret and translate these behaviors, to assume that the Etoro practice is best subsumed under the category of "sex," rather than, for example, "child rearing," would reflect ethnocentrism. Clearly, our choice of one translation scheme or the other will influence our attitude toward the Etoro practice. The point is that there is no practice, such as "sex," which can be morally evaluated apart from a cultural framework.

In general, historical and cross-cultural studies offer little reason to believe that the dominant forms of sexual practice in our society reflect psychological, biological, or moral absolutes that determine human sexual practice. Instead, such studies provide much evidence that, against a different backdrop of beliefs about the world, the activities we designate as "sex"—impersonal or otherwise—have an entirely different meaning and value. Yet, while we may choose not to condemn the "child-rearing" practices of the Etoro, we can nevertheless recognize that "penis-feeding" would be extremely damaging to children in our society. Similarly, though we can appreciate that making an occupation by the provision of sex may not have been oppressive to women in medieval France or ancient Babylon, we should nevertheless recognize that in our society it can be extremely damaging to women. What then are the features which, in our culture, render prostitution oppressive?

The Social Meaning of Prostitution

Let me begin with a simple analogy. In our society there exists a taboo against eating cats and dogs. Now, suppose a member of our society wishes to engage in the unconventional behavior of ingesting cat or dog meat. In evaluating the moral and political character of this person's behavior, it is somewhat irrelevant whether eating cats and dogs "really" is or isn't healthy, or whether it "really" is or isn't different than eating cows, pigs, and chickens. What is relevant is that, by including cat and dog flesh in one's diet, a person may really make others upset and, therefore, do damage to them as well as to oneself. In short, how actions are widely perceived and interpreted by others, even if wrongly or seemingly irrationally, is crucial to determining their moral status because, though such interpretations may not hold up against some "objective reality," they are part of the "social reality" in which we live.

I am not using this example to argue that unconventional behavior is wrong but, rather, to illustrate the relevance of cultural convention to how our outward behaviors are perceived. Indeed, what is wrong with prostitution is not that it violates deeply entrenched social conventions—ideals of feminine purity, and the noncommoditization of sex—but precisely that it epitomizes other cultural assumptions—beliefs which, reasonable or not, serve to legitimate women's social subordination. In other words, rather than subvert patriarchal ideology, the prostitute's actions, and the industry as a whole, serve to perpetuate this system of values. By contrast, lesbian sex, and egalitarian heterosexual economic and romantic relationships, do not. In short, female prostitution oppresses women, not because some women who participate in it "suffer in the eyes of society" but because its organized practice testifies to and perpetuates socially hegemonic beliefs which oppress all women in many domains of their lives.

What, then, are some of the beliefs and values which structure the social meaning of the prostitute's business in our culture—principles which are not necessarily consciously held by us but are implicit in our observable behavior and social practice? First, people in our society generally believe that human beings naturally possess, but socially repress, powerful, emotionally destabilizing sexual appetites. Second, we assume that men are naturally suited for dominant social roles. Third, we assume that contact with male genitals in virtually all contexts is damaging and polluting to women. Fourth, we assume that a person's sexual practice renders her or him a particular "kind" of person, for example, "a homosexual," "a bisexual," "a whore," "a virgin," "a pervert," and so on. I will briefly examine the nature of these four assumptions, and then discuss how they determine the social significance and impact of prostitution in our society. Such principles are inscribed in all of a culture's communicative acts and institutions, but my examples will only be drawn from a common body of disciplinary resources: the writings of philosophers and other intellectuals.

The universal possession of a potent sex drive.—In describing the nature of sexual attraction, Schopenhauer states:

> The sexual impulse in all its degrees and nuances plays not only on the stage and in novels, but also in the real world, where, next to the love of life, it shows itself the strongest and most powerful of motives, constantly lays claim to half the powers and thoughts of the younger portion of mankind, is the ultimate goal of almost all human effort, exerts an adverse influence on the most important events, interrupts the most serious occupations every hour, sometimes embarrasses for a while even the greatest minds, does not hesitate to intrude with its trash interfering with the negotiations of statesmen and the investigation of men of learning, knows how to slip its love letters and locks of hair even into ministerial portfolios and philosophical manuscripts, and no less devises daily the most entangled and the worst actions, destroys the most valuable relationships, breaks the firmest

bonds, demands the sacrifice sometimes of life or health, sometimes of wealth, rank, and happiness, nay robs those who are otherwise honest of all conscience, makes those who have hitherto been faithful, traitors; accordingly to the whole, appears as a malevolent demon that strives to pervert, confuse, and overthrow everything.[10]

Freud, of course, chose the name "libido" to refer to this powerful natural instinct, which he believed manifests itself as early as infancy.

The assumption of a potent "sex drive" is implicit in Lars Ericsson's relatively recent defense of prostitution: "We must liberate ourselves from those mental fossils which prevent us from looking upon sex and sexuality with the same naturalness as upon our cravings for food and drink. And, contrary to popular belief, we may have something to learn from prostitution in this respect, namely, that coition resembles nourishment in that if it cannot be obtained in any other way it can always be bought. And bought meals are not always the worst."[11] More explicitly, he argues that the "sex drive" provides a noneconomic, natural basis for explaining the demand for commercial sex.[12] Moreover, he claims that because of the irrational nature of this impulse, prostitution will exist until all persons are granted sexual access upon demand to all other persons.[13] In a society where individuals lack such access to others, but where women are the social equals of men, Ericsson predicts that "the degree of female frustration that exists today . . . will no longer be tolerated, rationalized, or sublimated, but channeled into a demand for, inter alia, mercenary sex."[14] Consequently, Ericsson favors an unregulated sex industry, which can respond spontaneously to these natural human wants. Although Pateman, in her response to Ericsson, does not see the capitalist commoditization of sexuality as physiologically determined, she nevertheless yields to the assumption that "sexual impulses are part of our natural constitution as humans."[15]

Schopenhauer, Freud, Ericsson, and Pateman all clearly articulate what anthropologists refer to as our "cultural common sense" regarding the nature of human sexuality. By contrast, consider a group of people in New Guinea, called the Dani, as described by Karl Heider: "Especially striking is their five year post-partum sexual abstinence, which is uniformly observed and is not a subject of great concern or stress. This low level of sexuality appears to be a purely cultural phenomenon, not caused by any biological factors."[16] The moral of this anthropological tale is that our high level of sexuality is also "a purely cultural phenomenon," and not the inevitable result of human biology. Though the Dani's disinterest in sex need not lead us to regard our excessive concern as improper, it should lead us to view one of our cultural rationalizations for prostitution as just that—a cultural rationalization.

The "natural" dominance of men.—One readily apparent feature of the sex industry in our society is that it caters almost exclusively to a male clientele. Even the relatively small number of male prostitutes at work serve a predominantly male consumer group. Implicit in this particular division of labor, and also the predominant division of labor in other domains of our society, is the cultural principle that men are naturally disposed to dominate in their relations with others.

Ironically, this cultural conviction is implicit in some accounts of prostitution by feminist writers, especially in their attempts to explain the social and psychological causes of the problematic demand by men for impersonal, commercial sex. For example, Marxist feminists have argued that prostitution is the manifestation of the unequal class position of women vis-à-vis men: women who do not exchange their domestic and sexual services with the male ruling class for their subsistence are forced to market these services to multiple masters outside marriage.[17] The exploitation of female sexuality is a ruling-class privilege, an advantage which allows those socially identified as "men" to perpetuate their economic and cultural hegemony. In tying female prostitution to patriarchy and capitalism, Marxist accounts attempt to tie it to particular historical forces, rather than to biological or natural ones. However, without the assumption of men's biological superiority, Marxist feminist analyses cannot explain why women, at this particular moment under capitalism, have evolved as an economic under-class, that is, why capitalism gives rise to patriarchy. Why did women's role in production and reproduction not provide them a market advantage, a basis upon which they could subordinate men or assert their political equality?

Gayle Rubin has attempted to provide a purely social and historical analysis of female prostitution by applying some insights of structuralist anthropology.[18] She argues that economic prostitution originates from the unequal position of men and women within the mode of reproduction (the division of society into groups for the purpose of procreation and child rearing). In many human cultures, this system operates by what Lévi-Strauss referred to as "the exchange of women": a practice whereby men exchange their own sisters and daughters for the sisters and daughters of other men. These exchanges express or affirm "a social link between the partners of the exchange . . . confer[ring] upon its participants a special relationship of trust, solidarity, and mutual aid."[19] However, since women are not partners to the exchange but, rather, the objects traded, they are denied the social rights and privileges created by these acts of giving. The commoditization of female sexuality is the form this original "traffic in women" takes in capitalist societies. In short, Rubin's account does not assume, but attempts to explain, the dominance of men in production, by appealing to the original dominance of men in reproduction. Yet this account does not explain why women are the objects of the original affinal exchange, rather than men or opposite sex pairs.[20]

In appealing to the principle that men naturally assume dominant roles in all social systems, feminists uncritically accept a basic premise of patriarchy. In my view such principles do not denote universal causal mechanisms but represent naturally arbitrary, culturally determined beliefs which serve to legitimate certain practices.

Sexual contact pollutes women.—To say that extensive sexual experience in a woman is not prized in our society is to be guilty of indirectness and understatement. Rather, a history of sexual activity is a negative mark that is used to differentiate kinds of women. Instead of being valued for their experience in sexual matters, women are valued for their "innocence."

That the act of sexual intercourse with a man is damaging to a woman is implicit in the vulgar language we use to describe this act. As Robert Baker has pointed out, a woman is "fucked," "screwed," "banged," "had," and so forth, and it is a man (a "prick") who does it to her.[21] The metaphors we use for the act of sexual intercourse are similarly revealing. Consider, for example, Andrea Dworkin's description of intercourse: "The thrusting is persistent invasion. She is opened up, split down the center. She is occupied—physically, internally, in her privacy."[22] Dworkin invokes both images of physical assault and imperialist domination in her characterization of heterosexual copulation. Women are split, penetrated, entered, occupied, invaded, and colonized by men. Though aware of the nonliteralness of this language, Dworkin appears to think that these metaphors are motivated by natural, as opposed to arbitrary, cultural features of the world. According to Ann Garry, "Because in our culture we connect sex with harm that men do to women, and because we think of the female role in sex as that of harmed object, we can see that to treat a woman as a sex object is automatically to treat her as less than fully human."[23] As the public vehicles for "screwing," "penetration," "invasion," prostitutes are reduced to the status of animals or things—mere instruments for human ends.

The reification of sexual practice.—Another belief that determines the social significance of prostitution concerns the relationship between a person's social identity and her or his sexual behavior.[24] For example, we identify a person who has sexual relations with a person of the same gender as a "homosexual," and we regard a woman who has intercourse with multiple sexual partners as being of a particular type—for instance, a "loose woman," "slut," or "prostitute." As critics of our society, we may find these categories too narrow or the values they reflect objectionable. If so, we may refer to women who are sexually promiscuous, or who have sexual relations with other women, as "liberated women," and thereby show a rejection of double (and homophobic) standards of sexual morality. However, what such linguistic iconoclasm generally fails to challenge is that a person's sexual practice makes her a particular "kind" of person.

I will now consider how these cultural convictions and values structure the meaning of prostitution in our society. Our society's tolerance for commercially available sex, legal or not, implies general acceptance of principles which perpetuate women's social subordination. Moreover, by their participation in an industry which exploits the myths of female social inequality and sexual vulnerability, the actions of the prostitute and her clients imply that they accept a set of values and beliefs which assign women to marginal social roles in all our cultural institutions, including marriage and waged employment. Just as an Uncle Tom exploits noxious beliefs about blacks for personal gain, and implies through his actions that blacks can benefit from a system of white supremacy, the prostitute and her clients imply that women can profit economically from patriarchy. Though we should not blame the workers in the sex industry for the social degradation they suffer, as theorists and critics of our society, we should question the existence of such businesses and the social principles implicit in our tolerance for them.

Because members of our society perceive persons in terms of their sexual orientation and practice, and because sexual contact in most settings—but especially outside the context of a "secure" heterosexual relationship—is thought to be harmful to women, the prostitute's work may have social implications that differ significantly from the work of persons in other professions. For instance, women who work or have worked in the sex industry may find their future social prospects severely limited. By contrast to medieval French society, they are not desired as wives or domestic servants in our own. And unlike other female subordinates in our society, the prostitute is viewed as a defiled creature; nonetheless, we rationalize and tolerate prostitutional sex out of the perceived need to mollify men's sexual desires.

In sum, the woman who provides sex on a commercial basis and the man who patronizes her epitomize and reinforce the social principles I have identified: these include beliefs that attribute to humans potent, subjugating sex drives that men can satisfy without inflicting self-harm through impersonal sexual encounters. Moreover, the prostitute cannot alter the political implications of her work by simply supplying her own rationale for the provision of her services. For example, Margo St. James has tried to represent the prostitute as a skilled sexual therapist, who serves a legitimate social need.[25] According to St. James, while the commercial sex provider may be unconventional in her sexual behavior, her work may be performed with honesty and dignity. However, this defense is implausible since it ignores the possible adverse impact of her behavior on herself and others, and the fact that, by participating in prostitution, her behavior does little to subvert the cultural principles that make her work harmful. Ann Garry reaches a similar conclusion about pornography: "I may not think that sex is dirty and that I would be a harmed object; I may not know what your view is; but what bothers me is that this is the view embodied in our language and culture. . . . As long as sex is connected with harm done to women, it will be very difficult not to see pornography as degrading to women. . . . The fact that audience attitude is so important makes one wary of giving whole-hearted approval to any pornography seen today."[26] Although the prostitute may want the meaning of her actions assessed relative to her own idiosyncratic beliefs and values, the political and social meaning of her actions must be assessed in the political and social context in which they occur.

One can imagine a society in which individuals sought commercial sexual services from women in order to obtain high quality sexual experiences. In our society, people pay for medical advice, meals, education in many fields, and so on, in order to obtain information, services, or goods that are superior to or in some respect more valuable than those they can obtain noncommercially. A context in which the rationale for seeking a prostitute's services was to obtain sex from a professional—from a person who knows what she is doing—is probably not a context in which women are thought to be violated when they have sexual contact with men. In such a situation, those who supplied sex on a commercial basis would probably not be stigmatized but, instead, granted ordinary social privileges.[27] The fact that prostitutes have such low social status in our society indicates that the society in which we live is not congruent with this imaginary one; that is, the prostitute's services in our society are not generally sought as a gourmet item. In short, if commercial sex was sought as a professional service, then women who provided sex commercially would probably not be regarded as "prostituting" themselves—as devoting their bodies or talents to base purposes, contrary to their true interests.

Subverting the Status Quo

Let me reiterate that I am not arguing for social conformism. Rather, my point is that not all nonconformist acts equally challenge conventional morality. For example, if a person wants to subvert the belief that eating cats and dogs is bad, it is not enough to simply engage in eating them. Similarly, it is unlikely that persons will subvert prevalent attitudes toward gender and sexuality by engaging in prostitution.

Consider another example. Suppose that I value high quality child care and am willing to pay a person well to obtain it. Because of both racial and gender oppression, the persons most likely to be interested in and suitable for such work are bright Third World and minority First World women who cannot compete fairly for other well-paid work. Suppose, then, I hire a person who happens to be a woman and a person of

color to provide child care on the basis of the belief that such work requires a high level of intelligence and responsibility. Though the belief
on which this act is based may be unconventional, my action of hiring a
"sitter" from among the so-called lower classes of society is not politically
liberating.[28]

What can a person who works in the sex industry do to subvert widely
held attitudes toward her work? To subvert the beliefs which currently
structure commercial sex in our society, the female prostitute would
need to assume the role not of a sexual subordinate but of a sexual equal
or superior. For instance, if she were to have the authority to determine
what services the customer could get, under what conditions the customer could get them, and what they would cost, she would gain the status of a sexual professional. Should she further want to establish herself
as a sexual therapist, she would need to represent herself as having some
type of special technical knowledge for solving problems having to do
with human sexuality. In other words, experience is not enough to establish one's credentials as a therapist or professional. However, if the industry were reformed so that all these conditions were met, what would
distinguish the prostitute's work from that of a bona fide "sexual therapist"? If her knowledge was thought to be only quasilegitimate, her work
might have the status of something like the work of a chiropractor, but
this would certainly be quite different than the current social status of
her work.[29] In sum, the political alternatives of reformation and abolition are not mutually exclusive: if prostitution were sufficiently transformed to make it completely nonoppressive to women, though
commercial transactions involving sex might still exist, prostitution as we
now know it would not.

If our tolerance for marriage fundamentally rested on the myth of female subordination, then the same arguments which apply to prostitution would apply to it. Many theorists, including Simone de Beauvoir
and Friedrich Engels, have argued that marriage, like prostitution, involves female sexual subservience. For example, according to de Beauvoir: "For both the sexual act is a service; the one is hired for life by one
man; the other has several clients who pay her by the piece. The one is
protected by one male against all others; the other is defended by all
against the exclusive tyranny of each."[30] In addition, Lars Ericsson con-
tends that marriage, unlike prostitution, involves economic dependence
for women: "While the housewife is totally dependent on her husband,
at least economically, the call girl in that respect stands on her own two
feet. If she has a pimp, it is she, not he, who is the breadwinner in the
family."[31]

Since the majority of marriages in our society render the wife the domestic and sexual subordinate of her husband, marriage degrades the
woman who accepts it (or perhaps only the woman who accepts mar-

riage on unequal terms), and its institutionalization in its present form oppresses all women. However, because marriage can be founded on principles which do not involve the subordination of women, we can challenge oppressive aspects of this institution without radically altering it.[32] For example, while the desire to control the sinful urges of men to fornicate may, historically, have been part of the ideology of marriage, it does not seem to be a central component of our contemporary rationalization for this custom.[33] Marriage, at present in our society, is legitimated by other widely held values and beliefs, for example, the desirability of a long-term, emotionally and financially sustaining, parental partnership. However, I am unable to imagine nonpernicious principles which would legitimate the commercial provision of sex and which would not substantially alter or eliminate the industry as it now exists. Since commercial sex, unlike marriage, is not reformable, feminists should seek to undermine the beliefs and values which underlie our acceptance of it. Indeed, one way to do this is to outwardly oppose prostitution itself.

Conclusions

If my analysis is correct, then prostitution is not a social aberration or disorder but, rather, a consequence of well-established beliefs and values that form part of the foundation of all our social institutions and practices. Therefore, by striving to overcome discriminatory structures in all aspects of society—in the family, at work outside the home, and in our political institutions—feminists will succeed in challenging some of the cultural presuppositions which sustain prostitution. In other words, prostitution needs no unique remedy, legal or otherwise; it will be remedied as feminists make progress in altering patterns of belief and practice that oppress women in all aspects of their lives. Yet, while prostitution requires no special social cure, some important strategic and symbolic feminist goals may be served by selecting the sex industry for criticism at this time. In this respect, a consumer boycott of the industry is especially appropriate.

In examining prostitution, I have not tried to construct a theory which can explain the universal causes and moral character of prostitution. Such questions presuppose that there is a universal phenomenon to which the term refers and that commercial sex is always socially deviant and undesirable. Instead, I have considered the meaning of commercial sex in modern Western cultures. Although my arguments are consistent with the decriminalization of prostitution, I conclude from my investigation that feminists have legitimate reasons to politically oppose prostitution in our society. Since the principles which implicitly sustain and organize the sex industry are ones which underlie pernicious gender asymmetries in many domains of our social life, to tolerate a practice which epitomizes these principles is oppressive to women.[34]

Notes

1. Nancy Hartsock, *Money, Sex and Power* (Boston: Northeastern University Press, 1985), p. 178.
2. See Rosemarie Tong, *Women, Sex, and the Law* (Totowa, N.J.: Rowman and Allanheld, 1984), pp. 37–64. See also Priscilla Alexander and Margo St. James, "Working on the Issue," National Organization for Women (NOW) National Task Force on Prostitution Report (San Francisco: NOW, 1982).
3. See Carole Pateman, "Defending Prostitution: Charges against Ericsson," *Ethics* 93 (1983): 561–65; and Kathleen Barry, *Female Sexual Slavery* (New York: Avon, 1979).
4. For example, see Gerda Lerner, "The Origin of Prostitution in Ancient Mesopotamia," *Signs: Journal of Women in Culture and Society* 11 (1986): 236–54; Lars Ericsson, "Charges against Prostitution: An Attempt at a Philosophical Assessment," *Ethics* 90 (1980): 335–66; and James Brundage, "Prostitution in the Medieval Canon Law," *Signs: Journal of Women in Culture and Society* 1 (1976): 825–45.
5. Pateman, p. 563.
6. Lerner, p. 239.
7. Emma Goldman, "The Traffic in Women," in *Red Emma Speaks,* ed. Alix Kates Shulman (New York: Schocken, 1983), p. 180.
8. Jacques Rossiaud, "Prostitution, Youth, and Society in the Towns of Southeastern France in the Fifteenth Century," in *Deviants and the Abandoned in French Society: Selections from the Annales Economies, Sociétés, Civilisations,* ed. Robert Forster and Orest Ranum (Baltimore: Johns Hopkins University Press, 1978), p. 21.
9. See Gilbert H. Herdt, ed., *Rituals of Manhood* (Berkeley and Los Angeles: University of California Press, 1982). Also see Harriet Whitehead, "The Varieties of Fertility Cultism in New Guinea: Part 1," *American Ethnologist* 13 (1986): 80–99. In comparing penis-feeding to breast-feeding rather than to oral sex, some anthropologists point out that both involve the use of a culturally erotic bodily part for parental nurturing.
10. Arthur Schopenhauer, "The Metaphysics of the Love of the Sexes," in *The Works of Schopenhauer,* ed. Will Durant (New York, Simon & Schuster, 1928), p. 333.
11. Ericsson, p. 355.
12. Ibid., p. 347.
13. Ibid., pp. 359–60.
14. Ibid., p. 360.
15. Pateman, p. 563.
16. Karl Heider, "Dani Sexuality: A Low Energy System," *Man* 11 (1976): 188–201.

17. See Friedrich Engels, *The Origin of the Family, Private Property and the State* (New York: Penguin, 1985); Goldman; Alison Jaggar, "Prostitution," in *The Philosophy of Sex*, 1st edition, ed. Alan Soble (Totowa, N.J.: Rowman & Littlefield, 1980), pp. 353–58.

18. Gayle Rubin, "The Traffic in Women: Notes on the 'Political Economy' of Sex," in *Toward an Anthropology of Women*, ed. Rayna Reiter (New York: Monthly Review Press, 1975).

19. Ibid., p. 172.

20. In his attempt to describe the general principles of kinship organization implicit in different cultures, Lévi-Strauss admits it is conceivable that he has over-emphasized the patrilineal nature of these exchanges: "It may have been noted that we have assumed what might be called . . . a paternal perspective. That is, we have regarded the woman married by a member of the group as acquired, and the sister provided in exchange as lost. The situation might be altogether different in a system with matrilineal descent and matrilocal residence. . . . The essential thing is that every right acquired entails a concomitant obligation, and that every renunciation calls for a compensation. . . . Even supposing a very hypothetical marriage system in which the man and not the woman were exchanged . . . the total structure would remain unchanged" (Claude Lévi-Strauss, *The Elementary Structures of Kinship* [Boston: Beacon, 1969], p. 132). A culture in which men are gifts in a ritual of exchange is described in Michael Peletz, "The Exchange of Men in Nineteenth-Century Negeri Sembilan (Malaya)," *American Ethnologist* 14 (1987): 449–69.

21. Robert Baker, " 'Pricks' and 'Chicks': A Plea for 'Persons,' " in *Philosophy and Sex*, ed. R. Baker and F. Elliston (Buffalo, N.Y.: Prometheus, 1984), pp. 260–66. In this section, Baker provides both linguistic and nonlinguistic evidence that intercourse, in our cultural mythology, hurts women.

22. Andrea Dworkin, *Intercourse* (New York: Free Press, 1987), p. 122.

23. Ann Garry, "Pornography and Respect for Women," in Baker and Elliston, eds., p. 318.

24. In "Defending Prostitution," Pateman states: "The services of the prostitute are related in a more intimate manner to her body than those of other professionals. Sexual services, that is to say, sex and sexuality, are constitutive of the body in a way in which the counseling skills of the social worker are not. . . . Sexuality and the body are, further, integrally connected to conceptions of femininity and masculinity, and all these are constitutive of our individuality, our sense of self-identity" (p. 562). On my view, while our social identities are determined by our outward sexual practice, this is due to arbitrary culturally determined conceptual mappings, rather than some universal relationship holding between persons and their bodies.

25. Margo St. James, Speech to the San Diego County National Organization for Women, La Jolla, California, February 27, 1982, and from private correspondence with St. James (1983). Margo St. James is the founder of COYOTE (Call Off Your Old Tired Ethics) and the editor of *Coyote Howls*. COYOTE is a civil rights organization which seeks to change the sex industry from within by gaining better working conditions for prostitutes.

26. Garry, pp. 318–23.

27. According to Bertrand Russell: "In Japan, apparently, the matter is quite

otherwise. Prostitution is recognized and respected as a career, and is even adopted at the insistence of parents. It is often a not uncommon method of earning a marriage dowry" (*Marriage and Morals* [1929; reprint, New York: Liveright, 1970], p. 151). Perhaps contemporary Japan is closer to our imaginary society, a society where heterosexual intercourse is not felt to be polluting to women.

28. This of course does not mean we should not hire such people for child care, for that would simply be to deny a good person a better job than he or she might otherwise obtain—a job which unlike the prostitute's job is not likely to hurt their prospects for other work or social positions. Nevertheless, one should not believe that one's act of giving a person of this social description such a job does anything to change the unfair structure of our society.

29. I am grateful to Richard Arneson for suggesting this analogy to me.

30. Simone de Beauvoir, *The Second Sex* (New York: Vintage, 1974), p. 619. According to Engels: "Marriage of convenience turns often enough into the crassest prostitution—sometimes of both partners, but far more commonly of the woman, who only differs from the ordinary courtesan in that she does not let out her body on piecework as a wage worker, but sells it once and for all into slavery" (p. 102).

31. Ericsson, p. 354.

32. Pateman argues: "The conjugal relation is not necessarily one of domination and subjection, and in this it differs from prostitution" (p. 563). On this I agree with her.

33. Russell informs us that "Christianity, and more particularly St. Paul, introduced an entirely novel view of marriage, that it existed not primarily for the procreation of children, but to prevent the sin of fornication. . . . I remember once being advised by a doctor to abandon the practice of smoking, and he said that I should find it easier if, whenever the desire came upon me, I proceeded to suck an acid drop. It is in this spirit that St. Paul recommends marriage" (pp. 44–46).

34. I am grateful to Sandra Bartky, Alison Jaggar, Elizabeth Segal, Richard Arneson, and the anonymous reviewers for *Ethics* for their critical comments and suggestions. Also, I am indebted to Daniel Segal for suggesting many anthropological and historical examples relevant to my argument. In addition, I would like to thank the philosophy department of the Claremont Graduate School for the opportunity to present an earlier draft of this paper for discussion.

Chapter 29

WHAT'S WRONG WITH PROSTITUTION?

Igor Primoratz

Over the last three decades the sexual morality of many Western societies has changed beyond recognition. Most of the prohibitions which made up the traditional, extremely restrictive outlook on sex that reigned supreme until the fifties—the prohibitions of masturbation, pre-marital and extra-marital sex, promiscuity, homosexuality—are no longer seen as very serious or stringent or, indeed, as binding at all. But one or two traditional prohibitions are still with us. The moral ban on prostitution, in particular, does not seem to have been repealed or radically mitigated. To be sure, some of the old arguments against prostitution are hardly ever brought up these days; but then, several new ones are quite popular, at least in certain circles. Prostitution is no longer seen as the most extreme moral depravity a woman is capable of; but the view that it is at least seriously morally flawed, if not repugnant and intolerable, is still widely held. In this paper I want to look into some of the main arguments in support of this view and try to show that none of them is convincing.[1]

1. Positive Morality

The morality of this society and of most other societies today condemns prostitution in no uncertain terms; the facts of the condemnation and its various, sometimes quite serious and far-reaching consequences for those who practise it, are too well known to need to be recounted here. But what do these facts prove? Surely not that prostitution *is* wrong, only that positive morality of this and many other societies *deems it* wrong. With regard to prostitution, as with regard to any moral issue, we must surely attend to the distinction between positive morality, the morality prevalent in a society and expressed in its public opinion, its laws, and the lives of its members, and critical morality, which is a set of moral principles, rules and values together with the reasoning behind them that an individual may adopt, not only to live by them, but also to apply them in judging critically the morality of any particular society, including his or her own.

To be sure, the importance, or even tenability, of this distinction has been denied; there have been authors (Emile Durkheim is a good example) who maintained that whatever a society holds to be right or wrong *is* right or wrong in that society. But the flaws of this position, which might be termed moral positivism or conventionalism, are obvious and fatal. One is that it implies that all philosophers, religious teachers, writers and social reformers who set out to criticize and reform the moral outlook of their societies were not merely wrong—all of them may, and some of them must have been wrong—but utterly misguided in what they were trying to do, for what they were trying to do logically cannot be done. There is no such thing as a radical moral critique of one's society (or any other society, for that matter). Another implausible implication of moral positivism is that the same action or practice can be both right (in one society) and wrong (in another). Thus prostitution was both morally unobjectionable (in ancient Greece) *and* a moral abomination (in nineteenth-century England). Finally, positive morality is often inconsistent. Prostitution is, again, a case in point. It has been pointed out time and again that there is no morally significant difference between the common prostitute and the spouse in what used to be called a marriage of convenience. This kind of marriage, said Friedrich Engels, for example, 'turns often enough into the crassest prostitution— sometimes of both partners, but far more commonly of the woman, who only differs from the ordinary courtesan in that she does not let out her body on piecework as a wage worker, but sells it once and for all into slavery.'[2] The word 'slavery' is too strong, and it may not be the spouse's body that is being sold, but otherwise the point is well taken. How can positive morality condemn mercenary sex in one case, but not in the other?

I am not saying that this inconsistency cannot be explained. It can, if we attend to the social meaning of marriage and prostitution.[3] Both can be called 'sexual institutions', as both have to do with sex, both are institutional frameworks for satisfying sexual desire. But their social meaning is not the same. Throughout history, the most important social function of sex has been reproduction. Marriage has always been seen as the best institutional set-up for procreating and socializing the young. Accordingly, marriage is the central, most respected and most strongly supported among the sexual institutions, while other such institutions, such as concubinage or wife exchange, are the less supported and respected the more they are removed from marriage. Prostitution is at the other end of this range, for in prostitution

> both parties use sex for an end not socially functional, the one for pleasure, the other for money. To tie intercourse to sheer physical pleasure is to divorce it both from reproduction and from the sentimental primary type of relation which it symbolizes. To tie it to money . . . does the same thing. . . . On both sides the relationship is merely a means to a private end. . . .[4]

Both money and pleasure may be very important to the individuals concerned but, as merely individual objectives, have no social significance. Therefore, society accords prostitution neither support nor respect. The traditional Western sexual ethic considers sex as in itself morally problematic if not downright bad or sinful, and thus legitimate only as a means of procreation, and perhaps also of expression and reinforcement of emotions and attitudes usually associated with procreation. It is easy to see how Western society came to condemn and despise the practice of prostitution.

However, the inconsistency of condemning mercenary sex outside marriage but not within it still has not been explained. The missing part is the fact that society is concerned with practices and institutions, not with individuals; social morality judges primarily practices and institutions, and deals with individuals simply, and solely, by subsuming them under the roles defined by practices and institutions. If it were otherwise, if social morality were interested in, and capable of, relating to the individual and his or her actions in their particularity and complexity, as all serious and discerning moral thinking does, it could not fail to condemn mercenary sex within marriage no less than outside it. For it does not consider marriage valuable in itself, but as the proper framework for reproduction and the upbringing of offspring, and also, perhaps, as the framework that best sustains the emotions and attitudes helpful in the performance of these tasks. Therefore marital sex is not legitimate simply as marital, but as sex that serves the social purpose of marriage. When a person engages in sex within marriage, but fails to live up to this normative conception of the institution and has sex merely in order to secure the economic benefits of the married state, that is no less mercenary than the sex sold on the street to all comers, and accordingly no less wrong from the point of view of the sexual ethic to which society adheres on the level of rules and roles, practices and institutions. Society does not see this because it cannot be bothered to look into the life, actions and motives of the individual. But that is surely reason enough not to bother with its pronouncements when attempting to settle an important moral question.

2. Paternalism

Paternalism is most commonly defined as 'the interference with a person's liberty of action justified by reasons referring exclusively to the welfare, good, happiness, needs, interests or values of the person being coerced.'[5] Philosophical discussions of paternalism have concentrated on paternalist legislation; for the most obvious, and often the most effective, kind of interference with an individual's liberty of action is by means of law. But paternalism can also be put forward as a moral position: one can argue that the wrongness of doing something follows from the fact that doing it has serious adverse effects on the welfare, good, etc. of the agent and, having made that judgment, exert the pressure of the moral sanction on the individuals concerned to get them to refrain from doing it. A popular way of arguing against prostitution is of this sort: it refers to such hazards of selling sex as (i) venereal diseases; (ii) unpleasant, humiliating, even violent behaviour of clients; (iii) exploitation by madams and pimps; (iv) the extremely low social status of prostitutes and the contempt and ostracism to which they are exposed. The facts showing that these are, indeed, the hazards of prostitution are well known; are they not enough to show that prostitution is bad and to be avoided?

A short way with this objection is to refuse to acknowledge the moral credentials of paternalism, and to say that what we have here is merely a prudential, not a moral argument against prostitution.

However, we may decide to accept that paternalist considerations can be relevant to questions about what is morally right and wrong. In that case, the first thing to note about the paternalist argument is that it is an argument from *occupational* hazards and thus, if valid, valid only against prostitution as an *occupation*. For in addition to the professional prostitute, whose sole livelihood comes from mercenary sex, there is also the amateur, who is usually gainfully employed or married and engages in prostitution for additional income. The latter—also known as the secret prostitute—need not at all suffer from (iii) and (iv), and stands a much lower chance of being exposed to (i) and (ii). A reference to (iii) actually is not even an argument against professional prostitution, but merely against a particular, by no means necessary way of practising it; if a professional prostitute is likely to be exploited by a madam or pimp, then she should pursue the trade on her own.

But it is more important to note that the crucial, although indirect cause of all these hazards of professional prostitution is the negative attitude of society, the condemnation of prostitution by its morality and its laws. But for that, the prostitute could enjoy much better medical protection, much more effective police protection from abusive and aggressive behaviour of clients and legal protection from exploitation by pimps and madams, and her social status would be quite different. Thus the paternalist argument takes for granted the conventional moral condemnation of prostitution, and merely gives an additional reason for not engaging in something that has already been established as wrong. But we can and should refuse to take that for granted, because we can and should refuse to submit to positive morality as the arbiter of moral issues. If we do so, and if a good case for morally condemning commercial sex has still not been made out, as I am trying to show in this paper, then all these hazards should be seen as reasons for trying to disabuse society of the prejudices against it and help to change the law and social conditions in general in which prostitutes work, in order radically to reduce, if not completely eliminate, such hazards.

However, there is one occupational hazard that has not been mentioned so far: one that cannot be blamed on unenlightened social morality, and would remain even if society were to treat prostitution as any other legitimate occupation. That is the danger to the sex life of the prostitute. As Lars Ericsson neatly puts it, 'Can one have a well-functioning sexual life if sex is what one lives by?'[6]

One way of tackling this particular paternalist objection is to say, with David A. J. Richards, that perhaps one can. Richards claims that there is no evidence that prostitution makes it impossible for those who practise it to have loving relationships, and adds that 'there is some evidence that prostitutes, as a class, are more sexually fulfilled than other American women.'[7] The last claim is based on a study in which 175 prostitutes were systematically interviewed, and which showed that 'they experienced orgasm and multiple orgasm more frequently in their personal, "non-commercial" intercourse than did the normal woman (as defined by Kinsey norms).'[8] Another, probably safer response is to point out, as Ericsson does, that the question is an empirical one and that, since there is no conclusive evidence either way, we are not in a position to draw any conclusion.[9]

My preferred response is different. I would rather grant the empirical claim that a life of prostitution is liable to wreck one's sex life, i.e. the minor premise of the argument, and then look a bit more closely into the major premise, the principle of paternalism. For there are two rather different versions of that principle. The weak version prevents the individual from acting on a choice that is not fully voluntary, either because the individual is permanently incompetent or because the choice in question is a result of ignorance of some important facts or made under extreme psychological or social pressure. Otherwise the individual is considered the sole qualified judge of his or her own welfare, good, happiness, needs, interests and values, and the choice is ultimately his or hers. Moreover, when a usually competent individual is prevented from acting on a choice that is either uninformed or made under extreme pressure, and is therefore not fully voluntary, that individual will, when the choice-impairing conditions no longer obtain, agree that the paternalist interference was appropriate and legitimate, and perhaps even be grateful for it. Strong paternalism *is* meant to protect the individual from his or her own voluntary choices, and therefore will not be legitimized by retrospective consent of the individual paternalized. The assumption is not that the individual is normally the proper judge of his or her own welfare, good, etc., but rather that someone else knows better where the individual's true welfare, good, etc. lie, and therefore has the right to force the individual to act in accordance with the latter, even though that means acting against his or her fully voluntary choice, which is said to be merely 'subjective' or 'arbitrary'. Obviously, the weak version of paternalism does not conflict with personal liberty, but should rather be seen as its corollary; for it does not protect the individual from choices that express his or her considered preferences and settled values, but only against his or her 'non-voluntary choices', choices the individual will subsequently disavow. Strong paternalism, on the other hand, is essentially opposed to individual liberty, and cannot be accepted by anyone who takes liberty seriously. Such paternalism smacks of intellectual and moral arrogance, and it is hard to see how it could ever be established by rational argument.[10]

Accordingly, if the argument from the dangers to the prostitute's sex life is not to be made rather implausible from the start, it ought to be put forward in terms of weak rather than strong paternalism. When put in these terms, however, it is not really an argument that prostitution is wrong because imprudent, but rather that it is wrong if and when it is taken up imprudently. It reminds us that persons permanently incompetent and those who still have not reached the age of consent should not (be allowed to) take up the life of prostitution and thereby most likely throw away the prospect of a good sex life. (They should not [be allowed to] become prostitutes for other reasons anyway.) As for a competent adult, the only legitimate paternalist interference with the choice of such a person to become a prostitute is to make sure that the choice is a free and informed one. But if an adult and sane person is fully apprised of the dangers of prostitution to the sex life of the prostitute and decides, without undue pressure of any sort, that the advantages of prostitution as an occupation are worth it, then it is neither imprudent nor wrong for that person to embark on the line of work chosen.[11] In such a case, as Mill put it, 'neither one person, nor any number of persons, is warranted in saying to another human creature of ripe years that he shall not do with his life for his own benefit what he chooses to do with it.'[12]

3. Some Things Just Are Not for Sale

In the eyes of many, by far the best argument against prostitution is brief and simple: some things just are not for sale, and sex is one of them.

It would be difficult not to go along with the first part of this argument. The belief that not everything can or should be bought and sold is extremely widespread, if not universal. The list of things not for sale is not exactly the same in all societies, but it seems that every society does have such a list, a list of 'blocked exchanges'.

The term is Michael Walzer's, and a discussion of such exchanges is an important part of his theory of justice. The central thesis of the theory is that there are several spheres of personal qualities and social goods, each autonomous, with its own criteria, procedures and agents of distribution. Injustice occurs when this autonomy is violated, when the borders are crossed and a sphere of goods becomes dominated by another in that the goods of the former are no longer distributed in accordance with its own criteria and procedures, but in accordance with those of the other sphere. The market is one such sphere—actually, the sphere with the strongest tendency to expand into, and dominate, other spheres of goods, at least in a modern capitalist society. But even this kind of society has an impressive list of things not for sale. The one Walzer offers as 'the full set of blocked exchanges in the United States today', but which would be valid for any contemporary liberal and democratic society, includes the sale of human beings (slavery), political power and office, criminal justice, freedom of speech, various prizes and honours, love and friendship, and more.[13] This is, obviously, a mixed lot. In some cases, the very nature of a good rules out its being bought and sold (love, friendship); in others, that is precluded by the conventions which constitute it (prizes); in still others, the dominant conception of a certain sphere of social life prohibits the sale, as, for instance, our conception of the nature and purpose of the political process entails that political power and office must not be bought and sold. (To be sure, some of the things listed as a matter of fact are bought and sold. But that happens only on the black market, and the fact that the market is 'black', and that those who buy and sell there do so in secret, goes to show both the illegitimacy and the secondary, parasitic character of such transactions.) There is, thus, no single criterion by reference to which one could explain why all these items appear on the list, and why no other does.

What of sex? It is not on the list; for sex, unlike love, can, as a matter of fact, be bought and sold, and there is no single, generally accepted conception of sex that prohibits its sale and purchase. 'People who believe that sexual intercourse is morally tied to love and marriage are likely to favour a ban on prostitution. . . . Sex can be sold only when it is understood in terms of pleasure and not exclusively in terms of married love. . . .'[14]

This is helpful, for it reminds us that the 'Not for sale' argument is elliptic; the understanding of sex that is presupposed must be explicated before the argument can be assessed. But the remark is also inaccurate, since it conflates two views of sex that are both historically and theoretically different: the traditional view, which originated in religion, that sex is legitimate only within marriage and as a means to procreation, and the more modern, secular, 'romantic' view that sex is to be valued only when it expresses and enhances a loving relationship. Let me look briefly into these two views in order to see whether a commitment to either does, indeed, commit one to favouring a ban on prostitution.

The first views sex as intrinsically inferior, sinful and shameful, and accepts it only when, and in so far as, it serves an important extrinsic purpose which cannot be attained by any other means: procreation. Moreover, the only proper framework for bringing up children is marriage; therefore sex is permissible only within marriage. These two statements make up the core of the traditional Christian understanding of sex, elaborated in the writings of St. Augustine and St. Thomas Aquinas, which has been by far the most important source of Western sexual ethics. To be sure, modern Christian thought and practice have broadened this view in various ways, in order to allow for the role of sex in expressing and enhancing conjugal love and care. Within the Catholic tradition this has been recognized as the 'unitive' function of sex in marriage; but that is a rather limited development, for it is still maintained that the two functions of sex, the unitive and the procreative, are inseparable.

Do those who are committed to this view of sex—and in contemporary Western societies, I suppose, only practising Catholics are—have to endorse the ban on prostitution? At a certain level, they obviously must think ill of it; for, as has often been pointed out, theirs is the most restrictive and repressive sexual ethics possible. It confines sex within the bounds of heterosexual, monogamous, exclusive, indissoluble marriage, and rules out sexual relations between any possible partners except husband and wife (as well as masturbation). Moreover, it restricts the legitimate sexual relations between the spouses to those that are 'by nature ordained' toward procreation. Prostitution or, more accurately, common prostitution, which is both non-marital and disconnected from procreation, would seem to be beyond the pale.

But then, even the legitimacy of marital and procreative sex is of a rather low order: as sex, it is intrinsically problematic; as marital and procreative, it is accepted as a necessary evil, an inevitable concession to fallen human nature. As St. Augustine says, 'any friend of wisdom and holy joys who lives a married life' would surely prefer to beget children without 'the lust that excites the indecent parts of the body', if it only were possible.[15] Therefore, if it turns out that accepting sex within marriage and for the purpose of procreation only is not concession enough, that human sexuality is so strong and unruly that it cannot be confined within these bounds and that attempts to confine it actually endanger the institution of marriage itself, the inevitable conclusion will be that further concession is in order. This is just the conclusion reached by many authors with regard to prostitution: it should be tolerated, for it provides a safety valve for a force which will otherwise subvert the institution of marriage and destroy all the chastity and decency this institution makes possible. My favourite quotation is from Mandeville, who, of course, sees that as but another instance of the general truth that private vices are public benefits:

> If Courtezans and Strumpets were to be prosecuted with as much Rigour as some silly People would have it, what Locks or Bars would be sufficient to preserve the Honour of our Wives and Daughters? For 'tis not only that the Women in general would meet with far greater Temptations, and the Attempts to ensnare the Innocence of Virgins would seem more excusable to the sober part of Mankind than they do now: But some Men would grow outrageous, and Ravishing would become a common Crime. Where six or seven Thousand Sailors arrive at once, as it often happens at *Amsterdam*, that have seen none but their own Sex for many Months together, how is it to be supposed that honest Women should walk the Streets unmolested, if there were no Harlots to be had at reasonable Prices? . . . There is a Necessity of sacrificing one part of Womankind to preserve the other, and prevent a Filthiness of a more heinous Nature.[16]

That prostitution is indispensable for the stability and the very survival of marriage has not been pointed out only by cynics like Mandeville, misanthropes like Schopenhauer,[17] or godless rationalists like Lecky[18] and Russell;[19] it was acknowledged as a fact, and as one that entails that prostitution ought to be tolerated rather than suppressed, by St. Augustine and St. Thomas themselves.[20] Moreover, it has been confirmed by sociological study of human sexual behaviour, which shows that the majority of clients of prostitutes are married men who do not find complete sexual fulfillment within marriage, but are content to stay married provided they can have extra-marital commercial sex as well.[21] Accordingly, even if one adopts the most conservative and restrictive view of sex there is, the view which ties sex to marriage and procreation, one need not, indeed should not condemn prostitution too severely. One should rather take a tolerant attitude to it, knowing that it is twice removed from the ideal state of affairs, but that its demise would bring about something incomparably worse.

Another view which would seem to call for the condemnation of prostitution is the 'romantic' view of sex as essentially tied to love; for mercenary sex is normally as loveless as sex can ever get. The important thing to note is that whatever unfavourable judgment on prostitution is suggested by this view of sex, it will not be a judgment unfavourable to prostitution as such, but rather to prostitution as a type of loveless sex. It is the lovelessness, not the commercial nature of the practice that the 'romantic' objects to.

One response to this kind of objection would be to take on squarely the view of sex that generates it. One could, first, take a critical look at the arguments advanced in support of the view that sex should always be bound up with love; second, bring out the difficulties of the linkage, the tensions between love and sex which seem to make a stable and fruitful combination of the two rather unlikely; finally, argue for the superiority of loveless, noncommittal, 'plain sex' over sex that is bound up with love. All this has already been done by philosophers such as Alan Goldman and Russell Vannoy,[22] and probably by innumerable non-philosophers as well.

Another response would be to grant the validity of the 'romantic' view of sex, but only as a personal ideal, not a universally binding moral standard. This is the tack taken by Richards,[23] who points out that it would be signally misguided, indeed absurd, to try to enforce this particular ideal, based as it is 'on the cultivation of spontaneous romantic feeling.'[24] My preferred response to the 'romantic' objection is along these lines, but I would like to go a bit further, and emphasize that it is possible to appreciate the 'romantic' ideal and at the same time not only grant that sex which falls short of it need not be wrong, but also allow that it can be positively good (without going as far as to claim that it is actually better than sex with love).

The 'romantic' typically points out the difference between sex with and without love. The former is a distinctively human, complex, rich and fruitful experience, and a matter of great importance; the latter is merely casual, a one-dimensional, barren experience that satisfies only for a short while and belongs to our animal nature. These differences are taken to show that sex with love is valuable, while loveless sex is not. This kind of reasoning has the following structure:

A is much better than B.
Therefore, B is no good at all.

In addition to being logically flawed, this line of reasoning, if it were to be applied in areas other than sex, would prove quite difficult to follow. For one thing, all but the very rich among us would die of hunger; for only the very rich can afford to take *all* their meals at the fanciest restaurants.[25]

Of course, B can be good, even if it is much less good than A. Loveless sex is a case in point. Moreover, other things being equal, it is better to be able to enjoy both loving and loveless sex than only the former. A person who enjoyed sex as part of loving relationships but was completely incapable of enjoying plain sex would seem to be missing out on something. To be sure, the 'romantic' rejection of plain sex often includes the claim that other things are not equal: that a person who indulges in plain sex thereby somehow damages, and ultimately destroys, his or her capacity for experiencing sex as an integral part of a loving relationship. This is a straightforward empirical claim about human psychology; and it is clearly false.

All this has to do with plain sex in general, rather than with its mercenary variety in particular. That is due to the general character of the 'romantic' objection to prostitution: prostitution is seen as flawed not on account of its commercial nature, but rather because it has nothing to do with love. Accordingly, as far as the 'romantic' view of sex is concerned, by exonerating plain sex, one also exonerates its commercial variety.

4. The Feminist Critique (a): Degradation of Women

In this section and the next I deal with what I have termed the 'feminist' objections to prostitution. This should not be taken to suggest that these objections are put forward only by feminists, nor that they are shared by all feminists. Contemporary discussion of the rights and wrongs of prostitution is for the most part a debate between those who hold that the sale of sex is just another service, in itself as legitimate as any other and not to be interfered with as long as no injustice, exploitation or fraud is involved, and those who deny this and claim that prostitution is essentially bound up with degradation or oppression of women. The particular concern for the role and status of women that motivates the latter position is clearly feminist; the former position can loosely be termed liberal. But there is a certain overlap: one of the currents of feminism is liberal feminism, and its adherents do not subscribe to the critique of prostitution advanced by feminists of other stripes, but rather think of it much as other liberals do, as morally unobjectionable in itself.[26] Incidentally, the position of liberal feminists seems to be more in tune with the way prostitutes themselves think of their occupation; but that may not count for much, as illiberal feminists are likely to dismiss the views of prostitutes as just another case of false consciousness.

One might want to take issue with the whole feminist approach to the question of prostitution as a question about women; for, after all, not all prostitutes are women. But this is not a promising tack; for, if not all, most of them are and always have been. So if prostitution involves either degradation or oppression, the great majority of those degraded or oppressed are women. But does it?

There is no denying that the belief that prostitution degrades those who practise it is very widespread. But this belief may be wrong. The question is: *Just why* should prostitution be considered degrading? There are four main answers: (i) because it is utterly impersonal; (ii) because the prostitute is reduced to a mere means; (iii) because of the intimate nature of the acts she performs for money; (iv) because she actually sells her body, herself. Let me look into each of these claims in turn.

(i) Prostitution is degrading because the relation between the prostitute and the client is completely impersonal. The client does not even perceive, let alone treat the prostitute as the person she is; he has no interest, no time for any of her personal characteristics, but relates to her merely as a source of sexual satisfaction, nothing more than a sex object.

One possible response to this is that prostitution need not be impersonal. There is, of course, the streetwalker who sells sex to all comers (or almost); but there is also the prostitute with a limited number of steady clients, with whom she develops quite personal relationships. So if the objection is to the impersonal character of the relation, the most that can be said is that a certain kind of prostitution is degrading, not that prostitution as such is. I do not want to make much of this, though. For although in this, as in many other services, there is the option of personalized service, the other, impersonal variety is typical.

My difficulty with the argument is more basic: I cannot see why the impersonal nature of a social transaction or relation makes that transaction or relation degrading. After all, the personal relations we have with others—with our family, friends and acquaintances—are just a small part (although the most important part) of our social life. The other part includes the overwhelming majority of our social transactions and relations which are, and have to be, quite impersonal. I do not have a personal relationship with the newspaper vendor, the bus driver, the shop assistant, and all those numerous other people I interact with in the course of a single day; and, as long as the basic decencies of social intercourse (which are purely formal and impersonal) are observed, there is nothing wrong with that. There is nothing wrong for me to think of and relate to the newspaper vendor as just that and, as far as I am concerned, nothing more. That our social relations must for the most part be impersonal may be merely a consequence of the scarcity of resources we invest in them. But it is inescapable in any but the smallest and simplest, so-called face-to-face society.

It may well be said that the selling and buying of newspapers and sex are quite different. While an impersonal attitude is unobjectionable in the former case, it is objectionable, because degrading, in the latter. But if this is the point, then the objection presupposes that sex ought to be personal; and that still has not been established. It need not be on any but the 'romantic' conception of sex; and I hope to have shown in the preceding section that the 'romantic' case against unromantic sex is not very strong.

The next two points are suggested in the following remarks by Russell:

> The intrusion of the economic motive into sex is always in a greater or lesser degree disastrous. Sexual relations should be a mutual delight, entered into solely from the spontaneous impulse of both parties. Where this is not the case, everything that is valuable is absent. To use another person in so intimate a manner is to be lacking in that respect for the human being as such, out of which all true morality must spring. . . . Morality in sexual relations, when it is free from superstition, consists essentially of respect for the other person, and unwillingness to use that person solely as a means of personal gratification without regard to his or her desires. . . . Prostitution sins against this principle. . . .[27]

(ii) Prostitution is said to degrade the prostitute because she is used as a means by the client. The client relates to the prostitute in a purely instrumental way: she is no more than a means to his sexual satisfaction. If so, is he not reducing her to a mere means, a thing, a sex object, and thereby degrading her?

If he were to rape her, that would indeed amount to treating her without regard to her desires, and thus to reducing, degrading her to a mere means. But as a customer rather than a rapist, he gets sexual satisfaction from her for a charge, on the basis of a mutual understanding, and she does her part of the bargain willingly. It is not true that he acts without regard to her desires. He does not satisfy her sexual desire; indeed, the prostitute does not desire that he should do so. But he does satisfy the one desire she has with regard to him: the desire for money. Their transaction is not 'a mutual delight, entered into solely from the spontaneous impulse of both parties', but rather a calculated exchange of goods of different order. But it does not offend against the principle of respect for human beings as such as long as it is free from coercion and fraud, and both sides get what they want.[28]

Most of our social transactions and relations are impersonal, and most are instrumental. There is nothing wrong with either impersonal or instrumental ways of relating to others as such. Just as the fact that A relates to B in a completely impersonal way is not tantamount to a violation of B's personhood, B's status as a person, so the fact that A relates to B in a purely instrumental way is not equivalent to A's reducing B to a mere means. In both cases B's informed and freely given consent absolves the relation of any such charge, and thereby also of the charge of degradation.

(iii) Sex is an intimate, perhaps the most intimate part of our lives. Should it not therefore be off limits to commercial considerations and transactions? And is it not degrading to perform something so intimate as a sex act with a complete stranger and for money?

It is not. As Ericsson points out,

> we are no more justified in devaluating the prostitute, who, for example, masturbates her customers, than we are in devaluating the assistant nurse, whose job it is to take care of the intimate hygiene of disabled patients. Both help to satisfy important human needs, and both get paid for doing so. That the harlot, in distinction to the nurse, intentionally gives her client pleasure is of course nothing that should be held against her![29]

It might be objected that the analogy is not valid, for there is an important asymmetry between pain and pleasure: the former has significantly greater moral weight than the latter. While it may be morally acceptable to cross the borders of intimacy in order to relieve pain or suffering, which is what the nurse does, that does not show that it is permissible to do so merely for the sake of giving pleasure, which is what the prostitute provides. But if so, what are we to say of a fairly good looking woman who undergoes plastic surgery and has her breasts enlarged (or made smaller) in order to become even more attractive and make her sex life richer and more pleasurable than it already is? Is she really doing something degrading and morally wrong?

(iv) Prostitution is degrading because what the prostitute sells is not simply and innocuously a service, as it may appear to a superficial look; actually, there is much truth in the old-fashioned way of speaking of her as a woman who 'sells herself'. And if *that* is not degrading, what is?

The point has been made in two different ways.

David Archard has recently argued that there is a sense in which the prostitute sells herself because of the roles and attitudes involved in the transaction:

> Sexual pleasure is not . . . an innocent commodity. Always implicated in such pleasure is the performance of roles, both willing and unwilling. These roles range from the possibly benign ones of doer and done-to, through superior and subordinate to abaser and abased. Thus, when a man buys 'sex' he also buys a sexual role from his partner, and this involves the prostitute in being something more than simply the neutral exchanger of some commodity.

More specifically,

> if I buy (and you willingly sell) your allegiance, your obsequiousness, your flattery or your servility there is no easy distinction to be made between you as 'seller' and the 'good' you choose to sell. Your whole person is implicated in the exchange. So it is too with the sale of sex.[30]

However, commercial sex need not involve obsequiousness, flattery or servility, let alone allegiance, on the part of the prostitute. These attitudes, and the 'role' they might be thought to make up, are not its constitutive parts; whether, when, and to what degree they characterize the transaction is an empirical question that admits of no simple and general answer. Indeed, those who, knowingly or not, tend to approach the whole subject of sex from a 'romantic' point of view often say that sex with prostitutes is an impoverished, even sordid experience because of the impersonal, quick, mechanical, blunt way in which the prostitute goes about her job.

Moreover, some services that have nothing to do with sex tend to involve and are expected to involve some such attitudes on the part of the person providing the service. Examples would vary from culture to culture; the waiter and the hairdresser come to mind in ours. Now such attitudes are undoubtedly morally flawed; but that does not tell against any particular occupation in which they may be manifested, but rather against the attitudes themselves, the individuals who, perhaps unthinkingly, come to adopt them, and the social conventions that foster such attitudes.

Another way to try to show that the prostitute sells herself, rather than merely a service like any other, is to focus on the concept of self-identity. This is the tack taken by Carole Pateman. She first points out that the service provided by the prostitute is related in a much closer way to her body than is the case with any other service, for sex and sexuality are constitutive of the body, while the labour and skills hired out in other lines of work are not. 'Sexuality and the body are . . . integrally connected to conceptions of femininity and masculinity, and all these are constitutive of our individuality, our sense of self-identity.'[31] Therefore, when sex becomes a commodity, so do bodies and selves.

But if so, what of our ethnic identity? When asked to say who they are, do not people normally bring up their ethnic identity as one of the most important things they need to mention? If it is granted that one's ethnic identity is also constitutive of one's individuality, one's sense of self-identity, what are we to say of a person who creates an item of authentic folk art and then sells it, or of a singer who gives a concert of folk music and charges for attendance? Are they also selling themselves, and thus doing something degrading and wrong?

The likely response will be to refuse to grant our ethnic identity the same significance for our self-identity that is claimed for gender. Although people typically refer to their ethnic identity when explaining who they are, there are also many exceptions. There are individuals who used to think of themselves in such terms, but have come to repudiate, not merely their particular ethnic affiliation, but the very idea that ethnicity should be part of one's sense of who one is. There are also persons

who have always felt that way (perhaps because that is how they were
brought up to feel). They do not think of their own sense of self-identity
as somehow incomplete, and neither should we. There are no analogous
examples with regard to gender; we all think of ourselves as either men
or women, and whatever particular conception one has of one's gender,
the conception is closely connected with one's sexuality. Gender is much
more basic than ethnicity, much more closely related to our sense of self-
identity than ethnicity and anything else that may be thought relevant.

Perhaps it is.[32] But if that is reason enough to say that the prostitute
sells her body and herself, and thus does something degrading and
wrong, will not we have to say the same of the wet nurse and the surrogate mother? Their bodies and gender are no less involved in what they
do than the body and gender of the prostitute; and they charge a fee, just
as the prostitute does. I do not know that anybody has argued that there
is something degrading, or otherwise morally wrong, in what the wet
nurse does, nor that what she does is selling her body or herself, so I
think she is a good counterexample to Pateman's argument.

The surrogate mother might be thought a less compelling one, for
there has been considerable debate about the nature and moral standing of surrogacy. I do not need to go into all that, though.[33] The one objection to surrogacy relevant in the present context is 'that it is
inconsistent with human dignity that a woman should use her uterus for
financial profit and treat it as an incubator for someone else's child.'[34]
However, it is not explained just why it should be thought inconsistent
with human dignity to do that. Indeed, it is not clear how it could be, if
it is not inconsistent with human dignity that a woman should use her
breasts for financial profit and treat them as a source of nourishment for
someone else's child. And if it is not, why should it be inconsistent with
human dignity that a woman should use her sex organs and skills for financial profit and treat them as a source of pleasure for someone else?

5. The Feminist Critique (b): Oppression of Women

The other main feminist objection to prostitution is that it exemplifies
and helps to maintain the oppression of women. This objection is much
more often made than argued. It is frequently made by quoting the
words of Simone de Beauvoir that the prostitute 'sums up all the forms
of feminine slavery at once';[35] but de Beauvoir's chapter on prostitution,
although quite good as a description of some of its main types, is short
on argument and does nothing to show that prostitution as such must be
implicated in the oppression of women.

An argument meant to establish that with regard to our society has recently been offered by Laurie Shrage. She expressly rejects the idea of

discussing commercial sex in a 'cross-cultural' or 'trans-historical' way, and grants that it need not be oppressive to women in every conceivable or, indeed, every existing society. What she does claim is that in our society prostitution epitomizes and perpetuates certain basic cultural assumptions about men, women and sex which provide justification for the oppression of women in many domains of their lives, and in this way harm both prostitutes and women in general.[36]

There are four such cultural assumptions, which need not be held consciously but may be implicit in daily behaviour. A strong sex drive is a universal human trait. Sexual behaviour defines one's social identity, makes one a particular 'kind' of person: one is 'a homosexual', 'a prostitute', 'a loose woman'. Men are 'naturally' dominant. In this connection, Shrage points out that the sex industry in our society caters almost exclusively to men, and 'even the relatively small number of male prostitutes at work serve a predominantly male consumer group.'[37] Finally, sexual contact pollutes and harms women.

The last claim is supported by a three-pronged argument. (i) In a woman, a history of sexual activity is not taken to suggest experience in a positive sense, expertise, high-quality sex. On the contrary, it is seen as a negative mark that marks off a certain kind of woman; women are valued for their 'innocence'. (ii) That sex with men is damaging to women is implicit in the vulgar language used to describe the sex act: 'a woman is "fucked", "screwed", "banged", "had", and so forth, and it is a man (a "prick") who does it to her.'[38] (iii) The same assumption is implicit in 'the metaphors we use' for the sex act. Here Shrage draws on Andrea Dworkin's book *Intercourse,* which invokes images of physical assault and imperialist domination and describes women having sexual intercourse with men as being not only entered or penetrated, but also 'split', 'invaded', 'occupied' and 'colonized' by men.

These cultural assumptions define the meaning of prostitution in our society. By tolerating prostitution, our society implies its acceptance of these assumptions, which legitimize and perpetuate the oppression of women and their marginality in all the main areas of social life. As for prostitutes and their clients, whatever their personal views of sex, men and women, they imply by their actions that they accept these assumptions and the practice they justify.

Now this argument is unobjectionable as far as it goes; but it does not go as far as Shrage means it to. In order to assess its real scope, we should first note that she repeatedly speaks of 'our' and 'our society's' toleration of prostitution, and refers to this toleration as the main ground for the conclusion that the cultural assumptions prostitution is said to epitomize in our society are indeed generally accepted in it. But toleration and acceptance are not quite the same; actually, toleration is normally defined as the putting up with something we *do not* accept. Moreover, prostitution is not tolerated at all. It is not tolerated legally: in the United States it is legal only in Nevada and illegal in all other states, while in the United Kingdom and elsewhere in the West, even though it is not against the law as such, various activities practically inseparable from it are. Some of these restrictions are quite crippling; for instance, as Marilyn G. Haft rightly says, 'to legalize prostitution while prohibiting solicitation makes as much sense as encouraging free elections but prohibiting campaigning.'[39] It certainly is not tolerated morally; as I pointed out at the beginning, the condemnation of prostitution is one of the very few prohibitions of the traditional sexual morality that are still with us. It is still widely held that prostitution is seriously morally wrong, and the prostitute is subjected to considerable moral pressure, including the ultimate moral sanction, ostracism from decent society. That the practice is still with us is not for want of trying to suppress it, and therefore should not be taken as a sign that it is being tolerated.

Furthermore, not all the cultural assumptions prostitution in our society allegedly epitomizes and reinforces are really generally accepted. The first two—that human beings have a strong sex drive, and that one's sexual behaviour defines one's social identity—probably are. The other two assumptions—that men are 'naturally' dominant, and that sex with men harms women—are more important, for they make it possible to speak of oppression of women in this context. I am not so sure about the former; my impression is that at the very least it is no longer accepted quite as widely as it used to be a couple of decades ago. And I think it is clear that the latter is not generally accepted in our society today. The evidence Shrage brings up to show that it is is far from compelling.

(i) It is probably true that the fact that a woman has a history of sexual activity is not generally appreciated as an indicator of experience and expertise, analogously to other activities. But whatever the explanation is—and one is certainly needed—I do not think that entails the other half of Shrage's diagnosis, namely that women are valued for their 'innocence'. That particular way of valuing women and the whole 'Madonna or harlot' outlook to which it belongs are well behind us as a society, although they characterize the sexual morality of some very traditional communities. A society which has made its peace with non-marital sex in general and adolescent sex in particular to the extent that ours has could not possibly have persisted in valuing women for their 'innocence'.

(ii) Shrage draws on Robert Baker's analysis of the language used to refer to men, women and sex. Baker's point of departure is the claim that the way we talk about something reflects our conception of it; he looks into the ways we talk about sex and gender in order to discover what our conceptions of these are. With regard to sexual intercourse, it turns out that the vulgar verbs used to refer to it, such as 'fuck', 'screw', 'lay', 'have,' etc., display an interesting asymmetry: they require an active construction when the subject is a man, and a passive one when the subject is a woman. This reveals that we conceive of male and female roles in sex in different ways: the male is active, the female passive. Some of these verbs—'fuck', 'screw', 'have'—are also used metaphorically to indicate deceiving, taking advantage of, harming someone. This shows that we conceive of the male sexual role as that of harming the person in the female role, and of a person who plays the female sexual role as someone who is being harmed.[40]

This is both interesting and revealing, but what is revealed is not enough to support Shrage's case. Why is 'the standard view of sexual intercourse'[41] revealed not in the standard, but in the vulgar, i.e. substandard way of talking about it? After all, everybody, at least occasionally, talks about it in the standard way, while only some use the vulgar language too. Baker justifies his focusing on the latter by pointing out that the verbs which belong to the former, and are not used in the sense of inflicting harm as well, 'can take both females and males as subjects (in active constructions) and thus *do not pick out the female role*. This demonstrates that we conceive of sexual roles in such a way that only females are thought to be taken advantage of in intercourse.'[42] It seems to me that the 'we' is quite problematic, and that all that these facts demonstrate is that some of us, namely those who speak of having sex with women as fucking or screwing them, also think of sex with them in these terms. Furthermore, the ways of talking about sex may be less fixed than Baker's analysis seems to suggest. According to Baker, sentences such as 'Jane fucked Dick', 'Jane screwed Dick' and 'Jane laid Dick', if taken in the literal sense, are not sentences in English. But the usage seems to have changed since his article was published; I have heard native speakers of English make such sentences without a single (linguistic) eyebrow being raised. The asymmetry seems to have lost ground. So the import of the facts analysed by Baker is much more limited than he and Shrage take it to be, and the facts themselves are less clear-cut and static too.

(iii) Shrage's third argument for the claim that our society thinks of sex with men as polluting and harmful to women is the weakest. Images of physical assault and imperialist domination are certainly not 'the metaphors we use for the act of sexual intercourse'; I do not know that anyone except Andrea Dworkin does. The most likely reason people do not is that it would be silly to do so.

What all this shows, I think, is that there is no good reason to believe that our society adheres to a single conception of heterosexual sex, the conception defined by the four cultural assumptions Shrage describes, claims to be epitomized in, and reinforced by, prostitution, and wants to ascribe to every single case of commercial sex in our society as its 'political and social meaning', whatever the beliefs and values of the individuals concerned. Some members of our society think of heterosexual sex in terms of Shrage's four assumptions and some do not. Accordingly, there are in our society two rather different conceptions of prostitution, which in this context are best termed (a) prostitution as commercial screwing, and (b) prostitution as commercial sex *simpliciter*. What is their relative influence on the practice of prostitution in our society is a question for empirical research. Shrage rightly objects to the former for being implicated in the oppression of women in our society, and one need not be a feminist in order to agree. But that objection is not an objection to prostitution in our society as such.

6. Conclusion

I have taken a critical look at a number of arguments advanced to support the claim that prostitution stands morally condemned. If what I have been saying is right, none of these arguments is convincing.[43] Therefore, until some new and better ones are put forward, the conclusion must be that there is nothing morally wrong with it.[44] Writing about pornography—another practice which has been condemned and suppressed by traditional morality and religion, and has recently come under attack from feminist authors as well—G. L. Simons said that in a society which values liberty, 'social phenomena are, like individuals, innocent until proven guilty.'[45] So is prostitution.[46]

Notes

1. I am concerned only with prostitution in its primary, narrow sense of 'commercial' or 'mercenary sex', 'sex for money', and not with prostitution in the derived sense of 'use of one's ability or talent in a base or unworthy way'. The question I am asking is whether prostitution in the former, original sense is a case of prostitution in the latter, secondary sense.

2. F. Engels, *The Origin of the Family, Private Property and the State,* trans. A. West (Harmondsworth: Penguin, 1985), 102.

The point was made as early as 1790; see M. Wollstonecraft, *Works,* J. Todd and M. Butler (eds.) (London: William Pickering, 1989), V, 22, 129.

3. Here I am drawing on K. Davis, 'The Sociology of Prostitution', *Deviance,* S. Dinitz, R. R. Dynes and A. C. Clare (eds.), 2nd ed. (New York: Oxford University Press, 1975).

4. Ibid., 328.

5. G. Dworkin, 'Paternalism', *The Monist* 56 (1972), 65.

6. L. Ericsson, 'Charges against Prostitution: An Attempt at a Philosophical Assessment', *Ethics* 90 (1979/80), 357.

7. D. A. J. Richards, *Sex, Drugs, Death, and the Law: An Essay on Human Rights and Overcriminalization* (Totowa, NJ: Rowman & Littlefield, 1982), 113.

8. Ibid., 146 n. 251. The study referred to is described in W. B. Pomeroy, 'Some Aspects of Prostitution', *Journal of Sex Research* 1 (1965).

9. L. Ericsson, loc. cit.

10. For an analysis of the two kinds of paternalism, see J. Feinberg, 'Legal Paternalism', *Canadian Journal of Philosophy* 1 (1971), 105–24.

11. Many authors who have written on prostitution as a 'social evil' have claimed that it is virtually never a freely chosen occupation, since various social conditions (lack of education, poverty, unemployment) force innumerable women into it. This argument makes it possible for Mrs Warren (and many others) to condemn prostitution, while absolving the prostitute. But even if the empirical claim were true, it would not amount to an argument against prostitution, but only against the lack of alternatives to it.

12. J. S. Mill, *On Liberty*, C. V. Shields (ed.) (Indianapolis: Bobbs-Merrill, 1956), 93.

It was clear to Mill that his rejection of paternalism applied in the case of prostitution just as in any other case, but the way he says that is somewhat demure; see ibid., 120–22.

13. M. Walzer, *The Spheres of Justice* (New York: Basic Books, 1983), 100–103.

14. Ibid., 103. (The parts of the quotation I have deleted refer to religious prostitution, which is not the subject of this paper.)

15. Augustine, *Concerning the City of God*, trans. H. Bettenson (Harmondsworth: Penguin, 1972), Bk. 14, Ch. 16, 577.

16. B. Mandeville, *The Fable of the Bees*, F. B. Kaye (ed.) (Oxford University Press, 1957), Remark (H.), I, 95–96, 100.

Mandeville discusses prostitution in detail in *A Modest Defence of Publick Stews: or, an Essay upon Whoring, As it is now practis'd in these Kingdoms* (London: A. Moore, 1724) (published anonymously). The argument I have quoted from the *Fable* is elaborated on pp. ii–iii, xi–xii, 39–52.

17. A. Schopenhauer, 'On Women', *Parerga and Paralipomena*, trans. E. F. J. Payne (Oxford: Oxford University Press, 1974), I, 623.

18. W. E. H. Lecky, *History of European Morals* (London: Longmans, Green & Co., 1869), II, 299–300.

19. B. Russell, *Marriage and Morals* (London: George Allen & Unwin, 1958), 116.

20. St. Augustine, *De ordine*, II, 4; St. Thomas Aquinas, *Summa theologiae*, 2a2ae, q. 10, art. 11.

21. H. Benjamin and R. E. L. Masters, *Prostitution and Morality* (London: Souvenir Press, 1965), 201.

22. See A. Goldman, 'Plain Sex', *Philosophy of Sex*, A. Soble (ed.) (Totowa, NJ: Littlefield, Adams & Co., 1980), in this volume, pp. 39–55; R. Vannoy, *Sex without Love: A Philosophical Exploration* (Buffalo: Prometheus Books, 1980).

23. Op. cit., 99–104.

24. Ibid., 103–104.

25. For examples of this kind of reasoning and a detailed discussion of its structure, see J. Wilson, *Logic and Sexual Morality* (Harmondsworth: Penguin, 1965), 59–74.

26. See J. R. Richards, *The Sceptical Feminist: A Philosophical Enquiry* (London: Routledge & Kegan Paul, 1980), 198–202.

27. B. Russell, op. cit., 121–122.

28. Here I find Russell's version of the principle of respect for human beings as such more helpful than the classic, Kantian one (H. J. Paton, *The Moral Law: Kant's Groundwork of the Metaphysic of Morals* [London: Hutchinson, 1969], 90–93); for Russell puts it forward as an independent principle, while in Kant it cannot function on its own, but only when accepted together with other tenets of Kant's ethical theory, which one may well find problematic (cf. H. E. Jones, *Kant's Principle of Personality* [Madison: The University of Wisconsin Press, 1971]).

29. L. Ericsson, op. cit., 342.

30. D. Archard, 'Sex for Sale: The Morality of Prostitution', *Cogito* 3 (1989), 49–50.

31. C. Pateman, 'Defending Prostitution: Charges against Ericsson', *Ethics* 93 (1982/3), 562.

32. But see A. Appiah, ' "But Would That Still Be Me?": Notes on Gender, "Race", Ethnicity, as Sources of "Identity" ', *The Journal of Philosophy* 87 (1990).

33. On the arguments pro and con see *Report of the Committee of Inquiry into Human Fertilisation and Embryology* (London: HMSO, 1984), Ch. VIII; M. Warnock, 'The Artificial Family', and M. Lockwood, 'The Warnock Report: A Philosophical Appraisal', *Moral Dilemmas in Modern Medicine,* M. Lockwood (ed.) (Oxford University Press, 1985).

34. *Report,* 45.

35. S. de Beauvoir, *The Second Sex,* trans. and ed. H. M. Parshley (London: Pan Books, 1988), 569.

36. By 'our society' Shrage most of the time seems to mean contemporary American society, but toward the end of the paper claims to have discussed 'the meaning of commercial sex in modern Western culture' (L. Shrage, 'Should Feminists Oppose Prostitution?', *Ethics* 99 (1989/90), 361). [This volume, pp. 435–50, at p. 447.]

37. Ibid., 354. [This volume, p. 442.]

38. Ibid., 355. [This volume, p. 443.]

39. M. G. Haft, 'Hustling for Rights', *The Civil Liberties Review* 1 (1973/4), 20, quoted in A. M. Jaggar, 'Prostitution', *Philosophy of Sex,* 1st edn., A. Soble (ed.), 350.

40. See R. Baker, ' "Pricks" and "Chicks": A Plea for "Persons" ', *Philosophy and Sex,* R. Baker and F. Elliston (eds.) (Buffalo: Prometheus Books, 1975).

41. Ibid. 50.

42. Ibid. 61.

43. I have not discussed those arguments against prostitution which I think have been effectively refuted by others. See L. Ericsson, op. cit., on the arguments that prostitution exemplifies and reinforces commercialization of society, that it is an extreme case of the general inequality between men and women, that sex is much too basic and elementary in human life to be sold, and on the Marxist critique of prostitution in general; and L. E. Lomasky, 'Gift Relations, Sexual Relations and Freedom', *The Philosophical Quarterly* 33 (1983), on the argument that commercial sex devalues sex given freely, as a gift.

44. That is, there is nothing morally wrong with it as long as the term 'morally wrong' is used in its robust sense, nicely captured e.g. by Mill: 'We do not call

anything wrong unless we mean to imply that a person ought to be punished in some way or other for doing it—if not by law, by the opinion of his fellow creatures; if not by opinion, by the reproaches of his own conscience' (*Utilitarianism,* G. Sher (ed.) [Indianapolis: Hackett, 1979], 47). This is the sense the term usually has in everyday moral discourse. When we say, e.g., that stealing is wrong, we normally do not mean to say merely that stealing falls short of the ideal way of relating to other people's property, or is not part of the good life, the best use one can put one's fingers to, or something one would recommend as a career to one's teenage daughter; we rather express our condemnation of stealing and imply that it is appropriate to apply the pressure of the moral sanction on those who steal. Of course, those given to using the term in some wider, watered-down sense may well come to the conclusion that prostitution is wrong after all.

45. G. L. Simons, *Pornography without Prejudice: A Reply to Objectors* (London: Abelard-Schuman, 1972), 96.

46. I have benefited from conversations on the subject of this paper with Carla Freccero and Bernard Gert, and from critical responses from audiences at Hull, Liverpool, Newcastle, St. Andrews and York, where I read this paper in December 1990/January 1991.

My greatest debt is to Antony Duff, Sandra Marshall, and Walter Sinnott-Armstrong, who read an earlier version of the paper and made a number of critical comments and suggestions for clarification and revision.

The paper was written during my stay at the Morrell Studies in Toleration project, Department of Politics, University of York, in the Winter and Spring terms of 1990/91. I would like to acknowledge with gratitude a research grant from the British Academy, which made that possible.

Chapter 30

WHORING IN UTOPIA

Pat Califia

Even people who are supportive of sex workers' rights often assume that prostitution would somehow wither away if women achieved equality with men or industrial capitalism fell on its blemished, bloated face. Whoring, like other deviant and thus "problematic" sexual behavior, is assumed to be an artifact of sexism, American imperialism, racism, insane narcotics laws, Christianity, or whatever institutionalized inequity has the pontificator's knickers in a twist. While large and sweeping social change would probably alter the nature of sex work, the demographics of sex workers, and the wage scale, along with every other kind of human intimacy, I doubt very much that a just society would (or could) eliminate paying for pleasure.

Prostitutes, both male and female, have been with us from the earliest recorded time. The "art of prostitution" and "the cult of the prostitute" are two of the *me* (sacred treasures) given to the Sumerian goddess Inanna by her father Enki, the god of wisdom. When Inanna takes the *me* back to the city of Uruk in the boat of heaven, the people turn out in droves to cheer in gratitude. A hymn to Inanna which describes the people of Sumer parading before her says, "The male prostitutes comb their hair before you. They decorate the napes of their necks with colored scarves. They drape the cloak of the gods about their shoulders." These poems are thousands of years old. In fact, Sumer is the first civilization from which we have written texts. And there's no reason (other than a

Pat Califia, "Whoring in Utopia," from her *Public Sex: The Culture of Radical Sex* (Cleis Press, 1994), pp. 242–48. Reprinted with the permission of Cleis Press.

certain wistful prudishness) to think that commerce and sex won't continue to intersect as long as either has meaning or a place in human culture.

In America today, the sex industry is shaped by several negative forces. First of all, because the work itself is illegal or plays pretty close to that edge, it attracts people who are desperate, who believe they have few or no other choices, and people who embrace the identities of rebel, outsider, and criminal. Very few sex workers are able to be open with their children, lovers or spouses, friends, and families about how they earn their livings. This need to hide puts enormous stress on people who are paid for relieving the stress of their customers.

The existence of prostitution as we know it is based on the compartmentalizations of male sexuality and female identity. There are women whom men marry and with whom they have children, and there are women whom they screw for a set fee. The wife-and-mother class is not supposed to acknowledge the existence of the whore class because that would destroy the "good" woman's illusion that *her* faithful, loving husband does not have an alternate identity as a john. The opportunity for paid infidelity (as long as it is hidden and stigmatized) makes monogamous marriage a believable institution. Of course not every married man has sex with hookers, but enough of them do to keep the black-market sex economy booming.

The illicit sex trade interacts and overlaps with other underground economies such as stolen merchandise and the circulation of illegal aliens. But the most influential of such economies is the narcotics trade. Street prostitution is the only occupation that provides most female (and more than a few male) junkies with enough money to support addiction to the overpriced, adulterated narcotics that our "Just Say No" social policy on drugs has caused to flood the urban environment.

Also, as technology grows more complex and educational opportunities for workers constrict, prostitution has become one of the few forms of employment for unskilled laborers. (Another slot for unskilled laborers, which is generated by laws against solicitation, is on the vice squad. Cops are often the socioeconomic counterparts of the people they harass, blackmail, bust, and control.)

So what would happen to the sex industry if some of these shaping constraints were lifted? What if narcotics were decriminalized and addicts were able to get prescriptions for maintenance doses of good drugs at decent prices? What if prostitution itself were decriminalized *and* destigmatized? If women had the same buying power that men do? If racism no longer forced so many nonwhite citizens into second-class citizenship and poverty? If the virgin/whore dichotomy and the double standard melted away? If everybody had sex education, access to contraception and safe-sex prophylactics, and we no longer believed sex was toxic? Wouldn't the free citizens of this wonderful society be able to get all the sex they wanted from other free agents?

Of course not! One of the dominant myths of our culture is that everybody longs to participate in romantic heterosexual love; that it is romance which gives life meaning and purpose; and that sex is better when you do it with somebody you love. We are also taught to assume that romance and money are mutually exclusive, even though the heroes of romance novels and neogothics are almost always as wealthy as they are handsome. It would be foolish to deny the existence of romantic passion and lust, but it would be equally foolish to ignore the people who prefer to fuck as far away as possible from the trappings of Valentine's Day. These people don't enjoy the roller coaster ride of romantic love. And there will always be people who simply don't get turned on in the context of an ongoing, committed relationship. Some of these people make trustworthy and affectionate, permanent or long-term partners as long as they're not expected to radiate a lot of sexual heat. But in a more sex-positive society, these folks might be able to have both marriage and paid sex without the guilt and stigma of being diagnosed as psychologically "immature" or "incomplete."

It's also possible that prostitution would become romanticized and idealized. The relatively new reality of women as wage earners has generated enormous tension in heterosexual relationships. This hostility has been exacerbated by divorce laws which continue to force men to pay child support and alimony while depriving them of their homes and custody of their children. In a world of prenuptial agreements and lawsuits for breach of promise and sexual harassment, the "good" woman who was once valorized by men as a suitable candidate for marriage and motherhood is increasingly perceived as a leech and a liability. More men may come to believe that "nice girls" are revolted by sex and will take all their money, while "fallen women" like cock, like sex, and want only a hundred dollars or so. The current media obsession with supermodels needs only a little push to turn into an image blitz popularizing glamorous courtesans and hookers with hearts of gold and ever available cunts-without-commitment.

Even in a just society, there probably would be plenty of people who were simply too busy to engage in the ritual of courtship, dating, and seduction. A person with a job that requires a great deal of travel, for example, may not have a stable enough living situation to connect with and keep a steady lover or spouse. Some of these harried businesspeople will be women. While male sex workers—whether they identify as gay or straight—today service an overwhelmingly male market, I can't imagine what would stop women who could afford it from beckoning the prettiest boys that money can buy to their executive limos, helicopters, and hotel suites. This new job market would have a tremendous impact on the parameters of male heterosexuality, identity, and fashion. Straight men are currently defined mostly by the things that they do *not* do (wear dresses or bright colors, get fucked, suck dick). But in a buyer's market, proactive behavior is at a premium. Female customers would prefer to be serviced by men who actively demonstrate their ability to please women and their arousal at the thought of doing so. The word "slut" would lose its gender.

There will always be people who don't have the charm or social skill to woo a partner. In a society where mutual attraction and sexual reciprocity are the normal bases for bonding, what would happen to the unattractive people, those without the ability or interest to give as good as they get? Disabled people, folks with chronic or terminal illnesses, the elderly, and the sexually dysfunctional would continue to benefit (as they do now) from the ministrations of skilled sex workers who do not discriminate against these populations.

The requirements of fetishists can be very specific. People who have strong preferences for specific objects, acts, substances, or physical types would probably continue to find it easier to meet their sexual needs by hiring professionals with the appropriate wardrobes or toolboxes of paraphernalia. Furthermore, a great many prostitutes' customers have fetishes for paying for sex. It's the sight of that cash sliding into a bustier or a stocking top that makes their dicks get hard, not the cleavage or the shapely thigh. Many festishist scripts are simply elaborate forms of sublimated and displaced masturbation that do not offer anything other than vicarious pleasure to the fetishist's partner. For example, a shoe fetishist's girlfriend may not be particularly upset about her or his need to be kicked with white patent-leather pumps with thirteen straps and eight-inch heels, but performing this act is probably not going to make her come. Especially in utopia, there would be no reason for someone to play the martyr and try to be sexually satisfied by an act of charity. Cash would even the bargain and keep the fetishist from becoming an erotic welfare case.

The first experience one has with physical pleasure has a dramatic impact on the rest of one's life as a sexually active being. In a better world, virgins and novices would probably resort to prostitutes who specialized in rituals of initiation and education. A talented sex worker could introduce brand new players to all of their sexual options, show them appropriate ways to protect themselves from conception or disease, and teach them the skills they need to please more experienced partners. This is a sensible antidote to the traumatic rite of passage that "losing your cherry" often is today.

An encounter with a hooker is already a standard part of the traditional bachelor party. The groom must pay tribute to the wild woman and subsidize her freedom before he is allowed to lay claim to a bride he can domesticate. If whoring were not stigmatized, it could be used to celebrate all kinds of holidays. A visit with an especially desirable and skilled sex worker would probably make a great lift for grandma when she came out of mourning for her deceased husband. A pregnant wife could thank her husband for being supportive and patient by giving him a weekend with the girl or boy of his dreams. Paid vacations could include sexual services. Bar mitzvahs and other puberty rites would be obvious occasions for incorporating orgasms for hire.

Since human beings are a curious species, and many of us need adventure, risk, and excitement, I would hope that the sex industry would continue to be available to fulfill those needs in positive ways. The thrill of arranging several sexual encounters with people you don't know very well certainly seems more healthy to me than big-game hunting or full-contact sports, which are high-risk activities sanctioned by our society. The story of the hero who meets a beautiful stranger and wins her favors is archetypal. If we are fortunate, we encounter the anima/animus in our beloved. But until that magical moment, those of us who require refreshment, insight, and sexual nourishment could pay for receiving that blessing. We may have an innate human need to take that mystical journey of transformation into a stranger's arms.

Perhaps sex work would even find its spirituality restored. Those who wished to worship icons of womanhood, manhood, or intersexuality could perform these sacred obligations with sex workers who were guardians of the mysteries of the human heart and loins. The Great Rite, the ancient sacred marriage between earth and sky, teaches us to respect the ecology of the natural world. Perhaps the Sierra Club could sponsor an annual *hieros gamos* as part of its major fundraising drive. Of course, the performers in such a majestic pageant would have to be compensated for their efforts.

It's obvious that the range of people who sought out sex for money would change dramatically in a kinder, gentler world. But what about the people who would do sex work? I wonder if the boundaries between whore and client might not become more permeable. The prostitute's identity is currently rather rigid, partly because once you have been "soiled" by that work you are never supposed to be able to escape the stigma, but also because such rigidity creates clarity for the heterosexual male. He is what the prostitute is not (male, moneyed, in charge, legitimate, normal). In a world where women were as likely to be clients as men; sex workers were well paid and in charge of their own lives; and prostitute were as valid a social identity as Senate majority whip, there would be less need for the high walls between "good" and "bad" people, "men" and "women." Everybody might expect to spend a portion of her or his life as a sex worker before getting married, if she or he didn't want to be thought of as sexually gauche. Perhaps there would be collective brothels where people could perform community service to work off parking tickets or student loans. A stint in the community pleasure house might be analogous to going on retreat.

The people who took up sex work as a profession would be more likely to pursue the erotic arts as vocations, just as priests and artists do today for their professions. They would be teachers, healers, adventurous souls—tolerant and compassionate. Prostitutes *are* all of those things today, but they perform their acts of kindness and virtue in a milieu of ingratitude. The profession would attract people who like working for themselves, who are easily bored, who want a lot of social contact and stimulation. It would also attract dramatic, exhibitionist performers and storytellers. As computer technology is used for sexual purposes, sex workers will need to be computer literate. The ideal sex worker might be somebody skilled at creating virtual realities, programming environments, characters, plots, and sensations for the client. This programming ability might become more compellingly sexy than a pair of big tits or a ten-inch dick.

Sex work would also attract stone butches of all genders and sexual orientations—people who want to run the fuck but are not interested in experiencing their own sexual vulnerability and pleasure. Often these people are the most adept at manipulating other people's experiences. They are more objective about their partners' fantasies and do not become distracted by their own desires, since their needs to remain remote and in control are already being fulfilled.

There are other social changes which would continue to alter the dynamics of the sex industry. In a society where everybody was doing work they enjoyed for fair wages, the meaning of money (and work itself) would change. It would cease to be a gender marker, for one thing (I am male, so I earn a paycheck; you are female, so men give you money). This change is already underway. In a postindustrial society where power was cheap or free and survival was no longer an issue, money might even cease to be a marker for social class. I believe human beings would still have the need to group themselves into smaller tribes or social units based on affinity and common interests, but the parameters of these groups would change. People would have new, now unforeseen, ecological slots as "those who pay/give" or "those who get paid/receive" for possessing certain characteristics or performing different activities.

Unfortunately, it's doubtful that any of these visions will be realized. As AIDS paranoia grows and nation-states continue to consolidate and extend their power, it's much more likely that sex workers will face harsher penalties and stepped-up law enforcement campaigns. In a few radical locales, prostitution might be legalized and subjected to strict government regulation as a social experiment to control AIDS and other sexually transmitted diseases. People seem to be suckers for anything that promises to make them safer, whether it's motorcycle-helmet laws or the Brady bill. But there is no guarantee that making the federal government the greatest pimp of all would do a goddamned thing to make sex work a better career or to protect the health and safety of the customer. In such a system, prostitutes would be like mill workers in late nineteenth-century England.

But a state that believes it has the right to send young men off to die in a war or conduct above-ground testing of atomic weapons in populated areas eventually will try to take over the hands, mouths, dicks, cunts, and buttholes that are sex workers' means of production. So the halcyon, golden days of prostitution may be happening right now. This may be as good, liberal, and free as it gets. So you might want to visit your ATM, take out a couple hundred bucks, and hurry to the red-light district now, before it becomes as antiquated as a Wild West ghost town.

SUGGESTED READINGS

General

Abramson, Paul R., and Steven D. Pinkerton, eds. *Sexual Nature Sexual Culture.* Chicago: University of Chicago Press, 1995.

Alexander, W. M. "Philosophers Have Avoided Sex." *Diogenes* 72 (Winter 1970): 56–74; rep. as pp. 3–19 in Alan Soble, ed., *The Philosophy of Sex,* 2nd edition. Savage, Md.: Rowman & Littlefield, 1991.

———. "Sex and Philosophy in Augustine." *Augustinian Studies* 5 (1974): 197–208.

Atkinson, Ronald. *Sexual Morality.* London: Hutchinson, 1965.

Baker, Robert, and Frederick Elliston, eds. *Philosophy and Sex.* 1st edition. Buffalo, N.Y.: Prometheus, 1975; 2nd edition, 1984.

Baker, Robert B., Kathleen J. Wininger, and Frederick A. Elliston, eds. *Philosophy and Sex.* 3rd edition. Amherst, N.Y.: Prometheus, 1998.

Belliotti, Raymond. *Good Sex: Perspectives on Sexual Ethics.* Lawrence: University Press of Kansas, 1993.

Brundage, James A. *Law, Sex, and Christian Society in Medieval Europe.* Chicago: University of Chicago Press, 1987.

Bullough, Vern L., and Bonnie Bullough. *Sexual Attitudes: Myths and Realities.* Amherst, N.Y.: Prometheus, 1995.

Bullough, Vern L., and Bonnie Bullough, eds. *Human Sexuality: An Encyclopedia.* New York: Garland, 1994.

Buss, David M. *The Evolution of Desire.* New York: Basic Books, 1994.

Davis, Murray. *Smut: Erotic Reality/Obscene Ideology.* Chicago: University of Chicago Press, 1983.

Dworkin, Andrea. *Intercourse.* New York: Free Press, 1987.

Foucault, Michel. *The Care of the Self.* Vol. 3 of *The History of Sexuality.* New York: Vintage, 1986.

———. *An Introduction.* Vol. 1 of *The History of Sexuality.* New York: Vintage, 1976

———. *The Use of Pleasure.* Vol. 2 of *The History of Sexuality.* New York: Pantheon, 1985.

Fuchs, Eric. *Sexual Desire and Love: Origins and History of the Christian Ethic of Sexuality and Marriage.* Trans. Marsha Daigle. New York: Seabury, 1983.

Gilbert, Paul. *Human Relationships: A Philosophical Introduction.* Oxford, Eng.: Blackwell, 1991.

Gruen, Lori, and George F. Panichas, eds. *Sex, Morality, and the Law.* New York: Routledge, 1997.

Gudorf, Christine E. *Body, Sex, and Pleasure: Reconstructing Christian Sexual Ethics.* Cleveland, Ohio: Pilgrim Press, 1994.

Hunter, J. F. M. *Thinking about Sex and Love.* New York: St. Martin's, 1980.

Jackson, Stevi, and Sue Scott, eds. *Feminism and Sexuality: A Reader.* New York: Columbia University Press, 1996.

Jeffreys, Sheila. *Anticlimax: A Feminist Perspective on the Sexual Revolution.* New York: New York University Press, 1990.

Laqueur, Thomas. *Making Sex: Body and Gender from the Greeks to Freud.* Cambridge, Mass.: Harvard University Press, 1990.

Leidholdt, Dorchen, and Janice C. Raymond, eds. *The Sexual Liberals and the Attack on Feminism.* New York: Teachers College Press, 1990.

LeMoncheck, Linda. *Loose Women, Lecherous Men: A Feminist Philosophy of Sex.* New York: Oxford University Press, 1997.

MacKinnon, Catharine A. *Feminism Unmodified.* Cambridge, Mass.: Harvard University Press, 1987.

Maglin, Nan Bauer, and Donna Perry, eds. *"Bad Girls"/"Good Girls": Women, Sex, and Power in the Nineties.* New Brunswick, N.J.: Rutgers University Press, 1996.

Marietta, Don E. Jr. *Philosophy of Sexuality.* Armonk, N.Y.: M. E. Sharpe, 1997.

Nozick, Robert. "Sexuality." Pp. 61–67 in his *The Examined Life.* New York: Simon and Schuster, 1989.

Nye, Robert A., ed. *Sexuality.* Oxford, Eng.: Oxford University Press, 1999.

Posner, Richard A. *Sex and Reason.* Cambridge, Mass.: Harvard University Press, 1992.

Primoratz, Igor. *Ethics and Sex.* London: Routledge, 1999.

Primoratz, Igor, ed. *Human Sexuality.* Aldershot, Eng.: Dartmouth, 1997.

Punzo, Vincent. *Reflective Naturalism: An Introduction to Moral Philosophy.* New York: Macmillan, 1969.

Radakovich, Anka. *Sexplorations: Journeys to the Erogenous Frontier.* New York: Crown, 1997.

Ranke-Heinemann, Uta. *Eunuchs for the Kingdom of Heaven: Women, Sexuality and the Catholic Church.* New York: Penguin, 1990.

Rubin, Lillian B. *Erotic Wars: What Happened to the Sexual Revolution?* New York: Farrar, Straus and Giroux, 1990.

Russell, Bertrand. *Marriage and Morals.* London: George Allen and Unwin, 1929.

Scruton, Roger. *Sexual Desire: A Moral Philosophy of the Erotic.* New York: Free Press, 1986.

Seidman, Steven. *Embattled Eros.* New York: Routledge, 1992.

Shelp, Earl E., ed. *Conceptual Roots.* Vol. 1 of *Sexuality and Medicine.* Dordrecht: Reidel, 1987.

———. *Ethical Viewpoints in Transition.* Vol. 2 of *Sexuality and Medicine.* Dordrecht: Reidel, 1987.

Singer, Irving. *The Goals of Human Sexuality.* New York: Schocken Books, 1973.

———. *Sex: A Philosophical Primer.* Lanham, Md.: Rowman & Littlefield, 2001.

Soble, Alan. *The Philosophy of Sex and Love: An Introduction.* St. Paul, Minn.: Paragon House, 1998.

———. *Sexual Investigations.* New York: New York University Press, 1996.

Soble, Alan, ed. *Eros, Agape, and Philia.* St. Paul, Minn.: Paragon House, 1989; rep. 1999.

————. *The Philosophy of Sex: Contemporary Readings.* 1st edition. Totowa, N.J.: Rowman & Littlefield, 1980; 2nd edition, Savage, Md.: Rowman & Littlefield, 1991; 3rd edition, Lanham, Md.: Rowman & Littlefield, 1997.

————. *Sex, Love, and Friendship.* Amsterdam: Editions Rodopi, 1997.

Solomon, Robert C., and Kathleen M. Higgins, eds. *The Philosophy of (Erotic) Love.* Lawrence: University Press of Kansas, 1991.

Stafford, J. Martin. *Essays on Sexuality and Ethics.* Solihull, Eng.: Ismeron, 1995.

Stein, Edward, ed. *Forms of Desire.* New York: Routledge, 1992.

Stewart, Robert M., ed. *Philosophical Perspectives on Sex and Love.* New York: Oxford University Press, 1995.

Thurber, James, and E. B. White. *Is Sex Necessary?* New York: Harper and Brothers, 1929.

Trevas, Robert, Arthur Zucker, and Donald Borchert, eds. *Philosophy of Sex and Love: A Reader.* Upper Saddle River, N.J.: Prentice-Hall, 1997.

Verene, Donald, ed. *Sexual Love and Western Morality.* 1st edition, New York: Harper and Row, 1972; 2nd edition, Boston: Jones and Bartlett, 1995.

Weeks, Jeffrey. *Invented Moralities: Sexual Values in an Age of Uncertainty.* New York: Columbia University Press, 1995.

————. *Sexuality and Its Discontents.* London: Routledge and Kegan Paul, 1985.

Weeks, Jeffrey, and Janet Holland, eds. *Sexual Cultures: Communities, Values and Intimacy.* New York: St. Martin's, 1996.

Whiteley, C. H., and Winifred N. Whiteley. *Sex and Morals.* New York: Basic Books, 1967.

Wojtyła, Karol [Pope John Paul II]. *Love and Responsibility.* New York: Farrar, Straus and Giroux, 1981.

Conceptual Analysis

Benn, Piers. "Is Sex Morally Special?" *Journal of Applied Philosophy* 16, 3 (1999): 235–45.

Frye, Marilyn. "Lesbian 'Sex.' " Pp. 109–19 in her *Willful Virgin: Essays in Feminism 1976–1992.* Freedom, Calif.: Crossing Press, 1992.

Giles, James. "A Theory of Love and Sexual Desire." *Journal for the Theory of Social Behavior* 24, 4 (1995): 339–57.

Jacobsen, Rockney. "Arousal and the Ends of Desire." *Philosophy and Phenomenological Research* 53, 3 (1993): 617–32.

Koertge, Noretta. "Constructing Concepts of Sexuality: A Philosophical Commentary." Pp. 387–97 in David McWhirter, Stephanie Sanders, and June Reinisch, eds., *Homosexuality/Heterosexuality: Concepts of Sexual Orientation.* New York: Oxford University Press, 1990.

Martin, Christopher F. J. "Are There Virtues and Vices That Belong Specifically to the Sexual Life?" *Acta Philosophica* 4, 2 (1995): 205–21.

Moore, Gareth. "Sexual Needs and Sexual Pleasures." *International Philosophical Quarterly* 35, 2 (1995): 193–204.

Ruddick, Sara. "Better Sex." Pp. 280–99 in Robert Baker and Frederick Elliston, eds., *Philosophy and Sex,* 2nd edition. Buffalo, N.Y.: Prometheus, 1984.

Shaffer, Jerome A. "Sexual Desire." *Journal of Philosophy* 75, 4 (1978): 175–89; rep. as pp. 1–12 in Alan Soble, ed., *Sex, Love, and Friendship.* Amsterdam: Editions Rodopi, 1997.

Sullivan, John P. "Philosophizing about Sexuality." *Philosophy of the Social Sciences* 14, 1 (1984): 83–96.

Taylor, Roger. "Sexual Experiences." *Proceedings of the Aristotelian Society* 68 (1967–68): 87–104; rep. as pp. 59–75 in Alan Soble, ed., *The Philosophy of Sex,* 1st edition. Totowa, N.J.: Rowman & Littlefield, 1980.

Sexual Perversion

Davidson, Arnold. "Conceptual History and Conceptions of Perversions." Pp. 476–86 in Robert B. Baker, Kathleen J. Wininger, and Frederick A. Elliston, eds., *Philosophy and Sex,* 3rd edition. Amherst, N.Y.: Prometheus, 1998.

———. "Sex and the Emergence of Sexuality." *Critical Inquiry* 14, 1 (1987): 16–48.

Denis, Lara. "Kant on the Wrongness of 'Unnatural' Sex." *History of Philosophy Quarterly* 16, 2 (1999): 225–48.

De Sousa, Ronald. "Norms and the Normal." Pp. 196–221 in Richard Wollheim, ed., *Freud: A Collection of Critical Essays.* Garden City, N.Y.: Anchor Books, 1974.

Gates, Katharine. *Deviant Desires: Incredibly Strange Sex.* New York: Juno Books, 2000.

Humber, James. "Sexual Perversion and Human Nature." *Philosophy Research Archives* 13 (1987–88): 331–50.

Kadish, Mortimer R. "The Possibility of Perversion." *Philosophical Forum* 19, 1 (1987): 34–53; rep. as pp. 93–116 in Alan Soble, ed., *The Philosophy of Sex,* 2nd edition. Savage, Md.: Rowman & Littlefield, 1991.

Kaplan, Louise J. *Female Perversions: The Temptations of Emma Bovary.* New York: Anchor Books, 1991.

Ketchum, Sara Ann. "The Good, the Bad, and the Perverted: Sexual Paradigms Revisited." Pp. 139–57 in Alan Soble, ed., *The Philosophy of Sex,* 1st edition. Totowa, N.J.: Rowman & Littlefield, 1980.

Kupfer, Joseph. "Sexual Perversion and the Good." *The Personalist* 59, 1 (1978): 70–77.

Levy, Donald. "Perversion and the Unnatural as Moral Categories." *Ethics* 90, 2 (1980): 191–202; rep. (revised and expanded) as pp. 169–89 in Alan Soble, ed., *The Philosophy of Sex,* 1st edition. Totowa, N.J.: Rowman & Littlefield, 1980.

Neu, Jerome. "Freud and Perversion." Pp. 175–208 in J. Neu, ed., *The Cambridge Companion to Freud.* Cambridge: Cambridge University Press, 1991.

———. "What Is Wrong with Incest?" *Inquiry* 19, 1 (1976): 27–39.

Priest, Graham. "Sexual Perversion." *Australasian Journal of Philosophy* 75, 3 (1997): 360–72.

Primoratz, Igor. "Sexual Perversion." *American Philosophical Quarterly* 34, 2 (1997): 245–58.

Slote, Michael. "Inapplicable Concepts and Sexual Perversion." Pp. 261–67 in

Robert Baker and Frederick Elliston, eds., *Philosophy and Sex,* 1st edition. Buffalo, N.Y.: Prometheus, 1975.

Soble, Alan. "Kant and Sexual Perversion." *The Monist* 86, 1 (2003), forthcoming.

Solomon, Robert. "Sex and Perversion." Pp. 268–87 in Robert Baker and Frederick Elliston, eds., *Philosophy and Sex,* 1st edition. Buffalo, N.Y.: Prometheus, 1975.

Steele, Valerie. *Fetish: Fashion, Sex and Power.* New York: Oxford University Press, 1996.

Vannoy, Russell. "The Structure of Sexual Perversity." Pp. 358–71 in Alan Soble, ed., *Sex, Love, and Friendship.* Amsterdam: Editions Rodopi, 1997.

Masturbation

Bennett, Paula, and Vernon A. Rosario, eds. *Solitary Pleasures: The Historical, Literary, and Artistic Discourses of Autoeroticism.* New York: Routledge, 1995.

Budapest, Zsuzsanna E. "Self-Blessing Ritual." Pp. 269–72 in Carol P. Christ and Judith Plaskow, eds., *Womanspirit Rising: A Feminist Reader in Religion.* San Francisco, Calif.: Harper and Row, 1979.

Burger, John R. *One-Handed Histories: The Eroto-Politics of Gay Male Video Pornography.* New York: Haworth, 1995.

Cornog, Martha, ed. *Self-Love/Self-Abuse.* San Francisco, Calif.: Down There Press, 2002.

Dodson, Betty. *Liberating Masturbation: A Meditation on Self-Love.* New York: Betty Dodson, 1978.

Engelhardt, H. Tristram Jr. "The Disease of Masturbation: Values and the Concept of Disease." *Bulletin of the History of Medicine* 48 (Summer 1974): 234–48; rep. as pp. 109–13 in T. Beauchamp and L. Walters, eds., *Contemporary Issues in Bioethics.* Encino, Calif.: Dickenson, 1978.

Fortunata, Jacqueline. "Masturbation and Women's Sexuality." Pp. 389–408 in Alan Soble, ed., *The Philosophy of Sex,* 1st edition. Totowa, N.J.: Rowman & Littlefield, 1980.

Francis, John J. "Masturbation." *Journal of the American Psychoanalytic Association* 16, 1 (1968): 95–112.

Groenendijk, Leendert F. "Masturbation and Neurasthenia: Freud and Stekel in Debate on the Harmful Effects of Autoeroticism." *Journal of Psychology and Human Sexuality* 9, 1 (1997): 71–94.

Haynes, James. "Masturbation." Pp. 381–85 in Vern Bullough and Bonnie Bullough, eds., *Human Sexuality: An Encyclopedia.* New York: Garland, 1994.

Kielkopf, Charles. "Masturbation: A Kantian Condemnation." *Philosophia* 25, 1–4 (1997): 223–46.

Moore, Gareth. "Natural Sex: Germain Grisez, Sex, and Natural Law." Pp. 223–41 in Nigel Biggar and Rufus Black, eds., *The Revival of Natural Law: Philosophical, Theological and Ethical Responses to the Finnis-Grisez School.* Aldershot, Eng.: Ashgate, 2000.

Sarnoff, Suzanne, and Irving Sarnoff. *Sexual Excitement/Sexual Peace: The Place of Masturbation in Adult Relationships.* New York: M. Evans, 1979.

Soble, Alan. "Kant and Sexual Perversion." *The Monist* 86, 1 (2003), forthcoming.
Tiefer, Leonore. "Review of Suzanne Sarnoff and Irving Sarnoff, Sexual Excitement/Sexual Peace: The Place of Masturbation in Adult Relationships." *Psychology of Women Quarterly* 8, 1 (1983): 107–9.

Homosexuality

Baird, Robert M., and M. Katherine Baird, eds. *Homosexuality: Debating the Issues.* Amherst, N.Y.: Prometheus, 1995.
Bersani, Leo. "Is the Rectum a Grave?" *October*, no. 43 (Winter 1987): 197–222.
Boswell, John. *Christianity, Social Tolerance, and Homosexuality.* Chicago: University of Chicago Press, 1980.
———. *Same-Sex Unions in Premodern Europe.* New York: Villard, 1994.
Bradshaw, David. "A Reply to Corvino." Pp. 17–30 in John Corvino, ed., *Same Sex: Debating the Ethics, Science, and Culture of Homosexuality.* Lanham, Md.: Rowman & Littlefield, 1997.
Calhoun, Cheshire. "Separating Lesbian Theory from Feminist Theory." *Ethics* 104, 3 (1994): 558–81.
Callahan, Sidney. "Why I Changed My Mind: Thinking about Gay Marriage." *Commonweal* (22 April 1994): 6–8.
Card, Claudia. *Lesbian Choices.* New York: Columbia University Press, 1995.
Colter, Ephen Glenn, Wayne Hoffman, Eva Pendleton, Alison Redick, and David Serlin, eds. *Policing Public Sex: Queer Politics and the Future of AIDS Activism.* Boston: South End Press, 1996.
Corvino, John, ed. *Same Sex: Debating the Ethics, Science, and Culture of Homosexuality.* Lanham, Md.: Rowman & Littlefield, 1997.
Dean, Craig R. "Fighting for Same Sex Marriage." Pp. 275–77 in A. Minas, ed., *Gender Basics.* Belmont, Calif.: Wadsworth, 1993.
Dreger, Alice Domurat. *Hermaphrodites and the Medical Invention of Sex.* Cambridge, Mass.: Harvard University Press, 1998.
Elliston, Frederick. "Gay Marriage." Pp. 146–66 in Robert Baker and Frederick Elliston, eds., *Philosophy and Sex,* 2nd edition. Buffalo, N.Y.: Prometheus, 1984.
Finnis, John M. "Law, Morality, and 'Sexual Orientation.'" *Notre Dame Law Review* 69, 5 (1994): 1049–76.
———. "Natural Law and Unnatural Acts." Pp. 5–27 in Igor Primoratz, ed., *Human Sexuality.* Aldershot, Eng.: Dartmouth, 1997.
Garber, Marjorie. *Vice Versa: Bisexuality and the Eroticism of Everyday Life.* New York: Simon and Schuster, 1995.
Halperin, David M. *One Hundred Years of Homosexuality.* New York: Routledge, 1990.
Hamer, Dean, and Peter Copeland. *The Science of Desire.* New York: Simon and Schuster, 1994.
Herdt, Gilbert. *Sambia Sexual Culture: Essays from the Field.* Chicago: University of Chicago Press, 1999.
Jung, Patricia, and Ralph Smith. *Heterosexism: An Ethical Challenge.* Albany: State University of New York Press, 1993.

Koppelman, Andrew. "Homosexual Conduct: A Reply to the New Natural Lawyers." Pp. 44–57 in John Corvino, ed., *Same Sex: Debating the Ethics, Science, and Culture of Homosexuality.* Lanham, Md.: Rowman & Littlefield, 1997.

LeVay, Simon. *Queer Science.* Cambridge, Mass.: MIT Press, 1996.

————. *The Sexual Brain.* Cambridge, Mass.: MIT Press, 1993.

Levin, Michael. "Why Homosexuality Is Abnormal." *The Monist* 67, 2 (1984): 251–83.

Mayo, David. "An Obligation to Warn of HIV Infection?" Pp. 447–53 in Alan Soble, ed., *Sex, Love and Friendship.* Amsterdam: Editions Rodopi, 1997.

Mohr, Richard D. "The Case for Gay Marriage." *Notre Dame Journal of Law, Ethics, and Public Policy* 9 (1995): 215–39.

————. *Gay Ideas.* Boston: Beacon Press, 1992.

————. *Gays/Justice.* New York: Columbia University Press, 1988.

————. *A More Perfect Union.* Boston: Beacon Press, 1994.

Moore, Gareth. "Natural Sex: Germain Grisez, Sex, and Natural Law." Pp. 223–41 in Nigel Biggar and Rufus Black, eds., *The Revival of Natural Law: Philosophical, Theological and Ethical Responses to the Finnis-Grisez School.* Aldershot, Eng.: Ashgate, 2000.

Murphy, Timothy F. "Homosexuality and Nature: Happiness and the Law at Stake." *Journal of Applied Philosophy* 4, 2 (1987): 195–204.

Murphy, Timothy F., ed. *Gay Ethics: Controversies in Outing, Civil Rights, and Sexual Science.* Binghamton, N.Y.: Haworth, 1994.

Nussbaum, Martha. "Platonic Love and Colorado Law: The Relevance of Ancient Greek Norms to Modern Sexual Controversies." *Virginia Law Review* 80, 7 (1994): 1515–651.

Prager, Dennis. "Homosexuality, the Bible, and Us—A Jewish Perspective." *The Public Interest,* no. 112 (Summer 1993): 60–83.

Reamer, Frederic G., ed. *AIDS & Ethics.* New York: Columbia University Press, 1991.

Rich, Adrienne. "Compulsory Heterosexuality and Lesbian Existence." Pp. 23–75 in her *Blood, Bread and Poetry.* New York: W. W. Norton, 1986.

Richards, David A. J. *Women, Gays, and the Constitution: The Grounds for Feminism and Gay Rights in Culture and Law.* Chicago: University of Chicago Press, 1998.

Ruse, Michael. *Homosexuality: A Philosophical Inquiry.* New York: Blackwell, 1988.

Soble, Alan. "Kant and Sexual Perversion." *The Monist* 86, 1 (2003), forthcoming.

Stafford, J. Martin. "Love and Lust Revisited: Intentionality, Homosexuality and Moral Education." *Journal of Applied Philosophy* 5, 1 (1988): 87–100.

————. "The Two Minds of Roger Scruton." *Studies in Philosophy and Education* 11 (1991): 187–93.

Stein, Edward. "The Relevance of Scientific Research about Sexual Orientation to Lesbian and Gay Rights." *Journal of Homosexuality* 27, 3–4 (1994): 269–308.

Strasser, Mark. *Legally Wed.* Ithaca, N.Y.: Cornell University Press, 1997.

Sullivan, Andrew. *Virtually Normal: An Argument about Homosexuality.* New York: Knopf, 1995.

Thomas, Laurence M., and Michael E. Levin. *Sexual Orientation and Human Rights.* Lanham, Md.: Rowman & Littlefield, 1999.

Weithman, Paul J. "Natural Law, Morality, and Sexual Complementarity." Pp. 227–46 in David M. Estlund and Martha C. Nussbaum, eds., *Sex, Preference, and Family: Essays on Law and Nature.* New York: Oxford University Press, 1997.

Abortion

Boonin-Vail, David. "A Defense of 'A Defense of Abortion': On the Responsibility Objection to Thomson's Argument." *Ethics* 107, 2 (1997): 286–313.

Cahill, Lisa Sowle. "Grisez on Sex and Gender: A Feminist Theological Perspective." Pp. 242–61 in Nigel Biggar and Rufus Black, eds., *The Revival of Natural Law: Philosophical, Theological and Ethical Responses to the Finnis-Grisez School.* Aldershot, Eng.: Ashgate, 2000.

Callahan, Joan C. "The Fetus and Fundamental Rights." *Commonweal* (11 April 1986): 203–7.

Nicholson, Susan T. *Abortion and the Roman Catholic Church.* Knoxville, Tenn.: Religious Ethics, 1978.

Paden, Roger. "Abortion and Sexual Morality." Pp. 229–36 in Alan Soble, ed., *Sex, Love, and Friendship.* Amsterdam: Editions Rodopi, 1997.

Shrage, Laurie. *Moral Dilemmas of Feminism: Prostitution, Adultery, and Abortion.* New York: Routledge, 1994.

Smith, Holly M. "Intercourse and Moral Responsibility for the Fetus." Pp. 229–45 in W. B. Bondeson, H. T. Engelhardt Jr., S. F. Spicker, and D. H. Winship, eds., *Abortion and the Status of the Fetus.* Dordrecht: Reidel, 1983.

Soble, Alan. "More on Abortion and Sexual Morality." Pp. 239–44 in Alan Soble, ed., *Sex, Love, and Friendship.* Amsterdam: Editions Rodopi, 1997.

Thomson, Judith Jarvis. "A Defense of Abortion." *Philosophy and Public Affairs* 1, 1 (1971): 47–66.

Kant and Kantian Sexual Ethics

Anderson, Clelia Smyth, and Yolanda Estes. "The Myth of the Happy Hooker: Kantian Moral Reflections on a Phenomenology of Prostitution." Pp. 152–58 and 231–33 in Stanley G. French, Wanda Teays, and Laura M. Purdy, eds., *Violence against Women: Philosophical Perspectives.* Ithaca, N.Y.: Cornell University Press, 1998.

Baumrin, Bernard. "Sexual Immorality Delineated." Pp. 300–311 in Robert Baker and Frederick Elliston, eds., *Philosophy and Sex,* 2nd edition. Buffalo, N.Y.: Prometheus, 1984.

Bencivegna, Ermanno. "Kant's Sadism." *Philosophy and Literature* 20, 1 (1996): 39–46.

Cooke, Vincent M. "Kant, Teleology, and Sexual Ethics." *International Philosophical Quarterly* 31, 1 (1991): 3–13.

Denis, Lara. "From Friendship to Marriage: Revising Kant." *Philosophy and Phenomenological Research* 63, 1 (2001): 1–28.

———. "Kant on the Wrongness of 'Unnatural' Sex." *History of Philosophy Quarterly* 16, 2 (1999): 225–48.

Estes, Yolanda. "Moral Reflections on Prostitution." *Essays in Philosophy* 2, 2 (2001), <www.humboldt.edu/~essays/estes.html>.

Gregor, Mary J. *Laws of Freedom: A Study of Kant's Method of Applying the Categorical Imperative in the Metaphysik der Sitten.* New York: Barnes and Noble, 1963.

Hampton, Jean. "Defining Wrong and Defining Rape." Pp. 118–56 in Keith Burgess-Jackson, ed., *A Most Detestable Crime: New Philosophical Essays on Rape.* New York: Oxford University Press, 1999.

Herman, Barbara. "Could It Be Worth Thinking about Kant on Sex and Marriage?" Pp. 49–67 in L. Antony and C. Witt, eds., *A Mind of One's Own.* Boulder, Colo.: Westview, 1993.

Kant, Immanuel. *Lectures on Ethics.* Ed. Peter Heath and J. B. Schneewind. Trans. Peter Heath. Cambridge, Mass.: Cambridge University Press, 1997.

———. *The Metaphysics of Morals* [1797]. Trans. Mary Gregor. Cambridge: Cambridge University Press, 1996.

Kielkopf, Charles. "Masturbation: A Kantian Condemnation." *Philosophia* 25, 1–4 (1997): 223–46.

Korsgaard, Christine M. "Creating the Kingdom of Ends: Reciprocity and Responsibility in Personal Relations." *Philosophical Perspectives* 6, *Ethics* (1992): 305–32.

Langton, Rae. "Love and Solipsism." Pp. 123–52 in Roger E. Lamb, ed., *Love Analyzed.* Boulder, Colo.: Westview, 1997.

———. "Sexual Solipsism." *Philosophical Topics* 23, 2 (1995): 149–87.

LeMoncheck, Linda. *Dehumanizing Women: Treating Persons as Sex Objects.* Totowa, N.J.: Rowman & Allanheld, 1984.

Madigan, Timothy. "The Discarded Lemon: Kant, Prostitution and Respect for Persons." *Philosophy Now,* no. 21 (Summer/Autumn 1998): 14–16.

O'Neill, Onora. "Between Consenting Adults." Pp. 105–25 in her *Constructions of Reason: Explorations of Kant's Practical Philosophy.* Cambridge, Eng.: Cambridge University Press, 1989.

Soble, Alan. "Kant and Sexual Perversion." *The Monist* 86, 1 (2003), forthcoming.

Sparshott, Francis. "Kant without Sade." *Philosophy and Literature* 21, 1 (1997): 151–54.

Waldron, Jeremy. "When Justice Replaces Affection: The Need for Rights." *Harvard Journal of Law and Public Policy* 11, 3 (1988): 625–47.

Rape and Date Rape (and Consent)

Archard, David. "'A Nod's as Good as a Wink': Consent, Convention, and Reasonable Belief." *Legal Theory* 3, 3 (1997): 273–90.

———. *Sexual Consent.* Boulder, Colo.: Westview, 1998.

Belliotti, Raymond. "A Philosophical Analysis of Sexual Ethics." *Journal of Social Philosophy* 10, 3 (1979): 8–11.

Bogart, John H. "On the Nature of Rape." *Public Affairs Quarterly* 5 (1991): 117–36; rep. as pp. 168–80 in Robert M. Stewart, ed., *Philosophical Perspectives on Sex and Love.* New York: Oxford University Press, 1995.

Burgess, Ann Wolbert, ed. *Rape and Sexual Assault: A Research Handbook.* New York: Garland, 1985.

Burgess-Jackson, Keith, ed. *A Most Detestable Crime: New Philosophical Essays on Rape.* New York: Oxford University Press, 1999.

Calhoun, Laurie. "On Rape: A Crime against Humanity." *Journal of Social Philosophy* 28, 1 (1997): 101–9.

Doniger, Wendy. "Sex, Lies, and Tall Tales." *Social Research* 63, 3 (1996): 663–99.

Estrich, Susan. "Rape." Pp. 158–87 in Patricia Smith, ed., *Feminist Jurisprudence.* New York: Oxford University Press, 1993.

———. *Real Rape.* Cambridge, Mass.: Harvard University Press, 1987.

Francis, Leslie, ed. *Date Rape.* University Park: Pennsylvania State University Press, 1996.

French, Stanley G., Wanda Teays, and Laura M. Purdy, eds. *Violence against Women: Philosophical Perspectives.* Ithaca, N.Y.: Cornell University Press, 1998.

Hampton, Jean. "Defining Wrong and Defining Rape." Pp. 118–56 in Keith Burgess-Jackson, ed., *A Most Detestable Crime: New Philosophical Essays on Rape.* New York: Oxford University Press, 1999.

Husak, Douglas N., and George C. Thomas III. "Date Rape, Social Convention, and Reasonable Mistakes." *Law and Philosophy* 11, 1 (1992): 95–126.

Kittay, Eva Feder. "AH! My Foolish Heart: A Reply to Alan Soble's 'Antioch's "Sexual Offense Policy": A Philosophical Exploration.' " *Journal of Social Philosophy* 28, 2 (1997): 153–59.

Leone, Bruno, ed. *Rape on Campus.* San Diego: Greenhaven, 1995.

Muehlenhard, Charlene L., Irene G. Powich, Joi L. Phelps, and Laura M. Givsi, "Definitions of Rape: Scientific and Political Implications." *Journal of Social Issues* 48, 1 (1992): 23–44.

Muehlenhard, Charlene L., and Jennifer L. Schrag. "Nonviolent Sexual Coercion." Pp. 115–28 in A. Parrot and L. Bechhofer, eds., *Acquaintance Rape: The Hidden Crime.* New York: John Wiley, 1991.

Murphy, Jeffrie. "Some Ruminations on Women, Violence, and the Criminal Law." Pp. 209–30 in Jules Coleman and Allen Buchanan, eds., *In Harm's Way: Essays in Honor of Joel Feinberg.* Cambridge, Eng.: Cambridge University Press, 1994.

Paglia, Camille. *Sex, Art, and American Culture.* New York: Vintage, 1992.

Parrot, Andrea, and Laurie Bechhofer, eds. *Acquaintance Rape: The Hidden Crime.* New York: John Wiley, 1991.

Pineau, Lois. "Date Rape: A Feminist Analysis." *Law and Philosophy* 8 (1989): 217–43.

Primoratz, Igor. "Sexual Morality: Is Consent Enough?" *Ethical Theory and Moral Practice* 4, 3 (2001): 201–18.

Remick, Lani Anne. "Read Her Lips: An Argument for a Verbal Consent Standard in Rape." *University of Pennsylvania Law Review* 141, 3 (1993): 1103–51.

Schulhofer, Stephen J. "The Gender Question in Criminal Law." Pp. 274–311 in Jeffrie Murphy, ed., *Punishment and Rehabilitation,* 3rd edition. Belmont, Calif.: Wadsworth, 1995.

———. *Unwanted Sex: The Culture of Intimidation and the Failure of Law.* Cambridge, Mass.: Harvard University Press, 1998.

Sommers, Christine Hoff. *Who Stole Feminism? How Women Have Betrayed Women.* New York: Simon and Schuster, 1994.

Warshaw, Robin. *I Never Called It Rape: The Ms. Report on Recognizing, Fighting, and Surviving Date and Acquaintance Rape.* New York: Harper and Row, 1988.

Pedophilia (and Consent)

Califia, Pat. "A Thorny Issue Splits a Movement." *Advocate* (30 October 1980): 17–24, 45.

Ehman, Robert. "Adult-Child Sex." Pp. 431–46 in Robert Baker and Frederick Elliston, eds., *Philosophy and Sex,* 2nd edition. Buffalo, N.Y.: Prometheus, 1984.

———. "What Really Is Wrong with Pedophilia?" *Public Affairs Quarterly* 14, 2 (2000): 129–40.

Frye, Marilyn. "Critique [of Robert Ehman]." Pp. 447–55 in Robert Baker and Frederick Elliston, eds., *Philosophy and Sex,* 2nd edition. Buffalo, N.Y.: Prometheus, 1984; rev. version, "Not-Knowing about Sex and Power," pp. 39–50 in her *Willful Virgin,* Freedom, Calif.: Crossing Press, 1992.

Kershnar, Stephen. "The Moral Status of Harmless Adult-Child Sex." *Public Affairs Quarterly* 15, 2 (2001): 111–32.

Primoratz, Igor. "Pedophilia." *Public Affairs Quarterly* 13, 1 (1999): 99–110.

Spiecker, Ben, and Jan Steutel. "Paedophilia, Sexual Desire and Perversity." *Journal of Moral Education* 26, 3 (1997): 331–42.

Sexual Harassment

Altman, Andrew. "Making Sense of Sexual Harassment Law." *Philosophy and Public Affairs* 25, 1 (1996): 36–64.

Dodds, Susan M., Lucy Frost, Robert Pargetter, and Elizabeth W. Prior. "Sexual Harassment." *Social Theory and Practice* 14, 2 (1988): 111–30.

Gallop, Jane. *Feminist Accused of Sexual Harassment.* Durham, N.C.: Duke University Press, 1997.

Hajdin, Mane. *The Law of Sexual Harassment: A Critique.* Selinsgrove, Penn.: Susquehanna University Press, 2002.

Klatt, Heinz-Joachim. "Regulating 'Harassment' in Ontario." *Academic Questions* 8, 3 (1995): 48–58.

LeMoncheck, Linda, and Mane Hajdin. *Sexual Harassment: A Debate.* Lanham, Md.: Rowman & Littlefield, 1997.

LeMoncheck, Linda, and James P. Sterba, eds. *Sexual Harassment: Issues and Answers.* New York: Oxford University Press, 2001.

MacKinnon, Catharine A. *Sexual Harassment of Working Women.* New Haven, Conn.: Yale University Press, 1979.

Paludi, Michele A., ed. *Sexual Harassment on College Campuses: Abusing the Ivory Power.* Rev. edition. Albany: State University of New York Press, 1990.

Patai, Daphne. *Heterophobia: Sexual Harassment and the Future of Feminism.* Lanham, Md.: Rowman & Littlefield, 1998.

Sanday, Peggy Reeves. *A Woman Scorned: Acquaintance Rape on Trial.* New York: Doubleday, 1996.

Stan, Adele M., ed. *Debating Sexual Correctness.* New York: Delta, 1995.

Superson, Anita M. "A Feminist Definition of Sexual Harassment." *Journal of Social Philosophy* 24, 1 (1993): 46–64.

Wall, Edmund, ed. *Sexual Harassment: Confrontations and Decisions.* Buffalo, N.Y.: Prometheus, 1992.

Prostitution

Anderson, Clelia Smyth, and Yolanda Estes. "The Myth of the Happy Hooker: Kantian Moral Reflections on a Phenomenology of Prostitution." Pp. 152–58 and 231–33 in Stanley G. French, Wanda Teays, and Laura M. Purdy, eds., *Violence against Women: Philosophical Perspectives.* Ithaca, N.Y.: Cornell University Press, 1998.

"Code of Ethics for Prostitutes." *Coyote Howls* 5, 1 (1978): 9.

Davidson, Julia O'Connell. "Prostitution and the Contours of Control." Pp. 180–98 in Jeffrey Weeks and Janet Holland, eds., *Sexual Cultures: Communities, Values and Intimacy.* New York: St. Martin's, 1996.

Ericsson, Lars O. "Charges against Prostitution: An Attempt at a Philosophical Assessment." *Ethics* 90, 3 (1980): 335–66.

Estes, Yolanda. "Moral Reflections on Prostitution." *Essays in Philosophy* 2, 2 (2001), <www.humboldt.edu/~essays/estes.html>.

Green, Karen. "Prostitution, Exploitation and Taboo." *Philosophy* 64 (1989): 525–34.

Jaggar, Alison. "Prostitution." Pp. 259–80 in Alan Soble, ed., *The Philosophy of Sex,* 2nd edition. Savage, Md.: Rowman & Littlefield, 1991.

Marshall, S. E. "Bodyshopping: The Case of Prostitution." *Journal of Applied Philosophy* 16, 2 (1999): 139–50.

Nussbaum, Martha C. "'Whether from Reason or Prejudice': Taking Money for Bodily Services." Pp. 276–98 in her *Sex and Social Justice.* New York: Oxford University Press, 1999.

Overall, Christine. "What's Wrong with Prostitution? Evaluating Sex Work." *Signs* 17, 4 (1992): 705–24.

Pateman, Carole. "Defending Prostitution: Charges against Ericsson." *Ethics* 93 (1983): 561–65.

———. "Sex and Power." *Ethics* 100, 2 (1990): 398–407.

———. *The Sexual Contract.* Stanford, Calif.: Stanford University Press, 1988.

Shrage, Laurie. "Is Sexual Desire Raced? The Social Meaning of Interracial Prostitution." *Journal of Social Philosophy* 23, 1 (1992): 42–51.

———. *Moral Dilemmas of Feminism: Prostitution, Adultery, and Abortion.* New York: Routledge, 1994.

Stewart, Robert M. "Moral Criticism and the Social Meaning of Prostitution." Pp. 81–83 in R. Stewart, ed., *Philosophical Perspectives on Sex and Love.* New York: Oxford University Press, 1995.

Pornography

Assiter, Alison, and Avedon Carol, eds. *Bad Girls and Dirty Pictures.* London: Pluto Press, 1993.

Baird, Robert M., and Stuart E. Rosenbaum, eds. *Pornography: Private Right or Public Menace?* Buffalo, N.Y.: Prometheus, 1991.

Baldwin, Margaret. "The Sexuality of Inequality: The Minneapolis Pornography Ordinance." *Law and Inequality: A Journal of Theory and Practice* 2, 2 (1984): 629–53.

Berger, Fred R. "Pornography, Sex, and Censorship." *Social Theory and Practice* 4, 2 (1977): 183–209; rep. as pp. 322–47 in Alan Soble, ed., *The Philosophy of Sex*, 1st edition. Totowa, N.J.: Rowman & Littlefield, 1980.

Brod, Harry. "Pornography and the Alienation of Male Sexuality." *Social Theory and Practice* 14, 3 (1988): 265–84; rep. as pp. 281–99 in Alan Soble, ed., *The Philosophy of Sex*, 2nd edition. Savage, Md.: Rowman & Littlefield, 1991.

Burger, John R. *One-Handed Histories: The Eroto-Politics of Gay Male Video Pornography*. New York: Haworth Press, 1995.

Burstyn, Varda, ed. *Women against Censorship*. Vancouver, Can.: Douglas and McIntyre, 1985.

Butterworth, Dianne. "Wanking in Cyberspace: The Development of Computer Porn." Pp. 314–20 in Stevi Jackson and Sue Scott, eds., *Feminism and Sexuality: A Reader*. New York: Columbia University Press, 1996.

Carse, Alisa L. "Pornography: An Uncivil Liberty?" *Hypatia* 10, 1 (1995): 156–82.

Christensen, Ferrel M. "The Alleged Link between Pornography and Violence." Pp. 422–48 in J. J. Krivacska and J. Money, eds., *The Handbook of Forensic Sexology: Biomedical and Criminological Perspectives*. Amherst, N.Y.: Prometheus, 1994.

———. "Cultural and Ideological Bias in Pornography Research." *Philosophy of the Social Sciences* 20, 3 (1990): 351–75.

———. *Pornography: The Other Side*. New York: Praeger, 1990.

Cohen, Joshua. "Freedom, Equality, Pornography." Pp. 99–137 in Austin Sarat and Thomas R. Kearns, eds., *Justice and Injustice in Law and Legal Theory*. Ann Arbor: University of Michigan Press, 1996.

Cornell, Drucilla, ed. *Feminism and Pornography*. Oxford, Eng.: Oxford University Press, 2000.

Dworkin, Andrea. *Life and Death*. New York: Free Press, 1997.

———. *Pornography: Men Possessing Women*. New York: Perigee, 1981.

Dworkin, Andrea, and Catharine A. MacKinnon. *Pornography and Civil Rights: A New Day for Women's Equality*. Minneapolis, Minn.: Organizing Against Pornography, 1988.

Dworkin, Ronald. "Women and Pornography." *New York Review of Books* (21 October 1993): 36–42; reply to letter, *New York Review of Books* (3 March 1994): 48–49.

Dwyer, Susan, ed. *The Problem of Pornography*. Belmont, Calif.: Wadsworth, 1995.

Easton, Susan M. *The Problem of Pornography: Regulation and the Right to Free Speech*. London: Routledge, 1994.

Garry, Ann. "Pornography and Respect for Women." Pp. 128–39 in Sharon Bishop and Marjorie Weinzweig, eds., *Philosophy and Women*. Belmont, Calif.: Wadsworth, 1979.

Gibson, Pamela Church, and Roma Gibson, eds. *Dirty Looks: Women, Pornography, Power*. London: BFI Publishing, 1993.

Gubar, Susan, and Joan Hoff, eds. *For Adult Users Only: The Dilemma of Violent Pornography*. Bloomington: Indiana University Press, 1989.

Hill, Judith M. "Pornography and Degradation." *Hypatia* 2, 2 (1987): 39–54.

Hoffman, Eric. "Feminism, Pornography, and Law." *University of Pennsylvania Law Review* 133, 2 (1985): 497–534.

Hunter, Nan D., and Sylvia A. Law. "Brief Amici Curiae of Feminist Anticensorship Task Force et al., in *American Booksellers Association v. Hudnut.*" Pp. 467–81 in Patricia Smith, ed., *Feminist Jurisprudence*. New York: Oxford University Press, 1993.

Itzin, Catherine, ed. *Pornography: Women, Violence and Civil Liberties.* Oxford, Eng.: Oxford University Press, 1992.

Jacobson, Daniel. "Freedom of Speech Acts? A Response to Langton." *Philosophy and Public Affairs* 24, 1 (1995): 64–79.

Jarvie, Ian C. "Pornography and/as Degradation." *International Journal of Law and Psychiatry* 14 (1991): 13–27.

———. *Thinking about Society: Theory and Practice.* Dordrecht: Reidel, 1986.

Johnson, Edward. "Beauty's Punishment: How Feminists Look at Pornography." Pp. 335–60 in Dana E. Bushnell, ed., *"Nagging" Questions: Feminist Ethics in Everyday Life.* Lanham, Md.: Rowman & Littlefield, 1995.

Kaite, Berkeley. *Pornography and Difference.* Bloomington: Indiana University Press, 1995.

Kappeler, Susanne. *The Pornography of Representation.* Minneapolis: University of Minnesota Press, 1986.

Kimmel, Michael S., ed. *Men Confront Pornography.* New York: Crown, 1990.

Kipnis, Laura. *Bound and Gagged: Pornography and the Politics of Fantasy in America.* New York: Grove Press, 1996.

———. "(Male) Desire and (Female) Disgust: Reading Hustler." Pp. 373–91 in Lawrence Grossberg, Cary Nelson, and Paula A. Treichler, eds., *Cultural Studies.* New York: Routledge, 1992.

Kittay, Eva Feder. "Pornography and the Erotics of Domination." Pp. 145–74 in Carol C. Gould, ed., *Beyond Domination.* Totowa, N.J.: Rowman & Allanheld, 1984.

Langton, Rae. "Love and Solipsism." Pp. 123–52 in Roger E. Lamb, ed., *Love Analyzed.* Boulder, Colo.: Westview, 1997.

———. "Sexual Solipsism." *Philosophical Topics* 23, 2 (1995): 149–87.

———. "Speech Acts and Unspeakable Acts." *Philosophy and Public Affairs* 22, 4 (1993): 293–330.

———. "Whose Right? Ronald Dworkin, Women, and Pornographers." *Philosophy and Public Affairs* 19, 4 (1990): 311–59.

Lynn, Barry W. "'Civil Rights' Ordinances and the Attorney General's Commission: New Developments in Pornography Regulation." *Harvard Civil Rights-Civil Liberties Law Review* 21, 1 (1986): 27–125.

McCormack, Thelma. "If Pornography Is the Theory, Is Inequality the Practice?" *Philosophy of the Social Sciences* 23, 3 (1993): 298–326.

MacKinnon, Catharine A. *Only Words.* Cambridge, Mass.: Harvard University Press, 1993.

———. "Pornography Left and Right." Pp. 102–25 in David M. Estlund and Martha C. Nussbaum, eds., *Sex, Preference, and Family: Essays on Law and Nature.* New York: Oxford University Press, 1997.

———. "Vindication and Resistance: A Response to the Carnegie Mellon Study of Pornography in Cyberspace." *Georgetown Law Journal* 83 (1995): 1959–67.

MacKinnon, Catharine A., and Andrea Dworkin, eds. *In Harm's Way: The Pornography Civil Rights Hearings.* Cambridge, Mass.: Harvard University Press, 1997.

Morgan, Robin. "Theory and Practice: Pornography and Rape." Pp. 163–69 in her *Going too Far: The Personal Chronicle of a Feminist.* New York: Random House, 1977.

Parent, W. A. "A Second Look at Pornography and the Subordination of Women." *Journal of Philosophy* 87, 4 (1990): 205–11.

Rea, Michael C. "What Is Pornography?" *Noûs* 35, 1 (2001): 118–45.

Rimm, Marty. "Marketing Pornography on the Information Superhighway: A Survey of 917,410 Images, Descriptions, Short Stories, and Animations Downloaded 8.5 Million Times by Consumers in over 2000 Cities in Forty Countries, Provinces, and Territories." *Georgetown Law Journal* 83 (1995): 1849–934.

Russell, Diana E. H. "Pornography and Rape: A Causal Model." *Political Psychology* 9, 1 (1988): 41–73; rev. version as pp. 120–50 in D. E. H. Russell, ed., *Making Violence Sexy: Feminist Views on Pornography.* New York: Teachers College Press, 1993.

Russell, Diana E. H., ed. *Making Violence Sexy: Feminist Views on Pornography.* New York: Teachers College Press, 1993.

Segal, Lynne, and Mary McIntosh, eds. *Sex Exposed: Sexuality and the Pornography Debate.* New Brunswick, N.J.: Rutgers University Press, 1993.

Skipper, Robert. "Mill and Pornography." *Ethics* 103, 4 (1993): 726–30.

Soble, Alan. "Pornography: Defamation and the Endorsement of Degradation." *Social Theory and Practice* 11, 1 (1985): 61–87.

———. *Pornography: Marxism, Feminism, and the Future of Sexuality.* New Haven, Conn.: Yale University Press, 1986.

———. *Pornography, Sex, and Feminism.* Amherst, N.Y.: Prometheus, 2002.

Stark, Cynthia A. "Is Pornography an Action? The Causal vs. the Conceptual View of Pornography's Harm." *Social Theory and Practice* 23, 2 (1997): 277–306.

Stoltenberg, John. *Refusing to Be a Man: Essays on Sex and Justice.* Portland, Ore.: Breitenbush, 1989.

Strossen, Nadine. *Defending Pornography: Free Speech, Sex, and the Fight for Women's Rights.* New York: Scribner, 1995.

Tong, Rosemarie. "Feminism, Pornography, and Censorship." *Social Theory and Practice* 8 (1982): 1–17.

———. "Women, Pornography, and the Law." Pp. 301–16 in Alan Soble, ed., *The Philosophy of Sex,* 2nd edition. Savage, Md.: Rowman & Littlefield, 1991.

Tucker, Scott. "Gender, Fucking, and Utopia: An Essay in Response to John Stoltenberg's *Refusing to Be a Man.*" *Social Text,* no. 27 (1990): 3–34.

Turley, Donna. "The Feminist Debate on Pornography: An Unorthodox Interpretation." *Socialist Review* 16, 3–4 (1986): 81–96.

Vadas, Melinda. "A First Look at the Pornography/Civil Rights Ordinance: Could Pornography Be the Subordination of Women?" *Journal of Philosophy* 84, 9 (1987): 487–511.

———. "The Pornography/Civil Rights Ordinance v. the BOG: And the Winner Is. . . ?" *Hypatia* 7, 3 (1992): 94–109.

Ward, David. "Should Pornography Be Censored?" Pp. 504–12 in James A. Gould, ed., *Classic Philosophical Questions.* New York: Prentice Hall, 1995.

Williams, Linda. *Hard Core: Power, Pleasure, and the "Frenzy of the Visible."* Berkeley: University of California Press, 1989.

———. "Second Thoughts on Hard Core: American Obscenity Law and the Scapegoating of Deviance." Pp. 46–61 in Pamela Church Gibson and Roma Gibson, eds., *Dirty Looks: Women, Pornography, Power*. London: BFI Publishing, 1993.

Sadomasochism

Airaksinen, Timo. *The Philosophy of the Marquis de Sade*. London: Routledge, 1995.

Califia, Pat. "Feminism and Sadomasochism." Pp. 230–37 in Stevi Jackson and Sue Scott, eds., *Feminism and Sexuality: A Reader*. New York: Columbia University Press, 1996.

———. *Macho Sluts*. Los Angeles: Alyson Books, 1988.

———. *Public Sex: The Culture of Radical Sex*. Pittsburgh, Penn.: Cleis Press, 1994.

Califia, Pat, ed. *The Lesbian S/M Safety Manual*. Boston: Lace Publications, 1988.

Gebhardt, Paul. "Fetishism and Sadomasochism." Pp. 156–66 in M. Weinberg, ed., *Sex Research: Studies from the Kinsey Institute*. New York: Oxford University Press, 1976.

Hopkins, Patrick D. "Rethinking Sadomasochism: Feminism, Interpretation, and Simulation." *Hypatia* 9, 1 (1994): 116–41; rep. as pp. 189–214 in Alan Soble, ed., *The Philosophy of Sex*, 3rd edition. Lanham, Md.: Rowman & Littlefield, 1997.

———. "Simulation and the Reproduction of Injustice: A Reply." *Hypatia* 10, 2 (1995): 162–70.

Linden, Robin Ruth, Darlene R. Pagano, Diana E. H. Russell, and Susan Leigh Star, eds. *Against Sadomasochism: A Radical Feminist Analysis*. East Palo Alto, Calif.: Frog in the Well, 1982.

Mann, Jay, and Natalie Shainess. "Sadistic Fantasies." *Medical Aspects of Human Sexuality* 8, 2 (1974): 142–48.

Noyes, John K. *The Mastery of Submission: Inventions of Masochism*. Ithaca, N.Y.: Cornell University Press, 1997.

Sade, The Marquis de. *Justine, Philosophy in the Bedroom, and Other Writings*. Trans. Richard Seaver and Austryn Wainhouse. New York: Grove Press, 1965.

Samois, ed. *Coming to Power: Writings and Graphics on Lesbian S/M*. 1st edition, Palo Alto, Calif.: Up Press, 1981; 2nd edition, Boston: Alyson Publications, 1982.

Shattuck, Roger. *Forbidden Knowledge: From Prometheus to Pornography*. San Diego: Harcourt Brace, 1996.

Vadas, Melinda. "Reply to Patrick Hopkins." *Hypatia* 10, 2 (1995): 159–61; rep. as pp. 215–17 in Alan Soble, ed., *The Philosophy of Sex*, 3rd edition. Lanham, Md.: Rowman & Littlefield, 1997.

Weinberg, Thomas S., ed. *S&M: Studies in Dominance & Submission*. Amherst, N.Y.: Prometheus, 1995.

Sex, Love, and Marriage

Carr, David. "Chastity and Adultery." *American Philosophical Quarterly* 23, 4 (1986): 363–71.

Cicovacki, Predrag. "On Love and Fidelity in Marriage." *Journal of Social Philosophy* 24, 3 (1993): 92–104.

Collins, Louise. "Emotional Adultery: Cybersex and Commitment." *Social Theory and Practice* 25, 2 (1999): 243–70.

Diorio, Joseph. "Sex, Love, and Justice: A Problem in Moral Education." *Educational Theory* 31, 3–4 (1982): 225–35; rep. as pp. 273–88 in Alan Soble, ed., *Eros, Agape, and Philia.* St. Paul, Minn.: Paragon House, 1989.

Geach, Mary. "Marriage: Arguing to a First Principle in Sexual Ethics." Pp. 177–93 in Luke Gormally, ed., *Moral Truth and Moral Tradition: Essays in Honour of Peter Geach and Elizabeth Anscombe.* Dublin, Ire.: Four Courts Press, 1994.

Gregor, Thomas. "Sexuality and the Experience of Love." Pp. 330–50 in P. Abramson and S. Pinkerton, eds., *Sexual Nature Sexual Culture.* Chicago: University of Chicago Press, 1995.

Gregory, Paul. "Against Couples." *Journal of Applied Philosophy* 1, 2 (1984): 263–68.

———. "Eroticism and Love." *American Philosophical Quarterly* 25, 4 (1988): 339–44.

Halwani, Raja. "Virtue Ethics and Adultery." Pp. 226–39 in David Benatar, ed., *Ethics for Everyday.* Boston: McGraw-Hill, 2002.

Higgins, Kathleen Marie. "How Do I Love Thee? Let's Redefine a Term." *Journal of Social Philosophy* 24, 3 (1993): 105–11.

Lesser, A. H. "Love and Lust." *Journal of Value Inquiry* 14, 1 (1980): 51–54.

Lodge, David. "Sick with Desire." *New York Review of Books* (5 July 2001): 28–32.

Martin, Mike W. "Adultery and Fidelity." *Journal of Social Philosophy* 25, 3 (1994): 76–91.

McMurtry, John. "Sex, Love, and Friendship." Pp. 169–93 in Alan Soble, ed., *Sex, Love, and Friendship.* Amsterdam: Editions Rodopi, 1997.

Shrage, Laurie. *Moral Dilemmas of Feminism: Prostitution, Adultery, and Abortion.* New York: Routledge, 1994.

Small, Meredith F. *What's Love Got to Do with It? The Evolution of Human Mating.* New York: Anchor, 1995.

Stafford, J. Martin. "Love and Lust Revisited: Intentionality, Homosexuality and Moral Education." *Journal of Applied Philosophy* 5, 1 (1988): 87–100.

———. "On Distinguishing between Love and Lust." *Journal of Value Inquiry* 11, 4 (1977): 292–303.

Steinbock, Bonnie. "Adultery." Pp. 187–92 in Alan Soble, ed., *The Philosophy of Sex,* 2nd edition. Savage, Md.: Rowman & Littlefield, 1991.

Taylor, Richard. *Having Love Affairs.* Buffalo, N.Y.: Prometheus, 1982.

Vannoy, Russell. "Can Sex Express Love?" Pp. 247–57 in Alan Soble, ed., *Sex, Love, and Friendship.* Amsterdam: Editions Rodopi, 1997.

———. *Sex Without Love: A Philosophical Exploration.* Buffalo, N.Y.: Prometheus, 1980.

Walsh, Anthony. "Love and Sex." Pp. 369–73 in Vern Bullough and Bonnie Bullough, eds., *Human Sexuality: An Encyclopedia.* New York: Garland, 1994.

Wasserstrom, Richard. "Is Adultery Immoral?" Pp. 93–106 in Robert Baker and Frederick Elliston, eds., *Philosophy and Sex,* 2nd edition. Buffalo, N.Y.: Prometheus, 1984.

Wreen, Michael J. "What's Really Wrong with Adultery." Pp. 179–86 in Alan

Soble, ed., *The Philosophy of Sex,* 2nd edition. Savage, Md.: Rowman & Littlefield, 1991.

Catholicism and Contraception

Anscombe, G. E. M. "Contraception and Chastity." Pp. 134–53 in Michael Bayles, ed., *Ethics and Population.* Cambridge, Mass.: Schenkman, 1976.

———. "You Can Have Sex without Children." Pp. 82–96 in her *Ethics, Religion and Politics.* Minneapolis: University of Minnesota Press, 1981.

Beis, Richard H. "Contraception and the Logical Structure of the Thomist Natural Law Theory." *Ethics* 75, 4 (1965): 277–84.

Cohen, Carl. "Sex, Birth Control, and Human Life." Pp. 185–99 in Robert Baker and Frederick Elliston, eds., *Philosophy and Sex,* 2nd edition. Buffalo, N.Y.: Prometheus, 1984.

Finnis, John M. "Law, Morality, and 'Sexual Orientation.'" *Notre Dame Law Review* 69, 5 (1994): 1049–76.

———. "Natural Law and Unnatural Acts." Pp. 5–27 in Igor Primoratz, ed., *Human Sexuality.* Aldershot, Eng.: Dartmouth, 1997.

Geach, Mary. "Marriage: Arguing to a First Principle in Sexual Ethics." Pp. 177–93 in Luke Gormally, ed., *Moral Truth and Moral Tradition: Essays in Honour of Peter Geach and Elizabeth Anscombe.* Dublin, Ire.: Four Courts Press, 1994.

Grisez, Germain, Joseph Boyle, John Finnis, William E. May, and John C. Ford. *The Teaching of "Humanae Vitae": A Defense.* San Francisco: Ignatius Press, 1988.

John Paul II (Pope). "Evangelium Vitae." *Origins* 24, 42 (1995): 689–727.

Martin, Christopher F. J. "Are There Virtues and Vices That Belong Specifically to the Sexual Life?" *Acta Philosophica* 4, 2 (1995): 205–21.

Noonan, John T. *Contraception: A History of Its Treatment by the Catholic Theologians and Canonists.* Enlarged edition. Cambridge, Mass.: Harvard University Press, 1986.

Paul VI (Pope). "Humanae Vitae." *Catholic Mind* 66 (September 1968): 35–48; rep. as pp. 167–83 in Robert Baker and Frederick Elliston, eds., *Philosophy and Sex,* 2nd edition. Buffalo, N.Y.: Prometheus, 1984.

Pius XI (Pope). "On Christian Marriage" ("Casti connubii"). *Catholic Mind* 29, 2 (1931): 21–64.

Watt, E. D. "Professor Cohen's Encyclical." *Ethics* 80 (1970): 218–21.

Wilson, George B. "Christian Conjugal Morality and Contraception." Pp. 98–108 in Francis X. Quinn, ed., *Population Ethics.* Washington, D.C.: Corpus, 1968.

INDEX

ABOUT THE CONTRIBUTORS

H. [Harriet] E. Baber received her Ph.D. from the Johns Hopkins University and is professor of philosophy at the University of San Diego. In addition to her interest in human sexuality, she has published in the areas of analytic metaphysics and theology, feminism, and the philosophy of mind.

Cheshire Calhoun is professor of philosophy at Colby College. She is the author of *Feminism, the Family, and the Politics of the Closet: Lesbian and Gay Displacement,* and the editor, with Robert Solomon, of *What Is an Emotion?* She has published widely in ethics, feminist philosophy, and lesbian and gay philosophy.

Pat Califia is "a feminist, a pornographer, a sadomasochist, a poet, a storyteller, an omnivore, a pagan, a social critic, a sex educator, a parent and an activist" (from her Website, <http://www.patcalifia.com/welcome.htm>). She is the author of *Sapphistry: The Book of Lesbian Sexuality, Doing It for Daddy, Macho Sluts,* and *Public Sex: The Culture of Radical Sex.* She is the editor of *The Lesbian S/M Safety Manual* and has also written many articles for San Francisco's *The Advocate.*

Sidney Callahan is the author of *The Illusion of Eve* (1965) and *Parenting: Principles and Politics of Parenthood* (1973). She is also the editor, with Daniel Callahan, of *Abortion: Understanding Differences* (1984) and, with Brigitte Berger, of *Child Care and Mediating Structures* (1979). She is a regular columnist for *Commonweal.*

Greta Christina is a writer whose essays have appeared in *On Our Backs* and the San Francisco *Times.*

John Corvino is assistant professor of philosophy at Wayne State University in Detroit, Michigan. He is the editor of *Same Sex: Debating the Ethics, Science, and Culture of Homosexuality* (Rowman & Littlefield, 1997), a member of the Independent Gay Forum, <http://www.indegayforum.

org>, and a frequent lecturer on gay rights issues. His other research interests include metaethics, business ethics, and Hume studies.

John Finnis is professor of law, Oxford University. Among his books are *Fundamentals of Ethics* (1983), *Moral Absolutes* (1991), and *Aquinas: Moral, Political, and Legal Theory* (1998). He is also the coauthor, with Joseph M. Boyle Jr. and Germain Grisez, of *Nuclear Deterrence, Morality, and Realism* (1987) and, with Germain Grisez, Joseph Boyle, William May, and John Ford, of *The Teaching of "Humanae Vitae": A Defense* (1988).

Alan Goldman is professor of philosophy at the University of Miami. He is the author of six books, including *Empirical Knowledge* and *Moral Knowledge* and, most recently, *Aesthetic Value* (2nd edition) and *Practical Rules: When We Need Them and When We Don't.*

Robert Gray has taught philosophy at McMaster University and the University of Richmond. His articles on Hume, Hobbes, and Berkeley have appeared in *Hume Studies,* the *Journal of the History of Ideas,* and the *Journal of the History of Philosophy.* In 1979, he switched to computer information systems. He is currently in the School of Business at Christopher Newport University in Newport News, Virginia.

Mane Hajdin has taught philosophy at universities in Canada, Papua New Guinea, New Zealand, and the United States; he now teaches at Santa Clara University. He is the author of *The Boundaries of Moral Discourse* (1994) and *The Law of Sexual Harassment: A Critique* (2002), coauthor, with Linda LeMoncheck, of *Sexual Harassment: A Debate* (Rowman & Littlefield, 1997), and editor of *The Notion of Equality* (2001).

Immanuel Kant (1724–1804) was a philosopher who studied and then taught at the University of Königsberg in Prussia (now Kaliningrad, Russia). Among his famous treatises are *Critique of Pure Reason* (1781, 1787), *Groundwork of the Metaphysics of Morals* (1785), *Critique of Practical Reason* (1788), *Critique of Judgment* (1790, 1793), and *The Metaphysics of Morals* (1797). A new edition and translation (by Peter Heath) of the *Lectures on Ethics* has recently been published by Cambridge University Press (1997).

Michael E. Levin teaches at the City College of New York and the Graduate Center of the City University of New York. He is the author of several books and articles on current events and general philosophical topics, including epistemology and the foundations of mathematics.

Thomas A. Mappes is professor of philosophy at Frostburg State University in Maryland. He is the editor, with David DeGrazia, of *Biomedical Ethics* (5th edition, 2001), and the editor, with Jane S. Zembaty, of *Social Ethics: Morality and Social Policy* (6th edition, 2002).

Janice Moulton (Philosophy Department, Smith College) is coauthor of *Scaling the Dragon* (1994), a whimsical story of her adventures while teaching in the People's Republic of China, *The Organization of Language* (1981), which was responsible for her going to China, *Ethical Problems in Higher Education* (1985), and *The Guidebook for Publishing Philosophy* (1986), which is available on the Internet at <http://sophia.smith.edu/~jmoulton/guidebook/>. Recently she completed *Heavy Metal,* an adventure thriller about a woman helicopter pilot in the U.S. Army.

Thomas Nagel is professor of philosophy and law at New York University. Among his books are *The Possibility of Altruism, Mortal Questions, The View from Nowhere, Equality and Partiality,* and *The Last Word.*

Martha C. Nussbaum is Ernst Freund Professor of Law and Ethics at the University of Chicago, appointed in the Law School, the Philosophy Department, and the Divinity School. She is the author of many books and articles on ancient Greek and Roman philosophy, including *The Fragility of Goodness* (1986), and on modern moral and political philosophy. Her recent books include *Cultivating Humanity: A Classical Defense of Reform in Liberal Education* (1997), *Sex and Social Justice* (1999), *Women and Human Development* (2000), and, edited with David M. Estlund, *Sex, Preference, and Family: Essays on Law and Nature* (1997). She has also written many reviews for *The New York Review of Books* and *The New Republic.*

Igor Primoratz is associate professor of philosophy at the Hebrew University, Jerusalem. He is the author of *Justifying Legal Punishment* (1989) and *Ethics and Sex* (1999), and the editor of *Human Sexuality* (1997) and *Patriotism* (2002).

Laurie Shrage is professor of philosophy at California State Polytechnic University, Pomona. She is the author of *Moral Dilemmas of Feminism: Prostitution, Adultery, and Abortion* (Routledge, 1994) as well as essays in a variety of philosophy and women's studies journals. Her writings on prostitution have brought her into dialogue with a number of sex worker organizations, and she is currently contributing to efforts to defend the civil and labor rights of sex workers. Presently, she is completing a book on the public abortion debate (forthcoming from Oxford University Press).

Irving Singer is professor of philosophy at the Massachusetts Institute of Technology. He is the author of many books, including *Sex: A Philosoph-*

ical Primer; Explorations in Love and Sex; Feeling and Imagination: The Vibrant Flux of Our Existence; The Goals of Human Sexuality; George Santayana, Literary Philosopher; Reality Transformed: Film as Meaning and Technique; and the trilogies *Meaning in Life* and *The Nature of Love.*

Alan Soble is University Research Professor of Philosophy at the University of New Orleans. He is the author of *Pornography: Marxism, Feminism, and the Future of Sexuality* (Yale University Press, 1986), *The Structure of Love* (Yale University Press, 1990), *Sexual Investigations* (New York University Press, 1996), *The Philosophy of Sex and Love: An Introduction* (Paragon House, 1998), and *Pornography, Sex, and Feminism* (Prometheus, 2002), and he has edited (in addition to four editions of *The Philosophy of Sex* [1980, 1991, 1997, 2002] the anthologies *Sex, Love, and Friendship* (Rodopi, 1997) and *Eros, Agape, and Philia: Readings in the Philosophy of Love* (Paragon House, 1989; reprinted, corrected, 1999).

Robert Solomon is Quincy Lee Centennial Professor of Business and Philosophy and Distinguished Teaching Professor at the University of Texas at Austin. He is the author of many books, including *The Passions; In the Spirit of Hegel; Love: Emotion, Myth, and Metaphor; About Love; A Passion for Justice; The Joy of Philosophy;* and, with Kathleen M. Higgins, *A Short History of Philosophy* and *What Nietzsche Really Said.* He is also president of the International Society for Research on Emotions.

Sallie Tisdale is the author of a number of books, including *Stepping Westward: A Long Search for Home in the Pacific Northwest; Talk Dirty to Me: An Intimate Philosophy of Sex;* and, most recently, *The Best Thing I Ever Tasted: The Secret of Food.*

Edward Vacek, S.J., is professor of Christian Ethics at the Weston Jesuit School of Theology in Cambridge, Massachusetts, and has taught courses in sexual ethics since 1979. He is the author of *Love, Human and Divine: The Heart of Christian Ethics* (Georgetown University Press, 1994).

Robin Warshaw, a freelance writer from Elkins Park, Pennsylvania, is author of *I Never Called It Rape,* a book about acquaintance and date rape. Her articles have appeared in many publications, including *The New York Times, The Nation, Woman's Day,* and *Ms.*

Alan Wertheimer is John G. McCullough Professor of Political Science at the University of Vermont. He is the author of *Coercion* (Princeton University Press, 1987) and *Exploitation* (Princeton University Press, 1996), as well as numerous articles.

Robin West is professor of law at Georgetown University Law Center, where she teaches jurisprudence, torts, law and literature, and feminist legal theory. She is the author of *Narrative, Authority, and Law* (University of Michigan Press, 1994), *Progressive Constitutionalism* (Duke University Press, 1995), and *Caring for Justice* (New York University Press, 1997). She lives in Baltimore, Maryland, with her husband and three children.

Ellen Willis, formerly a columnist for New York's *Village Voice,* is the author of *Beginning to See the Light* (1981) and *No More Nice Girls* (1992). She teaches journalism at New York University and is the director of that department's Cultural Reporting and Criticism Program.